My Days &

Ganesh Bagchi

For My Debuda, Rai, Sudarsana and Mark

*I wish to specially thank Aparajita Wiessmueller,
for without her initiative this book would not have been
published.*

Contents

Chapter   **Page**

1   Faridpur, where my life began   5
2   Father retires, Comilla   12
3   Calcutta, after a brief visit to Benaras   26
4   Back to Calcutta   82
5   University, Sudarsana, Shantiniketan   90
6   Calcutta riots, Independence, Regent Estate   106
7   'Birthday' visit to Tollygunge   116
8   Aparna and Aparajita. East Africa   141
9   Nondon is born, Teachers' course in London   207
10 Europe, the Middle East, India   248
11 Reunion with the Children, Kampala.   298
12 Demonstration School, Drama Festival, London   337
13 Shimoni Teacher Training College   360
14 Return to India, Julia   410
15 Teaching, Oxford University Press,
    Getting married, England   453
16 Living in England, Mark, Robert, Play   491
17 Thatcher - 'Immigrants go home!' - We go home   523

Chapter 1

Faridpur, where my life began

The streets of Faridpur didn't run wild the day I was born; after six siblings, it was a quiet advent onto this solid earth. What's more, I don't know which year I was born. But I do know that I was born at home, not in a hospital, and there was no birth certificate. None of my brothers and sisters had one. Life was simpler, and we got by without birth registrations and birth certificates. I did acquire a birth certificate of a kind – an official document – which was the matriculation certificate. It states, clearly and unequivocally, that my date of birth is the first of March, 1926. But it's a hoax. How did it come about?

My father and two of his brothers lived in a house on Harish Mukherji Road in Calcutta. Another brother, who lived in a village called Baliakandi in Faridpur, East Bengal, was visiting Calcutta, and he came to stay with his brothers. It was a weekday; so the schools were open, but I was playing with some of the boys from a less affluent part of the locality. These boys didn't go to school, nor did I. It wasn't unusual for these boys and their brothers and sisters, not to go to school. Their parents often couldn't afford to send them to school, nor did they think it was necessary. The visiting uncle came out of the house, smiled at me, said hello, and was walking away; but he suddenly stopped and came back. He was looking bothered. He came up to me and said, 'Don't you go to school?'

'No, I don't,' I said.

'Why is that?'

'I don't like school. I ran away twice from school in Faridpur. Father lets me stay at home.'

'These boys you are playing with,' he said, 'what are they doing here? Don't they go to school either?'

'No, they don't. Their parents don't mind.'

'You should all go to school. I can't do anything about your friends, but I'll certainly talk to my brother and make sure that you start school this week. I'm not at all happy that you should be playing when boys and girls your age are working hard in their schools, learning English and Maths.'

My Uncle looked serious. He looked at my friends critically and disapprovingly. I was slightly worried. Some of these boys, though quite young, could be cheeky and even cut up rough. 'Who is he?' asked one of the boys, when Uncle had left.

'My uncle; he's Headmaster of the school in the village where he lives.'

My friends were impressed. But it was a beautiful day with a clear blue sky, drifting clouds, the sun not too warm, and an unfinished game of pavement cricket. The idea of being cooped up in a classroom with thirty to forty children wasn't attractive.

But my uncle didn't drag his feet. Early the following week, I was marched off to South Suburban School, a local school with a good reputation and a large number of pupils. My uncle and I were ushered into the presence of the Headmaster, a large man sitting behind a large table. Uncle and the Headmaster were soon engaged in conversation about the state of education in the country, and I was temporarily forgotten. In the end the Headmaster did take notice of me, asked me a few questions and assured me that I would be happy in his school. The Headmaster's name was Binode Behari Chatterji. He was friendly, with a big but pleasant voice. I decided I was going to like the school, although I had seen very little of it and knew next to nothing about it.

We moved to the next room, which was larger than the Headmaster's office, with a few people typing away and a few others writing letters, dealing with files and generally looking very busy. Uncle was sitting at a desk, filling in a form. He turned to me and said, 'What's your date of birth?'

'I don't know,' I said.

'I find it incredible. You, a boy of ten or eleven, and you never really went to school, and you don't know your date of birth!'

Uncle was genuinely surprised, though he sounded more frustrated than angry.

'My mother knows when I was born,' I said.

'That's not much help, is it? I've got to fill in the form *now*. I'm not going back home to ask *Baudi,*' said my uncle. *Baudi* is sister-in-law in Bengali.

I took no interest in the date of birth my uncle allocated me. I was more interested in the new adventure which now lay ahead of me and which was going to start the very next day – in less than 24 hours.

For years I'd managed to escape the rigors of formal education. I did learn to read simple stories in both Bengali and English as a result of a little time I'd spent at a school in Faridpur and the sporadic interest one of my brothers had taken in my elementary literacy. But now it was going to be many subjects and many hours of learning with many boys in a large room in a large school. It was going to take some time for me to take it all in.

Saturday was half day, and Sunday was a holiday. I could play with my present friends at weekends. I didn't know yet how it was going to work out. It was going to be more exacting, but it could be exciting too. On the whole, I felt important because I was going to the big school.

'So, goodbye to loafing around with scruffy boys on a Monday morning! How do you feel?' asked my uncle.

'I feel happy,' I said truthfully.

That's the story of how I acquired a casually invented date of birth, which wasn't really the day I was born. What then *was* the true one? I still don't know

My sisters, two of whom were older than me, were 14 and 11. One was younger – only 5. The house we lived in must have been overcrowded – because there were so many of us – but I have no clear recollection either of the accommodation or the architecture of the place. It had a tin roof, so it must have been hot and uncomfortable in the summer months, but I have no recollection of discomfort. Nor did strong winds blow the roof away or heavy rain damage the foundation. I didn't feel either unsafe or uncomfortable in our house with the tin roof in Faridpur.

My father and my eldest brother were both clerks in a government office. A large family living on the salaries of a senior and a junior clerk had to be, I'm sure, extremely careful about the way money was spent. But I don't carry in my head any recurrent images of hardship or deprivation. I remember the huge mango tree in front of the house whose unique distinction was that it produced mangoes which were very sweet long before they were ripe. Our mango tree was now well past its prime, and had for many years stopped giving us a rich harvest, but its tall, strong, leafy presence in front of the house gave me a sense of security. We grew up under the watchful eye of this huge tree. It had become part of our life.

The most spectacular and dramatic time of the year was the monsoon months, when the rains came after the heat and dust of the summer months. They brought intense relief. But they could also create huge problems.

Heavy rain used to fill up the storm drains. I floated paper boats in the fast-flowing water. They moved along the surface if there was a wind, and though the voyage was usually short-lived, and most of my boats didn't last long, occasionally, a few were carried along rapidly until they were out of sight. It was a huge thrill, a great sense of achievement when that happened.

Other delights to which I thrilled were fishing and kite-flying. But I wasn't the protagonist in either of these activities. It was my brother, Debu-da, seven years older than me, who was an expert flyer of kites and had an uncanny skill at fishing. I watched him, fascinated, while he went about the business of making kites or flying them and "fighting" other kites while up in the air. Usually, it was a duel, a fight between two kites. The idea was to cut the thread of the other kite so that it was set adrift and fell down on the ground, on the roof of a house, on a tree, or just got lost.

Retrieving these kites was another sport, which some boys found equally exciting. With a little help from my brother, I was soon able to fly kites and engage in such minor skirmishes. I learnt enough about kite-flying and the aerial duels to enjoy the sport and appreciate its subtleties and intricacies. The ritual could become obsessive and demand a great deal of time and attention, but I loved it. Its special attraction for me was of course, that I could be with Debu-da, whom I loved and admired, and be initiated by him into the mysteries of this great sport. I lived in a world where nothing whirled past at a crazy pace. Fishing and kite-flying fitted in beautifully into my slow-moving life.

The roads were brownish, greyish and dusty in summer and muddy during the monsoon months. The chief means of transport were horse-carts, bullock-carts, *thelas* and bicycles. People walked long distances. It's possible that my memory is selective, but my boyhood days have lived on in my head as near-idyllic.

One unhappy recollection is that I fell out of my favourite mango tree. I could hardly breathe, and a neighbour, a friend of Debu-da's, came to my rescue. I was lying on the ground, greatly distressed, unable to move, gasping for breath, when

Biren-da carried me to his house. The next thing I knew, I was lying in my bed, being looked after by my mother.

To begin with, school was a bit too restrictive for me, although I managed to learn to read and write simple sentences in Bengali and English. There was noise and confusion in the classroom when the teacher wasn't there, and dull routine, conformity and obedience when he was – usually teaching things which I didn't understand – so I never really saw the point of my being there. It wasn't far from home, so when I had the opportunity, I would slip out of school and come home. Mother didn't worry too much about my missing school, nor did anybody else. I even walked into Father's office once or twice. He greeted me affectionately, suggested that I should walk back home or back to school carefully – it didn't seem to matter whether it was home *or* school – and, on one occasion at least, he even gave me money to buy some sweets! The teacher noticed my absence very rarely. And when he did, I was punished. But standing in a corner of the classroom wasn't too painful.

Mother would often read aloud to us – stories from the *Ramayana* and the *Mahabharata*. I don't know how much of these I understood when she *read* from the epics. I preferred it when she just *told* us stories from them, especially the exploits of Hanuman, who had once managed to set fire to Srilanka, Ravana's kingdom. There were two great collections of stories in Bengali which I loved: *Grandmother's Stories* and *Grandfather's Stories*. Actually, they were universally popular in Bengal. If they had ever been properly translated – I'm sure children living in various parts of the world would love them too. Sometimes one of my two elder sisters and some neighbouring children would join in the story-reading or story-telling sessions. These were memorable occasions.

My relationship with my parents was also very different from that of most of the other children's. There was very little show of affection, but at the same time, no bullying, no chastisement, and no attempt to discipline or regulate our behaviour. This wasn't because there was no need or occasion for controlling or restricting us, but it just worked out that way.

I wasn't old enough in Faridpur to understand the subtleties and complications of relationships, especially adult relationships, but I have a vague recollection that both my father and my eldest brother were worried about Debu-da's abundant interest in everything except school and studies. Debu-da had an extraordinarily good singing voice, so he was regularly surrounded by admirers of both sexes and various ages, and it's well- known that when that happens, the situation regularly gets out of hand. As far as I remember, however, there were no dramatic consequences for Debu-da or anybody else except for some gossip and curiosity.

It was about this time that I gathered that Father was going to retire, and we were going to Comilla, another large town in East Bengal, where Father's younger brother was a Subordinate Judge. My eldest brother and his wife were going to stay on in Faridpur and the rest of us were going to Comilla in a matter of weeks. It was disturbing news for me because I was born in Faridpur. This was the only town I knew. The only other place where I had lived for a few months was Baliakandi, a village where Father and his brothers owned a few acres of land. One of my uncles lived there. Father and his two other brothers visited the village occasionally – an obscure place not found in maps.

For me, too, Comilla was an unknown quantity, so the prospect of living there didn't have any familiar appeal. Quite a lot of discussion was naturally going on all around me. There was adventure and apprehension in the air. Although Mother and my sisters didn't say very much, it seemed to me that they were reconciled to the idea of change rather than being positively enthusiastic about it. Mother had always been the mistress of the house, so it must have been a disturbing – even distressing – prospect: the loss of authority in a shared household and the need to make many significant adjustments in the way we lived our lives. My two sisters just didn't want to go to this strange and terrible place. They'd decided that Comilla was some kind of purgatory or prison. They liked Faridpur. They didn't want to go to their rich uncle's house. 'Let's run away,' said Bula, the older of my two sisters.

But we all knew there was no running away; the wheels were moving inexorably in the direction of Comilla, towards a large, joint family of two brothers, their wives and children. What lay in store for us? What was the relationship between Father and my uncle? Were we going to be second-class citizens? Were the cousins going to patronize us because their father had a much larger income and our father had a small pension from a lowly job? The two older sisters discussed such matters, but I only half understood some of their sentiments. Most of these were totally obscure.

I was possibly even quite excited at the prospect of a new beginning in a new place with many people around, some of whom were about my age, though I don't really remember. I must also have felt that it wasn't going to be a seamless transition for me, at least emotionally. I would surely miss the patriarchal, ancient mango tree in front of our house, which had watched the rise and fall of many generations, sheltered many varieties of birds, harboured many and different kinds of lives, apart from gifting us some of the sweetest mangoes I'd ever tasted. Then there was the shimmering light before the end of a rain-washed day. But, perhaps most of all, I'd miss Badal, Bishnu and Bapi, three good friends.

Badal was the oldest – good at climbing trees and playing truant from school. We accepted his leadership without hesitation, as a matter of course, just as he took it for granted that he'd lead and we'd follow. He was good at sports. We played football and cricket with old tennis balls and Badal excelled in both.

Bishnu was the academic type, with a lot of interest in reading and writing. He got prizes at school. He had read books I hadn't heard of.

Bapi specialized in fishing. Even Debu-da discussed fishing strategies with him. He would dig worms out of a field or garden and use them as bait, usually with great success. I think I was accepted by them as part of the group partly because of my moderate skill in fishing and kite-flying, in spite of being much younger, and partly because I was Debu-da's brother. Debu-da was a hero to people in our age group – and also in his own.

One aspect of adventure is leaving the known for the unknown. I don't think I was quite ready for adventure yet. All around me at the time there was excitement, but also apprehension and uncertainty. My father had decided that we should go to Comilla to live with his brother. The word disorientated would probably best describe my emotional state, but I certainly didn't know the word at the time.

As usual, when in doubt, I turned to Debu-da, and as usual, he was unfalteringly optimistic about Comilla and our life in Comilla. He'd done his research. Our uncle was a sub-judge in Comilla, lived in a two-storey building with a veranda overlooking a small lake. The name of this lake was Rani Dighi. We could swim in the lake, he said, to make our life in Comilla sound exciting. But what was most important was that the uncle, the aunt and our cousins were all good people, kind people. There was nothing to worry about at all. Debu-da was an incurable optimist: we fell to rise, and slept to wake up to resplendent life.

It was always good to talk to Debu-da in times of uncertainty.

Chapter 2

Father retires, Comilla

I only vaguely remember the upheaval and commotion of moving to Comilla; the long journey, the exhaustion, and the disorientation on arrival. I had never met this uncle or his family before. Father talked about him with affection and pride, because holding the position of a Subordinate Judge in colonial Bengal was considered to be quite an achievement. When I arrived at the house where this uncle and his family lived, I must have been too confused and exhausted to remember any definite event or experience. I don't even remember any faces or snatches of conversation or affectionate greeting. All I have stored in my memory is impressions – impressions of exhaustion, disorientation and apprehension.

This uncle – the second eldest of four brothers – was a total stranger to me and so were his children and his wife. I have no recollection of any cordiality or affection from any one of them. Nor was there any open unpleasantness, rudeness or calculated indifference. Looking back, I realise that it's part of the culture of a middle-class Bengali family, not to be demonstrative. Even verbal expressions of love, affection or friendship were unusual, especially in public. More than anything else, I think it was the strangeness of the situation – the place and the people – that made me retreat, and withdraw, and made me feel lonely and forsaken. I went through a whole gamut of wretched emotions. One of the reasons for this was that Debu-da hadn't come with us. He was going to arrive a week or so later. The other reason was that my two sisters and my mother had very little difficulty in getting absorbed within the large community of women, doing various domestic chores and engaging in activities of common interest. But I didn't belong to any group; I had no sense of community; nor any common purpose or interest to lead to anything remotely resembling friendship or companionship, with any of my cousins.

Father must have noticed my loneliness and frustration, for he began to spend a little time with me, teaching me simple English words and telling me stories from Indian epics and Aesop's Fables. He must also have been lonely because he had left behind his friends in Faridpur. At his age it must have been rather difficult to make new friends.

I felt closer to Father in Comilla than I'd ever done in Faridpur. I try to visualize the two of us walking side by side to the temple, about half a mile away – he, a tall, well-built man with keen eyes and a big nose, and I, not yet ten, slender, and of average height, trying to keep pace with him and not succeeding. Father would often slow down and stop to point to things – a big banyan tree, a stray horse or donkey, monkeys gambolling in trees. Monkeys near the temple often descended from trees or roof-tops of huts or bungalows. I was always discouraged from offering any food to the temple monkeys because Father thought they were ill-mannered animals who snatched food from people, and had been known to turn nasty if they couldn't have their way. 'And if a monkey bit or scratched you, you could die', he said.

The God, who Father was devoted to, was Krishna, human incarnation of God. Krishna was human, Krishna loved, Krishna stood by those who needed him, in love and war. Krishna and Radha were lovers, but Radha was someone else's wife. Because Krishna was Father's hero, I also thought he was the greatest. His adulterous relationship with Radha didn't worry Father at all. Krishna also appears in the *Mahabharata*, where he drives the chariot of Arjuna. Father was taken up with the Krishna who was Radha's lover, and he wrote songs about their love, which were sung in temples. This particular kind of devotional singing is called *Kirtan*. Because of his interest in *Kirtans,* and his ability to write devotional songs, Father got both affection and respect from the priests as well as the devotees who regularly visited the temple. I basked in the reflected glory of my Father's popularity.

Before and after the singing, people came round to engage my Father in conversation, but he never forgot me, never ignored me. I knew he was always aware of my presence, whether or not he talked to me or bestowed any affectionate pat on the head.

'Do you like it here?' he asked me one evening, as we were walking back from the temple.

'Not as much as I liked it in Faridpur,' I said. 'I have no friends to play with'. Father just said 'Hmm', and we walked on.

I'm not quite sure how long it was – it could not have been more than a couple of months – before Debu-da arrived. The situation, the atmosphere, the feel of the place changed for me immediately. One of my cousins, Hambu-da, who was just a couple of years younger than Debu-da, became one of his most ardent admirers. In the evening a few of the cousins and one or both of my sisters would congregate on the large terrace of the house and Debu-da would sing. There was the most attentive silence as the summer air filled with the sound of his melodious voice.

Debu-da was not yet 20. His personality had an inexplicable charm, an inescapable aura. It was not only me, another of his many ardent admirers, who felt drawn towards him. Although it was going to be immensely difficult to compete against so many contenders for his affection, I felt good that all those cousins, who took very little notice of me, were such sincere admirers of Debu-da. They so much enjoyed his singing, as we sat beneath a summer sky at the end of a sizzling day, when the breeze was mercifully cool, and the sky was star-lit and cloudless, that nobody spoke, and we were often late for dinner.

In front of my Uncle's house in Comilla, was Rani Dighi, a small lake where people bathed and fished, and which they went around on their morning walks. Life around Rani Dighi started early in the morning. Because of the popularity of the place with bathers and those who came for their morning and evening constitutionals, a few vendors set up fruit and vegetable stalls. You could also buy flowers, balloons, soft drinks, nuts, crisps and colourful kites. In the early part of the evening, it had a fairground atmosphere. Rani Dighi was where I learnt to swim.

Father kept himself very much to himself in Comilla, and I would spend what time I could with him and Debu-da those days, but quite often I was at a loose end. Meanwhile my mother and sisters joined my aunt and some of my cousins in the kitchen, as they helped each other with various domestic chores.

At this time, two boys who lived at the end of our street invited me to play cricket with them – Gopal and Kartik. They were impressed with the skill I had acquired in Faridpur, playing with Badal, Bishnu and Bapi. I batted better than I bowled. Gopal was good at both batting and bowling. There was a small park not far from where we lived and we played there. Quite often other boys would join in, especially at weekends, and I began to feel part of the life in Comilla. Then about the same time, a cousin, Badal-di, introduced me to a game of Five Stones. It involved throwing a few pebbles or small stones up in the air and catching them according to certain rules and in a certain order. To impress my cousins, I practiced secretly whenever I could, and I became quite good at it. They admired my skill and began to take serious notice of me, to treat me like an equal. I found Badal-di attractive and friendly. She said she didn't want to get married. She wanted to be a doctor and look after sick women, especially women who were poor. She asked me what I wanted to be, and I said I didn't know. She was disappointed. But that was the truth. I hadn't spent a lot of time in school and I had no compelling ambition. I hadn't given the subject of my career any thought at all. Badal-di's question made me think, but as far as I remember, I couldn't decide.

Mother watched me, was concerned about my comfort and well-being, but wasn't demonstrative. I could feel her affectionate concern. I knew that if I turned to her at any time she would do all she could to relieve any anxiety and uncertainty. Of all the people I knew at the time she was probably the gentlest. I don't remember my mother ever raising her voice, even when she thought my father was being unreasonable. She managed to deal with very trying situations, with quiet dignity. Not once did she raise her hand against me, or talk to me in anger. She had been uprooted from Faridpur, a town which she knew well and related to, and where she had made a few good friends, and a town which she considered to be home. Yet I have no memory of any bitterness or resentment or grieving tears. If it was an emotional wrench, she showed no signs of it. No memory of meanness, anger or spouting malice spoils the memory of Mother's quiet dignity and gentleness.

Quite often we idolize those we love in retrospect, especially long after their death, when they are a distant memory. Is that what's happening? I really don't think so. I believe that my mother was a uniquely disciplined person, in whose presence I felt secure, comfortable and happy. She too, I'm sure, carried around with her marks of human weaknesses, but I can't recall them, however hard I try. She made me secure, like the earth beneath my feet. There was much more communication between my mother and my two sisters, Bula and Hena, although a lot of it was about mundane matters. There was nostalgia at times about Faridpur, which I shared, but there was a special feeling of camaraderie between the three women, from which I felt excluded, though I did not resent it. We were now part of a much larger unit – my uncle and aunt had four daughters and four sons – but we continued to be a closely knit unit with an even greater sense of solidarity than we had had in Faridpur.

Although my father was the eldest of four brothers, and after the death of my grandfather, played a crucial part in bringing up his younger brothers and sister; my uncle in Comilla was really the head of the family for all practical purposes. This was because he had status – in colonial India, an Indian Subordinate Judge was in a very small minority – and he had a much larger income than my father. To keep up appearances, my father was treated as the head on special occasions, but these occasions were quite rare. Mejokaka – Uncle – was rather reticent, and generally kept himself to himself – a remote figure who languished in the background, about whose existence I was only vaguely aware. The only bit of conversation which I remember, took place about a month after our arrival, and went something like this:

'Hello.'

'Hello.'

'How old are you?'

'Ten years, I think.'

'You think?'

'Which class are you in?'

'I don't go to school.'

'Oh, really? Why is that?'

'I don't know.' Mejokaka didn't worry that I didn't go to school.

I saw him from a distance after that – going out or coming in, or reading the newspaper in the living room. He didn't show much interest in me and I had no reason to seek his company. His wife, my aunt – Mejokakima – although much in evidence, telling servants what to do and telling the cook what she had decided people would want to eat – almost entirely ignored my existence. On the whole, my memory of the members of the two families, our family and my uncle's, is not very vivid, perhaps because the subject was an amorphous group of young and middle-aged people, engaged in routine tasks, living predictable lives. Only my father, with his interest in devotional music, and Debu-da, with his great singing voice and musical ability, were different.

Among my uncle's children, Hambu-da was somewhat eccentric, with an inordinate appetite for religious rituals, which perplexed and intrigued me. I didn't understand it, but was impressed with my cousin's ardour. He would get up early in the morning, sit cross-legged on the terrace in front of an image of some deity, and chant incantations with deep devotion. There was a college near Rani Dighi, and this college had a large garden. I had gone at dawn to fetch flowers for Hambu-da's early-morning worship of Krishna or Vishnu or Shiva – I forget who was his favourite – and was chased away by one of the men who looked after the garden. I fell trying to run away and hurt my knee, but managed to escape the wrath of the caretaker. Hambu-da carefully dressed the knee and gave me a few tips on the art of fleeing from chasing caretakers, which I never made use of. I don't think I was particularly adventurous at that age. And I don't think I changed at any point of time.

One morning after Hambu-da had attended to the rituals, he told me something nobody had mentioned before.

'Do you know,' he said. 'Father has been transferred to Calcutta?'

'I've heard of Calcutta,' I said, 'but I'm not sure where it is.'

'We live in East Bengal,' he said, 'and we're going to West Bengal. Calcutta is the largest and the most important city in Bengal.'

'Oh,' I said. I was impressed.

I took it for granted that we would all go to Calcutta. I didn't feel particularly excited, joyful or elated; nor did I worry about the upheaval, because Father and Debu-da would have to do most of the running around. I had little responsibility; I would do as I was told. Debu-da would probably ask me to run little errands for him, which I would do most happily.

But then I had to first find out from Mother if she had been told, and what she thought of the news.

'I don't like it,' she said. 'Just when I was beginning to feel settled, just when I was getting to know a few people, visiting a few places, making a few friends, I have to move again!' My mother wasn't particularly adventurous.

She did sound unsettled at the prospect of moving again, after having come to terms with leaving her home, and the environment in which she had spent so many years; where her children had been born; where she was the mistress of the house in a town whose roads and trees and rivers and sky she had come to love. Faridpur had been home.

To me also, Faridpur meant more than Comilla, because Faridpur was my town and Comilla was not. I knew the shops and houses of not only our street, but many other streets as well, and the streets always took me to where I wanted to go. Even the sky seemed a special sky, and the shapes and patterns and colours of the clouds seemed different from anything that I saw in Comilla. Then, there were the rivers, boats, boatmen, people, noise, excitement, when sometimes we travelled by steamer.

Even the trees of Faridpur had more life and character in them, because I and other children had climbed them, hid behind them, rested in their shade, eaten their fruit, if the fruit was edible, made them our silent companions. We related even to the derelict huts at the end of our street, where we often played hide and seek. Sometimes the crumbling, dilapidated huts became our pirate ships from where, with great courage and skill, we conquered our brutal enemies. Finally, there was the monsoon. The rain in Faridpur came with the beat of a thousand drums. Thunder and lightning frighteningly announced its advent. Darkness at noon, and gale-force winds whirling dust and dry leaves from the parched ground, round and round in a mad frenzy. After this dramatic introduction, equally dramatically, the heavens broke. It poured. After some time, the stormy wind and the clouds disappeared. The rain was heavy and long, creating its uniquely strong and steady monotone, bringing with it nature's reassuring message that it's there to sustain life, although sometimes it brought disastrous floods and destruction.

Nothing out of the ordinary, nothing dramatic or memorable happened to me or anybody else in Comilla. I think I went to bed fairly early, at about nine o'clock, and got out of bed at about seven, but the time between waking and sleeping was largely uneventful. Life must have been pretty humdrum, not only for me, but for others also. Only Rani Dighi, the lake in front of our house, played a part in my life, because I started off by bathing in it, then splashing about, and then gradually actually swimming, with a little help from Debu-da.

Occasionally, there were some agitated discussions about British rule in India between some of the cousins and their friends; these generated some heat, but I didn't understand their arguments, only registered their agitation. I gathered from the discussions that the British were in India to take as much as they could to make their country rich, and it didn't worry them that India was one of the poorest countries in the world, where only a small proportion of people had any education at all.

The name of Mahatma Gandhi was mentioned again and again, with the result that I thought of him as a superman, without understanding what he said, or what he stood for. I came to believe that British rule in India was something humiliating, and the sooner we got rid of it, the better.
Soon the transfer of my uncle from Comilla became common knowledge. There were discussions and speculation about how everything was going to work out; whether the change was desirable; whether it was an unwelcome disruption of the even tenor of our lives. But I was neither old enough nor wise enough to

understand the implications of the coming change. Like the move from Faridpur, this one brought with it both excitement and a little apprehension.

For Mejokaka, this was a promotion.   He was being transferred to the most important city of Bengal, and the challenges and complexities of the job had to be greater. My aunt and the cousins must have been pleased at the prospect because of what it must have meant to Uncle.   My Mother wasn't pleased because this upheaval was going to follow so closely on the heels of our move from Faridpur, after Father's retirement. I had no idea how the news affected my sisters. I think that they sympathised with Mother's disappointment and uncertainty. Only Mejda, my second eldest brother, and Debu-da reacted positively to the news, because they felt certain that Calcutta would offer much greater job opportunities for them. Especially for Debu-da, a career in music in Comilla was highly unlikely.

Plans had to be made and they were being made.   My father's youngest brother lived in Calcutta. He was a lawyer who practiced at the Alipore Judges Court. He would find a house large enough for himself and the two other brothers, Mejokaka and my father, when they moved to Calcutta.   My mother, with me and my two sisters would go to a village in Bihar, where my mother's eldest brother lived. He had retired from the Indian Railway Service. We would stay there until the house in Calcutta had been rented and generally set up.

Put like that, it sounds reasonably simple. Yet there were complications, decisions and revisions, frayed nerves, outbursts of bad temper and a great deal of uncertainty.

Mother, who very rarely questioned my father's decisions, did bring up the subject of relocation. Father had decided that we should spend some time with my mother's brother in Bihar, while joint-family life was being organised in Calcutta.

 "I don't see why we should have to go all the way to my brother's house in Bihar Why can't we all go to Calcutta directly from here?' Mother said.

'Kali, as you know, is the main player. He's renting a large house in Calcutta where we can all live. He says he wants to travel light to begin with. I'm going with Kali. When we have found the right house and a cook and one or two others to fetch and carry, we'll send for you,' Father said. Kali was my uncle.

'I don't like the idea of going alone with two daughters and my little son,' said Mother.

'I've talked to Debu,' Father said. 'He'll go with you.'

The news that Debu-da was going with us to Alkusha, made Mother feel better. I don't know what it was about Debu-da. His presence soothed nerves, gave people confidence, resolved conflicts. And his singing gave people great pleasure.

'I thought Debu was going back to Faridpur,' Mother said.

'No. He says he'll be happy to go with you,' said Father. Mother was at once at peace. She trusted Debu-da; idolized him. He could harness the wind, pluck the sun.

Travelling back to the events of a distant past, I realise that the definition of people and places becomes blurred. Comilla doesn't vividly stand out in my memory. The water of Rani Dighi does, and so do the bathers of different ages and sexes. Then there was the beautiful garden of the local college, which was looked after and protected by a fierce *mali* or gardener. The monkeys around the temple and in the trees near the temple were my favourite distractions. Their antics, their easy, fluid, confident movements in the most difficult and precarious situations, their protective and affectionate treatment of the smaller monkeys, made a great impression on me. They had chosen to live with us and yet they were independent. Apart from the monkeys, the temple, Rani Dighi and the college garden, there were a few trees, especially an old and large banyan tree, which I'll always remember when I think of the short time I spent in Comilla.

Of the people in Mejokaka's family, I liked Hambu-da best because he had many interests, and treated me with affection and consideration. Then there was Badal-di, who was friendly, and had taught me the game of Five Stones. I was going to say goodbye to them only temporarily, so there weren't too many reasons for me to feel any great emotional wrench. What is more, I hadn't noticed any sadness descending on anybody at the thought of having to leave. I think part of the reason for that was that we were going to Calcutta, towards which Bengalis had a very special attitude – one of affection and respect. It was like the Promised Land – the Land of Canaan.

On the day I was leaving, I must admit, there was very little in Comilla which would draw me back, although I had no idea about the place where I was now going.

The journey by train was pleasant because the people in the compartment were helpful, and the stations at which the train stopped were full of the noise of hawkers selling their wares – the vendors of tea making the most noise. When the train stopped at a station, I often had an impulse to get out and mingle with the milling crowd, to shout with the young tea vendors, 'Chai, Chai, Garam Chai.' But I stayed in the compartment, and looked and listened, while Debu-da did the fetching and carrying, buying Mother and my two sisters cups of tea, salted peanuts and boiled potatoes, which were sliced, salted and spiced, on improvised plates made out of banana leaves. I had access of course to all the food and drinks, except the really pungent food. When the train stopped at a junction, it waited much longer than at smaller stations and then Mejdi, Phuldi and I would quite often go out with Debu-da. Mother would usually stay behind in the compartment.

Mother was protective, watchful and concerned, but never over-anxious and didn't restrict our freedom to a point which was oppressive. She always managed to spend time with us when we sought her company, tell us a story or two from the *Ramayana* and the *Mahabharata*. Somehow Mother's relationship with the two daughters was different. Quite often, when they were amused by people and events, I didn't understand what they found funny or why they laughed. This worried me slightly, but not enough to cause me pain or resentment. On the train – it was a longish journey – we were literally closer because we were sharing a compartment in which we ate, slept and spent all our time. But we were also closer in other ways. Somehow there was a different quality to our relationship, brought about by the physical proximity and the movement of the train, and the uncertainty that awaited us at our destination. Mother hadn't seen her brother for a very long time and we hadn't ever met him.

'What's Uncle like?' I asked Mother.

'He used to be all right. I'm sure he still is. People don't change easily. Seeing him again will certainly make me happy,' she answered.

'And what about the aunt?' asked Phuldi.

'I've never spent any time with her. She's a good woman, I understand,' said Mother.

Then Mother looked a little pensive, a little serious. 'There's something about my brother I don't like. He goes out with his gun and shoots birds,' she said.

All that happened a long time ago – our arrival at a small railway station where there were no crowds of people waiting to get on to the train and nobody getting out, except the five of us – Mother, Mejdi, Phuldi, Debu-da and me. The weather was hot, the very height of summer. Uncle hadn't come to the station but had sent his son, who lived with him, and whose name I've forgotten. His meeting with Mother was affectionate. He had come with two strong, able-bodied Bihari men, who took charge of our luggage, and between them, loaded two bullock carts which they had driven to the station. Our cousin smiled at us and asked Debu-da and Mejdi how the journey was, and they replied that we had enjoyed it.

We all came out of the station where the two bullock carts, now partly loaded with our luggage, were waiting for us on a dusty road which seemed to stretch, shimmering, all the way to the horizon. We had had many rides in horse carts, but this was going to be our first ride in a bullock cart. Mother might have had the experience but none of us knew what it was like. I felt quite excited at the prospect and not at all apprehensive because the animals looked so strong and gentle. There was inexplicable excitement in the wide open spaces, where there was nothing between us and the horizon but some ancient trees and hazy outlines of hills.

As we were travelling in the direction of my uncle's house, the bullock carts creaking and clattering through wide-open fields on either side, the sun started to mellow, and soon hung just above the horizon. There is not a lot I remember, but this was really memorable, especially because the quality of light was quite extraordinary, compared to anything I had seen before.

When we arrived at our destination – a large bungalow in the middle of a field, with not many houses around – both Uncle and Aunt came out of the house to the open compound to greet us, while the two men who had driven the bullock carts, heaved our luggage out of the carts and carried it to the room to which they were directed. I liked the look of my uncle and aunt and the bungalow in which they lived.

The change was dramatic: the wide open spaces, the hills in the distance, the friendly tribal people, all slim, dark and elegant, the playful children, and women always ready to smile. They would do things for us, run errands for us, and help us in various ways – and although they had to work hard to survive, they were always able to find enough time and energy to enjoy themselves. They danced in large groups. Their sense of rhythm was natural, easy as breathing, I was told though I don't remember watching them dance.

The occasion my mother dreaded, however, was just round the corner. The next Sunday, my uncle announced, he was going bird-shooting, and any of us who wanted to go with him would be welcome. Sunday came. Debu-da and my cousin were going, and they weren't reluctant participants either. It didn't seem right to me – Debu-da, poet and musician, with a gun slung across his shoulder, going out with enthusiasm with our uncle and cousin to shoot down birds! It bothered me, but I don't think I could have put into words the reason for my discomfort.

This was happening in an environment of unusual beauty. The lake shone in the bright sunlight under a sky that was indescribably blue. Quite a few old trees, whose names I didn't know, were scattered around the lake, shelters at night, I suppose, for the birds we were out to kill. It was time for us to turn back. Everybody was returning to the bullock carts with their booty and they looked fairly pleased with their day's work, although a little tired. The shadows of the ancient trees around the lake were lengthening, the air was cooling down, and the sun had mellowed, but was still well above the horizon, when we started off on our way back home. I was tired and fell asleep.

I woke up a little before getting home. Mother was excited, but it was not because Uncle and my cousin had shot quite a few birds between them. She thought hunting and shooting were acts of barbarism. It was because Father had written, she said, and we would soon join him in Calcutta. Three brothers – Father and his two brothers – had rented a house with nine rooms. They had bought the essential furniture, the crockery, the cutlery and the other necessary items. All was well and they were waiting for us. At least Father was. I shared my mother's excitement, although I was happy here in Alkusha for various reasons. There was greater closeness during this time between Mother and me, and between me and my sisters. And Debu-da was quite happy spending time with me. He would tell me the names of stars at night and birds during the day, and I acquired some essential knowledge about flying kites during the few weeks we were there.

'Have you noticed,' he would say, 'the earth is reddish here? Its colour is different from that in Faridpur?'

'Yes, I have, and the grass isn't as green. But I like the shadowy hills over there,' I'd say, pointing to the horizon.

'They are shadowy because they're so far away,' Debu-da would say.

I don't think I missed Comilla. I hadn't really started relating to the place when I left. But Faridpur hadn't faded from my memory. Some people, places, events stay with you, make you who you are. Nature here was beautiful, but not in the same way as in Faridpur. The climate was dry, the air hot but not humid, the trees scattered rather than in groves, the grass more brown than green, and rain more an exception than the rule.

There was something reassuring about a downpour when the rains came in Faridpur – unless it caused floods, which I hadn't experienced. Then there were the rivers in and around Faridpur: Padma, Mara Padma, Gorai and Chandana. There was a feeling of relaxed certainty about the place. Faces were familiar. Streets took me where I thought they would take me, and trees stood where I expected them to stand. A bonding had taken place, and Faridpur would always remain a part of me.

Now Calcutta waited, Calcutta, the great metropolis, where everything happened. I knew very little about the history of Calcutta or anywhere else. I don't think it would have greatly impressed me if someone had told me, that just over two decades ago, Calcutta had been the capital of British India, and that in Calcutta was the beginning, of not only the British hegemony over India, but also of much of the Empire. Debu-da mentioned some of the features of Calcutta which excited my boyish imagination: the river Hooghly, the temple of Kali, the Victoria Memorial Hall, the Octerlony Monument, the Eden Gardens and the Zoo in Alipore. Another feature of the great city in which I was particularly interested was the trams. They were like small trains which ran on tracks like railway lines – through the length and breadth of Calcutta, Debu-da had said.

We said our goodbyes. Mother's eyes were moist. Was she ever going to see her brother again? Uncle said something about not giving up hope, for the unexpected did happen quite a lot of the time.
For me, travelling by bullock cart was an adventure. Travelling by train was a longer adventure, and I was fascinated by trains, by railway stations and by the hawkers and the innovative language they used to sell their ware. Debu-da was doing all the running around as usual, getting us cups of tea, organising our meals, buying Mother a Bengali newspaper to read. She was interested in politics, but not an active participant, only an ideological follower of Gandhi. Cooking, cleaning and bringing up several children, she didn't have much time for attending meetings or going on marches, but she had always taken a great deal of interest in what was happening in politics, especially in Gandhian politics of non-violent protest against the British imperial policy of subjugation, domination and exploitation. This was a recurrent subject, which I only half understood at the time. While in Faridpur,

Mother had started spinning to make *khadi*, indigenous cotton cloth, which, hopefully, could compete with British cotton fabric, made in Britain with our cotton, and then sold back to us.

Chapter 3

Calcutta, after a brief visit to Benaras

Father had come to the station with one of my cousins, Hambu-da, to meet us. Debu-da had spotted them first, and as soon as the train stopped, he opened the door and leapt on to the platform to go and meet them. Soon, my father, Debu-da and my cousin walked up to our compartment with two porters. There were the usual greetings, a show of respect, which included the touching of feet, carrying the dust there from to ones forehead, the so-called *'pranam'* and polite enquiries about each other's state of health. Meanwhile the porters, led by Debu-da, took charge of the luggage, and we all proceeded to the taxi stand.

Father asked me how I was. Father was tall for a Bengali, and had a light brown complexion. He had a longish nose, shaped a bit like a parrot's beak. His hair was short – it seemed to me even shorter than before – black hair streaked with grey. His eyes were black, neither large nor small, with something unflappable about them. He wanted to know if I had enjoyed myself, and I answered that I was well and that I had enjoyed going to, and staying with, my uncle and aunt. He did not ask whether I had missed him. Such questions were never asked. Looking back on those days it seems to me that my father was either unable, or unwilling, to show affection, either through words or gestures. A show of affection by word or action was usually avoided – very naturally and unconsciously. In some cultures this lack of display of affection might be considered unnatural or unusual, but this was how it was in my family and other families I knew. Yet I'm sure that my father missed my mother, me, Debu-da and my two sisters, and we certainly missed him. It was enough for me that Father had come to the station to meet us and welcome us. He looked well, but slightly thinner. We followed him to a taxi stand. Going through the crowd and noise of Howrah Station, I looked at my parents walking side by side, an unusual sight.

I find it difficult to separate what I actually remember from what I *think* I remember, but the impact of Howrah Station was powerful, and Howrah Bridge filled me with wonder. As the taxi drove through the streets of Calcutta, I felt bewildered by the noise, the traffic and the crowds. Debu-da had built up my hopes and had encouraged me to expect magic and adventure, but on first entering Howrah Station and then driving through the crowded streets, more than anything else, I felt panic, fear and bewilderment. The only sights which filled me with excitement and admiration were Howrah Bridge and the Ganges or the Hooghly River.

As we were approaching Harish Mukherji Road, where our new abode was to be, I was also able to take a good look at the Victoria Memorial, which I thought was a wonderful building.

Hambu-da had shown us pictures of the Taj Mahal while we were in Comilla, but that, though beautiful, was only a picture. This, the Victoria Memorial, was real – a magnificent building, the like of which I had never seen before. It stood right there for all of us to see as we sped past in our taxis. I was in a taxi with my parents when there was a gasp of wonder and admiration from Mother, followed by many questions addressed to my father. All that marble, where had it come from? When had this great building been completed? Where had they found all the money to build it? When had she, Queen Victoria, reigned? This must have been the kind of questions Mother asked. I'm clearly only reconstructing much of what happened so long ago.

Having exhausted her stock of questions about the Victoria Memorial, Mother turned her mind to the arrangements at 49/1C Harish Mukherji Road in South Calcutta, where we were going to live. How many rooms did it have? Which rooms were we allocated? But before Father had had time to answer Mother's questions, the taxis pulled up outside the large wooden door of a three-storey building. I looked up at it. I had never lived in a large building like this before.

49/1C Harish Mukherji Road, Bhabanipur, in South Calcutta was a house with three storeys. The first and second floors each had four rooms, and the third floor had one room which was the size of two rooms, and a terrace. Mejokaka, who was a Subordinate Judge at Alipore, had the major responsibility for setting up both money and organisation, though all those who had a regular income were expected to make a contribution. How much they contributed depended on how much they earned. The arrangement seemed to work. If there were undercurrents of resentment, and these led to tension, I didn't feel it. There were three separate groups which ate their meals, one after the other. First to eat were the children, then the men, and then the women. There was a cook and two others, a man and a woman, who did the general housework as well as helping with the cooking.

There was no question of picking and choosing for us children. We were given food that our mothers chose for us, and the cook cooked for us, and woe betides anybody who made a fuss. I don't remember what exactly was put in front of us. It is fairly certain that it was traditional Bengali food – rice, pulses, a vegetable dish, eggs, fish or meat curry and, occasionally, a milk-based dessert of some kind. Food was basic, healthy, balanced. We ate with relish; there were no restrictions on the quantity we ate. Some of my cousins did talk about the monotony of it, but I enjoyed it and looked forward to it.

The cooking, the distribution, the selection was almost entirely left to hired people, although my aunts and my mother did discuss what was going to be cooked. We children had no say in it, nor did we have any regrets that we did not. Food for so many hungry children was provided regularly, on time, and it was good. In any case, I don't think I was a connoisseur of food, and I had grown up in an environment where it was unusual to make a fuss about what was set before us. It was remarkable that so many children ate so many lunches, breakfasts and suppers, regularly, without any sign of frustration.

There were problems of a different and subtler kind. It seemed to me that my uncles, aunts and cousins were taking very little notice of me. It was as if they lived on a different planet, and their problems, priorities and preoccupations were totally different from mine.

This didn't affect me deeply because ours was a large presence in the establishment. There were my parents, my eldest brother, who was a step-brother, his wife, Debu-da, my three sisters, Mejdi, Hena and Kana, and I. For much of the time we kept ourselves to ourselves, but I had no sense of isolation, no feeling of loneliness. It was only very rarely that I had a feeling of being resented. I couldn't identify its origin, but it was unmistakably there.

Mejda, my second eldest brother, had come and gone before we had come to stay. The reason for his sudden departure was shrouded in silence. Why we should all stay there and Mejda live in a men's hostel was never discussed. Mejda did come to see us fairly regularly, but he never crossed the threshold to enter the house. For some reason that I didn't know about, a ban had been imposed on him. He was not allowed to come into the house at Harish Mukherji Road. Why not? I asked Mother again and again, but I never got a satisfactory answer.

Mejda's banishment or isolation never made sense to me. A deep sense of injustice and unfairness affected me, so I asked Mother, Debu-da and two of my elder sisters, but no-one would offer me an explanation that made the question disappear from my head. When Mother said Mejda didn't like the idea of living with so many people, I found that the most acceptable explanation: it was all right if it was *he* who had decided that he valued peace and quiet more than family solidarity.

However, some years later I gathered, as a result of the carelessness of one of my sisters, that Mejda had been thrown out when we were visiting Mother's brother. He was caught kissing one of his cousins. Any such intimacy between first cousins was taboo, totally unacceptable to my uncle and aunt, so Mejda had to go. There could be no argument about it. Such behaviour amounted to incest. There could be no acceptable explanation for such behaviour. No-one could expect to be forgiven for such transgression! Although my sisters were naturally sympathetic towards their brother, they didn't dispute Uncle's decision. Their brother had been punished for his sinful behaviour. What was there to say? In large joint families such attraction was bound to happen. But at that age I wasn't concerned.

School had started to play a significant role in my life. The first year in school was full of uncertainty because I hadn't coped with systematic learning before, although, somewhere along the line, I had acquired some skill in reading, writing and arithmetic. I was often asked to read out simple descriptions and stories in English and Bengali. My reading was good, the teacher said, although he corrected my pronunciation from time to time. The school believed in competition. I did well in most subjects, quite unexpectedly well, considering that in Faridpur and Comilla I hardly spent any time learning anything formally.

I came second in the annual examination. I had had no systematic schooling before this, but I had an unfair advantage over the others in my class: I was older by more than a year, through some mistake of my uncle's, who got me admitted to this school. Whether this was a decision that my uncle had made because he wanted to neutralize any disadvantages of my not having spent much time in school before, I don't know, but I didn't feel concerned about my examination results. The fact that I was almost top of the class, in spite of not going to school except for a few months, was not what mattered. What I did care a great deal about was the evident approval of my teachers and a little respect from fellow students.

One or two of my cousins were also impressed. Badal-di, one of my cousins, who was just a year older than me, and who I thought was an attractive and pleasant person, said to me one evening at dinner, 'I hear you came second among 60 students. That's very clever of you.' This made me feel good. It gave me immense pleasure that I could do something to impress Badal-di, who was a good student herself. Others were also impressed – some more surprised than impressed – that I had done so well. I kept a low profile because I usually felt like an alien, knew I didn't belong, thought my existence was hardly noticed by people outside my own family – my parents and siblings. I had also decided that I liked it like that way, but

I was wrong. The fact that my cousin Badal-di had actually looked out for me and congratulated me; that my uncle had stopped and smiled at me and said, 'Now who's a clever boy?', that another cousin, Bomda, who was about eleven years older than me, had said, 'What's this I hear? You've come second? Why second? Why not first? I want you to come first, and no excuses,' gave me great pleasure. I myself had started asking myself the same question: why can't I do even better?

There was one cousin, a year younger than me, who was not too impressed. He went to a different, more expensive school. He was heard to say, 'To come second in a second-rate school isn't such a great feat.' This cousin, Mejokaka's youngest son, was a bright lad who had followed in the footsteps of his father; he studied law and became a Subordinate Judge in Alipore later in life.

After my initial success, there was no stopping me. I remained in South Suburban School for another five years, and I was never second again in class. In class VI, I was awarded the Tirthapati Gold Medal and the Tirthapati Scholarship. The scholarship was six rupees a month, a princely sum for a twelve-year-old, except that I sometimes shared it with Debu-da, if he was broke.

It was about this time that there was some upheaval in our lives. Mejokaka, who earned the biggest income, and made the major contribution in the running of the establishment, let it be generally known that in three months' time he would be retiring from his job and would be going away to live in Deoghar. Deoghar was a hilly town of natural beauty in Bihar, a popular place for retirement for middle-class Bengali civil servants. This led to my father and my uncle being engaged in quiet discussions behind closed doors – sometimes for hours during weekends. There were times, however, when there were noisy disagreements, which we heard, in spite of closed doors. My father usually emerged from these discussions in an agitated state, and Mother had to make him a cup of tea, no matter what time of day. Father never drank anything stronger than tea.

Although of course, at the time I didn't understand what was going on, what those endless discussions were about or why there were recurrent debates. Uncle going away to live a quiet life... it wasn't quite as simple as that. I now know the central issue and understand the point that Father was making. Apart from the fact that it wasn't a brotherly act for him to disrupt the joint family, it wasn't legal to do so.

'It's strange, quite incredible,' Uncle had said, 'that you should tell *me* what's legal and what isn't.' Uncle was referring to the fact that he'd earned his living in the legal profession.

'I know what I'm talking about,' Father had said. 'You had the main responsibility in this joint family. If you walk out, you cause economic hardship and trauma. A joint Hindu family is protected by law against such disruption.'

'Let me tell you Borda,' Uncle had said, 'there's provision for an earning member of the joint family to quit when there's a change of circumstances.'

'And what's that change of circumstances? A selfish brother wants to leave his brothers and their families because he wants the best for *his* wife, *his* children and himself, never mind the others. I'm telling you, Kaliprasanna....' My Father sounded angry.

There was more than one occasion of such acrimonious altercation. Both Uncle and Father had now stopped being discreet and restrained, thrown caution to the wind, and dispensed with closed doors. The whole idea of standing by one another, of family solidarity, of the stronger members of a joint family taking care of the less able, the weak and vulnerable, had been abandoned. This was a painful and traumatic situation for me, especially disappointing because it came at a time when I had done well at school, and was beginning to be taken notice of by my peers at school and by my cousins at home, thus boosting my confidence. Now, I felt insecure again.

Though there was something remarkable about these arguments. Father and Uncle argued agitatedly about the legitimacy and legality of the action that my uncle was about to take, but their language never degenerated into insult or abuse, although voices did rise somewhat at times.

Anyway, the day did come when my uncle and his family were all packed and ready to leave. The leave-taking was a tight-lipped affair in which there was little evidence that the great physical and material disruption corresponded in any way to the emotional distress caused by it. Debu-da was especially unconcerned. He behaved as if Uncle and his family were going on a short holiday. He fetched and carried with some of his cousins, helped to load luggage into taxis, and went with them to the railway station to say goodbye. After they had left, Mother said, 'Is it a nice place they're going to?'

'I don't know,' said Father, 'those who run away do not interest me.'

He tried to sound casual, but he must have been very anxious. My other uncle, aunt and two cousins were also leaving at the end of the month, which meant that the entire responsibility of taking care of the rent and the maintenance of this large house was to be shared between Father and my eldest brother, Jogesh. Father had a small retirement pension. He also earned some money by acting as a middleman in financial transactions and property deals. My eldest brother was in the same business, and being younger and more resourceful, did better than my father. Between them, they managed to feed and clothe us, but the kind of money required for renting a large house like this was out of their reach.

Father was resourceful. He had worked out a strategy which he was going to use to deal with the situation. He filed a court-case against my uncle. He made the point that Uncle had acted illegally. By breaking up a Hindu joint family, he had caused psychological trauma and financial distress. This was against the law, which didn't allow such sudden and drastic disruption; therefore, my uncle should not only continue to pay the rent, but should also pay the abandoned members of the family sufficient compensation to rent another place and start life afresh. This was unusual and shocking; nothing like this could be found in the annals of the Bagchi family.

Friends, other members of the clan, well-wishers – all tried to persuade Father not to proceed with his plan to fight it out in a court of law, but he was adamant and quite certain that he would win.

There was also, however, another major problem: where was he going to get the money to fight the case? Court fees had to be paid, and lawyers were expensive. It so happened that a friend of Father was looking for a house to rent. He was a lawyer. Father made him an offer: fight my case and you can share this large house with me.

The offer was accepted. Mr Sanyal moved in with us. Mr Sanyal's youngest son, Amar, became a good friend of mine. He was very intelligent, played a good game of cricket and had a pleasant and friendly nature. Amar's mother was an excellent cook, and from time to time, after a game of cricket with Amar, I was a beneficiary of her great cooking. Father got on very well with Mr Sanyal. Everything was working well at the time. Father, my eldest brother and Mr Sanyal would discuss what went on in the court, the possible outcome, the arguments they had put forward, as well as what Uncle's lawyer had said.

The discussions were intense, friendly, and serious: three generals planning their onslaught on the enemy stronghold over cups of tea. Sometimes a game of chess followed: both Mr Sanyal and Father were keen chess players.

The lawsuit and the court proceedings came to an end after many months but the games of chess in the living room and the cups of tea and the discussion of the arguments continued. Father, my eldest brother and Mr Sanyal were all quite pleased with the outcome. The house had to be vacated and handed back to the landlord, which meant we had to rent new accommodation. We were allowed time to find suitable houses. My uncle was going to have to pay the arrears of rent.

There was no sense of victory, no jubilation, no clear winner or loser, but quiet acceptance of what seemed like even-handed justice. My father, my eldest brother and Mr Sanyal had expected this verdict, so they weren't thrown. My brothers had already looked at many houses, and there was one which had been approved by both my parents. Mr Sanyal's sons had also lined up a house for their family, to which they were going to move.

First the Sanyals left. Amar said he would keep in touch, but I met him next only about nine years ago, when I was visiting Kolkata. Between our departing from the house we had shared, and our meeting again, more than 50 years had passed, during which he had taught Physics in American colleges, and I had taught English in Africa, India and Britain.

We moved to a house farther down the road which had six rooms, three upstairs and three downstairs – 186 Harish Mukherji Road. I liked the house. An important reason for my liking it was that I was going to share a room with Debu-da. My eldest brother, his wife and two daughters were to have one room. My parents and three sisters were to have the largest room in the house, where Father had his bed on one side of the room, and Mother and my sisters had their beds on another side. Only Mejda, my second eldest brother, had a room to himself, which was downstairs.

My eldest sister, Buladi, had died about two year ago in the house we had just left. She was generous and affectionate. I had a lot of love and respect for Buladi. It had all started with a high fever which would not go away. She grew weak and was confined to bed for several days. I was standing by her bed one day, feeling helpless that my sister, who was so full of energy and did so much for anyone who turned to her, should lie in bed so helplessly. Not so long ago we were all getting excited because Father frequently talked about her marriage, which he was soon going to arrange, he said. I knew weddings were exciting, colourful and memorable events, where noisy people and noisy music were everywhere and you got excellent traditional food and sweets. All that, I thought, had to wait until my sister got well. 'My mouth feels dry. Will you get me some lozenges?'

'When?' I asked.

'Now,' she said. 'You can get some from the shop near Harish Park.'

'But I'm playing cricket in the park! I'm already late. My friends are waiting.'

'Forget it then,' she said, and closed her eyes.

Buladi, or Didi, my eldest sister, lost all interest in food. Talking was too much strain for her. When I went to her, she looked at me as if from a long way away. She had typhoid. She faded away, my sister, the tallest, strongest, the most attractive of all my sisters and cousins. She died when she was just twenty. I was playing cricket in the park.

And then finally, we moved house. There was a lot of activity; always a lot going on. Friends, relations and well-wishers visited us; we met a few neighbours; we began to settle down. One of the people who were very helpful to us was Bholada, whom I had introduced to the family. He lived in a house in School Row, a street parallel to Harish Mukherji Road, from where we had just moved. He wore glasses, had a thin, well-trimmed moustache, slightly curly hair, an earnest look and pleasant speech. He got to like me, and volunteered to teach me English and Mathematics. He lent me books to read which I wouldn't have read if he hadn't introduced me to them, and I wouldn't have been half as good in solving mathematical problems without the insights which I gained through his teaching. Yet, my eldest brother was deeply suspicious of his motives and relationship with me and my sister, Hena, who was two years older than me. He never entered into any serious discussion with him, and only acknowledged his existence with reluctant grunts and nods.

One day I was sitting on Bholada's knee while he was reading 'Treasure Island' aloud to me. A little later, my eldest brother, Jogesh, walked past and went out through the front door. He came back and told me to go to the park and play with my friends.

'But,' I protested, 'I'm listening to a very interesting story.'

'Never mind the story!' he frowned.

'But I want to know what happens to Long John Silva,' I protested

'Do as you're told! Get up and go!' He was not going to put up with any nonsense.

I had to go; that was the way of Borda, my eldest brother.

Bholada had to go too. He was told by Borda to go away and never come anywhere near our house, nor meet me anywhere outside the house. I was deeply disturbed by the way Borda treated Bholada, who was a gentle person, gentle and generous. He had come to Calcutta from Borisal, East Bengal, in search of a job. He hadn't found one, and just about managed to keep body and soul together by teaching. He had a degree in English. I continued to be distressed and puzzled, and one day I made bold to ask Borda why Bholada never came to the house any more.

To my surprise, the response to my question was very different from the one I expected. Borda didn't say it was none of my business. He didn't tell me to go away and do my homework, or play in the park. Without raising his voice, he answered my question seriously and explained why Bholada had to go. He told me that Bholada was an intelligent man with a degree, yet he didn't do a regular job of work and hung about in our house for many hours every day. He was over-indulgent with me and I was becoming too dependent on him. At last came his confession, 'And I didn't like him.' If I needed help he said, he would get me another tutor. Most unusually, his tone of voice was conciliatory. He knew what he was doing, and what he did was for my good. Bholada was probably a clever young man, but he wasn't sure that he was a good, honest, self-respecting young man. He said that I should forget him and get on with doing my work and living my life. It was unusual for Borda to spend so much time with me, talking about a serious matter, justifying a serious decision. I was flattered, I suppose, but I continued to feel unhappy. I missed the genuine affection and feeling of companionship, which Bholada managed to give me. He'd just got up and left.

Some years later, Debu-da brought up the subject.

'You remember Bholada?' He asked.

'Of course I do. Borda was very unkind to him. I didn't like the way he was treated,' I said.

'Borda felt certain that he was up to no good, that he was homosexual.'

'Why did he think that?'

'He had his reasons. He never explained it to anybody.'

Debu-da had great respect for Borda. Borda's decision had to be the right decision..

'Shall I ask you a straight question?' Debu-da suddenly said.
'Did he ever say anything or do anything which made you feel uncomfortable? Do *you* think he was homosexual?'

I thought for a bit, before I answered.
'Looking back, I think he probably was. He always sat very close to me or wanted me to sit close to him. To express his approval of any work I'd done well, he would give me a tight hug. Verbally and physically, he expressed his affection for me all the time, but he didn't do anything overtly sexual. My innocence might have discouraged him from doing anything which might have scared me,' I said.

'What you've said is most interesting, and I've listened to what you've said with attention, but you haven't really answered my question,' Debu-da said.

I thought for a moment. I was at that time just a juvenile and this man, Bhola Mukherji, an unemployed young graduate of Calcutta University, spent a lot of his time with me and gave me a lot of his affection. I also had a lot of affection for him. I didn't know about homosexuals then, and didn't care. Now I did, so I had to admit that I thought he was that way inclined.

'Yes, he was. He was homosexual,' I said.

'That's what I thought too,' said Debu-da.

Yes, it was the truth. His affection for me and his readiness to do so much for me and to give me so much of his time and attention had to have an explanation, but it hurt me to put a label on our relationship, to stereotype his feelings. I missed Bholada. What Borda thought of him didn't matter.

We had few books in the house. Phuldi, now my eldest sister after the death of Buladi, read Bengali novels from time to time: some she borrowed from the library, some from friends. I took up reading now more seriously, borrowed books from the public library as well as the school library. I also took my school work seriously with the result that I regularly came first in my class. Phuldi was much more affected by Bholada's departure. Looking back, I sometimes wonder whether she was in love with him, but I'll never know, because I've never asked her and never will.

Mother fell ill about this time. She had played no part in the little sub-plot of Bholada's departure. She lived in an uncomplicated world. It was quite remarkable how she managed to live her life without getting involved in the various complex episodes of life in the Bagchi household. She was an early riser, but one day when I had got out of bed and was ready to leave for school, Mother was still in bed.

'Aren't you feeling well?' I asked.

'I'm burning up with fever. Your father must be in the living room; please ask him to come and see me. You go to school and don't worry.'

The doctor came and went fairly frequently the whole of the following week. Her condition – the fever, the headache, the complete loss of appetite – was beginning to improve. Dr Mukherji looked more relaxed, the frown in his dark brown face slowly disappeared.

'Once Mrs Bagchi gets well, I'll come and play a game of chess with you,' he said to Father.

This was the first time Dr Mukherji had talked about Mother's recovery. Before that, he had looked almost as worried at times as my father. There was a general sense of relief all round. A few years back he had struggled to save the life of my eldest sister, Buladi, and failed. Buladi had died of typhoid. What did Mother have? It might have been the same, I'm not sure.

A few days after she had started feeling well, Mother decided she would pick up the threads, begin again from where she had left off.

'I can't tell you,' she said, 'how wonderful it is to feel normal again. It was a bad dream. It's over. Tomorrow morning I'll do my *puja* and thank Lord Krishna.'

Doing her *puja* meant getting up early – at around six o'clock – and having a bath and thanking the deity in the *puja* room. This was late November. It got quite cold, especially early in the morning. Mother had her bath, did her *puja,* but caught a bad cold. She started feeling ill again, weak and exhausted; coughed a lot, had high fever. Dr Mukherji came, examined her carefully, prescribed a few medicines, talked to Father in a serious and anxious tone of voice and left. Next week and the next, the doctor visited fairly frequently. Mother's condition was getting steadily worse. One morning, Dr Mukherji suggested to my Father that a well-known specialist, whom he had worked with before, should be consulted. Father agreed.

Before the specialist could be consulted, Mother died one night, a little before midnight. Father noticed she was quite still. He asked me to get the doctor. I ran all the way to his house and came back with him in his car. When Dr Mukherji examined Mother, he shook his head. Heart-rending sobbing and crying filled the air, for everybody was awake and everybody realised that Ma was not going to be with us any more.

My own deep sense of disorientation persisted through all the rituals: the visits of friends and relations, the partly social, partly religious ceremony on the tenth day after her death, when the priest came and chanted sacred verses from religious books, offered fruits and flowers to deities, and prayed for the peace of the soul of the departed.

Most of those who had come to attend the ceremony took notice of me and said comforting words, which included assurances that Mother's soul lived on. I found most of what was being said to me incomprehensible. All I knew was that nobody had remembered to light the lamp in front of the deity in Mother's *puja* room, and there was an empty space in the bed where Mother slept. At school, one or two of my teachers and several of my classmates came up to me and said they were sorry to hear the sad news. It didn't take very long, however, before everyone stopped making any references at all to Mother's death.

I continued to do well in school and Debu-da told everybody that his little brother was a prodigy. It was only my eldest brother whose expectations were unrealistic, and I was often tense and unhappy trying to live up to his demands. It wasn't enough for him that I always scored the highest aggregate marks; he wanted me to come first in every subject. He would find out if anybody had scored more marks in any of the subjects. A few of the pupils usually had, and this, my brother found difficult to accept.

'You haven't been taking your studies seriously,' he would say.

'Why do you say that?' I would ask.

'I've just looked through your report,' he said. 'Three boys have scored more marks than you – one in Geography, one in Sanskrit and one in Maths. How did this happen?'

'I draw maps badly. Ananda's strongest subject is Mathematics, and Sunil's father teaches Sanskrit,' I explained.

'They may be good, but I want you to be better,' Borda said, with a lot of emphasis on *you*. It wasn't much good arguing with Borda. I liked school. I enjoyed reading and writing, but I had little aptitude in drawing and Maths. The fact that I usually did very well in exams, and was genuinely interested in the knowledge and skills I acquired at school was accepted by my teachers. It gave me an identity. I felt good about it. It was important for me to do well, score high marks in the tests and exams because, apart from feeling good, I was also fulfilling the expectations of my teachers – and Borda.

Borda, I think now, was vicariously fulfilling his own ambitions. For various reasons, which had to do with family responsibilities and having to earn a regular income, he never went beyond the first year at University, and he would now like me to finish *his* unfinished business. I did feel flattered by his genuine interest in my academic achievements, but at the same time, I felt anxious not to let him down and I was afraid that I might let him down.

Father didn't show any obvious interest in how well or badly I was doing at school. Mejda, my second eldest brother, lived in a world of his own, and wasn't particularly concerned about the academic success or failure of his youngest brother. He had expressed the opinion, however, that Borda's interest in my studies and the level of my achievements in school amounted to persecution. Debu-da expressed interest in how well or badly I was doing at school, but I don't think it would have made a lot of difference to him if I hadn't stayed at the top. Father was inclined to extol the intelligence and academic ability of his youngest son, but made no demands. Mother used to put it down to the fact that one of the deities she worshipped had taken kindly to her youngest son, and before and after examinations, I had to go to her prayer room and thank them.

Father had found one of my two gold medals underneath her pillow after her death. There was some speculation about this. Debu-da thought that Mother did this to ensure that Father didn't sell it, for Father never hesitated to sell off valuables, including Mother's jewellery, if there was a financial crisis in the family.

My memory of Mother had already begun to fade. The sense of loss and loneliness was beginning to diminish, though it refused to disappear. The only time I ever cried over the death of Mother was when I was visiting a friend about a week after her death. When a parent died, it was our custom to wear a *dhoti,* a stretch of white cotton cloth – not trousers or pyjamas – and wrap another piece of white cotton cloth around our naked torso. We were not supposed to wear leather shoes or sandals. I was feeling at a loose end that Sunday morning, and I went to see Ananda.

Ananda's little sister, Usha, who was about six years old, looked at me puzzled, and said, 'Why are you wearing those funny clothes?'

I was going to explain. I was going to tell her that my mother had died just a week ago and that it was a religious custom which required us not to eat meat and fish, not to shave, and to wear those 'funny clothes'; but I choked, turned my face away and wept.

'Weep, my son,' said Ananda's mother, 'there are times when we must weep. It's the only thing that makes sense.' Over a period of time, the pain was replaced by a profound disbelief that Ma wasn't there, that her love had gone with her, had vanished with her ashes.

And then the coming event which demanded all my attention was the Matriculation Examination. I had some extra help from one of our Mathematics teachers: otherwise, I was on my own. In a few weeks' time it was all going to happen – the examination for which I'd prepared with such hard work and self-discipline. More than anything else, I was worried about letting my Borda down: he held his head high when his youngest brother outshone the others. I really wanted to do well and be told by Borda that he was really and truly proud of me. I thought of very little else in the weeks that followed – the Matriculation Examination of the University of Calcutta.

There was hard work, anxiety, elation, depression and sleeplessness. The examination came and went. I knew I hadn't done well in geography; otherwise I had done the best I could. But my best didn't add up to very much. At the time the results were about to be announced by the examination board, Calcutta newspapers used to publish the names of those 20 or 30 people who had done best in this

University Entrance Examination. The first ten or 15 were awarded the General Scholarship, and then the other ten or 15 received the District Scholarship.

I was waiting for the newspaper, which was delivered every morning. It came, and the list was on the front page. With fear and trepidation, I read the names. My name did not appear in the list for the General Scholarship. That was bad news. I was disappointed. I then read the names in the second list, trying to prepare myself for the worst. My name did appear in the second list. I did get a scholarship, but it was a District Scholarship. I would have accepted this with humility, rejoiced that I would be paid a certain sum of money each month for two academic years in college. Instead, I was afraid that my eldest brother would be thoroughly disappointed. He would probably consider it a disaster. It did not seem fair that I should feel that I had failed my brother. Ananda, my best friend in school, was good at his studies and highly intelligent. His father would have probably been very happy – would have thrown a party – if he had done well enough in his examination to get any kind of scholarship. Yet, I didn't know how I was going to face my Borda. I felt like running away.

Yes, that's what I'll do, I said to myself. I'll run away. I didn't think of the consequences; the practical problems of food and shelter didn't delay my decision. I walked out of the front door, in a *dhoti* and a vest, wearing my *chappals* and I had no money. I started walking towards the bridge across the canal in Kalighat, crossed it, and kept going up Judges Court Road, my eyes moist; the sky beginning to cloud over. I don't know how long I had walked. I came to a park. I was tired. My eyes filled up with tears, but I noticed that the rain had stopped, saw the sunlight on the green grass below my feet and on the green leaves of trees. There were children playing in the park, making a lot of noise. There was noise and laughter. Their sheer enjoyment of life made me feel a lot better. I began to think that what I was doing didn't make sense. Yes, I had tried hard, but others had tried harder. When hundreds of thousands of people are involved, there are bound to be quite a few who are outstanding. It's not my fault. Why should I cower? Why should I apologise? Why should I crouch and repent? I was going to face Borda, I decided, and started walking back home. It was past my lunch time. That made me walk faster.

When I reached home, there was no indication that anybody was particularly worried. Father and my brothers had all gone out. My sisters had finished lunch and gone upstairs. Baudi, was in the kitchen, tidying up. It looked as if my absence had not gone unnoticed, but nobody was particularly worried.

'Where have you been all this time? Your Borda was looking for you,' said Baudi.

'I've been out for a walk,' I said. And, of course, Borda was looking for me, I thought.

'It was a long walk,' Baudi said.

'Yes, it was,' I said.

I didn't reveal that the idea was never to come back home. I didn't tell her that I faltered. I didn't admit that between the idea and its realisation, fell the shadow of hunger. In short, I wanted to go away, but had to come home to eat. It was a bit of an anti-climax.

Baudi sat down and talked to me while I ate lunch. Since the death of Mother, she had played a greater part in my life and in the running of the house. She was in charge. She was the mistress of the house, and she fitted the part admirably. She asked me about my friends, wanted to know which college I was thinking of going to, and expressed anxiety about the quality of the education that her two daughters were getting at the local school.

Not a word was said about my performance in the Matriculation Examination. She wasn't bothered.

After lunch I went to the living room and picked up the newspaper, the harbinger of bad news, and looked at the list of scholars. I was relieved to see that nobody from our rival school, Mitra Institute, had got a General Scholarship, although someone had got a District Scholarship. I knew such things were taken seriously. I looked at some of the other news also; the most dramatic was Germany's invasion of Russia. The fact that Russia had probably the largest army hadn't made a difference to intrepid Hitler, or the fact that not so long ago he had signed a non-aggression pact with Stalin. Most literate Bengalis between the ages of 15 and 25 those days were pro-communist. Quite a few of them had read the Communist Manifesto in English or Bengali, and many had Marx's framed photograph on the wall or desk, prominently displayed.   We thoroughly disapproved of Germany's treacherous attack of Russia and hoped the seven million strong Red Army would destroy the German invaders in a matter of months.

There was also something about the Muslim League demanding the partition of India along religious lines. But for me, the most important news was the list, which

I looked through again and again, before I fell asleep sitting upright in a chair. When I woke up, there were still a few hours of sunshine left in the blazing tropical afternoon, so I walked across to the open space between our building and the next lot of buildings where some of our neighbours' children were noisily playing a game of cricket. When I got there, Arjun came up to me and congratulated me.

'I saw your name in the paper this morning; my father pointed it out to me. You've got a District Scholarship. Congratulations.'

This, at once made a difference to the way I looked at the news. After all, I did win a scholarship! Some had done better than me, but I'd done better than many more. I thanked Arjun most sincerely. He might have been somewhat taken aback by my pleasure and relief.

There was even more surprise in store for me. Borda was waiting for me when I got back. As I walked in through the front door, he came up to me and gave me a hug, an unusual gesture coming from Borda.
'Well done!' he said. 'I'm so glad I made you work hard!' He made it sound like his own achievement! I didn't mind. I was now sure I could relax.

Father did say 'well done' a few times. So did the others. Then it seemed it was all forgotten. But it wasn't. Later in the evening, Borda said in the presence of everybody, 'I've got a present for you!'

I opened the small parcel. A short-sleeved, blue-check shirt! This was beyond belief. What I thought was failure for me that morning was hailed as success by everyone in the family when we all met up for our evening meal. The Bagchis had something to celebrate. The atmosphere was almost festive.

A few days later I went to see my teachers at school to thank them. There was another surprise waiting for me. My History teacher congratulated me because I had secured the highest marks in his subject and had been awarded the Hrishikesh Goswami Scholarship – six rupees a month – and a silver medal.

I thought of Mother and how happy she would have been. There was something she would certainly have insisted on: the ritual killing of a goat to please the goddess Kali, in the temple in Kalighat, to thank her for the success of her son. I disliked the ritual sacrifice of a goat. The head of the goat was severed from its body with one fell stroke of a heavy sword which had a wide, curved blade, and the killing was accompanied by the chanting of sacred verses and the beating of drums.

This frightening and barbaric execution is still carried out, I'm sure, in the temple of the goddess Kali in Kalighat, Kolkata. Did I think it was a barbaric act when I was a little boy or in my early teens? I'm not sure. In retrospect, I'm glad I didn't have to live through that experience.

The next stop was college. Ashutosh College was five minutes' walk from our house. It was not the best college, but in the Humanities Department, the college had some outstanding teachers, and the university examination results were always good. Since the subjects I was going to study were English, Bengali, Sanskrit, Logic and History, there was no reason for me to travel several miles every day to St Xaviers, Presidency or Scottish Church College. There was another, and for me a more important, reason: the college offered me a free place, and when I decided I would stay in the college hostel, I was told that I could stay there if I made over to the college the scholarships I had been awarded, which totalled 16 rupees. I would still need a little pocket money for which I might have to depend on my father and three brothers. That would be all right, I thought, because I was never a big spender.

The college, the college hostel, new friends, a whole host of erudite, articulate and scholarly lecturers and professors – this unfamiliar world – was the most exciting experience for me in the first seventeen years of my life.

I had lived a sheltered life in Faridpur and Comilla, and after arriving in Calcutta, for seven or eight years, it was home to school and back most days. Now I felt I was in contact with a bigger and wider world. Quite a few of those who had come to stay in the college hostel were from other towns and villages of Bengal. Some came from quite an affluent background, but in the hostel I didn't find any consciousness of money or class. So, when I arrived at the hostel, which was situated on College Road, with my very few and modest earthly possessions – books, a few items of clothing and a badminton racket – I didn't feel any different from the others.

I made some good friends. Tarunjit – tall, slender, and sensitive – was intelligent and articulate, but unusually reticent. Kalyan Sen had won a General Scholarship, so all doors were open for him, but he had chosen Ashutosh College. Provat Guha was of average height, wore thick glasses and had a very pale complexion. He was already a dedicated communist, who took life and politics seriously. Then there was Robi Chakraborti, who had a room adjacent to mine in the hostel. He, too, was a General Scholar, which meant he was among the top ten or 15 of those who had passed the Matriculation Examination that year.

I lost touch with Tarunjit, but met up again with Robi, Kalyan and Provat at Calcutta University in 1945, where Robi and I studied English Literature. Provat read History, and Kalyan was a student of Economics. Tarunjit and Provat died in their late fifties or early sixties. I kept in touch with Kalyan until three years ago, when he died at the age of 82. Robi now lives in Kolkata, after spending most of his working years teaching at the University of California.

Some experiences stand out in my memory – experiences which happened during my stay at this hostel. The first experience was one in which I lost face and let my side down. There was a debate between the students of the First Year and the students of the Second Year, and the subject of the debate was the "Quit India Movement", which was mainly the brain-child of Mahatma Gandhi. The question was whether, in the middle of the war against Hitler, it was appropriate to launch our movement by opposing the alliance against Hitler, especially when hundreds of thousands of Indians had voluntarily joined the British Army, and were fighting against its enemies. Our civilisation was at a critical crossroads of history: the road taken or not taken might make all the difference between the preservation and the destruction of our cherished values. So we were debating the proposal, 'In the opinion of this house, the Quit India movement is ill-conceived and dangerous.'

I was going to say that the choice was clear. We should do nothing to deflect our attention and adversely affect the energy and resources which had to be used to overcome the fascists; therefore the "Quit India" movement should be abandoned.
But, after the preamble, and forceful and emotional introductory words, I quite unexpectedly received such loud and spontaneous applause that I lost the thread of my argument. I mumbled a few weak and incoherent statements, apologised, and sat down. The feeling that I had let the side down stayed with me, especially because when it came to the voting and the final decision was thrown to the house, we lost by a big margin.

Another experience I remember had elements of a spy-thriller. Provat came over on a Sunday morning and handed over a parcel to me. I had to give it to a man with a beard when he casually uttered a password as he walked past me. I had to wait near a tree beyond the Alipore Bridge. The Communist Party was still banned, and Provat was a committed member of the Party. I undertook the mission, duly delivered the parcel and got a rare taste of adventure. Though of course, this doesn't mean that life was dull and uneventful otherwise.

I looked forward to meeting the few friends I had made at college. In the hostel common room, I had the benefit of listening to the mature opinions and ideas of the senior students, some of whom impressed me greatly. A recurrent subject for debate and discussion at the time, quite naturally, was the war. We talked about the Blitz – in London, Liverpool, Southampton and Portsmouth. We sympathised, especially with the Londoners, who bore the brunt of the ruthless and indiscriminate bombing, weekly losing thousands of civilians and billions of pounds worth of property. It was clear to us that Britain was not meekly suffering: the RAF planes were shooting down German planes and the anti-aircraft guns were doing the German Luftwaffe further damage. Yes, we agreed, the British were a brave nation, making great sacrifices, and fighting bravely back, resisting German aggression without flinching, and were prepared to face them in their streets and on their beaches. But that was not the point, that was not what the excitement and the debate in the hostel common room was about.

What we could not agree about was whether it was moral to use this crucial, tragic and highly uncertain crisis of the British occupiers, to win back our independence. After all, some said, the British had exploited our country for more than two centuries; taken savage revenge against the freedom-fighters, whom they called "sepoys", in our First War of Independence, which the British called The Sepoy Mutiny. They had massacred innocent civilians in Jalian Wallabagh, and publicly hanged young Bengalis who had romantically and unrealistically been involved in trying to drive the British rulers out of India, by using a few dozen home-made bombs. Why should our hearts bleed for them? This was our opportunity. We should stake our claim and win back our independence. To have any scruples would be absurd and sentimental. Britain had entered this vast country into war without any consultation with the leaders, without so much as a by-your-leave, and when the Indian National Congress had asked for independence, and passed a resolution saying the British should quit India on the 8th of August, the British government had put all the leaders, including Mahatma Gandhi, behind bars, killed a few hundred protesters, and carried out public floggings. These unscrupulous and remorseless people, they said, must quit India.

Those who opposed the idea of India bringing immediate and colossal pressure to bear on the colonial masters were mainly communists and communist sympathisers. They drew attention to the possibility, indeed the certainty, of the destruction of all moral values, all our cherished ideals in the event of Germany and its allies winning the war. By withdrawing our support and depriving the allies of our vast resources, human and material, wouldn't we become an ally of a mindless, ruthless dictator? Did he or did he not break the non-aggression pact with Russia, this Hitler, this mad dictator in Germany? How many Russians had he killed in Leningrad, Stalingrad, Moscow and elsewhere? What would happen if German victory in Europe and

Japanese victory in Asia resulted in the Japanese occupation of India? Our primary concern should be the safety and security of the world, the preservation of moral and human values, and the promotion of human happiness. If, for all these worthy ideals, we were called upon to transcend personal and national interests, we should be prepared to do so.

Those in favour of co-operation were just as passionate and articulate as those in favour of confrontation. I was in favour of co-operation now, and confrontation afterwards, but I wasn't a major player, only part of a small minority. What was important for me was that I shared my ideology with a large group of intelligent and articulate young people, most of them older than me, students of languages and literature, history and philosophy, mathematics, chemistry and physics. I did very strongly condemn the violence of our rulers; at the same time, I believed that if Hirohito, Hitler and Mussolini had control of the world, life wouldn't be worth living. Whether many of the students in the hostel or college agreed or not, was not of overwhelming importance; the opportunity to interact with so many bright young men was. What's more, I made a few good friends.

The war was something that was happening *over there* – in Europe, in Singapore, in Burma. It had apparently no immediate and devastating impact on Calcutta in the way it certainly had on London, Dresden and Stalingrad. Yet, in a different way, it did.

The Great Bengal Famine happened in the middle of World War II – in 1943. According to one estimate, four million people died directly as a result of hunger, starvation, malnutrition, and indirectly as a result of criminal neglect, administrative inefficiency and indifference. Looking back, we can find many explanations for this great human tragedy, but at the time, not only did the British administrators fail – with tragic consequences – but so did the Indian, specially Bengali, politicians and administrators. The war was also partly responsible for the disruption of distribution and the scarcity of supply. Burma was a major supplier of rice and it had passed into the hands of the Japanese. The government had refused to declare Bengal a famine area, despite the stark reality of starvation and death in the villages on an unprecedented scale. A natural disaster – a cyclone – had hit the east coast of Bengal and Orissa, in October 1942, affecting severely the growing of rice in that area. But the most shameful part of this great human tragedy was the apathy and inefficiency of those – both Indian and British – who were in charge of our destiny.

The grim reality of the war was far away. It didn't affect me as badly as did the defenceless death and suffering of fellow Bengalis. About the middle of 1943 the mass migration to Calcutta from the impoverished villages of whole families and communities of emaciated men, women and children started. They patiently waited in long queues for a handout of rice, cooked vegetables and pulses at the food distribution centres in town, which most often could not cope with the needs of those who turned up. I was a volunteer at one of the centres. I don't remember any stampedes at the time of food distribution, nor was there any crying or cursing if the food ran out. Wordlessly they left. Was it dignity or total despair? Most of the refugees died quietly. The spectacle of misery was painfully haunting, that look of utter resignation on the faces of people who had once lived with pride and dignity.

Most historians, economists, sociologists and politicians, of quite different affiliations, accept that the tragedy of the Great Bengal Famine could have been avoided with better planning and greater concern about its possible consequences. Lord Wavell, Viceroy of India, was aware of the deficits in the administration's handling of this human tragedy, but he was more concerned about what the world was going to think about the British rulers.

'The Bengal Famine,' he wrote to Winston Churchill, 'was one of the greatest disasters that has befallen any people under British rule, and the damage to our reputation here both among Indians and foreigners in India, is incalculable.'

As far as I know, messages like Lord Wavell's about starvation and death in Bengal on an unprecedented scale did not make any impression on Churchill. He had more pressing business to attend to. At the time he was actually said to have said something to the effect that the spectre of dying Bengalis didn't give him sleepless nights.

But it was the most traumatic experience of my life. There were thousands of deaths from starvation. The emaciated faces and bodies of men, women and children were the apocalyptic images I had to learn to live with. People came across inert, skeletal bodies lying in the streets. Between three to four million Bengalees died. I was just about nineteen.

In Indian politics, the Famine did not become a big issue – as far as I can remember and on the whole, life went on as before. The question I asked, and couldn't answer, was: "Would a compassionate God see so many people die in such abject misery?'

A few years before this, I had acquired the sacred thread, the mark of a Brahmin, admitting me to the ranks of the Hindu priesthood novitiates if I so wished. A religious ceremony was carried out, attended by the family priest and friends and relations. I was "born again", and to mark my second birth, my head was shaved. From that day onwards, I was supposed to rise with the sun and chant *mantras* or religious verses, facing the divine orb of light. But as a mark of protest I tore off my sacred thread and threw it away. The Famine had made the sacred thread a symbol of divine indifference. Immature and melodramatic perhaps, the over-reaction of an emotional teenager, but it felt good.

This was 1943. Other important events were happening, events which were welcomed by the majority of the world's population. There was some good news in the world as a whole. The tide had begun to turn in the war. The Allied Forces had the upper hand. The German army had surrendered to the Russians in Stalingrad. Penicillin had started saving lives on various battlefronts. People had begun to hope that the end of the war might not be too far away. That was the good news. The depressing news was that the reprisal was vengeful, excessive, and sadistic. Allied bombings ripped the heart out of German industry and killed countless civilians in Berlin, Hamburg, Dusseldorf, Dresden, Munich, and other major cities, raising the question whether restraint and humanity are at all relevant in wars. The idea was to kill, kill, kill and cause maximum destruction, cowardly acts of destruction for revenge. That was certainly the consensus in the common room of our Ashutosh College, where not a day passed without a fairly in-depth discussion about the war, though it didn't affect our daily lives apart from the scarcity of food.

Some of us didn't have to pay for our board and lodging at the hostel, for two reasons: we had won scholarships and our parents could not afford to pay. The college took our scholarships, which amounted to much less than what we cost the college. Why did the college get involved in this unusual arrangement? What was there in it for the college? The Principal, I was told, was a great believer in academic excellence. He wanted to attract the more serious and academically ambitious and capable students to the college because he was certain that their presence would make a difference not only to the attitude of the students to learning but also to the standard of teaching. And if these students managed to live up to the expectations of the Principal, the reputation of the college for academic excellence would spread. The Principal's plan had started with us. We were the first group of scholarship winners. So I don't know how well the scheme worked. What I do know is that the arrangement suited me excellently well. I did not have to worry about food and shelter, and I didn't have to pay college fees.

Though of course, I had other needs – for simple necessities, not luxuries. I needed bus fare; money to buy an occasional book, stationery; and toiletries. I occasionally went with Nirmal to Sangu Valley Restaurant for a cup of tea and an omelette and a piece of toast. He was generous and usually paid. Occasional handouts from Debu-da and my father had kept me going but I wanted to be independent. Then, quite unexpectedly, and for the first time, my father came to see me at the hostel. Someone he had come across in the course of his business deals – an income-tax lawyer – was looking for a teacher for his two teenage daughters. He wanted the teacher to teach them English and Mathematics. They would write the Matriculation Examination in three years' time. Would I be interested? I said yes, yes, yes; took the address and telephone number of the lawyer, and told Father I would ring him in the evening and make an appointment. I also told him why this would make life a lot simpler for me.

I rang Mr Bhattacharya the next day, a Sunday, went and saw him in the evening, and was entrusted with the teaching of Chhobi and Kobi, 13 and 12 years' old. I was a teenager myself, but that didn't make any difference. It was agreed that I would teach five days a week for 15 rupees a month. I might have to help them with other subjects, but the emphasis was going to be on English and Mathematics. I met Chhobi and Kobi, two attractive girls; the older one was in a sari, the younger one in a dress. I said I was looking forward to teaching them, looked through their textbooks, had a cup of tea and left. I wanted to see my father and tell him how it all went, but it would soon be mealtime at the hostel, so I put it off. I would skip a lecture or two the next morning and give Father the good news.

The next day, as I was approaching our house, I could see movements of people and things – which filled me with apprehension. As I came nearer, I saw men in uniform moving furniture from inside the house to the front of the house, piling it all up on the path which led to the front gate. A man was supervising. He had in his hand what must have been the eviction order. We exchanged greetings. He was a pleasant, soft-spoken man, who asked me whether I belonged to the family that lived in the house there. Then, out of sympathy or fellow-feeling for a young man who was looking somewhat bewildered, he offered an explanation for the scene of chaos and confusion in front of us.

'I'm here to execute a court order, an eviction order. I certainly don't enjoy doing it. Sometimes it comes as a surprise. Women and children cry. But it's my job. I'm sorry if I've caused too much disruption.'

I said I understood his feelings. It was not his fault. I moved in the direction of a pile of books just outside the front door. I picked up the one on top. *Little Dorrit* by

Charles Dickens, said the dust jacket, which had a tear in the middle. I'd got it as a prize in class seven. The court-clerk came and stood next to me.

'All the things are still yours. You understand that, don't you? The eviction order only stipulates that you should give us vacant possession of the house.'

Debu-da came out from inside the house. When I asked him where he was, he said he was in one of the bedrooms upstairs. My eldest brother, Jogesh and father, he informed me, had gone to Alipore Court to get a stay order, but the landlord, obviously, had got in first and forestalled them. My three sisters had gone with Mejda or Bhabeshda, to stay with my father's youngest brother, who lived in a small house about half-an-hour's walk from where we lived. In short, our life was temporarily disrupted, turned upside down and nobody knew exactly how we were going to overcome the immediate problem of shelter. There was no solution, no redress for one very serious problem – loss of face. A neighbour came over to commiserate. I wish he hadn't. It was an insensitive intrusion.

Debu-da showed no outward sign of agitation or humiliation. He went round making sure that no damage was done to the articles which were being stacked or scattered outside the door of the house, which was ours only yesterday. He even engaged in friendly conversation with the crown clerk, who was supervising the eviction. Then, finding that I looked as if I was at a loose end, he came up to me.

'Your exams start next week, don't they?' he asked.

'Yes,' I said.

'You mustn't take all this to heart. Our life has always been a bit of an adventure, hasn't it? But we'll survive.' He was trying to be reassuring.

One of the habits that characterize Bengali speech is mixing English words with Bengali vocabulary. Debu-da and the clerk from the law court added to my stock of words: bailiff, eviction, stay order. It all added up to one word for me: humiliation. Boys from neighbouring houses with whom I used to play cricket gaped at our personal possessions heaped on the ground outside our front door as they walked past. One or two of them, quite unfamiliar with a sight like this, stopped and asked what was going on.

Debu-da came to my rescue and said to them that we really didn't want to talk about it. Then he turned to me.

'Don't take it to heart. Father wouldn't pay the rent for our last house either. He went to court and, in the end, lost the case against our uncle. But there was no legal eviction. Somewhere along the line, Father and Borda slipped up this time. The landlord wasn't a bit pleased with us. We didn't pay our rent on time, and then we didn't pay at all. I know this is very humiliating and depressing for all of us, but you mustn't be too upset. Will you promise you'll try to forget this unhappy business and concentrate on doing well in your exams?'

'Yes, I promise,' I said.

It was not for nothing that I had a great deal of love and respect for my brother, Debu-da. He had problems. He was a really outstanding singer and a very good teacher of music. But he didn't always do well because he refused to conform. And our society was relentless when it came to punishing and ostracising rebels. Debu-da refused to give in and suffered. It was not from intellectual conviction or some kind of romantic idealism that he refused to conform. He never made any policy statement nor got involved in polemics. He lived his life the way he wanted, without drawing attention to himself, without aggression, spite or jealousy. My eldest brother, Jogesh, recognised his musical talent, his excellence as a singer and his gift of song-writing and composing, but regretted that he lacked initiative. He said Debu-da was too trusting and modest to be successful in a highly competitive and quite ruthless society. I found him all right just as he was.

The exams came and went.

During our six or seven years in Calcutta we had moved from 49/1C Harish Mukherji Road to 186 Harish Mukherji Road and then to 91B Kalighat Road. This last house was at the end of a narrow lane in a crowded environment, an independent or detached house, with six rooms – three upstairs and three downstairs. Mejda had got married the year before we left our previous house. So Borda had a room, Mejda had a room, Debu-da had a room, the three sisters shared a room and there was a living room. Father had a room upstairs. I shared the room with Father. The house had to be made habitable. It fell short of even our modest expectations.

This house had no electricity, so I had to read and write in the light of old-fashioned hurricane lamps, a means of illumination which we hadn't used since our Faridpur days. The fact that my friends had fancy table lamps with fancy lampshades didn't give me the slightest sense of deprivation. I adapted to the use of hurricane lamps and small oil lamps, without any problems. I soon came to believe that the present arrangement resulted in greater concentration. I bounced back fairly quickly from the humiliation of the eviction and got quite involved in the challenges of the new environment at the college and at home.

I hadn't done outstandingly well in my Intermediate Art exam but well enough, I hoped, to get a place in Presidency College, to which it was the aim of the most ambitious students to go. Provat, one of my friends from Ashutosh College, was going to read History and had found a place in Scottish Church College. Sudangshu was going to try and find a place in St Xavier's College, where one of the Jesuit priests was an outstanding teacher of Physics. We took the tram to St Xavier's College. The idea was that Sudangshu would first go to this college, fill in the necessary forms, have his interview with Father Prefect, tie up his admission and then come with me to Presidency College. While he was having his interview, I sat on a bench at the rear of the room.

'Next,' said Father Prefect and asked me to move up for an interview with him. I went up. He asked me to sit down in one of the two chairs in front of him.

'I'm actually going to Presidency College for admission,' I explained.

Father Scheppers took no notice of what I'd said.

'Did you pass in the first division?' he asked.

'Yes, Father.' Father Prefect made a note of my name.
'What was your position?' I told him.

'What subject are you going to read?' he asked.

'English Literature,' I said.

'Have you heard of Father Bryan?' asked Father Prefect.

'Yes, I have. Most students of English have heard his name.'

'If you apply for a place in our College, Father Bryan will be your teacher. We could also give you a scholarship of six rupees a month. Do you want to come?'

'Yes, Father. Where can I get an application form?'

'Over there,' he said, pointing to the right. 'Next!'

So that was how I became a student of St Xavier's College. Sudhangshu was pleased, so was I. A scholarship was a most attractive proposition. Added to my 15 rupees from private tuition, it would make a difference in a financial situation which was insecure, at times quite precarious. I also liked the look of the place. I faced two problems: a minor one and a major one. The minor problem was sartorial. At South Suburban School, there was no prescribed uniform, but most of us wore shorts and short-sleeve shirts. At college, most of us wore dhotis and shirts or kurtas because the dominant culture there was middle-class Bengali. In St Xavier's College, the dominant culture was Anglo-Indian, so practically everybody wore trousers and shirts, and on special occasions a few jackets and neckties were also in evidence. I had no trousers and money in the Bagchi household was practically always in short supply. Mejda produced two or three pairs of trousers which he had grown out of but which were too long and too wide at the waist. I found a tailor who was ready to do the necessary alterations for a few rupees. After that for a week or so before the term started, I wore them to get used to them.

The other problem was much more difficult to overcome. There were a large number of Anglo-Indian students in this college and English was their mother tongue. The Indian students were mainly from St Xavier's School and La Martinaire. They also spoke English most of the time and a stilted variety of Bengali some of the time. For me English was a major subject which one had to learn. There were many exciting, interesting books in the language which one read for pleasure and information. In my school and at Ashutosh College if any of the Bengali students used English to speak to the other students, they had to put up with sarcastic remarks from outraged students. It was very much a written language for the likes of me. Very few of us were at home with spoken English – its idioms, its easy flow, its subtleties and, chiefly, its pronunciation. The result was that I stuck mainly to the Bengali-speaking students, some of whom were equally at home with English and Bengali. Ronu and Ajoy were fluent speakers of both Bengali and English. Mutu spoke excellent English, but his Bengali didn't measure up to his English in vocabulary, usage or pronunciation. Conversation between us took place primarily in English with occasional lapses into Bengali. My understanding of written English was much better than that of spoken English just as I wrote better than I spoke. I felt lost, excluded and puzzled when there were exchanges of jokes between my English-speaking friends, especially if these had undertones, or were couched in slangy or highly colloquial or idiomatic English, full of suggestive innuendoes. If these jokes were too obviously smutty, I was too embarrassed to laugh, which disappointed and irritated some of the students I got to know in the college. What they didn't appreciate was that my background was middle-class Bengali, and the content of the jokes shocked and surprised me, even if I had no feeling of revulsion or disgust. I still find it difficult to separate our conditioning from our acquired values. There were times when I found the rules, conventions and values according to which I was expected to live, too restrictive, demanding and unrealistic, and I felt liberated when I found myself enjoying bawdy jokes and smutty stories.

One afternoon, during a History lecture, I noticed that an envelope with a dozen or so postcard-size photographs was circulating among the students, who were looking at them surreptitiously but with intense interest. When Ronu had finished looking at the pictures, he passed them on to me. I had a quick look at some of them and I was mesmerised, transfixed. My heartbeat quickened. These were pornographic pictures – shamelessly explicit, deliberately provocative, the simulated acts of erotic love, incredibly realistic.

I didn't want to be caught poring over these pictures and I was afraid that the tell-tale look of concentration and excitement might give me away. I would never be able to live it down, the disgrace and the humiliation, I thought, if the lecturer suddenly stopped, looked at me and said, 'You seem to be engrossed in something much more interesting than my lecture. Do you think I can have a look?' So I quietly slipped out through one of the side doors of the lecture theatre to the lawn outside and stood under a tree and looked at the pictures with quiet intensity and put them in my pocket. I waited until lunch-break and then handed them back to Sunder.

'Did you like them?' he asked.

'Yes, I did. I was fascinated,' I said truthfully.

'I've got some more. Great stuff. I'll bring them along next week,' he said.

Sunder's father was a successful businessman. Sunder came to college in a large, shiny car, driven by a chauffeur. He fulfilled his promise, but the impact was not half as powerful.

The English Honours class had broken up into several groups of five or six students and, as always, there were a few loners. In our group we had Mutu, Ronu, Ajoy, Cuthbert and me. Mutu's father, Colonel De, had served in the army and later become the Principal of Calcutta Medical College. Mutu had started off as a medical student but, for reasons he never revealed to us, had abandoned the idea of a medical career and joined the English Honours course at St Xavier's College. Ajoy's father was a businessman who had something to do with either printing machines or printing presses, or both. Ronu and I had more in common with each other in that we were both more at home with Bengali than any of the others, read Tagore's poetry and were more at home in a *dhoti* than in trousers. Cuthbert's father, Mr Gomes, was into politics. He represented the Anglo-Indian community of Bengal in the Legislative Assembly. Cuthbert could keep his end up in a Bengali conversation on such subjects as women, the weather and popular music with his vocabulary of a few hundred words.

I haven't spoken here of an Anglo-Indian accent because there were many Anglo-Indians who spoke Bengali without the slightest trace of an accent. In other words the way they spoke Bengali was indistinguishable from the way the Bengalis spoke Bengali.

So in some ways my English – spoken English – was more of a problem than Cuthbert's Bengali – because Cuthbert was not likely to be required to comment in Bengali on some points which came up in a seminar on the subject of Literature and Morality *or* Shakespeare's Sonnets. On such occasions, I avoided participating in discussions or made very brief comments when there was no escape because I was directly called upon to say something. My hesitation or my reluctance was noticed by Father Bryan.

One morning he stopped me in the corridor on the first floor to talk to me. He said he had noticed my diffidence. He said he expected greater participation from me because my written work made sense. I explained to Father Bryan that my spoken English was too bookish and greatly flawed by bad pronunciation. He was sympathetic and offered to help.

Over a period of about six months he made me realise that I did not differentiate clearly between short vowels and long vowels; that my short vowels weren't short enough and my long vowels weren't long enough. I tended to use, he said, an intermediate length for both short vowels and long. As for the consonants, there were quite a few which I mispronounced – 'f' and 'v', 'th' as in *thanks* and 'th' as in *there*. My 'v' and 'w' were also suspect. But he said he would work on it and see what he could do to improve my English pronunciation, and he did. I have no doubt at all that Father Bryan did more than anybody else to create in me a real interest in the sounds of English, its large and varied patterns of stress and intonation. He introduced in his teaching words like phonemes and homonyms and explained what they meant, but their significance I understood only later. While he was teaching, I had responded regularly with, 'Yes, Father Bryan' or 'No, Father Bryan' and on one occasion he pointed out that in saying the word *Father* alone, I had made five mistakes. The way I said 'f' was wrong, my 'a' was too short, my 'th' was not a sound that could be found in English phonology, the final vowel sound, the most frequent vowel sound in English speech, I had mispronounced, and, finally, I had pronounced the terminal 'r' which was preceded by a vowel. He would rather I didn't pronounce the 'r'. This was depressing. But my teacher did not let me feel discouraged. He assured me that I was making astonishing progress.

After about six months of occasional lessons and discussions, I had gained enough confidence to open my mouth from time to time in everyday personal conversation as well as literary seminars and college debates. It wasn't a great deal of time that Father Bryan managed to spend with me, but in that little time he gave me insights, and created my lifelong interest in English, especially English speech. Father Bryan was a great teacher, a caring teacher. He profoundly influenced thousands of young men.

My lack of understanding of fast English conversation was the problem I thought I needed to focus on. I had little difficulty with literary English, with the lectures I attended, with the books I read, but fast English conversation, especially with topical jokes, irony and innuendoes was baffling. Watching English films could be a frustrating experience – not the likes of "Tarzan the Ape Man", or "The Thief of Baghdad", where Douglas Fairbanks was the *thief,* but films with a lot of social and personal interaction and rapid speech, casual understatements and throw-away remarks. I was impressed with Noel Coward's slick dialogue – when I understood it. But there was a very special occasion – *Gone with the Wind* with Vivien Leigh as Scarlett O'Hara, Clark Gable as Rhett Butler, Leslie Howard as Ashley Wilkes and Olivia de Havilland as Melanie Wilkes – was coming to Metro Cinema, and Mutu, Ronu, Ajoy, Cuthbert and I were going to see this film, about which we had read and heard quite a lot.

To ensure that I understood enough of the dialogue to enjoy the film, Mutu sat on my left and Cuthbert on my right. I had to turn my head slightly to the left or right, when I didn't understand the dialogue, and either Mutu or Cuthbert would explain in an undertone what was said and what was going on. I was most impressed with the performance of Vivien Leigh as Scarlett O'Hara. On the screen inside my head, her images came back again and again, as well those of the spectacular scenes. It was a great experience for me, this film with its superb acting, its colours and its spectacles. After some time, we got too absorbed in the messages the moving images were communicating to us to worry about the verbal messages. The impact was powerful and the experience memorable.

There was something unequal, arbitrary and disproportionate in our system of education, because there was greater emphasis not only on the English language – the medium of instruction in a large number of schools and the only medium in practically all colleges and universities – but also on Western art, literature and history. The students of St Xavier's College were certainly more at home with the English language and the culture and values it represented than with Bengali, Hindi or Sanskrit and the values and culture enshrined in them. We knew how Henry VIII broke away from the Catholic Church and how the Church of England was born. We also had at least some elementary knowledge about the major differences between the Catholic and the Protestant faiths. But very few of us knew about even the fundamental differences between the Hinayana and the Mahayana forms of Buddhism. I didn't know a great deal about the historical background of the *Mahabharata* or about its legendary author, Vyasa, but I had read a Bengali version of the great epic and I had certainly come across the name of its author many times. I'm fairly certain that neither Mulu nor Cuthbert would hesitate for a second if they were asked who wrote the *Odyssey* and the *Iliad,* but I'm not so sure that they would remember the name of Vyasa, the author of the *Mahabharata*, although this epic, written by Vyasa, is eight times as long as the *Odyssey* and the *Illiad* put together.

Our teacher of Bengali was particularly critical of our cultural leaning towards the West. He gave us simple questions on the history and culture of India and he looked positively triumphant if we failed to answer any because here was proof positive that our obsessive interest in Western art, literature, history, religions, philosophy and politics was directly responsible for our ignorance of everything Indian. 'Name three main Hindu gods,' he would say. 'What are the main Upanishads?' 'Which Hindu god resembles Zeus?' 'What is Dharma, Varna, Ashrama?' When did Ashoka reign?' 'When was the Taj Mahal built?' This was a diversion and a challenge. We quite enjoyed answering these questions.

In course of time we became quite good at it. This did not, however, disprove his contention that many of us, who had been born in Bengal and had grown up there, knew a lot more English than Bengali, and had read Shakespeare, Shaw, Hardy, Dickens and Jane Austen, but couldn't even name half a dozen Bengali novels by Bankimchandra, Saratchandra, or Tagore.

All in all, the experience of college-life was positive and enjoyable, and I wasn't looking forward to the day when I would have to leave. The time for university examinations were approaching and with it the anxiety which always besets the minds of students, for they have to prove that they hadn't spent their time in college or university in self-indulgent dalliance, but had made good use of their time, and the money their parents had spent on them. I had some uncertainty about how well or badly I was going to fare, but I suffered from no chronic or debilitating anxiety. During the day there were lectures and seminars. In the evening I gave private lessons to earn a little money for my bus fare and the odd cup of tea in a restaurant, so it wasn't a lot of time that I had for preparation. I didn't allow myself to engage in frenetic study, staying up till midnight and beyond. There were some modern poets whose messages I couldn't decode. So, from time to time, I did seek Mutu's help, inviting myself to lunch at his Loudon Street flat. It was business mixed with pleasure, for Mutu's mother was an excellent cook.

The modern poets' very individual way of looking at life, their very personal and original imagery and their introspective use of language often led to obscurity, and I found two minds better than one for grappling with these poems. Mutu was much more confident in his interpretation and perfectly credible. I couldn't have done without his help in getting an insight into some of the poems. The very important BA examination was round the corner but, except for a little help from Mutu, I was totally on my own, since neither my father nor any of my brothers had the slightest interest in anything academic. My sisters were all literate, but they hadn't spent any time at all in a school or college. There were practically no English books in the house and certainly no reference books except an English-Bengali dictionary. So when I sat down and started my preparation, after teaching Chhobi and Kobi earlier in the evening and having had my supper, I often felt rather lonely – apart from being quite tired.

I had to go from Kalighat Road to College Street by bus, for the examination was going to be held at the main hall of the Calcutta University. Examinations are a unique institution. Years of reading, writing, thinking, listening, and learning by various other ways are assessed by experts, by learned people and specialists – and, no doubt, by some imposters – on the basis of fairly predictable questions to which we produced fairly predictable answers. For both information and ideas, most of us depended on standard textbooks. When we answered questions on the history of English literature, it was natural and unavoidable that we should look up the facts and use them in our answers. But we tended to do the same when we were asked to do a critical assessment of a character or a piece of writing: we turned to critics who told us what to think and we passed off someone else's ideas as ours. We knew very little about the tools of assessment, so most of us never learnt to use them. What we wrote down in our answer papers was largely derived from standard sources. In other words what I thought of *King Lear* or *Hamlet,* the plays and their heroes, wasn't what *I* thought, but what Bradley or Wilson Knight told me to think. It was unsatisfactory, but that is how it was, by and large. This, I think, was the general picture and, probably, still is – except that there are always some odd characters, eccentrics, geniuses, makers of history who don't fit the general description. There were some outstanding students, I'm sure, who thought for themselves and used their own criteria and judgement in their essays. I wasn't one of them.

When the results came out, there were no surprises. None of us had got a first. In our group, only Mutu had done better than me. I got a second-class honours, nothing brilliant, but nothing too depressing. The good news was that my eldest brother had stopped taking the kind of interest he did before – when I was at school. He knew I wouldn't get a first, and if I didn't, he wasn't interested. My own attitude to academic excellence and achievement had also changed. I was more relaxed and, therefore, enjoyed my life at college and the society of friends much more than I had done at school.

World War II had already started before I left school, yet it made very little impact on me. Though both in the hostel and at college, we regularly discussed the war, and the successes and failures of the Allied forces made a difference to us in a way they never did while I was at school. My last years at school and my six years at university were some of the most disastrous years in the history of mankind. First, there was the Second World War 1939-45, in which more than sixty million people died and the damage to the property and infra-structure of some of the great and historical cities of the world were incalculable. Each of the other disasters, all connected with the war, was uniquely horrific. I have already talked about the great, man-made famine of Bengal in which, all agree, almost four million people, mostly villagers, died in 1943-44. One curious aspect of this great tragedy is that very few people in Britain, let alone Europe, know anything about it although it is comparable to the great human tragedy of the Holocaust. It is in books and films that I have seen the emaciated bodies of the victims of the Holocaust. But the skeletal bodies of the victims of the Great Bengal Famine, queuing up for a handout of gruel, I had seen before me in the flesh. There were dead bodies of villagers, victims of the famine, in the streets of Calcutta. Both were of the stuff of nightmares, the Famine and the Holocaust.

When I was a student at university, I didn't know a great deal about the Holocaust, the extermination of six million Jews in Germany, and another estimated ten million people of various descriptions and nationalities – Ukrainians and Poles, Russian civilians, Romanies, socialists and homosexuals. This was planned mass-murder – cruel, sadistic, bizarre and mindless – carried out mechanically and systematically over a period of more than ten years. We hadn't even heard of Belsen, Buchenwald or Dachau. "Concentration camps" hadn't entered our vocabulary. While Jews and Gypsies were being gassed and murdered in Germany and more Jews were being slaughtered in Warsaw ghettos, we were celebrating Monty's triumph at El Alamein and the Germans' humiliating defeat near Stalingrad. The Holocaust came into focus much later in my life.

The most imaginative writer of horror stories couldn't have invented anything more gruesome than the planned destruction of men, women and children in the various concentration camps in Germany and Poland.

Another act of mass destruction, carried out with ruthless precision, after years of research and planning, and quite unique in human history, was the bombing of Hiroshima. It was unique because it was no ordinary bomb but an atomic bomb and it was detonated <u>above</u> Hiroshima. It was dropped from Enola Gay in the early hours of August 6, 1945, another day in our history when science and technology triumphed, humanity failed. There were various reactions – relief that the war wouldn't drag on, disbelief that such a powerful bomb could be used in a city so thickly populated, with the certainty that countless innocent people would die in an instant and others die slow, painful deaths after suffering for a long time. Hardly two weeks had passed, and the death toll was 92,000 and rising. After the immediate reaction of stunned disbelief, people started discussing the morality of the bomb. I didn't think there could be anybody who was prepared to offer any kind of rationalisation or justification for this, the most powerful single act of mass destruction in World War II. But there were people who were, within a week or so, justifying the dropping of the bomb as an act of desperation. Japan hadn't surrendered. The only way to make them bend, and if necessary break, they said, was extreme and unprecedented measures like the bomb. Just three days after the bombing of Hiroshima, on the 9th of August, another atom bomb was dropped – on Nagasaki. This time 40,000 people were killed in a matter of minutes. The second bomb was dropped – because it was there.

More than any other act of violence or atrocity that we discussed among ourselves; Hiroshima and Nagasaki caused heated arguments and bad-tempers and frayed nerves, because, quite unexpectedly, a group had emerged to defend the bomb.

Cuthbert, to our astonishment, held the view that the atomic explosions had saved lives because, had the war dragged on for longer, more lives might have been lost – our lives.

In the event, Japan surrendered or decided to surrender on the 10th of August 1945. That was the day the Second World War really ended. Or did it? In what sense does a war that kills more than 60 million people, and destroys what our civilisation has taken a few millennia to build and create, really end?

In comparison with the direct and palpable destruction which happened to so many of the world's great cities, what happened to Calcutta was negligible. But there was an unmistakable economic downturn which affected people in Calcutta, especially lower-middle class people like us. My father and my eldest brother, Jogesh, were again spending quite a lot of time together, discussing a case which was coming up in Alipore court. Did this case have anything to do with the non-payment of rent? Yes, it did. Was it the rent for the house at 91B Kalighat Road? Yes, it was. How is it that in spite of two earlier evictions, it was allowed to happen again? It was because the protagonists – my father and my eldest brother – had no regular source of income. Father had a very small pension which could buy bread, but not both bread *and c*heese. As for Jogesh, my eldest brother, he seemed to work hard, but it wasn't clear to what purpose. So, once again, there were long conferences. The vocabulary of those conferences was familiar – eviction, bailiffs, court fees, stay order, appeal, etc. The spectre of homelessness began to haunt me again.

Where would we go this time? Would these faceless people from Alipore Judges Court – the bailiff and his assistants in khaki coats – pull out the furniture, clothes, books crockery, cutlery and pictures from the walls, shoes from the shoe racks, the gramophone and the gramophone records, and pile them up in front of the entrance and make us leave our house yet again? Would the passers-by look at the officials going about their business of evicting us with derision and amusement, or concern and compassion? Did I want to go through that humiliating experience yet again?

It was at about four in the afternoon that I returned from work – I'd got myself a job in one of the American army supply centres after the BA examination. Debu-da was waiting in the living room of the Kalighat house, sitting in an old, rickety chair. There was no other furniture in the room; the pictures had disappeared from the walls. He greeted me with a smile and explained.

Borda (Jogesh) had found out that the eviction order had been passed and in a day or two would be executed. So Father and he had decided on a plan of pre-emptive action. It was all very sudden. There was very little time for planning. Father and our three sisters moved in with Debu-da's mother-in-law who was a widow. She had a small house in Shambazar. Debu-da, his wife, Father and the three sisters went to live in a house which could accommodate only four people with difficulty. Borda, his wife and four daughters moved in with Borda's brother-in-law in Manicktolla, also in the north of Calcutta. I was to move in with Bhabesh, my Mejda, who lived in Shambazar, also in North Calcutta.

Mejda lived in Star Lane, behind Star Theatre, which was made famous at one time by the great Bengali actor, Sisir Bhaduri. Mejda lived in a fairly large room with his wife and three children, two daughters and a son, all teenagers. When I moved in, there were six of us. I don't remember how we all managed to sleep in one room. There was another family, with whom we shared a common courtyard. There were five of them too. We had a separate kitchen but for all of us – eleven in all – there was a common bathroom and two toilets. It seems incredible that we survived in the circumstances, but we did, without any tension, without falling out, without getting in each other's way. Baudi (sister-in-law) was a great cook. I got on well with her – not because she was such a good cook, but because she was a friendly and generous person, unassuming, caring and efficient.

One of the great advantages of living with Mejda was that the university was a ten minutes' bus-ride from Star Lane. But one of the problems was that both my students, Chhobi and Kobi, lived in Southern Avenue, which took almost an hour to reach. So the time and energy and bus fare – which I spent to earn 20 rupees – was disproportionate. I could not really go on teaching Chhobi and Kobi. It was a decision I would have to make fairly soon.

In the end, I did nothing. The money I received from Chhobi and Kobi's father, however little, was useful. There were the university tuition fees and the bus fare to the university and to South Calcutta. A helpful friend found me two students – a girl who went to Loreto College and a boy of 12 or 13 who went to St Xavier's School. This time I undertook to teach Bengali. Whereas I thoroughly enjoyed teaching Nomita, who went to Loreto College, my teaching of the teenager was very frustrating, and I wasn't sure I was making a great deal of progress. But I couldn't afford to give up any of the tuitions because it was extremely important, quite crucial as a matter of fact, that I should earn enough to pay for my needs. For, who was I going to turn to?

I had saved some money from a job I had done after my BA examination and before the Masters degree course had started. The American army was in Calcutta and they had army stores. I managed to get a job in one of them that sold K-ration and uniforms to officers.   I was the cashier.   Their recruiting officer sent me to Lieutenant Golden, who asked me a few questions, rang up the Principal of St Xavier's College, and in the course of an afternoon, I had got a job. They paid well in comparison with other employers. I managed to save a little from this job, out of which I was able to pay my admission-fee and buy a few books. What's more, a little money was left over.

I could present this financial tightrope walking, this travelling by bus from North Calcutta to Southern Avenue to teach four students of different levels of ability and aptitude; the sharing of a small room with two other adults and three children; and eating an inexpensive meal at about ten at night in a small Punjabi vegetarian eating-place as real hardship.   But I had no feeling of deprivation and no resentment. There were problems and there were challenges, but none so large and overwhelming that I couldn't deal with it. Sometimes unexpected help came my way, which I gratefully accepted.

I'd got to know Lalit while I was still at St Xavier's College, an intelligent, handsome and helpful young man, just a couple of years older than me. I met him again in College Street Coffee House, which was the favourite haunt of not only the students of Calcutta University and local colleges, but also of ex-students and the general public. During our conversation over a cup of coffee, I said to him that I could do with a room of my own. He said he might be able to help and he did. One Mr Roy, a wealthy businessman, had a spare room in one of his houses in Bhim Ghosh Lane. I could have it if I agreed to help one of his nieces with her English. I moved in. The arrangement worked beautifully. If anything, it worked too well. My pupil was an attractive and intelligent young woman in her first year in college. Quite early in the morning, often before the break of dawn, she would go out for a walk, usually with a friend from college, a girl of about the same age.   Then one morning there was a knock on my door before I was out of bed, and who should be outside the door but Bina, all ready and waiting to go out for an early morning constitutional with me. 'Come in,' I said. I explained to her that it wouldn't do for me to be seen going out alone with her, which she accepted. I do not know whether she was unrealistic, adventurous or unthinking. She certainly had a lot of affection for me. She made it quite clear that she was attracted to me, after which there was a little petting from time to time, when we felt completely safe from prying eyes, but not much more.

I had a close and affectionate relationship with Chhobi and Kobi as well, especially Chhobi, but that too was circumscribed by considerations of propriety and lack of opportunity.   Before this, while I was at the Kalighat Road house, there was

Jamuna, the neighbour's daughter, who had once come to our house, having slipped out through their back door. We had kissed and cuddled until we heard footsteps – my father's footsteps – in the corridor. I was in my twenties, yet my physical and emotional relationships with young women were brief, perfunctory and frustrating. When there are gaps in real life, fantasy fills the void. I read avidly, getting vicarious pleasure and excitement from the lives and loves of fictional characters. Among my friends, Ronu was most successful in his relationships with women, but he too was not too excited or fulfilled by the relationships. Women had come into his life and gone, but no one had left a lasting memory of brightness and sweetness.

Our cultural background made a difference, and because of that, our experiences with women were by no means similar. Ronu belonged to the Brahmo Samaj, whose roots were firmly in the Upanishads but which had dispensed with the traditional gods and goddesses worshipped by Hindus along with their rituals.

The influence of Western culture and Christian religious practice was much more prominent in the Brahmo religious faith than in Hinduism. The Hindus worshipped innumerable gods and goddesses – who differed widely in shape, form and colour, whereas the Brahmo god had no shape or colour. The Hindus indulged in various complex rituals the significance of which was obscure. Their language of worship, the language of all the slokas and mantras, was Sanskrit. Very few people understood the language. On many occasions, as I watched Hindu priests performing their rituals and reciting Sanskrit, it was quite clear to me that they were mouthing some kind of obscure gobble-de-gook which carried no comprehensible messages. The preachers of the Brahmo faith used Bengali or English or some other language, depending on the participants, something people understood.

Then there was the relationship between men and women in Brahmo society and Hindu society. Brahmo society encouraged the association of men and women as a result of which young people were able to choose their own partners. In Hindu society, certainly in the society in which I was growing up, it was the parents who chose their children's partners and arranged their marriages. When a young man met a young woman, decided they liked one another and affection and love led to marriage, it was called a love-marriage; when parents or guardians selected partners and they married, it was referred to as an arranged marriage. The Brahmos and the Westernised sections in our society had opted for love-marriages; the traditional Brahmins and Hindus generally who believed in the caste system, preferred arranged marriages. Their parents mostly believed in traditional values and the children believed in modern and democratic ways of living and thinking. So there was a regular source of conflict between one generation and another, conflict which has been regularly exploited in fiction and films, especially in popular Hindi films.

Ronu was Brahmo and came from a family which had acquired Western values. I listened to the stories relating to his amorous adventures with so much interest that he loved telling them. In my retrospective assessment of some of his narratives, I have found certain inconsistencies, wondered about their credibility, but at the time, I found them riveting. What I'm fairly certain about is that he couldn't have invented it all. There was some embellishment. There were probably some flights of fancy, but it didn't really matter. Some of Ronu's romantic heroines were larger than life; some of his experiences were of the stuff that dreams are made of. Yet, I never felt I had to try hard to believe him. I liked his company and enjoyed his stories. I enjoyed his stories probably because I liked him. It doesn't really matter.

While I was settling down in my new environment, Father, my eldest brother, my three sisters, my sister-in-law and three nieces were settling down in Benaras. They had managed to rent a house in the holy city, where the antecedents of my brother and my father as non-paying tenants would not be easy to trace. Both men were impressively tall and good looking. They both had an air of authority and the easy confidence of men who led rather than being led. Father's hair was beginning to grey. He had an impressive moustache which he trimmed at the edges. He wore traditional clothes and, on high days and holidays, wrapped a shawl round his shoulders. He used a heavy walking stick with a silver top, not because he had to lean on it or depend on it in any way but because it made him feel good. Borda, my eldest brother, was clean-shaven, had black hair – adequate but not abundant – quite a light complexion for a Bengali, big brown eyes and an aquiline nose. He was equally well at home in a dhoti and punjabi and in Western clothes. They were an impressive duo. A landlord had to have a third eye or a sixth sense to be able to conclude that they wouldn't pay rent after some time and he would have to go to court to throw them out.

My sister-in-law, hard-working and self-effacing, fitted into our disorganised and insecure set-up in Shyambazar in Calcutta without showing any anxiety, and coped with the day-to-day existential problems with equanimity and resourcefulness. Whether she expressed her anger and frustration late at night, when she was alone with her husband and the children were asleep, I cannot tell. But I never saw Baudi having an unseemly row with her husband. Nor did I see her being unduly restrictive with her daughters, of whom she had four. Hashi, the eldest, died when she was 15. She had tuberculosis, which was incurable in those days. Both Baudi and Borda, my sister-in-law and my eldest brother, did their best by her, gave her all their care and attention and all their love. The family was capable of great solidarity, love and sacrifice. My other nieces were affectionate and helpful about the house. What I regretted was that their education was totally neglected, although they were all literate in Bengali and could do elementary arithmetic. I supposed they would do the housework, read a few Bengali novels, go to the cinema occasionally and do a bit of shopping and socializing until they got married. And I didn't suppose the pattern of their lives would change very much after they got married either. There would be the additional responsibility of childbearing and childrearing after that. However, I saw no great sign of frustration in their lives, though they did dull and repetitive domestic chores which demanded little skill. Only my sister-in-law and my sister, who was two years older than me, had to do most of the housework all week, month, and year. They seemed to enjoy each other's company; they laughed and joked, had a sense of companionship. Sometimes my sister-in-law would go out with my eldest brother, Jogesh, but more often she would go out with my eldest sister for a bit of shopping or to watch a Bengali film. I hoped that life hadn't changed very much, that Boudi was still cooking her delicious curries; Father was writing his love-songs about the holy love-affair of Radha and Krishna; Hena was keeping the house tidy with meticulous care and devouring Bengali novels, and Radha, the younger sister, managing to find something to do, although I didn't know exactly what. On the whole I believed the new beginning in Benaras was working. And I desperately hoped Borda and Father were paying the rent.

Looking back, Father and Jogesh, my eldest brother, between them, had always managed to keep the family fed and clothed and sheltered, but they had always found it difficult to pay the rent. I have already described those traumatic evictions in Calcutta. My father married my mother after the death of his first wife. Borda – Jogesh – was from Father's first marriage. My mother bore my father eight children – five daughters and three sons – of whom two daughters died in their late teens, leaving six of us, three brothers and three sisters. We had all lived together in Calcutta, but now the family had split. Father, Borda and Baudi and their three children, and my three sisters lived in Benaras and Mejda, Baudi, their three children, Debu-da, his wife and I lived in Calcutta. Debu-da and his wife lived in Shambazar, where Debu-da's mother-in-law had a small house. Mejda – Bhabesh – had no steady job but he managed to feed himself, his wife and three children, though their shelter was rather small: a single room on the ground floor, a kitchen, and a bathroom, which they shared with the landlord and his family. It's here that I had found shelter when we were evicted from our Kalighat Road house. Mejda and Baudi treated me well while I was there. They were generous and affectionate, hard-working and organised. They were also very disciplined: they *had* to be, living in those difficult circumstances and that limited space, as they did.

Debu-da, the third eldest brother, was the one I really felt close to, because we did things together from our days in Faridpur – the fishing, the kite-flying and the plucking of mangoes from trees in other people's gardens. Debu-da sang beautifully. He was naturally gifted with a golden voice, which was greatly admired not only by his friends but also by total strangers who heard him sing. The greatest admirers were his young women students.

I don't remember exactly how many months had passed between Father's departure from Calcutta for Benaras, and my receiving an urgent telegram from him – to say that no matter what I was doing at the time, I should take the next train to Benaras because urgent business awaited me over there. My summer holidays had just started but I had other plans for this long break, plans not for pleasure but work. A few extra tuitions during the holidays would bring in much-needed cash, books I needed to buy and a few essential items of clothing. But telegrams had a psychological impact. They were also quite expensive compared to a postcard, so people didn't normally resort to them. In short, telegrams were for really urgent messages. So when the telegram arrived my neighbour's wife, Mrs Guha, registered the fact and enquired whether all was well. I said it was, although I myself had asked that question many times already. Although there was no suggestion of death or disaster in the wording of the message, the word "immediately" was suspect. What's all the hurry about? Well, I would have to wait and see.

There was a close association for me, and I think for many others, between telegrams and occasions for celebration and mourning; births, marriages, deaths. Nobody was born in Benaras, nobody was getting married, and nobody was dead. Then why was this telegram sent to me? I was intrigued, curious, and apprehensive. But, at the same time, I was excited at the prospect of seeing my sisters again, and Borda, Baudi and my Father. Besides that, I was interested in visiting the great and historic city of Varanasi or Benaras, an ancient city on the left bank of the holy river, Ganges. I'd heard of the famous temples and ghats with their long flights of wide stone steps – and seen many pictures of them. I knew that Sarnath, where Buddha had preached his first sermon, was just ten or so kilometres from the city of Benaras. In Benaras, there was the Benaras Hindu University, a great and ancient seat of learning.

More than anything else, I was looking forward to the experience of going down the endless steps of one of the ghats, and bathing in the sacred river, not because I took the sacredness of the river or its purifying function seriously, but because I thought it would be a memorable experience. One of my friends at the university recommended going out in a boat on the river and viewing the great spectacle of Dasaswamedh Ghat, from a distance, of the hundreds of bathers in the river, and of people on the steps of the ghat; of pilgrims and holy men; of pedlars, beggars and sightseers. Mejda's wife, Mejobaudi, when she heard of the telegram and my plan to go to Benaras, said, 'Please buy me a Benarasi sari or two'. That was a joke, of course. Benaras was famous for its silk saris, *Benarasis,* but there was no way I could afford to buy one. A Bengali bride looked forward to wearing a Benarasi silk sari on her wedding night. It was often a dream unfulfilled.

The main attraction in Benaras was my two sisters – Hena, who was two years older, and Radha, who was almost ten years younger. We belonged to a world of our own, which would be largely incomprehensible to the others. When we were evicted from our last two rented houses in Calcutta, we stuck together, feeling equally frustrated, equally humiliated, wanting to cry but unable to do so because strangers in khaki uniform were milling around the place, removing things. Mother wouldn't have let them touch the pictures of the gods and goddesses in the prayer room, so I'd put them in a suitcase which I carried around with me. Father and Borda must have felt profoundly humiliated and undermined because they couldn't stop the eviction orders. Anyway, because of shared misfortune, I felt very close to my sisters. Apart from that, they were caring, loving sisters.

Then there was the fact that my sisters, like most women in our kind of families with a low income, probably had pretty low self-esteem and very little to look forward to except a life of cooking and bringing up children. None of my sisters went to school, but they weren't illiterate. Their knowledge of Bengali was above average. They could read the Bengali versions or translations of the epics *The Ramayana* and *The Mahabharata.* All three of us loved reading the Bengali translation of *Les Miserables.* Phuldi and I quite regularly read Bengali novels, both the classical and the contemporary ones. Very few women were literate in India at the time and there was little opportunity for higher education for them. My sisters hadn't done too badly. For me, what was important was that my sisters were sensitive, affectionate people, and I felt good that I was soon going to see them. I arrived in Benaras almost a week after I'd received my eldest brother's telegram. I had to borrow money from a friend, for the money I had was not sufficient for train fare and other likely expenses. Travelling by train, so long as I had a reserved seat, was pleasant and interesting. And I always found it rather exciting – the sights and sounds – the porters in their red shirts, the masses of people milling around on the platform, the guard with his red flag and whistle, the vendors of tea, shouting – *Chai, garam chai!*

When I arrived at the house I was looking for, a two-storey house tucked away at the end of a quiet street in a suburb of the city, neither my father or my elder brother was at home. Baudi, my sister-in-law, and my two sisters were pleased to see me. They asked me about the journey, about my two brothers in Calcutta and their families. Elder sister, Phuldi, asked me how I was enjoying being at Calcutta University and whether I'd met any nice girls. I said I really liked most of my teachers – there were some outstanding ones like Amiya Chakraborty – but I hadn't met the love of my life – not yet.

'Good,' said Baudi.

'Why good? Don't you want me to meet anybody I like?' I asked.

'Not in the present circumstances,' she said.

'What circumstances?' I asked.

'My husband and your father have decided that it's time for you to get married, and they've chosen the girl you're going to marry. I haven't seen her yet but I've seen her photograph. She has a pleasant and intelligent face and a much lighter complexion than yours.' Baudi thought all this was great and exciting news for me. I think that in the uneventful lives of Baudi and our sisters, weddings were exciting events, more so for them than for the men.

So that's what all this was about! This was sudden, almost dramatic enlightenment. When I got the telegram, I was worried that Father might be ill, because telegrams in my life had usually been harbingers of bad news.

'But, Baudi, I'm just beginning my sixth year. There's a whole year to go before I finish university.

'What's the use of telling me that? Marriages in our society are arranged by parents. When your brother and I got married, what do you think happened? I saw a photograph of your brother and he saw mine. Then we saw each other on our wedding day. As it happens, we've loved each other, cared for each other. But it could have been disastrous. Do you know how many women in Bengal alone put an end to their lives within the first two years of their married life?'

'No, I don't,' I said. 'But that's mainly on account of disputes over dowry, isn't it?'

'Not entirely. When there's a marriage and no bonding, tragedies happen.'

'So why should I and this young woman…'

Baudi interrupted. 'Debika,' she said. Her name's Debika.'

'Why should Debika be thrust upon me and I upon Debika? She might find life intolerable with me. She may be in love with some very sensitive, intelligent young man.'

The arguments for and against arranged marriages were robust. I needed a rest in any case, so I excused myself, went to the room allocated to me and tried to sleep. But the conversation I'd just had with my sister-in-law wasn't exactly sleep-inducing. Of the four brothers and three sisters, I was the only one with a university degree, and there was one more year to go before I finished my MA. Why couldn't this wait for another year? The whole course of my life might change after this marriage. I was managing reasonably well, living in my rent-free accommodation provided by a friend's friend and earning a less than modest income from a few underpaid private tuitions. But I was getting by.

That evening I spent a little time with my father and Borda, neither of whom gave me the slightest indication of why I was here instead of in Calcutta. I slept, woke up the next morning, and spent the day mainly in the company of my sisters and my sister-in-law. The lunch was divine, representative of traditional Bengali cooking: my sister-in-law was a great cook. Then in the late afternoon, when Baudi had just made some tea, quite unexpectedly, Debu-da came in through the front door, which wasn't locked, except at night.

We were all excited, and when Bengalis are excited, they tend to talk – often all at the same time – loudly and noisily. We all wanted to know the same thing, of course. To what did we owe the pleasure…? And he explained. He always enjoyed coming to Benaras. His wife was going to spend some time with her mother and her sister was going to a wedding of one of their cousins. Their cousin's family could afford an expensive wedding party, so all their friends and relations were invited. Debu-da's mother-in-law, his wife and sister-in-law were going to stay with the family for a few days. Debu-da's wife and the bride were good friends, Debu-da was invited, but he hadn't felt like being involved in the jamboree. Also, he'd really come because he wanted to spend time with us.

Debu-da also had problems with Father. He had married for love, depriving Father of the dowry and, for a time, there was estrangement between them. Yet he dutifully saw Father, visiting Benaras as often as he could afford to. It was most opportune for me that Debu-da was here. I wanted to talk to him about my impending interview with Father. When I told him I wasn't looking forward to it, he said it was a conflict between the ideas of two generations, one much older than the other. Father's generation did what was good and acceptable for the family and the community, we do things *we* want to do, and which don't conflict with our ideology.

'I don't want to give you any brotherly advice. It's obvious that what happens when you see Father tonight isn't going to make a lot of difference to you. But I want you to decide what you're going to say, what you're going to do.'

Then he suggested that we went out to explore the city, which was exciting, not because it was holy but because it was human and colourful with a lot of history. Two religions flourished in and around here, the essence of which was humanity – Hinduism and Buddhism.

'More than anything else I like the ghats with their wide, never-ending steps from near the city streets right to the edge of the river,' he said.

So to the ghats we went, through crowded streets, some wide and some narrow, and wherever we went there were people, masses of them, going about their business, often noisily, but rarely getting in each other's way. We stopped at a roadside eating place to enjoy some really hot, spicy food and drink cups of sweet, milky tea.

The ghats are really spectacular. It was late afternoon but people were still bathing. The steps leading to the edge of the river were nearly empty, those hundreds of steps which, according to Debu-da, were usually full of people – bare-bodied men, coming out of the water or going into it, and sari-clad women, pilgrims and priests, beggars and sadhus, devout wives and prostitutes, the rich and the poor. If you bathed in the water of the Ganges, all your sins were washed away. The ghat in front of us was Dasaswamedh Ghat, a popular one. If I were a film-maker, I thought, I'd make a film of this ghat. Debu-da and I sat on the steps of the ghat and

I resolved to revisit it in the morning when most people came to bathe in the sacred river.

We visited a temple where the priest was chanting *slokas,* ringing a bell and offering the deity fruit and flowers, while people standing around were praying, hands joined together, eyes shut. It's amazing how in the minds of these devout people, and also in the minds of a few billion others, some kind of god exists. The colossal injustice all around them and the spectacles of dire poverty, deprivation, humiliation and death, of which they themselves are often the victims, do very little to shake their faith! It had all the air of a millennium ago.

Then we wandered around the city without a sense of direction or a fixed destination.

'This is the way to absorb the spirit of a city like Benaras – to wander around without a shopping list of famous monuments and landmarks, without a diary, map or camera. This way you don't fail to hear the heartbeat of a city,' Debu-da said. He was a chronic romantic. Debu-da was also absent-minded and unpractical. Exploitable. Vulnerable. And although I was a lot younger, I felt quite protective.

'To absorb the spirit of a sprawling city with so many historical and religious landmarks, you certainly need a little more than a week, don't you?' I asked.

'Time helps. But an open, receptive mind is more important. There's abundance here, human and divine.' Debu-da often waxed quietly philosophical in my company.

We returned home at dusk, walking through crowded streets, lazily watching people, cars, crowded buses, *thelas*, cows. Phuldi greeted us from the kitchen and said, 'Just in time for a nice cup of tea.' We sat down on stools outside the kitchen to have tea, while my elder sister got on with the cooking. Radha, our younger sister, came along and asked us many questions about what we'd done and seen. Then Baudi came and two of her three daughters, and soon everybody was talking and nobody was listening.

I knew there was something on everybody's mind which nobody was talking about – the likely outcome of my meeting with my father later in the evening. It had disappeared from our conversation because both my sister and sister-in-law had noticed my reluctance to discuss the subject and my lack of enthusiasm. I appreciated their restraint. Debu-da and I went to our room. Debu-da commented on my reticence – with understanding. Then he went to the bathroom to have his "bucket bath", which consisted of pouring mugs of water out of a bucket over your head, sitting on a wooden stool, soaping your body, and then washing away the soap by pouring more mugs of water over your head.

I went in after Debu-da. This was the first time in a long time that I had been on my own and I couldn't help feeling oppressed at the thought of the impending confrontation. I couldn't, and I wouldn't, get married now. I had both love and respect for my father, but that didn't mean he could expect me to surrender my values. I was getting ready to meet my father later on, but not with the happy tremble of anticipation.

It was now meal-time for the adults at the Bagchi household – the children had eaten. It was fish curry and rice for supper – my favourite food in those days. Much later in life I converted to vegetarianism. Halfway through the meal Boudi, who believed in arranged marriages and knew I opposed the idea, could not restrain herself any more. And, I suppose, she didn't see why she should: she was old enough to be my mother!

'Would you say,' she said, 'it's the way you think that makes the difference?'

'Yes,' I said. 'At least, most of the difference, most of the time.'

'I grew up thinking that when I was between 17 and 20, my father would find a young man who – he thought – would take me to wife, love me, respect me and look after me as best he could. I married your brother when I was 20. The two of us were brought together according to the tradition of our society. We were expected to live together on the basis of mutual respect. Love could not be taken for granted, nor could it be ruled out. I haven't felt reduced by my relationship with your brother. Your emphasis is on the individual, our emphasis is on the community. Who is to say which is better?'

I'd never before seen Boudi so agitated, never heard her uttering so many words with such deep conviction. I didn't doubt her sincerity, nor did I suspect that she was speaking out of self-interest. But it did cross my mind that she had little choice. My sisters also were going to be victims of the same system because, without money or education, they couldn't go out and choose their partners. It's the lack of choice that I objected to.

I'd kept quiet for too long. I had to respond. Baudi was waiting. A wedding in the family – and a fairly generous injection of money – would brighten up the lives of the Bagchis of Benaras for a few months, but I just couldn't convince myself that it would be a noble act of selflessness and not abject compromise on my part and opportunist exploitation on the part of my father. And how did I know that Debika wasn't being coerced into accepting something abhorrent to her? What if she despised me for wilting under pressure, for collusion, for not having the courage to reject something that didn't make sense to either of us?

I tried not to show any emotion. I said with quiet conviction, '*All* our customs and traditions do not deserve our respect. If I do something which I think unjust, unfair, humiliating and exploitative, I won't be comfortable. I live with myself all the time, and during any of that time – early in the morning, in the middle of the day or late at night – I do not want to feel really and truly uncomfortable because one evening in Benaras I failed to articulate with conviction what I believed, because I couldn't stand up to my single-minded, authoritarian father and allowed myself to succumb under pressure.'

Baudi wasn't pleased, I thought. She looked thoughtful. Did I revive in her the memory of some old passion, some lost love, the memory of something she cherished? Her face brightened, her attitude changed.

'You know, Ganesh, I've really liked talking to you. I wish you the best. You've had a good rehearsal with me. Now go on to the stage and don't forget your lines. And don't believe your Baudi believes in the same ideas and values as your father or your brother.'

Did this amount to Baudi saying, 'You've my blessing but not my approbation,' or, 'You've my blessing *and* my approbation'? I wasn't sure.

Debu-da had kept quiet all through the discussion and at the first opportunity, slipped away into our bedroom. Now he reappeared to remind me that it was time for me to see father.

When I entered the room, Father was pleased to see me.

'So how are you?' he said with warmth and affection. 'Did you have a good day?'

I said I was fine and I had a very pleasant day, visiting the ghats, some temples and some very old suburbs of Benaras.

'There's so much to do, so much to see that I don't think you can fit it all into ten days. Yes, it's a great city, but I'd rather be in Calcutta than anywhere else,' he said, looking into space.

'Calcutta is my city too,' I said.

'You must have wondered why I wanted you to come here so urgently. Your Baudi must have given you some idea. Well, I've arranged your marriage, and certain formalities have to be attended to before we can go any further. First of all, you've to meet the family, and I've fixed up tomorrow evening for us to go there,' Father said with quiet confidence. I felt that it'd be cruel to point out how absurd it all was: for I wasn't once asked whether I wanted to get married, nor had I ever met my prospective bride. I also knew that Father would find it both incredible and unacceptable if I insisted that I ought to have been consulted first about whether I was ready to get married at all, and that I should have had a say in who was going to be my wife.

My father wasn't too worried by my silence; it was quiet approval, he must have concluded.

'It's a highly respected family here. Mr Maitra is a solicitor and Debika, his daughter, is doing an honours degree in English. I've been offered a large dowry which will make a lot of difference to our lives.'

There wasn't any beating about the bush. Father was matter-of-fact. He was saying he had made certain decisions on my behalf, without asking me even once, *before* he made his commitments. What I thought of the idea of getting married to someone *he* had chosen for me just didn't matter. My father's world-view and values were different from mine. He believed in God; I didn't. He believed in caste; I didn't. He believed in arranged marriages; I didn't. He accepted the dowry system; I found it abhorrent. The reconciliation of our two worlds was nearly impossible. Yet he'd made for me this very important decision of the woman I should marry.

'I'm not thinking of getting married yet,' I said.

'I'm not thinking of your marriage in the immediate future, either. You meet them and leave the rest to me,' said my father.

'I don't want to get married before I've finished university. That apart, the idea of getting married to a total stranger isn't acceptable,' I said and waited for an explosion.

The explosion didn't happen. Father's tone of voice was conciliatory, his expression relaxed. He thought my hesitation was legitimate, entirely understandable. I was an adult; why shouldn't I have my unique way of looking at such important aspects of life as love, marriage, friendship, career and life's values in general? But what we call principles can be another name for selfishness, a way of promoting self-interest. Had I thought of that?

'I hadn't thought of that. But I want to finish my present course of studies without any further distractions. Without any real qualifications, without a job, and much against the values I believe in, why should I take the responsibility which marriage invariably brings? I don't want any more change of circumstances before I finish university.'

'Most of the important decisions we make in life have a strong element of uncertainty,' Father said philosophically in elegant Bengali. 'Most relationships can go either way. How can you be sure that if you turn down this proposal, you'll meet your ideal partner? . What's on offer? In a country where women's literacy is appallingly low, your wife will have a degree in English by the time you get your MA. I told Mr Maitra about your academic ambitions. He said he'd be delighted if he could help in any way.' Father now waited for my reaction.

'How can Mr Maitra support me? How can I get married and then depend upon my father-in-law?' I asked.

'It's false pride. I know many people who've done it in my generation and the next. Your mother was a daughter of a friend of my father. She was 20 and still not married. He turned to my father for help because he was subjected to social disapproval for keeping at home an unmarried daughter who was 20. My first wife had died the year before and I married your mother. I had three children by my first wife, one of whom died young, and nine children by your mother, two of whom died. You were number seven. I had a good relationship with both your mother and the mother of Jogesh.' Jogesh was my eldest brother, virtually the head of the family, my stepbrother.

'Baba,' I said. 'I really don't want to get married now and depend on my father-in-law to support me and my wife... And if I don't want to depend on anybody other than myself, I'll have to quit my studies and get a job. I don't want to do that either. I'd really like to wait.'

I hadn't stood up to my father before and I don't know how I managed to defy him now. But I couldn't afford to do anything else. Yet I hadn't told him the whole story. I'd put forward mainly practical objections, without getting involved in ideological differences between his generation and mine.

Father realised that I seriously believed what I was saying, so he explained why my decision was central to the essential needs of food and shelter for the Bagchi family in Benaras.

'You know that it's an established practice in our society to give and take dowry. Whether I like it or not, I'll have to pay fairly large sums of money to the fathers of whoever marry Hena and Radha. But that can wait. What can't wait is the payment of rent. We owe our landlord six months' rent. If we can fix a date for your marriage with Debika, Mr Maitra will advance enough money for me to pay the rent and attend to a few other important matters.'

My father was now able to create a conflict within me. Am I abandoning those I care for in the hour of need? The system of giving money and property to one's son-in-law, which I thought was humiliating for women, had started with good intentions at a time when women didn't go out to work. So parents gave their daughters a little money so that they could feel independent to a certain extent and do a little shopping – buy presents for their husbands on their birthdays, for example – without turning to others. This was called *streedhan,* "a wife's wealth".

This, in course of time, degenerated into dowry, which the father of the son demanded from the father of the daughter, and it was often extortionate, especially for parents of small means. Like the caste-system in certain parts of India, it was an atrocious and ugly feature of our society. Would it be right for me to co-operate, to promote a tradition I abhorred?

'But Baba, I don't believe in the dowry system. And I've read many credible reports of harassment of young wives by their mothers-in-law because the dowry, they thought, wasn't enough…'

Father interrupted me. He was losing patience, I thought, but he was still in control.

'I'll have to find husbands for Hena and Radha. Do you think the fathers aren't going to demand money and gifts from me? Will you undertake to find two high-minded rebels who'll defy their parents and marry your sisters? Do you realize you're indulging in your ideology at the expense of me and your sisters? Now, I don't want to go on about this. I want to ask you a simple question: will you or won't you marry Debika?'

I kept quiet. I wanted to help. I didn't want my father to lose face. I didn't want my sisters to remain spinsters. But I kept quiet.

'I take it that your silence does *not* indicate consent,' Father said, trying not to show his anger and disappointment.

I still didn't say anything. It was quite clear that I didn't want my father to make Mr Maitra pay for the privilege of his daughter getting married to a young man about whom he or his daughter knew very little; nor did I want to marry a stranger. The people I'd met, the books I'd read, the thoughts I'd thought had made me what I was. How could I suddenly become somebody else to please my father?

'Are you really going to do this to me, Ganesh?' Father said after a long pause 'Never in my life have I been in a situation like this. There'll be practical problems of money. And I'll lose face. I don't know how I'll justify myself. Mr Maitra will have little respect for me after this.'

'I'm sorry, Baba. But…'

Father didn't let me finish.

'No. Don't say another word. It's not necessary. I don't want you to give it another thought. But I don't want to see your face again. I've always been very fond of you, Ganesh, but you've humiliated me. It sounded as if I was beginning to whimper. I've decided that I'll not ask you for anything ever again. But I can't bear to see you around any more. There's a train tomorrow afternoon which will take you back to Calcutta. And please don't come to say goodbye. Good night.'

'Good night, Baba,' I said and got up to leave.

'If Hena is still awake, I'd like a cup of tea.'

'Yes, Baba.'

Father never drank anything stronger than tea. Hena, my elder sister, hadn't gone to bed, so I told her Baba would like a cup of tea.

'How did it go?' she asked.

'Not at all well,' I answered.

'I didn't hear father raise his voice once.'

'He was in control throughout. But he was angry.'

'I'll make Father his cup of tea and then come and join you.' Hena or Phuldi disappeared into the kitchen. Debu-da came out of the bedroom which he and I were sharing. He was used to going to bed much earlier than I was, but tonight he was waiting to hear the outcome of my encounter with Father.

'So when is it all happening?' Debu-da had come to the wrong conclusion. He thought, I was looking pensive and depressed because I'd given in and Father had had his way.

'No, Debu-da, nothing is happening. I've told Father that I wouldn't marry before I'd finished my studies and got a job. And I was against the practice of taking money and gifts from the father of the bride and arranged marriages,' I said all that quickly – as if I wanted to get it all off my chest. Hena came in quietly.

'How did Father take it?' Debu-da asked.

'He's angry and disappointed that his carefully laid plan had come to nothing, and that he was going to lose face. Actually, what Baba's most upset about is losing face. Then there was the dowry. I don't think Borda's doing too well in his business and money has been scarce. He needs the dowry.'

Hena now joined the conversation. She'd listened and got the drift. 'So what happens now?' she asked.

'I've been thrown out. I've to take the train to Calcutta tomorrow afternoon.'

'That's a bit drastic,' Hena said, 'isn't it?'

'Not really. I've created a crisis. Instead of being the solution, I'm the problem. Father turned to me for help and I've let him down. I think it's best that I leave tomorrow,' I said.

I'll come with you. It's best that I come with you. I'm sure Father thinks that I'm partly responsible. But I know I had nothing to do with it,' Debu-da said.

'No, you didn't,' I confirmed.

Soon after that, we went to bed.... I'd stood my ground, but it hadn't brought me great satisfaction; only a deep feeling of sadness.

Chapter 4

Back to Calcutta

Indian railway stations – the large and important ones – are crowded, noisy, extremely busy and frenetic places, especially at the time of the arrival and departure of trains. Some of the porters were carrying half a dozen pieces of luggage each, on their heads and in their hands, and walking very fast, even running, without dropping a single piece. And they were the people who found the compartment allocated to you, put your luggage in the appropriate place, and thanked you and smiled at you when you'd paid them the standard amount of money, which is quite small. I'd always thought they were extraordinarily patient and efficient people, although I'd seen them getting cross if someone was deliberately and intolerably mean.

As soon as we'd settled down in our compartment, Debu-da went out and got us some sweet, milky tea, which is made only in the railway stations of India, and is usually served in tiny pots of baked clay, which you threw away and broke after you'd drunk the tea. I'd drunk that tea as a little boy, as a teenager, and was drinking it now as a young man in his twenties. The tea tasted the same and was served in the same disposable clay pots. It's the same even now. The sweet tea in earthenware pots that you get at Indian railway stations has remained the same since people first started travelling by train in India, I'm sure. It's almost part of the history of the Indian Railways.

Debu-da told me how he courted his wife and how he got married. His wife, one of two daughters of a widowed mother who lived in Shambazar, North Calcutta, was his music student to begin with. They got married and Debu-da supported his mother-in-law as best he could. Then Debu-da and his wife moved to South Calcutta, where they lived now. I'd met Debu-da's wife briefly but hadn't got to know her at all well.

Their lives were financially precarious, Debu-da said. He taught a few students to sing. That was his only regular income, not enough for food and shelter, let alone luxuries of any kind. Occasionally, there was a windfall, like when a film director made a film about a young Bengali revolutionary, Khudiram, who was hanged by the British, and he was music director. The film was not a hit, but it was fairly successful.

Then the subject of love, marriage and a dowry came up. The dowry system had a great deal to do with the absence of any significant scope for women's education and their economic dependence on their husbands. Women's literacy hovered round one per cent at the time and national literacy wasn't more than about twelve per cent. A great many changes had to happen in society to make this shameful custom obsolete.

'Then there's the physical and emotional need of young people in a conservative society where free association is discouraged and sex outside marriage is taboo. So most young people in conservative middle class families go along with established practice.

Some don't, like you and me, and some have the best of both worlds – have their relationships outside marriage, and when appropriate, get married to the man or woman their parents choose for them. And money and property change hands. The whole transaction for many is exciting business and is taken seriously. But things are beginning to change – slowly. At this rate, however, it'll take us at least half a century.'

Debu-da wanted to talk. He was in a serious frame of mind.

'I don't really feel altogether certain that what I've just done was fair. My father, like everybody else, is subject to the same social pressures. At his age, he isn't going to undertake to change society. He was depending on me, and I've let him down. Is my sense of principle really more important than the sense of security of my father, my elder brother and my sisters?'

Debu-da didn't say anything reassuring. After Father, my eldest brother and two sisters had gone to live in Benaras, he didn't have a lot to do with the family. He was managing – not too well – on his own, and whether he did well or badly, sank or swam, he wouldn't turn to the family. He didn't answer my question for a minute. Then he said,' It's all right to help; it's rotten to compromise.'

The train had stopped. The familiar noises of an excited Bengali crowd and the feverish activities of fellow passengers meant we'd reached Howrah Station. Debu-da went south and I north – to Shambazar, my home, my Egypt, Rome, Hellas, Byzantium.

I returned to Bhim Ghose Lane in a confused state of mind. I had no hard feelings about my father. Love, respect, obedience, following the traditions of the family and the community: these came in the society of his generation as a compact package. One couldn't be separated from another.

But that wasn't how it was with me. I couldn't marry the girl he'd chosen for me. That didn't mean that I had lost either my love or respect for him. I was partly affected by the knowledge of the tragic consequences of one such arranged marriage: the girl had taken her own life, possibly because the idea of such intimacy with a stranger was frightening and repugnant.

Though millions of men and women in our society were conditioned to accept what some thought was a fate worse than death – I felt disturbed and unhappy about the conflicts and contradictions in our attitudes and behaviour – within the space of just two generations.

The bus had gone past the university buildings and the Coffee House. Dusk had descended. Street lights had been lit. Crowds of people were going about their business with seemingly unhurried steps. People in the streets of Calcutta rarely give us the impression that they're in a hurry, unlike Londoners, for example – just doing some weekend shopping on Tottenham Court Road.

Star Theatre – my bus stop. Time to get out.

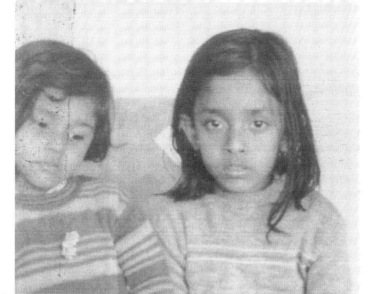

Chapter 5

University, Sudarsana, Shantiniketan

I first went to my room in Bhim Ghose Lane in Shambazar, read a little and rested, and in the evening went to see Mejda, my second eldest brother, and my sister-in-law. They welcomed me and wanted to know about Father and the rest of my family.

'Is Father beginning to look frail at all?' Mejda asked. Father was almost eighty.

'I don't think so. What impressed me was the way he kept his temper in check. You can't have forgotten his fits of temper. I thought he would rage when I said I wasn't going to get married to the girl he'd chosen for me, but he didn't. Instead of that, he asked me to leave the next day. He didn't want to see my face again, he said.'

'Incredible. Just threw you out? I didn't spend a lot of time in the joint family, so I never experienced his fits of temper, but your brother tells me he can be fierce,' said Baudi.

'I felt that sometimes he put on an act, like some primitive tribes wear masks to frighten their enemy. I never had a show-down with my father,' Mejda said. From Mejda's gloomy mood and pensive face, I got the message that he sympathised with my father.

'One reason why there was no confrontation between you and Father was that you didn't live under the same roof with him for many years, and both you and Borda married those he chose for you,' I said.

'We haven't regretted it. And, quite frankly, I don't understand what the fuss is about,' said Mejda. There wasn't a deluge of sympathy for me.

'Times have changed,' said Baudi, 'And I don't think it's changed for the worse. I certainly don't approve of the dowry system. My father is a post-master and he had to spend a lot of money getting my sister and me our husbands.'

'Thank you,' I said.

I ate my evening meal with Mejda and Baudi and came back to my small room in Bhim Ghose Lane, where I lived rent -free. I was supposed to teach a distant cousin of my benefactor, Mr Khunni Roy, a landlord and businessman, but Ruby wasn't extraordinarily keen on having English lessons. Our relationship at the time was undefined. I liked Ruby, found her attractive and intelligent. But she found it difficult to take me seriously as a tutor. Tutors had to be older, with a greying head of hair. They had to inspire feelings of fear and respect. I lacked these and several other qualities. These, I think, are some of the reasons why I didn't succeed in my role as Ruby's tutor. Also, we lived in a society dedicated to the suppression of free association between young men and women.

Our MA at Calcutta University those days wasn't awarded on the basis of post-graduate students writing dissertations on their chosen subjects under the supervision of a tutor. They had to study English poetry, plays, novels, the history of English literature, and understand the principles of literary criticism. There were recommended textbooks which they were expected to study in depth, and there were regular lectures, a certain proportion of which it was obligatory to attend. At the end of two years there was an examination. Now we had reached the sixth year and there was an intake of new students for the fifth year. It was a well-established tradition for the students in the sixth year to ceremonially welcome the newcomers.

Food and entertainment were the responsibility mainly of the sixth year students, but when it came to entertainment – singing, a play, jokes – the newcomers also made their contribution. One of the newcomers got on to the stage. She was going to sing. She was from Shantiniketan. She had done her BA Honours degree in English from Visva-Bharati, Tagore's university. We expected her to sing one of the poet's songs, and that's what she did – sang one of Rabindranath's songs which I'd always loved. It was a powerful voice. The singing was spontaneous, inspired, riveting. Its impact was immediate and powerful.

The words of the song were those that only Rabindranath could have written - about the transience of life, about laughter and tears, hopes and fears; about feelings in search of expression; about my life, everybody's life. It was an unexpectedly powerful experience. I hadn't been affected by any singer or song quite like this before. I was 22 years old. To fully understand why I felt the way I did, I have to be young again. The name of this young woman who had just joined the Calcutta University as a student of English and who sang the songs of Tagore so beautifully was Sudarsana Roy. After the first song, she sang two other songs at the request of the audience.

After that I saw her from time to time from a distance, standing in the corridor or sitting in the women's common room, chatting with friends. Once she approached me for some subscription. She and a few others had decided to start a society for the understanding and appreciation of the works of Tagore – his poetry, his songs, his plays, his novels, short stories and essays. Was this necessary in Calcutta, where Tagore was so central to our intellectual and emotional life? But I was happy to become a member of the society, not only because I was an ardent admirer of Tagore, but also because I hoped to see Sudarsana from time to time when the Tagore Society had meetings. She was really unlike any other woman I'd met before—utterly relaxed in the company of both men and women and unmistakeably warm and friendly. I did think she was special, but what about her? What did she think of me? It looked unlikely that I'd made any impression on her. There was no way of knowing, no alternative to living on the banks of uncertainty.

It's obvious why I was asking these questions, and various problems, real and imaginary, began to disturb my sleep. Then Provat Guha, a good friend, told me that he had been at a students' steamer party on the River Hooghly, as a guest of a friend, and found her flirting outrageously with someone called Shankar. That was disturbing news. But why should I worry? She probably came from a Westernised background where having a fling or two before one settled down to a steady boyfriend and contemplated marriage was common practice. In any case, what she did was her business. I was a face in the crowd, one of several hundred students milling around the university campus. And one way of coming to terms with the unattainable, for me, was to pretend I wasn't interested.

Sudarsana had a lively face; a brown complexion – a shade or two lighter than mine; a swan's neck, but not quite as in Modigliani; a strong, sharp nose that fitted her face perfectly, and lips which were neither too thin, nor too full. She had long brown hair, with which she did various things. She was slim, of average height, wore glasses. She walked with long strides, in spite of her sari. There was something in her movements and gestures which made me think of her as a very independent individual.

I did not always get to see her even when there were regular lectures. We didn't share a common room, nor were there lectures which were attended by both the fifth and the sixth year students. When we met, it was usually by accident. And a meeting by chance did happen that evening, when the lectures were over and we were all wending our way home.

I, however, was <u>not</u> returning home like my fellow students. I was going to Southern Avenue to teach Chhobi and Kobi, two sisters who lived in South Calcutta. So I boarded a 2A bus, which went all the way from Cornwallis Street in the north to the Lakes in the south. The bus was crowded, as it always was this time of the day, when students from the university and its different affiliated colleges got on to return home. There was nowhere I could sit down, so I was standing near the front of the bus, holding on to the bar just above my head, which was provided for the purpose. A ladies' seat was vacant near where I was standing but I couldn't sit there, unless there were no ladies around. And if a lady was sitting in one of the two seats, a man could occupy the seat next to her only if she requested him, loudly and clearly, to sit there. The lady's explicit permission was obligatory. Women had to have certain privileges. They had to have some specific rights which had to be protected. This was positive discrimination. Nobody minded. The last time I went to Calcutta from England in 2004, more than 58 years after this occasion, the rules hadn't changed.

The young woman, who was sitting next to the empty seat and looking out of the window, turned her head towards me and said, ' Why don't you sit ?'
It was Sudarsana, returning to her home in South Calcutta. I couldn't believe my luck. I was slightly nervous. I sat down.

'I live in Lansdowne Road now. I used to live in Park Circus. Where do you live?'

'I live in Bhim Ghose Lane, which is quite near Star Theatre in North Calcutta. I regularly go to Southern Avenue, where I teach a couple of girls, who are in secondary school,' I said.

'A long way to go. How often do you teach them?'

'Five days a week.'

'That's a lot of travelling.'

'I'm afraid it is. But I don't mind.'

Sudarsana was very natural and relaxed and that helped me not to betray my excitement. We talked shop for a bit. Dr Amiya Charaborty was our favourite lecturer, not only for the content of his lectures but also for the quality of his English. She had gone to Visva-Bharati University for her Intermediate Arts and her BA. That was four years of free association with young men of her age group as well as older and younger men. So she found the whole business of separate common rooms for the girls, and reserved seats in the front of the classroom, quite ridiculous. What's more, she belonged to the Brahmo Samaj where social and religious conservatism was quite energetically discouraged, and the free mixing of men and women was considered natural and healthy. Raja Rammohan Roy was the original founder of Brahmo Samaj. Since his time, many highly erudite and intelligent people, people of outstanding spiritual and intellectual calibre, have come from the minority community of the Brahmos of Bengal. Before she got off the bus in Bhabanipur, Sudarsana said she'd like me to meet her parents and her sister and that it had been great talking to me. A travelling companion made a difference. Normally, I stood quietly most of the way.

'We must do it again,' she said, smiling, and left. I watched her go. I watched her walk away with her long, loping strides. She did not look back. The bus moved and she was out of sight. In that fleeting moment when she was disappearing from view, I decided that I loved Sudarsana.

This meeting was not long, but it was the longest and one without any interruptions. Between attending to Chhobi's problems with decimals and Kobi's confusion over fractions, I thought of Sudarsana's natural and unaffected way of speaking, her interest in what I had to say, her lack of self-consciousness and her spontaneous laugh. She was also quite outspoken. She didn't like the formality and the impersonality of the teachers at the University.

'The lecturers and professors here are remote. They live on a different planet. At each lecture, they dole out a dollop of information and ideas and disappear – until their next lecture. There are no tutorials, no discussions and no interaction. If you asked Professor Das, 'What does Ganesh Bagchi look like? Who's Sudarsana Roy?' do you think he'll be able to tell you?' She was critical without being harsh.

'One of the problems, I think, is large classes,' I suggested.

'That *is* a problem, but not to know who you're teaching and their strength and weakness should be frustrating – if you're a teacher. I'd like to have some idea what my teachers are like. For them, we're post-graduate students who come and go every two years. In Visvabharati, we knew our teachers and they knew us.' Sudarsana was beginning to sound slightly agitated. She hadn't quite settled down in Calcutta, I thought. She was missing Shantiniketan. 'Our university has a great library,' I suggested. It was time, I thought, I stood up for my university. 'Yes, it's a great library. The number of books here probably exceeds that of our library in

Shantiniketan. But we usually got the books we wanted there. Professor Lahiri recommended Wilson Knight's *The Crown of Life* and Lionel Trilling's *The Liberal Imagination* as compulsory reading. I've been trying to get hold them for more than a week. Can I get them?'

'*I* was able to borrow them,' I said.

'And have you still got them?' she asked.

'Yes, I'm afraid I've had them for about two weeks.'

'You need to keep them for a bit. They're not easy books to read. Tell me when you're ready to return them and I'll try to get them issued to me. But shouldn't the library have multiple copies of books which are essential reading?'

'Yes, it should, and I think it has.'

I used to teach Chhobi and Kobi in Mr Bhattacharya's office, where he met his clients during working days. At the end of a lesson, I always got a cup of tea. After fractions, decimals and the cup of tea, I came away and waited at a bus stop for a 2A bus to Shambazar.

I went up and sat in the top deck of the double-decker bus – where there were about a dozen people – because I wanted to think about what was happening to me. I had no previous experience of being in love. I'd thought about love, read about love, but I'd never *been* in love. None of the relationships had meant much. They were more in the nature of brief encounters than relationships. I hadn't kissed Sudarsana, nor held her hand, but she meant more to me than anybody I had met before. The bus had reached the stop opposite the Star Theatre, so my reverie was interrupted.

Now we met more often, but not as often as I'd like – between lectures, during the lunch break, at the end of the lectures and on the bus. It was only occasionally that I was able to sit next to her because there were usually more ladies than there were seats. One afternoon when we met in the corridor, I told Sudarsana that Chhobi and Kobi's aunt had invited them to spend a few days with her, so I wouldn't be teaching them.

'Why don't you come and have tea with us?' she said. I said I'd love to. We skipped a lecture and took the usual 2A or 2B bus, which went to South Calcutta. Because students, lecturers, professors and the office staff at the university and the affiliated colleges were all hard at work – it was just coming up to three o'clock – the buses were not crowded, and we were able to sit together. Sudarsana told me a little about her family. Their ancestral home was in East Bengal, she said, in Arkandi. 'My ancestral home is also in East Bengal. The name of our village is Baliakandi. I was born in Faridpur,' I said.

'There's a river between our two villages,' she said. 'Do you know what it's called?'

'Chandana,' I said.

'Beautiful name, don't you think?' she said.

'Yes, it is,' I said, 'but I don't remember having seen it.'

'That is a coincidence – a remarkable coincidence,' she commented. 'Baliakandi and Arkandi. With the river Chandana flowing in between.'

I was also thinking. She's so friendly, so good at communicating her ideas. But she wanted to remain friends. Not once had she even grasped my hand with affection and warmth. This is also something rare, something I've never experienced before – this relaxed friendship into which physical love didn't come at all. It was partly her background, I realized. People she had grown up with were relaxed about friendship between the sexes. Also the last four years in Visvabharati, Tagore's university, had an influence on her personality and her outlook on life. It was also there that she had learnt to sing so beautifully.

'Why don't we stop at Victoria Memorial? I love the gardens surrounding the Memorial,' said Sudarsana. 'My father and my sister won't be home yet, I'd like you to meet them as well as my mother.'

'I think it's a great idea,' I said. 'I haven't visited the Memorial except once. I wasn't impressed with the memorabilia.'

'We should reject the Memorial on principle,' she said. 'First of all it falls far short of the great building which inspired Curzon.'
'Which building?'

'The Taj Mahal, of course. Even the marble came from the same quarries – Markana in Rajasthan.'

I was impressed with her knowledge. I'd no idea the marble of the Taj Mahal and that used in building the Victoria Memorial was from the same source. The bus stopped outside a building just past Theatre Road. We got off the bus and walked to the Memorial and sat on a bench by the pool nearest to the front gate.

'I don't find the Memorial ugly. It certainly doesn't rival the Taj but it's not a monstrosity,' I said.

'It's not the aesthetics of the building which bothers me. It's the ethics. This memorial monument was built at a time when famine and disease were killing millions. Every disease you can think of was endemic in some part of India, and there was no planned effort to do anything to reduce the colossal Indian poverty. Right in the middle of death and disaster, Curzon decided to build this memorial as a visible monument to imperial glory. You should hear my cousin, Montu-da, on the subject.'

Sudarsana spoke excellent Bengali and her English was unselfconscious and fluent. Her political ideas were largely influenced by her cousin, Montu-da or Subroto Sengupta, who was a well-known communist, a leader in Bengal of the Communist Party of India.

'But Sudarsana,' I said, 'Why was our country taken over? Because we were weak and divided. Why have we been exploited? Because powerful people in our own society have collaborated in the exploitation of the weak and vulnerable, and the weak and vulnerable have served the British in order to survive. My father and my eldest brother worked in a government office in Faridpur. They were low-paid civil servants. Our whole family depended on their income. But there was one thing they could take for granted – their salaries at the end of the month, although they were mean handouts. Jobs and salaries were secure. There was also security of life and property. But if you stepped out of line…'

'There was hell to pay,' Sudarsana said with conviction. 'And you couldn't be sure that your uncle or cousin or friend wasn't helping the police to keep a watchful eye on you.'

'That's just it. Why were the Americans able to throw the British out when they found that colonial exploitation was intolerable, but we couldn't? Because Mirjafar let his master – Siraj-ud-Daula - down and colluded with the British, who promised to put him in charge. But America was united enough to throw out the British. The two events happened within twenty-odd years of each other. Our problem was that we weren't a nation but tribes, large and small. What happens to a nation is what it allows to happen.'

'I agree with most of what you say,' Sudarsana said. 'I'm sorry. I didn't suggest coming here for a political discussion. But politics is important, I think. We discuss politics quite a lot.... But let's have a look at the gardens, shall we?'

We got up and started walking. Sudarsana was quiet. It was a week-day but there was quite a crowd of people. I was hoping we might find a quiet corner in the large gardens. We had never been entirely on our own, so I was interested to see whether that made any difference.

'One particular difference between Bolpur, where I went to university as an undergraduate, and Calcutta is that over there you could be on your own. You wandered away from the campus, and there were the wide open spaces. Here in Calcutta there are people everywhere,' Sudarsana said.

'I don't know about Bolpur,' I said. 'But here it's certainly difficult to find anywhere without noise, people and prying eyes,' I responded. I said this quietly, trying not to show my frustration.

'I'll tell you what,' she said. 'Would you like to come to Shantiniketan for the celebrations which happen on the campus on the first of Baishakh?'

I said I'd love to go. The first day of Baishakh is the first day of the Indian calendar, widely celebrated in India. It usually falls between the last week in April and the first week in May.

'Yes, I'll come,' I said, immediately worrying about how I'd manage to find the money for travelling … and accommodation. The two new tuitions were a help. Perhaps I could manage, I thought. 'Do you know I've never visited Shantiniketan, although I've wanted to. I always marvel at Tagore's greatness as a poet, musician, artist and human being.'

'I like Tagore's songs most of all,' Sudarsana said.

'You don't have to tell me that. Your love comes through in your singing. It's when I heard you sing at the university that I decided that I must get to know you,' I said.

We didn't take the train or the bus. We came out of the rear gate of Victoria Memorial and started walking. Sudarsana gave me some idea of the family. Her father was an electrical engineer who had a degree from Sheffield University. Now he was Lighting Superintendent, for the Calcutta Corporation. His name was Tarun Roy. Her mother, Uma Roy, was quite content to stay at home and look after her family. She had a younger sister, Sunanda, who was doing a science degree at Presidency College. We walked down Lower Circular Road and turned right on to *Lansdowne* Road. *Victoria* Memorial, *Cornwallis* Street, *Lansdowne* Road, *Dalhousie* Square. There was no way we could forget who our rulers were.

You couldn't wish to meet a more pleasant family. Sudarsana's mother made the biggest impression on me – she was so quiet and dignified. She'd be the kind of person I'd turn to in a crisis. The father was informal, pleasant and unassuming. He discussed politics, wanted to know whether I thought the partition of India was a possibility or a certainty. I didn't want India to be divided but it looked like a distinct possibility, I said.

Sunanda gave me the impression that she was sizing me up. She attended to tea and cakes. She was an attractive young woman, confident and probably critical. These were my first impressions. How true they were, I thought, was difficult to say.

It was almost seven o'clock by the time I left for Shambazar. I was wondering why Sudarsana had kept in the background practically the entire time I was there. Did she want her sister and her parents to make their assessment independently and then compare notes? Why should she want to do that? She had so far shown no signs of deep and lasting affection, made no commitment; given away nothing. But were these questions not a sign of my immaturity? I had never before spent so much time with any woman outside the family. I didn't doubt that I had a friend now – a woman – intelligent, forthright and companionable. Why did I want to spoil it all by being anxious and insecure?

We were going to Shantiniketan a day before the Baishakh celebrations. The train was due to leave about 12 o'clock in the afternoon. I had to wait a long time for a taxi and the traffic on the way to the station was heavy. I was in a panic. Was I going to make it? It was almost time for the train to leave. I paid the taxi and ran. An anxious group of young men were standing outside a compartment. I could see they were waiting for me. 'Run,' they said.

I was already running, but I ran faster. I threw my bag to a young man about my age who was still standing outside the door. He caught it, threw it to someone waiting at the entrance.

The train had started. The young man who'd caught my bag extended a helping hand and lifted me into the carriage. There was a universal sigh of relief. Someone clapped, and then everybody clapped. Sudarsana came forward and clasped my hand in both her hands. Were her eyes moist? I couldn't tell. Then Kalyani was the first to speak – Kalyani was Sudarsana's closest friend – tall, confident, attractive.

'Now that the excitement is over,' Kalyani said, 'Mr Ganesh Bagchi will be tried by the people's court for causing pain and panic to innocent people. The judge and the jury in this case is Sudarsana Roy.'
'Release the prisoner. Let him go. On grounds of diminished responsibility,' the judge said.

'Why diminished responsibility?' asked Kalyani, pretending to be the counsel for the prosecution.

'The accused is a very confused young man,' the judge declared. Everybody laughed.

I didn't mind being made fun of.

Bolpur looked festive on account of the arrival of visitors, mainly from Calcutta, most of them ex-students and their families. The students of Shantiniketan had a love and loyalty for their institutions which we didn't feel for our schools and colleges. Many of them were meeting a long time after leaving the campus, so there was greeting, reminiscing, exchanging of news, laughter, even spontaneous singing. I suddenly found myself among joyful people, giving uninhibited expression to their love of life. I wished I could join in. I was no older than most of the revellers, but I didn't know anybody and I didn't have their spontaneity. And, having met old friends, Sudarsana had abandoned me. It seemed every other person among these visitors knew her. Was she some kind of celebrity? After what seemed like a millennium, she emerged from among her friends and admirers and came to me.

'Will you forgive me?' she said. 'I had to abandon you because many of these people you see here are old friends. I spent my four years at the university with some of them. One of them is married. Some have jobs. Some are looking for jobs. Some are at different universities. I meet even more old friends at the Paush Mela – the fair which takes place on the campus in winter.'

I was genuinely happy to see Sudarsana so relaxed and happy. She had a natural ability to relate to people, especially in her own age-group. I was in love with her, which she might or might not reciprocate. But her warm-hearted friendship, her spontaneity and her beautiful singing voice always inspired my admiration. And although I'd love to be loved, I wouldn't want to lose her friendship – neither because she was already in love with somebody else, nor because I wasn't the kind of person she could love. I remembered Debu-da, the brother I loved and respected. He'd once said to me, 'You can only love, and hope for the best. Being loved isn't in your hands. Take it from me - you don't lose anything by loving.' Wise words, but what about the pain? It wasn't a philosophy of life easy to practise, but I was ready to give it a go.

Sudarsana took me to the Guest House. She was staying at the women's hostel. Even if we were deeply in love, we couldn't share a bed or a room in those days. We would have <u>had</u> to be married. The manager recognised and greeted Sudarsana. She introduced us. I settled for a room which I'd share with three others because it was the cheapest.

We walked down the main road on the campus lined with flowering trees, and arrived at a restaurant with a small covered area and a lot of open space in front with some large tables and portable chairs around them. This was obviously the most popular haunt of the students and other campus-dwellers. The place was crowded when we arrived with quite a few of the visitors and a few locals, sipping their tea and indulging in 'adda', which means unfocused, chance-directed conversation in which you discussed a wide range of subjects – serious and trivial, sublime and ridiculous – without coming to any conclusions. It was usually a social, not an intellectual, exercise – although it could reach unintended heights.

Once again, it was obvious to me that Sudarsana was a popular member of the community. They were happy to see her, just as she was happy to see them. Her zest for life had a positive impact on them, which expressed itself in animated conversation and genuine, spontaneous laughter. Someone thumped a table and announced that Sudarsana was going to sing. She obliged without the slightest hesitation. It was about the tide of love flooding both sides of the river, the river of the heart. I loved that song. Then a young man sang a song about the soul's restless aspiration for the infinite. Bivash sang very well – but it was one of the songs that Sudarsana sang especially well, a song which had moved me so deeply when she first sang it. There was another request for Sudarsana to sing, but she declined because it was almost time for our evening meal and she was keen for us to go and eat with the first batch of guests at the canteen.

Sudarsana chose a table in the corner of the room to avoid attention. She was sorry, she said, that she hadn't talked to me very much. I said I didn't feel neglected.

'What can you do?' I said sympathetically. 'When old friends demand your attention, you have to neglect your new acquaintances.'

'I wouldn't call you an acquaintance,' she said.

'I mean they've known you much longer than I have.'

'How long is not the only thing that matters,' she protested. 'You don't really understand a lot, and demand even less.' What was all this about? I was puzzled.

I didn't think my casual remark would be taken so seriously.

I said I was sorry I'd said what I'd said. I knew she thought of me as a good friend. Her other friends she'd known longer and she had lost touch with most of them, so it was important for her to spend time with them. I hadn't taken it to heart.

'Good,' she said, laughing. 'Let there be no hard feelings.'
We were walking down the fairly wide central road of the campus, flowering trees on either side in bloom, with moonlight shining on them. The scene was kind of romantic... yet neither of us did anything. I wanted to hold her hand, but what if she should discreetly withdraw it to casually scratch her nose and say, 'I think we should now go back and meet up with our friends?' And if she wanted to be more explicit, she might say, 'Why do men think that it's absurd to be just friends with women? What I learnt in Shantiniketan is that friendship between men and women is natural and rewarding.' No, I didn't want to force the moment to its crisis. The clear blue sky, the fragrant air, the moonlight, the gentle breeze – all the conventional stage props for a romantic scene were there, but it was clear neither of the characters involved was ready to respond to the stimulus.

Instead we talked casually about people and events: Kalyani's ambition to be a nurse, although she'd done an honours degree in English; Bibhash's hope to become a writer; the Cripps Mission; and Jinnah's provocative statements, which might incite the Muslim population. Much of what we were talking about was inconsequential. We walked past houses in Purbapalli and headed towards nowhere, for beyond us were wide open spaces, leading to the horizon – wide open spaces, where nothing grew, and where there were only a few trees scattered around. And soon there were just the two of us, walking towards the horizon, under the friendly eye of the moon.

Sudarsana stopped, put her arms round me, and kissed me long and hard. We said nothing, kissed again. We sat down. The ground was dry and hard. I touched her, kissed her, and drew her closer to me. She passed her fingers through my longish hair.

'I love your hair,' was the first thing she said after the long silence. She shut her eyes and played with my hair. 'Do you know, Ganesha, I have waited for this for months,' she continued. *Ganesha* is the way my name is pronounced in Sanskrit. Ganesha is the god with an elephant's head in Hindu mythology. 'I wanted to tell you of my love *here,* in Shantiniketan, under the open sky, in the middle of these wide open spaces, with the moon shining above our heads. Silly? Romantic? If I told my sister, who has now a degree in Zoology, she'd laugh her head off. But I don't care. Now I've achieved my ambition and I want to tell you again: I love you. Not being able to tell you this before wasn't easy. Do you love me?'

'I do,' I said, 'and I will *Till a' the seas gang dry.'*

'Mission accomplished,' she said light-heartedly. 'Let's go back and join the others.' Suddenly she was matter-of-fact. For me it was like waking up with a start. But I knew why it was important for us to go back.

We got up and walked back towards the campus. We were back in the real world and tried to sound businesslike, but there was nothing businesslike in my head. I think we were aware that being on our own for too long in that magical location wouldn't be a sensible thing to do. There couldn't be any other explanation. Our friends wouldn't grudge us a little time on our own.

The next day we started off on our way back. The journey wasn't the anti-climax that I feared it might be. Initially, everybody was busy organising where they were going to sit and sleep and put their luggage, and even when our carriage had started rolling towards Calcutta, many in the group we were travelling with were busy attending to various matters relating to the return trip. But soon they settled down and started talking about the highlights of the festival, a very important one of which was the music and drama laid on by the entertainment committee for the visitors. It was of a remarkably high quality, someone said. I don't think I saw you there, Bibhash said to Sudarsana. No, she wasn't there. She would have liked to have been, but... She was sitting next to Kalyani in whom I was certain she had confided, because Kalyani, I thought, had looked at me and smiled a friendly smile.

Soon after people felt settled, the singing began and the effect was immediate and joyful. It was amazing how many of the ex-students sang and sang very well.

Practically everybody participated in the group singing. There were songs about life and love, about earth and sky, about spring, summer and the onset of the monsoon. One song followed another, songs sung by many voices, practised voices of competent singers, full of youthful enthusiasm and vitality. And Sudarsana, it seemed to me, enjoyed nothing better than singing. There was something special in the quality of her singing today. I wanted to believe that I might have had something to do with it. I felt good. The journey, even after last night, wasn't an anti-climax.

Listening to the singing both on the way to Shantiniketan and on the way back to Calcutta, I decided, rightly or wrongly, that Tagore's songs reflected the richness, variety and humanity of life in a uniquely Bengali as well as universal way. I still believe that.

Apart from Tagore, the Bengalis had another passion – politics. After the singing, we turned to politics. Not unusually, the Raj was at the centre of all debate, discussion, rage and criticism. Did the British spend at least one out of every four rupees in India on the instruments of repression? Did they use their repressive agents to kill innocent civilians in Amritsar? Did they flog publicly many who demonstrated against their atrocities? There was general agreement. The colonisers were cruel and callous. Not a single voice of dissent. But when the discussion moved to Mahatma Gandhi's Quit India campaign of 1942, the group was divided. Wasn't the weakening of the war effort a dangerous gamble? Wouldn't Japanese occupation mean transition from the frying pan into the fire? Who was responsible for the death of more than three million people in the Bengal Famine and why was there so little publicity on this man-made disaster? Even the rest of India didn't know about it, let alone the world. Other subjects that came into the discussion were the role of Communists in India's struggle for freedom and who was really responsible for the present muddle over the Partition of India. Were the decisions about the Partition hasty?

There wasn't a moment's boredom or weariness during the journey. Sudarsana and Kalyani had commented, criticised, elaborated – with interest, but intermittently. They hadn't really taken part. The singing and the discussions had certainly speeded up our journey. The last few days were quite different from those of my routine-bound existence. I said goodbye to everybody, already feeling a little nostalgic for the days just gone by.

I said goodbye to Kalyani and Sudarsana. We were in Calcutta. We were back home.

Chapter 6

Calcutta riots, Independence, Regent Estate

We returned to Calcutta – Sudarsana to Lansdowne Road in South Calcutta and I to Bhim Ghose Lane in North Calcutta. We met in the English Department of the University briefly from time to time, and spent an hour or so at the YMCA restaurant, if it was possible to do so. One of the attractions of this place was that its curtained cubicles ensured a modicum of privacy in an environment where everything was public. The students usually moved in groups rather than ones and twos. Holding hands was as far as we could go – and we did. Kissing would certainly be considered deviant behaviour, bordering on the scandalous. Nobody we knew or knew of had indulged in such behaviour and neither Sudarsana nor I had any immediate plan to burst into notoriety.

At home or in the world outside home in Calcutta, it was frustratingly difficult to organise even a brief period of privacy for Sudarsana and me. At Lansdowne Road, there were Sudarsana's mother and aunt, who were always at home. The cook and the cleaner were also milling around – with a few children thrown in for good measure. My little room in Bhim Ghose Lane was on the ground floor, only a few yards away from the main road, with the caretaker of the property coming and going most of the time, especially when he was least expected or wanted. And all public places – parks, restaurants and the area around the Lakes in South Calcutta – were always, or practically always, busy. Our highest ambition at the time was holding hands, one that we could manage to fulfil only at times in the cubicles of the YMCA Restaurant or when the house lights were off at the Metro or the Lighthouse Cinema. Our problem was our problem and we didn't want to take anybody into our confidence. For now, the knowledge that we loved each other – to the exclusion of all the other potential rivals, present and future – seemed to be sufficient, although both of us, I think, lived in the hope of a place where we could be alone, all on our own.

Both Sudarsana and I were focused on politics. There were at the time a few political events of quite some importance, we thought. Clement Attlee, who became the Labour Prime Minister of Britain in 1945, had introduced a significant programme of nationalization and social welfare for Britain. Nothing like this had happened before. The National Health Service, a truly free health service, for both the rich and the poor, was introduced during Clement Attlee's time. But what was most important for me was that Attlee had declared that one of the major objectives of his government was to ensure that India was independent – as soon as possible, without preconditions. The news of civil war in China, between the Communists and the Nationalists was, again, a most significant political development of the time.

When news like this came through, the Coffee House was the place to visit for this restaurant was where Kumar, Tapan, Amal, Robi, Ashok and several other university luminaries congregated and discussed various current problems and events. Sudarsana's interest soon began to dim and then disappeared. She found some of these students pretentious and boastful. We soon returned to the YMCA Restaurant.

The overall reaction to the news that India was going to be independent after nearly 200 years of the *Raj* was, naturally, positive. There were several questions which began to be asked. Such questions are always inevitable on the eve of a change as important as this. The very first question in the minds of most people was why? The British were a pragmatic race. They were already spending at least 25 per cent of their annual budget on the army and the police. The naval mutiny, the Quit India movement and various other instances of disaffection and rebellion must have indicated to the rulers that ruling India against the wishes of the people was going to be inordinately expensive, and the country that was such an asset at one time might cost the British taxpayer money. In the case of this Labour Government, there were idealistic reasons too. After an excessive amount of expense and bloodshed, and endless anxiety and tension, it might have been possible for the British to hold on for a few more years. 'Would it have been worth it?' was the pragmatic question many would ask. In addition, I believe that the Attlee government was also asking the moral question, 'Would it be right?' Their answer was an unequivocal no.

We had had many debates in the past about the exploitation and the benefits of colonial rule. Suddenly, all that became irrelevant because the transfer of power was an impending reality, and a matter for universal rejoicing. The transition to independence we'd hoped would be marked by joyful celebrations, popular processions and singing in the streets. But when Mohammed Ali Jinnah, leader of the Muslim League, demanded a separate Muslim State – Pakistan – there was fear of repercussions. Pakistan would comprise Muslim-majority areas of the Punjab, Kashmir, the North-West Frontier Province, Assam and Bengal.

To reinforce this demand, a day of direct action was declared: August 16, 1946. Demonstrations took place all over India. They were, by and large, peaceful in the rest of India, but in Calcutta things got out of hand completely and disastrously.

Nearly 5,000 people died, according to reliable estimates, and 15,000 were wounded during four days of indiscriminate violence. I'd lived through one nightmare – the Bengal Famine – when poor, destitute, hungry villagers died in the streets of Calcutta and at the doorsteps of its citizens. This was another. Quite innocent people in the streets and houses of Calcutta were battered, burnt, slashed to death because of their religion, because some people had decided to make political capital out of who people worshipped - Bramha or Allah or ...

I started travelling with Sudarsana from College Street to Lansdowne Road, because it gave Sudarsana's parents and me a sense of security that she wasn't travelling alone through some Muslim areas, where violence had erupted and lives were lost.

I looked forward to going on the bus with Sudarsana. I hoped I was being useful, although she never confessed to any fear or sense of insecurity. Nor was there a great deal of risk for those who lived in the affluent localities of Calcutta, especially South Calcutta. Also there were many more Hindus than Muslims in Calcutta. One of the standard practices of the unscrupulous trouble-makers was to spread rumours. The Hindu rioters went round telling people in Shambazar about murder, arson and rape in Chitpur; and the Muslim followers of Jinnah and Suhrawardy in Chitpur made similar accusations about the Hindus. Even after the worst was over, various rumours – credible and incredible – went around, resulting in mindless acts of revenge. Many tragedies, confrontations and conflicts continued to happen, vitiating the air we breathed.

Most offices remained open most of the time, but academic life was seriously affected. Schools and colleges and the university had poor attendance and then closed down. Debu-da suggested that I moved to his flat in South Calcutta, near Southern Market, and I did. My income from the tuitions was very small. Debu-da also depended mainly on his tuitions although he managed to get a film contract occasionally. The flat was really one room, but there was a small passageway between Debu-da's flat and the other flat on the first floor. Debu-da talked to the landlord and the tenant on the first floor so that I could sleep in the passageway at night. During the day I spent most of my time in Debu-da's flat. Days, weeks went by. There wasn't any sign of the university resuming regular classes. I started writing to Sudarsana, who had in the meantime moved from Lansdowne Road to Regent Estate in Tollygunge.

I went there one Sunday, stayed for lunch and came home after tea. It was a large house divided into four flats. Sudarsana's parents, Sudarsana and her sister Sunanda had one of the two upstairs flats and one of Sudarsana's uncles and his three children had the other flat. This uncle was a widower. It was a beautiful house in the middle of a large field, with wide open spaces all around and nothing between the house and the horizon on two sides. All day, we were surrounded by the family, but after tea, we went up to the terrace and enjoyed the physical closeness which we didn't have all day. We sat close to each other, held hands, embraced, kissed, talked about our love, which we were sure at the time would go on forever – though we were always worried our tryst might be interrupted.

'This is really the first time since Shantiniketan that we've been on our own', Sudarsana said.

'It's a beautiful place – but not quite like the moonlit open fields of Shantiniketan. What's important is that we can be on our own here.'

Just then one of Sudarsana's cousins came up. Early dinner had been arranged for my benefit for it was a long way back to Shambazar.

I liked them all – her parents, Sudarsana and Sunanda. Sunanda also had an excellent singing voice, and before I left to catch a bus or take a cycle-rickshaw to the tram depot in Tollygunge, there was often a brief session of singing Rabindranath's songs, which we all liked. It was usually Sudarsana and Sunanda who sang.

Many months went by. We met and parted at the university during the week, and at Regent Estate during weekends. My examinations had been postponed because lectures had been disrupted and, for a time, the university and other educational institutions had to close down because of the political situation and the Hindu-Muslim riots. But, after the trauma and disruption of the Great Calcutta Killing, and several months of insecurity and dithering, classes were resumed. What was worse, our examinations were looming ahead. I hadn't – for various reasons – managed to do much work. Sudarsana – about two hours away – was the major distraction over weekends. During the week, when I returned from university, Debu-da was either teaching or composing music or having a musical evening with fellow musicians. Debu-da's flat consisted of just one large bedroom, which was also our living room and dining room. It wasn't a place appropriate for serious study before an important examination. What was I going to do?

'What about your room at Bhim Ghose Lane?' Ronu asked, when I told him of my predicament.

'When I spent two days there quite recently, I felt I wasn't wanted,' I said.

'Let me think and explore. I may have a solution. But you'll have to wait until after the next weekend.'

I didn't ask him what his solution was. It was obvious that he didn't want to raise expectations until he had explored. I felt at the time that I was out on a limb... Returning to North Calcutta wasn't an attractive idea because, for some reason I knew very little about, I'd fallen out of favour with Khunni Roy, who had provided my rent-free accommodation. So I didn't return there. Sudarsana and I did meet from time to time at the YMCA restaurant in College Street and talk about various things – other than our separation. We were trying to be mature, I suppose. Indian independence and the partition of India was at the time an important and universal topic for discussion, not only between Sudarsana and me but everywhere. There were sections of the population of our subcontinent in which suspicion; anguish and deep resentment were the dominant emotions on the eve of independence. In the Punjab, the Sikhs were most apprehensive about their part of India being ruled by the Muslim League and took pre-emptive action on the second of August, killing sixteen Muslims, thereby starting a cycle of killing and counter-killing – in Amritsar, Lahore and elsewhere. Though at the time, such occurrences were distant thunder for us. We were so much in love.

Despite the unprecedented outbreak of violence in some parts of India, and fear and apprehension in others, the British Empire's sun did set at last at the midnight hour of the 15th of August, 1947.

Nehru became the Prime Minister, dedicating himself 'in all humility' to the service of the people of India. Pakistan had become independent a day earlier, so there were a few hundred million people rejoicing and celebrating across the entire sub-continent.

How long would it be before India really began to feel different? To what extent would our lives change? What kind of change would I see in my lifetime? A people's reaction to occupation is rarely positive, and I had very little doubt that the India that was born on the 15th of August 1947 rejoiced almost universally – except, perhaps a proportion of the Anglo-Indian community and the heads of Indian states – the *rajas,* the *maharajas*, the *nawabs* and others – who had felt protected by the British, and had had power and privileges which they might now lose.

In Britain, at least one person must have been profoundly unhappy – Winston Churchill – because 'the British lion, so fierce and valiant in bygone days, so dauntless and unconquerable…' had been 'chased by rabbits from all the fields and forests of his former glory'. Churchill wasn't the only unhappy witness of this retreat of the British from India. The transition to independence was one of the most tragic events of the century – with the country divided and countless citizens dead. Yet the consequences of Churchill's plan to hold on to India, whatever the cost, might have been far worse. It's a matter of speculation, and I'm glad that it is. While the majority of people in India and Pakistan were rejoicing over their countries' independence, events of tragic proportions were taking place in many parts of India. A cold-blooded, calculated and cowardly massacre of unarmed Muslims travelling from Delhi to Pakistani territory was carried out in Amritsar by armed Sikh civilians. It was reported that a large number of Sikh soldiers also participated in this mass killing. This was one of the worst tragedies of the time of transition, but by no means the only one. The Muslims also retaliated with savage brutality whenever they could.

In Noakhali, East Bengal, countless Hindus lost their lives. In Bihar, Muslims were slaughtered. Half a million people died, most of them killed. There was mass migration – the Hindus moving in the direction of India, full of fear and trepidation, and the Muslims headed for Pakistan. An estimated eight and a half million Hindus and Muslims migrated, uprooted from the land where, in most instances, they had lived for generations. The world knows very little of this great tragedy. At the time, the independence of India and Pakistan created problems and resulted in tragedies the like of which undivided India had never experienced. And we were all caught up in our national misfortune - some more and some less, some directly but indirectly – everyone without exception.

This was the year of my final MA examination. Sudarsana's would come next year. Because of the troubled times, the dates of the examinations had to be changed more than once. Finally it was decided that it would happen in December that year, which meant we were to be the first batch of students of Calcutta University to write this examination in free India. This delay, I knew, was for tragic reasons, but for me it was a boon, for I was really unsure of my scattered knowledge of the various authors and their works that we were expected to study in depth. The other problem was my natural habitat at the time – Debu-da's one-room flat, a popular resort of his students and other musicians, not only during the day but also for part of the evening, was certainly not the most appropriate place for serious study.

Some months back I had discussed my problem with Ronu and he had said that he might be able to suggest a viable alternative. He did just that. Quite often on Sundays Ronu and I used to meet up, and then go to a local restaurant and have a cup of tea and some *samosas* – which the Bengalis call *singaras* – and talk about various matters, including Ronu's current girlfriends. Ronu was good-looking, had a good singing voice, and played a great game of tennis and badminton. Above everything else, he was a pleasant and charming young man. It was no wonder, therefore, that he was popular, with both men and women seeking his company.

This particular morning, Ronu revealed his plan to make it possible for me to do enough work before December to bluff my way through the examination. I would go with him the following weekend to Dum Dum on the outskirts of Calcutta, where his eldest sister and his brother-in-law lived. They had no children. They had a spare room. It was only half-an-hour's journey by bus to the university. Everything sounded just right. The very next Sunday, we would go there and I would stay with Robi-da and Didi until my examination was over. What I found most remarkable was that he gave me the news quite casually, although finding a place where I could do some serious work was truly important. I said thank you, making it sound as casual as I could.

Robi-da and Didi were probably in their forties – Robi-da tall, dark and slightly grey, and Didi of medium height, light brown colour, with a good head of black curly hair. Robi-da was always alert and active, interested in sports, politics and people, ready to help and eager to participate. Didi also had a lively interest in life and politics, but she was reticent, ready to participate but wanting to keep a low profile. We ate a light lunch and had our dinner only after Robi-da had returned from his office, had his cup of tea, read the newspaper and spent some time with Didi. I was usually in the background, desperately doing work that I should have done a long time ago. We did spend a little time together after dinner, but I returned to work as soon as possible. In short, it was the most uneventful time in my life in many ways and it was a good thing too, that I was able to quietly get on with my work and wasn't distracted. The routine was fixed, the rhythm regular and my life for the next few months leading to my examination clearly mapped out. I was actually most impressed with my discipline and dedication.

I did meet Sudarsana, but the event needed careful organisation. I didn't have easy access to a telephone. So I wrote to tell her that I'd go to the library on a particular day and time. Usually she would also come, and we'd meet, have our tea at the YMCA and return home, Sudarsana to Tollygunge and I to Dum Dum. Sudarsana's family had now moved from Regent Estate in Tollygunge to Golf Club Road, also in Tollygunge. This situation wasn't very satisfactory but examinations were a fact of life, and even those in love were not exempt from doing them. But discontent and rebellion were building up within me. There was only so much that the soul could take and flesh could bear!

One weekend I took the bus to Shambazar, then another bus to South Calcutta, and the tram to Tollygunge. I *had* to see Sudarsana. Even she didn't know I was coming. There are times when precipitate action is indicated and if you hold back, there's no way you can retrospectively put things right. At least, that was my moral and philosophical justification for defying the tyrannical monster – examination, and arriving, unexpectedly and unannounced, at Golf Club Road, Tollygunge, in the late afternoon one weekend in October 1947.

Sudarsana had just washed her hair and was waiting for it to dry. Sudarsana's mother was doing some complicated crocheting with a hooked needle; her father was reading *The Statesman*; her sister, Sunanda had gone out ... Sudarsana's father pushed his glasses down towards the tip of his nose and looked over them at me.

'Hello', I said.

'Hello', he replied. 'What brings you here? Khuku told me you weren't coming again till your exams were over in December. You were, she said, working like one totally committed, totally dedicated, and somewhat demented.' Khuku was Sudarsana's pet name.

I didn't respond to the question. The answer was obvious, wasn't it? I hadn't spent much time with his daughter for a long time, and I had got bored and frustrated and had travelled for over two hours to come and see her. I couldn't quite decide whether Sudarsana's father was being somewhat insensitive and unsympathetic – or pulling my leg I didn't understand the intention of his question. Somewhat confused, I lied.

'I am rather anxious and uncertain about my preparation. There have been so many interruptions the whole of this year! Sudarsana is quite right. I <u>have</u> been tied up with my work. *But tomorrow is my birthday and I wanted to be here.*'

Tomorrow, of course, was just another day, not my birthday.

'I see,' said Sudarsana's father. 'I <u>am</u> glad you decided to spend your birthday with us. Does Khuku know?'

'No, I don't think I ever mentioned it to her,' I said. I hadn't mentioned it to her because I didn't know myself that the 24th of October was my birthday – until a few minutes ago. I'd told a spontaneous, unpremeditated lie.

Sudarsana was making tea. She came in and was handing out cups of tea when her father told her that the next day was my birthday. She looked at me with surprise, with incredulous eyes.

'You never told me!' she said.

'I never thought of it,' I said.

'Do you know my date of birth?'

'Yes, I do, because we celebrated your birthday at the YMCA Restaurant.'

The matter was temporarily dropped. Then Sudarsana's mother, who'd withdrawn to the adjoining room for a brief break from her exacting crochet-work, joined us, and Sunanda returned home at the end of a long day of gallivanting. She'd gone out with some of her friends from Presidency College. As soon as she heard about my birthday, she took over.

'How old are you going to be?' she asked.

'Twenty-four,' I said.

'Then it's not important,' she said.

'I don't think so either,' I said.

'But,' she said, 'I think we should celebrate. I've decided that even your twenty-fourth birthday is important enough to celebrate. Baba, what do you think we should do?'

Before her father had time to answer, her mother responded. 'Why don't we take a boat to the Botanical Gardens? We'll take a picnic lunch with us, and spend some of the time sitting under my favourite banyan tree. Then a leisurely and quiet walk along the banks of the river just before sunset. That's what I want to do.'

'It's a great idea,' I said. 'What do you think?' I asked Sudarsana.

Sudarsana was enthusiastic. The river Ganges was the eternal river, the sacred river. We all loved it. It was the river which didn't only flow out there in Calcutta, but also in Benaras, Haridwar, and many sacred places. I would indeed love to spend my 'birthday' on the river and by the river and under the ancient banyan tree in the middle of the Botanical Gardens on the 24th of October.

That evening we sat around in the living room and there was spontaneous singing. Sudarsana's mother joined in from time to time but neither Sudarsana's father nor I sang a single note. Some must listen.

Chapter 7

'Birthday' visit to Tollygunge

Although I'd at last managed to be alone with Sudarsana, there was always the chance of Sunanda or Sudarsana's mother coming up to say goodnight. I lay in bed, thinking about the spontaneous lie I'd told everybody here, including Sudarsana. Why couldn't I say, 'I've come because I wanted to spend a little time with Sudarsana, whom I haven't seen for some time, whom I've missed? Surely I can't be expected to wait until the end of my examination in December?' Would I have the courage now to tell either Sudarsana or Sunanda or their parents that I had lied to justify my unexpected visit? That night I tried to justify my lying to myself. 'I'd never before celebrated my birthday. I had to have a birthday so that I could celebrate it. One date of birth was just as good as another'.

But nothing helped. I was full of contrition, and for a time, I couldn't sleep. But I had woken up early that morning and travelled for at least a couple of hours, tense with expectation and fearful of disappointment. After that, I must have fallen asleep. I woke up at about three o'clock, maybe even later, and went to the toilet. When I came out, Sudarsana was waiting near the door of her bedroom.

'I couldn't sleep. I was lying awake, so I saw you,' she whispered.

I was going to say something, but she put a finger to her lips. She slipped into the room between the toilet and the kitchen, where coal and firewood were stored for lighting the kitchen fire. The darkness in this small room when I shut the door was impenetrable. We kissed. We made love in the darkness – inexperienced lovers, finding their way into an unexplored world. What was going on in Sudarsana's mind? Did she feel closer to me than before? There was no way of knowing, and I'm not sure I worried about it. We got up in the darkness, got dressed in the darkness, clung to each other a very short time, and went back to our separate beds, in separate rooms. It was early morning. My sleep must have been profound after that. I woke up squinting into the shafts of sunlight coming in through the open window. I was engaged in fondly and lazily recalling everything that had happened the night before, or rather earlier that morning, when my reverie was loudly interrupted by the unique sound of the blowing of a conch shell just outside my door.

First Sunanda and then my mother-in-law came in. After the demonstration of genuine affection and expression of sincere good wishes, I was told that nobody should expect an elaborate breakfast that morning because an early start was important. I didn't waste any time at all, got washed and dressed and ready to go across the river I loved. It was a welcome break from the obsessive work that I was doing to overcome my fear and dislike of examinations. I had no doubt, as a student, that examinations were introduced by malevolent people in order to destroy our happiness.

One of the great experiences in Calcutta is a boat trip on the Ganges. A gentle breeze, the wide expanse of the river, the clear blue sky and the rhythmic sound of the oars as they dipped in and out of the water, created a euphoric feeling, further deepened by the presence of Sudarsana. We reached the gardens and walked to the great banyan tree, had our picnic and walked round the gardens. The banyan tree in the gardens is very old and occupies a large area, with its aerial roots growing down from its spreading branches. The roots form supporting pillars, making one tree look like a colony of trees. Countless people have had picnics in the shade of this benign old tree. I felt like a pilgrim visiting a sacred site. Sudarsana's father was a scientist, an engineer, well-informed and interesting to listen to. He gave us a lot of information about when and how the Botanical Gardens came into existence. He also talked about the Royal Botanical Gardens in Kew, Surrey, in England, which he'd visited when he was an engineering student at Sheffield. Kew Gardens was founded much earlier but given to the nation by Queen Victoria in the middle of the 19th century.

'How old is this banyan tree?' I asked.

'More than 200 years,' he said. 'It's probably the largest of its kind. These gardens are very old too. There's a large collection of orchids here.'

I had enjoyed the picnic, the scenery, and the company. I'd acquired information I didn't have before. The world around was bright and beautiful, but my recurrent problem was beginning to raise its recurrent head - Sudarsana and I found it difficult to leave the company of a loving family. We were never alone.

As if Sudarsana could hear what I was thinking, she wandered off towards the river in the direction of some trees and hedges. Maybe she was looking for those orchids that her father was talking about. I followed.

'What are you looking for?' I said.

'Not orchids,' she said. I was beginning to believe Sudarsana could hear my thoughts.

Shibpur Botanical Gardens seemed to be one of those places to which couples came to hold hands. Kissing in public would shock and surprise, but lovers holding hands seemed to be the norm. So we too held hands. Our conversation was casual, matter-of-fact. Just being together and feeling close was enough. It wasn't the done thing in College Street or in Tollygunge to walk around, holding hands. But here in the Botanical Gardens, under the open sky and surrounded by ancient trees, it was a natural thing to do.

After some time, we sat down on a bench under a tree. I asked Sudarsana to sing some Tagore songs. She sang softly but with her usual passion. Although she was singing for me, keeping her voice right down, there were a few people standing a few paces away, quietly listening. Sudarsana had a beautiful voice. I think I've said this before. I might say it again.

Sunanda had walked across to us to say it was time to go. We walked back to where Sudarsana's parents were waiting for us, all packed and ready. Sudarsana's mother asked me whether I'd had a good birthday. I said, truthfully, that it was the best birthday I'd ever had.

On the way back we watched the sun set across the river. Sudarsana's parents asked me whether I was happy where I was staying in Dum Dum, whether I found it a good place for doing my work, what Ronu's sister and brother-in-law were like and so on. Then we turned to politics. This was mainly conversation between Sudarsana's father and me about the aftermath of Partition and Independence, the Marshall Plan, the bloodbath of communal riots. He came through as caring and humane, as someone who was able to keep an open mind. He disapproved of the witch-hunt for communists in Hollywood, but, at the same time, couldn't reconcile himself to the single-party system of communist governments. The two sisters and their mother were having a relaxed conversation a few feet away from us. We'd now crossed the river. We got into Sudarsana's father's Austin and he drove us back to Tollygunge. There was some singing in the evening as usual, spontaneous, natural singing, without any musical accompaniment, in which I was persuaded to join in once or twice. After dinner, Sudarsana, Sunanda and I spent a little time together on the terrace before going to bed. It was a very pleasant day. 'A pity,' I thought, 'that you can have only one birthday a year.'

Returning to Dum Dum and settling down to work was less difficult than I thought it was going to be. It was the old routine – working with might and main all morning, before and after breakfast, visiting the library on Wednesday afternoon, when Sudarsana also would often come to work in the library, and then going for a cup of tea at the YMCA Restaurant. We were both less restless now, more certain of the fact that we were going to get married, waiting for the day when we'd start our life together. Nothing was said about the future. There was, however, unspoken certainty that we would soon be husband and wife and begin life together. We'd walked into each other's space, and the idea was to remain there.

The examination was now fast approaching. I had another practical problem to do with shelter. It would be hazardous to depend on public transport to bring me every morning to the university. Buses picked up their passengers for College Street at long intervals and they weren't always reliable. I'd practically left Bhim Ghose Lane, and space was a major problem at Mejda's little place. As soon as I'd solved one problem, there seemed to be another. The feeling I was beginning to experience was alarmingly similar to self-pity. So I decided to put it out of my mind.

Then one Wednesday, my day of visiting the library and meeting up with Sudarsana, I met Tapan, a highly intelligent, caring and sensitive friend. He asked me how I was getting on in Dum Dum. I told him how well I was looked after by Ronu's sister and brother-in-law. I also told him what was uppermost in my mind – accommodation near the university during the examination.

'Come and share my room in the hostel,' he had no hesitation in saying. 'Strictly speaking, it's against the rules, but if we're careful, we can manage.'

Tapan had a room in one of the hostels of Scottish Church College. He was excellent company, and I couldn't have asked for a better solution. But I had to be careful. I couldn't, for example, laugh out loud at night, especially after dinner, for fear of being discovered by the hostel superintendent, a Scotsman. Nor could we indulge in agitated discussions about controversial subjects. I managed to keep a low profile and slip in and out of Tapan's room in the hostel over almost two weeks. Tapan insisted that I had the bed and he slept on the floor on an improvised one.

There were no surprises. There were no unlikely or difficult questions in the examination to cause me any problems. There were no political or communal disturbances either to disrupt or disturb us during the period, although we had, not so long ago, experienced some of the worst horrors and unforgettable nightmares ever in the history of our sub-continent. Those we had to forget, at least for the time being. Without some selective lapse of memory, life can become unbearable.

Although my relationship with Mr Roy, the landlord of Bhim Ghose Lane room, was neither cordial nor particularly strained, I had a feeling of unease when I moved back into my single room abode. The caretaker of the place was quite pleased to see me. He actually spent some time talking to me that afternoon, whereas he had in the past always been too busy to waste his time. Part of the reason, I think, was that he knew that his employer was my benefactor and I stayed there without paying rent. My long absence seemed to have changed his attitude for the time being. He even made me a cup of tea which was hot, strong and sweet, the kind I liked those days. The homecoming to Bhim Ghose Lane was pleasant. This made a huge difference because it took away my feeling of homelessness. What's more, freed from the worries and anxieties of writing an important examination without adequate preparation, I was eagerly waiting for the time when Sudarsana and I could meet up again. But before we met up, there was something very important to attend to. I hadn't been doing my tuitions. I'd been living on the little money I'd saved, which was soon going to run out. Just when life was beginning to look full of promise, was this perpetual and awkward problem going to turn life upside down?

In this rather reflective frame of mind, I went to Mejda and Boudi to have my supper. Mejda told me that I was to see someone by the name of Sinha the next day because he might organise a job for me. I had no experience, no expertise and very little confidence, but I was ready to do my best, provided the job I was offered wasn't way beyond my ability to cope with it. At the time, I had practically no professional skills or specialist knowledge.

Mr Sinha lived in an upstairs flat in a two-storeyed house. The living room was lined with bookshelves full of books of mainly travel and literature, both Bengali and English. I registered the fact that he liked Tolstoy, Dickens and Victor Hugo. I can't recall them all. I think there was also Romain Rolland, Thackeray, George Eliot and Agatha Christie – many more books by her than by anybody else. There was a photograph of Gandhiji out on his Salt March on one wall – just one photograph – on one wall.

Mr Sinha was tall, had thinning hair and wore glasses. He was polite, pleasant and friendly. He asked me several questions about my education and interests, and then wrote a letter to one Mr Neogy, whose name was familiar. He'd come to South

Suburban School once while I was a student there to give a talk on his travels in the Himalayas.

'Give Mr Neogy this letter. He'll ask you a few questions. Then he'll either recommend you for a job or he won't. I wish you the best of luck.'

I held the letter in my hand and got up to go. He said I should give Mr Neogy his best regards. 'Goodbye,' he said, 'and good luck.'

Mr Sinha also lived in Shambazar, in North Calcutta, but I can't recall the name of the street. This was in the middle of a week and I wasn't going to see Mr Neogy until the morning of Monday the following week. I didn't think that I stood any real chance of landing a job so soon after my examination. People had to be in and out of many interviews before they landed a job, and I had to be prepared for such eventualities and make contingency plans. 'It will probably be necessary to go back to the pupils I was teaching,' I said to myself, hoping that some inconsiderate interloper hadn't usurped my place during my long absence.

I still had a little money left from what I'd saved from before my examination. Ronu's Didi or older sister and her husband, Robi-da, didn't let me make any contribution for the months I'd stayed there, so I could hold out for a little longer. I had toast and tea and an omelette for lunch, wandered around in the New Market and in the evening turned up at Golf Club Road. Everybody was at home and they were all genuinely pleased to see me. The conversation flowed. Sudarsana's father was particularly interested to know how I thought I'd fared in the examination, and when the results were going to be published. Her mother was more interested about my physical well-being. Where was I living at the time? Where was I eating? Was I now travelling again from north to south to teach students?

'I haven't been doing my tuitions since before the exam. I may have to go back to teaching, but I'll wait first to see what happens on Monday, when I go for an interview for a job,' I said.

Sudarsana's father was immediately interested. When I told him I was going to see one Mr Neogy for a job in an advertising company, The Scientific Publicity, he said he had known Mr Neogy for a very long time. He wished me luck. '... And do give Mr Neogy my regards,' he said.

Sudarsana was uncharacteristically pensive this evening, pensive but not distant. She sat close to me, gave my hand a friendly squeeze or two, but didn't join in the conversation with her usual enthusiasm. She was quite content to let life pass her by, to be a spectator, not an actor. I had no doubt at all that she loved me, and she was feeling close to me. Yet her reticence created within me a slight anxiety, a sense of unease. Sunanda made up for her sister's silence by talking about the few young women in Presidency College and the overwhelming number of young men, and about the relationship between the majority and the minority. What did worry me somewhat about Sunanda was the certainty with which she assessed values, ideas and people. A little doubt, a slight uncertainty would have, I thought, made her more credible.

Dinner was a simple affair with *dal* and fried aubergine, rice and fish curry, followed by sweet curds and *sandesh*, a sweet made out of milk. Rice and fish curry was my favourite food and I usually got it when I visited Golf Club Road. Sudarsana, who had spent most of the evening sitting next to me while Sunanda held forth, now joined in, wondering about the condition of the refugees on both sides of the newly-created borders of India and Pakistan; for the subject of discussion in most houses, clubs, offices, factories, streets and restaurants was still this great migration.

'Just think of these millions of people, deprived of their homes, uncertain of their future, often travelling through hostile country, in search of security and shelter and a little food in order to survive,' Sudarsana said, trying to keep her emotions in check.

Sudarsana's father said it was probably the greatest mass migration in history. Sudarsana's mother wondered how long it was going to take before these hapless refugees had a life with some semblance of normality and Sunanda didn't understand why the international community didn't come to the aid of these refugees at all. But international help wasn't available in those days, certainly not on a scale which could have made a real difference.

After dinner, Sunanda and the parents went to the living room. Sudarsana and I didn't. We hadn't been together on our own since making love in the early morning of my "birthday", more than two months ago. My examination had come and gone, events of great national and international importance had happened, but we had only met a few times in one of the cubicles of the YMCA restaurant and held hands behind the curtains, with Sudarsana saying she missed me and I saying I missed her. Then Sudarsana went to her room, put on a warm sweater and brought along one of her father's woolen shawls for me. We went up to the terrace.

'December is quite cold on the terrace,' she said. But because it was cold, we had some privacy. The neighbours rarely went up to the terrace during the cold months. We kissed. We remained in each other's arms. We didn't say anything for some time. Then I said the obvious thing.

'I missed you,' I said.

'I missed you too,' she said.

We both went quiet again, feeling happy just from our closeness. She ran her fingers through my long hair: she liked my hair long.

'I'm carrying your baby,' she said, quietly but with pride and pleasure

'Are you sure?' I asked breathlessly.

'I've missed for two months. Yes, I'm quite sure.'

I embraced Sudarsana, I kissed her and I told her that the idea of being the father of her child was overwhelming. It made life special. It made me special. It made us special.

'I felt quite certain that I was pregnant after the first month but I didn't tell you anything because I'd already caused a lot of distraction before your exam. You were spending time with me when you should have been in the library. Excitement and distraction wouldn't have been good for you. You might have forgotten who wrote King Lear,' she said.

I asked her why she had looked pensive earlier in the evening when we were all sitting in the living room. She said she did feel anxious about how her father would take it. Her mother wouldn't say anything to hurt her – she would almost certainly rejoice. But her stringent father might be disappointed that we'd acted against convention when there was no real need to do so.

'I respect your father. I'll be disappointed if there is a conventional response from him,' I said.

Sudarsana pointed out that there were some very conventional people that her father had to reckon with – his sister, for example, who lived in Park Street.

'There's something I must tell you. I didn't once think that you might react with doubt or misgiving, go quiet and frown, or worry about consequences. You proved me right. You've made me happy.'

It was getting late and the temperature had fallen a few degrees. It was time we went to bed – our separate beds. But before we did that there were two decisions we made: Sudarsana must see her cousin, Tutu-da, who was a gynaecologist at Eden Hospital, for confirmation of her pregnancy, and I must go and see Sudarsana's father in his office during his lunch-break to break this news to him.

The chasm between the individual and society won't disappear in a hurry. Out there, in our own familiar world, there were people who felt threatened by deviations from the norm – their norm… I was thinking many things before I went to sleep. But what was uppermost in my mind was what Sudarsana had said just before we parted that night.

'I want you to remember that nothing in my life – no previous experience – compares with my love for you. And nothing has ever given me more joy than this baby in my womb'.

The next morning, both Sunanda and her father were out. Sudarsana, her mother and I were at home, drinking tea, quite late in the morning. Sudarsana said that we'd known each other for more than one and a half years, yet she knew very little about me. I'd told her of my great escape from Benaras, and in the context of that, mentioned my father, my mother, my sisters, brothers and their husbands and wives. She wanted to know about my friends at college. I told her about Cuthbert, who was always falling in and out of love. Most of my friends in college were quite indulgent about Cuthbert's boastful behaviour because he was friendly and amusing, totally devoid of malice and aggression. At this point Sudarsana's mother excused herself and went to see about lunch. The friend in St Xavier's College who was closest to me was Ronu, whom Sudarsana knew quite well because they both belonged to the Brahmo Samaj. I told Sudarsana that I admired Ronu, he was a role-model, a mentor – especially when it came to relationships with women.

Once he'd said to me, 'They like to give you the impression that they're unavailable, unassailable – all women, whether they're young or old. But they're just as vulnerable as you or me. I really believe they like you to take the initiative. So give it a go and see what happens.' Ronu was always trying to pump a little initiative into me.

I did give it a go, I told Sudarsana, and succeeded. Young women – younger than me – came to Debu-da to learn to sing. Sometimes Debu-da wasn't at home and my sister-in-law was in the kitchen. On three separate occasions, I tried to kiss three different music students of Debu-da and each time I succeeded.... We were in a reminiscing mood.

'I was, I thought, desperately in love with a cousin of my aunt, a tall, strong young man, several years older than me. But it didn't work,' she said.
'I was seriously involved,' Sudarsana said. 'I was hurt but I survived. That too was before, long before we went to Shantiniketan. And now I love life in general and this life in particular.' she said, pointing to where our baby was.

After lunch Sudarsana walked down with me to the tram stop to say goodbye. We had a heavy and important schedule ahead of us. She had to tell Tutu-da that she was expecting a baby and fix up an appointment for the necessary test. And she had also to take care of herself, as much for herself as for the baby. I would first attend my interview and let her know how I'd fared. I'd also arranged to see her father as soon after the interview as he found it convenient to see me. The tram came and I got on to it and left, waving goodbye. She didn't look desolate at all. She had company which probably mattered more to her than I ever did, a life that would live and grow inside her womb.

I went for my interview on Monday morning. Mr Neogy asked me questions about my family and about my education. I told him I had listened to one of his talks about his travels and seen the magnificent pictures which were projected onto a screen – of the Himalayas and some Himalayan regions when he gave his talk

'Did you like my talk?' he asked.

I told him it was a popular talk and my friends and I as well as others discussed the talk and the film for weeks. We did like it.

What I liked about this interview was that it didn't feel like an interview. Mr Neogy wasn't so much interested in what information I'd hoarded during the twenty odd years of my life. It was more about who I was. I thought that the interview had gone well. It had.

'How soon can you start work?' he asked.

'Whenever you want me to,' I replied, startled and then relieved.

'I'd like you to come along next Monday by 9 o'clock. I wear my clothes Bengali style. Most wear shirt and trousers. There isn't any dress code, but you'll have to deal with people, go out and meet clients and potential clients, so you've to be presentable. See you on Monday.'

I said thank you and left. The relief was immense. The little money I had saved was running out. Now I wouldn't have to depend on anybody. I went to the receptionist and gave her Sudarsana's telephone number. She connected me and I gave her the good news. She was delighted and relieved and wanted to see me. I wondered, I said, if she could meet me at the entrance of the Metro Cincma about three o'clock. We could have some tea somewhere and talk and she could go back to Tollygunge and I could go back to Shambazar. I'd have to go to Shambazar because Mejda, my second eldest brother, who was instrumental to my getting this job, was waiting to know how I'd fared, and I'd promised to go and see him and tell him personally how the interview went. He wouldn't expect to know the result because normally it took at least a week before one was told.

Sudarsana came. We had tea and cake at a restaurant quite close to the cinema. She said she'd made an appointment to see Tutu-da the next day. Would I want to go with her? We arranged to meet in the waiting room of the gynaecological department of Eden Hospital. When I arrived, Sudarsana had already seen Tutu-da.

'I spoke to Tutuda. He said there is no doubt. The baby's fine. All's well. Regular checks are a good idea, he said. He's given me the next appointment,' Sudarsana said. Tutu-da was now busy doing his round. I didn't get to see him.

Then she said she'd changed her mind about my going to see her father now. She didn't think it'd serve any purpose to tell her father about her pregnancy because it would only upset him. She suggested that we get married and then let her parents know that our first baby would appear on the scene about three months before anybody would expect him or her to be there. After the birth, she'd like to be with her mother for two or three months and then we'd set up our own home. Now that I had a job, she didn't see any problems.

'And well done, Ganesh,' she said.' Your getting this job will make all the difference. And you must come over this weekend and give my parents and Sunanda the opportunity to congratulate you personally. What's more, I wouldn't mind seeing you either,' she said.

We went to see Tutu-da again a few days later. He took us to the Medical College canteen, where he gave Sudarsana some appropriate advice and said that all being well, the baby should be born some day during the third or fourth week of July. Then he talked about diet and exercise and the necessity for regular check-ups, and we left, pleased with ourselves because it was now confirmed that our baby was doing well, and should be with us in a matter of months.

Mejda and Baudi were happy that I'd got this job. Mejda had a special reason for being pleased because he had initiated the process by talking to Mr Sinha. I bought some special sweets to celebrate the occasion. We'd heard about champagne but never tasted it. In any case, it would be unthinkable. Alcohol and physical love outside marriage were equally reprehensible in our Bengali middle class culture. I never mentioned Sudarsana to either Mejda or Baudi because they wouldn't approve. Arranged marriages, in which the whole clan could participate, were popular in our families because it was an occasion the community waited to celebrate. When one chose one's own partner, it was called 'love marriage'. It was considered a selfish act. It displayed an egocentric obsession which the community didn't want to promote, because it went against the greater common interests of the family, the extended family and the community. At least that's the way many people thought and felt. Their active participation would also alienate Father, incur his wrath, especially when I'd rejected his plan of an arranged marriage for me. I also hadn't discussed my relationship with Sudarsana with either Debu-da or his wife either, although Debu-da was a rebel, who didn't believe in such nonsense as family loyalty, clan-solidarity or Hindu tradition. I would tell a few friends about the coming event, especially those like Ajoy, Ronu and Mutu, who knew both Sudarsana and me.

Excitement was writ large on the face of Sudarsana's mother. It was obvious to me that, apart from my getting a job, there was some other reason for the general atmosphere of excitement. Our marriage was discussed, and the primary reason for everybody's excitement was the prospect of a wedding in the family, which meant the reunion of nephews, nieces, cousins, uncles and aunts, apart from close friends. Sometimes even friends and relations we'd given up as missing or dead would turn up at a family wedding. My landing a job was incidental. The excitement was mainly about the wedding. But neither Sunanda nor her Mother forgot to congratulate me on having landed a job at this particular time.

When I met Sudarsana's father, he congratulated me. The job was briefly discussed. Then we soon got on to the subject of the wedding. Our wedding had been discussed and tentative decisions made about when we were getting married. He then congratulated me for having got the job – because it fitted in perfectly with his plan.

'I don't suppose you have any problems about getting married in January, have you?' he said.

Then he suggested a date in January. I'm not sure which date it was, but it was in the third week of January. I think it was the same date on which Sudarsana's father's parents were married. There would be only one reception, not two. Sudarsana's parents would have a reception on the day of the wedding, but my father and brothers were not expected to reciprocate after a few days according to the tradition of our families. Everybody knew that my father would be hurt and angry when he came to know about my marriage, and because of my father, none of my relations would want to participate in the ceremony or come to the wedding party. Then there was the problem of my homelessness. Where was I going to take Sudarsana after the wedding? Problems existed, but we were going to get wed!

Then one day many guests – men and women – men wearing their traditional *dhuti* and *punjabi* with, quite often, a shawl tossed over their shoulders, and women wearing silk saris – arrived to participate in the wedding ceremony of Sudarsana Roy and Ganesh Bagchi. There were flowers in the women's hair and in scores of vases. The *sanai* or *sehnai,* a kind of bagpipe, was playing to the accompaniment of percussion music - a tradition for Bengali weddings. The fragrance of flowers and perfume hung in the air. And the whole atmosphere was livened up by human voices – people laughing and talking.

A South-Indian lay-priest performed the wedding ceremony in English. The ritual was punctuated with the songs of Tagore, which both Sudarsana and I loved. At the end of the chanting of *slokas* and the singing and the taking of marriage vows, when we were centre-stage, the main ritual was over. After that, we stood around, Sudarsana and I, not far from each other, and received the blessings of older people and the good wishes of friends and younger people. The felicitations were warm and friendly. We loved everybody, everybody loved us. It was as if we'd acquired a new dimension that evening. It felt good, but both Sudarsana and I were beginning to feel very tired. Sudarsana's mother was probably watching us – she was always alert and caring. She asked whether we shouldn't give it a break and quietly wander away into our bedroom. I said that's really what we wanted to do. Our friends and well-wishers rapidly began to disperse – as if they'd heard what we'd said. Some had to go and have their dinner and some to go home. And Sudarsana and I did exactly what my mother-in -law had suggested – retired to our bedroom.

I shut the door. We'd waited for this moment for a long time, although I did enjoy being the centre of attention of people, many of them attractive young women in silk saris with flowers in their hair. But after the music and the excitement were over, and the guests had either departed or were eating their dinner, what was there to wait for?

We were on our own, quite unexpectedly. We sat close to each other – the newly-married on our brand new bed decorated with flowers.

'How does it feel?' I asked Sudarsana.

'It's difficult to say. I think music, flowers, excited voices, happiness – these make a difference. I have been happy and excited. But now I'm tired,' Sudarsana said.

She asked me if I'd enjoyed getting married, and I said I did, although the wedding party was larger and noisier than I was prepared for

'I'm feeling tired,' Sudarsana said again. 'I did feel excited and happy, but towards the end I was beginning to feel weary. Don't forget there are two of us.'

She ought to have a good night's sleep, I said. She didn't need much persuasion.

While Sudarsana slept peacefully, I was awake, going over the events of the day in my head. When I was about twenty, I started smoking. I didn't smoke heavily, but occasionally got some pleasure out of it. I didn't have the opportunity to smoke all evening because to smoke in front of people who were older – parents, uncles, older brothers, for example – was to show them disrespect. I went on to the veranda, wrapped my shawl around me, lit a cigarette and smoked while watching the stars flickering in a clear night sky and thinking about the eventful day. When I came back to the room to go to bed, Sudarsana was fast asleep. She looked vulnerable. She'd had a tiring day. Being the centre of attention is both exciting and exhausting. For one evening, friends, relations and strangers treated us as celebrities, the main protagonists in a noisy play, and then disappeared. Sudarsana had to cope, which wasn't easy for her, and now she was fast asleep, exhausted. I too felt tired and lonely and wondered whether all this social meeting and parting, all the hard work, noise and expense was really necessary. What purpose did it serve? It was well past midnight. Most inhabitants in our half of the world must have been asleep.

Morning came with the smell of bacon and eggs from the kitchen and the sound of laughter outside our window. We were beginning to take it all in, still lying in our new bed, trying to get used to the idea that we were now husband and wife.

It was a weekend. Everybody was at home. Sudarsana's two younger cousins hadn't gone to school and Sunanda and my father-in-law were trying to give the place some semblance of order. There was a distinct change in the attitude of everybody towards me. The young man who visited the house every now and then had overnight become family – after having taken part in a time-honoured ritual. The affection, attention, warmth and friendliness came through because of everybody's casual but unmistakable assumption that the occasional visitor had now become integrated; acquired rights and privileges denied to him before. I think I noticed a definite reorientation, a slight change in attitude and behaviour.

Tonight we didn't go to bed to sleep and we decided that my father-in-law should be told without any more delay that our baby would arrive in just over six months. Yes, I'd see my father-in-law in his Calcutta Corporation office and tell him that our child was well on the way. Back in the office of Scientific Publicity Company, business was as usual until one of my colleagues asked how it felt to be a married man. Then others remembered, and congratulated me, most of them married men and women. Mr Neogy also congratulated me and later, asked me to go with him to Eden Gardens, where the Industrial Exhibition was going to take place. The stalls were at different stages of completion. Some had made very little progress and Mr Neogy wanted me to note down their names so that he could ring them and request that they should aim at greater progress. I was impressed to see the scale and ambition of this exhibition, although what I saw was just the beginning. Some stalls had been finished or nearly completed: a few of them very impressive. All kinds of national industries – including cottage industries – were going to be represented in this exhibition on an unprecedented scale. I was proud to be part of this organisation. Someone in the office who was very pleasant and friendly gave me the impression that he was disappointed that he wasn't one of the wedding guests, so I took him out to lunch. I'd borrowed some money from Krishna Shroff, a friend, to buy the wedding ring and to tide over the weeks before I received my first month's salary. I had to be careful. My salary was a few hundred rupees.
In one particular respect, this was an important day because I was leaving my office early to see my father-in-law to tell him that Sudarsana and I were going to be parents, and that he and my mother-in-law would be grandparents, about three months before tradition and custom sanctioned that to happen; that Sudarsana became pregnant in October and the baby should be born in July.

I was impressed with my father-in-law's large room in the office, his enormous secretariat table – Mr Neogy's was only about half its size – and the general feeling of tidiness and efficiency around the place. He knew I was coming but had no idea what it was about. He asked me whether I wanted tea. I said I didn't.

'Actually,' I said, 'I've come to tell you that Sudarsana is pregnant. The baby is expected in July.' I'd rehearsed the sentence several times in my head. I tried to sound as natural as possible, natural but not casual. But right then I was less concerned about how I said it. What mattered was what effect it had on my father-in-law.

'That's almost three months earlier,' he said.

'That's right,' I said.

'Who else knows about this?' he asked.

'Tutuda has known from the start. He has examined her, carried out necessary tests and confirmed that the baby's due in July,' I answered.

My father-in-law frowned. My progressive, Brahmo, engineering- graduate -from-Sheffield- University father-in-law didn't smile with pleasure, didn't show any excitement, didn't jump out of his swivel chair to come and hug me or shake my hand, but frowned. I was disappointed. But why was I disappointed? Did I really expect him to be ecstatic, cry hosanna, or sing for joy? Not at all. But I did expect a positive response, even if it were muted – since he was sitting in an executive engineer's chair in an office at the time. But a frown? Signs of anxiety? Those were the last things I'd expected.

'I'll tell Sudarsana's mother, of course, but nobody else at this stage, and I'd rather you didn't either,' he said.

So were we to be partners in a conspiracy? I wasn't going to accost neighbours and tell them about this very important and significant event in my life, but why should I treat this as my guilty secret? Why shouldn't Sunanda know and Ronu and Debuda? The suggestion was, unmistakably and overwhelmingly, that my first-born was going to be an embarrassment for respectable citizens like Mr Tarun Roy. I'd begun to have a great deal of affection and respect for my father-in-law, which silently began to wither as I sat opposite him and watched his growing anxiety about his loss of face.

'We'll talk things over when we're back home. Don't feel too stressed and anxious. On no account must we say or do anything to make Sudarsana worry. Your mother-in-law is really the person to talk to.' That was better. I relaxed a little. There was no word of reassurance, no expression of happiness, no upsurge of tenderness; but by showing concern about his daughter's well-being, he'd made amends.

In the evening, my mother-in-law's reaction was spontaneous. She called out to Sudarsana, who was making tea, and asked her to come to the living room. The moment Sudarsana had come into the room; she embraced her with great love and tenderness and said, 'This is what we've been waiting for – a grandchild. Friends and relations younger than us, have half-a-dozen, some of them. Now I feel equal to them.' She kissed her on the side of her head and then hugged her. There were tears in Sudarsana's eyes too. Why cry when you're happy?

Father-in-law was better at being practical, expressing concern about health, diet, exercise and things like that.

'You're in the third month. You ought to have a medical check-up immediately. I'll talk to Dr Dasgupta.'

Sudarsana told her parents that that was something we wouldn't neglect, hadn't neglected. 'We've been in touch with Tutu-da right from the beginning. It was Tutu-da who confirmed that I was pregnant, and I've been going to him for check-ups.'

Both her parents were reassured. Sunanda was visiting a friend after college because it was her friend's birthday. She noisily expressed her delight and approbation. Famous in the family as one who always went for precipitate action, Sunanda at once told us what we should call our baby if we had a boy and what names would be appropriate if we had a girl. Father-in-law said he also had a few ideas. When we went to bed that night we were a much relieved, a much happier couple, Sudarsana and I.

Work at the Industrial Exhibition was progressing well. Some of the stalls and temporary buildings were beautifully designed and constructed. It seemed like a waste of money because, after the exhibition was over, all the structures had to come down, leaving the Eden Gardens as pristine as they were before, and it was our responsibility to ensure that they were. We had our own office in the gardens to monitor progress, provide information, and to meet representatives of various organisations. I regularly spent a little time there.

Mr Majumdar, who was our General Manager, had financed the entire enterprise, and Mr Neogy was the man with ideas, the Chief Executive Officer. Between them they had planned the venture, which was ambitious and financially hazardous. Therefore they must have been greatly relieved when they found that the response was deep as well as wide.

Not only did most of the local industries respond, but organisations from farther afield – Bombay and Delhi – also wanted to participate. Our responsibility was to provide the infrastructure, which included water, electricity, sanitation and other essentials, and to ensure that visitors could stop somewhere for a cup of tea and something to eat or just to rest their tired limbs. We had meetings for discussing various aspects of our responsibility. We were also encouraged to make suggestions for undertaking duties and extending the sphere of our activities. I suggested the making of a film which would be in three parts: stage one – events leading to the exhibition; stage two – the exhibition itself, and stage three – events after the exhibition. The exhibition itself would have to be filmed with creative imagination.

My life was now on an even keel. I was busy all day, and in the evening, when I returned to Golf Club Road, Sudarsana was always there, because she'd abandoned the idea of doing an MA. In a few months it'd be somewhat difficult for her to concentrate on what learned professors at the university had to say about Blake's poetry or Hardy's novels if the baby inside her, bored by learned generalizations, decided to kick. In any case, she was beginning to feel rather weary at the end of the day. So when I came back I'd tell her what was happening at the Eden Gardens, and she'd tell me how she'd spent the day. Then, quite often, she would sing in the evening. Sometimes my mother-in-law would join in and, sometimes, Sunanda. Some people might designate my life as humdrum, devoid of drama and excitement. Others might find my bourgeois existence 'weary, stale, flat and unprofitable'. For me this was bliss – a wife I related to, a loving environment, food and shelter, and a job that guaranteed a regular income at the end of the month.

About this time, came the news of the assassination of Mahatma Gandhi. The violence, death and destruction which had marred the joy of independence for so many million people in undivided India, and then in India and Pakistan, had continued. Mahatma Gandhi had made it known that the violence and the killing had made him desperately unhappy and that he was going on a fast, as he had done many times before, to register his protest, his sadness and his disapproval. He did go on a fast on the 12th of January, but after about a week he was persuaded to give it up because leaders of both Hindu and Muslim communities had assured him that they would intervene to prevent further carnage and stop all kinds of violence.

Gandhiji was looking very weak. If he'd continued for any longer, his frail body wouldn't be able to take the strain. But at the very first prayer meeting after the fast, a bomb went off in the Garden of Birla House in Delhi where the prayer was taking place. It didn't seem to those who were attending the prayer meeting that the blast had made any impression on Mahatma Gandhi. It was business as usual for him, who had quietly and without any panic, defied death many times before. Neither he nor those attending his prayer meeting had panicked: they had prayed and sung and dispersed in their usual way.

Two days had passed, just two days. Gandhiji was walking to the prayer meeting as usual in the garden of Birla House in Delhi, rather weak from his recent fasting. A young man emerged from among the people waiting for the meeting, greeted him and shot him three times at close range. The name of the young man was Nathuram Godse, who belonged to a fundamentalist Hindu organisation which believed in perpetual confrontation with the Muslims until all Muslims were annihilated – a rather unrealistic vision of the future. The young man was quickly removed from the scene by someone from the Indian air force, thus preventing further violence, which could have been ugly and brutal: inappropriate reprisal for this great man of peace.

Jawaharlal Nehru made a moving speech. There was a day of mourning. The nation grieved. It was the end of an era.

The assassination of Gandhi made a profound impact on all of us. The nation was in a state of shock as never before in my lifetime. At the first meeting at our office after the tragedy, it was decided that the Industrial Exhibition would have to be postponed. 'Our beloved leader,' said Jawaharlal, 'is dead'. People had to say it again and again to believe it, to come to terms with it. Sudarsana and I had decided that after I'd got my salary, we'd go out for an evening – watch a film, eat out and celebrate by ourselves. We hadn't gone out together for some time. We cancelled our plan. Many people I knew were quietly mourning. It was as if a close relative, someone they genuinely loved and respected had suddenly and unexpectedly died. In spite of his greatness, Gandhiji had managed not to have become an inaccessible icon. His way of living and thinking was simple and human. Even his political philosophy was fairly straightforward: We shall not co-operate with an administration that exploits us, humiliates us, and rules us by force.

The imperialists believed in and practised one kind of fundamentalism, the conservative, caste-ridden Hindus practised another. Churchill had stated openly that he'd have dearly loved to have this *'half-naked fakir'* out of the way. He didn't mind if the means were violent. Nathuram Godse had merely been the instrument of execution dearly and devoutly wished by many in whose way Gandhi stood. But the people of India missed him and would miss him for a very long time to come.

The cruel irony of it all was that the man who had prevented the death of so many, for whom all life was sacred, whose religion was peace, had died at the hands of an assassin. But then, this was not the first time this had happened, nor was it going to be the last time. There'll always be people who will worship *Ravana,* the demon of malevolent destruction.

And then a sudden upheaval of a positive kind took place in our lives. One of Sudarsana's uncles brought the news that someone he knew was offering his very decent one-room flat in Chandni Chowk for 70 rupees a month and he was going to let it out for a year. Sudarsana showed great interest because she wanted an independent household where she was in control although her loving parents were totally unobtrusive. She spoke to her mother. Originally, our plan was to continue to live with Sudarsana's parents till the baby was born and a few months old. But here was a flat on offer that we could move into at once – a flat at an affordable rent. When the baby was born, Mother-in-law could come and stay with us for a month or two to initiate Sudarsana to the challenges and mysteries of motherhood and then visit us from time to time. We discussed our plan in the evening the next day, and since there didn't seem to be any major objections, and both Sudarsana's parents agreed that it was worth a try, we arranged to see the flat that weekend. It was a fairly new building, well-appointed, with a large bedroom, an attached bathroom, a living room opening out onto a small balcony and a kitchen leading out of the living room. We decided we'd rent the flat from the following week.

It took us an amazingly short time after we'd moved into our flat to get settled, and for me to feel like the lord of the manor. Sudarsana was indefatigable: the move seemed to have increased both her mental and physical energy. Then we had an incredible bit of good luck – someone by the name of Ishwar turned up at the door of the flat and said that since we were moving into a new place, we might need someone to do the cooking and keep the place clean, and he offered his services. The wages for which he was ready to work for us seemed reasonable, and since he was a man of pleasant aspect, we appointed him – without any references whatsoever. Ishwar turned out to be a pleasant and responsible partner in our new adventure. A tall, strong young man of thirty-odd years – Ishwar was older than both of us. Though a total stranger – he slept at night on the floor of the living room and was Sudarsana's sole companion during the time I spent at Scientific Publicity and Eden Gardens. Ishwar was a naturally good, honest and responsible person.

Mother-in-law would spend a day occasionally with us. Sudarsana's father would drive her up to the flat and then go to Corporation Street to his job. Occasionally, he'd turn up for lunch. I didn't come home for lunch. In the evening Father-in-law would collect my mother-in-law from our flat and return to Tollygunge. The regular rhythm of my life, our own independent establishment and a regular income with which we could just about manage had created in me a sense of well-being which bordered on euphoria. Dependence, however convenient or comfortable, created a sense of spiritual unease, even if the people one depended on were most considerate and unobtrusive – like my parents-in-law.

However it wasn't plain-sailing all the way. After a long wait, mainly on account of the assassination of Gandhiji, we were now ready to open the exhibition, and since we were a publicity company and aware of how to make a product or an event known widely, there was a very large crowd of visitors on the opening day. They were impressed with the exhibition and very surprised to see how many different industrial products were now being manufactured in our country. Britain had at one time imposed restrictions on various products for fear of competition with British goods, but during the two wars – the First World War of 1914-18 and the Second World War of 1939-45 – the colonial masters had relaxed controls which they hadn't imposed again after the end of hostilities. And in the last few years it just wouldn't do to take regressive steps when Indian independence was being discussed seriously. Yes, the response to the exhibition was unmistakably positive, and the visitors were enjoying themselves and, at the same time, becoming much better informed about India's achievements in the manufacturing industries.

What a good proportion of the young visitors were not impressed with was the admission fee, which they, mainly students, found colossally unfair. A group of young men and a few young women stood outside the main entrance of our office and started shouting slogans. We were called anti-people profiteers. A young man stood on a wooden box, in which various articles for our temporary office had been transported when the exhibition was being set up, and asked how we could expect students to pay such a high entrance fee. More people crowded round the speaker and applauded him. I thought the situation was becoming menacing, and on the spur of the moment, I made a conciliatory speech without asking the permission of either Mr Neogy or Mr Majumdar. I said, truthfully, that we expected mainly people from the business community and the offices of industrialists to come to the exhibition. They wouldn't find the admission fee prohibitive. Although we were pleased and flattered that so many young people, mainly students, had turned up, we hadn't expected them. We would from the very next day introduce a much lower admission fee for students. Students who produced their ticket at the entrance or in our office would be refunded the extra money we'd charged.

'What kind of concession are you offering?' asked a tall young man from the back of the crowd.

'It'll be about 50%,' I said, again without consulting anybody.

There was consultation between the young people in different groups. Many of them had calmed down but some dissident groups still looked unhappy and menacing and jeered when I suggested that the exhibition was presenting to us the nation's achievement in the field of industry and we should be proud of ourselves.

I'm afraid the assembled crowd didn't find my speech riveting, so they were beginning to disperse. Though it wasn't a disappointment for me – more than anything else, I wanted them to go away and look at the few thousand exhibits – admire them and enjoy themselves. As they went their way, laughing and chatting, their angry mood already a thing of the past, I slipped out of our enclosure to a small restaurant near the entrance gate for a hot cup of tea and a quiet reflection on the unexpected crisis and its equally sudden resolution.

Wasn't it presumptuous of me to address the crowd on behalf of the organisers and hold forth as if I was some small time Mark Antony? Would it not have been better for me to go into our office and tell Mr Neogy or Mr Majumdar that there was trouble brewing, so that one of them could go out and face the crowd? And what if the situation had got out of hand?

Prakash came through the door: Mr Neogy was looking for me, he said. He walked past me and joined some friends a few tables away. I was expecting Mr Neogy or Mr Majumdar or both to send for me so that they could ask me who I thought I was. Did I not realize that things hung in the balance? One angry word, a high moral tone, a raised voice and the crowd could have gone on the rampage. It was a huge and unnecessary risk I'd taken. But the situation did <u>not</u> get out of hand. The crowd did <u>not</u> go on the rampage. So why was I worried? Because I was unsure. Because I thought I was presumptuous.

It was quite late. I should have got back home an hour ago. Mr Majumdar had gone home. Mr Neogy didn't keep me waiting, so there was no suspense, no palpitating heart thumping against my rib cage. Mr Neogy wasn't frowning either, or looking anxious and bothered. He was smiling.

'Well done, Ganesh. What you did was admirable. There wasn't the time to wait. When the crowd gets into an ugly mood, there is no time to wait. Someone had to do something quickly and you did just that. Timing was important. And the other important thing was age. How old are you?' Mr Neogy asked.

'I'm 24,' I said.

'Most members of the protesting crowd were in their twenties. They found you credible. They trusted you. If Mr Majumdar or I had talked to them, they'd react like young people do when confronted with the representatives of the establishment, especially in Calcutta, with distrust. You spoke their language. I appreciated your immediate reaction to the crisis. Thank you.'

Then Mr Neogy suggested that I went with him in his car because it was quite late. I gratefully accepted the offer and arrived back at our flat about one and a half hours late.

Sudarsana was distraught. We had no telephone at home, so I couldn't inform her. The reason why she was so anxious was that I had never been so late before, and I wasn't able to ring her. She had sent Ishwar out to look for me. It was an unrealistic thing to do because he had no idea where to go and how to find me. But in a crisis, real or imagined, there's an inner compulsion to act. When Ishwar came back, he was relieved to see me. He said, 'There was such a crowd coming out of the Eden Gardens that it was impossible to find you. People were here one moment and gone the next. You probably walked past me and I didn't see you.'

'That's quite possible, but there's no need to think about it now. Why don't you fix us a cup of tea? We can then tell you why I'm late,' I said.

As I was telling them about the day's events, I saw Sudarsana's casual interest deepening into anxiety, and anxiety changing into relief and pride. Exactly what we ate I don't remember, but we went to sleep talking about our unborn child who had now started to remind us about his or her impending arrival by various means. We weren't going to have to wait for long, we said. There was in me excitement and tenderness as well as anxiety and fear. My child will soon be here, I kept thinking and saying to myself, with a lot of emphasis on *'my...'* But it wasn't ego. It was a genuinely and incredibly wonderful event – that I could become a father. This feeling was more akin to humility than ego. I was sure of that.

Our first child, our daughter, our first-born – Sudarsana's and mine – was born on the 21st of July, 1948 in Eden Hospital, Calcutta, and I saw her the same evening, lying fast asleep in a baby cot by her mother, who was wide awake and waiting for me, happily smiling.

'A girl,' she said, sitting up and turning her head towards the baby in the cot.

'I know,' I said. 'She's fast asleep. She's beautiful. And how are you feeling?'

'I'm all right. A little tired,' Sudarsana said. 'Tired but happy.' She gave my hand a squeeze.

I was happy too. Life is about life. How can we question that!

My daughter slept practically the entire time I was there. She did seem to open and close her eyes a few times, make some faint, indeterminate noises. She wasn't particularly concerned that from the warm comfort and security of her mother's womb, she had been catapulted into our insecure world of danger and deceit.

But then there was love and warmth too. We'll surround her with our love, I said to myself. We won't let any harm come to her. But how can I make such promises? In the world out there, she's bound to be exposed to pain and loss, disloyalty and deception, cruelty and selfishness. How could I, with the best of intentions, prevent her from suffering...

'You look thoughtful, almost solemn, what's the matter?' Sudarsana interrupted my thoughts.

'Believe me, I'm really happy. But I was thinking it's a difficult world we live in. It's a cruel world in which our baby is going to grow up,' I said, 'but what can we do about that?'

Sudarsana put a hand on my arm and said all was going to be well. There was no reason to believe that our baby wouldn't grow up into a beautiful, intelligent and caring woman, who would not only be happy herself but bring happiness to others.

Tutu-da came in, looking very professional in a white gown, the stethoscope hanging from his neck.

'So what do you think of your baby?' he asked.

'My daughter is beautiful and unique. And she sleeps a lot,' I said.

'Good thing,' Tutu-da said, 'that you reminded me of her uniqueness. After some time, we tend to forget because newborn babies seem all too similar.'

Tutuda, a gynaecologist.,was going to spend the rest of his professional career supervising the well-being of mothers and ensuring the safe arrival of babies. So he had to be caring about mothers and their babies... My daughter blinked and stirred. I picked her up, held her close to my body, looked at her, felt like I was the only father in the world and gently put her down. Holding one's new-born baby close to one's body must be one of the most wonderful feelings there is.

Sudarsana's parents came. Their happiness was good to watch. My mother-in-law picked up my daughter with perfect ease and confidence, great love and tenderness. Mothers, I thought, were a class apart. I kissed my daughter's mop of hair, said goodbye to everybody, thanked Tutu-da once again and left. There was a report I had to write for Mr Neogy.

At the flat, Ishwar was waiting for the news. He was glad to hear that all was well. I asked him if he had any children and he said he wasn't married. This was unusual, I thought, but didn't ask him why he was still a bachelor. I wanted everybody to know that I was now the father of a beautiful daughter, but I couldn't tell the world because I didn't have a telephone.

Chapter 8

Aparna and Aparajita. East Africa

Sudarsana and our new-born daughter came home. There were four of us to welcome mother and daughter: Sudarsana's parents, Ishwar and I. I couldn't concentrate on the conversation because I kept looking at my daughter. I was a besotted father – nothing original about that. Was it all too sudden for her – the light, the noise, the taste of mother's milk, the feel of the bed where she slept? Much of my thinking was incoherent. They were feelings rather than thoughts, difficult to recall. What I do remember was that this little daughter, who took very little notice of us, made a difference to all of us in ways which are difficult to describe. She ate, slept, woke up, and lay there, her life moving in a fairly regular circle. Friends and relations came and went. Some lifted her out of her cot to feel the warmth and softness of her body, to speak to her, to gaze at her. She enriched us just by being there

Father-in-law had chosen our daughter's name. I hadn't thought of one, nor had Sudarsana. He said he was going to call her Aparna. Both Sudarsana and I liked the name. So our first-born was called Aparna, who was Lord Shiva's consort in the Hindu Pantheon. Shiva is an important god, one moment the preserver, the destroyer the next. I wasn't a particularly devout Hindu, but I liked the sound of the name. What was quite astounding was that my little daughter had moved centre stage and acquired her separate and unique identity in the course of a few days.

We often connect events which are disparate because a coherent world is a safer world. It's the incomprehensible that's unsettling. The direction of my life suddenly changed after the birth of my daughter. And I couldn't get rid of the irrational belief that Aparna had brought me luck and was going to make a difference to our lives.

I received a letter from Calcutta University to say that I had during my last year at the university done well enough at an interview to be short-listed for a job with the Port Commissioners, and I should attend further interviews at their head office. The Commissioners for the Port of Calcutta was an old and respected organisation which had been in charge of the Calcutta port for a long time and established a reputation for efficient administration. The job of Traffic Inspector, for which I'd applied, was considered desirable by middle class aspirants because it was stable and reasonably well-paid. The Commissioners also provided decent accommodation in colonial bungalows. When I told Mr Neogy at Scientific

Publicity, he thought I was fortunate to have been invited to an interview and wished me good luck. The alacrity with which he encouraged me made me wonder whether he wanted me to seek employment elsewhere because I was neither irreplaceable nor indispensable. It was also possible that Mr Neogy didn't worry too much because he knew that securing employment with the Port Commissioners wasn't easy.

Apart from the element of chance, which always played a part at interviews, there were other factors – influence and nepotism, for example. I wasn't particularly anxious. It didn't really matter immensely because I had a stable job – a job, what's more, that I liked.

We were asked to wait in the waiting room when the interview was over, and after the last candidate had been met and assessed, one of the staff of the head office came to us and announced the names of those who'd qualified for round two. My name was among them. It was too late to go back to Scientific Publicity, so I returned home, full of excitement and rather pleased with myself. Sudarsana didn't share my excitement.

'I'm not too sure that I like the idea of your leaving an interesting job like publicity and advertising to go into an organisation like the Port Commissioners. I don't see how Shakespeare, Shaw, Dickens or Hardy is going to be relevant to a job with the Port Commissioners. What has English literature got to do with ships and cranes and cargo?' she said.

'Come to think about it, what has Shakespeare got to do with publicity? I'll be writing copy to promote the business interests of fat cats in the world of film and industry,' I replied.

'Not entirely satisfactory,' she said. "But better than Port Commissioners,' she said.

'I haven't got it yet,' I said.

'I hope you don't,' she said casually. Women, I thought, didn't like change.

Sudarsana could be obstinate. But one of the problems was that she didn't understand, and therefore didn't appreciate, my chronic sense of insecurity, which had arisen out of my experiences as a boy and a young man when bailiffs turned up with court orders to throw us out of our rented accommodation in Harish Mukherji Road and Kalighat Road. Compared to me, Sudarsana had a secure childhood and she'd grown up into an adult without ever having to worry about food and shelter, with the result that she had little understanding of why stability and security were so immensely important for me.

'A stable job, a regular income and subsidized accommodation are really important for me, Sudarsana, for reasons which I've never had the opportunity to explain. I want to take this job if I get it. And if it's dull, I think I can take it, because the compensations are quite considerable and important for me,' I said. Jobs in the government departments, Customs and Port Commissioners were considered desirable by most of my friends. I'd have liked to teach, but I hadn't acquired the right qualifications for that.

'In the end,' Sudarsana said, 'you have to decide because I'm not going to look for a job yet. My daughter will need all the attention I can give her. And if you think you can cope with this job without getting bored, I'll give you all the support I can.'

'Thank you,' I said. 'But what we're both forgetting is that I haven't got the job yet. I've just got through the first round. If in any of the subsequent rounds I'm eliminated…'

'*I* won't cry my heart out,' she interrupted.

The trouble with Sudarsana was that she was as obstinate as she was romantic, and she found it difficult to reconcile her romanticism with pictures of me trudging up and down the quayside, supervising the loading of jute and tea, and the unloading of assorted cargo from incoming ships. Why did I have to have an MA in English literature for, if I was going to settle for this kind of mindless work for the rest of my life?

'I find the idea of working at a busy port and having a lot to do with ships and cargo rather exciting,' I said.

'I hope you like it. But the ships won't bring in cargo, you can be sure, which will be exciting or exotic: no diamonds and emeralds, amethysts, topazes or cinnamon!'

'I'll survive. My present job's financed by private small capital. Its future depends on a single entrepreneur. I feel insecure,' I said.

'Well,' said Sudarsana, 'I'm worried that the job might turn out to be dull and soul-destroying, and I'll have a neurotic, frustrated and bad-tempered husband to live with for most of the rest of my life.'

'If it does, I can look out for another job. Doors blow open, doors blow shut.'

'In the end, I'll stand by you, whatever you do,' she said, casually.

Aparna had woken up and had to be fed. I sat in a chair in one corner of the room, watching mother and daughter. Sudarsana looked happy and relaxed as she breast-fed Aparna, who had a good appetite. Now Aparna was beginning to register and respond, to show pleasure. I don't remember her crying at all, but that could be my selective memory. I was watching my wife and my daughter, oblivious of struggle and conflict.

I felt confident. I was in control. I was master of my fate, captain of my soul – that kind of feeling. I had this feeling occasionally, which was just as well – for I couldn't have dealt with it all the time… the feeling of being merely a spectator.

The second interview also happened at the head office of the Port Commissioners and once again I wasn't eliminated. At the third and final interview, each one of us spent more time with the panel, which included the Traffic Manager, Mr Majumdar, who must have been either a student of English literature, or an avid reader of English poetry and fiction. He asked me questions which had largely to do with English literature. This was a great help. I came away from the interview and waited. I was one of the people who were selected along with five others. I've always hated interviews, so I was glad it was over. I wasn't expected to report for duty yet. First, in a week's time, there was going to be a medical test and, only after that, if there wasn't any problem, would I receive a letter of appointment, setting out the terms and conditions of my job. I would then have to write a formal letter of acceptance, agreeing to the terms and conditions, following which I'd become a Traffic Inspector, one of the Commissioners for the Port of Calcutta.

Sudarsana did not jump for joy, but she decided to take over the cooking from Ishwar that evening and provide a treat because I had stood up to the rigours of the interviews – and managed to be selected. She knew I hated interviews and yet I'd weathered three of them, taken them seriously, and even managed to get selected; so she was going to cook for me and I was going to get a meal, the main feature of which was going to be a moderately hot fish curry with plain white rice and the Bengali variety of rice pudding. This was most generous of Sudarsana because I knew for certain that she didn't fancy being the wife of a Traffic Inspector of the Port Commissioners. But I wanted one of those bungalows by the river. I'd get one – sooner or later.

My colleagues at Scientific Publicity congratulated me, all except somebody, whose name I've forgotten, who said, 'And what about your soul?'

'If I'm barred from Heaven because I'm a Traffic Inspector,' I said,' so be it.'

I was going to have my medical tests, and if my body wasn't flawed, I'd live, love and strive to make a *good* Traffic Inspector of the Commissioners for the Port of Calcutta, I resolved.

It was Sunday afternoon. Lunch was over. Ishwar had gone away to wherever he went on a Sunday afternoon. Aparna was asleep, and Sudarsana and I were talking in an undertone for fear of waking her up. I loved those lazy afternoons – my daughter usually fast asleep, and Sudarsana, full of zest for life and plans for the future, telling me exactly how our life was going to shape out.

Shantiniketan was always the ideal place to live because that was where she came into her own at a time when she felt rejected by her aunt's cousin, when she was very young and vulnerable. Wasn't it possible for me to get a teaching job there at the school or the university some day?

If she had the opportunity to go to Shantiniketan, she said, that's where she wanted to go – a place of peace and happiness, a place without a trace of terrestrial stress. I knew that this romantic, almost utopian, recollection of Shantiniketan might be dispelled by the realities of life, the back-biting and competitiveness of academics and campus pettiness of all kinds. But on a Sunday afternoon after lunch was over, and Ishwar had gone to spend the rest of the afternoon with his brother, and Aparna was fast asleep, it was time for Sudarsana and me to plan and dream and pretend that all we ever wanted was at our beck and call. Nights and days of grief and strife might lie ahead, but here and now, in our one-bedroom flat in one of the most crowded parts of one of the most crowded cities of India, I felt secure.

Knock, knock, knock. The knocking at the door was insistent, loud and clear, very different from the gentle and tentative knocking of Ishwar, and it interrupted the tranquillity of our afternoon. Knock, knock, knock. I hurried to the door and opened it. My father, looking frail and tired, was standing outside the door. With him was a young man of twenty-odd years, who was carrying his large case.

'I've come to spend a few weeks with you. I really want to see my granddaughter. What's her name?'

'Aparna. My daughter's name is Aparna. Father, please come in,' I said. Father liked the name Aparna.

Father and the young man came in. The young man was related to my eldest sister-in-law. With his help, Father had found our flat, and he'd carried Father's large case. He stayed for a while and then left. Sudarsana came out of the bedroom, carrying Aparna in her arms. Sudarsana and Father greeted each other. When Sudarsana tried to touch his feet to show respect in the traditional way, Father prevented her doing that, and said, 'I've come here to welcome my granddaughter and you. We lived in Baliakandi, a village in Faridpur and your grand-uncle, Tarini Roy, lived in Arkandi. He was not only a good doctor, but also a helpful person. He treated the poor in the villages free of charge. I was one of his admirers. So when I heard that you were so closely related to Tarini Roy, I felt good that Ganesh had married you.'

So I had been forgiven. It surprised me that Father knew so much about someone in Sudarsana's family. It was amazing how relaxed father was. He'd come to our flat just over an hour ago and already he was in control, not in the least apologetic. What impressed me most was the way he held Aparna in his arms, without uncertainty, wholly loving.

I didn't remember seeing this side of my father before. I don't think I ever saw my father holding a little baby in his arms and looking at it adoringly. But the most startling surprise was yet to come. 'I'm glad to be here. I'm glad to meet Sudarsana and hold my granddaughter in my arms. And I'm happy to be in Calcutta, which is my city. We shouldn't have gone to Benaras in the first place, where history repeated itself. Jogesh's business didn't prosper. My miserable pension is hardly any help, and once again, we couldn't pay the rent and we were evicted,' said my father, without any embarrassment. He sounded human, vulnerable.

'Father,' said Sudarsana, 'please relax. I think you need to rest. You'll have our bed to sleep in. We'll move into the living room. Your granddaughter will be beside you in her cot. We'll keep the door to the bedroom open and make sure that Aparna doesn't disturb your sleep. She sleeps peacefully most of the night. If she wakes up, we'll take care of her. Stay here, Father, as long as you like. We're happy to have you here. Would you like some tea?' I was overwhelmed. I wanted to embrace Sudarsana there and then and tell her she was a good woman.

It was a memorable day. How was Father going to react to my wife, who I'd married for love, after totally disrupting his plan to get me married to a stranger? How was Sudarsana going to live with a father-in-law, who'd asked her husband to get out of his house and catch the next train to Calcutta? But everything ran counter to my apprehensions. Father was genuinely happy that I'd married into the family of Tarini Roy, who he had admired as a young man. And Sudarsana offered my father our bed to sleep in. We'd sleep on the floor of the living room. It was all quite incredible. Father went into the bedroom to rest.

'Where's Ishwar going to sleep?' I asked Sudarsana.

'I've had a quick word with him. He'll have no difficulty moving in with his brother, who's also a bachelor like him, and works for a rich businessman in South Calcutta.'

So the situation was under control. Sudarsana, my father and Ishwar, between them, had resolved all problems. Yet I, being young and foolish, was full of anguish. It was a particularly eventful day in my life, eventful and confusing.

My father, who'd thrown me out of the house in Benaras because I wouldn't marry the girl he'd chosen for me, had arrived at the door of my flat, had come to stay with me, had obviously forgiven and forgotten. He'd shown genuine affection for Aparna and Sudarsana. I was happy. I was relieved. I was glad I was useful to Father, whom I'd deeply offended and betrayed. Yes, betrayed, because, although he'd unilaterally taken my consent for granted – he hadn't done anything most fathers in our society didn't do. It was established practice. It was *my* conduct which was deviant. But what impressed me more than anything else was the natural cordiality with which he related to us. I was his son. Sudarsana was his daughter-in-law. Aparna was his granddaughter. He had come to stay with them. He had had no hesitation. He'd had no doubt that he'd receive from us the love and respect which were due to him. And I gave him my love and respect because of who he was and the way he related to us, with dignity and affection.

'I've come to see my granddaughter. That's my main mission, but Sudarsana and you are no less important in my life. I'm glad I'm here,' is more or less, what he said.

I didn't really know my father. But I was beginning to feel a closeness to him that I hadn't felt before. For almost twenty years, I saw him most days of my life, yet I hardly knew him. Another aspect of this unusual and unexpected meeting which made me feel good and compelled my respect towards him was the completely relaxed, almost casual way in which he told both Sudarsana and me that they'd been thrown out of the house in Benaras because he and my eldest brother, between them, had failed to pay the rent for the house there and had, once again, been evicted. He needed shelter, which he'd no doubt we'd provide, but it was a great joy for him to see us. There was no prevarication or glossing over the reason why he'd suddenly appeared at the door of our flat. There was no pretence or play-acting. This was my father. I'd hardly known him before.

Father usually went to bed quite late, but tonight he was ready for bed much earlier than usual. Aparna was awake, making incomprehensible noises, wanting to be fed. Father spent a little time with her. Then grandfather went to bed in our double bed and Aparna was soon fast asleep in her cot. We kept the bedroom door open, made our makeshift bed on the floor of the living room, discussed the unusual and unexpected events of the day for a few minutes and went to sleep.

Father was up uncharacteristically early. He was standing near the window, gazing pensively at the unseasonable rain.

'Would you like a cup of tea, Father?' I asked.

'I'd love a cup of tea,' he said. 'Your daughter is extraordinary. She sleeps so peacefully,' he remarked about Aparna with admiration.

Ishwar and Sudarsana were attending to breakfast. Soon Sudarsana was going to have to feed Aparna and I'd have to leave for Scientific Publicity – according to our daily routine.

There could have been awkward and long embarrassed silences in our life with Father, so it was heartening to see the absence of any feeling of discomfort. How could anyone not be soothed by the gurgling and chuckling and other baby noises that Aparna made and by the perpetual movement of her limbs when she was awake and alert? She seemed to be fascinated by Father's prominent nose, which she grabbed, on one or two opportune occasions. It seemed to me he was disappointed if Aparna left his nose alone! For much of the time when Aparna was awake, they took each other over, quite oblivious of everybody else. Sudarsana and I agreed that after the trauma of eviction, the long train journey from Benaras to Calcutta, and the present uncertainty about the future, his granddaughter was doubtlessly his ideal companion, so Sudarsana left them alone as much as possible.

There was a small problem at this time. Actually, I didn't know if it was a big or a small problem. I had a bad cold that weekend and I was due for my medical examination for the Port Commissioners' job on Monday. Should I take a chance and go for the test, or should I inform the appropriate officials that for reasons outside my control – it could be a common cold or a bout of influenza – I couldn't attend the medical examination that Monday morning? I told Sudarsana about the conflict. She had no problem, and took no time at all in making her decision.

'They want good people, right? They've taken a lot of time and trouble to select a young man, Ganesh Bagchi, for the rather dull job of Traffic Inspector. Do you think they're even going to consider turning you down because you have a sniffle?' said Sudarsana.

I went for my medical examination. Before the end of the week, I received my letter of appointment. Father positively and unequivocally approved of my decision. Sudarsana reluctantly and hesitantly decided to celebrate by organising a special dinner, just for ourselves. When I rang my father-in-law in his Lighting Superintendent's office in Calcutta Corporation, his reaction was positive and spontaneous – Approval! I said Sudarsana, Aparna and I would soon come and see him and my mother-in-law in Tollygunge.

It seemed to me that he wasn't too keen on meeting my father.

Father showed great interest in everything that was going on around him, especially in my career. He was most supportive of me. He said to Sudarsana that he was at peace with himself and others when his income as a clerk in a government office was small but regular; when his ambition didn't go beyond providing food and shelter to those who depended on him; and when he was unlikely to lose his job unless the Empire turned upside down. He also pointed out other possible advantages of the job in order to allay Sudarsana's fear that I might get depressed and unhappy doing this job.

'I think,' Father said, 'Ganesh should take this job, do it as honestly and efficiently as he can, and look out for an alternative if he finds that it's a dead-end job and depression is about to set in. Millions do boring jobs every day. But, quite often, there's no option.'

Sudarsana seemed to feel reassured. Father's relationship with Sudarsana continued to be pleasant and friendly, and Aparna continued to be fond of grabbing Father's prominent nose. Father continued to sleep in our double bed. Aparna continued to sleep in her cot next to the double bed and Sudarsana and I continued to sleep in an improvised – but not at all uncomfortable – bed on the floor of the living room.

There was a drop in my salary. As a probationary Traffic Inspector I was to get a salary, I think of one hundred and fifty rupees, whereas I used to be paid two hundred rupees by Scientific Publicity. I bought a second-hand bicycle and undertook to teach two teenage brothers for forty rupees. It was one of the busiest three months of my life. I wasn't coping particularly well with the situation, when events took a turn.

Sudarsana's uncle – the one who was just three years younger than her father – was going to move in with Sudarsana's father in the downstairs flat at Golf Club Road. So he offered me the rented flat which he was about to vacate. The rent was within my means. It had three bedrooms and there wasn't going to be a problem of accommodation. Father could have his own room. This was in Congress Exhibition Road in Park Circus. With some contribution from Father and Borda, there was no reason why we shouldn't be able to settle down and restore some much needed privacy to our lives. Father was enthusiastic. Sudarsana thought it was a good idea. I looked forward to sleeping in a bed again with Aparna by our side in a cot. I saw Sudarsana's uncle and the terms and conditions were worked out. We could move in immediately.

During the morning and the afternoon when we moved out, everything worked without any untoward incidents, and we were installed in a clean and spacious first floor flat in Congress Exhibition Road in Park Circus, where the majority community, was Muslim before the Calcutta riots. But at the time we acquired our flat there, the Muslims were there in smaller numbers and there was no chronic apprehension of a riot breaking out suddenly, causing loss of life and property. What I liked about this particular street was that, although it wasn't lined with large leafy trees, there were quite a few ancient trees to give it a pleasant and shady appearance. There were a few car owners, who drove ancient Fiats and Ambassadors. It wasn't a traditional set-up; at the same time, it wasn't totally westernised. The men wore trousers and shirts, and occasionally a suit without a tie, but most women wore *saris*. I looked around, making a mental note of things, because we were going to come and live here. There's no reason why we shouldn't live here a long time, I thought.

Sudarsana was apprehensive about problems of adjustment. Though she agreed there was going to be ample space – that was an attraction. Whilst an important reason for my happiness was that I was going to be able to be of some use to my father.

We started well. Getting used to a new environment has its challenges as well as excitement. Once Sudarsana got involved in organising our new home, she grew more optimistic about the future and generally more confident. I too had the general feeling that things were looking up.

But the feeling of euphoria didn't last long. My eldest brother, Jogesh, came to see us. He spent some time with Father. At one point I was sent for. Father said Borda was having problems finding a suitable house or flat in Calcutta. Would I have any objection if he and his family moved in with us? There was no question of my saying that it was not realistic. We'd be too many people. And too many people frequently meant too many problems. I told Sudarsana. She was emphatic. It wasn't realistic, she said.

Once Borda and Baudi, that is my eldest brother and his wife, with their three grown-up children - two daughters and a son - came to stay at Congress Exhibition Road, the infrastructure, we thought, would soon crack. It was my belief that chaos was what we'd have when nine people, including a baby still in the mother's arms, tried to live in a flat meant for at most five people. So Sudarsana and I talked about it and took no time at all to decide that for the sake of the greatest good of the greatest number, it would be best to move out of the flat at Congress Exhibition Road, leaving it to Father, Borda and his family – and move in with Sudarsana's parents at Golf Club Road, Tollygunge.

And so we did, one drizzly weekend in late December in 1948, when Aparna was about six months old.

We'd visited Golf Club Road on several occasions but not as often as we'd have liked for the simple reason that we had to travel by taxi – public transport would be hazardous for Aparna – and taxis cost more money than we could afford. We'd consulted everybody there. My parents-in-law were enthusiastic. I was convinced that they'd waited for Aparna a long time and they'd like nothing better than having her around. She would be loved and cherished. And so she was. Aparna seemed to have made a difference to their lives. Her comfort and well-being were central to everything they did... The only negative aspect of the situation was that I had lost my freedom to run my household the way I wanted to. The idea of the loss of freedom irked me, but there was no doubt about the congeniality of the environment.

The status of the 'kept' son-in-law – *ghar jamai* – was ignominious in our middle class Bengali society but that didn't create profound unease in me – for at least two reasons that I can think of – the natural, affectionate and gracious behaviour of my parents-in-law; and the fact that I wasn't totally dependent on them.

I had an income from my job and a couple of tuitions, which took care of our personal needs. Sudarsana bought general household articles from time to time when she thought they would be useful. Sometimes she would leave Aparna with her mother and go shopping for food for a special treat. In short we'd now settled down to a regular rhythm of life. I had no anxiety about my relationship with Sudarsana's parents. Sudarsana's sister, Sunanda, might have been disappointed that she hadn't been the centre of attention of both parents for very long when we returned and moved centre-stage, partly because of our longish absence, and partly because of Aparna. But she didn't show any prodigious signs of resentment. In short, life was peaceful.

For a time, I did shifts: morning, afternoon and night. Quite often during those days, I slept in the day and worked at night. I had to learn about stacking goods in sheds and the hatches of ships. I had to learn a little about ships. Small trains carried goods from one part of the docks and jetties to another. I learnt to drive a railway engine – in case there was an emergency and I had to transport goods by train from one point to another. We even had a course in first-aid. But mainly my job of Traffic Inspector was to make sure that various operations in the port were taking place as expected, and the supercargoes, the crane operators, the train drivers and others were doing their jobs efficiently. And they were. During this period, I rarely came across instances of gross negligence or inefficiency. This made my job quite pleasant. What's more, there wasn't a strict hierarchy which was taken too seriously.

Then, quite unexpectedly, I was appointed as the Allotment Officer. The Allotment Officer's job was to allot to different companies and individuals railway wagons to move goods from the port to various destinations. There were at least two reasons – railway stock was not always available; and the dispatch of too many wagons could create congestion at junctions. Therefore, the movement of wagons had to be planned and phased, and I was the person to control the dispatch of wagons through busy junctions and to ensure the rolling stock was being used fairly and economically. I had to learn a few facts, which the senior clerks with many years of experience were only too glad to teach me. I had no trouble learning from Mr Paul and Mr Banerji because I didn't believe in hierarchy and both these senior clerks were excellent teachers.

One great advantage of being appointed as Allotment Officer was that it was a job which started at nine in the morning and finished at five, with a break for lunch. After the shifts, this was a welcome change. I could now work during the day and sleep at night, spend time with Aparna who was laughing, talking, relating to people, finding ways to amuse herself and others, and at just over two, had already become quite a personality with her likes and dislikes, her attachments and indifferences.

I forget the names of my colleagues at the Port Commissioners – except for a few. There was William, who was Anglo-Indian and from Calcutta. There were two Majumdars – a tall one and a short one. There was Keshuv Dutt, an Olympic hockey player and badminton champion. There was Claudius and Glacken and Jansen – great Olympic hockey players. They were all, by and large, easy-going people – friendly, with a good sense of humour. Pradip Sen was an efficient and highly intelligent colleague, whom I hadn't got to know yet.

As far as I can recollect, we didn't have a canteen where we could congregate for lunch and discuss news – local, national and international. Instead, we often met up at people's offices and had lunch and talked. On the whole, it seemed to me, that my Anglo-Indian colleagues were loyal to the Crown. Quite a few of them didn't look Indian at all. They had British connections. One or several of their ancestors were British with often an Indian ancestor somewhere along the line. Many Anglo-Indians looked more European than Indian. They spoke English as a first language, they were Christian, and they were much more loyal to the ex-colonial power – the British – throughout their hegemony in the Indian sub-continent – than the Indians. A fair proportion of Anglo-Indians left India and emigrated to Britain, Australia, New Zealand and Canada just before and soon after independence, which is a pity because their presence in the country would have been something positive. They were an asset; also, I'm sure, to the countries to which they emigrated.

By and large, Calcutta Port Commissioners was run by people who were Anglophile, who spoke English and regretted the transfer of power from the reliable British administrators to the inexperienced Indians. We didn't have many opportunities for relaxed extended conversation, and most often when we met, the exchange was incidental and insignificant. Sport came into it because there were many outstanding sportsmen, past and present, who had worked for our organisation, and at the time, there were G Singh, Keshuv Dutt, Jansen, Glacken and Claudius, all Olympic hockey players I've just mentioned. They'd played for the winning Indian team, and Sumant Mishra, had represented India at Wimbledon. Films, women and politics were the other topics which appealed to us, but I'm not sure in exactly what order. There emerged a rather uniform and, to a certain extent, fairly predictable, pattern when it came to politics. Most Anglo-Indian colleagues and some senior Indian ones were not certain that India governed by Indians wouldn't run into chaos and confusion because the administration of this vast country required expertise. Internecine strife marked the history of India before the advent of the British and at the time of their departure. As for Indian poverty, Indians in vast numbers have always been poor and always will be. There was an inevitable causal connection, as it were, between being Indian and being poor: the British had nothing to do with it. How could just about two centuries of British rule reverse the fortunes of a nation which had been poor for many centuries, before the British had even stepped onto the soil of India?

They would then point to the benefits, the chief among which was 'parliamentary democracy'. A question which they'd ask with confidence was: did the British system introduce the idea of one law for everybody or not? Then there was the huge network of railways, beautiful colonial buildings, universities which produced outstanding scholars, and the administrative system which produced efficient and gifted administrators. The list was endless. The pro-British lobby was at their triumphant best at the end. They would ask: Who gave us Shakespeare; who gave us Milton, Blake, Keats, Dickens and Hardy? Who gave us the English language?

Although I accepted some of their arguments, my sympathy was unequivocally with the other group, dominated by the Bengalis of Calcutta. The sole Anglo-Indian member of this group, William, had decided never to emigrate because he liked Calcutta. Our strongest objection to British rule was that the foreign administrators – whether they were based in Westminster or in Delhi – were indifferent to the massive poverty in India and they presided over some of the most disastrous famines that the world had ever witnessed, including the Bengal Famine of 1943, in which between three and a half and four million people died. Poverty and hunger were perpetuated by the greed of the colonialists who made rules which were always weighted in their favour. The gap in prices, for example, between the manufactured products which we bought from Britain and the agricultural products which Britain bought from us was most disproportionate because we, being the colonised, had little say in the matter, at a time when the most unequal forms of price-fixing passed muster.

At the time, that greatly publicised western commodity, democracy, really affected less than ten per centre of the population. And what proportion of the population was literate when the British left India? It was a lot less than twenty per cent. Was every disease known to us endemic in some part of our country? Yes, it was. We'd little doubt about the fact that it was a ruthless and brutal age and that British administrative policy was exploitative and self-serving. Although I didn't accept some of the statements some of the members of our group made in their anger and frustration, I agreed with most of their premises. And when I did a little research to examine some of the statements that this group of colleagues made about the *Raj,* I found that they'd done their homework. They were knowledgeable and honest, and they were saying that it wasn't a question of what the British rulers should or shouldn't have done; it was what they *did* do. Nearly 200 years of British administration did create colossal poverty, the statistics for which exist, and they haven't been contested by even the most ardent believers in colonisation and imperialism – because indisputable records are quite easily available.

Opportunities for such discussions were few. But they were a welcome diversion because the duties and responsibilities of the Allotment Officer didn't include any exciting activities. Controlling the movement of goods was necessary, but not much more.

It was equally necessary that this movement should be efficient and economical in spite of the limited rolling stock and over-crowded routes. There was a certain challenge because of the need for planning, but very little excitement and absolutely no sense of adventure. There were times, while signing the endless piles of railway forwarding notes, when I remembered Sudarsana's warning at the time of my interviews for this job – that she couldn't believe, however hard she tried, that I would ever enjoy working for the Port Commissioners. I'd argued that aiming single-mindedly at enjoyment is not only self-indulgent but can also be dangerous and self-defeating. The conflict within went on, although it wasn't allowed to get out of hand.

Sudarsana was expecting again. We were excited, but the news wasn't received with as much happiness as the news of Aparna being on the way. Sunanda made appropriate noises. My father-in-law got down to taking care of the practicalities: the right food, exercise, regular check-ups. But, rightly or wrongly, I perceived a certain lack of warmth. To make up for the lack of enthusiasm, people often became efficient, practical, and businesslike. Planning for our second child's arrival started. Names were selected. In a matter of a few days, half a dozen names had already been compiled and more were being discussed.

Because I registered a marked lack of enthusiasm in the case of my second child compared to my first, I began to feel protective about the baby on the way. Was it practical to have a second child so soon after the first? Certainly it was a question for Sudarsana and me to ask and answer? Maybe not – because a baby needs attention and care. It also needs space and it needs people's time. It costs money. If we were living on our own, we could decide how many children we were going to have and when, but while we lived in a joint family, the convenience of others had to be important, if not paramount. In retrospect, I can think of these as relevant points. If I thought hard enough, I might even think of numerous other questions, problems and issues.

But at the time I was unhappy and at times, angry. I had never felt like this before in Sudarsana's parents' house and certain ideas began to form in my head. I felt defiant. I didn't want anybody else to have control over my life and the lives of those who mattered most to me. I had applied for one of those bungalows by the river which I'd looked at many times with possessive lust. And since I was now confirmed in my job, I was, theoretically, entitled to one of them. I say 'theoretically' because many others, most of them senior to me, also wanted those bungalows and the waiting list was long. But then to hope was human. Before very long, I was sure, I was going to be allocated one of those houses.

I'm partial to Calcutta for many reasons, only some of which I can rationally justify. It's a densely-populated large city with problems of various kinds, too numerous to discuss in detail, but held together, I think, by its basic humanity. It is chaotic, sometimes violent, obstinate, creative, irrational, sentimental and parochial – but human. Yes, I loved Calcutta, but ideas were forming in my mind which had to do with leaving.

Of all the things I liked about Calcutta, the monsoon was high on my list. One moment everything looked pretty normal – the earth and the sky, people going to work, children going to school, roadside shops selling their wares, a few retired people walking down to the local teashop or to a friend's house to discuss politics or sports. Then, out of nowhere, dark, threatening clouds began to appear in hordes and obliterated the sun, and it poured and it poured... and then it all just as suddenly – stopped. It didn't take long before the sun shone, crowds of people walked up and down pavements, street-side traders sold their wares, retired men sat on park benches reading newspapers, and business went on as usual.

In May and June, before the regular monsoon of heavy downpours started, we often had a dark, threatening sky, thunder and lightning, strong winds sweeping across dusty roads scattering dry leaves, and then the rain, which was often heavy but didn't last long. There was often something rather dramatic, rather spectacular about these rains, the so-called Nor' Westers. I'd always found it exciting. Afterwards, Lychees were a lot sweeter, though no-one really knows why. It was like nature doing an act, giving a performance, presenting a curtain raiser before the real play began.

Then, when the real monsoon set in in Calcutta, the rain could be heavy and last a long time, flooding the streets, bringing traffic to a halt. It was early September, the eleventh day to be precise, I'd come back home from the docks in Kidderpore, where my office was. It had rained all day, but it wasn't too heavy, though still a nuisance. When it rained heavily, water built up under Tollygunge Bridge, which was about three miles from where I lived. And heavy rain often made it impossible for traffic to go through. I was lucky. There was water under the bridge but not so much water that traffic couldn't go through. I was home, sipping hot tea and smoking a cigarette. I didn't smoke when either of Sudarsana's parents was around. One didn't, in front of ones elders. I was on my own in the house. That made me think: 'Why am I alone in the house?' Where's Sudarsana? Where's mother-in-law? They're usually here when I come home from the office.'

The phone rang. It was my father-in-law at the other end. While I was in the office of the Allotment Officer in the Kidderpore docks, the world hadn't stood still. Significant events had taken place, not only in the world at large, but in my life also. Sudarsana's labour pains had started in the morning. She and her mother had taken a taxi and gone to Eden Hospital. Tutu-da was there and had taken charge. My second daughter was born that afternoon. Did I want to come over? My father-in-law would wait and give me a lift back home. I said I'd leave the house at once and get to Eden Hospital as soon as possible.

While I was having my tea and then talking to my father-in-law on the phone, it had rained heavily. The streets were flooded. Public transport had disappeared from the road. It always did after a heavy downpour because so much water collected under Tollygunge Bridge that you could swim in it. I stopped a private car and asked the driver whether I could have a lift to somewhere near the bridge. I had no luck because the driver wasn't going in that direction at all. I stopped a taxi, but it was going in the opposite direction. In any case, he wasn't going to risk driving through the 'lake' beneath the bridge: taxis couldn't be made to swim. What about an alternative route? That was possible, but that would cost me twice the normal fare.

So be it, I said, and climbed in and sat next to the driver, who was from Bihar but spoke Bengali quite well, except for occasional lapses. I told him I was going to Eden Hospital and he was to take me to the entrance facing Central Avenue because the maternity ward was nearer to Central Avenue than College Street. Why the maternity ward? I explained that my second daughter had been born in the early afternoon, and I was going to see her.

Tutu-da was there and my parents-in-law. And there was Sudarsana, in the same ward as the last time, sitting up in bed and talking, without showing any signs of strain. My daughter was asleep. She must have been woken up by my mother-in-law, who couldn't have resisted the temptation of taking her in her arms. I too took her up in my arms. She kind of looked at me and then went to sleep. My worst enemy couldn't dispute the fact that my daughter was beautiful. I loved her – she looked so delicate, vulnerable and fragile. There and then I decided what I was going to call her. She was going to be called Aparajita, the unvanquished. This delicate-looking daughter was going to be strong, stand up to the ghastly, unforgiving world and do her thing, live her own life – independent, creative and full of the love of life.

'What are you thinking?' said Sudarsana.

'I'm thinking of a name for her,' I said, without revealing the name I'd decided on.

'I'm also thinking of what I'm going to call her,' said my father-in-law. I don't know why my father-in-law thought it was always his prerogative to name my children.

'I'd like to call her Aparajita,' I said – with pre-emptive haste.

My father-in-law wanted to call her Krishna, but he accepted my choice gracefully. .

'Where's Aparna?' I asked.

She's with Uncle and Aunt in Landsdowne Road,' Sudarsana said. Soon it was time for us to leave. I said goodbye to Sudarsana and Aparajita and left.

Unexpected events often determine the course of our lives. Even when we think that what we're doing is spontaneous action, there's often a connection between today's events and yesterday's input. Family-planning was not on my agenda. I didn't look before and after. I had another beautiful daughter and I was hurt by the insufficiency of spontaneous and joyful response from people around me. It was a great relief for me that my mother-in-law was just as welcoming with Aparajita as with Aparna. In a few days Sudarsana and Aparajita were home. My new-born daughter didn't discriminate against anybody. She was always ready to respond with delight to anybody who picked her up and held and cuddled her.

Aparajita thoroughly enjoyed the company of people. It was my initial perception that Sunanda had reacted with muted enthusiasm when Aparajita was born, but now, soon after returning from college, she went to Aparajita, picked her up and spent time with her. She even gave Aparajita zoology lessons before her examination. When asked to explain her madness, she explained that my daughter frequently made noises which led her to believe that she understood what she was being taught and appreciated the trouble her aunt was taking to teach her biology. What Aparajita liked most, according to Sunanda, was zoology.

Because I'd had this perception initially that my father-in-law and my sister-in-law might have thought and felt that it was self-indulgent of us to have had a second child so soon after the first, I felt alienated from them for the first time in four years. And I said silently to my new-born daughter, 'Forgive me. It didn't seem to me that you were welcomed completely without reservation by everyone in the family. But I love you more for that, not less.' Sudarsana seemed unaffected by what either her parents or her sister had said or done. She didn't see any need for deconstruction. There wasn't anything at all in the attitude of either her father or her sister which she found unusual. Her parents had a grandchild after many years of waiting, so their enthusiasm for Aparna was really great. They hadn't expressed quite the same excitement at the birth of their second grandchild. Wasn't that only to be expected? I imagined reactions and motives in people which were non-existent and took them so seriously that I made myself miserable. I was somewhat prone to negative thinking, she concluded.

Such speculations could neither be proved nor disapproved, I said. But it was my impression – that there was a difference and I'd registered it with sadness. Sudarsana made more reassuring noises and I began to wonder whether I'd overreacted. Aparajita, however, had no problems: she ate and slept and showed no sign of neurotic anxiety.

Aparajita was born on the 11th of September, 1950. I'd by then worked for more than two years in the Port Commissioners, and for about a year as the Allotment Officer. I wasn't altogether happy although my life was fairly uncomplicated. First of all there was very little in my job which was challenging or exciting. There was hardly any scope for any communication with anybody. Representatives from various companies – Brooke Bond, Liptons, Imperial Chemicals, Imperial Tobacco and others – would come for the allocation of wagons and I'd sign their railway forwarding notes, assess their needs and their eligibility, and allot wagons if they were available. The job had no real challenge in it. What there was, however, couldn't be treated with casual indifference: security, a reasonable salary and accommodation at a highly subsidized rent. The problem was that, day in and day out, I had to do predetermined tasks along set lines with little or no scope for creativity or innovation. But I was determined to carry on, for the sake of stability and security.

This was the time when Mao was establishing the communist regime in China, when Bernard Shaw died at the age of 94 and Bertrand Russell was awarded the Nobel Prize. The French were engaged in a do-or-die confrontation with the Viet Minh guerrillas, and for a time it didn't look as if the Vietnamese were going to have it all their own way. The North Korean offensive was difficult to contain: they had taken Seoul for a second time... But all this was happening over there, far away from Calcutta, and our involvement in international affairs was casual. I missed our coffee-house discussions and debates. I felt isolated. I lived in a narrow world – the two poles of my existence being office and home. Yet I did nothing to alter the situation. And because I couldn't think of an alternative lifestyle, I didn't do anything to change the status quo; and since I didn't try, I neither succeeded nor failed. The desire for taking up some new challenge to alter the course of our lives, wasn't a dominant emotion, but it was there, however dormant.

At his phase, Sudarsana had mentioned that one of her aunts – her father's sister – was coming to spend her overseas leave of three months in Calcutta. Her husband, K. D. Gupta, widely referred to as KD by his equals and superiors, was coming with her. They lived in Uganda. Sudarsana's aunt was a teacher there and her uncle was the Indian Education Officer. Uganda was, at the time, a British Protectorate. Ideas began to form in my head. I had wanted to teach but, for various reasons, I didn't explore the possibility. I was married and I had a child right at the beginning of my career. I couldn't set up our home on a lecturer's salary. For teaching in a school, I needed teaching qualifications, which I didn't have. Then there was my extraordinary luck: I got one job after another without any preparation and without any real competition. I forgot all about teaching.

Africa, from the time I was ten or eleven, had attracted me. It was, I'd gathered, a country of adventure, of frenzied dancing to the beating of drums, of lions and elephants, zebras and giraffes. It was where Tarzan performed his extraordinary feats of skill and strength. Rider Haggard and *She* and *King Solomon's Mines* also had played their part in creating in my mind a romantic image of that continent. Boys and girls and young men and women of my generation had an incomplete conception of the people and the country. Nothing was ever said of the massive colonial exploitation of its natural resources. As a result, my idea of Africa in general, and of Uganda in particular, was limited. Right then, however, I was more focused on Uganda than on Africa, so I looked it up in reference books and collected some elementary information.

Uganda was a landlocked East African country, a British protectorate, which was accessed from Mombasa through Kenya. If we went to Uganda, we would go from Calcutta to Bombay by train and then from Bombay to Mombasa by ship, probably stopping at a beautiful group of islands, the Seychelles. The train journey from Mombasa to Kampala was said to be most picturesque and at times the experience was dramatic. There was a sizeable Asian population there, mainly from India, Pakistan and Goa. They were traders and clerks and teachers but there were some rich businessmen and entrepreneurs among them who controlled practically all transactions to do with the growing and marketing of tea, coffee, cotton and sugar. What was of interest to me was the fact that the children of the Indians, Pakistanis and Goans went to schools to which African children didn't have access, just as the children of Ugandan African parents didn't go to Asian schools. I didn't aim high. I would be content to teach English in a secondary school, but I wouldn't know whether I was eligible until Sudarsana's uncle and aunt arrived in Calcutta.

Mr and Mrs KD Gupta arrived. They stayed with an uncle's brother but regularly visited us at Tollygunge. I was the newcomer to the family, so they were both curious and interested to give me the once-over and then, perhaps to get to know me. Sudarsana's uncle was a confident and well-informed person, the type that believed that their kind was born to lead. There was no occasion for me to question his authority or dispute his ideas on art or science, life or education. One evening when he was having a drink – he liked brandy and ginger ale – he happened to ask me what it was that I did at the port of Calcutta.

When I described my duties and responsibilities, he made the highly predictable and polite comment, 'Quite interesting.

'Not at all interesting, really,' I said. 'There are times I feel like a zombie. I make my decisions quite mechanically. I don't have to think.'

Uncle KD's reaction was extraordinary. He wasn't at all worried about my frustration. He held forth on the West African origin of the word zombie, its etymology and the fact that it had something to do with some snake-god in West Africa.

'English is such a rich language,' he concluded, 'because of its extensive borrowing from other languages. You said you often felt like a zombie: the word comes from West Africa.'

There the discussion ended. My mother-in-law came in, and then Sudarsana and Sunanda. My father-in-law was going to Park Street, where he was going to collect his younger sister from the flat of his older sister. It was frustrating. Now I would have to wait for another occasion when I could bring up the subject of the government of Uganda using my services as a teacher of English. There will be a time, I hoped, there will be a time.

The opportunity did come in the end. The first question I asked was whether the government of Uganda insisted on a teaching qualification for their teachers. Uncle KD's response was most encouraging. A teaching diploma or degree was most welcome but not compulsory. The Government of Uganda did employ teachers who had no teaching qualifications but a good degree in the subject which they wanted to teach. He interviewed people in India who wanted to teach in Uganda and decided whether their qualifications, ideas and personalities were suitable for teaching posts in Ugandan schools for boys and girls whose parents were from the Indian subcontinent. He wanted me to think it over, talk to Sudarsana and her parents and anybody else who's ideas and opinions I valued and then ring him. He would have to talk to me, he said, ask me questions and decide whether I was suitable for the profession. The next decision he would have to make was whether I was the kind of person to take the emotional strain of living so far away from friends and family and work in a largely alien environment. He would also interview Sudarsana, then let us know his honest opinion, first about our competence and suitability, and then about the advisability of such an upheaval in our lives. He'd also have to have a really long discussion about the proposed move from one continent to another – from free India to a British Protectorate. And, finally, he'd discuss the matter with Sudarsana's parents.

Sudarsana came through as a positive and clear-thinking person whenever we approached a crossroads. She had decided a long time ago that the job at the port was a good job for security, prospects and stability, but the post of Traffic Inspector or Allotment Officer and I weren't made for each other. Now that we knew that a teacher's diploma was not compulsory, there was no insurmountable problem in the way of getting the job.

So she wanted me to resign from my present post and go to Uganda. She hoped that she might also qualify as a teacher because she had an honours degree in English.

Sudarsana's uncle, the Indian Education Officer of Uganda, gave us an interview; asked us questions on our subject and about education and recommended us. The response came through so quickly that I began to feel disorientated: I was appointed a teacher of English in Kampala Secondary School and I would be expected to start teaching soon after I arrived in Kampala. Sudarsana would be offered a renewable contract after arriving in Kampala. This was the year 1951 – Aparna was three and Aparajita was one. So Sudarsana couldn't be expected to start teaching before she had found someone competent to look after them while she went out to teach. We were really impressed with the efficiency of the Department of Education in Uganda.

I resigned. Our passage to Uganda was booked on a ship which left Bombay for Mombasa once a month and arrived there in ten days, stopping briefly at the Seychelles Islands. I think the ship was SS Kampala, the agents for which were Messrs Mackinnon & Mackenzie Ltd. We were all excited. It was a matter of a few weeks before we started our long journey for the unknown territory of Uganda. We're ready, we're coming, we said to the dark blue sea over there in Bombay.

Resistance came from unexpected quarters. When I tried to enthuse Aparna with the idea of a new life in a new country, she said categorically and without any hesitation that she didn't want to go. Her attitude wasn't difficult to understand. Her grandparents loved her dearly and she loved her grandparents, so she resisted the idea of ever leaving them. She wasn't old enough to have developed romantic ideas about the magic and mystery of Africa, nor was she looking forward to a great adventure in the wilderness of that great continent. Her perception was that going somewhere else meant being separated from her grandparents and that particular idea was quite intolerable. There was nothing I could think of which could make the slightest impact on her resolute mind. A new continent lying beyond the luminous waves of the Indian Ocean, a new country whose language and culture were unknown to us, a people whose way of living and thinking we hadn't come into contact with before – all that added up to a most powerful attraction for me. But none of this made the slightest difference to Aparna. We could only hope that she might be impressed with Uganda and change her mind – and even come to love it. But in her present state of mind, that seemed like a most unusual development. Our best strategy was not to mention the subject in her presence. For Sudarsana and me, the foremost reason for excitement was that independence with a house of our own beckoning us became bigger by the day...

My only teaching experience was through my tuitions – Chobi, Kobi, Ruby, Namita and a young lad of twelve, whose name I can't recall. But I'd enjoyed my teaching for two reasons – I didn't undertake to teach any subject I couldn't handle, and I related well to my students. Sudarsana had no experience of teaching, but she was fairly certain that she would do well because, she said, she related well to her teachers. I wasn't fully convinced that being able to relate well to one's teachers was proof positive that one would make a good teacher. Though I also thought she'd make a good teacher, albeit for a different reason: she related well to people and her knowledge of English – both the language and the literature – was good. She was also a confident speaker. So, despite the uncertainty, the break in the continuity of our lives, and separation from friends and relations and my favourite city, we were positively excited at the prospect of our new beginning. And right now nothing was in the way: the appointment was finalised; the passage booked; everybody who needed to know about our impending arrival was informed. And it all happened so easily and quickly that it was difficult at times to believe that it had actually happened. There wasn't much paperwork; nor many forms to fill out, or letters to write. We had got our passports, keys which opened the doors of a world that lay beyond. There was quiet contentment, alternating with sudden apprehensions and misgivings... Sudarsana and I would sit on our little balcony in silence or speaking quietly, oblivious of everything except the flickering stars in the blue October sky and the children sleeping in the bedroom just behind us.

We heard a little movement in the bedroom. Aparajita, who was now just over one year old, wasn't sleeping very peacefully. She was restless, coughing between fitful spells of sleep. She woke up, wanted to be picked up by Sudarsana. After a short cuddle, she felt comfortable in Sudarsana's arms and fell asleep. She was burning up with fever, asleep, and lying beside Sudarsana, who was now wide awake. Aparajita looked small, frail and vulnerable. Sunday morning always began slowly. My mother-in-law always got out of bed before anybody else and made sure everybody had their breakfast when they wanted.

But this Sunday was different. Aparajita was her first priority, her only concern this morning.

Dr Dasgupta had moved in with his family to the ground-floor flat, after Sudarsana's uncle had moved out of there and gone back to his flat in Park Circus, then a predominantly Muslim area, which he'd left during the Hindu-Muslim riots in the wake of Partition. I went and saw Dr Dasgupta, a pleasant and friendly man, who said he'd come and see Aparajita in half-an-hour. Father-in-law looked anxious, he and Sunanda, the two scientists in the family, talked agitatedly about diphtheria, anti-toxins and antibiotics. Dr Dasgupta also looked concerned and decided that a laboratory test was necessary to check whether it was diphtheria because of the inflamed throat and the high temperature. In any case, he was going to treat her for diphtheria because he was not comfortable when he saw Aparajita's degree of discomfort and her loss of appetite. The treatment wouldn't do her any harm, but would prevent serious damage. Some changes might have to be made, he said, after he had received the report. The report didn't confirm diphtheria, much to everybody's relief.

It was, however, a serious throat infection and for a time, with a high temperature, with the result that Aparajita was looking quite frail, although she'd looked delicate but strong at birth. Yet the relief was immense; she'd suffered and was still suffering but her life was not at risk. There was no certainty about what shape events were going to take when Aparajita fell so seriously ill. We had no idea about how long it'd be before she would be fit to travel, so we thought it best to prepare for a longish delay in our departure. We cancelled our passage on SS Kampala and booked on SS Karanja, which was due to leave Bombay for Mombassa in about three weeks. Dr Dasgupta was quite certain that it'd be safe for Aparajita to travel. After all, what could be more appropriate for convalescence than a voyage on the Indian Ocean from Bombay to Mombasa? Most of the preparation for our departure was already in place; the delay wasn't going to make a great deal of difference nor cause additional upheaval. The dates of train and hotel reservations had to be changed. Some people Sudarsana's uncle knew well in Mombasa were going to meet us when the ship berthed there. They'd give us shelter and look after us for a day or two and then put us on the train to Kampala. They also had to be informed about our unavoidable delay.

Sudarsana's uncle and I, between us, did all that, and then we were ready to depart. Aparna still refused to give in. Never once, by word or gesture, did she show the slightest sign of relenting or changing her mind. She didn't cry, throw tantrums or tearfully refuse to cooperate, but she made it clear that her heart wasn't in it. The reason she was going was that her grandparents had promised to come over to Kampala as soon as they could and spend a month or two with her. It seemed to me that Aparna was closer to her grandparents than to either Sudarsana or me. But neither of us felt jealous. The unquestioning love which had grown between my daughter and her grandparents, and the grandparents' dedication to the comfort and happiness of their granddaughter was a good thing to see.

From the beginning, my father-in-law had decided to come with us to Bombay and stay around us until we sailed away. Sudarsana's uncle and aunt had for a long time wanted my mother-in-law and my father-in-law to visit them in Uganda but they couldn't do it for various reasons, one of which was that my father-in-law was still working as the Lighting Superintendent of Calcutta Corporation, a job which he took seriously. First, it'd take more than a month to travel from Calcutta to Kampala and back, and another month would go by, travelling in Uganda, spending some time with Sudarsana's uncle and aunt and returning home. He might be able to do this after a year or so – after he had retired. So when my father-in-law promised his granddaughter a visit, he meant it. He said to Aparna more than once that he'd come and see her in Kampala. This calmed her down. She was suddenly interested in the sea, the ships, and the country to which we were going.

Her grandfather answered all her questions, satisfied her curiosity, and encouraged her to know about Africa, the continent and the people, but in the simplest language and with patience, because Aparna was only three years and four months old. Exactly how much of the information she either understood or was interested in I don't know. But her sense of insecurity seemed to be less and she looked altogether a happier little girl. I too felt happier, pleased that the conscientious objector had taken the oath of allegiance and settled down.

Towards the end of the train journey, Aparajita had started fretting and whining and intermittently scratching her head. Now, on the way to the quayside of the Bombay port – where SS Karanja had berthed – she was scratching her head quite furiously and crying. Father-in-law was looking lonely and disconsolate at the thought of the long separation. Now, added to that was this anxiety about his little granddaughter, with whom he hadn't yet bonded, suffering from some great discomfort, the source of which hadn't been traced. I was temporarily distracted by the sights and sounds at the quayside, which brought back memories of my three years at the Calcutta port – the Kidderpore docks and the Calcutta jetties – the cranes, the long hands of the jibs, the feverish activities when a ship was berthed, the desolate look of the quayside when berths were empty.

We said goodbye to father-in-law, who didn't show any signs of pain or anguish, but immersed himself completely in the business in hand – the luggage, the travel documents, the money. We walked up the gangway, Aparajita still uncomfortable, crying from time to time, whining, settling down for a while – half awake – and then crying again. She was still scratching her head quite furiously when we got to the cabin – two upper berths and two lower ones. Aparna and Aparajita were going to have the lower berths and we the upper ones.

Quite suddenly and unexpectedly, Sudarsana started speaking, loudly, rapidly and excitedly:
'What a fool I am, what an utter idiot. I never thought about it, and think of all the suffering and anxiety I have caused by my sheer stupidity!'

She opened her bag and took out a small case, out of which emerged a bottle of liquid. She was now talking to herself in an undertone – she did this in situations of stress – muttering lethal imprecations aimed at herself. She took out a towel. And now, armed with a towel and her bottle of liquid, she proceeded to the wash basin in the cabin. She took off Aparajita's frock and asked me to hold her tightly, her head over the basin, while she washed her hair with a medicated shampoo. Aparajita complained, cried, whimpered and then suddenly stopped. It was now almost as if she was enjoying her mother's messing about with her hair. Sudarsana dried her hair, put on some fresh clothes on her, combed her hair carefully and kept talking to her.

'I've killed the monsters which were bothering you – with my witches' brew. Now you won't itch, you won't suffer: it was all my stupidity. Will you forgive me?' She'd indeed forgiven her mother. Aparajita was fast asleep.

Aparna was still missing her grandparents. She was always helpful, mature for her age. She hardly ever threw tantrums or demanded attention because she was at a loose end. It seemed to me that she was sufficiently distracted by her new environment to forget the fact that this was the beginning of a long journey away from her grandparents. I wondered what she was thinking.

'What's Dadu doing?' Aparna asked.

'You and I must go and see. He's waiting, I'm sure. He won't leave before the ship starts moving,' Sudarsana replied.

We couldn't both leave the cabin because Aparajita was fast asleep in one of the lower berths of a cabin of SS Karanja, after a very restless train journey from Calcutta to Bombay. She had had lice in her hair, not an unusual thing to happen in India in those days when travelling on a train. After her mother had got rid of them, she had fallen asleep. We couldn't disturb her sleep. In any case, we would never leave the children on their own.

Sudarsana returned to the cabin. She said she'd tried to communicate to her father, by shouting as well as miming, that Aparajita had had lice in her hair and she'd managed to get rid of them with the result that she was now sleeping peacefully. She thought Father-in-law had managed to decode her message, because her father looked pleased and said something like, 'Thank you for telling me.'

The ship would soon pull out of the berth. It was quite clear from all the hectic activities which were happening all around us. So I left the cabin, went up to the deck and looked down to see if Father-in-law was there. He was sitting on a bench, opposite the middle of the deck, looking small, frail and lonely. It seemed incongruous to me because he'd always impressed me as a strong man of deep loyalties and unswerving principles. I waved to him and he waved back, getting up from the bench and moving towards the ship. It struck me that to be human was to be vulnerable. He loved his daughter and his two granddaughters, and all three of them were leaving for an unfamiliar destination in preference to the security of a stable environment and loving parents, grandparents and friends. I'm sure he didn't understand my eagerness to quit my job and travel a few thousand miles to earn a living by teaching, when my experience of teaching was very limited indeed.

I was quite certain that our decision didn't have his wholehearted approval. Yet, not once did he express his disappointment... He helped in any way he could: he travelled all the way from Calcutta by train with us and looked after his granddaughters with devotion. And now he was going to have to travel back quite a distance all by himself – from Bombay to Calcutta. I waved again. He waved back. Then he turned round and walked away. The ship began to move from the quayside, the cranes, the goods sheds, and the quayside crowds. I followed my father-in-law as long as I could with my eyes, and then he disappeared.

I continued to stand on the deck as the people; the buildings and Bombay's coastline began slowly to recede. I thought about my father, who had suddenly looked old. He was increasingly dependent on people around him, a situation which he must have found painful and humiliating because he was a proud man. He was still managing to get around but had slowed down quite considerably. I was going away for at least four years: would I see him again? Then there was Debu-da who was always precariously poised on the brink of destitution because he was unworldly, and a creature of unrestrained emotion. There were also my other brothers and their families.   Finally, there were my friends –Ronu, Mutu, Ajoy.   I said goodbye to them all – silently – as the coastline of Bombay receded from sight.

I also said goodbye to my three sisters.   Only the second one of my three sisters was married.   I worried about my unmarried sisters because neither my father nor my brothers were capable of raising enough money to provide a sufficient dowry for a conventional marriage.   Wasn't I being selfish?   Wasn't I running away from my responsibilities to look for a better life, thinking only of myself and my wife and children?   Was I going to be able to live with myself if poverty, ill-health and other kinds of misery plagued the lives of those I had grown up with and who'd done their best for me?   It wasn't an easy choice.   What if I proved unequal to the challenge of the new environment?

The coastline of Bombay had by now receded out of sight.   There was the sea all around us and the horizon beyond – but there was no answer there. At the time of leaving the shores of India, I was still looking back.   It was going to be a long time before I saw my father, my brothers, sisters, friends.   I wouldn't see Calcutta either.

But Sudarsana's parents were coming in a year or so: that was something to look forward to.   The coastline of the country where I'd grown up had now vanished, creating in me the feeling that I was in the middle of nowhere.   I turned around to look in the direction of where the sea met the sky.   I also began to notice lots of movement of people around me.   That was reassuring.

The SS Karanja moved slowly away from the shores of Bombay; the coastline fading, disappearing, merging into the horizon.   There was nothing between the ship and where the sea met the sky but deep blue water.   The sky arching above us was clear blue with banks of white, floating clouds.   The only sound was that of the engine as the ship chugged through the Indian Ocean, the third largest ocean of the world, which washed the shores of many countries and continents.   Never before had I been surrounded by vastness like this.   It was like nothing I'd ever seen or felt or experienced before, humbling and exhilarating.   I went down in the direction of our cabin.   I tried to tell Sudarsana about the way I felt.   She said she too had had similar feelings and thoughts.   Aparajita was wide awake, chuckling, laughing, reacting and responding to her sister and mother, who were trying to amuse and entertain her.   It was a relief to see Aparajita playful and happy.   I joined in.   I picked her up.   I cuddled her, tickled her, and made her laugh.   She grabbed my nose.   Children have always loved grabbing my big nose.   It's not as large as Cyrano's, but large enough to attract their attention.   Things were now back to normal.   I wanted to thank somebody, hug somebody.   Thank you, I said, not knowing who I was thanking. Then I hugged and kissed my daughters and Sudarsana, who felt overwhelmed and puzzled by my sudden ardour.

'What you've done is magical,' I said to Sudarsana.

'Always glad to be of use,' she said smiling. 'It was those beastly things in her hair. I shouldn't be praised but called an idiot for not realizing that a long time ago.'

Now that Aparajita was her usual self again, I suggested going up on to the deck to look at the sea, the sky, and the uncluttered horizon far away. So that's what we did; we went up to the deck, two young parents and their two little daughters. It was unlike anything Sudarsana and I had experienced before – overwhelming and hypnotic. The hardly perceptible throbbing, the barely audible reverberations from the engine, the steady movement of the ship, the vaulting sky and the endless ocean had a similar effect on both Sudarsana and me. We quietly watched, listened, contemplated. Aparajita was *not* quiet; apart from using her entire repertoire of sounds, she managed to invent and improvise new ones which took us by surprise. She was not impressed by infinitude.

'Why aren't Dadubhai and Dida going with us?' Aparna, quite unexpectedly, wanted to know. My daughter didn't know life often went one way when we wanted it to go another.

'I'm going out to Uganda to teach. Most fathers and some mothers have to work. I'm going to work in Uganda, this new country we're going to.'

'But you had a job,' she said.

'I didn't like my job,' I said.

'Why didn't you like it?' she asked.

'It was dull,' I said.

'Why was it dull?' she asked.
'I did the same things every day. I didn't enjoy that.'

'I wish they were coming with us,' Aparna said, looking wistful and sad. She was thinking of *Dadubhai* and *Didibhai.*

'They've promised to come,' I said.

Aparna went quiet.

The engine's steady and ubiquitous reverberations had a soporific effect on me much of the time while I was in the cabin. On the deck, there was a steady, invigorating breeze, which smelt of the sea; cleared the cobwebs in the head and filled me with energy. We loved going on to the deck whenever we could. Aparajita was an extrovert without a doubt, so she loved company. She would go to whoever wanted to hold her and cuddle her. She was quite popular on the deck. Aparna would often engage in conversation with total strangers without any self-consciousness. Sudarsana and I would also look out for people who were interested in talking to us because, apart from the fact that we liked meeting people from a different environment, some knowledge of the country we were going to inhabit for at least the next four years was important.

The ship was going to Mombasa. Yet we saw no African passengers on board SS Karanja. The immigration was one-sided: Indians and Pakistanis had come away to live and work in East Africa, but East Africans hadn't come to settle in India. We met families of Patels, Desais, Mehtas and Naiks. There was a family of Khans and at least two families with the surname of Singh. Most of them were friendly, but some were more communicative than others. Sudarsana had less success communicating with the women than I had with the men. This was partly because not many of the women could speak English and discuss subjects which needed more than just basic English. Fortunately Sudarsana's Hindi was quite adequate for coping with simple ideas and information, so she was able to talk with some of the women about various problems relating to setting up home in East Africa. From time to time she would join us men to discuss politics – especially race-relations. It was our impression that the Indian community in East Africa – mainly a business community – had the same attitude towards the Africans as the colonisers. By and large, the attitude of the Gujarati passengers I talked to was politically and racially neutral. They hated the idea of political turmoil. They liked nothing better than being left alone to ply their trade; but in the event of a conflict between the colonisers and the colonised, they were more likely to stand behind the masters. They weren't too concerned, they let me understand, whether the colonisation of another people's country was right or wrong. They weren't particularly disturbed by the assumption of racial superiority implicit in the exercise of colonial authority when the people of one country go over to another and run the lives of those who live there. What happens to an individual has to do with his personality and background. What happens to a nation, similarly, connects with its history and culture. But what about the use of power, of disproportionate force? Doesn't that disturb the process, distort the natural course of events? The dominance of the strong was also natural, they argued. I was disappointed with some of the people I met on the deck. I had some problems with some of the sweeping generalisations Mr Naik and a few others made about Africans, remarks which were biased and racist. At the time, I wasn't too upset by such remarks because I hadn't come into personal contact with the Africans of Uganda, Kenya or Tanganyika. And because of this total absence of experience and contact with the Africans, I had to restrict my dissent to such expressions as, 'It seems unlikely,' or 'I don't believe in the myth of racial superiority.'

Yet it was not really a situation which would justify dismay. Quite a few of the people from Kenya and Uganda were easy to discuss life and politics with, and their attitude, by and large, was friendly. I got the impression that some of my fellow passengers and I were ideologically poles apart and, because both Sudarsana and I were years younger than Mr Naik and others, they probably put our ideas down to the naivety of young people. People like us were full of romantic idealism – just as children had mumps and measles.

Mr Desai was different. He was interested in history, philosophy and literature. He had a music shop in Nairobi in which he and his much younger-looking wife worked, selling musical instruments, records, radios, gramophones. He was interested in the evolutionary process which can be observed throughout history. One of his favourite theories was that the empire-builders became the victims of what they created. The Romans gave the Britons organisation, created social cohesion and made a nation out of disparate elements.

Then they found it difficult to control the people whom they'd given an identity and a sense of nationhood to. Similarly, the British in India, through their organised administration, a common system of law and justice, and the elaborate network of railways, had created a sense of cohesion which led to and strengthened the Indian sense of nationhood. As a result, the Indians had wanted an independent country.

'But wasn't it the policy of every imperial power to divide and rule?' I asked.

'That's true. That was their deliberate, calculated policy to stay in power. But, without wanting to, they united us by giving us all the same courtrooms, the same railways, the same policemen on the beat, the same currency. Then the English language played a very significant part because we could now speak to each other in a common language – especially people with a university education. So, I think, the British, our rulers, played a part in welding us into a nation. Many of our leaders were steeped in Western culture.'

Both Sudarsana and I found Mr Desai excellent company. We were flattered that he and his wife always made us feel comfortable and gave us the impression that we were welcome to spend time with them. They were much older than us. This did not make any difference, for we didn't feel that they had any prejudice against youth, nor did we register in them any tendency to patronise us or talk down to us. Another important aspect of our brief relationship was that we could disagree without it making any difference to our relations. In some ways Mr Desai made me think of my father-in-law: his wide range of interests, his equable temper, his ability to treat other people's ideas and ideology with respect. There was just one disconcerting aspect of our meetings: Mr Desai would sometimes doze fitfully in his deckchair just when I felt the discussion was getting exciting. But then he had no difficulty in starting where – or nearly where – he'd left off. He had a special interest in the history of the British Empire in India, starting with the East India Company, the Battle of Plassey in 1757, the Sepoy Mutiny, or the First War of Independence, in 1857. He was interested in the deep-down compulsions behind conquests: money, power, proselytizing, and adventure. Peace was, by and large, considered an unnatural state of affairs. History and politics were not his only interests. He would also talk with great insight on other subjects – but always in a monotone and without passion, even when he was dealing with a volatile crowd of memories. We didn't find him any less interesting for that.

We also met other people with a variety of interests. Golf, race horses, philately were beyond our ken, but we managed. There were some young boys and girls from various East African schools from whom we tried to get a picture of the secondary schools in East Africa. It didn't seem to us that either the content of education or methods of teaching were a great deal different from what we ourselves had experienced in the schools of India.

What Mr Joshi, a secondary-school teacher, told us about what went on in the schools of East Africa also confirmed our earlier impressions that teaching meant teaching the prescribed syllabus for the school-leaving examination through traditional teaching methods. There was little scope for innovations or experiments. A. S. Neill wouldn't get a teaching job in any of these schools. And if he managed to get a job, he would soon lose it. The only teaching experience I'd had was derived from private tuitions, in a one-to-one situation, and Sudarsana had no experience of teaching at all. Nor did we have any professional teaching qualifications. Therefore, any opportunity we had of discussing the content of education in the schools of East Africa, the methods used, the attitude of pupils and the general atmosphere in the schools was of immense interest to us.

Mr Joshi was the only teacher we met and he was a teacher of Physics in Tanganyika. He'd assured us on more than one occasion that, by and large, the students were well-behaved and discipline was no problem. The only negative message which he conveyed to us was that in his subject, Physics, the proportion of interested students was pitifully small. We sympathised with him, but at the same time wondered whether his expectations from his students were realistic. It was good to meet Mr Joshi. He was nearer our age group than Mr Desai, always friendly, glad to be of use, helpful and jovial, with a good sense of humour. There were also many others – men and women – whom we got to know. We discussed various subjects, but mainly aspects of East African life, which was obviously of immediate interest to us.

There were also inevitably long breaks in our discussion because we spent time with the children. Mr D'Souza, the steward, had the responsibility of attending to us in the cabin. On a few occasions, we entrusted him with looking after our two daughters and went up briefly to a party or to have dinner at the captain's table. The infra-structure of the ship was compact and efficient. Whether it was the captain or the bursar or the attendants, they all went about their business with impressive seriousness of purpose. Strict discipline was in evidence everywhere. And what was most important for us, inexperienced, first-time voyagers, was the helpfulness of the crew, officials and fellow passengers.

Apart from this everybody, at some time or other, responded to the mesmerising attraction of the ocean and the great concave blue sky… It was a feeling unlike any feeling I'd experienced before. There was water all around. Beyond all this water, there was land, but there was no evidence of it yet. A certain longing for land was beginning to grow within me, although my sense of wonder over the beauty and grandeur all around remained undiminished.

Mr Naik on the other hand, said he got bored with travelling by sea after the first few days because of the sameness of the sights and sounds and the limited space around us.

He sometimes felt claustrophobic in the cabin. Fortunately, the feeling was transitory. Neither Sudarsana nor I had any such problem: we were always aware that we were surrounded by a vast expanse of water, and above the sea was the infinite sky. We certainly hadn't felt bored by their sameness.

When we next met Mr Naik, he looked happier than he'd done the last few days. The reason was that the ship was going to stop at Seychelles, an island country of less than 200 square miles, comprising two groups of islands. He had stopped at Seychelles before and been taken on a conducted tour of some parts along the coast, which he had enjoyed. It was a British colony. The name of its capital was Victoria. Seychelles was a popular stop for the passengers of ships which sailed between Mombasa and Bombay. It was much closer to Mombasa. We decided against going ashore because we didn't feel too adventurous and there was still a distinct feeling of insecurity about the health of Aparajita. But we stood on the deck and looked at the islands and they looked beautiful: green, verdant, tropical. We watched the excitement of those who were going ashore but we ourselves were quite content to stay aboard SS Karanja and wait to go ashore at Mombasa.

In Mombasa we said goodbye to Mr and Mrs Joshi, Mr Naik and a few others whom we had got to know well. We also said a special goodbye to Mr D'Souza, who had taken care of us in various ways and looked after Aparna and Aparajita on a few occasions when we had to leave them on their own. The ship had now berthed in Mombasa. I needed to concentrate on the here and now.

We were about to disembark, go through immigration, identify our luggage, get customs clearance and meet our host and hostess, Mr and Mrs Patel.

The efficiency of colonial administration was undeniable. Impressive and rather impersonal in their approach, both the European and African officials checked documents, stamped passports, examined luggage selectively and let people go to where their friends and relations were waiting for them.

Immigration and customs formalities didn't take much time. After coming through, as we didn't know Mr and Mrs Patel, we were vaguely and generally looking for a middle-aged couple – about the same age as Sudarsana's uncle and aunt. We didn't have to wait long. I could see a couple confidently walking in our direction, the man with ample hair tinged with grey, tall and plump, with a friendly face, and his wife, not so tall but also slightly plump, both smiling confidently at us. They introduced themselves – they were Mr and Mrs Patel.

Mr and Mrs Patel greeted us and welcomed us to Mombasa and wished us a happy stay in Kampala and a successful career. They had no difficulty identifying us, they said, because of Aparna and Aparajita. What's more, we looked more or less like what they'd expected us to look like. Uncle had written to them and reminded them about our arrival, although they certainly didn't need any reminding.

Both Mr and Mrs Patel thought our daughters were lovely. They had a large Ford with ample space to accommodate us and our luggage. Mrs Patel sat with the children and Sudarsana at the back and I sat in front with Mr Patel. Mr Patel was interested to know what made us decide to come to East Africa, what our interests were, how long we were planning to stay in Africa, and whether, apart from Mr and Mrs Gupta, we knew anybody else in Kampala. I asked him his opinion of the people and the country. His views were pro-British but not anti-African. The British administration was good for both Kenya and Uganda because it had opened them up to the rest of the world both culturally and economically. The colonisers' main interest was exploitation, but the incidental benefits were too many to count. I wanted to know whether there were political movements to drive out the British. There certainly were. Paradoxically, it was those with a good British education who were the main agitators for independence.

I said that I was impressed with the efficiency of the Customs and Immigration officers at the port of Mombasa and the discussion turned to the ancient port. Mr Patel at once warmed to the subject. Even as early as the twelfth century, if not earlier, it was a prosperous place full of rich merchants and their money and merchandise. It was a centre of maritime trade. Not only India, but also China had trade links with Mombasa. For centuries, Africa had been a major source of ivory, and much of its exports took place through Mombasa. This port was quite central to the prosperity of East Africa.

In the back seat of the car, Mrs Patel was telling Sudarsana about more practical aspects of life in East Africa. Most immigrants from Britain, India, Pakistan, Goa and elsewhere depended on African cooks, cleaners, *ayahs,* gardeners and other manual workers. I was familiar with the economic divide. Though Mrs Patel did her own cooking now that there were just the two of them – her daughter and two sons were all married and had set up their own homes. She did have help - a maid who kept the house clean and a gardener who looked after their garden. From time to time Mrs Patel turned her attention to Aparna and Aparajita. Although they knew neither English nor Gujarati and Mrs Patel didn't know Bengali, she managed to have some communication with them. Once or twice, Sudarsana was called upon to do some interpretation; otherwise they managed fairly well. Aparajita, with hardly any vocabulary in any language, seemed to be managing best of all by drawing upon her large repertoire of noises and improvising whenever necessary. Aparna asked a question or two from time to time in Bengali, which Mrs Patel answered in

Gujarati, and it seemed to me that they didn't have much difficulty in decoding each other's messages.

Mr and Mrs Patel lived in a large bungalow with a large garden. It had four or five bedrooms. Our bedroom was large. During the two nights we were going to spend in Mombasa, we'd decided to sleep in the same room with the children.

Although we'd enjoyed travelling by ship, we were glad to be back on land. We had tea in the garden. The Patels were vegetarian. A few vegetarian savouries which were served with the tea were exquisitely tasteful. I said to Mrs Patel that I'd often felt sorry for vegetarians because I'd been brought up on fish and meat, but I'd just discovered that vegetarians certainly weren't the deprived people I thought they were. The truth of my observation was even more firmly established in the evening when we had a purely vegetarian meal, which tasted subtle, delicate, and delicious. The range and variety of vegetarian cooking couldn't be established at just one meal. What's more, Mrs Patel wasn't trying to prove anything. Yet I found this a memorable experience; so much so, that after a considerable number of years, I still remember the food we ate at the Patels.

After the children went to bed, Mr and Mrs Patel sat in the living room and talked about the lifestyle of people in East Africa. Mr Patel mentioned Jomo Kenyatta, who had emerged as the leader of Kenya's political movement for independence which the colonial power had naturally condemned as completely unacceptable and illegitimate. There was going to be trouble, he thought. We asked several questions; he answered them quite comprehensively. I, more than Sudarsana, was eager to know which way the world had moved in the last two weeks, when we hadn't heard or read a lot of news, so I asked Mr Patel many questions. He thought Egypt was heading for trouble over the Suez Canal, the use of which it had refused to ships bound for Israel. He also mentioned the fierce Soviet delegate to the United Nations, Andrei Vyshinsky, who wanted the UN forces in Korea to leave immediately. Both Mr Patel and I regretted the return of Winston Churchill to No. 10, Downing Street because he was a dyed-in-the-wool imperialist, and like all imperialists, a rabid capitalist, who would certainly damage the nascent socialism of Attlee's Labour administration. We stayed up both nights which I spent at Mr Patel's and talked about politics, political morality and international events. The life he lived and his intellectual convictions and ideology seemed to be in conflict. I was curious how he reconciled some of the ideas he believed in with the life he lived, but I asked no probing questions. I was happy that I'd spent two evenings talking with him about matters which I took seriously.

Mr Patel, a much older and very well-informed man, had taken me seriously and treated me as an equal. There were times when I'd feared that I was going to have to spend a disproportionate part of my life with blinkered businessmen whose main objective was to make as much profit as possible. But that was arrogant and ill-informed. I felt certain that I'd meet other people among businessmen who were interested in sports and politics, life and literature. There would also be our colleagues, a community of teachers, among whom we would certainly find like-minded men and women, whose company we'd enjoy. Our minds, both Sudarsana's and mine, were certainly more full of expectation and excitement, than apprehension, though we didn't expect our students-to-be to line the streets ringing bells and beating drums.

On the second day, we went out with Mrs Patel to the city centre after Mr Patel had left for work. Mrs Patel drove her husband to his shop and came back and took us to look at the market and various other places of interest. The market was a picturesque place, noisy and vibrant. The traditional clothes which the women wore had all the colours of the rainbow. There were some large African women but most of them were tall, slim and elegant. Quite a few of them wore Western outfits. Then there were shops for fruit and vegetables, shops for meat and fish, spices and local specialities. In the outer circle, there were various kinds of shops bicycle shops, shops for handicrafts, clothes, general stores, wines and spirits, toys for children and hundreds of other items of merchandise. But the most memorable part of that morning's trip to the marketplace and the shops around the market were the marvellous multi-coloured, long, flowing robes which the African women were wearing and the tall, elegant women themselves. We'd come out to get a feeling of the city, not for sight-seeing; for there was so much to see in this historical city that we would need considerably longer than just a day or two to acquire any idea of its past glory and present variety and importance. We talked about it and decided that since it was such an important and interesting part of East Africa, it would certainly be worthwhile to come back and explore. Mrs Patel said we would be most welcome to return and spend some time with them, meet her son and daughter, and get to know the city.

Mrs Patel was going to take us to the railway station because Mr Patel was tied up with some important business commitment. Aparna and Aparajita didn't show a great deal of enthusiasm about our journey to Kampala on the celebrated East African Railway trains. Mr and Mrs Patel related well to them and they related well to Mr and Mrs Patel. Why were we in such a hurry to leave? It seemed to me that in a very short time, Mr and Mrs Patel had become their surrogate grandparents, so they wanted to spend more time in Mombasa. Aparna said so, and Aparajita, I'm sure would have said so too, if she had been articulate like Aparna.

So we set out for Kampala, the capital of Uganda, though the administrative headquarters was Entebbe, situated beside Lake Victoria. We were equipped with very little knowledge of East Africa as a whole, and what we knew about Uganda wasn't particularly remarkable. We knew that the capital of Kenya was Nairobi and the capital of Tanganyika was Daresalam. We knew the name of Kenya's political leader, Jomo Kenyatta, and the name of Mt Kilimanjaro. The Kabaka of Buganda had royal status and ruled a fragment of the country with pomp and ceremony, but real power was vested in the colonial administration. Educational standards were fairly high.

It was a segregated system with different schools for the Asians, Africans and Europeans.

I was going to teach English in Kampala Secondary School, which was Asian. Sudarsana would also teach there, it was expected, but her appointment hadn't been finalised as yet because the children were only three and one. We would have to make safe and reliable arrangements for our two daughters being taken care of before Sudarsana could think of teaching at the school.

Right now this was a decision we just couldn't make. We were both old enough to know that a new career in a new country was going to create a sense of adventure and apprehension, and that the two feelings were related. We were going to live in a community of teachers. It would be most unusual if we didn't find some interesting, well-informed and companionable people among them. But there was also the equally important question of whether they would find our company tolerable. There was a lot we could not tell.

Mr K. D. Gupta – Uncle KD – who was married to Sudarsana's aunt, was the Indian Education Officer. It was he who'd encouraged us to come to Kampala, and we'd come, full of expectations and a sense of adventure, and there was no question of looking back. We'd liked what we'd seen so far of East Africa and liked the people we'd met, so our minds were full of hope and positive expectations as Mrs Patel was driving us to Mombasa railway station.

The construction of the railway line had started more than fifty years ago. The Mombasa-Kisumu section was finished in 1901. The fundamental purpose of the railway line wasn't travel but commerce: the transportation of raw materials from various parts of the colony to the port of Mombasa and the carrying of manufactured British goods to the towns and villages of East Africa. It was a system of give-and-take, here as in India, which was of great advantage to the British because it was unequal. But there were aspects of the great networks of railway lines in India and Africa which were profoundly positive: fragments were put together; what was divided became whole; far-flung little villages and towns became a country. This might sound like an overstatement of the part played by the railways in welding together fragments into a whole, but I do believe its role was most significant.

Then there was the Indian connection. The railway lines over which we were going to travel to Kampala were mainly built by Indian labourers, shiploads of them, brought in from our subcontinent. Therefore, I had a right to take some pride in its existence and its great usefulness. The economy of both Kenya and Uganda would collapse without the East African Railways.

The Indian and African workers suffered many hardships. Many lives were lost in 1898 when two lions attacked and killed Indian and African workers busy building a bridge across the Tsavo River. The story of the man-eaters of Tsavo is well-known because of the great numbers of lives lost. In the end, one Colonel Patterson shot and killed the pair of killers. Sudarsana and I were looking forward to travelling by Uganda Railway for mainly two reasons: it was the last lap of our journey; and both Mr and Mrs Patel had talked most enthusiastically about the legendary beauty of the terrain through which the train would pass. Even on the way to Mombasa railway station, Mrs Patel was telling us what to look out for – the sights of outstanding beauty and the flora and fauna. When we reached the railway station, she was most helpful and we were soon installed in our compartment, which we had all to ourselves. We thanked her for the care with which she'd treated us and the affection she'd shown us – Sudarsana, the children and me. We said goodbye. She didn't wait for the train to leave.

Here was colonial administration at its best: efficient and unobtrusive. Everybody knew what they were supposed to do and they did it well. The compartment and the attached toilet were impeccably clean. The attendant, dressed in a long, flowing white Kanzu, turned up soon after the train had started, to say hello and to introduce himself. He would see us at meal times in any case, and he'd come at other times as well, he said. There was something reassuring about his personality. It's a pity I've forgotten his name, just as I've forgotten so much else. Names have been a recurrent problem, and I've had to invent quite a few of them.

Now the journey for the country for which we were bound had started in earnest. The train would take us through Kenya and then to Uganda. My mind made its adjustments. The events of the past receded. The carnage and upheaval preceding and following Indian independence, which had upset and saddened me for a long time, disappeared from my consciousness and so did the unhappy memory of Churchill's victory at the general election of 1951.

The conflict between communism and capitalism in Korea, Vietnam and Europe – in which not so long ago I'd had an obsessive interest – also faded away from my memory. I was now focused entirely on what lay ahead of Sudarsana, Aparna, Aparajita and me.

We ate and chatted and looked out of the window at the world which lay out there, always including the children in what we did. We told them stories which Aparna enjoyed and Aparajita listened to with seeming interest. When our two daughters went to sleep, we talked to each other in an undertone. When the dusk of evening deepened, nothing was visible outside the window unless we were passing or stopping at a station. During the day, especially early morning and before darkness fell, we saw some spectacles of breathtaking beauty. It was when the darkness of night was very slowly making way for the dawning day and Sudarsana, Aparna and Aparajita were all asleep, rocked gently in their beds on the bunks, that I woke up. The train was speeding through the savannah, past intermittent clumps of bushes and shrubs, patches of woods and a scatter of trees here and there. Dawn appeared. It was my first African dawn. I felt as I hadn't felt for a long time. Nature hadn't figured in my life since I'd been to Shantiniketan about four years ago, when Sudarsana and I were both students. Now here I was, surrounded by mile upon mile of open space of unusual beauty and exotic flora and fauna.

And then, suddenly, there was the sun. Its crimson glow tinged the edges round the clouds. It brought to my mind the picture of a very large, red hibiscus, slowly opening its petals, an image I came across in a Sanskrit verse. The sun rose, large and clear, in a blue African sky, and as it grew stronger, it dispelled some of the delicate colours that had been there before. Under the great blue, tropical sky and surrounded by the vast space of the savannah, I felt like a figure on a Chess board travelling in a toy train. The tops of the occasional tree now caught the light of the early morning sun. The outlines of bushes and shrubs became clear. I could see some early herds of impala, generally frisky and nervous, moving like ripples one moment and freezing the next, turning their heads from right to left, and from left to right, as if trying to listen to some urgent message in the air. The train moved on. We came to a station where people were already awake and alert and going about their business in a matter-of-fact manner, and the contrast between the world which had just passed away and this one was difficult to adjust to. Aparna, Aparajita and Sudarsana woke up and took their places by the windows as the train was pulling out of the station – as if nothing mattered except the sights outside.

For weeks before we'd left Calcutta, we'd read about the part of world we were now visiting. We'd read about the amazing Rift Valley of 5,000 kilometres with its many beautiful lakes. We'd also heard of the very large area where the very small amount of rainfall created problems for both man and beast and was therefore inhabited by about ten per cent of the population, a very tough ten per cent. Then there were the highlands with mountains including Mt Kenya, much of it lush green and beautiful. But none of this was of any great interest to our daughters. What they were looking for were the animals: not the mountains, not the beautiful and some very special and unusual trees, not the most incredible number and species of birds which could be seen in these regions – but animals. Aparajita wasn't quite sure what she was looking for, but Aparna was definitely looking for animals as she sat at the window, eagerly looking out at the savannah: the lions, leopards, cheetahs, rhinos, elephants, zebras and giraffes.

Just as I had seen earlier, the first herds of animals we saw were impala, and both my daughters looked at them fascinated by their delicate beauty, playfulness and graceful movements. We saw no elephants, lions or rhinos but we did see a giraffe, that unique animal, that animal like no other animal, busy eating leaves from the tallest branches of a tree. Aparna was delighted, and watched its every movement. She had seen giraffes in the Alipore Zoo, but this was different – a giraffe in its natural habitat, eating leaves from the taller branches of an acacia tree. Later on we came across herds of zebras, uniquely African animals, and spectacularly beautiful in their unusual way. We were also told about the extraordinary variety of birds to be seen in the savannah, but travelling by train didn't seem to be the best way to watch birds. The idea of watching birds hadn't occurred to me, nor had I come equipped with a pair of binoculars. But I made a mental note of the fact that, apart from the birds that belonged there, there were others which flew in their millions from far-away countries, and a really interested ornithologist could spend years here, exploring the beauty and variety of the local as well as the migratory birds.

The names of stations sounded exotic: Mombasa, Voi, Mtito Andes, Makindu, Nairobi, Naivasha. From the savannah, we were moving on to the highlands – towards Nairobi, the capital of Kenya, situated at a height of 5,450 feet – a large and prosperous city of more than a million people. The administration and power was in the hands of white colonisers and the land and money was in the hands of the white farmers. Asian businessmen were also affluent citizens of the country. Segregation was widely practised in clubs, swimming pools and other private places of recreation with total impunity. In other areas of activity, too, there was segregation and discrimination – for example, clubs or law courts. Much of the incentive and inspiration for the segregationist policy and practice in Nairobi came, without doubt, from South Africa. It suited the privileged to isolate themselves. They had guns and prisons to deal with dissent.

Because of the children, especially Aparajita, who was just over a year old, we had our meals in the cabin. But mainly for the experience, we did go to the dining car once or twice and were impressed with the clean white outfit of the waiters, the silver cutlery, the spotlessly clean tablecloths and the attentive service. The diners were almost entirely European, mostly British, who had ensured that their lifestyle didn't change as a result of their contact with a different culture, which most of them considered to be inferior. If one's way of life is more efficient, is there any harm if one wants it to be replicated? It was a pity, however, that it was unusual for the conquerors to appreciate and admire the culture and lifestyle of the conquered people. The potential for conflict was inevitably there.

What came to my mind in British history was the Peasants' Revolt in 1381, when the feudal system was as oppressive as it was unjust. Rome had its slavery; England had its serfs. The oppressed gladiators and other slaves as well as the English peasants accepted their oppression and humiliation for a long time before they rebelled. They had initial success but in the end they succumbed to superior force and strategy. The pattern had a tendency to repeat itself in the oppression of the weak and vulnerable; protest followed by suppression, protest and suppression. If the protest was cruel and violent, the suppression was infinitely more so. Being Indian, I thought of the Indian soldiers' protest against their British oppressors' disregard of their culture, religion and self-respect, which had led to what the British rulers called the Sepoy Mutiny and the Indian historians refer to as the Indian Rebellion, the Indian Revolution or the First War of Independence of 1857.

The French Revolution was also the result of a similar insensitivity of the ruling classes. The poor, the oppressed and the humiliated couldn't take it any more and there was a bloody revolution. This is a process, I'm sure, that will be repeated many times even in our days. But the repressive measures today are more powerful and effective.

In all these protests, there were leaders, and one of the most powerful incentives for them and the rebellion or revolution was ideology: equality, justice, freedom and the right to live with dignity.   The deeply felt sense of humiliation in a large community of people with a common cause usually produced a leader – Spartacus, Wat Tyler and John Ball, the Rani of Jhansi, Robespierre and Danton.   None of these revolutions was wholly successful.   None of them resulted in the banishment of injustice.   Jomo Kenyatta was the emerging leader in Kenya.   Would he be able to lead the country to a peaceful resolution of the Africans' conflict with their colonisers?

We'd decided to work in Uganda because of circumstances which were causing me frustration and a loss of self-esteem.   My job was dull and repetitive.   I saw the same faces, made the same or almost the same decisions; signed the same railway forwarding notes.   I didn't like having to depend on my father-in-law after the birth of a second child; I was going to sink deeper into dependence.   So partly for practical reasons and partly for that elusive, immanent entity, the soul, I'd got up and left Calcutta.   It was precipitate action.   And Sudarsana had co-operated in all this, not because she was determined to be a good wife, but because she'd shared my sense of frustration.

Anyway – whatever the reasons - we left without much preparation and very little knowledge of Uganda, in particular, and of Africa, in general.   One of the great gains of this decision was that Sudarsana and I had felt closer.   We were talking about ideas and events we'd never done before.   She was discovering my areas of interest and I hers.   We'd spent almost a fortnight together when she hadn't had to do anything except mind the children, who demanded little attention, and I hadn't had to travel up to Kidderpore Docks to allocate railway wagons.   Now we could gaze with fascination at the plants and animals of East Africa during the day and look at the dark velvet African sky in the evening, and talk about our future.

As well as Spartacus, the Peasants' Revolt, the First Indian War of Independence and the French Revolution.   The reason Sudarsana and I found ourselves talking about these things was because of a discussion we'd had – Mr and Mrs Patel, Sudarsana and I.   Whilst we were busy planning our new beginning in Uganda and giving very little thought to the political future of East Africa in general, and of Uganda in particular – we were naturally hoping that nothing would crack the sky or start a bloody revolution in Uganda in the years to come.

The political future of Kenya, they pointed out, was not just uncertain; it showed every sign of real conflict between the settlers and the people of the Kikuyu tribe. Mr Patel's perception was that the situation was hurtling towards real disaster because of the settlers' conviction that the principles of justice and fair play were relevant in their Western countries, but not here in black Africa. The settlers believed that they were a race apart, which indeed they were. They'd helped themselves to the central highlands of the most lush and beautiful parts of Kenya – without any regard to law and tradition. It was a case of misappropriation on a massive and mindless scale, which had made a very large proportion of the people of the Kikuyu tribe landless. Many of them had moved into Nairobi, roaming the streets and resorting to crime. A commission was appointed and its partisan report published. It had made a bad situation worse by according official approval to the criminal misappropriation of Kikuyu land by settlers.

'The situation can only get worse, not better,' Mr Patel had said.

'Can't the dispute be settled through the mediation of a powerful, non-partisan third party? A Commission of some sort?' I had asked.

'The settlers don't want any mediation. Why should they? To each square mile of land live 625 Kikuyus, whereas only 2.5 settlers occupy the same area. And the settlers have the best land. Why should they want change?' Mr Patel had said.

And Sudarsana and I had concluded that real and deadly conflict couldn't be far away. There was in this crowd of bitter, disenchanted and violent people, someone who, Mr Patel thought, might steer the country out of trouble. Jomo Kenyatta, a man of courage, integrity and real qualities of leadership, had become the president of the Kenyan African Union and was able to instil a sense of commitment into its members. He might forestall the disaster which was waiting to happen. We sincerely hoped he would.

Nairobi railway station was clean and people who administered the day-to-day running of the place were extremely efficient. It was, after all, their organisational and administrative ability which had made it possible for the British to hold their large empire together – just fire power wouldn't have been enough. And the railways in India and Africa were very good examples of that ability. What we saw for the most part – the busy, clean, affluent and efficient Kenya – impressed us deeply. But what made us feel insecure was the rumbling discontent and resentment just below the surface, which we'd heard of.

Now we were leaving Nairobi Station and thinking of the country which was going to be home for Sudarsana, me and our two daughters: Uganda. Kampala, the capital of Uganda, was 500 miles north-west of where we were. It was a journey of almost two days on the narrow-gauge line on which trains moved at less than 50 miles an hour. I don't remember exactly how many hours it took to reach Kampala or exactly when we left and when we arrived.

Outside Nairobi, not far away from the railway lines, we could see improvised temporary dwelling places, semi-permanent huts as well as large, old, shabby buildings, each of which was parcelled out between several families. Beyond the poverty-stricken suburbs lay open fields, Kenya's rich and fertile lands, where grew a variety of vegetables. But alongside, there were other signs of human habitation, of communities living together over a stretch of a few miles. It is always these destitute people, living on the periphery of affluent cities and societies, who create a sense of unease, make us question our political morality and our humanity. We have formidable nuclear arsenals and yet death by starvation of countless faceless people is a daily fact. Bombay was, even at the time I'm writing about, the most affluent city of India, where businessmen millionaires and film stars abounded, but Bombay also had – and Mumbai still has – the most appalling, crowded and poverty-stricken slums in and around it. Nairobi was, and I am sure still is, the largest and richest city in East Africa. It was full of impressive buildings. Life in the city was rich, colourful, exciting, multi-national, and full of embassies, night clubs and five-star hotels. Yet, just on the outskirts, there was poverty and human degradation which made a mockery of civilisation and affluent lifestyles.

But there were times when we could get away from it all – the urban affluence and the suburban squalor, the arrogance of the colonisers and the anger of the colonised. There were trees, open fields, the Rift Valley. Then there were hills and blue mountains and neat little village huts surrounded by a fence. There was the African sky, the banks of nimbus clouds, the various species of birds in flight. I know Sudarsana admired the unique beauty of the landscape. Aparna was interested, which we gathered from her sudden bursts of enthusiasm. And Aparajita kept using her limited vocabulary and a wide range of sounds, I think, to express her admiration, approval and disapproval. Most of the time she was happy and gave the impression of participation in what was happening around her.

Now we were in Uganda. I got the feeling of rich, lush abundance as I looked out and saw banana trees, palm trees, umbrella tress and other tropical vegetation. Then Lake Victoria came into view in all its glory, the lake that's inseparable from the life and culture of the East African people. Lake Victoria is certainly at the centre of Uganda's life, for without it Uganda wouldn't be the rich, verdant land it is – with its cotton, coffee, bananas and a large variety of vegetables. Water is Uganda's greatest friend, richest asset – the water from lakes, rivers and the 'long' and 'short' rains. Water not only provides the country with all the food it needs but also cash crops vital for its economy.

Since leaving Nairobi, we'd moved through towns and railway stations, again with exotic names like Thika, Naivasha, Nakuru, Kisumu, Eldoret, Tororo, Mbale, Bugamba, Jinja – and Sudarsana enjoyed rolling these off her tongue.

We'd seen beautiful trees the names of which we didn't know. There wasn't anybody to tell us what they were. I don't think knowing names was all that important; their glorious beauty was what mattered. And we did register that Uganda had beautiful trees and forests and birds and animals we wouldn't be able to see in India. What we had experienced in the short time we were in Uganda was already more than I'd hoped for. There was a lot more to see – the lions, the elephants, the buffaloes, the hippos, the rhinos. Then there was the crested crane, the national emblem of Uganda. There were still some gorillas to be found in Uganda, but I didn't know where. Some day I wanted to climb Mt Elgin and Mt Kilimanjaro and visit Murchison Falls. Some day... The train trundled into Kampala Station.

The station was neither too large, nor too small. It wasn't either too crowded or too noisy. It was clean. There was a feeling of quiet, friendly efficiency. It felt good to be here. I didn't feel tired or anxious. I looked out of the window of our coach for Sudarsana's uncle or aunt or both. We found no familiar faces eagerly looking out for us. Instead, there was a group of four adults confidently walking towards us as we were looking out of an open window. One of the adults talked to Sudarsana and me. He was Naresh, a Bengali, who'd come from Calcutta a year or two before us to teach art at the Government Indian Secondary School in Old Kampala. He brought us the message from Sudarsana's aunt and uncle – that they were waiting for us in their house in Old Kampala, where we were going to stay until we moved into our own bungalow. Then there was Ramen Bhattacharya, a teacher of English, and his wife Mira, who taught in a primary school. There was another teacher from the same school, John Caneiro. Naresh Sengupta was tall and lean, with a longish face and longish hair. Ramen Bhattacharya, with his thick, curly mop of hair and emphatic way of speaking, looked like a rabble-rousing revolutionary, waiting for the day of direct action. John Caneiro was from Goa. He dressed tidily and spoke English clearly and confidently. Naresh, John and Mira were in the same age group as me and Sudarsana; Ramen was a few years older.

We came out of the station and piled into two cars. Sudarsana, Aparna and Aparajita went with Naresh and John in John's car. I went with Ramen and Mira.

We had a common destination – the bungalow of Mr and Mrs K. D. Gupta in Old Kampala. It was clear that the arrangements were common knowledge because there was hardly any discussion about what was happening next. We arrived at the quite large bungalow of Sudarsana's uncle and aunt, *Pishemashay* and *Pishima*, in Bengali. They greeted us with affectionate warmth. Sudarsana, Aparna and Aparajita were received not only with words of affection but also hugs and kisses by Pishima. Pishemashay said words of welcome to us, persuaded everybody to stay for a drink and then came over to talk to us. He first talked to the children, gave each a hug and then sat down briefly beside Sudarsana to find out how the journey went – from Calcutta to Bombay, Bombay to Mombasa, and from Mombasa to Kampala. Sudarsana couldn't have given him much more than a very brief account of the journey. But she didn't forget to give Pishima and Pishemashay the regards and good wishes which Mr and Mrs Patel of Mombasa had asked her to convey to them. After the usual small talk and a single round of drinks – of brandy and ginger-ale, Coca-cola and orange juice – everybody left except the Guptas and the Bagchis. Within minutes of the guests leaving, Aunt proceeded to spoil Aparajita, who'd woken up after a longish sleep. It was quite clear that she'd taken to Aparajita, although I wasn't sure that she quite was ready to reciprocate yet. She looked somewhat bewildered and overwhelmed. I felt comfortable, both physically and emotionally, in the new environment.

The four colleagues who'd turned up at the station to meet us were all pleasant and friendly people. Both Uncle and Aunt showed genuine affection for all of us and Aunt was particularly happy in the company of my two daughters. There was, however, a small problem. Uncle was the Indian Education Officer, on whose good opinion depended the careers of a large number of Indian teachers, both men and women. As a result, a certain amount of restraint and formality had crept into their communication.

The school where I was going to teach was Old Kampala Secondary School. The students took the Cambridge School Certificate examination in their final year of school. There were, as far as I remember, three sections of each form of thirty children – so the total number of students in the school was about 550. I was going to teach English mainly in the final year of the school. First, I walked round the school campus to get some idea of the size and atmosphere of the school. It was much smaller than an average secondary school in Calcutta. The school I went to about 15 years ago was twice its size. The grounds of the school here were thoroughly clean, the classes weren't noisy, and the teachers looked businesslike. The school building was surrounded by green fields where tall, old, leafy trees provided ample shade on hot, sunny, tropical afternoons for the students to have their packed lunches in the school break or just sit around chatting. At a level slightly higher than where the school was, I found the playing fields on which there was a cricket pitch and goal posts for football. The tennis courts were nearer the school at a level lower than the cricket and football field. Just a few hundred yards behind it, overlooking the school, was Old Kampala Hill. From the top of it, you could get a good view of the surrounding hills, which were quite spectacular. Kampala is a city built on seven hills. How many I was able to see from the top of Old Kampala hill, I really can't now recall.

I wandered back a few minutes before 11 am, when I was expected to see the headmaster, Mr B. D. Gupta, who was one of the two younger brothers of Sudarsana's uncle. Mr Gupta was shorter than Uncle. He had a lighter complexion and a shiny, balding head.

He blinked from time to time behind his thick glasses and made little noises repeatedly which suggested that he was trying to clear his throat. He greeted me formally in English, and the conversation which took place after that was also entirely in English. He was the headmaster and I was an inexperienced junior teacher in his school. If I took my work seriously, did what I was told, behaved in a responsible way, and came to him from time to time for advice and guidance, unconditionally accepting his leadership, all would be well, he seemed to be saying. Arrogance, irresponsibility and a lack of commitment often ruined the careers of young people. It was a pity, he commented... I didn't feel bored. I was genuinely interested in what Mr Gupta had to say. I had no real experience of teaching. I wanted to learn. I couldn't be offended if he sounded superior – he was an older man with many years' experience.

The meeting was brief. Mr Gupta had allocated senior classes to me on the assumption that since I had an honours degree in English and an MA from Calcutta University, I should be able to cope. But passing examinations is largely – almost entirely – a matter of writing down answers to questions asked by people one doesn't know and marked by people one's never met. I didn't have to be particularly personable to do well in examinations, but a teacher had to communicate in a way which was both interesting and well-informed. Then there were the most important aspects of teaching – relationships, group dynamics and mutual respect. Nobody knew which way things were going to go.

Was I likely to have a pleasant relationship with my students? Was I creative, was I competent? A single interview of half-an-hour or so wasn't long enough for Mr B. D. Gupta to find indisputable answers to these questions. But he had to try to make an assessment. I suppose that's what he was trying to do. And he did it with pleasant informality. What's more, he made me a good cup of tea.

Mr Gupta wanted me to go away and come back in half-an-hour or so – during the break – when he was going to introduce me to the other teachers. I went back to the top of Old Kampala hill, which I'd decided might become one of my favourite haunts, and came back. It was amazing what I could see from the top of Old Kampala Hill – other hills, hilltops, groups of buildings scattered around hillsides and in the valleys; church spires and trees, a lot of trees, all over the place. There were roads looping the hills and running through the valleys which looked like wide ribbons. And there was always the clear blue African sky, full of sunny clouds.

I returned to Mr Gupta's office. The staff room was now full of people, men and women, who taught at the school and had assembled for an hour's relaxation before going back to teach. Mr Gupta and I walked in. Mr Gupta addressed his colleagues and said that my name was Ganesh Bagchi and that I'd arrived recently from Calcutta, and that I would be teaching English from the next week.

Everybody was friendly. They welcomed me. There were two familiar faces – those of Naresh and John Caneiro. There were others who came and greeted me and said pleasant, welcoming words. I had some tea with Naresh and John. It was at dinner time that both Sudarsana's uncle and aunt wanted to know my impressions of the school. I said I couldn't say anything significant at this stage. I liked the look and the feel of the place. I was excited as well as apprehensive. On the whole, my feelings were positive.

'What do you think of Bhabesh?' Sudarsana's aunt asked me. By Bhabesh, she meant Mr B. D. Gupta.

'He takes education seriously, the academic side of education. He's for efficiency and he's for results – measurable results. He's happy that the results of the school's external examinations have always been good,' I said.

I did think he was a practical man of education because he talked to me of practical aspects – the syllabus, the textbooks, the external examination and the school results. He made it quite clear that he'd assess the quality of any teaching by the results in the external examination.

Teaching alone couldn't produce excellent results. The quality of the pupils and their commitment also made a difference, I'd suggested.

'There's the trading community and there's the professional community. The boys and girls from professional families do better than those from trading families. There are exceptions of course,' said Sudarsana's aunt.

Aparna and Aparajita seemed settled and relaxed. Aparajita laughed and chuckled and made noises which were difficult to understand. Aparna at three years' old spoke with amazing maturity. Those who talked to her, including Uncle and Aunt, were amused as well as impressed to see such maturity in one so young.

'Let's go for a walk,' I said to Sudarsana.

'Aparajita will soon be awake. I must stay around to feed her,' she said, so Aparna and I walked up to the top of Old Kampala hill, where I'd been a few hours earlier. I wanted her to see the tops of other hills, the trees, the church spires, the people and the cars, which looked so much smaller from the top of the hill. She looked interested to begin with and asked questions about the names of the hills and their heights, the names and types of trees, which I didn't know. But Aparna soon lost interest.

'Didibhai and Dadubhai – when are they coming?' Aparna suddenly asked.
'I'm not sure,' I said.

'Why aren't you sure?'

'Your Didibhai and Dadubhai did say they'd come but they didn't say when,' I said.

'I want them to come soon,' she said.

'I'll write to them, I'll tell them that you want them to come soon,' I said.

'Very soon,' she said.

'Very soon,' I repeated.

It was getting late. It'd soon be dark. We turned round and started walking in the direction of the bungalow. Aparna looked quite thoughtful.

'Why are we here?' she asked, my irrepressible daughter.

'We've got jobs here, your mother and I. And soon we'll have our own house,' I replied.

'But you <u>had</u> a job, and we <u>had</u> a house,' Aparna wouldn't give up.

'I didn't like my job, and the house wasn't ours.'

Aparna became thoughtful again. Then she asked me the name of one of the big, leafy trees on the hill. Again, I didn't know. I must put this right, I thought; I must acquaint myself with the names of these beautiful trees. I didn't want Aparna to think that her father was ignorant. When we came home, lights were blazing in the living room, Uncle had returned from work and Aparajita was showing off her vocabulary, which was increasing by the day. I told Uncle about how I'd lost face with my daughter by not being able to tell her the names of trees at the top of Old Kampala hill.

Uncle had in the past said once or twice that he was a teacher for a time and he'd enjoyed his teaching. I could see that he liked being in charge of the education of a whole community: he enjoyed having the responsibility, and the power which went with it. But I didn't know about his interest and ability as a teacher.

Now, as soon as I'd told him about my ignorance of African trees and my predicament when Aparna asked me about them, Uncle went and fetched a book from his small office-cum-library in the house, asked for a pot of tea for us and sat down to educate me. I've forgotten most of what he taught me but he showed me pictures of elder trees, canopy trees and acacia. There were trees with Swahili names of which I remember Muali and Murule. Bamboo and palm trees were familiar: we saw many of those in India. What impressed me was the interest Uncle took in educating me.

Mr and Mrs Hira came to dinner that evening. They were impressed with our daughters and Sudarsana and Mrs Hira seemed to have a few common interests, Indian music being one of them. They were from Sindh, a region in West Pakistan, but had emigrated to Uganda, and considered Uganda to be home, unlike many Indians and Pakistanis, who had lived in Uganda for several generations and yet wouldn't call themselves Ugandans. This was my first social encounter with people outside the greater family and the school. They were a highly sophisticated couple who spoke English fluently and well, had a good sense of humour, and a certain zest for life. I was impressed with them except for the fact that they talked slightingly about Ugandan Africans – African politicians as well as the car mechanic, people in high places and low... There weren't many occasions when Africans came into the conversation, but when they did, they weren't important.

I had the same feeling when I talked to Mr B. D. Gupta, the headmaster, not so long ago. We lived in Uganda, but did not think of ourselves as Ugandans, Asian businessmen had the money and the colonial masters from Britain had the power. I hadn't yet come across anybody who was a Ugandan African *and* a professional or a businessman or an administrator. There was the clerk in the headmaster's office, who gave me the impression of being a quiet, self-effacing man. The man who went about with Uncle and fetched and carried for him was another Ugandan African I'd come across.

Did Uncle have an African friend with whom he could discuss problems of his personal or professional life? Did Mr B. D. Gupta go out for a drink with an African friend? Am I likely to have African friends who would take me seriously? It was too early to worry about such imaginary problems. I tried to put them out of my mind.

There was good news. We'd been allocated a house on the same stretch of wide, leafy mud road where uncle lived, along the side of the school. On one side of the road – along the entire length of it – was the school, and on the other side were half-a-dozen houses, all bungalows. The houses were at different levels: Uncle's house was at the highest level, at the top of the road and our house was going to be at the bottom. There was a large acacia tree at the corner of the sloping land outside the house. Nobody had attempted to organise a garden on this land, probably because it sloped so steeply. Our front door was a few yards away from the main road. Our next-door-neighbour was Mr B. D. Gupta. Our house had two bedrooms, a large living-cum-dining room, and a study. Sudarsana and I were pleased with it. Aparna made no comment. Home to her meant 37C Golf Club Road; anywhere else was a temporary refuge.

This was a big occasion for Sudarsana and me. The last home of our own, the only one we'd had until now, was the flat at Chandni Chowk near Dharamtollah Street in Calcutta. We had to abandon that in circumstances over which we'd had no control. So we longed for a place of our own. There were times I fantasized about it. Calcutta Port Commissioners, the organisation for which I had worked, had beautiful houses by the river and one of the great attractions of the job had been that I'd expected to live in one of those bungalows some day...

Yes, it was important for me that now we had a house in Kampala near the top of Old Kampala hill – a house for the Bagchis at last. It certainly was a memorable day. The furniture – beds, the dining table, desks, chairs – were provided by the Public Works Department, and so were mattresses, pillows, mosquito nets and many other household essentials. We found someone to cook for us and someone to look after the children as well as do some housework. The cook was Okello; Mary was going to look after the children. Sudarsana was due to begin teaching in a few days. I'd already started. What was for me a welcome change was that Aparna hadn't mentioned her grandparents for quite a few days. Our preparation to face life in Africa, to live with a sense of security and in reasonable comfort, was progressing well, and our two daughters hadn't yet shown any signs of restlessness or insecurity.

Sudarsana was going to start teaching the lower forms in the afternoon the week after, and she was excited, but at the same time rather apprehensive, because she had absolutely no experience of teaching. Learning-by-doing may be a good way of acquiring skills, but not when an employer is paying you a reasonable sum of money every month. Though of course, such discussions were futile because it was not possible to change the situation. She had got hold of the textbooks and decided how she was going to go about presenting the lessons. What she was going to teach wasn't a problem; how she was going to present the material for learning was. She was tense, although the anxiety didn't exactly keep her awake.

It was almost a fortnight now since I'd been teaching. I felt quite strongly that my students had accepted me as their teacher and thought that they'd benefit from what I taught and how I taught. Shakespeare is always a challenge for both teachers and students in secondary schools. Many secondary school students found him wordy, boring and difficult to understand. The proposal that Shakespeare should be abandoned because he didn't make sense to by far the greater proportion of the students had often been seriously discussed, but the point of view of the traditionalists that Shakespeare was such an important landmark in not only English literature but also in world literature that to deprive the students of our secondary schools the opportunity of having some idea of his plays would be short-sighted and unfair. I didn't think that Shakespeare should be abandoned, but that the way Shakespeare was taught should be changed. My own experience was that teachers of Shakespeare tended to paraphrase Shakespeare – reduced good poetry to indifferent prose, adding a running commentary of their own or derived from literary critics such as Bradley and Wilson Knight. There were also writers of notes who guaranteed to help students to get good marks in examinations. So students often only half understood the text and then read up notes on Shakespeare which told them of the social, moral and political implications of the play, examined critically the nature of the conflict and provided them with a study of each character. This kind of approach destroyed the students' interest in Shakespeare. Not so long ago, when I was at the receiving end of that kind of teaching, I hadn't liked it. So I wanted to devise a strategy to make Shakespeare interesting for students.

I was teaching *As You Like It*. First of all, instead of reading and paraphrasing, I gave the students a general idea of the situation, a loose paraphrase of the lines in question, I'd say, 'Where in this speech does Jaques talk about a young man with a beard like a leopard's, who doesn't always use polite language, who isn't worried about dying, and who wants to be remembered for his courage, and so defies death?' I expected someone to read out the lines:

'...Then a soldier,
Full of strange oaths, and bearded like the Pard,
Jealous in honour, sudden and quick in quarrel,
Seeking the bubble reputation
Even in the cannon's mouth.'

On another occasion I might do a more general explanation and paraphrase and ask someone to read the relevant lines. 'Juliet is shocked and surprised and torn between her love of Romeo and her affection for and loyalty towards Tybalt, her cousin. Romeo has killed Tybalt in circumstances about which she knows very little, Juliet doesn't understand how such a sensitive, loving and tender person could take the life of her cousin. She couldn't condone murder, but at the same time, she couldn't give up Romeo. Here's an instance of a very real and human conflict, the essence of drama. The co-existence in Romeo of good and evil puzzles and upsets her. How can this man, full of loving-kindness, have the heart of a snake, she asks? How can her Romeo be beautiful and tyrannical at the same time? A series of other similar questions follow, by which she tries to solve the puzzle, the paradox of good and evil living together in the person of Romeo. 'Please read out these lines,' I would say.

Then one or more of the students would find and read the lines:

Juliet: 'O serpent heart, hid with a flow'ring face!
Did ever dragon keep so fair a cave?
Beautiful tyrant! Fiend angelical!
        Dove-feather'd raven! Wolfish-ravening lamb!
Despised substance of divinest show!

Just opposite to what thou justly seemest,
A damned saint, an honourable villain!
O nature, what hadst thou to do in hell,
When thou didst bower the spirit of a fiend
In mortal paradise of such sweet flesh?
Was ever book containing such vile matter
So fairly bound! O, that deceit should dwell
  In such a gorgeous palace!'

Finding the relevant lines and reading them gave the students a sense of participation. When the teacher did the reading, explaining and commenting, single-handed, the students invariably lost their concentration at some point. Some teachers even asked and answered questions all by themselves. It was then obvious that the teachers were enjoying themselves, the question being *were the students enjoying themselves?*

The students' own initiative is often destroyed when teachers tell them all the answers: I was for preserving and encouraging their initiative. I didn't point out the many instances of the *'conjunctions of contradictions'* in Juliet's speech that I've just quoted, but encouraged them to discover and point them out. I would then explain words like *paradox* and *oxymoron*, if none of the students knew them. But I'd first find out if any of the students knew them already.

From time to time we would do a loose paraphrase – using modern language and modern idioms – of a scene or two. It was a combined effort – we did it together and the scribe we'd selected would write it down. We would then act it all out. Unfortunately, there wasn't a lot of space for movement, but we used what space we had. The students enjoyed the acting. Sometimes we created so much noise – legitimate noise of fun and enjoyment – that people walking past in the corridor would stop and look curiously, and sometimes disapprovingly, at what was going on. Once the headmaster, Mr B. D. Gupta stopped and peered through the glass door, but he didn't later send for me and ask questions about the noise and laughter which a scene from *As You like It* had generated. One of the students, Sadruddin, had a loud and raucous voice, so the fact that he particularly enjoyed this kind of activity created a problem. But what was important for me was that the students were beginning to enjoy Shakespeare. We used an annotated edition. I didn't want unfamiliar and archaic words to get in the way, so I wrote them on the blackboard with their meanings alongside them. If we wanted to know the meaning of a word, we'd refer to the blackboard for ready reference – although annotated editions provided the meanings of most of the unfamiliar words. Finally, after this initial preparation, we'd act out selected scenes, with me often taking a minor part.

For writing essays, I introduced the idea of research and library work followed by discussions: the students found that this kind of preparation made the writing easier and more interesting. Rita wrote an excellent essay on gypsies. It was published in the school magazine... I was really beginning to enjoy my teaching, especially because I'd convinced myself that my students liked me and enjoyed my teaching. Some would come and see me at home – purely social visits. Sometimes, Srilekha Ahluwalia, Minakshi Mehta, Ravinder Maini, Surinder Singh and a few others came to my house. These were just friendly visits. They were happy if I spent a little time with them, talking about matters of common interest. Ravinder was an outstanding student. He came a few times to listen to long-playing records of Shakespeare's plays. He won prizes for the school in inter-school competitions in debate and elocution. Quite a few of the boys and girls were intelligent, gifted and motivated people. This made my launching into a teaching career both interesting and exciting.

Later on in life, quite a few of them had successful careers. I'm still in touch with Ravinder, who went to Cambridge to study medicine, became Professor of Immunology at Charing Cross Medical College, did ground-breaking work on rheumatoid arthritis and was knighted for his contribution to medical science. Yasmin Alibhai Brown is another student who's well-known in England in the world of journalism I had quite a few bright, intelligent students whose company I enjoyed, and if I did my research properly, I'd probably find that quite a few of them have made considerable contributions in their fields of work. But what's relevant for me isn't whether they've become rich and famous, but that they related well to me and I to them and the sterile environment of my previous employment was now beginning to recede from my memory.

I hadn't kept my distance from my students, so I had to pay a price for it from time to time. Inder Chawla criticised my handwriting in the middle of a lesson one day. He said half the time he couldn't understand the comments I'd written at the end of his essays because my writing was hardly legible. I said I'd do something about it and I did.

I think my handwriting was quite legible, but I accepted that when I wrote in haste, it could be difficult to read. I bought a book on handwriting and practised from the models and made sure that Inder Chawla understood what I'd written. There were three reasons why I did this. If I didn't take Inder seriously, he wouldn't read my comments with attention and interest. In short, he wouldn't take me seriously. Secondly, it was important that my relationship with students should be based on mutual respect. And, finally, I took the trouble to improve my handwriting because I took teaching seriously. My problem was that I now wrote rather slowly.

'Are you beginning to be able to understand my handwriting and my comments?'

'Yes, sir, I am,' Inder said, with a broad grin.

I particularly liked the fact that Inder wasn't afraid of speaking out, partly because he was Inder Chawla, and partly because my students related to me well enough to ask me why I did what I did. I was beginning to get somewhere.

But my relationship with my students, which was a major source of pleasure for me in my new profession, was precisely what the headmaster objected to. I was summoned to his office and advised to be less matey with my students. He'd had a long career in teaching, he said, and he was certain that students lost respect for teachers who treated them as their equals.
'Especially in *our* culture,' he said, 'it is most unusual.'

There was more to come.

'I've been looking at the way you mark the written work of your pupils. I'm afraid I don't like it,' Mr Gupta said.

'If you tell me what it is that you find unacceptable, I think I can explain why I do what I do,' I said.

'First of all, we underline the wrong word or spelling and write *v* for vocabulary, *sp* for spelling, *gr* for grammar, *p* for punctuation and so on in the margin. You use a different set of textual and marginal marks. Why is that?' he said. He wasn't unpleasant or aggressive; it was as if he really wanted to know.

'I once worked as a copy writer in a publicity company. There we used a set of marginal and textual symbols. The system is comprehensive and is understood by everybody in the literary and advertising world. I think it's more efficient,' I said.

'I *know* these symbols,' he said, 'they're used for proofreading. Proofreading has one objective, marking essays has another,' he said. 'There is something else I don't understand. You correct spelling and grammar one week, and punctuation and sentence structure the next, and something else the week after. It's our tradition here to correct *every* error in *every* essay *every* time. I'm not in favour of these deviations from our standard practice.'

'What I do isn't entirely original,' I said, ' It's because I read an article in a language teaching magazine and I found what the writer said made sense.'

Quite naturally the headmaster wanted to know about the article and I told him what I remembered. It said that if there were too many corrections, the students lost interest and were disheartened. If there were a few mistakes, they felt good. In neither situation was there any obligation or necessity for the students to do anything. So all they did was to look at the assessment at the end: A+, A, A-, B+, B-, C+, C, etc. But if the correction of a particular kind of error is made and then discussed and the students do their own correction, the whole exercise is much more effective. What's more important for the teacher is to ensure that our students understand how to handle *discourse*. And I pointed out at the end of every essay what I thought about the content and about the shape and substance of the discourse. Whole lessons were devoted to discussing their stylistic deviations and the nature of discourse – in language that they understood. I felt certain, I said, that this was an effective way of encouraging students to write good essays.

The headmaster listened to everything I had to say with patience, interrupting from time to time for clarification or to express disagreement. It was soon clear that he wasn't convinced. Although, he said, he liked some of the ideas, on the whole it wasn't practical.

Another – and for him the most important point – was uniformity. Unless all teachers in a school followed the same system of marking, he remarked, there was going to be almighty confusion on account of my deviations. He directed me to see one of my senior colleagues, Robi Banerji, and discuss the subject seriously.

Robi Banerji was a friendly, intelligent, knowledgeable and gentle person. He told me that he didn't always agree either with the methods of teaching which the headmaster so devoutly relied on or his philosophy of education. But certain compromises had to be made. I said I couldn't accept his commitment to uniformity because individuality has to be at the core of any educational philosophy. One of the aspects of the school which I liked was the absence of school uniforms. He saw my point - but said with regret that some compromises are unavoidable in life. I liked Robi Banerji, our senior English teacher. He was a much older man. Dissent or discord, open confrontation however, wasn't something he was used to.

Another week or two went by without anything untoward or dramatic happening. I was always quite excited, however, by just the ordinary events of life – Aparna's interest in her new environment, her sudden surge of affection for her little sister, Sudarsana's total involvement in her teaching.   Sometimes one of the senior students would drop by and we'd discuss sports, politics and school. Quite often they'd come in groups of two or three. Because of my interest in cricket, I was asked to take charge of this. I was to make sure that our cricketers had regular net-practice and won matches against rival schools.

Then came a week of inter-school competitions in which my team did very well. Ravinder won the elocution prize, reciting Antony's oration in *Julius Caesar* beginning, *'Friends, Romans, countrymen, Lend me your ears ...'* – a popular and predictable choice. We also won the cricket matches against Jinja and Mbale. And since I was the teacher in charge of both elocution and cricket, I had to be taken notice of. The weather was lovely, the sunshine was golden and the frangipani in the garden was in bloom. I felt good.

Mr B, D, Gupta, the headmaster, sent for me. 'Not again! What is it this time?' I wondered.

First of all, he congratulated me. He had to. But what followed wasn't pleasant.

He'd noticed, he said, that my classes were noisy and I disturbed lessons in adjoining classes. Had he received any complaints? I asked. No, he hadn't, he said. He himself had noticed that the students were moving around in front of the class, being noisy. I pointed out that the teaching of drama generally, and Shakespeare particularly, needed to be acted out. The speech and the movement made the class look rowdy and noisy, but this was not for lack of discipline. Students moving around the classroom de-claiming, wasn't his idea of discipline, he said. I could have pointed out that creative work in the classroom produced the right kind of involvement and excitement, leading to valuable motivation. But I held back because he had already made up his mind, and our relationship wasn't going to improve if I had the nerve to start propounding the rationale of my method.

I did point out however, that I considered acting out selected portions of a Shakespeare play in the classroom was essential for the understanding of it.

However, I would, I said, make sure from then on, that my students were less noisy. I was beginning to feel persecuted, but I couldn't think of a civilised solution.

I was angry. I wanted to scream. Why was it, I was asking myself, that people with a limited view of things are always sure of themselves? I was doing what I was doing for a reason. Shouldn't he have asked me for the rationale of the methodology? Wasn't it important that a teacher of English literature should discourage their students from reading Shakespeare in the way the secretary of the teachers' union reads the minutes of their annual general meeting?

But in the end I didn't rebel. I went quiet. I indicated that I wasn't going to engage in a debate with him about Shakespeare-in-the-classroom. Mr B. D. Gupta needled me for a minute or two without much success. Then I got up and left.

A week or two went by. I carried on teaching the way I'd always done.

Then, one morning, I entered one of the senior classes to find that Mr David Gregg, the Deputy Director of Education, had already installed himself at the back of the class. He had a human and reassuring face, and that made a difference. Apart from that, he smiled, said good morning and waited as I began my lesson. It was literature on Monday morning and I was doing a scene from *As You Like It*. This was the lesson, during which the class was at times somewhat noisy, but the noise wasn't deliberate disruption – it was a natural reaction. We had only a few girls in the class, and some of them had opted out of acting. Therefore, from time to time, one of the boys would do the part of Rosalind, Celia, Phoebe or Audrey. And when Sadruddin, acted as Phebe and declared his love for Ganymede, there was much laughter.

That week we were doing Act V, Scene IV, a happy-making episode, the resolution of conflicts, the triumph of truth and reconciliation. The exchanges between Touchstone and Jaques dragged a little, but the students were involved in what they were doing. The vocabulary of Shakespeare, with its archaic words, did pose a problem. I dealt with it by providing the meanings of difficult words on the blackboard to which we referred when we needed to, but word meanings weren't of paramount importance. By introducing some acting and movement, we were able to establish the importance of other elements in the play. It's a long scene. We could deal with only a part of it.

Mr David Gregg sat in on a few more lessons, during one of which we dealt with a prose text, and during another, prepared material for writing on the flora of East Africa. The subject of this essay resulted from the fact that the previous week, one of my women colleagues and I had taken the class to the Botanical Gardens in Entebbe. My colleague and one or two students knew a lot more about trees than I did, so I learnt to identify certain trees and also learnt the names of other trees. I'd seen the flame-of-the-forest trees before; now I learnt that their origin was in Australia and that several different trees with vivid scarlet flowers were referred to as flame trees. Another tree that interested me was the baobab, an African tree with a barrel-like trunk of a large diameter – a most unusual-looking tree.

We also saw acacia, frangipani and bougainvillaea with its brilliant flamboyant magenta and fuchsia flowers, a beautiful climbing plant. I've forgotten quite a few other species. Mr David Gregg was drawn into the discussion. He made several contributions, especially when our discussion turned to the usefulness of trees. We decided that we'd need at least another day's discussion before writing was attempted.

I had a free period during which Mr Gregg and I sat in the staff room and discussed the lessons. Mr Gregg pointed out a few lapses in my pronunciation, mainly to do with stress. He approved that I always encouraged student participation, but thought that I'd missed a few opportunities to do so. On the whole, it was my impression that, instead of being thoroughly disappointed, he was pleasantly surprised.

I suspected that Mr David Gregg's visit was initiated by Mr B. D. Gupta. He'd come to investigate my ineptitude, but he wasn't over-critical. He took me seriously, treated me as an equal. I didn't feel anxious. I didn't toss about in bed without being able to sleep. And Sudarsana, without being anywhere around, without even discussing with me how the lessons went, assured me that Mr Gregg was impressed.

'You have a big advantage,' she said.

'What's that?' I asked.

'Your voice. Even if you talk rubbish, it sounds good,' she said.

'Thank you very much,' I said, while she mischievously grinned.

We were approaching the end of 1952. It was, I think, September. A fortnight had passed. I did wonder from time to time whether David Gregg was going to write a comprehensive critique of the lessons he had observed. If I was doing something which went against the grain of pedagogy, I thought, I ought to know before I did further damage to the students. And if he found that my teaching contained creative ideas which resulted in effective learning, that too I ought to know. Apart from that, I was afraid that too many adverse remarks from the Deputy Director of Education would encourage the headmaster to be even more oppressively critical of my teaching. Finally, it was natural human curiosity. I took my teaching seriously. So I was interested to know what an erudite and experienced educationalist like David Gregg thought of my teaching and my potential as a teacher.

Although it had seemed very long to me, it was only a few days. One Monday morning during my free fourth period, I was summoned to the office of the headmaster, who smiled cordially. 'Would you like a cup of tea?' he asked.

'Yes, please, I'd love one,' I said.

'While we're waiting for the tea, why don't you read Mr Gregg's report?' he said.

Mr Gregg had said in his report that I did make some mistakes, but I was able to keep my students interested, and that was more important for him than minor errors. What was most important, however, and really encouraging, was that he felt quite certain that my relationship with my students was one of mutual respect and co-operation. He had used words like 'creative' and 'innovative' in his report. It wasn't just exoneration. It was approval, it was praise! I felt relieved, elated, choked with emotion. The headmaster must have noticed happiness and relief on my face. He smiled. 'Have you read it all?' he asked.

'Very nearly,' I said.

'Read the last paragraph carefully,' he said. I did. In it Mr Gregg had said that I had the makings of a good teacher, but I lacked training and experience. He recommended that I should have teacher training and that training should be provided as soon as possible.

'Yes, I have now read the final paragraph of the report,' I said.

'But do you understand what it means?' he asked.

'Mr Gregg is recommending that I should have some teacher training, like B.T. in India,' I said.

'For training, you go to Britain. His recommendation means that you're going to the Institute of Education in London. I'll recommend that you do your post-graduate training at the Institute of Education. Professor Pattison was my professor. I think he's still there.' He sounded enthusiastic.

'Lil' will be glad to hear the news,' he added. Lily was his wife, whom he affectionately called Lil'. He had a daughter, who was ten or eleven. There seemed to be little tension in the relationship between husband and wife, and both parents adored their daughter, an only child.
'The education department usually sanctions just two bursaries a year between our three schools. It's always good for our school and its reputation when a teacher from our school gets the bursary,' he said.

My brain buzzed. My head was crammed with intricate and complex pictures of things to come. I was surprised, elated and apprehensive. I wasn't sure that all this was happening. Was I really going to the country of Shakespeare and Clement Attlee? They were my heroes at the time – Shakespeare for writing *King Lear* and Attlee for making India independent! Was I really going to London, a city I'd loved from afar, and where so many exciting and tragic events had happened? Could it really be true that in just about a year I'd be going to London?

'Would you like to come to dinner with us this Saturday evening?' Mr Gupta asked.

'Certainly. Thank you very much,' I said. Life's fun, I thought, for it's unpredictable.

'Bring your two daughters along,' he said.

'That's kind of you.' I thanked Mr Gupta and left.

Mr Gupta said that our conversation was to remain between us. It shouldn't be public knowledge. Not yet.

I went to the staff room and waited for the bell to go. A few minutes after our discussion of the restrictive and descriptive functions of adjective clauses, Inder Chawla said, 'You're quite thoughtful today.'

'Am I? You may be right,' I said.

When Sudarsana returned from the school, we sat down to have a cup of tea and I revealed to her the day's events. She was very pleased but congratulated me thoughtfully.

'It's not official yet. So we're supposed to keep it strictly to ourselves,' I said.

Sudarsana got up and so did I. She held me in a tight embrace and said, 'I've always known you'd make an excellent teacher. Congratulations!' Sudarsana's happiness was entirely sincere. I took my teaching seriously and my skill and dedication had been officially recognised and rewarded. She was happy and she said so. But wasn't I forgetting something? If I went away for a year, it'd mean Sudarsana being abandoned for a year to fend for herself in a new country, largely dependent for help on her uncle and aunt. Would that be fair?

'What's the matter? One moment you embrace me, then you go all pensive, pucker your eyebrows, crinkle your forehead and look at me through thoughtful eyes. Why?' she asked.

'I *am* feeling thoughtful,' I said.

'I don't want you to be pre-occupied or worried,' she said.

'We'll talk about that when I've got my thoughts together. I'm not obsessed with ambition. I'm not chasing after fame. Why should I go away to London, leaving Aparna, Aparajita and you here?' I asked.

'Let's talk about it when we're together, you and I, tonight, after the children have gone to bed,' she said. 'Would you like a cup of tea?'

Yes, please,' I said.

So we had tea. We always had tea—when we were tense and when we were relaxed. Nothing like a cup of tea!

The air smelt of rain. Our two daughters returned from their running around and playing on the hillside. They always came back before it rained or got dark on the hilltop. They were happier now, more adjusted to their new environment.

I was happy to see them, and seeing them set in motion my conflict again. I thought of loneliness, of the feeling of being abandoned. It grew darker, the drizzle turned into a downpour. Sudarsana came back from the kitchen and we had tea, several cups of it...

Chapter 9

Nondon is born. Teachers' course in London.

You've been rather quiet the last few days,' Sudarsana said.

You're right,' I said, 'I don't want to go away for a year.'

'Our lives are tied up with yours. If you do well, we do well. If you want to teach, you need a good teaching qualification. This is chance of a lifetime. How can you even think of letting it go?' she said.

'Of course I can. What I can't do is to leave you, Aparna and Aparajita. If you went back and stayed with your parents in Calcutta, I'd think it over. But you don't want to give up your job, do you?' I asked.

'I wasn't thinking of giving up my job. If you change your mind, I'll go and ask my aunt if we can stay with her for the academic year when you're in London. But, right now, I can't do that because we're not supposed to know,' she said.

We agreed that a change of circumstances can lead to a change of decision. So we ought to wait, give it time. Sudarsana insisted that my lack of ambition was neither good for the children, nor for her, nor for me. She said I was short-sighted in spurning what others crave. After some more discussion and arguing – during which we got agitated, talked at cross purposes and let our voices rise – we stopped with spent emotion.

The expected letter duly arrived but the news was available only at the staff meeting. The headmaster offered me congratulations on behalf of himself and his colleagues. After the meeting, he fixed a time next day when I should see him in his office to discuss matters relating to the Education Department's decision to send me to Britain for further experience and training in teaching, which in my case meant teaching English. My colleagues, especially those I'd got to know well, came and congratulated me. That afternoon I'd become the centre of attention.

During early evening, I told Sudarsana about the letter. She said she'd heard about it because her colleagues were talking about it. Some had congratulated <u>her</u> – as if she'd got the bursary.

'But you never said anything to me!' I said.

'I've already congratulated you, but I'll do it again – congratulations!' she said. There was no lack of warmth, but she looked thoughtful. What was she thoughtful about?

I thought she was making a point. What was her point? She'd enthused but I'd argued against going away. Had she now come round to my point of view? Was she giving it more serious thought, now that the offer was official?

'Are you still cross with me because I reacted against your suggestion that I should be more positive and go away?' I asked. 'I was, and still am, worried about the long separation.'

'No, I'm not angry but I'm thinking about things. Of course I'm happy that Mr Gregg saw your potential and recommended you and the offer is now official. Do you have to write to the Department saying that you accept the offer?' she asked.

'I don't think so... The next step is to fill in forms, which will come through in a few days,' I said.

'I'll approach Uncle and Aunt just before you do all that. They'll have thought about the problem of my living on my own in a new country – where I don't speak the language that everybody understands – with two such very young daughters. Yes, I think I want to wait a bit,' she said.

We waited. Colleagues came up to me and congratulated me. Various thoughts, fears, expectations kept crowding in my mind. I was beginning to think that it might not be such an absurd idea, but a lot would depend on the reactions of Uncle and Aunt. But Uncle must have known about it all along.

We'd finished dinner. The children were in bed, fast asleep. I was writing my notes for the lessons I was teaching the next day. Sudarsana was reading something. She got up, ruffled my hair affectionately and said, 'I'm expecting another baby.' She said it quietly but not casually, and came and stood close to me.

'Yes, Ganesha, I'm pregnant. And I'm happy, but a little afraid this time,' she said. Sudarsana called me 'Ganesha' on special occasions. Ganesha is the Sanskrit version of Ganesh, which is Bengali. Both words refer to the elephant god.

'Why afraid?' I asked.

'There were some problems after Aparajita was born. I'm not sure I should have another baby,' she said.

'We'll see Dr Ruperalia,' I said. 'He has a good reputation. He's honest, dependable and his son is one of my students.'

Dr Ruperalia examined her carefully. There wasn't anything life-threatening, he said. There was no reason why Sudarsana couldn't have a safe delivery and a healthy child.

I was relieved. I felt like embracing him, but Dr Ruperalia wasn't the kind of person one could embrace. We thanked Dr Ruperalia, paid his fees to the secretary, and left.

Sudarsana also looked relieved and happy to begin with, but then she was pensive and quiet.

'Are you worried?' I asked. 'Are you unhappy?'

'No, I'm not,' she said emphatically. 'I found Dr Ruperalia thorough in his examination. I trusted him. He rid me of my fear. I'm grateful to him. What I feel is relief.'

We'd walked to Dr Ruperalia's surgery, which was on old Kampala Hill, and we were walking back. It was getting dark: darkness fell on the hill quickly. I told Sudarsana that I'd noticed recently that she was so lost in thought from time to time that I felt I couldn't reach her.   It was as if she was having some serious conflict within herself, or trying to puzzle out some complex existential problem.   It didn't seem to me that Dr Ruperalia's reassurance had done anything to remove her anxiety. I had no doubt that she was happy but the expression of her happiness was muted.

She held my hand, leaned her head against me and remained quiet for a time as we stood on Old Kampala Hill while it was beginning to get dark.   Then she said, looking away from me, 'I'll tell you, Ganesh, why I've said so little of late. I'm not as strong as I want to be. I don't want to have your baby here while you're in England. I want to see my baby in your arms. That's my moment of fulfilment.' Then turning to me, and looking straight into my eyes, she said, 'I don't want you to go.'

I told her that I'd already put the whole business out of my head.   My excitement and happiness, mixed with undefined apprehension, had crowded out other ideas. 'I'll be here to welcome our newborn,' I assured her. I was happy that our unborn baby had made her acknowledge her anxiety.

That evening we walked up to the bungalow of our uncle and aunt. Aunt was happy to hear the news, but Uncle looked somewhat disorientated at its first impact. Then he took it all in and reacted positively.

'One of your colleagues in this or some other school will be the beneficiary of your decision.   If you want to be here when your baby comes, so be it.   We'll send another teacher for training,' Uncle said.

There were many months to wait. When a baby's on the way, happiness is always mixed with anxiety. Boy or girl was a question which rose in our minds. Some friendly colleagues took bets. Boy was the more popular choice.

It's remarkable how waiting for a really significant event makes other happenings less important.   It really didn't matter much to me that I'd missed out on the opportunity to be trained as a teacher at a university in England.   What mattered was my relationship with people around me and my teaching.   I made friends among my colleagues. Robi Banerji, our Senior English Teacher, was most pleasant to spend time with. He was friendly but not a friend – he tended to be a little too serious and formal most of the time. Then, there were my three friends – John, Ted and Naresh. For one thing, they were my age group, and we had quite a few common interests. From time to time, we'd meet at Naresh's house, which was three or four houses further up the hill from ours, and talk politics, literature and art; discuss people and events, and probably even indulge in some gossip. John Carneiro, Ted Fernandes and I would sometimes write a short story or a poem in English and discuss their content and style. All three of us taught English. Naresh Sengupta would occasionally talk about painting in general and about his paintings in particular. He would, almost always, make us a cup of tea. Alcohol wasn't taboo but we rarely had anything that inebriated. We did drink at parties, but such parties were very occasional and our drinking was very much within limits.

One morning at school I was teaching *Macbeth* in one of the senior classes when Napoleon D'Souza – or Nap – gently knocked on the transparent glass door. I took my eyes off the page and looked in the direction of the knocking. Nap's genial face was behind the glass door. He was looking at me with some urgency. When I opened the door, he informed me that he was selling lottery tickets for the Irish Sweep. He'd sold all but one. It was most important that I should buy the ticket because it was the last day for posting. That meant that if he didn't post all the counterfoils that very day, the tickets wouldn't count. Would I be ready to buy that last ticket? I said yes and he went away. Soon after that he came back and knocked on the door a second time. He'd forgotten to ask me what *nom de plume* I'd like. I said, '*Macbeth*.' He thanked me, apologised, and went away.

A few weeks passed; another knock on the door, another face behind the glass – this time that of the Office Clerk, who was part of the general set-up of the headmaster's office and attended to various chores like delivering and collecting the post, carrying round the book in which notices were posted for us to sign, and delivering messages. I've forgotten his name. He addressed me as Mr Bagchi, except that when he said my name, it sounded different. I soon discovered that he wasn't actually saying Bagchi but *Bagichi*. The reason was that in his language consonant clusters didn't exist. A consonant was followed by a vowel. He also addressed Mr Gupta as *Mr Gupita*.

The Office Clerk came through the door and handed me a telegram. Telegrams had unhappy associations for me, so I was apprehensive. I forgot the exact words of it but I remember the content. It said that my Irish sweep lottery ticket had come up in the draw. The name of my horse was 'Glen Fire'. If it came first, second or third,

I'd receive some astronomical sum of money. During break, I showed Nap the telegram.

'Don't be too excited,' he said. 'One of these fantastic sums of money will be yours only if your horse wins one of the first three places. But even if it doesn't you'll get a certain sum of money, however small. And I'll get a small share of it. Not bad for a first attempt,' Nap said.

After some more time, another letter informed me that I'd won not hundreds of thousands but six hundred and something pounds, which, for Sudarsana and me was a large enough amount of money. I'd never had that kind of money, nor had Sudarsana. We decided that the unborn baby had brought us good luck.

Soon after this, one weekend, Sudarsana felt that the baby was on the way and Uncle drove her to the hospital. I went along, saw her installed in her bed in the maternity ward, held her hand, said reassuring words and came away. On Sunday morning I went over to see uncle and aunt – we did most Sundays, giving aunt the opportunity to spoil her granddaughters – an occupation she thoroughly enjoyed. The telephone rang.

Aunt was told that Sudarsana had given birth to a baby boy. The impact of the news was so powerful that I behaved like someone possessed and banged on the first thing I saw – a door – with my clenched right fist so many times in quick succession and so hard that the wrist swelled up soon after, and Aunt wondered whether it was a brief spell of insanity that had taken hold of me. It was a sudden flush of joy too strong to control. She wasn't cross but amused and indulgent. She decided we ought to go to the hospital at about tea-time.

Sudarsana was awake, and the baby asleep. She looked content, rested and at peace with the world. She greeted us with a smile and looked at the baby, whom we were all looking at. The baby blinked and slept on. Sudarsana told us that he weighed seven pounds and a bit and liked nothing better than sleeping. 'He wakes up fairly punctually to appease his hunger, which means it won't be long before he blinks and opens his eyes,' she said.

It all happened the way Sudarsana had said. Then I picked up my son and held him close to my body, feeling like the only father with the only baby in the world – a feeling I'd had before.

Uncle went and saw Dr Gopal, the gynaecologist, and came back and reported that it was a birth without any complications. On a bright and beautiful morning, my son was born. It was a very special day for me, the kind of day when one notices what's bright and beautiful in life and forgets the misery and squalor.

We returned to Old Kampala. We talked about mother and baby who, it seemed, were doing well. Uncle said he'd sent a telegram to Sudarsana's parents, but I had no one to send telegrams to because I'd lost contact with my father, brothers and sisters. In any case, they wouldn't be interested because they'd felt alienated and abandoned when I'd left India. We sat round the table drinking tea and talking about the great occasion. Aunt asked me to stay to dinner but I said I'd decided to see Naresh and tell him the good news. They knew he was a good friend, so they appreciated my eagerness to see him. Uncle offered me a brandy and ginger ale. We had a celebratory drink.

Naresh was glad to see me. John and Ted were also there. We tried to meet up most weekends. I valued my relationship with these three friends in a foreign country and an unfamiliar environment. They were happy to know that my baby son had arrived safely and wanted to celebrate his arrival. John had an old Ford and he and Ted drove away, and returned with a bottle of red wine and Naresh rustled up some *kebab*. We sat and drank and ate and talked under the open sky and discussed the Mau Mau movement, racism, colonial administration and the unholy alliance between local rulers and their colonial masters; sex, death and the super ego. I thoroughly enjoyed the evening – the conversation, the companionship, the *kebab* and the red wine.

We used to discuss the Mau Mau movement quite often, and we weren't the only ones. It had started before I'd come to Africa. A year after my arrival, an estimated 20,000 Kikuyu tribesmen were incarcerated in makeshift concentration camps behind huge barbed-wire fences, where torture was routine and murders could be committed with impunity, in an African Gulag, administered by British colonisers. At least 11,000 Kikuyu rebels were killed and 2,000 loyalists, according to one estimate. A hundred or so Europeans died. More death and destruction have happened in other uprisings, mutinies and revolutions, but what made the Mau Mau so infamous was the brutal, savage and relentless cruelty of the Kikuyu rebels and the even more brutal and ruthless suppression of the rebels. The excesses of this tribal violence and cruelty were reported at great length and frightening detail, but not the cruelty and barbarism of the British reprisals. It was all about the survival of the pitiless. The reports we frequently received of atrocities committed by both the Kikuyu tribesmen as well as their colonial masters were outrageously inhuman.

But we had to pretend that they were sick fantasies of diseased minds. To preserve our sanity, we avoided the subject. Fortunately for us, although we'd come to East Africa at a time when the Mau Mau movement was reaching its peak, life in Uganda wasn't greatly affected by what was going on in Kenya – though it regularly featured in our discussions.

It was mainly on account of our fairly regularly meetings at Naresh's house that I didn't feel isolated from the rest of the world. The Mau Mau Uprising was the recurrent topic for East Africans at the time. But we also discussed Stalin's death and Khrushchev's emergence as his possible successor; the conquest of Everest by Edmund Hillary and Tensing in May 1953; the coronation of Elizabeth II; the end of the Korean War, and the signing of the Armistice; England's winning back the Ashes after a gap of 20 years and so on. I lived in Kampala, the capital of Uganda, not one of the most exciting capital cities of the world, but the four of us managed to keep in touch with what was going on out there – in the big mad world. Ted was perhaps the most well-informed of us, because he listened regularly to BBC news. The *Uganda Herald* was my source of information. Their coverage of international news couldn't compare with that of the BBC, but their reporting of East African news was, not unexpectedly, more comprehensive than that of the BBC. I found the *Uganda Herald* a quite impressive newspaper. In spite of their limited resources, they managed to provide authentic information about what was happening in and around Uganda as well as in the world at large. What I learned about the ongoing political development in East Africa in general and in Uganda in particular, I owed mainly to the *Uganda Herald.*

A significant difference between Kenya and Uganda was that Kenya was a colony and Uganda was a protectorate. Whereas Kenya was dominated by white farmers, Buganda's long line of *Kabakas* or Kings constituted a tradition of governance which wasn't easy to change without violent upheavals. From the very beginning of the twentieth century, it was quite clear that Britain and Uganda had chosen the principle of mutual co-existence, based on treaties with the different kingdoms, the most powerful and privileged of which was Buganda. Buganda's jewel-in-the-crown status was resented by other kingdoms, especially Bunyoro, but there was no redress.

There was another reason for the privileged status of Buganda. The wealth generated by cotton had made it economically independent so that it could manage without any colonial subsidies, and its economic stability had also contributed to the establishment of educational institutions in Buganda, resulting in greater availability of educated man-power. By coming to Uganda instead of Kenya, we'd escaped the tension and trauma of the excesses of the Mau Mau Rebellion and its brutal suppression, and by coming to Uganda in 1951, we'd avoided being caught up in the riots of 1949, during which the Buganda burned and pillaged to protest against the government policy of price controls on cotton export and Asian monopoly taking over. The riots had taken place before we'd even thought of coming to Uganda. I. K. Musazi's Uganda National Congress was founded after our arrival in 1951.

When we first came to Kampala, Sir John Hall was the governor, but he was replaced by Sir Andrew Cohen in 1952. Sir Andrew's objectives were radically different from Sir John Hall's because the British government's approach and attitude to colonies had undergone a sea-change. Sir Andrew's remit, quite clearly, was to pave the way to transition to independence, and the devolution of power was to start from the time of his arrival. The four of us who used to assemble at weekends – Naresh, Ted, John and I – decided that under this man's administration, far-reaching changes – changes for the better – were likely to happen. For a newcomer to this country, it was a good feeling.

Sudarsana came home with the newborn baby – a healthy, happy, beautiful baby. His impact on all of us was immediate and positive. His two sisters gazed at him with wonder and affection. His mother had already deeply bonded with him, judging by the look of adoration on her face. She had had two babies already, but each time, she said, it was altogether a new experience. When I first heard the news of his birth, I banged so hard on a door that happened to be in front of me that I damaged my wrist. That excitement was replaced by quiet satisfaction and pride.

We did nothing much to celebrate the birth of our little boy. We had a quiet little family party at Uncle and Aunt's, where we also named our baby. Sudarsana wanted to call him 'Gautam', the name of the Buddha. I wanted to call him 'Nondon'. *Nondon* has to do with aesthetic pleasure – but it also means a son. In the end, we compromised. His real or official name was to be *Gautam* but his everyday name was going to be *Nondon.* I hadn't felt so good for a long time. My own separate establishment and my economic independence added immensely to my happiness.

Sudarsana's uncle, her father's elder brother, came to Uganda to spend a few weeks with his sister. So of course, Uncle and Aunt had parties, took him around everywhere and showed him off. He was a good-looking man with gentle, civilised manners, who spoke with precision and simple elegance. He was connected with the film world. He was the General Manager of the New Theatres' Film Studios. On a few occasions, while I was living with my father-in-law, I'd seen famous film stars visiting him at the Film Services, where the laboratory work was done for films, and above which this uncle had his flat.

He had a plot of land near where his business was and he was building some flats there. I could have one of these flats, he said, if I let him have the £600 which I'd won on a lottery. I thought it was a good idea and gave him the money. The money was sitting in the bank and we had no plans for spending or investing it, so we were glad that we'd been offered the opportunity for an investment which was safe, and was in my favourite city. Our flat, what's more, was going to be next to my father-in-law's.

Sudarsana's uncle, Mr P N Roy, came and went. Visits from friends and relations from India were memorable landmarks in the lives of us immigrants, occasions for celebration. Aunt, who was excited and happy during her brother's visit, now looked depressed, although she knew all along that he was only coming for a few weeks.

The family was central to our lives those days, and I found myself at variance with some of my communist friends who condemned it as a bourgeois institution. What was bourgeois about the way I felt about Sudarsana, Aparna, Aparajita and Nondon? At the time, Nondon was causing a great deal of distraction, especially when I needed to concentrate on my teaching and write tidy lesson notes, because the inspectors were on the way.

No teacher has ever liked inspectors and lesson observation. My colleagues and I certainly didn't look forward to this annual ritual. At the same time, we realised these served some quite important purposes: the selection of teachers for training abroad, interacting with teachers, especially the less experienced ones, participating in a general discussion about motivating students. A recurrent theme of Mr Gregg's advice to us was self-help – encouraging students to find information for themselves from an early age was a much more effective way of teaching, he repeatedly said to us, a much more effective way of achieving our goal, than telling them all they wanted to know.

Each boy and girl in a secondary school must know, he insisted, how to use a dictionary, an encyclopaedia, a thesaurus and other reference books. They had also to be encouraged to make their own experiments and exploring and observing to make the whole experience of learning more exciting. A teacher, he would say, must set out from the very beginning to make himself redundant. I don't think I fully understood the meaning of what he said in the beginning; I understood and appreciated the significance of his remarks as I continued my teaching.

Mr David Gregg added to the problems of our lives by recommending Sudarsana also for a teacher-training course in Britain. Nondon wouldn't be much more than a year old by the time we were due to leave the year after. Why didn't inspecting officials take people's personal circumstances into consideration before making their recommendations? Yet we were both thrilled. Sudarsana said that we'd think about the practical problems later; right now we should both walk on air because she had been selected and my offer renewed. We celebrated by putting flowers in vases, eating a special dinner and spending time with our children, who didn't understand why we were so excited. They certainly wouldn't rejoice if we explained. Aparna would understand at once that our going to Britain for further studies would mean separation from them. Aparajita and Nondon wouldn't understand the implications.

Sudarsana and I discussed the various problems of our accepting the offer. The situation made one decision unavoidable. I had to go, because if I turned down the offer a second time, the Director of Education probably wouldn't keep it open for a third time. Any further vacillation or postponement would certainly mean losing an opportunity which was the dream of many of my colleagues. So both Sudarsana and I decided that I had to go. But how did we know that the Department would make the offer to Sudarsana again?

There was no dearth in the schools of Uganda of young, ambitious and gifted teachers.   So turning down the offer would destroy Sudarsana's prospects for progress and promotions in the years to come without any doubt.

But how could we both abandon our three children – the eldest would be just over six and the youngest just over one – and go thousands of miles away to acquire educational qualifications to improve our career?   To what end?   The question certainly didn't have an easy answer.   That weekend, we did what we both knew we'd do sooner or later – saw Uncle and Aunt, especially Uncle, to discuss the impact of our selection for teacher's training on our immediate future.   The problem was our separation from three very young children.   Both Uncle and Aunt began by congratulating us.   Then Uncle took us to his study to discuss the situation as he saw it.   First of all, he made it clear that both Sudarsana and I had won the approbation of the inspecting team purely through merit – our proficiency in English, especially spoken English, and our teaching.   It was most likely that some of our fellow teachers should say that we were selected because he'd influenced the inspectors' decision.   These are people of integrity, so we could be quite certain that they wouldn't be influenced by anything other than the merit of the teachers, their personality and their ability to teach.   As for the practical ramifications of the situation, he had thought of a plan of action.

Aunt joined us and we carried on the discussion.   It appeared that Uncle and Aunt had already discussed the situation and worked out a tentative solution.   My father-in-law was retiring that year.   While Aunt and Uncle were last in Calcutta, they had discussed with my father-in-law the possibility of him and my mother-in-law visiting Kampala for a few weeks after his retirement.   So Uncle was going to write to Sudarsana's parents that they should come next year for a few weeks before we left for England – and take the children back with them to Calcutta.   We would then go to Calcutta from London on completion of our course of studies and return to Kampala with the children.   Both Sudarsana and I agreed that this was a sensible arrangement.   Sudarsana's parents were the two most caring, affectionate and dependable people we knew.   They would be the best people to leave the children with.   Aparna would love the reunion with her grandparents, and Aparajita and Nondon would soon like nothing better than being with their *Dadubhai* and *Didibhai.*   Nobody was immune to the magic of their Didibhai's unadulterated goodness and a capacity to love.   Nondon hadn't been under the spell, and Aparajita was too little to realize the uniqueness of her grandmother's character.   Therefore, my worry wasn't that the children would have some kind of trauma at the absence of their parents, but that *we* would miss them and regret the decision to leave them for so long to go so far away...

Sudarsana's parents arrived. It was decided that we'd attend the Post Graduate Certificate in Education course at the Institute of Education, University of London. Both Sudarsana and I were students of English literature; so London, apart from being one of the most important cities of the world, was a place of some special significance to us. Shakespeare, Milton, Dr Johnson, Shaw, Wilde and a whole host of other poets and dramatists had lived and died here, Karl Marx had made London his home during the latter part of his life. Then there was Virginia Woolf and the Bloomsbury Group. We'd visit Shakespeare's birthplace, Stratford-upon-Avon, and watch a play or two at the Royal Shakespeare Theatre... We were both excited and couldn't stop discussing famous Londoners, famous English people and places. The list was very long and growing longer by the hour. When I got very excited, Sudarsana would take matters in hand.

'And what about the Post Graduate Certificate of Education?' she asked.

'What about it?' I said.

'When are we going to work? When are we going to attend lectures, do our assignments, prepare our lesson notes and teach?' she asked.

'We'll also do those things,' I said.

'No,' she said. 'We'll attend lectures, do our assignments, make a success of our teaching practice, and *also* think of all the distractions. We'll go to Stratford-upon-Avon, watch ballet, go to the theatre, go dancing, go to parties, but not without first attending to our course of studies,' she said, assuming the voice of a stern headmistress.

'Yes, madam,' I said.

'Good boy!' she applauded.

Uncle and Aunt took charge of Sudarsana's parents and ensured that they got some idea of Kampala and the surrounding areas. But Sudarsana's parents were more interested in spending time with their grandchildren. So they spent as much time as possible with them, especially Nondon, to make sure as far as possible that separation from their parents for almost a year didn't cause them any misery or trauma. I could see that my two daughters sought the company of their grandmother just as eagerly as she sought theirs, and Nondon seemed just as happy with his grandmother as with his mother. Every weekend, Uncle and Aunt took Sudarsana's parents out to meet their friends and to go sightseeing. They visited Ripon Falls, Lake Victoria, the Entebbe Botanical Gardens, the Kabaka's Palace and a few other places which Aunt and Uncle had decided they ought to see. The people they met – most of them friends and acquaintances of Uncle and Aunt – were impressed with these two gentle, kind and sensitive people, who were genuinely interested in other people and interesting places.

So Sudarsana's parents came, and after spending enough time with Nondon to ensure that he trusted them and felt secure with them, collected the children and then left for India. The simplicity and affection with which they volunteered to come, travelled from one continent to another and spent a large sum of money travelling to make it possible for us to take advantage of the opportunity to acquire professional qualifications from the University of London made a deep and lasting impression on me. Sudarsana, who was used to their extraordinary generosity, probably didn't find anything unusual about their behaviour.

Now we turned our attention to preparing to leave for England. It was a time of exciting events. In 1953, Edmund Hillary and Tenzing Norgay had climbed Everest under the leadership of John Hunt. Elizabeth II had been crowned queen; a British and an American scientist had both identified DNA. In 1954, the connection between smoking and lung cancer had been scientifically established, and Roger Bannister had run a four-minute mile. Sudarsana and I started taking much more interest in British and international events. We'd already moved, figuratively speaking, out of the backwater of Kampala into the thick of things, into the wider world of money, excitement and power, where the destinies of nations were fashioned mainly by men in pinstripe trousers and bowler hats. Whether there was any definite evidence for the kind of ideas we had I did not know. What we did know was that both Sudarsana and I were getting rather excited as the day of our departure for the great metropolis approached.

There are, quite often, problems and difficulties one doesn't take into account or forgets to consider. While we were getting organised to go, I discovered that our passports needed to be renewed. One of the Assistant Directors of Education was supposed to take care of the administrative problems of those going to Britain for further education. He was friendly – he said call me Norman – and efficient and helpful. He said that Indian passports had to be sent to Nairobi for renewal, but it would be hazardous to do so because it was uncertain whether they would let me have my new passport before my day of departure. And if they didn't, there would be serious complications.

'What's the solution? What do you suggest?' I asked.

'Get British passports,' he said.

'But Sudarsana and I are both Indian citizens,' I said.

'Become British citizens,' he said.

'But that's bound to take longer,' I said.

'Not at all,' said Norman casually. 'First of all, you'll have to swear an affidavit that you'll be loyal to the Queen and the country. Then you'll have to apply for citizenship, which should come through in a week or so. Then you'll apply for your passport.'

All this seemed incredibly simple. How was it possible to get British citizenship and British passports in a matter of weeks? But it happened exactly as Norman had said. We did as we were told and both Sudarsana and I got our brand new British passports. Whenever we've told people about this later in life, they've found it quite incredible that British citizenship was given away so easily. About 20 years later this generosity caused the British government serious problems when more than 30,000 Indians and Pakistanis thrown out by Idi Amin had to be accommodated in Britain. Most of them held British passports.

Now there was a lot of excitement and a little apprehension. Neither Sudarsana nor I had seen the inside of an aeroplane before. This was going to be our first experience of flying. We were flying BOAC via Cairo. Maggie – I think that was her name – one of the secretaries at Makerere University was then in London on home leave and she was going to meet us at Heathrow, take us to the accommodation temporarily allocated to us by the Institute of Education, and later help us to find a flat in or around London for the academic year at the Institute. I had met some very friendly and erudite people on Makerere University campus – Professor Alan Warner, Alan Greenslade and Alan Wiltshire – all of them from the English department. It was Alan Wiltshire who'd introduced me to Maggie.

I found flying a very pleasant and exciting experience. The service was excellent, the food good and the people friendly. Sudarsana and I talked animatedly to each other as well as to others.   Then I must have fallen silent, because Sudarsana commented on it.

'You've gone very quiet,' she said.

'It must be the aftermath of all the excitement,' I replied.   It was a false explanation. I missed the children.   I didn't know how this long separation was going to affect us. Various other thoughts also crowded into my head.   Why guilt, the pain of separation, uncertainty, hopes and fears should suddenly flood my consciousness when we were flying through the clouds was beyond me to explain.   At the same time, the entire experience of flying was unique and filled me with a sense of adventure – the take-off, the landing, the moving above the clouds and the mere consciousness that we'd left solid earth hours ago and were flying above it and the clouds, beneath us only the clear blue sky, thrilled me.   Sudarsana shared my feelings and we both wondered whether touching down in London wouldn't be an anti-climax.

But then, without ever visiting London before, we'd both decided that it would be one of the most exciting experiences of our lives, so the idea of London being anything but rewarding and exhilarating, we abandoned at once.   Even sitting on the plane among strangers, doing humdrum things like reading, chatting, eating and sleeping, were not at all dull because we were flying in the direction of London.   So when the passengers around us spoke to us about London in a matter-of-fact manner and ate, slept, and generally looked bored, we didn't quite understand how that could happen.   We decided that most of the other passengers flew so often that there wasn't anything magical or exciting about it any more.   It was almost like a daily bus ride from home to work.   For us both flying and Europe were unknown territory.   Europe fascinated me with its abundant energy to plunder and kill – but also create.

The next stop was LHR – London, Heathrow.   Maggie was going to be waiting for us.   We had got to know her through Alan Wiltshire, who was a lecturer in French at Makerere University College, but who also had a genuine interest in English literature.   The closer we flew to Heathrow, the more excited we were.   We found it increasingly strange that people around us showed no sign of excitement.   The young lady with red hair in front of us was still engrossed in her fashion magazine, and the man sitting next to her was still engrossed in crosswords.   The expression on their faces seemed to say, 'We've seen it all already, seen it all'. Most of them probably had, whereas Sudarsana and I were flying for the first time. We'd washed and tidied ourselves up and were looking out of the window as the plane slowly began to descend. Buildings came into view down below, and streets with toy men and women appeared between rows of buildings. Soon, we were able to make out the movement of cars and saw the air-terminal at Heathrow.

Then the plane touched down. We had landed safely. We unfastened our seat belts, got up, collected our hand luggage and stood in the aisle with other passengers, moving slowly towards the exit. The customs and immigration formalities were soon over, and as we came out of the demarcation zone, we found the lean figure of Maggie, who welcomed us with a friendly smile and enquired about the flight and some of our mutual friends – Alan Warner, Alan Wiltshire, Paul and Valerie Vowels, Margery and Murray Carlin. The Institute of Education had provided us with temporary accommodation at one of their hostels and we were expected to find our own place within a certain period of time. Maggie found the warden, introduced herself and us to her and told her that she would help us to find a suitable place – a room or a flat – not too far from the Institute. The warden, a pleasant, efficient-looking woman, in her mid-forties, polite but matter-of-fact, offered us tea and biscuits. We discussed the terms and conditions of residence and went back to our room – Maggie, Sudarsana and I.

It wasn't a large room, but clean, tidy and well-appointed. The most remarkable feature was the economical and imaginative use of space. Long before we came to London, however, we'd decided that we'd have a place of our own because our situation was different. I was 30 and Sudarsana 29. We were parents of three children and we'd acquired teaching experience for more than three years. We belonged to the category of mature students. There was another respect in which we were different from most of our fellow students: we were Indian.

'Would that make any difference?' We asked Maggie.

'Unfortunately, yes,' said Maggie, unexpectedly. 'Many Londoners don't want tenants who have a dark skin – even if they're Nobel Laureates. And I don't want either of you to be hurt or surprised. You're more likely to face problems than I am. So I've decided that I'll find you a flat.'

Indeed our understanding of people's attitude in this part of the world to colour was most inadequate. Later on we found that racially discriminatory language wasn't illegal and did appear in certain advertisements for flats and houses. We were relieved that Maggie had decided to bear the brunt of the attendant hazards of flat hunting for us. She was a most unusual person. She hadn't married, lived alone on Makerere University campus, and helped everybody – the deserving and the undeserving. She was a highly efficient and caring person who lived an uncomplicated life. She had the reputation of being an excellent secretary and a loyal friend.

It didn't take Maggie long to find a place which she thought would be right for us. Both the landlord and his wife were into teaching. She was a teacher of geography at a state secondary school, and he a lecturer at the London School of Economics. The landlord was Asher Tropp and his wife's name was Lynn. Sudarsana and I went over to Finchley Central with Maggie one Saturday morning and found the house, the last house on the left in a cul-de-sac, quite close to railway lines. It turned out not to be a flat but a single room with a kitchen alongside – and a bathroom – on the first floor of a double-storey house. The accommodation was much smaller than we expected, but the rent also was a lot less than we were ready to pay. After a quick word with Sudarsana, I said to Asher Tropp that we would hire the place if he'd have us. Maggie was talking to Lynn Tropp while I was settling with Asher Tropp the terms and conditions of the tenancy. Dr Tropp was businesslike and clear-thinking. We had no disagreements, so I said we could move in the next day. Maggie had said she'd drive us down. Her leave was coming to an end, so the sooner we were settled in our room in Finchley Central the better for us all. At the end of our transaction, Dr Tropp suggested that we should call him 'Asher' and Mrs Tropp 'Lynn' and we reciprocated by requesting that they should also call us by our first names. They had a little difficulty saying our names – Sudarsana and Ganesh – but practice soon made them more adept. We were offered tea, which was most welcome. Bengalis share with the English their love of tea and, believe it or not, although it was many years ago, I distinctly remember that it was an excellent cup of tea.

Maggie went to London University and knew London well, so conversation between her and Asher was spontaneous and friendly as they reminisced about their student days. We also learned a little about our Institute of Education, which had celebrated its fiftieth anniversary two years ago. We gathered that Sidney Webb was primarily responsible for the founding of not only the Institute of Education, originally called London Day College, but also the London School of Economics, where Asher was a lecturer. The Institute, Asher told us, had moved into the North Wing of Senate House in Bloomsbury before World War Two.

The mention of Bloomsbury led to some talk about Virginia Woolf, John Maynard Keynes and E.M. Forster, and the conversation had the potential of turning serious when we discovered that it was lunchtime and immediately decided not to overstay our welcome. On the way back, not far from Finchley Central tube station, we found a Cypriot restaurant. We stopped, had a simple lunch there and then started off in the direction of Bloomsbury.

Now, Sudarsana and I had a room of our own and a kitchen and a shared bathroom – for the next nine months. The anxiety over shelter was now out of the way, thanks to Maggie's positive intervention. Looking back at the past few days, I realised what an extraordinary person Maggie was. We'd got to know each other through a mutual friend in Kampala, and hadn't really spent more than, say 10 hours altogether at parties and meetings, and here she was, giving up a large chunk of her holiday to organise for us a place to stay and trying to protect us from any nasty shocks or surprises.

Do we not, I wondered sometimes, tend to remember selectively the few unpleasant instances of discrimination, racist innuendoes and harassment – and forget an infinitely greater number of acts of kindness, consideration and generosity? Apart from Maggie's consistent and friendly helpfulness, there was another instance of spontaneous generosity which I must not forget to put on record. Two days after we had moved into our temporary accommodation at the hostel, Sudarsana and I had gone for a walk and window-shopping past Goodge Street tube station. We'd gone quite some distance away and got altogether lost. We hadn't just got lost but we'd begun to <u>look</u> lost and frightened, when a well-dressed, middle-aged man, observing the look of distress and desperation on our faces, had walked us all the way back to our hostel.

Something that Asher had said in passing worried me, and I brought it up as Maggie was driving us from Finchley Central to our temporary abode, near the Institute of Education. Asher couldn't stand the strong smell of Indian spices which hung in the air as curries were being cooked. What were we going to do about it?

'He can't have it both ways, can he?' was Maggie's response. 'You can't be expected to live on roast beef and Yorkshire puddings for the next nine months! Keep the kitchen door shut and briefly open a window. I shouldn't worry too much about his remark.'

There was yet another problem. Sudarsana and I had no other experience except of a tropical climate and had, as a result, got used to having a shower or a bucket-bath every day. If the weather was too oppressive, we'd have two showers or bucket-baths, one in the morning and one in the evening. Even slum-dwellers wouldn't miss out on a bucket-bath: a thorough wash with soap and water. A bucket-bath was convenient. All we needed was a large bucket of water, cold water most months of the year, and a mug. We immersed the mug in the water and poured the water over our head. When the body was fully wet, we soaped ourselves as thoroughly as we could. How thorough the soaping was depended on how public the place was where we were having our bath. When I was between 16 to 18 years old, I bathed and swum in a canal which was connected with the River Hooghly. It was a tidal canal and I remember having seen dead animals, usually the smaller variety – cats, dogs and sheep – floating by. A few thousand people in Calcutta used the canal every day for washing themselves clean and having a bath. Rich or poor, young or old, Hindu, Christian or Muslim, having a 'bath' was obligatory. And it had to be every day unless one was ill or travelling, although the bath didn't always make one cleaner.

So when Asher said that hot water for baths would be provided every weekend – either Saturday or Sunday – I was distressed at the idea of not having a bath seven days a week, and Sudarsana was horrified. When I told Maggie about our problem, she explained that this kind of arrangement had to do with expense – the expense of heating up bath water every day for several people is unaffordable for most families. In the end, we agreed to pay for the extra days and Asher said we could have five baths each week. In winter we found skipping a couple of baths a week a sensible thing to do and not at all painful!

Maggie left in a few days. What she'd done for us had given us confidence. We also understood certain aspects of life in London a little better.

We used to take the tube from Finchley Central and get off at Goodge Street and walk to the Institute. There was - at the very beginning of the course - a reception at which the Director made a speech, welcoming us and then we had tea and coffee and introduced ourselves to each other and tried to get the feel of the place. I forget who'd made the speech, which was interesting, well-informed and funny. He started off by suggesting that we should make the most of the bright and beautiful weather of his country – the clear sky, the warm sunshine, the trees laden with flowers and fruit all round the year. Then he abruptly stopped and apologised: he made believe that he'd, by mistake, picked up the notes of a lecture he'd delivered in some exotic tropical country. Then he mentioned the fact that the weather could be inhospitable. He then proceeded to give us a brief outline of the course, wished all of us the best of luck in the country and with the course and stopped. There was spontaneous applause. Sudarsana and I were both impressed with the speaker and the speech. If a fair proportion of the lectures during our course of studies were anything like this one, we wouldn't have anything to complain about. It's a pity that I can't remember the name of the speaker.

During the lecture, I was somewhat distracted by the different colours of hair of my fellow students - red, gold, auburn, ginger and various shades of brown. In our classrooms and lecture theatres in India and Africa, all heads were the same kind of colour – dark brown bordering on black. All those different coloured heads still stand out in my memory... But what made a much bigger impression on me: was the naturally relaxed and friendly relationship between the students. If anybody self-consciously tried to be loving and giving towards us, we wouldn't have liked that. Similarly, if anybody was deliberately aloof, patronising or superior, we wouldn't have liked it either. Neither Sudarsana nor I had any problems. Michael – a tall, blonde, handsome young Englishman – invited us over for dinner right at the beginning of term, gave us an excellent English meal and a friendly, relaxed evening. Michael lived with his parents and his sister. The parents were not aloof but fairly formal. They were pleasant and asked us predictable questions about sights we'd seen, and what we'd thought and felt during the two months we'd now spent in England. It was Michael's sister, Debbie, who was centre-stage most of the evening with her witty comments on university life, her interest in politics – she was an ardent socialist – and her refreshingly young and iconoclastic humour. She gave me quite a bit of attention, I thought, in an off-hand, whimsical way, which pleased me no end. It was an evening both Sudarsana and I enjoyed very much. And the fact that it was our first evening out in England with an English family, an evening that was friendly, relaxed and interesting, made it a memorable occasion. Sudarsana and I talked about the evening over a cup of tea after we were back at the flat in Finchley Central and decided that the English, when they're good, were very, very good; how horrid they could be when they were bad, we hadn't yet found out. We hoped we never would.

The PGCE course was going on well both at academic and human levels. Professor Bruce Pattison, Professor Elliott, Professor Vernon, Geoffrey Barnard – were all highly erudite people. Their lectures held our attention; their tutorials solved individual problems in a friendly way. Geoffrey was younger than the others, not a lot older than Sudarsana and me. He was most informal and friendly. He took his tutorial group out on one occasion to Shah's Restaurant, which was not far from the Institute. We all enjoyed the evening. The food and the company made the occasion extremely pleasurable. Some of us were amused and impressed by the performance of someone with a handlebar moustache, who looked every inch an ex-colonial colonel, sitting at a table near ours. He asked the waiter for some green chillis in his loud, rasping voice. He looked rather lost and lonely without his Indian empire.

For Sudarsana and me, the significant player of the evening was our host, Geoffrey, with his ideas and anecdotes and his relaxed relationship with us, his students, who came from various countries and continents. An evening like this with one of our lecturers was inconceivable in our days in India, because they were expected to keep their distance. Mr B D Gupta in Kampala had reminded me after I'd been teaching in the secondary school for a few months that it was against the tradition of the school for teachers to be too friendly with the impressionable and vulnerable teenagers who were our students. Our teachers in school certainly didn't fraternize with us, nor did our lecturers at St Xavier's College or Calcutta University. I thought it was good practice to discourage close friendship between teenagers and their teachers but I never understood why our lecturers and professors at our colleges and at the university were so remote, not only at the beginning but throughout our courses.

Not everybody, however, at the Institute of Education was as friendly as Geoffrey Barnard. We hardly ever saw the professors except at lectures. There was something unique about Professor Pattison's lectures: he rarely used the entire time allocated for his lectures, but set apart time for questions, and if we didn't hurry up, he wouldn't wait patiently and attempt to cajole a few questions out of us. He'd just leave. All our lecturers were good, and some brilliant. Neither Sudarsana nor I missed lectures. We enjoyed what we did, completed our assignments on time but I didn't take this course of studies as seriously as I should have done. I didn't think I'd ever again visit London: therefore we were doing a few interesting things which we could only do in London. Sudarsana started attending a course in dancing sponsored by the Indian High Commission, of which the celebrated Indian dancer Ram Gopal was the teacher.

Before Sudarsana had started going to the Indian High Commission building for her lessons in Indian classical dancing, we joined classes for a course in ballroom dancing. Now, one of these classes every week clashed with Sudarsana's dancing lessons in London, so I was without a partner. One of the girls who served at the bakers was very friendly and I'd occasionally communicated with her about the state of the weather. Would she agree to help me out, I wondered...

Then one late afternoon when I was returning home from the Insitute of Education and Sudarsana had gone to the Indian High Commission, I found the bakery not at all busy and I walked in. Would Susie mind being my partner for one day a week at the dancing class for the next three weeks if I asked her? I walked in, explained the situation and nervously asked her if she'd like to come along to help me out. Her response was, 'Not half!' I was very embarrassed and apologised for my brashness because I thought Susie's response was negative – she'd turned me down. I hurried home and debated with myself whether I should tell Sudarsana about it when she came back home. I didn't. But at the Institute I mentioned it to Jack, whom I'd got to know well.

'That wasn't a turn-down, you idiot,' he said, 'It was a resounding yes.'

I used to pass the bakery regularly on my way back from the Institute and I waited for an occasion when she was on her own again. I went in and explained that I'd caused some confusion through ignorance and hoped she'd forgiven me. We had a good laugh and I continued to meet her in the shop and buy bread and pastry fairly regularly. Nothing was ever said again about the muddle. Sudarsana and I attended a few classes at the school of dancing after she'd finished her course, but my skill at the end of it was far from impressive. Though as a result of a few lessons at the school and a lot of help from Sudarsana, who danced well, I was able to keep my end up on the few occasions on when it was necessary for me to dance – in London.

Something I remember with a certain mixture of guilt and pleasure is that on a few of these occasions, there were mutual expressions of affection between my partners and me – experiences totally new to me, experiences I still remember from time to time. Sudarsana was a better and more popular dancer, who genuinely enjoyed dancing. Did she also have similar experiences? We never compared notes, and none of these incidents were really significant as relationships – but exciting all the same.

We did take our course of studies fairly seriously, but neither of us allowed ourselves to be disproportionately preoccupied with it, or particularly worried about examination results. We attended lectures and tutorials, did our assignments, read some of the recommended books and hoped for the best. We'd come to an unknown, new country; it'd be wrong and short-sighted if we devoured all the recommended books on education, did a lot of research for every dissertation we wrote, and conscientious, in-depth preparation for every lesson we taught. We didn't want to let life generally pass us by. We'd come to spend about a year in the England of the fifties, during which all kinds of exciting things had happened and were happening.

A highly accentuated theoretical conflict between capitalism and communism; rock'n roll, Mao, the conquest of Everest, Dien Bien Phu, the anti-segregation legislation in the USA and other significant events gave us the feeling that it was all happening in the fifties. There were two peace deals within a month or so before we'd arrived in England – the Sino-French pact which ended the Indo-China War and the Anglo-Egyptian agreement leading to the evacuation of British forces from the Suez Canal zone, both of which I'd welcomed. Then there were the communists in China who seemed to have the upper hand over the nationalists. And in Hanoi the Vietnamese celebrated their victory over the French as Ho Chi Minh, the Communist leader, returned there after coming out of many years of hiding. In the world of sport, art and culture also exciting events were taking place all the time and in London we felt their impact more than we would have done in Kampala. We felt excited, we felt part of the wider world in a way we wouldn't have done in East Africa. But we didn't allow our interest in art, culture, sport or politics to interfere too much with our academic work.

We only occasionally watched a film or went to the theatre. Our opportunities for socialising were limited. There were only about half-a-dozen students at the Institute whose company we sought and who sought ours. About a dozen or so of us that year were interested in Marxist ideology. One morning I was selling communist literature in the foyer of the Institute. The supervisor of foreign students —I think his name was Mr Holland – let me understand the next time I met him that Das Kapital or the Communist Manifesto wasn't his literature of choice. He seemed to disapprove of my political affiliations. He suggested that I should do more education and less politics.

I continued to sell The Communist Manifesto in the foyer of the Institute.

The fifties were exciting for other than political reasons as well. Marilyn Monroe, Elvis Presley, Brigitte Bardot, Dean Martin, Sophia Loren, Diana Dors; all belonged to the fifties. Other big players were Fellini, Kurosawa, Ingmar Berman, Camus, Russell, Pasternak, Gamal Nasser, Fidel Castro, Ho Chi Min. There were so many outstanding personalities in the fifties that it would be unrealistic to try to mention their names or chronicle their achievements. Politically, the fifties were marked by some memorable successes, achieved by the leaders of Communism – Chairman Mao, Fidel Castro and Ho Chi Min had achieved revolutionary successes, and in Korea there was unfinished business. In Europe, Russia's sphere of influence had widened; as in Eastern Europe and East Berlin. It was therefore not unnatural that the world that followed the capitalistic ideology of production, distribution and governance was seriously disturbed by the growing power and influence of Communism. In London, at the Institute, Mr Holland gently expressed his disapproval; in Hollywood and elsewhere in America, Mr McCarthy was far from gentle or sensitive in handling the growing influence of Communist ideology.

In less than a year, England seemed to have made an impact on the way I perceived what was happening in the world around me. I was also more aware of world events because I lived in Finchley Central, doing a PGCE at the Institute of Education, London, reading the Manchester Guardian and the Socialist Worker, and had friends like Sheila Bose, Jack, Michael, Eunice, Gill, Robert, Nilakshi and others – all clear-thinking, humane and highly intelligent people, without any major prejudices and preoccupations. Gill and Robert were active members of the Communist Party and they'd go about their business on Robert's motorcycle – which had seen better days – for business, pleasure and party work. They were a unique couple; Gill's parents were middle-class academics, Robert's parents were working class, with nothing more than working class ambitions. Gill was training to be a teacher and Robert, like his father before him, worked in a factory. They travelled from somewhere near Islington on their nearly clapped out motorbike to have dinner with us in their spacemen outfits, and we had one of the most pleasant evenings with them in our little place in Finchley Central. Robert admired Nehru but was, at the same time, most critical of him because, he said, Jawaharlal was one of those leaders who raised enormous expectations but were unable to fulfil them.

Gill was more restrained than Robert and didn't believe as much as Robert did in the power and dynamism of four-letter words. She wondered about the malignant growth of McCarthyism and McCarthy's anti-communist hysteria, which led to the witch-hunt of good people, sensitive artists, actors and writers. Twenty-or-so million people died in Russia fighting a common enemy. What recognition did they or their leaders get for the demise of Fascism from Europe? That led to the topic of the rise of Franco. We didn't have time to find a satisfactory answer to the question, 'What went wrong with the revolution?' We were totally absorbed in our problem-solving when Robert was shocked out of any further discussion having looked at his watch. They had quite a way to go. Fortunately it was a pleasant spring evening – and they had enjoyed Sudarsana's curry.

We'd made some good friends, been exposed to some new ideas, attended some good lectures, visited some interesting places, and at times found ourselves puzzled and bewildered and out of our depth. However, we agreed, unequivocally, that our coming to London had been worth it. We hadn't encountered anything particularly painful or shocking. That doesn't mean that there was *nothing* painful or shocking. Privilege in all its ugliness was starkly there, and unnecessary poverty, squalor, violence and human degradation side by side with it. Why, in spite of all our wealth and modern technology, we hadn't been able to solve these problems in India, Africa and even in Britain was a question we never attempted to answer – except as an academic exercise. Post-war London – we were there almost a decade after the war – was an exciting place to live in because Britain had survived the war without loss of self-respect, and the optimism which had resulted from that still pervaded the atmosphere. We could have found traces of imperial arrogance if we'd looked for them but we didn't see any good reason for going out of our way to make ourselves miserable. We saw little evidence of it around us. And we didn't see why during our short visit to England, we should undertake serious research to make ourselves miserable.

We were thinking of all this because the time to go was looming closer and an assessment of our time in England was happening in our minds and in our discussions. Had our time in Britain, mainly in England, changed us at all? I think it had. I won't speak for Sudarsana, but there were changes I noticed in myself. I'd gained in confidence generally, but particularly in my relationship with women. I was more relaxed, less self-conscious and inhibited. Yes, my time in England had made a difference, but how profound the change was… I didn't know.

There was a great deal of unfinished business. Time was running out. examination was drawing closer every day. We'd been to Madame Tuss visited the London Zoo, watched the Changing of the Guard, seen Karl M residence in Soho, and St Paul's Cathedral. We'd done quite a few other intere trips and visits which I can't now recall. Both Sudarsana and I were now begin to feel apprehensive. Was the work we'd done so far sufficient for the kin examination results which would be acceptable to the Director of Education an uncle, the Indian Education Officer? Then, there was Mr B D Gupta; he'd prob rejoice if our results were below par, partly because of our profess disagreements and partly because his brother had a closer and more affection relationship with us than with him and his wife. We had to do well, devote time to educational psychology, the history of education, the principles of teach Since both Sudarsana and I had come to attend this course after a few year teaching experience, we weren't obsessively fearful about the assessment of teaching practice, which was a constant source of anxiety for our younger frie I'd always hated examinations and interviews. Fortunately, I didn't have to ap before three, four or more wise men to be asked relevant as well as irrele questions about a wide range of subjects – from cricket to Confucius – for the jo Uganda. And this examination wouldn't involve any kind of interview either. was good news.

We'd done one session of teaching practice in Wales. The reason was that for m of us on this course, English was a second language, and we'd be going bach different parts of the world where English certainly wasn't the first language. certain parts of Wales, the Welsh liked to think that English was the sec language and Welsh was their first; but Mike who was with us in Porthmadog, to his teaching practice, said that this was a fantasy generated by Welsh nationali and that he had still to come across a Welshman who was more at home in We than in English. He had met a Welshman or two who appeared to be as proficien Welsh as in English, and there must have been a small number of Welshmen in north who, not having been exposed to the wider world, managed to get by with having to speak a lot of English. But English at the time I went to Blaen Ffestiniog Grammar School to teach was certainly not the *second* language of th I taught, judging by the level of their proficiency.

There was, and is, something incongruous about Blaenau Ffestiniog. Situated rig in the middle of Snowdonia National Park, it was a shabby little industrial town, stark contrast with the great beauty of its surrounding landscape. At one time, tl unprepossessing aspect of the town was partly compensated for by its affluenc

which was based on slate extraction. It was known to the people in and around Snowdonia as 'the town that roofed the world'. The evidence of its great stony past was in the slate steps and slate roofs of houses and various slate products still available in shops. It is true that the slate industries had created an eyesore in the middle of so much natural beauty, but those who wanted aesthetic excitement could always stand in Blaenau Ffestiniog and look around at the Manod and Melwyn Mountains and enjoy the magnificence of nature.

I couldn't say exactly how old the buildings were, nor what the style of their architecture was. But I do remember that Blaenau Ffestiniog Grammar School was a well-organised school where deviant behaviour in the classroom was not just rare but almost non-existent. The grasp of English in the senior classes was rather impressive.

I remember a discussion with one of these senior students. I think her name was Phyllis. She made the point that *Macbeth* wasn't really a tragedy because a man who was ambitious, ruthless, disloyal, dishonest and cruel had got what he deserved. The punishment was proportionate to the crime. She would have been disappointed if he had lived to a ripe old age, continuing to enjoy his power and glory. I conceded that Phyllis had a point, but I pointed out that we could also look at the situation differently. Wasn't it tragic that Macbeth, who was a brave and loyal subject, a great general, a loving husband, a man whose language showed that he had an extraordinary and powerful imagination, could behave like a common criminal, capable of the most brutal crimes and senseless cruelty? The tragedy, I suggested, was in the contrast between what could have happened and what did happen. I don't think I was able to convince Phyllis that Macbeth, in spite of his terrible lapses and fatal flaws, emerged for me as a tragic hero, lonely and defeated, but still not devoid of dignity and greatness.

What was exciting was that in remote Blaenau Ffestiniog there was a grammar school where a senior girl was not cowed by her teacher's age and experience. On the contrary, she stuck out for her point of view and made a reasonable case for considering Macbeth not a flawed, tragic character, but a weak, impressionable man whose criminal conduct didn't rouse her compassion. We didn't have to agree, I said. She found Macbeth revoltingly weak and cruel and unworthy of her pity. I found his weakness human and his degeneration tragic, for potentially he was an honourable man of courage and imagination. He caused death and misery to others and himself through delusions of power. I found that tragic. It was good to be able

to engage in a discussion of this kind, to meet someone like Phyllis who thought for herself and wasn't impressed by Aristotle or Ganesh Bagchi. Ten or eleven years later, I met Phyllis in Calcutta. She'd married a Bengali doctor and settled there. She was principal of a school. It was she who reminded me that many years ago, she'd disputed my interpretation of *Macbeth*.

Living and teaching in North Wales was pleasant. My school had a high standard. My colleagues and my students were friendly and helpful, and when it was time for me to leave, the students organised a group photograph which I carried around with me for quite some time. I also got to know some of my colleagues better – Sheila Bose, Michael Knight, a Chinese friend – whose name I have forgotten – who always took Sudarsana's side whenever there was an argument between Sudarsana and me, or Sudarsana and someone else.

Soon it was time to return to London. The Rotary Club of Porthmadog gave us a farewell party. The members of the club were friendly and hospitable. Apart from us, there was Geoffrey Barnard at the party. Geoffrey had come over from London to see how we were shaping up and he sat in on the lessons of all those from the Institute who were doing their teaching practice in Wales. Geoffrey Barnard was one of those teachers who were able to have a close and friendly relationship with their students without being thought any the less for it. He praised without patronising, criticised out of a genuine desire to make us better teachers. The president of the Rotary Club spoke briefly about how Porthmadog looked forward to the brief advent of the students from the Institute of Education every year. Usually the students were from various parts of the English-speaking world and their presence in North Wales gave them a sense of being connected. He and his colleagues also appreciated the good work we did in the schools. Geoffrey had asked me to acknowledge the goodwill and hospitality of the club. I spoke about the friendly environment, the good food, the beautiful countryside. I had a sense of homecoming in Wales and that feeling was further enhanced by the hospitality of the Rotary Club.

I can't really think of anything else that happened in Wales which I particularly want to report – unless it is our group's attempt to climb Snowdon. The scenery all around it was breathtakingly beautiful. But, like all special tourist attractions, it had been blighted somewhat by commercial enterprises trying to make capital out of people's love of adventure and beauty. I didn't climb to the top of Snowdon; I think

Sudarsana, Mike, Sheila and our Chinese friend did. After that, all that remained to do was to return to London.

I, like all the other students at the Institute, did two lots of teaching practice. I did one at East Ham Grammar School, and another at Blaenau Ffestiniog Grammar School. I did some junior classes in East Ham Grammar School, but most of my teaching was in the school-leaving year. East Ham Grammar School, founded in 1965, was in Barking Road, East Ham, Essex – just over 12 miles from Charing Cross. It was a large school in an old building with both age and character. Apprehensive in the beginning, I soon settled down in an environment which was organised and efficient, but not rigid. Whereas Blaenau Ffestiniog was co-educational, East Ham Grammar School was for boys only.

Here I taught 14 year-olds grammar and composition in the junior classes and 16 year-olds English literature in the senior classes. I discussed the structure and content of discourse: the sentence, the paragraph, the whole piece of writing, the connecting of ideas, the transition from one idea to another, relating facts to ideas – in language which I thought was comprehensible. To begin with, everyone wrote on the same topics, but quite soon each student chose their own subject for composition. The students liked choosing their own subjects. I thought that my approach was fairly successful.

There were two memorable occasions in East Ham Grammar School for me. Mr Shannon, the head of English, was a friendly colleague, quite a few years older than me. He was tall, had black hair, and wore dark-rimmed glasses. He liked playing chess, and whenever he couldn't organise one of his colleagues who fairly regularly played chess with him, he would turn to me, who had a lighter timetable compared with the regular teachers on the school staff. Mr Shannon was an experienced chess player, whom other chess players in the school treated with respect because of his skill. It was no wonder, therefore, that he regularly beat me – except that the more I played the longer I was able to keep my end up. But in the end, I'd lose. I'd be defeated, vanquished, check-mated. Then, one afternoon, I won – dramatically, unexpectedly and decisively! I was totally surprised by my success. But Mr Shannon was amused and most gracious in defeat. It was beginning to be interesting to play a game of chess with me because, he said, I'd now acquired skills and gained insights which I didn't have before. During the rest of the time that I was there, I never again managed to beat Mr Shannon. That's all the more reason why my single victory was so memorable.

The other occasion at East Ham Grammar School that I remember clearly and with affectionate indulgence had to do with *Macbeth* again, which was the prescribed textbook that year. I entered the class where I was teaching *Macbeth* that morning and found a class which had transformed itself. The students looked really alert; the desks and chairs were all arranged neatly, and all the students were sitting in their appropriate places, bolt upright, with a look of serious concentration on their faces. *And* not one of them was talking. I was impressed but apprehensive.

'Good morning,' I said.

'Good morning, sir,' they said together, with precise timing as if in a play, pretending to simulate the behaviour of an ideal class of students. They seemed to know exactly what they were doing, but I had no idea, because they had no intention of showing their hand. I would have asked them not to be silly, not to play games, to be their age, to take Shakespeare seriously, but I decided to let their plan unfold.

I was also going to pretend that I'd noticed nothing unusual in the behaviour of the class, and teach exactly as I'd done before. So I started off by saying something like this:

'At the heart of drama, there has to be conflict and Macbeth is at war with himself before he commits the murder of his king and his kinsman as well as afterwards.' Every one of the students, all sitting bolt upright, gave me the impression that they were listening with rapt attention, but that was a hoax. As soon as I finished making my generalization, each pair of students, in slow motion, turned their heads and torsos to each other, bowed deeply to signify assent, and then, again in slow motion, straightened their heads and torsos to look at me. The whole class did this charade with a straight face, without giving the game away. They produced the same act, performed the same charade, each time I made a generalization. I could react in one of half a dozen ways, I was thinking. I could get angry and leave the classroom in a huff. I could report these cheeky boys to the headmaster. But none of this appealed to me. I was desperately looking for a solution which would match their creative way of taking the Mickey.

I've got it, I said to myself. 'The next time, they do their cheeky act, I'll join them and see how they react.'

'Macbeth's conflict is both in the world without and in the world within. It's the conflict within which produces some of the most memorable lines in Shakespeare.' I paused. The charade started. I joined my students. Just as they were bowing to each other in slow motion to indicate assent, I too bowed deep to the class in slow motion. When I slowly straightened my torso and looked at the class, they were all laughing. We'd resolved our supposed conflict amicably, and all was well. I congratulated them on their innovative strategy. It was good theatre, I said, and meant it. Then, for the rest of the time, we had a general discussion about Shakespeare's tragic heroes. They didn't know the plays but knew the stories of Hamlet, Julius Caesar, King Lear and Romeo and Juliet. The tragic story of Romeo and Juliet had moved them most. It was for them pure tragedy because neither Romeo nor Juliet had really done anything to deserve their untimely death. It's probably Hamlet's indecision and inaction which led to his death. Lear was stubborn, self-centred, vain- glorious and short-sighted. Macbeth had abandoned all moral principles, lost all his compassion, considered himself above any human weakness like fear. He said.' direness cannot once start me.' But there was nothing in their own persona to which the tragedy of Romeo and Juliet could be ascribed. It was pure tragedy ... I felt good that my students were sensitive, intelligent and imaginative people. I felt sad that I was going to stop teaching them in a week or two, and it was unlikely that I'd ever see them again. I was for comprehensive schools, but I liked this grammar school.

At the Institute, everybody was getting agitated over the examination, which was just weeks away, whereas a fatalistic calm had descended on me. Once or twice, Sudarsana expressed anxiety because she mistook my refusal to get agitated over the impending examination as overconfidence. It was nothing of the sort. More than anything else, it was a feeling of disorientation and desperation. There was so much I didn't know – about methodology, the principles of education, the history of education, the psychology of education and other aspects of education – that I had no alternative to hoping that the compassionate examination paper-setters would ask me just those questions which I would be able to answer. In most of the written assignments I'd done reasonably well, but in Professor Vernon's assignment, in which I had to do a case-study, I'd got a C+, which had hurt my ego, especially because I found Educational Psychology a most interesting subject.

The examination came and went. I had no idea how well or badly I'd fared. Sudarsana felt fairly confident that she'd done reasonably well; and that although she hadn't done brilliantly, she was above average. At the time, since there was no way of finding out the outcome of our efforts, we decided not to speculate about the which was based on slate extraction. It was known to the people in and around Snowdonia as 'the town that roofed the world'. The evidence of its great stony past was in the slate steps and slate roofs of houses and various slate products still available in shops. It is true that the slate industries had created an eyesore in the middle of so much natural beauty, but those who wanted aesthetic excitement could always stand in Blaenau Ffestiniog and look around at the Manod and Melwyn Mountains and enjoy the magnificence of nature.

I couldn't say exactly how old the buildings were, nor what the style of their architecture was. But I do remember that Blaenau Ffestiniog Grammar School was a well-organised school where deviant behaviour in the classroom was not just rare but almost non-existent. The grasp of English in the senior classes was rather impressive.

I remember a discussion with one of these senior students. I think her name was Phyllis. She made the point that *Macbeth* wasn't really a tragedy because a man who was ambitious, ruthless, disloyal, dishonest and cruel had got what he deserved. The punishment was proportionate to the crime. She would have been disappointed if he had lived to a ripe old age, continuing to enjoy his power and glory. I conceded that Phyllis had a point, but I pointed out that we could also look at the situation differently. Wasn't it tragic that Macbeth, who was a brave and loyal subject, a great general, a loving husband, a man whose language showed that he had an extraordinary and powerful imagination, could behave like a common criminal, capable of the most brutal crimes and senseless cruelty? The tragedy, I suggested, was in the contrast between what could have happened and what did happen. I don't think I was able to convince Phyllis that Macbeth, in spite of his terrible lapses and fatal flaws, emerged for me as a tragic hero, lonely and defeated, but still not devoid of dignity and greatness.

What was exciting was that in remote Blaenau Ffestiniog there was a grammar school where a senior girl was not cowed by her teacher's age and experience. On the contrary, she stuck out for her point of view and made a reasonable case for considering Macbeth not a flawed, tragic character, but a weak, impressionable man whose criminal conduct didn't rouse her compassion. We didn't have to agree, I said. She found Macbeth revoltingly weak and cruel and unworthy of her pity. I found his weakness human and his degeneration tragic, for potentially he was an honourable man of courage and imagination. He caused death and misery to others and himself through delusions of power. I found that tragic. It was good to be able

There was a great deal of unfinished business. Time was running out. The examination was drawing closer every day. We'd been to Madame Tussaud's, visited the London Zoo, watched the Changing of the Guard, seen Karl Marx's residence in Soho, and St Paul's Cathedral. We'd done quite a few other interesting trips and visits which I can't now recall. Both Sudarsana and I were now beginning to feel apprehensive. Was the work we'd done so far sufficient for the kind of examination results which would be acceptable to the Director of Education and our uncle, the Indian Education Officer? Then, there was Mr B D Gupta; he'd probably rejoice if our results were below par, partly because of our professional disagreements and partly because his brother had a closer and more affectionate relationship with us than with him and his wife. We had to do well, devote more time to educational psychology, the history of education, the principles of teaching. Since both Sudarsana and I had come to attend this course after a few years of teaching experience, we weren't obsessively fearful about the assessment of our teaching practice, which was a constant source of anxiety for our younger friends. I'd always hated examinations and interviews. Fortunately, I didn't have to appear before three, four or more wise men to be asked relevant as well as irrelevant questions about a wide range of subjects – from cricket to Confucius – for the job in Uganda. And this examination wouldn't involve any kind of interview either. That was good news.

We'd done one session of teaching practice in Wales. The reason was that for many of us on this course, English was a second language, and we'd be going back to different parts of the world where English certainly wasn't the first language. In certain parts of Wales, the Welsh liked to think that English was the second language and Welsh was their first; but Mike who was with us in Porthmadog, to do his teaching practice, said that this was a fantasy generated by Welsh nationalism, and that he had still to come across a Welshman who was more at home in Welsh than in English. He had met a Welshman or two who appeared to be as proficient in Welsh as in English, and there must have been a small number of Welshmen in the north who, not having been exposed to the wider world, managed to get by without having to speak a lot of English. But English at the time I went to Blaenau Ffestiniog Grammar School to teach was certainly not the *second* language of those I taught, judging by the level of their proficiency.

There was, and is, something incongruous about Blaenau Ffestiniog. Situated right in the middle of Snowdonia National Park, it was a shabby little industrial town, in stark contrast with the great beauty of its surrounding landscape. At one time, the unprepossessing aspect of the town was partly compensated for by its affluence, to engage in a discussion of this kind, to meet someone like Phyllis who thought for herself and wasn't impressed by Aristotle or Ganesh Bagchi. Ten or eleven years later, I met Phyllis in Calcutta. She'd married a Bengali doctor and settled there. She was principal of a school. It was she who reminded me that many years ago, she'd disputed my interpretation of *Macbeth*.

Living and teaching in North Wales was pleasant. My school had a high standard. My colleagues and my students were friendly and helpful, and when it was time for me to leave, the students organised a group photograph which I carried around with me for quite some time. I also got to know some of my colleagues better – Sheila Bose, Michael Knight, a Chinese friend – whose name I have forgotten – who always took Sudarsana's side whenever there was an argument between Sudarsana and me, or Sudarsana and someone else.

Soon it was time to return to London. The Rotary Club of Porthmadog gave us a farewell party. The members of the club were friendly and hospitable. Apart from us, there was Geoffrey Barnard at the party. Geoffrey had come over from London to see how we were shaping up and he sat in on the lessons of all those from the Institute who were doing their teaching practice in Wales. Geoffrey Barnard was one of those teachers who were able to have a close and friendly relationship with their students without being thought any the less for it. He praised without patronising, criticised out of a genuine desire to make us better teachers. The president of the Rotary Club spoke briefly about how Porthmadog looked forward to the brief advent of the students from the Institute of Education every year. Usually the students were from various parts of the English-speaking world and their presence in North Wales gave them a sense of being connected. He and his colleagues also appreciated the good work we did in the schools. Geoffrey had asked me to acknowledge the goodwill and hospitality of the club. I spoke about the friendly environment, the good food, the beautiful countryside. I had a sense of homecoming in Wales and that feeling was further enhanced by the hospitality of the Rotary Club.

I can't really think of anything else that happened in Wales which I particularly want to report – unless it is our group's attempt to climb Snowdon. The scenery all around it was breathtakingly beautiful. But, like all special tourist attractions, it had been blighted somewhat by commercial enterprises trying to make capital out of people's love of adventure and beauty. I didn't climb to the top of Snowdon; I think

Sudarsana, Mike, Sheila and our Chinese friend did. After that, all that remained to do was to return to London.

I, like all the other students at the Institute, did two lots of teaching practice. I did one at East Ham Grammar School, and another at Blaenau Ffestiniog Grammar School. I did some junior classes in East Ham Grammar School, but most of my teaching was in the school-leaving year. East Ham Grammar School, founded in 1965, was in Barking Road, East Ham, Essex – just over 12 miles from Charing Cross. It was a large school in an old building with both age and character. Apprehensive in the beginning, I soon settled down in an environment which was organised and efficient, but not rigid. Whereas Blaenau Ffestiniog was co-educational, East Ham Grammar School was for boys only.

Here I taught 14 year-olds grammar and composition in the junior classes and 16 year-olds English literature in the senior classes. I discussed the structure and content of discourse: the sentence, the paragraph, the whole piece of writing, the connecting of ideas, the transition from one idea to another, relating facts to ideas – in language which I thought was comprehensible. To begin with, everyone wrote on the same topics, but quite soon each student chose their own subject for composition. The students liked choosing their own subjects. I thought that my approach was fairly successful.

There were two memorable occasions in East Ham Grammar School for me. Mr Shannon, the head of English, was a friendly colleague, quite a few years older than me. He was tall, had black hair, and wore dark-rimmed glasses. He liked playing chess, and whenever he couldn't organise one of his colleagues who fairly regularly played chess with him, he would turn to me, who had a lighter timetable compared with the regular teachers on the school staff. Mr Shannon was an experienced chess player, whom other chess players in the school treated with respect because of his skill. It was no wonder, therefore, that he regularly beat me – except that the more I played the longer I was able to keep my end up. But in the end, I'd lose. I'd be defeated, vanquished, check-mated. Then, one afternoon, I won – dramatically, unexpectedly and decisively! I was totally surprised by my success. But Mr Shannon was amused and most gracious in defeat. It was beginning to be interesting to play a game of chess with me because, he said, I'd now acquired skills and gained insights which I didn't have before. During the rest of the time that I was there, I never again managed to beat Mr Shannon. That's all the more reason why my single victory was so memorable.

The other occasion at East Ham Grammar School that I remember clearly and with affectionate indulgence had to do with *Macbeth* again, which was the prescribed textbook that year. I entered the class where I was teaching *Macbeth* that morning and found a class which had transformed itself. The students looked really alert; the desks and chairs were all arranged neatly, and all the students were sitting in their appropriate places, bolt upright, with a look of serious concentration on their faces. *And* not one of them was talking. I was impressed but apprehensive.

'Good morning,' I said.

'Good morning, sir,' they said together, with precise timing as if in a play, pretending to simulate the behaviour of an ideal class of students. They seemed to know exactly what they were doing, but I had no idea, because they had no intention of showing their hand. I would have asked them not to be silly, not to play games, to be their age, to take Shakespeare seriously, but I decided to let their plan unfold.

I was also going to pretend that I'd noticed nothing unusual in the behaviour of the class, and teach exactly as I'd done before. So I started off by saying something like this:

'At the heart of drama, there has to be conflict and Macbeth is at war with himself before he commits the murder of his king and his kinsman as well as afterwards.' Every one of the students, all sitting bolt upright, gave me the impression that they were listening with rapt attention, but that was a hoax. As soon as I finished making my generalization, each pair of students, in slow motion, turned their heads and torsos to each other, bowed deeply to signify assent, and then, again in slow motion, straightened their heads and torsos to look at me. The whole class did this charade with a straight face, without giving the game away. They produced the same act, performed the same charade, each time I made a generalization. I could react in one of half a dozen ways, I was thinking. I could get angry and leave the classroom in a huff. I could report these cheeky boys to the headmaster. But none of this appealed to me. I was desperately looking for a solution which would match their creative way of taking the Mickey.

I've got it, I said to myself. 'The next time, they do their cheeky act, I'll join them and see how they react.'

'Macbeth's conflict is both in the world without and in the world within. It's the conflict within which produces some of the most memorable lines in Shakespeare.' I paused. The charade started. I joined my students. Just as they were bowing to each other in slow motion to indicate assent, I too bowed deep to the class in slow motion. When I slowly straightened my torso and looked at the class, they were all laughing. We'd resolved our supposed conflict amicably, and all was well. I congratulated them on their innovative strategy. It was good theatre, I said, and meant it. Then, for the rest of the time, we had a general discussion about Shakespeare's tragic heroes. They didn't know the plays but knew the stories of Hamlet, Julius Caesar, King Lear and Romeo and Juliet. The tragic story of Romeo and Juliet had moved them most. It was for them pure tragedy because neither Romeo nor Juliet had really done anything to deserve their untimely death. It's probably Hamlet's indecision and inaction which led to his death. Lear was stubborn, self-centred, vain- glorious and short-sighted. Macbeth had abandoned all moral principles, lost all his compassion, considered himself above any human weakness like fear. He said.' direness cannot once start me.' But there was nothing in their own persona to which the tragedy of Romeo and Juliet could be ascribed. It was pure tragedy ... I felt good that my students were sensitive, intelligent and imaginative people. I felt sad that I was going to stop teaching them in a week or two, and it was unlikely that I'd ever see them again. I was for comprehensive schools, but I liked this grammar school.

At the Institute, everybody was getting agitated over the examination, which was just weeks away, whereas a fatalistic calm had descended on me. Once or twice, Sudarsana expressed anxiety because she mistook my refusal to get agitated over the impending examination as overconfidence. It was nothing of the sort. More than anything else, it was a feeling of disorientation and desperation. There was so much I didn't know – about methodology, the principles of education, the history of education, the psychology of education and other aspects of education – that I had no alternative to hoping that the compassionate examination paper-setters would ask me just those questions which I would be able to answer. In most of the written assignments I'd done reasonably well, but in Professor Vernon's assignment, in which I had to do a case-study, I'd got a C+, which had hurt my ego, especially because I found Educational Psychology a most interesting subject.

The examination came and went. I had no idea how well or badly I'd fared. Sudarsana felt fairly confident that she'd done reasonably well; and that although she hadn't done brilliantly, she was above average. At the time, since there was no way of finding out the outcome of our efforts, we decided not to speculate about the results... We left our Indian address with a friend, who undertook to let us know our results when they were out.

Apart from our examination results, there were other matters of interest and importance. I was taking driving lessons but failed the test twice. I wanted to buy a car in England and use it in England and then export it to Uganda. The idea of buying a car gave rise to plans, the architects of which were Joy and Tutu-da. Tutu-da, Sudarsana's cousin, was a good friend of mine. He was in England for work and study which would lead to Membership of the Royal College of Gynaecology (MRCOG). Tutu-da had also delivered our two daughters, Aparna and Aparajita. Joy was his wife. Tutu-da had finished his course and was ready to return to India with Joy, but there was no immediate hurry. Sudarsana and I had completed our course of studies and were also going to spend our leave in India but we could spend some of our leave in England and Europe... The similarity of our situations led to discussions from which emerged a plan of action.

But before it could be finalised, there were several little problems or impediments. The car we would have liked to buy – a Volkswagen – wasn't immediately available. There was a waiting list which would entail a delay or two or three months. There was nothing wrong with a Morris Minor, Tutu-da suggested, and it was a lot cheaper. What's more, we could buy it immediately. We settled for a Morris Minor. A Morris Minor, believe it or not, would cost me less than £300 because, as since it was for immediate export, I wouldn't have to pay any purchase tax. But there was another problem: just then we didn't have enough money to buy a car and have a holiday in Europe and India. Without the slightest hesitation, Joy offered to lend me the money. I could pay it back after I'd returned to Uganda, she said. Was that the end of the problem? No, it wasn't. Tutu-da needed a driver who could provide some relief. It was important for me to acquire a licence, but bad luck, or rather a combination of bad luck and bad driving, had already led to two failures.

I bought a black Morris Minor. Its registration number was PLR 844. We called it 'Poor Little Rabbit' – affectionately. I started taking driving lessons again and became a member of the Automobile Association. Tutu-da was at the time attached to Birmingham Hospital. He fixed up a driving test with the Automobile Association for me. In those days the Automobile Association was authorised to give driving tests to its members. The man who took the test was very different from the two others who had administered it before him. They were men of few words and frowning faces, men who were strict and unsmiling.

But the examiner in Birmingham actually smiled as he said good afternoon and asked a few questions. Then we set off, drove through some busy streets, parked, started again, reversed around a bend, I answered a few more questions and we returned to the office of the Automobile Association in Birmingham. I had passed!

It was one of my most memorable days in Britain. I was now authorised to drive our Morris Minor here in Britain as well as elsewhere. That weekend, we met up at Joy's house in Holland Park to celebrate my success and plan our trip. None of us drank regularly. I occasionally drank a peg or two of whisky, but I knew nothing about wines. Joy had bought a bottle of red wine. Tutu-da opened the bottle and we drank to our holiday in Europe and the Middle East.

Then Joy produced a map of Europe and we pored over it as we discussed our plans and tried to decide on countries we were going to visit and the route we were going to take. How much time we were going to spend at the places we'd visit was something we didn't have to decide in advance because we were fairly independent in that respect – since we were driving our own car and staying in our own tents on camping sites, or in youth hostels. Sudarsana and I had bought a nylon tent which could be carried in one hand without any difficulty because it was small as well as light. Joy had travelled in Europe before, so we depended on her to tell us about money, documents and other essentials, while we drank our red wine. There were suggestions and counter-suggestions, but we all agreed that we couldn't indulge in fantasies, and it would not do to be too ambitious and ignore the constraints of time and money. We wanted to do everything: go to the top of the Eiffel Tower and look at Paris; visit the Notre Dame and other churches; the Versailles Palace, the museums and art galleries. We'd all like to drive up and down the Swiss mountains. Why not go to Spain, someone suggested. The fortified palace, Alhambra in Granada, which went back more than 600 years, would be a fascinating place to visit. We must go to Italy, it was generally agreed. It was Joy who was the most enthusiastic supporter of the idea. The Coliseum, the amphitheatre in Rome, 615 feet long and 160 feet high, which seated 50,000 spectators, was one of our chosen destinations.

And if we are going by rail to Basra, should we miss the opportunity to visit Damascus? I asked. We hadn't yet finished discussing our plans in Europe, Tutu-da pointed out, so we returned to Italy. Wouldn't it be a good idea, Joy suggested, to go to Yugoslavia, come back to Italy and then take the train to Turkey? Nobody objected. Although, theoretically, we were equal partners in this democratic discussion, Joy, by virtue of her greater experience of travelling in Europe, was really our leader. It was to her credit that at no time did she make us feel that we were less than equal partners. The real leaders have always known how to make people feel that the decisions *they* made, were really made democratically.

In the end the route to Bombay which we'd worked out was fairly straightforward, Joy insisted, although to us it looked quite ambitious and complicated. From London we'd drive down to Dover and then cross over to Calais and then go to Paris and spend a few days there. From France we'd drive up to Switzerland. From there we'd drive off to Austria, and then from Austria to Italy. From Italy we'd drive off to Tito's Yugoslavia, spend some time there, and return to Italy. From Italy, we'd ship the 'Poor Little Rabbit' off to Bombay and take the train to Turkey, Syria and Iraq. From the Iraqi port of Basra, we'd go to Bombay, and then by train to Calcutta.

If the outline seemed like a challenge, what kind of impression would the completed travel-plan have on me? I felt excited but apprehensive. Fortunately, however, what mitigated my anxiety and uncertainty was Joy's cool confidence and businesslike approach to the project. She'd already prepared a tentative list of visas which we'd require and calculated the approximate amount of money we'd require for the journey. Our wardrobes would have to be basic and we'd have to live within a strict budget. Each of us was allowed a set of presentable clothes in case we were caught up in some formal or semi-formal event. Because our plan was to camp whenever possible, unless youth hostels were within easy access, we'd have to restrict our ambitions, Joy said. Then there was the question of space. The small boot of our Morris Minor and the roof rack would have to accommodate our earthly possessions; therefore what we took with us had to be cut down to a minimum. We'd have to do some shopping, pay our bills, sort out travel documents and see our friends or ring them to say goodbye.

It was the idea of saying goodbye to friends and to London which often made me feel sad and pensive during the last days of our stay in Finchley Central. I hoped to come back to London because I found it an exciting city, but I had little hope of meeting my friends again: Michael Knight, Sheila Bose, Eunice and Nilaskshi... Then there was Jack, who was in many ways different from others. I visited him in his small rented place one evening when he was getting ready to eat his dinner – which he had just cooked in a saucepan while he talked to me. He detached the handle of the saucepan – I hadn't seen one of these before – put it down on his dining table and ate out of it. Economy, he explained... He was interested in philosophy – especially in his own theories.

Everything overlapped, he said, but philosophers loved drawing lines between ideas and concepts to make them cut and dried. You couldn't, he insisted, differentiate between existence and essence, or between appearance and reality. What the mind creates is just as real as what's out there in space. He said things like that... Philosophy was never my forte, so I was quite happy to agree with him.

In the years to come, when I thought of London, I felt certain I'd think of Jack and the few other friends I'd made there. We sought some of them out to say goodbye, and behaved casually, talking about politics, the weather, job prospects and the possibility of meeting up again, but there was unspoken and genuine sadness. It was good to be in London. Friends are people we feel most comfortable with, people who, if they miss the train and stay the night, make us rejoice.

We didn't pay a lot of attention to British politics because it didn't matter to either Sudarsana or me whether it was Churchill or Eden who ran Britain. It was a pity, we thought that Attlee was not in power – he was our favourite Prime Minister. The rail and dock strikes were on and the Tory government was seeking draconian powers to crush the insolent workers who had dared to strike.

Going away from London was going to be painful also because we'd come to love the city, which we'd found exciting and where we'd made some good friends. But more powerful than any other emotion was our desire to be with our three children in Calcutta – Aparna, Aparajita and Nondon. Once we started our journey, every mile away from London would bring us closer to our children. Various interests and a few good friends – Tutu-da and Joy among them – had made London the memorable experience it was. Sudarsaa was also eagerly looking forward to meeting up with her parents and some friends.

We were now waiting for the beginning of our great adventure, for names to turn into exciting places – Paris, Rome, Florence, Istanbul, Baghdad. We'd seen our friends, paid our rent, done most of our packing and were all set to go and explore what to us was a whole new world, and we had no idea what shocks and surprises were waiting for us. We wrote letters to India – to the children, to Sudarsana's parents and to friends. Sudarsana cooked lunch, I read the newspaper, we talked about India, did some last minute shopping. In the evening I'd exercise my recently acquired right to drive the Morris Minor, test my skill and acquire confidence through unsupervised driving by visiting various restaurants around Finchley Central. This was a relief for Sudarsana, for she didn't have to think about the cooking. A Cypriot restaurant – which had an eccentric owner, who also did most of the cooking – was our favourite eating place. Then one morning Tutu-da came over, and after a quick coffee, we set off for Holland Park. We'd put our things in the car but hadn't done proper packing. We spent the day in the Holland Park flat, did some last minute shopping, ate out, did a proper job of packing, and quite early in the morning, set off for Dover.

244

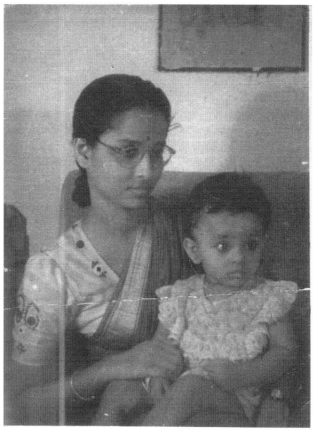

Chapter 10

Europe, the Middle East, India.

We came to Britain and lived in Finchley Central at a time when the nightmare of the Second World War was long over and the general outlook of people around us was relaxed. As we were leaving Holland Park, where we'd assembled to set out for the ferry in Dover, images of the past year floated in and out of my mind, creating a sense of nostalgia. England had given me a feeling of liberation. People, especially young people, were talking of Black Power, women's freedom and various other issues for the rejection of bourgeois values. I had no idea where it'd take us, nor was I speculating about it. All I knew was that there was something intoxicating about the fact that during the decade which had gone by, the trauma of the cruellest, most devastating and no-holds-barred war had faded from memory, and people were looking for ways of enhancing the quality of life. Freedom from some established traditional values was at the centre of that quest.

I found it incredible that I'd just lived about a year in London and was going to Paris. Other capitals to follow would be Rome, Istanbul and Baghdad – apart from numerous cities and places of interest in Switzerland, Austria, Italy, Yugoslavia and Turkey. We would go through Syria and Iraq as well, but it wouldn't be much more than the railway stations that we would be able to see. Before I came to live in Finchley Central and study at the Institute of Education, London University, I'd lived in a state capital, Calcutta, and the capital of Uganda, Kampala. Nothing that I'd experienced before compared with what I was exposed to here in London. What we could have done was so much more compared to what we actually did that I'd certainly look back with some regret and compare the little done with the undone vast in the years to come. But right then what I was experiencing was the excitement of the unknown as Tutu-da drove our black Morris Minor with three passengers and a surfeit of luggage towards the ferry and the white cliffs of Dover, while the morning mist was clearing away and the sun was waiting in the wings. For me the excitement was in the journey itself, in the movement towards destinations whose names for me were no more than printed words in books and maps. Now we were actually crossing the Channel, the scene of great happenings – dramatic, tragic, heroic – full of great expectations and a distinct feeling of adventure.

Absorbed in the procedure of getting ourselves and the car on the ferry, I'd forgotten about the White Cliffs of Dover, which we were at the time sailing away from. I was looking towards the coast of France when Sudarsana cried out in an agitated voice, 'Ganesh, turn around. There, over there, are the White Cliffs of Dover.'

It was a magnificent sight, an unforgettable spectacle of cliffs rising out of the water, white, vast, jagged, still. How many millennia did it take – the formation of the rocks, and then how many millennia for the sea to erode the sides of the cliffs to make them look the way they were? This magnificent coastal site in Kent, the rocks rising out of the Channel, was the first great source of visual excitement of the five weeks of travel we'd planned. We were looking forward to more.

After arriving in Calais, we set out for our camping site in Bois de Boulogne in the west of Paris on the River Seine. We arrived in time for a late lunch at the canteen. The food was fairly basic. What exactly we ate I don't remember, but I don't think it had very much to do with the famous French cuisine. Joy was the only one among us who'd lived on different camp-sites in Europe, and it was her experiences which were of interest to us. Her view on the subject was that food at camp-site canteens and restaurants were unique, in a class by itself. It wasn't French or Spanish or Greek cuisine but camp-site cuisine. The eating places on camp-sites catered to the needs of young men and women with healthy appetites, usually too hungry to worry about subtlety or delicacy. I certainly enjoyed what I ate. It was a vast, green leafy camp-site with enough space to build a palace, so our nylon tent looked like a not-too-large anthill; but Tutu-da and Joy's tent, pitched a few yards way, seemed quite adequate... After that, we explored the site for a very short time, used some of its facilities – which were quite basic – and went to a small restaurant where we had coffee and sandwiches. After that, by general consent, we went for a drive to familiarise ourselves with some of the sights and sounds of Paris. We drove round for a time. I was trying to imagine what Paris looked like at the time of the Revolution nearly 160 years ago. It is possible that Danton and Robespierre had walked these streets and made revolutionary speeches about liberty, equality and fraternity not too far from where we were. But just as my mind was about to graduate to the bloody and violent images of the storming of the Bastille and the almost indiscriminate and frenzied beheading of Parisians by the guillotine, Tutu-da declared that he had no idea where he was. In other words, he was totally lost. Joy had spotted a traffic policeman and she suggested that Tutu-da stopped the car somewhere so that he and Joy could go and ask him how to get back to Bois de Boulogne. Tutu-da parked the car and he and Joy went up to the man to ask for directions. Tutu-da also needed a toilet and he was going to ask where he could find one. They came back. She looked amused. I asked her what had amused her.

'Tutu asked the policeman where he could find a toilet. Do you know what he said? The whole of Paris is a toilet, Monsieur. Just find a convenient corner.'

This wasn't particularly helpful, so we found a small cafe, had coffee there and laughed over the extreme helpfulness of the traffic policeman. But he wasn't totally useless. He'd told us how to get back to the camp-site. That evening we talked vaguely and generally about the shape of things to come, and after a rather indifferent meal at our camp-site restaurant, we went to our tents. In the morning, the first question we asked each other was which places of interest we were going to visit. There were several options – the Eiffel Tower, the Louvre Museum and Art Gallery, the Palace of Versailles, the streets and cafes of Paris, some of the bridges over the River Seine, the Notre Dame Cathedral, the Champs-Elysee Avenue leading to the Arc de Triomphe, and so on. There were so many landmarks to choose from that we were quite at a loss and confused but excited. In the end we settled for the Eiffel Tower, the great iconic landmark on Champs de Mars, the tallest tower in Paris, built as the entrance arch of the World Fair in 1889. Gustav Eiffel was the name of the designer, an engineer, and it was named after him.

We ate our lunch in the restaurant at the second level and admired the towers, steeples and spires, and tops of skyscrapers. Joy, who'd visited Paris before, was able to identify some of the buildings. I'd never before experienced anything like the view which spread out in front of me – its spectacular variety was mesmerising. We ate in silence – a meal which was both delectable and expensive. The immense distraction all around was exciting but confusing. Hardly anyone spoke. Occasionally there was a slight outburst of excitement when someone recognised a steeple, turret, spire or skyscraper, or an ancient building or famous landmark. Otherwise, the assembled crowd, including us, watched in silence, as the sun glittered on the buildings below. For me, it wasn't so much what I saw that special day from the great height of the Eiffel Tower, but how I felt. In North Wales, when I'd looked down from near the top of Snowdon, I'd had an extraordinary sensation. What I experienced here also was a feeling of exhilaration but of a different kind.

The visitors to the Eiffel Tower were an international crowd with more middle-aged and older people in it than young men and women. There were people from many parts of the world, and people of different colours. In the initial stages of our holiday, I didn't get to know anybody at all. It seemed to me that tourists were a special tribe of people who were more interested in places and spectacles than fellow human beings. We, too, were focused on places of interest rather than people. To be close to great human creations and historical achievements and wonder at our ancestors' creative genius is important, but how long does the effect of a few minutes in front of Mona Lisa last? I was thinking along these lines because the next day we were visiting the Louvre. Yet another source of frustration for me – and Tutu-da and Sudarsana – was that we didn't know the language – didn't have even a basic French vocabulary, let alone its grammar and syntax. No communication which was natural and spontaneous could happen between us and native speakers of French. I wouldn't settle in a country where my ability to communicate with people around me was really limited.

It was now quite clear that the few days we spent in Paris would be mostly away from the camp-site at Bois de Boulogne, which we'd leave immediately after breakfast, and where we'd return for a drink, and to compare our impressions before we went to bed.

We agreed that our day at the Eiffel Tower was full of surprises, because we had no idea about the kind of experience it was going to be. It was not so much what the Tower is as what it stands for; not what's in it but what's around it. But the Louvre, once the royal palace, was going to be different – a great building, with a great and famous museum – and we were looking forward to the experience.
It's a most spectacular building – the Louvre Palace – but what makes it so famous and important is the great art treasures it houses. The museum and the art gallery are situated on four sides of the Palace and house some great works of art, Venus de Milo and Mona Lisa, for example. We'd read up a little about the Louvre and I was immensely impressed; but what I saw when we were at the site was incomparably larger and more impressive than I'd imagined it to be. For example, I had no idea that it occupied an area of more than 650,000 square feet, or that it had existed as a national museum since the French Revolution. The status of the Louvre had changed several times. During the Republic, it was the people's museum. But with the return of the monarchy, it received royal patronage and built up a really great collection of art treasures. The Venus de Milo was added to the Louvre's collection during the reign of Louis XVIII. During the two world wars, the Louvre, like many other museums and art galleries in the world, wasn't able to add many great art treasures to its collection. But the end of the World War II saw the beginning of a resurgence of interest and creative enterprise in the art world from which the Louvre benefited; but to what extent exactly, I couldn't measure.

The collection at the Louvre was too large and occupied too many centuries for me to attempt a comprehensive account of my impressions of all that I saw. It was an experience which was exciting, but at the same time, there was a feeling of surfeit, of too much information and too many sensations jostling in my brain for accommodation. We'd started early. The time had passed quickly; and it was soon past lunch-time. I was too hungry to take in anything I declared, and we went looking for a place where we could have some lunch. After lunch we returned to the museum and at last I was standing within a few feet of the Mona Lisa, Leonardo da Vinci's painting in oil, completed at the beginning of the 16th century, viewed regularly by millions of visitors from all around the world, mostly with rapt attention and admiration. What did I really feel? I felt it was a great moment of my life because the experience was of the kind which made me part of the hundreds of millions of admiring spectators who had gazed in amazement at this oil portrait before me and the millions who would follow. It was, without doubt, a most beautiful and quite unique piece of painting, and by admiring it, by standing in front of it and gazing at it for the first time – and perhaps also the last – I'd become one of a great multitude of people who had experienced similar feelings. Certain feelings united us; it was one of them.

Another masterpiece was the ancient statue of Venus de Milo, carved by a Greek sculptor over 2,000 years ago, found on the Aegean island of Melos in 1820 – a piece of sculpture genuinely representative of the Hellenistic tradition.

The experience of wandering through the Louvre was a mixture of satisfaction and frustration. The fact that we could rest our gaze on the works of some of the world's greatest artists gave us a sense of fulfilment. The frustration arose from the fact that there was so much to see and admire and so little time. There were priceless, beautiful and timeless artefacts from Egypt, the Near East, Greece and Rome – statues of man and beast, caskets, carpets, textiles, stained glass panels. Never before had I been exposed to so much great art; never before had I felt so excited and exhilarated by visual experiences – and all that was within the walls of a building. But I couldn't take in any more: I was ready to return to our campsite at Bois de Boulogne. To stand in silence and admire *Venus de Milo*, the *Mona Lisa*, *The Lacemaker* and various works by the likes of Michael Angelo and Rembrandt should be more than enough for one day, and it was. The others were also ready to return to base – relax, discuss our experiences, compare notes, have some supper and go to bed. The next morning, we were going to visit the palace at Versailles.

When after driving through the great avenue of trees which led to the Versailles Palace, we arrived at our destination, I felt humbled by the majestic building which stood in front of me, and entranced by the beauty of the palace gardens. The kings of France in the 16th, 17th and 18th centuries certainly believed in thinking big. A symbol of royalty so aggressively ostentatious, so shamelessly exhibitionist, so defiantly selfish and self-indulgent, was hard to imagine. It was perhaps the brainchild of Louis XIII, but it was Louis XIV who shifted royal residence to the

Versailles Palace in 1688. Each room was lavishly decorated and contained art objects worth a king's ransom. Then there was the Hall of Mirrors, where huge mirrors, specially manufactured at huge expense, placed strategically, created a dazzling illusion of endless light and space. Generations of French citizens and millions of tourists had admired the extravaganza that the French monarchs indulged in until perhaps the French Revolution called into question the morality of such mindless, dazzling, wasteful and exploitative high-living. Marie Antoinette's question, 'Why don't they eat cake?', in retrospect, was tragically funny, but I'm fairly certain that the grim reality behind her singular naiveté was that she really had no conception of real poverty. The queen was as much a victim of the institutionalised inequality and injustice as anybody else in the sense that she was born into it; she didn't create it. If you or I were born into a rich, profligate and self-indulgent family, the chances are that we wouldn't ooze the milk of human kindness. Buddha was born nearly 2500 years ago.

The French aristocracy, which ought to have known better, completely ignored the possibility of a backlash to their way of living and thinking. They continued to use their wealth and power to further pillage and plunder, without ever seriously considering the possibility of lifting people out of poverty and creating a just society. In other words, things weren't a lot better there then than in most countries of the world today. If Louis XIV, XV, or XVI had heard in the cry of misery of every man and child the mind-forged manacles that Blake talked about, the French Revolution might not have happened. It is interesting that William Blake was a contemporary of the French Revolution. It is appropriate, I think, to wonder whether there's a connection between the certainty of omnipotence that absolute power engenders in our rulers and the revolutions which follow. Without the Louis's, would the French Revolution have happened? Without the Stuart Kings, would Oliver Cromwell have played such a significant role in the history of Britain's parliamentary democracy?

Although Louis XIII initiated the project, it was Louis XIV 'the Sun King', who was credited with the creation of the Palace of Versailles. Louis XV and Louis XVI were also beneficiaries. They also made their contribution. They also lived there, in the palace with the famous Hall of Mirrors, with its huge state apartments and more than 2,000 rooms; its immense park and gardens. Were these and other historical characters looking down at us, wondering what we were doing there? For the first time since my arrival in Paris, I had a real awareness of this city's past and found myself quietly contemplating the impact that the city of Paris had made on European history. Various European sovereigns were inspired by the Versailles Palace and the Hall of Mirrors. Some of them had even tried to copy both the

Palace and the Hall of Mirrors. In January 1871, Bismarck was in the Hall of Mirrors, after France's defeat in the Franco-Russian war, to gloat, to add insult to injury. The Treaty of Versailles at the end of World War I between the Allies and the Germans was also signed in the Palace of Versailles – in 1919.

There are places in the world – a city, a village, an open field, a graveyard, a palace, a monument – where we, temporarily, feel part of history; we feel the ebb and flow of world events. We become citizens of the world. That's how I felt in Versailles.

At the Palace of Versailles, we were overwhelmed by the sheer size and expanse of the place, the magnitude and the magnificence. The most impressive aspect of the palace for me was, that despite the size of the buildings and the gardens, and the huge sum of money spent on it, I didn't find anything loud and vulgar. Nothing grated on my aesthetic nerves. The question buzzing in my head was how the same kind of morality evolved among the really rich and powerful families all over the world – Shajahan in India was no more concerned about the poor and the destitute than Peter the Great was worried about the homeless and starving in Russia. Nor was Louis XIV aware that he was probably creating a condition which would get out of hand and that desperate people would commit desperate acts of violence, the like of which France had never witnessed before.

After returning to the camp-site at the end of our foray into places of historic and aesthetic interest, we'd go to one of the modest eating places and compare our reactions during the day's outing. By and large, the areas of disagreement were small. We were all immensely impressed with the avenue lined with beautiful ancient trees which led to the Palace of Versailles. We were all in favour of the rich creating beauty for the world to enjoy – beauty that is visual or intellectual. What we disapproved of was the ruthless exploitation of labour which was an integral part of the great monuments and buildings which have withstood the ravages of time, and still fill us with wonder, admiration and awe – Stonehenge, the Pyramids, the Coliseum, the Taj Mahal, the Parthenon, the Alhambra, St. Peter's Cathedral. There was, however, an absence of consensus over whether the end justified the means. We also argued about whether it was exploitation at all, if those who laboured on the sites of ancient buildings and memorials and places of worship considered themselves fortunate to have the opportunity to build great edifices, and, at the same time, earn enough to keep themselves fed and sheltered, and warm in winter.

Tutuda didn't get too involved in these discussions. When he got dragged into an argument, he rarely became agitated. Sudarsana was quite firm in her beliefs, less prepared to compromise than anyone else. I did get agitated, but I believed that I wasn't inflexible. Joy trod the middle path. She was neither on the side of privilege nor for revolution. Every dispute under the sun, she believed, could be settled by sitting around a table, if only people tried long enough and hard enough. If there was a leader in the team it was Joy. Here in Paris, I don't know what we would have done without her. She was a good leader – except that we had no leader as such. She would have objected, I suspect, if we had called her the leader, or even treated her too obviously as the leader.

It was Joy who interrupted our discussion about the rich and the poor and suggested that we spend the next day at Montmartre. Montmartre is a hill which gave its name to the surrounding district. We agreed it was a good idea to visit the district for many reasons. Montmartre belonged more to the present than did the Palaces of Louvre and Versailles. We'd so far seen Paris by day. Our visits to the Eiffel Tower, the Louvre and Versailles were between nine o'clock in the morning and five o'clock in the evening. But Montmartre <u>had</u> to be visited for its night life. So we decided to leave our camp-site early and return late the following day. We'd visit the Sacre Coeur on top of Montmartre hill and admire its white dome during the day and at night try and get some idea of the much-talked-of night-life at Montmartre – without spending a lot of money.

The white-domed Sacre Coeur was a most memorable sight – tall, white and prominent against a clear blue sky, on top of Montmartre hill, away from the thousands of buildings on the plains below, emphasizing its solitary majesty. We found some artists painting away, producing impressive paintings. I was tempted to buy one or two, but I had to remind myself that we had no money for such indulgences. We hung around the place, not only because of its spectacular surroundings but also because of its history. The famous cabaret, the Moulin Rouge, was here. It was well-known, Joy said, that world-famous artists – Modigliani, Dali, Monet, Picasso and Vincent van Gogh had all, at one time or other, lived and worked here. Montmartre was certainly more representative of modern Paris than any other place that we'd visited. So we were trying to get the feel of the place by roaming the streets, doing some window-shopping, buying small gifts, having coffee at a roadside cafe. What was important was that we'd switched over to contemporary Paris from its historical past. We wandered around, quite aimlessly, looking at people, and window-shopping, and speculating about whether Vincent van Gogh and Henri Matisse, Pierre-Auguste Renoir, Edgar Degas and Henri de Toulouse-Lautrec had walked the same streets as us, eaten at the same restaurants, shopped at the same shops and looked up at the same sky. I got a thrill out of imagining that they probably had. The years that separated us didn't seem to matter. Would I ever return to Paris again, I who was born in Bangladesh, grew up in Calcutta and was teaching in Africa? Our few days in Paris certainly gave us the feeling of unfinished business, a feeling quite common, I think to tourists. A week, even a month, wouldn't be sufficient to take away the feeling that we hadn't really got into the spirit of the place. A feeling of regret, of dissatisfaction, of vulgar haste was inevitable. We all knew Montmartre by reputation. It was the place, outside the city, where a deviant culture flourished and artists had congregated to celebrate life, often in their deviant ways. We were intrigued, fascinated, but I can't pretend that I'd discovered during the day anything that was particularly extraordinary.

Physically and mentally exhausted, I returned to our camp at Bois de Boulogne. We'd spent more time and walked more miles at Montmartre, than at any other place that we had visited since arriving in Paris. That night, I distinctly remember, we didn't stay up very long comparing our impressions of Montmartre and planning our visit to Notre Dame de Paris the next day. I knew very little about church architecture. Joy had told us a little about the Notre Dame Cathedral. Its place was very high in the hierarchy of cathedrals. The architecture was Gothic; it had been damaged during the French Revolution but later restored to its former glory. The construction of this famous cathedral started towards the latter part of the twelfth century but wasn't completed before about the middle of the fourteenth. That was, I thought, some kind of record in cathedral building. The fame of Notre Dame Cathedral was so great and its size, beauty and history so impressive that I felt overwhelmed when I first looked at it as I was approaching it. It was a good thing, I thought, that there have always been people – in different cultures and countries – who weren't afraid to think big. I was overwhelmed as I looked at the cathedral from a distance and then at close quarters. But my admiration was uninformed. I had only elementary knowledge of church architecture, so Joy filled me with admiration when she very naturally and casually used words like apse, transept and nave. We saw the famous organ which, I was told, had a few thousand pipes. And this great organ had attracted great organists. The cathedral also received the wrong kind of attention: statues were beheaded during the French Revolution and church furniture set alight during the Paris Commune. But now it stood there, more than 600 years after its construction, magnificent and serene, without any battle scars, without any visible signs of the impact of wars, revolutions – and time.

Then there were the celebrated bells of Notre Dame – one of them weighed more than 13 tons and tolled to mark the hours of the day, and some special occasions. Apart from this bell, there were four other bells which were rung to mark services and festivals. Sudarsana and I were especially interested in the bells because of Victor Hugo's *The Hunchback of Notre Dame*, which we'd read when we were still at school and were moved by the story of Quasimodo's unrequited love for beautiful Esmeralda. Quasimodo, we remembered, was the bell-ringer of the Cathedral, a hunchback, immensely strong and incredibly ugly, who lived a lonely life in the cathedral – the bells and statues his only companions. His loneliness was temporarily relieved by Esmeralda but it all ended tragically.

There might have been other places of interest that we visited, but nothing of major importance. The daily schedule of frenetically moving from one important, historical, artistic site to another was beginning to affect us all. There was too much to see, experience, register and understand, so a little weariness was setting in. Then, after Paris, there were so many places to visit, so much to do! Normally I'd feel excited, but after returning from the Cathedral, I had a strange feeling of being disconnected. Was this the loneliness of the long distance runner? The last day in Paris, we decided, we'd spend in Bois de Boulogne, talking about our experiences so far, and planning the next leg of the journey.

It was almost a year that we had been separated from our three children. When we were on our own, Sudarsana and I speculated about how they'd adjusted to their environment, especially Aparajita and Nondon. Aparajita left Calcutta when she was just a little older than one, and Nondon went to live with his grandparents when he was, similarly, a little older than one. There were times when I'd have to deal with Sudarsana's moist eyes.

In the middle of being exposed to a new and exciting world, my mind would travel to Golf Club Road, Tollygunge, Calcutta, where my three children were being looked after by their grandparents. Did Nondon remember me? Aparna and Aparajita, I'm sure, thought about us, and wondered when we were going to meet up again. But had we become strangers to Nondon? Would he leave his grandparents with reluctance and apprehension? We didn't have similar anxiety about our two daughters, although when we left Calcutta, Aparna was unhappy about leaving her grandparents and had, at least on two occasions, demanded an explanation from us why it was necessary for us to leave Calcutta and go and live in a country where she wouldn't be able to see Didibhai and Dadubhai. We didn't talk about our two daughters and Nondon very often because of the feeling that it was futile to do so. Thinking about them was a source of pleasure, being so far apart, a source of pain.

'You must be missing the children,' Joy would say.

'Yes, I am,' Sudarsana would say.

'Now it's just a matter of weeks,' Joy would say.

'Yes, 46 days,' Sudarsana would say.

Quite early in the morning of the next day, the day after our visit to Montmartre, we left for Zurich. We were visiting Zurich, not because it was the largest city in Switzerland, but because of various other reasons. One of those reasons was that someone we had got to know in Finchley Central lived there. Susie was the girlfriend of a young Bengali, Manab, who also lived in Finchley Central, and Sudarsana and I had got to know them. Susie had said she would be in Zurich when we visited there and she'd like to put us up. So we were on our way to Zurich through the most picturesque terrain – the Swiss Alps – the beauty and majesty of which isn't easy to describe. We were all quiet, looking out of windows at what was around and above us. I do remember that I was entranced, but I've no clear memory of exactly what it was that so completely held my attention.

What I do remember is that Tutu-da slowed down the car and then stopped. The steep climb in low gear was heating up the engine. Tutu-da opened the bonnet letting out an outburst of smoke. The water was boiling. He left the bonnet open to let the engine cool down and stopped passing cars to enquire whether there was a garage anywhere around where we could take the car to check whether there was any serious, mechanical problem. It was the driver of the third or fourth car who gave us relevant information and directed us to a small garage not far from there. He spoke fluent English so Tutu-da could discuss the problem with him... It wasn't anything serious, they decided, but this very helpful man directed us to a garage.

After the engine had been attended to, we continued in the direction of Zurich. We drove on through terrain so beautiful that it seemed unreal, especially the snow-clad mountains and mountain peaks. When we arrived in Zurich, we met up with Susie at an appointed place and then followed her to her flat on the outskirts of Zurich. It was a modest flat, spotless, everything in its place, without the slightest suggestion of clutter. The idea was that she would sleep that night in her all-purpose room – dressing room, study and small library – let Tutu-da and Joy have her bedroom for the night, and offer us the floor of the living room. There was no problem. We had an adequate supply of sleeping bags.

It was pleasant to meet up with Susie because we could talk about London and Manab and the landlord at Finchley Central, Asher Tropp and his wife, Lyn Tropp. She said she'd enjoyed being in London; the Tropps were formal with them but never unpleasant. Manab had gone back to India for personal reasons, but would return in a few weeks. They were thinking of getting married as soon as legal formalities were completed. Manab's wife had no objection to a divorce. Actually, she wanted one; the sooner the better. It was a welcome change for all of us to shift our attention from the impersonal to the personal, from history, art, architecture and sculpture to people we knew and found interesting. Susie had made up her mind to settle in Calcutta. It was now a question of time. Now, talking about time, we decided that we shouldn't miss the opportunity of looking around this illustrious city and we should start at once. So we put our heads together and decided to get some idea and carry some images of this beautiful city back with us in our heads. We had only to look around to discover the most enticing and memorable features of Zurich - its woods and hills, and the River Limmat and Lake Zürich, which is its source. We drove alongside the river, taking in as much as we could of this wonderful city. We'd set aside very little time for Zurich, for the next day we were setting out for Innsbruck.

We'd developed an addiction for roaming around city streets in Montmartre and we did a lot of that on that day in Zurich. The backdrop of magical mountains, the church spires and scores of beautiful buildings, trees and gardens made wandering the city streets a memorable experience.

We took Susie out to an upmarket restaurant in Zurich, which she had to choose for us. The food was excellent and the atmosphere friendly, and we ate, talked and laughed in that restaurant in Zurich one late afternoon in the summer of 1955, feeling relaxed, interested in living. I was glad that I wasn't rushing around this city – although it was so spectacular and though the time we'd spent in Zurich was absurdly short, we had no regrets because we had decided that we'd look at the famous buildings and museums from outside, and when we came the next time, we'd explore all the treasures that they contained. When the next time was going to be, we had yet to decide.

Susie was tall, even by European standards, with shoulder-length brown hair, which she often tied up in a pony-tail. She was naturally attentive during a conversation, in which she participated with honesty and clarity, and without intellectual pretension. But when she got involved in the subject, she was usually well-informed. What Susie had to say about the Swiss – the people and the culture – was both amusing and interesting.

Susie had met Manab at a friend's house two years ago, and for most of the time since then, they'd been partners. Manab was married. He'd gone back to India to get his divorce. Susie was waiting to join him when he wrote to her that he'd done all that he needed to do and it was now both appropriate and convenient for her to go there and start her new life in chaotic Calcutta, about which she didn't know a great deal, apart from what Manab had told her.

'And what has he told you?' I asked.

'Manab feels good in Calcutta. It's overcrowded. Certain areas are quite dirty and noisy. The weather can be beastly – hot, wet and sticky. We're at least five times more likely to fall ill in Calcutta than in Zurich...'

'All that is true, an honest and truthful description,' I interrupted. 'But it's not the whole truth.'

'I know it's not. Manab says that it is warm, friendly and human. Some good poets, musicians, film-makers and scientists have lived, worked and died there. I'm really hoping to live in Calcutta from this winter,' Susie said, with obvious enthusiasm.

'Manab's comments are entirely fair. I do hope you like it there, get into the spirit of Calcutta,' I said.

Sudarsana and Tutu-da also made their comments. Joy was interested in the same way as Susie. Two women, one from London, another from Zurich, were going to make Calcutta their home, the reason being their love for two Bengali men from Calcutta, which for many Western men and women, has been for a long time, the city of slums, starving children and Mother Theresa. After Susie had told a little about the way she felt about going to live in Calcutta, Joy told us about her mother's reaction to the news that Tutu had proposed marriage and she had accepted.

'How well do you know this young man?' she'd asked.

'I know Tutu well enough to love, respect and trust him entirely,' Joy had said.

'All your love and trust may not be enough to live in a city like Calcutta,' Joy's mother had said. She'd probably heard about the Black Hole of Calcutta and the Great Bengal Famine and the race riots of the forties.

'I am getting married and I am going to Calcutta this summer,' Joy had said.

'So be it,' Joy's mother had reacted with resignation, and then she'd become quite detached: 'Please remember that you have my blessings but *not* my approbation...'

The next morning we left for Innsbruck, bright and early, driving through landscapes of extraordinary beauty: the ubiquitous, snow-capped Alps turned everything for miles around into something bright and beautiful.

'I suggest that you take over. I find what's around distracting,' Tutu-da said.

'Yes, of course. You should really relax and look before it all disappears,' I said.

I was glad to be of use. Joy and Sudarsana were looking out at the glory of the Alpine environment with rapt amazement.

When we set out from Zurich, our main destination was Innsbruck, Austria, capital of Tirol, known for its enthralling beauty as well as its history and culture. But we couldn't have negotiated nearly 850 miles in one day – the new *autobahn* and the *Europa Brücke* hadn't been built yet – so we must have spent the night of the first day in a hotel on the country road – and started off the next morning, although hotels were places we usually avoided because of our lean purse. We arrived at the camp-site in Innsbruck quite late. We registered at the office, put up our tents, ate at the camp-site restaurant and were ready to retire for the night. We chatted briefly about the sylvan surroundings, the Alpine background, the charm, the entrancing, exhilarating effect of the place on us and then went to bed.

It wasn't for long that we were able to sleep or dream. We'd noticed earlier that the wind in the trees was somewhat stronger than usual but hadn't taken much notice of it. We hadn't once thought that there was a storm brewing. But there was. At about two o'clock in the morning a storm raged and nearly blew my small nylon tent away. The rain came down in torrents and before that there was a clap of thunder and flashes of lightening. There was something incongruous about this tropical rain and storm with the Alps looming in the background. Clutching our sleeping bags and our money, we ran, not very fast, through the pouring rain, to the camp-site office where other campers had also assembled. We appreciated the hot coffee provided by the manager. Most of the campers opted for something stronger.

One of the by-products of the unseasonal storm was that all the holidaymakers at the site converged towards the solid brick built office and were, for the first time, able to meet up with each other, communicate, share a joke and get an idea who the others were. There was a sense of camaraderie. Groups of three or four people were talking agitatedly about the unexpected onslaught of the storm which was still raging quite noisily outside our closed doors. The noise generated by these different clusters of people speaking different languages was like the Tower of Babel, because people generated a lot of noise but didn't understand each other. There was a group of Swiss people to whom we were drawn because they spoke English. They were surprised that we were in Zurich and hadn't visited places which are their pride and joy. Did we see the clock face at St Peter's church, the largest in the world? How could we spend two days in Zurich and not visit *Kunsthaus Zurich*, where we could see original Picassos and Braques? The questions came thick and fast. We liked these fellow travelers.

The storm had gone. The heavy rain was replaced by a slight drizzle. Everyone was leaving for their tents to check the damage and salvage whatever wasn't beyond repair. The damage, as a matter of fact, was far from catastrophic. A day of summer sunshine would take care of the soggy clothes and dry the ground in and around our tents. We could start living as if nothing had happened: that was the consensus. Now we were sufficiently relaxed to look back and discuss the drama on the very first day of our arrival. What we found incongruous was the tropical storm and rain in this popular Alpine resort, and perhaps for the first time during the first week of our holiday, we had a sense of adventure. We'd weathered the storm.

Now we put our heads together to decide where we were going to go, what we were going to do. The frenetic pursuit of too many objectives, especially when the time was limited, would be counter-productive. That was how Tutuda reflected. So we set out to carefully consider how we were going to spend our time. Innsbruck, capital of Tyrol, is in a valley, surrounded by snow-capped mountains. For a true lover of natural beauty, it would be enough to stand in the valley and look at the magnificent mountain peaks all around. But we wanted to do a little more than that, because the city, especially the old city, was full of great historical buildings as well as elegant, modern ones. A lot of the time, we drove round the city looking at houses, shops, office buildings and historic mansions. We also walked about, stopping to eat, shop, watch people – local people as well as tourists. The tourists were distinguishable from local people, I thought, by the clothes they wore, their cameras and the way they looked, which signified a seriousness of purpose – although there were exceptions.

Some people – like me – also must have looked lost. I had a habit of looking and feeling lost. What impressed me most was some of the old buildings, the names of which I couldn't pronounce at the time and now can't remember. Then there were always the Alps in the background. I must have seen the Golden Roof. Everyone who visits Innsbruck must see the Golden Roof, but I don't clearly remember having seen it. The impression I carried in my head when I left Innsbruck was that of an extremely tidy, modern city with beautiful old buildings everywhere, especially in the old city centre. One of the most remarkable aspects of Innsbruck was that modernity hadn't affected the natural old-time beauty and charm of the place. Our camp-site, with green grass below and blue sky above, the tall trees and the Alpine background was a place of natural beauty and charm in a plateau above the valley. There were many villages around the city like that in the valley and above it. We all thanked Joy, the mastermind of our trip, for bringing us to Innsbruck while we had supper at the camp-site restaurant and discussed our plans for Italy. Early next morning we were to set out for Florence.

Our Poor Little Rabbit, the Morris Minor, stood up to the punishing schedule very well. It wasn't the car but the drivers and passengers that were showing signs of wear and tear. Although we were driving through beautiful Alpine country most of the time, weariness would set in and we'd stop the car, sometimes to look at the scenery of breathtaking beauty and sometimes to get out into the fresh air, to have a cup of coffee at a roadside cafe, or just to stretch our legs. I felt important –and useful - when Tutu-da let me drive. I'd by now driven many more miles on the right of the road than I had on the left because I'd only driven short distances through crowded streets in an urban environment while I was in England. Here distances were long. It would've been heroic if Tutu-da had done all the driving, heroic and dangerous. I'd already gained a great deal in confidence, which meant I was much less tense compared to how I was at the beginning, and was therefore enjoying the experience much more. It was a beautiful summer in Europe that year. We were all enjoying the sunny, crisp and warm days and the beautiful environment. The distances we'd planned to cover on those winding country roads were formidable. We had to spend the occasional night in a hotel. It's just not realistic to attempt to chronicle everything we did, every place big or small that we visited, every interesting encounter that we had during our holiday. So I or my memory has had to make a natural selection.

I'll start with *Firenze* or Florence. Starting back from Innsbruck, once again, we drove through terrain that was as exhilarating as it was spectacular. If it hadn't been for a lean purse, lack of time and the fact that we were eagerly waiting to meet up with our three children, Sudarsana's parents and my father, my brothers and sisters, we would have wanted to spend more time in Europe, especially this part of Europe, which had everything – snow, mountains, rivers; tall, elegant and leafy trees; the green of the forests, the blue of the sky. Although many of the cities of Europe also had a great attraction for once-in-a-lifetime tourists like us – cities like

Paris, Zurich, Florence, Rome, Pisa, Venice, Trieste and Istanbul – and London... I still looked back on our time in London and regretted not having seen and done enough to have felt part of that great metropolis. I wished I'd gone to Hyde Park and listened to some fiery lectures ; visited the Globe Theatre; watched some plays at Stratford and elsewhere; stood in a corner of Oxford Street and watched the people, so fascinatingly diverse. pass by.

Now we were in Florence; great Italian city, the capital of Tuscany, famous for, among other things, its Renaissance art and architecture; its ruling family, the Medici and their palaces and gardens; the Duomo, the domed cathedral, and the River Arno. First of all, we said to ourselves, it was a most memorable event – our being in the city the name of which we would always associate with those of Dante, Galileo, Michelangelo, Boccaccio, Botticelli, Leonardo da Vinci and Raphael. Their work all lay around us, but of course, we had to find it, though we couldn't see it all. We had to select. We put our heads together and decided that we'd visit the cathedral, Santa Maria del Flore (the Duomo), gaze at Michelangelo's David, spend some time at the Uffizi Gallery and visit a palace and a museum or two. A lot of the time we'd roam the streets and get the feel of the city. And to get the feel of the city, it would also be a good idea to drive across the Ponte Vecchio, the bridge on stilts on the edges of which were a large number of shops.

I think we managed to do what we wanted to do, see what we wanted to see – by and large. Like millions of others before us, we gazed with reverence and admiration at the famous dome, an architectural achievement of many centuries ago, the Duomo. We also went to Ponte Vecchio and mingled with the window-shoppers, most of them tourists like us. Then we were in the *Academia* and it was difficult for me for a time to believe it was all real; that it was really me and it was really Michelangelo's David that I stood in front of. Then at the Uffizi, we were surrounded by a collection of art treasures the like of which few art galleries or museums in the world would dare to dream of – Giotto, Botticelli, Leonardo da Vinci, Michelangelo, Donatello, Raphael and others. They were all priceless. Any one of them would cost more than a king's ransom – in the unlikely event of any of the paintings or sculptures ever being offered for sale. They are part of our heritage – not just Italian. There were other places of interest also which we must have visited, explored, found exciting, but they've dimmed and disappeared. There was one activity we all enjoyed – roaming the streets of the towns we visited: London, Paris, Zurich, Innsbruck and now Florence. It's not at all unusual to find people of more than a dozen nationalities in any of the streets of these cities. They speak different languages, dress differently and have their different cultures. But they all have a common objective – to explore other cultures, discover a common human identity. Tourists seemed a happy bunch of people. The summer sun helped.

Our budget just wouldn't rise to our staying in a hotel, or even a modest bed-and-breakfast place. We'd find accommodation either on a camp-site or in a youth hostel. We stayed in a youth hostel, where a hot shower was available at no extra expense; where the food was good. We met some Italians as well as non-Italians to talk to and exchange ideas with. There is, at any given time, a multitude of people floating around the globe: some watching the vast mass of cascading water of the Niagara Falls at the Canadian-US border; some gazing at the magic marble mausoleum of the Taj Mahal in Agra, Northern India, uniquely commemorating marital love; some visiting the tomb of Tutankhamen in the Valley of the Kings in Egypt, or looking up at the amazing pyramids at El Giza near Cairo. This large and various population, interested in other countries, other people and their cultures, promote our vision of one world. I liked being a tourist, I liked being part of a nation without a country, being in motion, being rootless and restless, looking out for the next surprise, the next sensation – which for us was going to be Rome.

All day we went from one tourist landmark to another – looking, learning, admiring, storing information in our head. In the evening, when we had our big meal of the day, we sat and chatted and compared our reactions to various buildings, paintings, sculptures and other landmarks. If anything out of the ordinary happened, to any or all of us that too came up for comment. Sudarsana had been briefly accosted by an Italian, a young man who wanted to know how she managed to wind round her 'such a long and wide piece of cloth' – by which he meant her sari. She'd said that Camillo Cavour was hardly the place to give a demonstration, but she explained the mystery verbally as clearly as she could. He thanked her, but didn't go away.

'I was getting slightly alarmed,' she said. She'd heard the same as us, that Italian tricksters were cool customers who committed fraudulent acts in the streets of Florence, Rome, Venice, Milan, Pisa and other large cities and small towns, tourist attractions, with sophisticated skill. Their methods of deception were so artistic that one might consider it a privilege to be their victim.

'Would you mind terribly if I asked you another question?' the young man said.

'Go ahead,' she said.

'Do Indian women wear underwear beneath their saris?'

'Some do and some don't. Most Indian women don't. At least, I don't think they do,' Sudarsana replied.

The young man had thanked her and then melted into the crowd. We wondered whether it was that young man's response to the challenge thrown out by some of his friends. Being teachers, both Sudarsana and I were sympathetic to young people and weren't thrown by this bit of what was, in those days, decidedly impertinence.

We often went our separate ways and then compared notes when we met up. Tutu-da had met a young Italian with whom he'd had a comprehensive discussion about Italian cars. This must have been interesting for him because he had a possessive lust for Italian cars. Joy had done some essential shopping. And *I* had been conned. A pleasant, smiling, friendly young Italian had sold me a Parker 51 a prized fountain pen in the fifties, before the advent of the ballpoint advertising give-aways. I'd wanted one of those for a long time, but couldn't afford the price. So when I was able to buy one at half the price, I thought I'd done well – only to discover that, although it looked like a Parker 51, it was a completely useless fake.

By now we'd done what we'd wanted to do and seen all we'd wanted to see, or could afford to see in Florence, and were ready for a new destination – Rome, the eternal city. Rome in 1955 was a city where revolutionary changes were happening everywhere. This was more than ten years after the fall of Rome to the Allies in 1944. The Romans had shaken off the humiliation of defeat and were now busy transforming their lives on both the economic and the cultural front. Rome was an exciting city in the past and it was an exciting city now, and we set off quite early in the morning in the direction of the capital of Italy, which, only a few centuries ago, was the most important city in Europe, the epicentre of the vast Roman Empire. Rome evoked images of wealth and power which few other cities did anywhere in Europe. We were looking forward to visiting some of the ancient monuments, Renaissance places, medieval churches, palaces and fountains. We hadn't made a list – we rarely did. The distance we were going to drive was 250 miles – give or take 20 – and most cars did it, I think, in less than five hours. We had a small car and we were slowed down by the large roof rack which carried some of our heavy luggage. We were in Rome about tea time, after having stopped briefly at Narni. Our first objective, almost always, was to find shelter – a youth hostel or a camp-site. We found a youth hostel, unloaded the car partially, set ourselves up, had some coffee and then went out for a walkabout and something to eat. We then returned to our rooms and discussed our plans for the following day. The unanimous and quite predictable decision was that, before we did anything else, we must visit the Sistine Chapel in the Vatican City, not for any religious reasons, but because it was a magnificent building and the frescoes by Michelangelo, Raphael and Botticelli have no parallels anywhere else in the world.

We went as planned, found the chapel and gazed spellbound at the building, restored from an older building towards the end of the 15th century. But the frescoes on the ceiling, the most amazing artistic achievement, were so vast and so incredibly beautiful that it was difficult to work out how exactly frescoes of such magnificent quality and immense proportions could have been painted – by some of the finest artists who have ever lived – Botticelli, Michelangelo, Raphael and Bernini. I'm thinking of the physical challenge and the strategy to overcome it. Michelangelo alone was supposed to have painted 12,000 square feet of the ceiling of the Sistine Chapel between 1508 and 1512. About 30 years before that, Botticelli had created frescoes which had to do with the life of Moses and the life of Christ. Joy was the most knowledgeable person in our group of four because she was interested and had lived in England and travelled in Europe. What artists like Michelangelo and Botticelli had achieved wasn't through artistic ability alone but also dedication and religious faith, I'd felt sure.

The Sistine Chapel, brick-built and rectangular, was a very impressive building, but I didn't know enough about church architecture and its different styles and traditions to appreciate its subtleties. I looked at the vaulted ceiling of the chapel and felt privileged to have the opportunity to have this great experience. This was the ceiling that Michelangelo took four or five years to paint. One always feels privileged on occasions like these – here I was in the presence of one of the most glorious examples of artistic conception and creation in the world, in the Vatican City in Rome, I who'd grown up in Calcutta and worked in a small town in Uganda!

We found out facts about these paintings, only some of which I remember. I'd also looked up reference sources. The famous paintings have to do with *God's Creation of the World, God's Relationship with Mankind* and *Mankind's Fall from God's Grace,* all completed by Michelangelo about 450 years ago. Some of the walls also have paintings created by great artists like Botticelli and they're even older. I thought of the millions of people killed in a war which had ended just ten years ago, a war in which more civilians had died than soldiers, and wondered how the same human animal can create the wonders of the Sistine Chapel, and fight a war in which more than 50 million people die as a direct result of ruthless, vengeful and murderous acts of aggression. It's a question which others have asked as well.

Although we'd read about Michelangelo's paintings on the ceiling of the Sistine Chapel, we knew very little of the great paintings on the walls, which were also unique, and compared favourably with those on the ceiling. A whole host of the top-ranking artists of the time had painted the walls. The only name that I was familiar with was Sandro Botticelli. The history of any one of the paintings at the Sistine Chapel would require the writing of a whole book. I found the whole experience totally riveting, quite overwhelming. We'd all been somehow humbled by our experience. It was much bigger than we'd expected. And what was our next experience going to be? The Colosseum was where we were bound for.

There were two reasons why our next stop had to be Rome: we were all interested in the Colosseum on account of its reputation as a significant symbol of the great Roman Empire; but also because Joy had booked seats for us at the open-air theatre at the Colosseum, also known as the Flavian Amphitheatre, where Verdi's opera, *Aida,* was going to be performed that evening. I had very little knowledge, experience or understanding of opera, but it was a chance of a lifetime and I was excited about it.

It was an incredible experience: sitting down under the open sky with many thousands of other spectators on one of the many semi-circular tiers which went up from the ground to a height of more than 150 feet, and listening to some of the world's most outstanding opera singers in one of Verdi's operas.

Because for me the opera was a new, and partly strange, experience, it didn't have the same impact on me as it did on Joy, who had grown up with it, and remembered having shed tears over Carmen's cruel fate when she was a girl. I think Joy and Sudarsana got more out of the opera than either Tutu-da or me.

Tutu-da wasn't particularly involved in art and literature. His main interests were science, surgery, medicine and motor cars. He was very human and helpful. His friendship meant a great deal to me, and his quiet confidence made me and others feel safe. Joy was also a natural leader and an efficient organiser whose foresight prevented our ever being caught on the wrong foot. Sudarsana was good with people, relaxed and friendly. She was largely in charge of the food and drinks department. My role was undefined. I was the relief driver. I would often run errands. I was in charge of keeping a diary – a job I did indifferently well. And oh, yes – I was also in charge of our money and documents.

The experience of the evening was *Aida* in the Colosseum Amphitheatre. During the day, we explored other areas around the Colosseum, Rome's most popular tourist attraction.   We gathered that Emperor Vespasian had started off the construction of the Colosseum, but at the time of his death it wasn't anywhere near completion: it had only reached the third level.   His son, Titus, completed the project, and his younger son, Domitian, added refinements, improvements and surprises.   The citizens of Rome loved spectacles and here was a spectacular building which was consciously created to be spectacular.   This is where gladiatorial fights took place, a mindlessly cruel sport, and here it was that the early Christians were martyred. The idea that a fight to the death between man and man, and between man and beast was a pleasurable sport, most exciting to behold, was accepted unquestioningly by millions of Roman citizens.   People raising serious objections might well have been thrown to the lions in the gladiatorial arena of the Colosseum.   Apart from being a building of massive proportions, a great engineering feat, a sports stadium to beat all sports stadiums, it was a monument to commemorate the power and the glory of Emperor Vespasian, founder of the Flavian Dynasty.

We learned a great deal that day and enjoyed the opera that evening. But when after dinner we sat down to mull over the events of the day, our body, the mortal frame, told us it had had quite enough. The next morning we discussed over coffee how best to use the last two days of our stay in Rome. While we went around looking at streets and buildings, monuments, museums and art galleries, there was in each of us the feeling that there was too much to do and too little time, a lethal combination which invariably led to a feeling of frustration. And at the end of our stay in a city like Rome – one of the most visited tourist destinations of Europe – there was also the feeling of unfinished business. So what could we do to still the voice within which kept saying, 'Do more! Stay longer!'? There was indeed a vast area of great and historic achievements by the Romans of old which we hadn't even set eyes on. Buildings representing the excellence of Renaissance architecture like *The Tempietto.*   There was *The Pantheon*, which went back to ancient times and the Mausoleum of Augustus.   There were also Medieval, Renaissance and Baroque buildings, which were popular tourist attractions.   I admired them for their architecture, the utilitarian dimension of art, which is of such great importance. A church has to be an appropriate place for prayer and a theatre, for the presentation of plays.   This fact was very efficiently demonstrated by the great architects of Rome.   We found names and listed them: *The Pantheon,* the *Quirinal Palace, Piazza del Campidoglio* and many others. What the brochure for tourists had was a formidable list. We decided that we'd visit the places that we'd listed. If we still had time we'd visit a few more sites – the city's parks and gardens, and probably some fountains and bridges. We'd have a quiet evening, and early next morning, we'd set out for Pisa, which was just over 160 miles away. Then we'd drive from Pisa to Venice – 150 miles or so. After that there was Trieste, a mere 72 miles.

Having pored over the map, and more or less worked out our itinerary, we were all exhausted, so we settled for another cup of coffee. In England the drink of choice was tea; in Italy, it was coffee: white and black coffee, iced coffee, cappuccino coffee. There was also Viennese coffee. I don't think Turkish coffee was either popular or universally available.

Before setting out on our last day's foray into the Eternal City at the end of our Roman holiday, I had a confession to make. I said to Joy – and Tutu-da and Sudarsana – that I knew very little about Italian architecture. Joy said she'd visited some of the cities before and had found out a little about the architectural styles which flourished in Rome and the other ancient cities of Italy. The style of architecture which went back to the fifth century, and was older than other styles, was the Byzantine, a mixture of the oriental and the classical. Then there were the Romanesque, Gothic, Renaissance, Baroque and Neo-Classical styles of architecture, one style chronologically following another every two or three centuries, with a significant amount of overlap. Renaissance architects like Brunelleschi, Michelangelo, Bramante and others had made outstanding contributions to the architecture of not only Italy but also of other countries. In the field of art also, Italy was streets ahead of other countries in Europe and elsewhere.

Our last day in Rome was going to begin later than we'd planned because we got caught up in the discussion about architectural traditions. We set out late morning to look our last on all things Roman. No, not all things but a building or two, gardens, public squares, a monument, a bridge and a famous approach road which would take us to St Peter's Square. We did all we wanted to do but, unfortunately, we weren't able to spend as much time at any of the places as we'd have liked to. One of Tutu-da's priorities was to drive through *Via della Conciliazione,* which takes you all the way from the River Tiber to St Peter's Square. We did that and found it a great experience. The Pantheon was another memorable experience, because it was, without doubt, one of the great monuments of ancient Rome. We skipped the medieval period, although it was replete with remarkable churches and towers, and drove on to the *Piazza del Campidoglio* by Michelangelo which, according to experts, is the most remarkable of the architectural creations during the Renaissance. We spent some time at the Monument of Vittorio Emmanuel II, had a quick look at the Villa Borghese and the gardens and, at some point, drove across the Bridge of Angels. I say in my account of our last day in Rome that these are places we visited, when I should really say these are the places which I seem to remember, think we must have seen or at least passed through.   What I do remember is that our last day in Rome was a most successful day, when we managed to do most of the things we wanted to do. We ate at an Italian restaurant, and returned to our base, exhausted but happy.

We were off again the nest day. Tutu-da was driving. I normally took over when we were well on our way to the destination, the wind in our sails and no storm brewing. By now I'd become quite used to driving on the right side of the road and registering road signs sufficiently in advance to act appropriately – with the result that I enjoyed driving much more than I did in the beginning. The roads were well laid-out and wide, well-lit and carefully sign-posted. So driving was made easy and comfortable, by and large. Yet when some large car overtook my little Morris Minor at great speed, I did still felt a little nervous, because I felt the car shake.

We arrived in Pisa soon after lunchtime and went to a restaurant and had a late lunch of pasta. I can't tell how many times since our arrival in Italy we'd had pasta for lunch and supper. The pasta is good in Italy. I was beginning to get addicted. Whether there is anything addictive is doubtful but there's something creative, something innovative about Italian pasta as its numerous names, shapes and sizes indicate.

Right now our destination was the Leaning Tower of Pisa; for as far as tourists like us were concerned all roads led to the Bell Tower of the city's cathedral square, in the Piazza del Duomo.

We stayed in a youth hostel, where a hot shower was available at no extra expense; where the food was good. We met some Italians as well as non-Italians to talk to and exchange ideas with. There's, at any given time, a multitude of people floating around the globe, some watching the vast mass of cascading water of the Niagara Falls at the Canadian-US border; some gazing at the magic marble mausoleum of the Taj Mahal in Agra, Northern India, uniquely commemorating marital love; some visiting the tomb of Tutankhamen in the Valley of the Kings in Egypt, or looking up at the amazing pyramids at El Giza near Cairo. This large and various population, interested in other countries, other people and their cultures, promote our vision of one world. I liked being a tourist; I liked being part of a nation without a country, being in motion, being rootless.

The Tower of Pisa was assaulted by wind and rain, partly destroyed, but fortunately, not bombed during World War II after all; the story goes that but for a visiting general who was impressed by its beauty and decided to spare it the planned heavy artillery attack, for it was a German military base at the time, it would have been blasted away. Years of study and consultation by engineers and scientists and architects and several years of stabilisation from 1989 onwards – when it was closed to the public – led to its progressive inclination being halted. It was repaired and opened to tourists and visitors in 2001 and now the devout can continue to believe that it is God's hand that's holding up the Leaning Tower of Pisa. It was a curious situation, we thought: some ancient engineer's lack of foresight in giving a 180 feet bell-tower a shallow foundation made it more famous than the magnificent cathedral of which it is the bell tower. We were privileged, we thought, that we were trudging up and down Piazza del Duomo or Piazza del Miracoli. Facing the main cathedral, a magnificent building, we found the Baptistry on the left of the main cathedral and the Leaning Tower on the right. Each building was an architectural achievement, the city's main cathedral being a really noble building, within the walls of which the Divine Presence would be most appropriate. We spent our time on the day we arrived in and around these buildings and the Piazza and then went looking for a place to stay.

I don't always remember whether we stayed in a youth hostel or a camp-site. Both kinds of accommodation were usually fine-tuned to the basic needs of the less affluent tourists, the majority of them students trying to make the most of their summer holidays by satisfying their desire for knowledge and adventure. We were older than most of them, but not so much older that we couldn't relate. Before visiting Pisa, I had no idea that Pisa was such an old city and its history went back to antiquity and is even mentioned in Virgil's Aeneid. It was an important Mediterranean port through which passed massive loads of merchandise, and where many historical battles were lost and won. For Pisa was a city state fighting other city states to ensure its survival, Genoa being one of them. There was a lot more history to learn, but a very superficial knowledge of Pisa's past was all we could hope to acquire. I was going to find out a lot more about Pisa's past once we stopped rushing around, I decided.

The churches in practically all important Italian cities were numerous and the architecture was, almost always, magnificent. If you asked me, 'How many churches did you see in Pisa?' I wouldn't be able to give you the exact number, but I'd say that they were numerous, many more per square kilometre than in London or Paris, some of them famous worldwide. What did we do in the three or four days which we spent in Pisa? We certainly went to Piazza dei Miracoli, but we also visited the Palazzo della Carovana, its facade designed by a famous architect, Giorgio Vasari, whose name I'd never heard before. We also visited the Church of St Francis and the Medici Palace.

We didn't visit any museums, because we'd found that going round a museum took much longer than visiting churches and palaces. In all of us there was a feeling that we'd have to leave behind a great deal of unfinished business because we could only reconnoitre, not research – the time was too short. If we spent the entire time that we'd allocated to this tour in just one of these splendid historical cities – Rome, Florence, Venice, Pisa, or Trieste – we'd still feel frustrated. So we decided that we'd do the best we could in the time that was left and not allow ourselves to feel frustrated: rejoice that we'd seen the palaces and the churches and the monuments round the ancient streets and squares; met some interesting people and eaten some delicious food – rather than moan about what we hadn't been able to do.

Having initiated ourselves into this philosophy, we set out the next day for Lake Garda, where nature rather than art and architecture would be centre stage. The three weeks or so which we'd spent in Europe had been taken up with learning about creative human achievements. What I'd found out, for example, about architecture, especially church architecture, was quite considerable compared to what I knew before. For the first time in my life, words like *font, lectern* and *nave, pew, pulpit* and *belfry* found their way into my conversation. After so much education and enlightenment, we needed to relax and Lake Garda was our next, and I thought, most appropriate, destination. We wanted to turn from the wonderful art, architecture and sculpture created by man to wonderful sites created by nature, and when we arrived at Lake Garda, we all marvelled at what lay in front of us – a magical expanse of water and magical mountains that seemed to rise out of the water of the lake, canopied by a clear blue sky, with white clouds floating around without purpose. We found a camp-site, and for the first time, we were able to slip into our swimming costumes. And we also had a feeling of relaxed well-being. Many more people were sunbathing than swimming or splashing about in the water, and on the shore of the lake, there was a friendly, civilised sense of togetherness. Some spoke English in sentence-fragments with accents which could be easily identified as foreign; some spoke their own languages – Spanish, German, Italian - using appropriate gestures and hoped for the best, and some spoke English excellently well. Sometimes in the evening, someone would sing in Italian, Spanish, German or English. More often a group of three or four would sing in a language which we didn't understand, but we enjoyed listening to these songs when the evenings were fairly warm and the sky above was blue. 1955 was a good summer and we were sitting by Lake Garda in Northern Italy and enjoying the company of other young people – friendly, generous people with an obvious love of life. One evening we sang a song in Bengali – Sudarsana and I – about life renewing, refreshing rain after a long drought which brought relief to all the tillers of the soil. The song was very popular. Sudarsana tried to teach the song – some young men and women were interested – and we were all amazed at how well they managed to sing it. Not all the words sounded like Bengali words, but that didn't take away from the competent rendering of the song. In short, Lake Garda had already turned out to be a completely different kind of experience, a very positive one. Sudarsana, for the first time ever, was wearing a swim-suit – not the more adventurous type – and sitting out in the sun, and so were we. Joy was used to wearing swimming costumes and sun-bathing, but none of the others were, including myself. We were young, with youthful bodies, so we were quite happy to sit exposed to the warm sun and the eyes of others, occasionally swimming in the not-so-warm water of the lake – not very warm but quite pleasurable after the initial shock. Anyway, what was important for me was lazing in the sun, getting to know a few fellow tourists, and briefly relating to people from different countries whom I didn't expect to see again.

One of the characters, an Italian, a young man called Tony, was a popular figure, especially with the women, because of his youthful charm and, more importantly, his youthful, athletic body. He was tall, bronzed by the sun, with a shock of brown hair and ripples of muscle in his bare torso: a young Jupiter wandering around on the beaches of Lake Garda. I thought Sudarsana was under his spell too. He, like Tutu-da, was interested in cars in general, and fast cars in particular, so they got on very well. He also managed to charm Sudarsana by asking her questions about arranged marriages, the very idea of which they both abhorred. What made Sudarsana really happy was Tony's interest – real or simulated – in Bharatanatyam – a style of dancing in which Sudarsana had considerable skill. So his presence among us was welcomed by Tutu-da and Sudarsana. Joy and I were fairly detached.

It was, I think, to the south of the lake that we spent our few days, totally relaxing – eating, swimming, sunbathing and behaving as if we had all the time in the world. We didn't seek education or enlightenment. We didn't even go anywhere near Sirmione on the south of the lake, which is visited by hordes of tourists on account of its spa complexes. Nor did we bother to drive to Gardaland, the famous theme park. The voice of the tourist said, 'Do not miss out on the opportunity to go to Sirmione. Drop everything and go to Sealiger Castle. The theme park in Gardaland is one in a million. You may not have the chance again to see it.' But we ignored the voice and ate at a nice restaurant, did some window shopping at fashionable stores, walked around some streets and a market and returned to base to get organised for a very early start the next morning – for Venice.

For anyone who'd come under the spell of Western culture, however briefly and inadequately, Venice would be a most attractive and romantic city to visit because of its numerous associations – historical, literary, technological. It is an ancient city that was rich, powerful and independent, and even today it is famous as a City of Water, City of Light, City of Bridges and City of Romance. When I first came into contact with Shakespeare, one of the plays I read was *The Merchant of Venice*. We'd all heard of this City of Water for other reasons as well. It is a nexus of 118 islands. When lights from these numerous islands are reflected in the very wide expanse of canal water in the evening, there's a spectacle the like of which, I am sure, can't be found in any other city in the world. It's beautiful, spectacular and romantic, but the most appropriate description is that it is unique. From the moment we entered Venice – we had driven just 100 miles from Lake Garda – we found it an incredible city. We had been told it was an incredible city. We had read many times that it was an incredible city. Yet, when we actually saw it, we were still surprised that a city like this could be conceived and constructed in such a difficult and watery terrain. The City of Water was at one time the refuge of Romans fleeing from invasions by Germans and Huns. It was inhospitable to people who wanted to live here, so the population was sparse. Its beginning as an independent city probably goes back to the second half of the eighth century, when the ducal seat was transferred to Venice, and the palace of the Duke was built and the basilica of St Mark. St Mark was the guardian saint of Venice and St Mark's Square was, perhaps, the most famous, most popular and important place in Venice, and our first destination. We organised accommodation, unloaded our luggage, consulted the warden of the youth hostel, and left for St Mark's Square and St Mark's Basilica.

We went by gondola to St Mark's Square, which was the principal Venetian square, very important and very large. I didn't know how large, but I did know it was by far the largest in Venice. In this piazza or square, human voices could be heard all around; warm human voices, matter-of-fact human voices, excited human voices. There were thousands of pigeons, occasionally making their characteristic noises, but in St Mark's Square it was predominantly the human voice that one heard, without any interference from machine-made noises, which one heard when travelling through the waterways. The square was unique, pulsating with life. Pigeons were all over the place. There was St Mark's Basilica, an outstanding example of Venetian architecture. There were superb restaurants, fashionable shops and beautiful buildings. But if I had to give it a name, I'd call it the People's Square, because wherever I looked there were people – women, men and children; Russian, German, American, Indian, French and Italian – basking in the sun, playing with children, reading the newspaper, sight-seeing with single-minded determination or just relaxing.

We went to eat at a restaurant which didn't look too expensive. We enjoyed the food. Sudarsana caused some amusement by mistaking some special pickle for a main dish and eating it all up. When the waiter first found the entire bowl of pickle empty, consternation was written all over his face. Then Sudarsana told him how much she'd enjoyed the side dish. The waiter spoke fairly good English. He asked Joy what had happened to the bowl of pickles.

'I ate it all. It tasted very good,' Sudarsana answered.

'But it was a pickle. It was hot and pungent, to be eaten a little at a time with food,' said the waiter. At least that's what he seemed to mean, when he spoke excitedly with lots of gestures.

'I like hot and pungent food. So I thought it was a side dish and ate it all,' Sudarsana said, not a bit apologetic.

The waiter laughed. He was amused and a little surprised; but not shocked. A waiter at a restaurant in St Mark's Square met all sorts of people, encountered all kinds of eccentricities. He couldn't afford to lose his sense of humour. He said he was impressed. He wouldn't be able to eat more than a spoonful of that stuff with his dinner.

The sunshine and Chianti made me sleepy. I sat on a bench and watched the people – an international crowd with a few locals. I think I was by now able to distinguish the Italians from the others. Most of the young women, it was my impression, were Italian. There were quite a few Germans and Americans. Italy, I thought was a great tourist attraction for the British also. I don't remember having seen people from my sub-continent. While watching, I must have fallen asleep. Someone was ruffling my hair.

'Wake up,' Sudarsana was saying. The siesta time is over. You're in St Mark's Square in Venice and it's the chance of a lifetime.'

'What am I missing?' I asked. 'I'm making the most of the occasion. How many people in India and East Africa are you likely to meet who have snoozed in St Mark's Square in Venice?'

The world-famous St Mark's Basilica, she explained, was a Byzantine architectural masterpiece, which had required centuries of dedicated and inspired work to complete. If I didn't visit this Basilica and failed to be inspired by its spectacular domes, its famous facade, its paintings and mosaics, I'd have proved that I was the greatest Philistine around. Sudarsana was forceful and I, vulnerable. I went into the Basilica with the others, and I <u>was</u> impressed, but I can't really recall the details of my experience. But I was glad I'd visited the Basilica.

Now the Square was beautiful with lights, people and shops, and a summer sky above. So this was St Mark's Square in Venice, and I was there with my wife and friends, and people from all over the world milling around us. We went around and visited a few shops. We might have bought a few items here and there, before we visited a small shop where a motherly-looking middle-aged lady with a smiling aspect and cheerful temperament was selling mementos. We'd already bought a few souvenirs in Florence and Rome but we had an appetite for more. I bought some replicas of Venetian gondolas for the children. I also bought a few other modest gifts. There were many attractive items, but I had little money. The smiling lady talked the others into buying a few touristy items. I paid – I carried the money and documents in a bag from which I never allowed myself to be separated.

It was a pleasant evening; the moon was out; and it was reflected in the canal water. The smart, young gondolier rowed us back to the other shore of the canal from where we'd left in the morning. The gondolier, in his fairly adequate English despite the Italian accent, was giving us a running commentary on the environment through which we were passing. He'd point to one building and tell us that Shylock had lived there. He'd also point to a veranda and say Othello had paced up and down there before strangling Desdemona to death. I wasn't quite sure whether he expected us to take him seriously. We arrived at the point of the canal where we had to alight. We thanked the gondolier and I looked for the special bag where I kept money and documents, and from which I wouldn't allow myself to be separated at any time. Hotels, camp-sites and youth hostels provided facilities for the safe-keeping of documents, but I'd volunteered to take care of them, and had so far caused no anxiety. There was, as a matter-of-fact, a bonding between the black leather bag and me. I'd felt good all along that I had this special responsibility. But now I couldn't find it. The bag had disappeared.

'Tutu-da,' I said. 'We've to return to St Mark's Square. I've left the black bag there.'

'But where do you think you left it? It's a large place and we rushed around a bit,' said Tutu-da.

'I must have left it in the last shop we visited. I'm sure I left the bag on the counter after paying the lady,' I said. But I wasn't really sure. One's never sure on such occasions.

I requested the gondolier to turn back and take us to St Mark's Square. It was getting late, but this time of the year summer shopping extended well into the evening. I held my breath. I suddenly panicked. The gondolier wasn't moving fast enough. Quite by chance, I realised what Einstein's Theory of Relativity was all about.

The lady at the shop – I never found out her name – was waiting.

'I should have left 20 minutes ago,' she said. 'But I had to wait for you. I knew you were coming back.' She held up my black bag with a partly triumphant, partly mischievous smile. I loved her at that moment. I loved her slightly tilted head, the twinkle in her eyes, her simple natural honesty and her affectionate smile. I'll love her always. This incident made my entire tour worthwhile, I thought. It's not often in a lifetime that such events happen; that an Italian shop assistant waits to deliver a black leather bag to an anxious, young Indian man – without any expectation of praise or reward. It wasn't locked, but it didn't once occur to me to check if the contents, including money for the rest of the Italian tour, were intact. We rarely drank, but on this occasion we returned to the camp site with a bottle of Chianti, to celebrate.

We set out for Trieste the next morning – a distance of just over 70 miles. It was still a long way to go – by car, by train, by boat – before we reached Calcutta, which was beginning to loom more and more prominently on the horizon.

We had no camera. We'd brought with us no pictures of the children and we weren't taking back any photographs of our exciting trip. I don't think photography was such a popular hobby for people like us as it is today. Now, towards the end of the journey, I felt very strongly from time to time that a few photographs of the children to look at occasionally would help and it would also make it possible for our friends and relations in Calcutta and Kampala to see us in front of the Sistine Chapel or trudging 2,000 feet towards Snowdon.

Whereas Rome, Florence and Venice had a history full of excitement and achievement, both political and artistic, Trieste had a more recent and exciting past, because of the conflicts of Austro-Hungarian and Italian interests, which were political, economic and cultural. It was important especially as a trading port and a ship-building centre both in the past and now. In 1955 when we were in Trieste, it might not have been at its most glorious best, but it was still a cosmopolitan city, to which converged philosophers, poets and artists from different parts of Europe. It had a prosperous economy and the population was growing. The fifties were a good time to be in Trieste and we were going to look round.

It was only the previous year – in 1954 – that, after some political squabbling and bargaining, Trieste had been restored to the sovereign state of Italy. It had a chequered past.

In Trieste we found, some distance away from the city centre, a small hotel run by an Italian couple in their fifties. Apart from us, there were two other couples there who were away at the time we arrived. The husband did the cooking and the wife looked after the guests. He was proud of his cooking. He'd spent several years in Hong Kong, cooking in a large hotel, but he had come back to the city where he'd lived before and where his children were born. He wore his immaculate, white apron quite often even when he wasn't actually cooking. He took his culinary occupation seriously and had the kind of pride professional people often have when they know they've been fairly successful in their pursuit of excellence. He was a perfectionist. We chose our fish for dinner individually from a small tank where they were swimming, unaware of what was in store for them. I never had an experience like that before, nor have I had one since. The owner of the hotel was friendly, knowledgeable and articulate, so we asked him which places of interest we should visit during our short stay in Trieste.

Trieste in the mid-fifties had a population of 270,000 thousand or so, with a large minority group of Slovenes. Added to that were the Balkans, and in summer, a goodly number of tourists. During this mini tour of Europe, mainly Italy, what I'd noticed was that my attention and interest had moved slowly from cathedrals, basilicas, museums, art-galleries and shopping centres to people – people of different colours, shapes and sizes, cultures and convictions. The problem was that I couldn't get to know a person the way I could get to know a cathedral.

I had, I'm ashamed to admit, a certain anxiety about my relationship with my children. I wanted them to be happy in Calcutta with their grandparents, but at the same time, I was slightly worried that they, having lived for such a long time with their loving grandparents, might feel uncertain and unhappy about returning to Kampala with their parents who, being working people, wouldn't be able to do for them half as much. I also worried, secretly and silently, about the final written examination and the assessment of our teaching practice at the Institute of Education. If the result was below par, how would I face the music, the snide remarks that would come wafting in the wind from various directions? I'd always hated examinations and interviews and had often said to my students and to Sudarsana, that if I ever became the Minister of Education of an independent country with the power to decide how to assess the ability of students to learn and apply their learning to real-life situations, I'd look for ways which were less painful and more reliable. But I also suspected that these alternative methods might not be easy to devise or discover.

It was time for dinner. It was one of the best, if not the best, dinner I'd had on this trip. Fish at the time being my favourite food, I was looking forward to it anyway, and what I got far exceeded my expectations. The cook, who was also the owner of the small hotel, didn't seem too surprised at our appreciation of his cooking – he had heard all that before but conceded a gracious smile. He joined us briefly for coffee and recommended that we should visit *Piazza Unita d'Italia*, both by day and night the next day, and have a look at the Miramare Castle before we set out for *Crikvenica* in Yugoslavia. We followed his advice and left Trieste with the feeling that we'd spent the time there the way we wanted to. *Piazza Unita d'Italia* had a delicate, floating quality in spite of its many massive, beautiful buildings. Have any other people since the beginning of our civilisation built so many beautiful buildings with so much care and skill? Where else have so many survived so majestically and in such pristine condition, and enjoyed the admiration of generations as in Italy? Although I hadn't yet left Italy, I found myself often looking back on the days we'd just left behind.

We occasionally got hold of an English newspaper, and this one said that some of the world's most eminent scientists – seven of them Nobel winners – had made a declaration stating that disputes between nations ought to be settled not by bullying and war but by peaceful means – discussion, reason and forbearance. War, according to them, must not be resorted to as a method of solving problems, not even as a last resort. They also stated that the atom bomb must be abandoned without the slightest hesitation. Bertrand Russell was the man who'd taken the initiative for the declaration and one of the many eminent signatories was Albert Einstein. And there was a clash in Gaza between Israel and Egypt. There was hardly any Indian news in these newspapers. There were times when we felt isolated.

From Trieste to Crikvenica was no distance at all. We'd said goodbye to our pleasant hotel-keeper and his wife, stipulating that we'd return for a day or two from Crikvenica before we left by train for Istanbul – after having handed over our Morris Minor – our Poor Little Rabbit (PLR 884) to a ship's agent for delivery at Bombay. We started off a little late, stopped and ate at a roadside restaurant in a pleasant environment. After all it was a good summer, a Mediterranean summer, and the light and heat lasted a long time. We were all relaxed – so far a successful, exciting and highly enjoyable holiday, in which four people had lived together without any bickering or perceptible tension. In Crikvenica we were going to relax – put up our tents somewhere along the Adriatic coast and bathe in the sea, sleep or lie in the sun most of the day and gaze at the stars, lying flat on our backs at night. We all allowed free rein to our imagination and described, for our mutual benefit, competing images of indolent physical indulgence and enjoyment. For after Crikvenica, we'd be without our car and dependent on the railways to take us all the way from Trieste to Basra. Crikvenica had become an attractive health resort. The pictures we'd seen and the accounts we'd read had made a great impression on us: so we were on our way with great expectations. We'd already decided to stop briefly on the way somewhere, as we so often used to do, have something to eat and drive on to this very attractive part of the North Adriatic coast.

I was driving, making steady and relaxed progress, when I noticed that the warm, friendly sun, more or less our constant companion throughout the holiday, had lost its shine. Dark and heavy clouds were moving in, transforming the sky and the horizon. It got darker and the wind rose. I requested Tutu-da to take over because I felt the wind was making an impact on the movement of the car; threatening to blow it off the road, which was now dark and slippery. The wind rose and whooshed away and threatened to land our small car in a roadside ditch. Now there was heavy rain added to the strong wind, a tropical downpour the like of which I hadn't expected to experience in Europe. Tutu-da stopped the car where he thought the car and its passengers would be safe until the storm blew over. One fortunate aspect of this unexpected and violent disruption of our steady progress was that though it started dramatically, it stopped just as suddenly and it hadn't done any damage. While it lasted it was a spectacle which only nature could so quickly and dramatically conjure – the darkness, the high winds, and the huge whiplash of fire flashing across the gloomy expanse of the sky. When the rain came, there were no half measures. It was a deluge. The four of us, huddled together in our little car while the storm raged and the rain threatened to deluge the ground all around, must have felt like Noah's animals.

Then the raging storm and heavy downpour suddenly disappeared. Joy broke the silence.

'I think the worst is over. It did give me a fright.'

'You're not the only one. I think it shook us all,' I said.

There was a drip, dripping of rain water from the twigs and leaves of the tree under which we were parked on to the roof of the car and the roof-rack. Tutu-da started the car and drove along at a steady speed towards the border. Somewhat sobered by the experience of a freak storm and the relentless downpour, we'd all gone quiet, but now we felt sufficiently relaxed to plan our seaside holiday in Crikvenica.

Both Joy and Sudarsana had bought themselves colourful swimming costumes in Trieste. We'd also provided ourselves with tinned food – tuna, corn beef, sardines, ham, peas, tomatoes and tinned milk. Our bathing trunks – Tutu-da's and mine – were ancient. We'd now recovered from the storm and the scare, so we were planning our week or so in Crikvenica with a positive frame of mind and a strong desire to enjoy ourselves. It was quite late because we'd lost hours because of the storm. So when we arrived at the border, the border guards were not at all pleased to see us. There were two or three of them. They grunted. They didn't look a bit friendly. It was quite clear that they weren't expecting anybody to disturb their sleep this stormy night, especially when they'd coped with the storm and gone to sleep. They grumbled, they grunted. They asked us a few questions in good, standard English, stamped our passports and opened the barrier to let us through. They didn't even forget to wish us a happy holiday in Crickvenica.

We arrived at a part of the coast quite late at night when all was quiet. There was no sign of human presence anywhere along the coast where we were driving at 20 miles an hour to find an appropriate place for setting up our tent. But there was no stretch of land along this coast which struck us as a good place for camping. So, following the logic that when there is no choice, one alternative is as good as another, we just stopped our car and put up our two tents in the middle of nowhere, but within striking distance of the sea. I don't remember what we ate and drank that evening: it really didn't matter. What mattered was sleep and I, at least, didn't have any problems falling asleep there and then, and waking up bright and early the next morning. I walked to the beach, but the seafront was deserted; nobody was even walking a dog along the beach. A sacred silence reigned, as if it was still the hour of meditation and prayers. It was a brief and memorable experience – nothing but the sea in perpetual motion between me and the horizon, the dawn about to break to start the cycle of waking and sleeping.

I returned to the clan. They were all up and about. There was no clutter inside the tents. Everything was pristine, the work mainly of Joy and Sudarsana. Sometimes I felt Joy and Sudarsana did a disproportionate amount of cooking and cleaning and coping with the clutter; but they did all that so naturally and unobtrusively that we didn't always realise how much they did. Real efficiency is unobtrusive. I admired efficient people. We were fortunate in having Joy and Sudarsana with us, not only because of who they were, but also because of their practical good sense.

'We're all ready for breakfast,' said Joy. 'There is, however, a little problem – we need some water for our coffee.'

For big crises we depended on Tutu-da. When the car was about to roll off the wet surface of the road in the storm the previous evening, we all depended on him to do the right thing and find an appropriate solution. But when problems were small, the other members of our unique venture usually turned to me. I had to go forth and beg, borrow or steal some water so that we could make coffee and have some drinking water in reserve.

I set out. There were only a few people around. After some time I came across a man, probably in his forties, and said, pointing to my lips and simulating drinking, 'I want some drinking water.' I thought he didn't understand, so I repeated, 'I want some drinking water,' again pointing to my lips and pretending to drink. The man looked at me, shrugged and walked on.

The next person I met in a matter of minutes was a woman in her forties who smiled at me, so I was encouraged to ask her the question which had led me nowhere – so far. She stopped. She realised I had some kind of problem and she was ready to help. I repeated my act, pointing to my lips and simulating the act of drinking. What exactly she thought I was asking I don't know. A few hundred yards from where we were standing, there were at least 20 tents scattered around and there was a tent a little distance away from the rest on a small hill. This very pleasant woman pointed to that tent and said, Mila. I thanked her profusely. I thought the word 'mila' meant water, which would be available at or near the tent on top of the hill. There was movement inside the tent but nobody outside.

'Hello', I said, looking at the opening of the tent.

'Hello,' said a woman's voice from within.

'Can I see you for a minute?' I said.

'Certainly,' she said and emerged from the tent. She was wearing her swimming costume, getting ready for the sun, sand and sea. She was a lovely young woman with a friendly, sympathetic smile

'I want Mila,' I declared pointing to my lips again and simulating the act of drinking.

'I am Mila,' she said. We laughed.

There was confusion because I thought that 'Mila' wasn't the name of a person but meant 'drinking water'. I explained why. She laughed. She was friendly and ready to help.

She gave me a jug of drinking water to take back with me. I'd have loved to spend more time with her but I knew my thirsty companions a few hundred yards away from us were waiting anxiously for the jug of water which Mila had just given me. I thanked Mila several times and was rushing off in the direction of our two solitary tents in Crikvenica somewhere on the Adriatic coast when Mila stopped me and said.

'Ganesh, you have to be careful. You can't pitch your tent anywhere you like. I'm sure the police will ask you to move on – several miles to the east where there's a large camp site near one of the bays of the Riviera.'

Quite spontaneously and without any ulterior motive, I said what I felt, 'Now that I've got to know you Mila, and you're not water but a friendly and helpful person, I don't want to go away to one of the wide bays of the Riviera and live among large crowds. We'll be here – I and three others – for a little over a week. Can't we stay somewhere near so that we can spend a little time together?'

Mila gave me a hug which lasted a few seconds longer than I expected – a warm hug to a stranger who was born in India, worked in Uganda and had come to Tito's Yugoslavia for a brief seaside holiday towards the end of a fairly comprehensive tour of some of the cities of Europe.

'There's no problem,' she said. 'I and a colleague of mine are in charge of these young people, all students of a secondary school. As teachers in charge of this camp site, we can allow you to come and live here and share our amenities. That open space at the foot of the hill should do nicely for you. But I'm afraid my students are rather noisy.'

This was great good luck. I thanked Mila once again.

'Many thanks, Mila! Bye! My wife, Sudarsana, and my two friends will be wondering whether I have lost my way or been kidnapped, I must go now. See you soon,' I said.

Mila stood at the opening of her tent and waved goodbye just as I was about to disappear. Mila and I lived on two continents, spoke different languages and had different hopes and aspirations. But none of that mattered. She treated me with friendly warmth.

Coffee was ambrosia. We had more than one cup each and we all commented on the beauty of the sea and the beach and congratulated Joy on the imaginative planning of the trip.

'There's another problem,' said Joy. 'A policeman turned up not long after you'd left and told us to move to one of the camp sites several miles east of this place.'

This was my moment. I was going to prove that I was a far-sighted young man who thought not only of the present but also what lay farther ahead.

'Mila warned me this might happen and has come up with a solution. She'd like us to move in with her and the students on their camping site. Then there won't be any problem,' I said.

The suggestion was received with relief. We moved to the students' camp-site. It had a relaxed atmosphere, based on mutual respect and some simple rules of discipline. One of the teachers, a young man in his twenties surprised me by showing his familiarity with songs sung by a Bombay film star. Raj Kapoor was a popular film-maker in Yugoslavia and, when we were there, quite a few young people were singing *'Mera juta hai Japani Yeh patloon Englisthani, Sir pe lal topi Russi, phir bhi dil hai Hindusthani':* my shoes are Japanese, my trousers English, my red hat from Russia, but my soul is Indian.

It was quite amazing how much pleasure these young Yugoslavs got out of Hindi films and Hindi songs. That our film industry, having produced a film in Bombay, should provide pleasure and entertainment on the Yugoslavian coast of Crikvenica made me feel good. Daniel, pronounced *dah-nee-al,* was not the only one who liked Bombay films and the songs in them. They had a large following. I knew the opening lines of *juta hai japani* but I let Daniel teach me the rest of it. It was good to be with these younger people and share their interests.

Daniel had his eye on the Morris Minor. He thought it was a beautiful car. I'd given him and others several lifts to different places, including the town centre. I got the impression that he wanted to drive it.

'Have you got a licence to drive?' I asked.

'Yes, I have, but I haven't driven a car because I haven't got one,' he said. He wanted to have a go at the wheel. He'd love to have the opportunity to drive the 'Poor Little Rabbit...'

I'd refused to entertain the idea, especially because driving along the hillside needed special skill and control. My own driving license was only a few months old. So I had to be careful. But one afternoon, I relented.

'Try going round the hill,' I said. 'If you have any problem, stop at once. There's hardly any traffic this side of the hill.'

Daniel started off well, but before very long, the car juddered and stopped. He started again. This time the car swayed dangerously.

'Stop Daniel, stop,' I shouted and ran after the car. The car stopped but at a slight angle from the road.

'You need practice. The co-ordination went a bit wrong. Maybe you should take a few more lessons.' I was trying not to embarrass him because he looked so very apologetic – although I was shaken.

Daniel agreed and the matter ended there. I'd describe what happened as a serious averted accident. At the time I didn't mention the trauma I'd experienced to anyone. It was business as usual. Not even Daniel, the author of the crisis, suspected that there might have been very tragic consequences to our irresponsible experiment.

There was excitement at the camp-site. The end of the holidays was approaching and there were plans afoot to make the last few days an exciting experience.

Some of us – Mila, Joy, Sudarsana, Tutu-da, Daniel and I among others – were bound towards a hotel in a nearby town, a hotel which was popular with the local people as well as tourists for its good food and good music. The others were going to have their party at the camp-site, for which there was a great deal of feverish activity. When the time came, Mila, Joy and Sudarsana piled in at the back of the Morris Minor and Tutu-da drove us to the hotel which had a very festive atmosphere with people of different nationalities – mainly young – milling around in casual as well as semi-formal clothing. We found ourselves a table, got ourselves a drink – and despaired because, unless the music stopped, there could be no conversation, only snatches of it.

'What do you think of the music?' Mila asked.

'I like it,' said Joy.

'Just right for the occasion,' said Tutu-da.

Daniel hadn't in the end come with us, but stayed on at the party at the camp-site. He liked my company, but in the end his wish to stay with his friends was stronger. There was another reason. He would ask me questions about love, sex, morality and women – especially women – which he wouldn't have been able to ask in the presence of others. I often found myself acting like an oracle, pretending to know answers to questions which have been blowing in the wind since the beginning of time.

'Do things like love and sex mean as much to women as to men?' he'd ask.

'I think they do. But it varies from person to person,' I'd say. 'I don't really know.'

There would be others questions about selfishness, fidelity, friendship and the quality of life. I tried to be as honest as I could, making sure that he understood the fact that what I said to him was from a 31-year-old Bengali who had conflicts and uncertainties of his own.

Mila had got up from the table and gone reconnoitring. She knew some local people and some tourists who were so fond of the place that they came year after year. We were complimenting Joy at the time because she'd worked out for us a wholly rewarding holiday, which had not only made us better informed, but also more appreciative of the fact that life holds for us exciting surprises. It was good, towards the end of our holiday, to be able to acknowledge the creative planning which had gone into the success of the trip. I said so.

'We haven't finished yet,' said Joy.

'We're nearly done,' said Sudarsana.
'What worries me,' said Tutu-da 'is that we'll be separated from the 'Poor Little Rabbit'. We'll have to depend on the railways.'

'That's a new experience to look forward to,' I said.

I looked up from our conversation and found Mila hurtling towards us.

'Come,' she said to me, 'dance with me.'

'Yes, of course,' I said, and got up to dance.

Ambling towards us was the Frenchman who'd visited Mila once or twice at the camp site. The tall, clean-shaven Frenchman was quite an attractive young man. He sat down at the table and we moved on to dance.

'He's quite an attractive man,' I said.

'I don't find him attractive. He's a bore,' Mila said.

'Why is that?' I asked.

'Because he thinks he's irresistible. He chases me because I haven't succumbed to his good looks and charm. He'll lose interest as soon as he finds his magic has worked. I don't want to be rude, so I avoid him.' Mila was warm and friendly. She danced with me in a close embrace. But we didn't kiss.

The Frenchman was dancing with Sudarsana. Tutu-da was dancing with Joy. Tutu-da only danced with Joy because he didn't guide her; she guided him. He looked happy when dancing with Joy. I've very rarely come across such quiet and undemonstrative devotion between a husband and wife. Mila had moved close to me. I felt her warm breath on my neck as she rested her head on my shoulder. She held me tightly in her arms as we moved across the dance floor among the other dancers – all participating in the same joyful experience of dancing, in a small hotel in Crikvenica, on that far away Adriatic coast of Croatia, way back in 1955.

'I'll miss you,' Mila said unexpectedly.

'I'll miss you too,' I responded, entirely truthfully.

It was a good, warm feeling. Two strangers had briefly but strongly bonded.

It was time for us to pack up and leave. Daniel came and helped us with the packing. Many students and most of the teachers came to say goodbye. This was the first time that people, rather than places, had become central to our holiday. We'd visited the town and seen some impressive buildings. We'd lazed on the beach, swum in the sea, gone out to eat once or twice, but the most cherished memory of my Crikvenica trip is the friendly, warm and human people and the generosity of those young people.

Tutu-da was driving – he looked at the rear view mirror from time to time to see our camp-site companions waving goodbye. Sudarsana, Joy and I watched and waved as long as it was possible to do so. Then we drove on back in the direction of Trieste.

From now on the emphasis was going to be on travelling, on returning to Calcutta and meeting up with the children. Crikvenica had temporarily suppressed my anxiety and longing, but it was only a diversion. We returned to the hotel run by the Italian chef and at once requested fish for dinner. Add fresh fish to real professional cooking and the result is something quite irresistible. Everything was open until quite late in the evening in Trieste. We all went to the shipping agent to hand over the car to be shipped to Bombay. The agent brought us back. We said goodbye temporarily to our Morris Minor. We were all a little emotional when we saw her being driven off. We took the train at Trieste the next day after saying a relaxed goodbye to Frederico – I think that was the hotelier's name – and his wife. We promised to spend time in his hotel whenever we came to Trieste. We never went back because none of us visited Trieste ever again. But at the time we meant what we said because this was an exploratory trip, and the next time we came, we'd know how exactly to spend our time to our best advantage, and Frederico's clean and comfortable hotel and his cooking skills would certainly have been a powerful incentive for us to visit Trieste.

The train was comfortable, the dining room was sumptuous. Even the very rich often chose the train as their preferred mode of travelling. We relaxed. We spent quite a lot of time in the dining room. I think the train went through Athens at night, so we didn't even catch a clear glimpse of the Parthenon, but I had the illusion of having seen the remains of the building, a shadowy presence in the background, rather than a solid structure built nearly 2,500 years ago to Athena, the blindfolded Goddess of Justice, and a perfect example of Doric architecture. The Elgin Marbles which we'd seen in London in the Victoria and Albert Museum, had been part of the Parthenon... Did I imagine it?

It was certainly a most frustrating experience to pass through the great ancient city and not even to set eyes on the Parthenon. It was a pleasant trip, with plenty of leg-room where we sat, and good food and company in the restaurant car. We relaxed, read English newspapers, spent much of the time between sleeping and waking, trying to visualise what the children now looked like. My daughters couldn't have changed much, but Nondon certainly had.

'I'm quite certain that Aparna, Aparajita and Nondon have been well looked after and genuinely loved. Do you think they wonder how we could abandon them and go away?' I asked Sudarsana.

'That's an adult way of thinking. Our children are happy with my parents. They aren't the problem, we are,' Sudarsana said, thoughtfully. '*We* miss them. *We* feel guilty.'

We were now approaching Istanbul, known as Constantinople before 1930, the largest city and chief port of Turkey, situated on the Straits of the Bosphorus. Where I'd chosen to live and work, the city of Kampala, was built on seven hills; so was Istanbul, although there the likeness ended. Istanbul had been in the centre of Christian and Islamic civilisations for centuries. Kemal Ataturk had shifted the capital from Constantinople to Ankara. But our interest was mainly in Istanbul and we'd decided to explore this city before we moved on.

We'd responded to the request of a particularly importunate taxi-driver who'd offered to drive us to the 'cheapest and best' hotel in Istanbul. He brought us to the hotel of his choice, a place without frills, but that's all we needed for a break of two nights. The taxi-driver had mentioned a sum of money for taxi-fare. I went to the manager and owner of the hotel and changed money to pay the taxi-driver.

'How much fare is he asking for?' he asked and I named the sum.

'Oh, really?' It was a comment, not a question.

The manager came out with me.

'How much have you asked for?' he asked the driver. The driver mentioned the sum.

'Is that fair?' the manager asked.

'In summer we make a little extra,' said the driver.

'In summer you cheat tourists,' the manager said. 'You give our city a bad name.'

'It's between me and this man,' the driver said. 'You keep out of it.'

Before letting anybody think, the manager slapped the driver across the face. 'This is your legitimate fare,' said the manager, eyes flashing with anger.

The taxi-driver accepted the money I paid him and left in grim silence. What repercussions there might be on account of the manager's angry and insulting behaviour, I couldn't tell, but it could spark off problems of violence in the days to come. Fortunately, none of the others witnessed this because they were in the reception room devouring news from English papers. After the event – I didn't say anything to anybody at the time – we went to our two modest rooms which we'd hired for two nights at a very reasonable rate. We thanked the manager and went out to explore.

This great historical city has one unique characteristic – the western part of the city is in Europe while the eastern part is in Asia. In Istanbul the East literally meets the West. One of the most memorable pictures that I'll always carry around in my head was what suddenly appeared around us and ahead of us: the great mosques and minarets which overwhelmingly dominated the landscape in front of us as the train came round a bend – the sea on one side and all this inspiring architecture on the other – mosques, churches, synagogues, palaces, castles and towers.

It wasn't part of Joy's planning that the last large city we visited and explored would be one in which different cultures and religions had co-existed and flourished in spite of being antagonistic and antagonistic towards each other. The Greek occupation was ended under the leadership of Mustafa Kemal Ataturk, and a new, progressive government was more interested in welding together a new nation than in encouraging fragmentation. It was nearly 30 years ago that the Greeks were defeated and Kemal Ataturk's programme of radical change and Westernisation had started. It had made a difference. A new city and a new nation had been created by Ataturk. We felt somewhat disorientated. We didn't have a car, and so were entirely dependent on public transport. Taxis were a menace because all drivers preyed on the tourists. But we managed to visit the Maiden's Tower, a visible monument from any part of Istanbul and therefore a symbol of the city. We also visited Hagia Sophia, first a church, then a mosque, now a museum and the largest ever cathedral for a thousand years. We wandered the city streets and were amazed at the variety of people, costumes and languages – the result of the coexistence of different cultural, religious and linguistic groups over centuries in the same city under different names. There was a lot more we wanted to do but decided to get back to our "Istanbul Hilton" as we'd dubbed it, relax and read newspapers. One interesting aspect of English newspapers which we had access to was that there was hardly ever any mention of India.

I liked the meal I ate. Nobody complained, so the others might have enjoyed it too. My impression was that it was quite a lot like North Indian food, rich and spicy. We went to bed. I slept well for most of the night but then woke up because I thought I was sharing the bed with very small creatures which crept and crawled around. I got out of bed and switched on the light. Sudarsana woke up, her eyes heavy with sleep.

'Didn't you feel little creatures scattered around the bed?' I asked.

'No, I didn't,' she said, turned round and went to sleep. There were bedbugs, I was sure. I couldn't sleep.

Another feature of this Turkish hotel was the noisy ceiling-fans whirring around. How Sudarsana or anybody else could sleep through that almighty racket was another puzzle I was never able to solve.
I told the manager that there might have been creatures in my bed and that they had kept me awake. The manager froze. Never, he repeated, *never* had anybody made a complaint like that. If this was true, he'd sell his business next week, go away on a *hadj* and never come back from his pilgrimage and self-imposed penance.

'I didn't mean to insult you,' I said.

'I'm not insulted because it isn't true,' he said.

We had fresh sheets that night. In the morning I thanked the manager who looked as if he'd forgiven me. He suggested some places like the Sultan Ahmed Mosque and the Istanbul University for adding to our itinerary that day. They were beautiful buildings, which have carried their age well and added to the rich and varied traditions of the great schools of architecture. On the last evening at dinner, the manager joined us and talked about visiting India some day – the Taj Mahal, the Agra Fort, and various places and palaces in Rajasthan. He showed us pictures of his family – wife, two daughters and two sons – and talked about their future. He didn't want his sons to go into business because it led you into crooked ways. He wanted his sons to be doctors – his first preference. People who healed had the blessings of Allah. Lawyers were all right as long as they protected the poor against the rich; the weak against their immoral and powerful adversaries. Our hotel manager, who had a framed photograph of Kemal Ataturk on his desk, was an idealist – fairly placid, pleasant, peaceful and friendly. What made him erupt the way he did when the taxi-driver had overcharged me will always remain a mystery. I've often wondered whether there were any repercussions. When we visit a place certain events and images often make a deep and lasting impression on us. One of these was the violent and spontaneous outbreak of anger of a good, honest man. And the other was the spectacle of Istanbul from the train as it turned a corner and I looked round to see a great city – Byzantium, Constantinople or Istanbul – with its domes, spires, pillars, turrets, minarets, churches, mosques, synagogues, and buildings, ancient and modern – revealing itself suddenly and spectacularly – a city rising out of the sea.

I don't know what kind of railway ticket or booking Joy had organised for us, but we seemed to be able to stop and start when we wanted. Now we were on our way to Syria. We weren't going to stop in Damascus for sight-seeing, although it was such a great and ancient city. Apart from that we didn't have Syrian money. A young German, just out of university, was travelling with us in the same compartment. He had Syrian money which we bought with our English money. Peter didn't want to accept any money, but Joy was able to persuade him to be reasonable. Peter was a well-informed young man whose company we enjoyed because he was for some reason quite deeply interested in English culture and some of my heroes: Bernard Shaw, Sidney and Beatrice Webb, H.G. Wells, Bertrand Russell. We were talking with great interest when I saw a water tap on the station platform from which people were collecting water in bottles and buckets. I waited until I had access to the tap and then collected handfuls of water from it and wet my bare torso. The heat in the compartment was quite unbearable, and so the relief was immense. I wondered why others didn't follow my example.

It didn't take me long to find out why others hadn't followed my example. A uniformed railway policeman had materialized out of thin air. He was making noises, which certainly were not polite, and pointing to my bare torso with the barrel of his gun. He urged me loudly to put on my shirt at once. He was speaking English rapidly and with anger, and pointing to the Muslim women around. The message I got – the deconstruction wasn't difficult – was that men shouldn't expose or parade their bare torso in the presence of women just as women would never dream of doing anything like that. In our society the rules are unequal; in Muslim society, at least in Damascus, the men and women had the same restrictions: women couldn't take off their blouses, nor men their shirts. That was fair enough. But, for a moment, I was scared. Never before had anybody pointed a gun at me. In our compartment, there was a mixture of amusement and indignation.

'It's absurd that policemen should point their guns at tourists for an offence so small,' Joy was indignant.

'I found something rather comic about the whole incident,' said Peter.

'It was completely unnecessary,' I commented. 'He could have just asked me.'

Anyway, we settled down in the compartment. The consensus was that the equal rights idea was progressive – if that's what it was – but the method of enforcing it was excessive. When we got to Baghdad, Peter left us for his posh hotel. We had nothing booked, but found a cheap one not too far from Baghdad railway station. Peter was youthful, full of fun, helpful, full of certainties. He radiated confidence... It'd been good to have him with us as a travelling companion.

So here we were in Baghdad, *the Beautiful Garden, the Gift of God*, but we had no plans for exploring the city. We'd quietly come, and would quietly go. I was really beginning to feel distressed by the long separation from the children. But we were, at the same time, excited by the fact that we were in this ancient city, with its own unique culture and civilization. At one point of its history, Baghdad was called 'Madinat as-Salam' which, I understand, means the City of Peace. The tragic irony of that name today would be too much to bear. Baghdad, Babylon, Harunal-Rashid, and the Thief of Baghdad – we'd all grown up with fact and fiction which came out from this part of the world. Sir Richard Burton's 16-volume edition of *The Book of the Thousand Nights and a Night: A Plain and Literal Translation of the Arabian Nights Entertainments*, published between 1885-1888, opened up to its readers a world the like of which they hadn't visualised even in their wildest fantasies. There were few boys and girls in middle-class schools in Calcutta whose life hadn't been made a little more pleasurable and whose imagination enriched by *Sinbad the Seaman (or Sailor), Ali Baba and the Forty Thieves* and *Aladdin and his Wonderful Lamp*. We hadn't read Sir Richard Burton's 16-volume edition of *The Arabian Nights* but I think the famous and fascinating stories which have provided pleasure and entertainment to generations of readers were made more accessible because of him.

We visited the Bazaar in Baghdad but found very little magic or mystery there, with large crowds of people milling around, selling many kinds of fruit, many kinds of vegetables, very colourful, very noisy and quite smelly – as in Delhi or Calcutta. As far as I remember, I was disappointed.

I left Iraq with a few regrets. We didn't visit the famous National Museum of Iraq. On the whole our visit to Baghdad wasn't too memorable. Were we travel-weary? Was it the longing for Calcutta which was distracting? The night before we left Baghdad, we had an excellent meal in one of the restaurants. It was different from our kind of cuisine in India – but, I thought, there was a lot in common.

'Some day, we'll have to come back,' Tutu-da said. Joy thought so too.

Sudarsana said nothing. She was withdrawing more and more into herself. It was obvious that she was now finding it a little difficult to wait to see the children. Quite often, the closer we are, the more difficult it becomes to wait. I'm not sure I know the reason why.

We went looking for SS Dwarka before we did anything else. SS Dwarka was a passenger ship owned and operated by the British India Steam Navigation Company. It was due to leave the next day from Basra, sail through the Persian Gulf and the Gulf of Oman and then through the Indian Ocean to Bombay. It took, I think, ten days. The captain was Iraqi. He said the ship was due to leave two days later instead of the next day. But we could be his guest and move in immediately. That evening before dinner, we were introduced to *arrack*, a strong alcoholic drink distilled from either rice or molasses. Ours, I think, was from rice, judging by the colour and flavour. I coped; Tutu-da enjoyed it and had more than one or two; Joy was slow and didn't finish. Sudarsana declared she didn't drink. It was a friendly crew and the voyage, we thought, was going to be pleasant. But it takes more than a friendly crew to make a voyage safe and pleasant. In the Persian Gulf, not long after we'd left Basra, I felt sick from the rocking. I didn't throw up, but felt I couldn't eat. Many other passengers were in a similar predicament. Whether it started at the Persian Gulf and continued through the Gulf of Omar, or whether the feeling of sickness and nausea began and ended in the Persian Gulf, I don't remember. But whatever the length of the suffering, it was unpleasant, an anti-climax after the great excitement of our carefully planned tour through Europe, Turkey and now the Middle East.

By the time we reached the Arabian Sea, all was well, and we were able to relax, without having to worry about food and shelter, shopping or a haircut or work. Sudarsana read Agatha Christie; Tutu-da read every English newspaper and magazine, of which there weren't many. Joy knitted and I, by and large, did nothing except read a little and sleep a lot, lulled by the relentless thudding of the engine – which was always there in the background. Stretched out on a deck chair, out of the strong sun, I watched dolphins arching in and out of the sea, kites flying lazily – gliding rather than flying – and large masses of white clouds floating across the sky. It was as if the world around and I on the deck of SS Dwarka had made a temporary pact that we'd move slowly and lazily and peacefully across the surface of the world. I thought at the same time that there was no act as peaceful and refreshing as a quiet and long snooze on the deck of a ship, after breakfast or lunch. I loved to sleep on the deck of SS Dwarka. It wasn't always possible because various activities were often organised by the ship's officials to ensure that the passengers didn't die of boredom, but most of these were after-dinner activities and didn't interfere with my shameless cultivation of idleness.

Neither Sudarsana nor I mentioned the subject which we wanted to talk about more than anything else – the children. We assumed they didn't miss us a lot because that was the way we felt at peace.

In Old Kampala, the maid, Mary, had been, in many ways more important to them than we were – because it was she who made sure they had clean clothes on every day and that they went out for a walk and ate on time. We always ate together. We also spent as much time together as we could, but it wasn't a lot of time. Over in Tollygunge, Calcutta, they would be looked after by their grandparents – every inch of the way. I couldn't speak for Sudarsana, but I was a little worried that the grandparents, having looked after my children and given them what only they could offer, would have made us redundant. But such fears were neither recurrent, nor obsessive. The positive aspect of separation is the thinking, the hoping and the dreaming of reunion, which wasn't very far away. That must have been uppermost in Sudarsana's mind also, but we talked about Bertrand Russell and Albert Einstein's declaration that wars must for ever be relinquished and the bomb destroyed. We discussed Portugal's decision not to give up their colonial possession in India – Goa. I mentioned the failure of the staging of Samuel Beckett's *Waiting for Godot* in London. We wondered what was for dinner, but usually kept off the subject of the children. Before the ship berthed and the passengers dispersed, there were various specials: special dinners, dances and a children's evening. We participated in whatever was happening, got to know the bursar and the captain and a few fellow passengers. And before long, the Port of Bombay loomed ahead on a clear afternoon. Home at last!

Chapter 11

Reunion with children in Calcutta, Kampala

Nobody was waiting to meet us as we arrived back in India, but the feeling of homecoming was strong because this was Bombay, the most important port and industrial centre of India. The surroundings were familiar – the goods sheds, the boxes, the bales and packages – all stacked in rows; the porters in their uniform, bestriding the quayside; the ships from various countries carrying various merchandise, sheltering in the port. After all, it was for three and a half years that I'd worked at the Kidderpore Docks and Calcutta Jetties!

The arrangement in Bombay was that Sudarsana and I were going to find ourselves a room for two nights at one of the seaside hotels and Joy and Tutu-da were going to stay with Tutu-da's friend and his wife, Harisadhan Dasgupta and Sonali Dasgupta. We collected our luggage and piled into two separate taxis. Tutu.-da said he'd inform his parents as well as Sudarsana's of our safe arrival using the phone at the Dasgupta's. That evening we were on our own in a room at Seaview Hotel, which had clean and pleasant surroundings, reasonably good food – mainly Indian – and excellent service. We didn't do much, didn't *want* to do much; we'd mastered the art of *relaxation* almost to perfection. We had some tea, went for a walk along the promenade, full of people, old and young, men, women and children. It's a famous promenade where every evening hundreds of vendors of a large number of different articles opened their stalls just as the sun was beginning to mellow and kept them open until an hour or so before midnight: balloons, various kinds of street food, some of which were immensely popular with many of the visiting families. There was one item which raised the seafront to aesthetic heights: flowers. Probably every thousand square yards, a florist had set up his temporary stall of fresh flowers – jasmine, *champak*, roses – yellow, red and white. There were other varieties – all exotic, fragrant and beautiful, and one of the first objectives of Indian women, both young and not-so-young, was to put flowers in their hair. How was it, I wondered, that in so many cultures and religions, flowers play such a significant role! Sudarsana put a young bud of *champak* in her hair, which made the air beautifully fragrant and slightly heady in our hotel room. We hadn't been together, on our own and so comfortable for a long time. And, inexplicably, tears welled up in my eyes that we were still more than a thousand miles away from the children. Sudarsana was carefully fixing her single blossom of *champak* strategically in her hair and I was watching.

'The day, a long time ago, a woman put a flower in her hair,' Sudarsana said, 'civilisation started.' I thought it was a credible idea.

The next day we had lunch with Tutu-da's friend, Harishadhan Dasgupta and his beautiful wife. Nobody could dispute that Shonali Dasgupta was a beautiful woman. Shonali and Harishadhan had a son. They called him Raja. Sudarsana said that I'd take a long time to recover from Shonali's impact on me. I don't remember what I said.

We'd selected a train which would take us to Howrah Station about midday. That would make it possible for their grandparents to bring Aparna, Aparajita and Nondon to the station. We were travelling a distance of over 1,200 miles, but there was something special about railway journeys in India. It has a human dimension which is unmistakable. The porters who carry your luggage are knowledgeable and helpful. The chicken curry and rice which comes from the railway restaurant is enjoyable. The breakfast is always good, and the travelling companions are usually interesting to talk to. It's home and it feels like home.

Nobody baulked at the idea that we were travelling more than 1,200 miles over a period of 38 hours. For the first time in a long time, I was thinking rather sentimentally that we'd hear Bengali spoken all around, confirming our home-coming. Travelling by train in India was always a special experience for me. And I was more excited, for various reasons, than I'd been in a very long time. We could see Howrah Bridge long before we arrived at the station – a magnificent bridge which replaced the old one. Whereas the station building was colonial, 19th century, the bridge was very much a twentieth-century gift to the citizens of Calcutta from the British colonialists. The British built the Victoria Memorial Hall to make Calcutta look beautiful. It also – much later – built the New Howrah Bridge, a cantilever bridge which was considered to be one of the best of its kind. It was not its beauty but its usefulness which was the main consideration. But for me, Howrah Bridge, which was completed in 1945 and linked Howrah to Calcutta, was not only useful – it accommodated traffic of many thousands of vehicles and hundreds of thousands of pedestrians – but a very beautiful structure, more beautiful than anything else that I can think of in Calcutta. Whenever I came back by train from somewhere to Howrah, I looked out for this great cantilever bridge, strong and beautiful, connecting the two banks of an ancient river. Howrah Bridge was iconic for me, the symbol of the city, and whenever I saw it from a distance before the train entered the appropriate platform, the uncertainty and waiting was over: I had arrived back home in my city. I had only to cross the bridge and I'd be there...

There were gasps of happiness, relief and excitement among my fellow passengers. I've often wondered whether we'll ever fully realise that life is overwhelmingly about people and their relationships. Take care of your relationships and everything else will fall into place. I looked out of the window – there were faces at every window, looking out for a familiar face. And just half a minute before the train stopped, faces flashed past, faces I'd been waiting to see, faces which meant so much. There was Aparna and Aparajita, standing next to their *Dadubhai*, their grandfather. There was Sudarsana's mother, and standing next to her – Nondon, who looked so different from the way I remembered him. Children's looks change rapidly at that age. He was barely a year old when we'd left for England. Now he was walking along, holding his *Didibhai's* hand.

Tutu-da's father, mother, younger brother and sister were all there. His older brother wasn't. After the excitement of reunion and homecoming, they left for their Park Street flat. We were still standing around our luggage and talking. I hugged my children several times: they were all there. Sudarsana embraced them, kissed them, looked at them, felt their faces, held their hand, but was in control. In many situations in our lives, I found Sudarsana was the more resilient and pragmatic of us two. We were now back with the children – that was all that mattered!

Nondon moved up close to me, held my hand and looked up into my face.

'Are you my Baba?' he asked.

'Yes, Nondon, I am your Baba'.

'You lived in England?' he asked.

'Yes, I did, 'I said.

'You won't go back again?'

'No, I won't.'

'I'm your son, Nondon.'

'Yes, I know. You're my son, Nondon, and I haven't seen you for a long time.' I was holding back my tears. I picked him up, held him, then put him down.

The introduction was over. The waiting was over. Nondon never moved from my side until we reached our destination in 33 D, Golf Club Road, Tollygunge, South Calcutta.

For Sudarsana and me it was a family reunion – meeting up after a year with the children, Sudarsana's parents, sister and others – as well as a reunion with our city, Calcutta. Sudarsana had divided loyalties – she loved Shantiniketan, where she went to college, at least as much as she loved Calcutta, but no other place in the world had any rival claims on *my* loyalty. I wholeheartedly, spontaneously, compulsively, loved Calcutta. I identified myself with this city, and still do, and it won't matter whether you call it the City of Joy or the City of Sorrow, heaven or purgatory. Here I had lived from the age of about ten to about thirty, when I left for Uganda, East Africa. Here I grew up, watching the advent of the *Kaal Boishakhi,* for me the event of the year, when intense dark clouds floated in from nowhere in huge masses, obliterated the sun, changed noon into night. Quite often, there was thunder and lightning. And then it often poured, and in a matter of minutes you could find yourself ankle-deep in water. *Kaal Boishakhi* has always fascinated me. It's one of Nature's ritual acts. I couldn't think of Calcutta without *Kaal Boishakhi.*

It was now almost four years since I'd left Calcutta for Kampala, capital of Uganda, and since then I'd lived in that city for about three years, and in London for nearly one. Yet Calcutta has remained part of me, and there will always be a feeling of homecoming when I return to Calcutta.

It was a radical city and the centre of the independence movement in the late nineteenth, early twentieth century. But it wasn't Calcutta's history but its humanity which has always appealed to me, and what makes it human is the suffering which it has faced, internalised and sublimated. It can't be an accident or a mere coincidence that one city in the Ganges Delta, in the east of India, on the banks of the River Hooghly, called Calcutta, should produce poets, dramatists, novelists, musicians, film-makers as well as folk-art the like of which isn't easy to come by in any other city in India. Of the musicians with the closest connection with Calcutta, I'd like to mention Ghulam Ali, Ali Akbar Khan and Ravi Shankar. Among Calcutta's well-known film-makers, the most outstanding and creative, indisputably, was Satyajit Ray. For me, the other outstanding film-makers were Mrinal Sen and Ritwik Ghatak. The greatest name of all among writers, of course, was Rabindranath Tagore. The names of some of the other great Bengali writers with the closest association with Calcutta are Bankim Chattopadhyay, Sarat Chandra, Kazi Nazrul and Jibanananda. Then there was the traditional folk music of the Bauls and folk-theatre known as *Jatra.* Yes, I was now in Calcutta – after an absence of four years – the city where I'd grown up, the city where I'd first met Sudarsana, who was now the mother of our three children. Not everything that happened here was ideal or even desirable, but it didn't matter.

Right now what was important was that we were with the children on our way to Tollygunge. Tollygunge, Ballygunge, Kalighat, Bhabanipur, Shambazar, Chowringhee, Harish Mukherji Road, Southern Avenue, College Street, Cornwallis Street, Dharamtolla Street, Park Street, Bhim Ghose Lane – are all places where I'd either lived or spent a lot of time. Calcutta was home.

The old, familiar landmarks came and went as we drove along – Howrah Bridge, Dalhousie Square, the Esplanade, the Maidan, and the Victoria Memorial Hall. Then through Bhabanipur we drove towards Tollygunge Bridge, the infamous bridge under which so much water collected after a long, heavy downpour that neither man nor machine could negotiate an area of about 200 square yards, and all traffic between Tollygunge and the south came to a standstill. This was the last of the prominent landmarks which confirmed that I was back home, for Tollygunge had become home for me before I left for Uganda, East Africa. It was my going away which I thought had made a difference: I was rediscovering Calcutta.

After lunch, we sat round and answered questions, mainly from Sunanda – Sudarsana's sister – and my father-in-law. My mother-in-law joined in only occasionally. There was so much interest in our course of studies at the Institute of Education, in post-war Britain, in British politics and our tour in Europe, Turkey and the Middle East that we could have gone on talking into the middle of the night. But my mother-in-law intervened. She suggested that we had some tea and then spent some time exclusively with the children. We didn't need much persuasion. I borrowed my father-in-law's car and went to the Lakes, where in the late afternoon and early evening there was the atmosphere of a busy fairground with hundreds of temporary stalls doing brisk business, selling all manner of wares – flowers, balloons, toys of various kinds; tea and certain kinds of cooked food to go with it, sold in *Saal* leaves folded into a bowl and pinned in place by its own stem, soft drinks, cigarettes, some popular magazines. There were actually so many different kinds of articles available there by the Lakes in the early evening of a summer's day that some people came specifically for the purpose of shopping and looking round. The balmy air and the opportunity for discussing politics – a favourite Bengali conversation topic – were extra attractions.

It was a good idea – bringing Aparna, Aparajita and Nondon to the Lakes. They had us all to themselves and they were enjoying the relaxed atmosphere, with many other children playing, laughing and running around. Sudarsana and I were getting a lot of joy just watching them. We'd brought each one of them a gas balloon. Nondon had taken charge of them. Each balloon was attached to a fairly long piece of string so that Nondon was able to let them go up to a particular height and then bring them down again by lengthening and shortening the pieces of string to which they were attached to. It was like flying kites. I could see that he was really enjoying flying his three balloons. And while we were approaching the car, he was still engrossed in flying his gas balloons, each one a different colour. He let the balloons – red, green and blue – fly up and up by releasing a little more of the strings at the end of which they were tied, and then he pulled them back, letting out little chuckles of satisfaction and then laughing joyfully. He came to the door of the car and started pulling back his beloved balloons so that he could enter the car, an old four-door Renault. And then it happened.

The strings slipped from his grasp and the balloons flew away. Quite quickly they rose higher and higher and nearly disappeared in the deepening dusk as my little son, not a lot older than two years, looked up full of disbelief and despair and said:

'Baba, look, my balloons, they're gone!'

His voice broke. His eyes filled with tears. Disconsolate, he started crying. Sudarsana took him in her arms, kissed his tear-stained cheeks and said,

'Tomorrow, we'll buy you some more. You've lost nothing that we can't buy again. Tonight I'll read you some great stories.'

The trauma was short-lived. Sudarsana managed to divert his attention to matters more important than escaping balloons.

We had a flat of our own now in Tollygunge, not far from where we'd lived before we had left for East Africa. I'd won a few hundred pounds in a lottery and with that money Sudarsana's uncle had built us this small flat of two bedrooms and a living room on land which he'd bought a long time ago. Although our colonial bungalows were much larger with quite a bit of land around them, this was *our* flat and the very first piece of property that we'd ever owned.

'So, you're now a man of property?' Sudarsana said.

'No more than you are a woman of property,' I said.

'How does it feel?' she asked.

'Gives me a sense of security. Let's face it, our outlook on life is purely *bourgeois,* and it's important for most us to own property,' I said.

'I just like the feeling. At last we've a place of our own,' said Sudarsana.

We realised that the flat was immediately useful because we had our six weeks' holiday ahead of us and during this time our privacy was easier to organise, when we really wanted it, with a flat of our own, than if we were sharing a place with Sudarsana's parents or somebody else. But, on the whole, on a short holiday after a long absence, we certainly didn't want to lock ourselves away. It gave us pleasure when friends and relations came to visit us in *our* flat, but it was only a peripheral pleasure, derived from the pride of ownership.

I went out to see Debu-da and Baudi, who had now settled down further north of Tollygunge from where we lived. Their domestic and financial situation hadn't changed. Debu-da still only very occasionally – with gaps of years in between – got the opportunity to direct a low-budget film at a fee which most music directors considered derisive. Baudi had neither the education nor the temperament to earn even a modest living. The result was insecurity and humiliating dependence on occasional loans from helpful friends and students. But the incredible fact was that on the few occasions I managed to spend some time with Debu-da, I found him the same friendly, unworldly, uncomplicated and generous person he'd always been. Success was always going to elude him because he lacked the discipline and the determination to face up to the dull routine of a humdrum life, which we all have to face up to a lot of the time. Most critics of Debu-da put it more simply – he had no discipline. But for me Debu-da was still one of the most interesting and companionable people I knew, and Baudi was as ever long-suffering, uncomplaining, and affectionate.

At least a fortnight had gone by but I hadn't seen my father; Mejda and Borda, and their families. Sudarsana had no sense of loyalty towards them because they'd objected to my getting married to her and my three children hardly knew them. But I wanted to see them. It was really pleasant spending one Sunday at 5 Star Lane with Mejda, Baudi and their three children, and answering their questions about life in East Africa and England. They were also curious – Mejda and Baudi – about the cities I'd visited on our way back from London to Calcutta, the sights we'd seen, the people we'd met. There was no change at Number 5, Star Lane.

At Borda's place, I was welcomed wholeheartedly with a great cup of tea. Father looked frail. His bed was in one corner of the living room, not far from the main bathroom. He spent quite a lot of time in bed, reading a little and sleeping a lot. He sat at the edge of the bed and held me in a long embrace.

'I can't remember, my son, when I last saw you. The next time you come, there mustn't be such a long gap. Your father is now old and infirm. You must come and see him more often. How are you? Are you well?'

I said I was fine. I explained that I lived a long way away; it took me more than a fortnight to get back to Kampala, where I lived, and it was only once every four years that we had leave to come and spend a few months in Calcutta.

'The next time you come, I may not be around,' my father said, in a matter-of-fact voice, without self-pity.

My eyes filled with tears. My father, who used to tell me that one must banish the fear of mortality and live, always, as if one was the master of one's destiny, was now trying to face up to the ultimate reality. He was not the tall, straight-backed, confident man he used to be. He said that he was very cold the last winter. I suggested that we went shopping that morning and he responded positively.

'I rarely go out these days,' Father said, 'but when I do, I enjoy the sights and sounds of Calcutta.'

Father was bent up, but there was no pain, he said; only a feeling of discomfort. He walked slowly down the stairs and then got into the taxi with some difficulty. We were setting out for Dharamtollah Street. He bought some underwear, a shawl and a warm coat. It was a large store that sold only clothes. Father looked around, walked about, showed interest in various items of clothing, even looked animated, but was soon exhausted. Age had taken its toll. No signs of the soul clapping its hands and singing.

When we returned to Borda's in Park Circus, Father went straight to bed for a rest and I went to spend some time with my eldest brother's wife. She was very cordial as usual and worrying about how to get her daughters married. This was an obsessive problem leading to the constant preoccupation of parents, especially mothers. 'Who is my daughter going to marry? Is he going to be a good man who'll love and cherish my daughter, or is he going to give her a terrible time?' These are questions parents frequently asked themselves. Then there was the problem of dowry. How much was legitimate? How much was adequate? Parents of grown-up daughters worried regularly and masochistically about such matters. Nobody said, 'No more dowry for our daughters. Our daughters don't need to marry any more than your sons do!' It would be better still if young men and women who wanted partners insisted that this pernicious system wasn't allowed to cast a shadow on their relationship. Those who give and those who take inducements of money and presents for getting into a human relationship which is important for enriching and creating life should be persuaded to discontinue the practice. We discussed the subject quite seriously, and we both remembered that almost ten years ago we had a similar discussion and I held the view that the practice was unworthy of those who paid and those who received and should be immediately discontinued. But one's ideal can be another's ruin.

Father had just woken up. I went and sat on a stool next to his bed.

'It's good you're still here,' he said. 'I was exhausted.'

'You did very well, Father,' I said.

'When are you coming again?' he asked.

'In about five years, I hope,' I said.

'That's a long time,' he said.

I explained that teachers recruited from overseas – mainly Britain and India – had overseas leave: the British every three years and those from the Indian sub-continent once every five years. Father wanted to know why British expatriates had better terms. I tried to explain: demand and supply, market forces, etc. He wasn't convinced.

The British made their rules in our country as well.' he remarked, 'and they were usually in their favour. Anyway, come back and see me again as soon as you can. And don't forget, I've only ever met one of your daughters.'

It was a good day for me. I returned to Tollygunge soon after teatime. The children made no comments whatsoever on my long absence. I wondered whether they'd noticed that I was away all day. I must have been disappointed that they didn't once say anything about it. Sudarsana did ask how everybody was at Congress Exhibition Road in Park Circus, how Father was keeping, whether my big brother was earning enough to feed so many mouths and whether my sister, two years older than me, whose name was Hena, was ever going to get married. This last question was one which I hated being asked because I held myself responsible, without ever wanting to do so, for the fact that she was still unmarried. The idea had been that the dowry I received from my bride would pay for the wedding of my sister. I told Sudarsana that neither my elder sister, Hena, nor my younger sister, Radha, was at home and I didn't discuss the prospect of their getting married.

'My uncle has been taking a lot of interest in your sister, Hena,' Sudarsana said. 'Practically every weekend, your two sisters visit my uncle's house in Park Circus, ostensibly to spend time with Ira and Arati, my two cousins. But the real incentive comes from my uncle. It's he who organises these meetings.'

I took some time to respond. Most of the information was news to me. What I was just told was about the beginning of a relationship between two adults. I wouldn't be in Calcutta long enough to see it mature or come to an end. But I wanted them to marry, have children, and have a life together. I knew my sister hated her dependence on her older brother and would love to have her own life, her own partner, her own children, and her own independent establishment. And if Sudarsana's uncle, a widower, had sufficient means to support his three grown-up children – two daughters and a son – and my sister – why should anybody object? Sudarsana was ambivalent.

'It seems to me,' I said to Sudarsana, ' that you aren't particularly enthusiastic about your uncle getting married to my sister.'

'I don't think I have any strong feelings either way. It's my cousins, Ira and Arati, who don't like the idea of anybody taking their mother's place. Aunty Mary was a good wife, a good mother and a popular member of the Roy clan. It'll be difficult for your sister to take her place,' Sudarsana said.

'I think speculating about their future is a futile exercise. What two adults decide to do with their lives is entirely their business,' I said.

'I agree whole-heartedly,' Sudarsana said, loudly and dramatically, in a pre-emptive effort to diffuse any tension which might result from the discussion.

I wasn't particularly interested in discussing a hypothetical situation, especially when I knew that we'd soon be out of the country and wouldn't have the slightest influence on the lives of those we were leaving behind in Calcutta. I wanted my sister to get out of big brother's hegemony and start life in a different and more congenial environment, where she was mistress of the house, and a wife and mother. Sudarsana's uncle was at least 15 years older than Hena, my sister. But if the age difference was not an issue for them, why should we worry? But I felt that there was hostility in both camps and I didn't know how the conflict was going to resolve itself. I didn't want it to affect our relationship – Sudarsana's and mine. But I was beginning to feel that Sudarsana was partisan – more concerned about her cousins' petulant and interfering sentiments than two adult, lonely individuals' need to live together in a meaningful relationship.

I had enjoyed the last fifteen months or so. The memory of mainly London, but also of Paris, Rome, Trieste and Baghdad, among other exciting cities, would take a long time to fade from my memory. Meeting up with my children, my father and brothers and sisters and Sudarsana's parents and sister was certainly the climax of the time I was away from Kampala. But I'd also realised that that unique city, built on seven hills, the capital of Uganda had come to mean more to me than I'd realised. I was now ready to return to my friends, my students, my new life.

Aparna was amazingly mature, sensible and responsible. It was already clear that she had to be taken seriously. She was seven but woe betides anyone who should try to give her the little-girl treatment. She was affectionate but quite critical for her age. She loved books, enjoyed listening to what she found interesting – with an intensity which was unusual for someone her age. One misfortune for my daughter was that she had asthma and it came upon her unexpectedly and caused her suffering. Sudarsana's father also was a victim of recurrent attacks of asthma, especially after his retirement. And it's a tragic fact of life that we often pass on to those we dearly love some of our worst infirmities and afflictions. I had no doubt that Aparna's asthma was genetically connected with her grandfather's. Aparajita, who for reasons of her own has always preferred being called Pinki, which was her nickname, was always quietly and unobtrusively good at whatever she was doing. She was naturally gifted, creative and imaginative, but not particularly dependent on attention, adoration or approval. She must have noticed that Nondon and Aparna got a disproportionate share of adult attention, but it didn't make her in the least bitter or resentful. My children were always good to have around because quite early in life they had started enjoying what they did and being themselves. My overwhelming feeling at the time was that I wasn't spending as much time with my children as I wanted to. But one of my problems has always been that I'm easily distracted.

Pronoti lived a few houses away, an attractive young woman, tall for a Bengali, with the slim figure and litheness of a dancer. She had abundant black hair, which she displayed with careful inattention, and a friendly smile, which she flashed at me – and probably others – quite generously. One morning when I was driving in the direction of Park Street on some minor errand, I found Pronoti walking in the direction of the tram stop on the main road, in Tollygunge. I drove ahead of her, waved and stopped.

'Would you like a lift?' I said.

'No thanks,' she said immediately and automatically. I started the engine. Then she started running towards the car. I stopped and got out.

'Are you all right?' I asked politely.

'Yes, thanks. I think I will come with you. Will you be going past Southern Avenue?' she asked.

'Yes, I will,' I said. 'Hop in. I'll be driving to Park Street.'

Pronoti sat down next to me and thanked me. She was a pleasant and attractive young woman. She'd heard that Sudarsana, the children and I lived in Uganda. So she asked me questions about our life there and, not unexpectedly, about the animals in the National Parks. I got the impression that our neighbours in Tollygunge were curious about us. It was pleasant to get to know Pronoti. It was a pity we knew so few of our neighbours.

I liked Pronoti. It was a chance encounter. I never met her again. I'd have liked to have got to know her better.

I went to Park Street, met Sunit, an old friend from university days, had some coffee with him, bought some books and returned to Tollygunge.

Sudarsana was waiting. She had news for me, she said, but she wanted to know first where I'd gone.

'I went to Park Street to meet a friend. I thought I'd told you,' I said.

'Never mind,' she said. 'Jack has written. We've both passed our exams. Both you and I now have the Post Graduate Certificate in Education from the University of London,' Sudarsana said with genuine enthusiasm.

For me, it was immense relief. I couldn't count the number of times when I'd felt really anxious about the outcome of the examination and wondered what should happen if I'd done badly. How could I face my colleagues? Would I be asked to quit? I never liked examinations and interviews. I was always surprised and relieved when I passed an examination or did well at an interview. I wanted to take Sudarsana in my arms, and dance round the furniture in the living room, but I couldn't. The room was too small and cluttered. So I turned to Sudarsana, held her hand and said, 'Thank you. I can't tell you how relieved I am.'

'Some think they can do more than they actually can. Some think they can do much less,' she said. 'Why do you always underestimate your ability to do things?'

'OK, I get the message,' I said.

I expected to do badly in examinations and it was always a relief if I did well or somehow got by. Probably because of this irrational, ingrained fear of being examined, tested, assessed and classified, I'd take these occasions seriously and work and worry – often quite unnecessarily. And I usually coped. It was a relief when I passed an examination or managed to keep my end up in an interview. It was therefore natural that I should want to celebrate when there was a positive outcome after all the fear and trepidation.

Sudarsana agreed. No, more than that – she was enthusiastic. I took her shopping list, borrowed my father-in-law's car and went shopping. It was a typical Bengali meal, with emphasis on fish and vegetable dishes and sweet curds, and *sondesh* for dessert. As far as food was concerned, I was a totally gastronomically conditioned Bengali, who would settle for good traditional Bengali cooking any day in preference to any other kind. My appreciation of the various kinds of food available in India and elsewhere wasn't highly developed. My favourite food then, and for years to come, was boiled rice and fish curry. Dull and predictable, Sudarsana would say. Sudarsana and Sunanda sang. The children's eyes were heavy with sleep, so they went to bed. We too soon followed– after an eventful day and a pleasant evening.

Tutu-da and Joy were finding it difficult to settle down in Calcutta. When we all returned to Calcutta, we found that Joy was coping better with the weather than she did in Baghdad and Basra. She often used to get tired in the heat in Italy, Turkey and Baghdad because she was unaccustomed to heat. We could take a lot more of it. Her present problem had to do with Tutu-da's medical practice. Women in Calcutta – and most places in India – would rather go to a woman gynaecologist than a man. This made life difficult for both Tutu-da and Joy. Tutu-da tried to make a living as a general practitioner, which he didn't like. His first qualification was Member of the Royal College of Gynaecology; now he was a Fellow: FRCOG. But this didn't make a great deal of difference. In desperation he was thinking of taking up an appointment in one of the tea gardens – a dead-end job. So Sudarsana and I felt concerned but helpless.

The time for leaving for Kampala was getting closer. Although the children were very settled in their grandparents' house, much loved and very well looked-after, none of them was against the idea of returning to Kampala. Especially Nondon's devotion and loyalty to me was inexplicable – he'd go to the end of the world with me with love and unquestioning trust.

The time had come for visiting friends and relations to say goodbye. There were problems... Father was getting weaker and frailer by the day; my elder sister Hena's future hung in the balance; Debu-da still didn't know when the next opportunity for earning a reasonable income would come. These were problems which I could do very little about – I had neither the means nor the time to attend to them.

There was unfinished business which I had to attend to. The Morris Minor, which I'd shipped out from Trieste to Bombay, had to be cleared and rebooked to Kampala. I went by train to Bombay, contacted the agents and took delivery of the car. I was told I could use it in Bombay while I was there and then hand it back to the agents. Once again, I stayed at the Seaview Hotel.

I found that I had Shobha's telephone number. Shobha had been a young student of mine in Old Kampala School. She was going to college in Bombay. I rang her and she and a friend of hers came to the hotel. Shobha was mature and friendly. I was both pleased and flattered that she'd taken the trouble to come to see me. I always had a problem with my young students. I was never able to keep the traditional distance between myself and my students. I have to confess that I was often more friendly than convention was ready to countenance, though during my more than fifty years' teaching career my friendly or over-friendly relationships never gave rise to any problems or scandal, pain or alienation.

Shobha was pleased to see me, she said. And was I pleased to see her? Yes, of course, I said. She'd grown a little taller and leaner since I'd seen her last. The fact that she'd brought along a friend indicated to me that she'd started thinking like a far-sighted woman. It wouldn't do to meet me in a hotel room all on her own, she must have said to herself. It was a hot, sticky afternoon. Both, Shobha and her friend had a shower in the bathroom attached to my hotel room. Then we drove several miles away from the centre of Bombay to a beach which wasn't too crowded, had a meal in a restaurant and drove back to the hotel. It was a pleasant outing, a day of relaxed enjoyment in the company of two women, full of youthful zeal and fun and mischief. Shobha's friend's name, I think, was Urmila. When we were at the beach, she hitched up her dress and waded into the sea. She walked further and further, and at one point she was almost waist-deep in water. Both Shobha and I were amused to begin with but amusement soon changed into anxiety.

'Does Urmila swim?' I asked Shobha.

'I don't know,' she said.

'Come back, don't go any further,' I shouted.

'Come and get me,' she said, her voice full of mischief.

'I quickly took off my shoes and socks, rolled up my trousers and waded through the gentle waves to where Urmila stood laughing in the water. When I was close to her, she hung on to me as we came to the shore.

'What was that about?' Shobha said.

'I wanted to be carried,' Urmila said, simply.

'I see,' said Shobha. She didn't at all look pleased.

Life has many beginnings without a middle and an end, I was thinking, philosophically.

I never met either Shobha or Urmila again.

In Bombay I did some paperwork and paid for the transportation of the car, business that had to be attended to. It was important that this business was transacted without much fuss or any bureaucratic issues. The man who was dealing with the transportation of the car, a friendly Welshman, was helpful and efficient. He not only attended to the business of transporting my car to Kampala, but also invited me to dinner at his hotel. He was unusually and embarrassingly friendly and generous. I enjoyed the evening to begin with, but felt relieved when the dinner and the postprandial generosity and bonhomie were over. A likely explanation for my unease is that his sexual orientation was different from mine.

After returning to Calcutta, I concentrated on preparing to go back to Kampala. We saw friends and relations, checked on the date and time of the departure from Bombay, wrote to Sudarsana's aunt and uncle in Kampala. We saw Ronu, my friend from St Xavier's College, and Reba, his wife, who lived in Tollygunge at one time, but now lived in a flat in Chowringhee. They had a daughter, Runki. Ronu, Reba and Runki – they constituted one of those ideal families which live happily ever after. Sudarsana knew Ronu long before she met me because they both belonged to the Brahmo Samaj, which had moved away from the popular idol-worshipping and holy-water-bathing version of Hinduism. It was inspired by the principles outlined in the Upanishads and promoted by some of the Bengali middleclass intellectuals. The Brahmo religious practices had some things in common with Christianity, group-worship being one of them. It was on the occasion of celebrating one of the most important days of their religious calendar that I was formally, ceremoniously introduced to Sudarsana – at the time, almost a first step towards getting engaged to be married. I always enjoyed the celebration which I attended because of good company and excellent singing. The food was an anti-climax for the critical. I found it quite fun – the communal eating, dollops of food – a spicy stew made of rice, lentils, potatoes and onions called *khichuri* – dished out in a great hurry to people sitting on mats on the ground in an open field with a makeshift, projecting canopy overhead called *chamianas*. The whole arrangement was actually fairly effective. Socially, there was a lot more in common between Sudarsana and Ronu and they were good friends. I enjoyed the company of Reba and Ronu. I was glad we went. It was like renewing or revitalising a relationship because we hadn't written to them or set eyes on them for more than four years. We took our time when saying goodbye. It was going to be at least another four years before we met up again. We probably talked casually about the crisis in Goa, England's victory in the test series and the death of Thomas Mann – and left. I've noticed men often talk about sports and politics when they feel emotional.

I wasn't only saying goodbye to Ronu and Reba but also to Calcutta, a city which was part of my identity. I was going to go away again for five years. But it didn't really affect me so much. I'd grown up. I wasn't sentimental about people and places or anything else any more. I was quite casual when I left my father and my brothers and sisters. Yes, it's grown-up to be casual. It is sophisticated, civilised behaviour. What is more, nothing gets done if you let emotions get in the way.

'You're very quiet,' remarked Sudarsana.

'I was thinking about saying goodbye to people who matter to me and to Calcutta,' I said.

'I wondered briefly why we'd gone away so far – when we were leaving Ronu and Reba's flat,' she said.

'I too have known Ronu a long time,' I said.

Now all the goodbyes were over and we were ready to go. I only wanted to look forward, and not regret all the unfinished business here in Calcutta. I felt guilty that I hadn't spent enough time with my father, my sisters, Debu-da and Mejda. There were friends in Calcutta who didn't even know that I was in Calcutta. Now my mind was focused on returning to Kampala to catch up with my students and colleagues and doing a good day's teaching.

'Are we going to go back to our old house?' asked Aparna.

'I don't think so. Both Sudarsana and I will probably have different jobs in different schools, and where we live will depend on where we work,' I said.

'It's a pity,' Aparna said. 'I liked the tall tree at the back of the house.'

Aparna didn't like leaving her grandparents when we set out for Uganda four years ago. This time she didn't show any resistance, and didn't ask any difficult questions although, at the same time, she didn't demonstrate any great enthusiasm. She was now seven plus – still too young to have evolved a philosophy of life, yet mature enough to realise that certain courses of events are pre-determined; parents work to make a living and work involves travelling, sometimes to the next postal district, sometimes to another continent. Aparajita was quietly getting ready to go, making sure she didn't leave anything behind and always helping her mother in any way she could. It was Nondon who was walking six-foot tall. He was going back to Africa – not East Africa, not Uganda, not Kampala, but to Africa. He was born in Africa. He was African. The African elephant was bigger and stronger than the Indian elephant. The African lion had no equal. Then there were leopards and cheetahs and the spotted hyena. There were black and white rhinos. There were hippos and many kinds of monkeys. He was most interested in two animals – the zebras and the giraffes. Most of his love and knowledge of African animals he got from his grandparents who talked to him about African animals and showed him pictures of them. It was they who told him that Africa was the country of his birth and he should be proud of that because Africa was a great continent. That was why Nondon, who loved his grandparents dearly, couldn't wait to get back to Kampala. Grandma and Grandpa had prepared him for the journey back to Kampala.

There was more in favour of looking forward than looking back at this stage. I hadn't seen John, Ted and Naresh for a year and we hadn't written, so I was most interested to see how things were with them. These three friends helped me to adjust to my new environment in a way which was natural, unselfconscious and congenial. I know we had a great many common interests. All four of us believed that power and privilege still had the upper hand in our society to an extent which was unacceptable. We read a lot of poetry and fiction – John, Ted and I – and Naresh painted. I was the only married man among bachelors. I was also looking forward to teaching again. I had learnt a few skills and wanted to try out some new ideas. It would be wrong, however, to compare me to an actor who had acquired new skills and insights, waiting for the curtain to rise. For, this time round, I wanted my students to act.

I'd always thought that teachers tend to teach too much. They tell students all there is to know and get in the way of their finding out. They talk, the students listen. They act, the students observe. Teaching would be a much more dynamic, interesting and creative experience for students if students could be made active partners in the experience of learning, exploring and discovering. I had to find a practical and viable approach to release the energy locked up in the students and direct it to the supremely important business of learning. To find this approach and make it effective, I needed to return to the classroom.

There was also the need to be together as a family again. The family doesn't work for everybody, but it had worked for me. I couldn't think of it as a bourgeois institution which had outlived its usefulness. My father-in-law was going to come with us to Bombay again – my father-in-law, who loved quietly and gave all he could afford to give without people realising how much he was giving. My mother-in-law and Sunanda, my sister-in-law were coming to Howrah Station to say goodbye. We were all more relaxed this time because we knew where we were going, what we were going to do, what kind of house we were going to live in and, what's most important, what kind of people we were going to live with. My father-in-law was also relaxed because just over a year ago he had come to Kampala with my mother-in-law and they had liked what they'd seen. All three children were fighting fit; Aparna wasn't so resistant to the idea of leaving behind her Dadubhai and Didibhai; we'd both acquired highly-rated, professional qualifications. In short, travelling back to Kampala was proving to be more enjoyable this time without the uncertainties and anxieties of the 1951 experience. We arrived in Bombay and went to the hotel we were familiar with – the Seaview Hotel – which we'd found perfectly comfortable as well as affordable on our earlier trip.

One small anxiety did exist in a corner of my mind. Ronu had taken me into one corner of the living room, away from Sudarsana and Reba, and shown me an article in which the writer had described, with admirable impartiality, the events of the Mau Mau rebellion against colonial oppression and exploitation. When we went to Uganda in 1951, Mau Mau was already in the air. Members of the Kikuyu tribe were meeting in secret and planning brutal violence against their colonial masters. The storm was brewing. While we were living in Kampala – before we went to London and the children came to India – we had heard of great atrocities being committed by both the Kikuyu tribesmen and the Kenyan police. Then the British troops arrived in 1952 after savage atrocities had been committed by the Mau Mau. In 1953 the death penalty was declared by the British Governor for anyone who administered the Mau Mau oath. All this we knew. And we knew about the arrest of Jomo Kenyatta in 1952. Now what I learnt from this article was that the rebellion was far from over. Some Mau Mau activists were hanged, thousands imprisoned and killed. The situation was quite critical, fraught with consequences the nature of which nobody could predict. The article had caused me some anxiety. I kept it to myself. And even when the subject came up during a discussion – my father-in-law was a well-informed person – I showed no sign of unease or fear. I remembered that the Mau Mau rebellion and its ruthless suppression had caused us anxiety while we were in Kampala but the agitation for an independent Uganda was entirely or almost entirely non-violent compared to what was happening in Kenya. I really had no serious misapprehensions about returning to Kampala. My expectations were positive. I felt at the time that life was going my way. I lived in an orderly universe.

I can't recall the name of the ship which was going to take us to Mombasa. It was either the SS Karanja or the SS Uganda. Father-in-law came to say goodbye to us and waited until we were all on board. He wasn't tense. He didn't look anxious. He didn't wait until the ship had left the quayside as he had done four years ago. He smiled, waved and left. I do tend to go on about my father-in-law, I'm sure he too had his share of human weaknesses. But he was the person who gave

Sudarsana, me and the children all he could give from the very beginning. That was his way of dealing with us: the only way he knew. Three men who until then had made a significant impression on me – between the age of 14 and 30 – were Bhola-da, Debu-da and my father-in-law, all gentle people, who related well to people and life. There was also my mother-in-law. Yes, I was leaving the shores of India this time chock-full of positive feelings. My reunion with the children, I'm sure, had quite a lot to do with the way I was feeling.

Life on board the ship also was more enjoyable and relaxed. We ate our meals in the dining room instead of our cabin. The children played on the deck and made friends with other children. We got to know some like-minded people with whom we could discuss even such inflammable subjects as politics and religion: the connection between colonial exploitation and the Kikuyu uprising, the relentless and obsessive proselytizing zeal of Christian missionaries, Islam's insistence that Allah is the only god, the systematic refusal to let poor people live with dignity in a healthy environment. The majority of these friendly and articulate acquaintances were teachers from Kenya, Uganda and Tanganyika.

We were all looking forward to our day out any time during the next 48 hours in Seychelles, one of the smallest countries in the world, an isolated country comprising two island groups – one group where the islands are quite close together, one quite accessible from another, and another where the islands are far apart. Originally a French colony, it became a British colony at the end of the nineteenth century. Our ship berthed at the port of Victoria, which is also the capital of Seychelles. There was frantic activity all around the ship, with men and women approaching the ship and trying to sell their wares. We went ashore, like the majority of those travelling on this ship and we were taken around in coaches to visit places of interest, to do some shopping, to be frantic tourists for a day. Seychelles is probably the greenest country I've ever seen, with coconut trees everywhere. It grows various agricultural products I was familiar with, products which were in abundance in India and Africa – coconuts, bananas, sugar cane, cassava, potatoes and tea. Articles which the cottage industry of these islands produce were largely made of coconut shells, sea-shells and certain kinds of leaves, woven into baskets. Bamboo grew here in abundance and many fancy articles which attracted tourists were made out of bamboo. After a modest bit of shopping and feasting with our eyes on the beauty of the islands, we had a meal by a seaside restaurant where crab, prawn, lobster, octopus and other kinds of seafood were in plentiful supply. We ate fish. We liked fish. Bengalis are fish eaters. The children did their shopping with great interest. They walked, shopped, and watched with interest the sea, the sky, the islands, the various groups of people, tourists as well as local inhabitants of the islands. Apart from us, there were tourists from various parts of the world, or people who looked like tourists and behaved like tourists. The local population was largely identifiable because they were mainly Creole, of mixed African and Asian descent. A small section of the population was British and French, settled there for generations. A long time after this, a good friend and a good artist, Michael Adams, settled in Seychelles. He may still be there. Just as the islands were fascinating and colourful, so were the people.

We returned to the ship towards evening. Everybody who went ashore was talking about the day's experience with excitement, wishing they could spend longer there, wondering how many such wondrous countries existed on planet earth about which we knew little or nothing. Some of the ship's passengers had visited this country of many islands several times and were talking knowledgeably about it. It was one of the smallest, independent, sovereign countries of the world with between 70 and 75 thousand residents with an area of almost 110 square miles. The smallest independent state in the world was, of course, the Vatican, also known as the Holy See. The reasons for the Vatican being independent are religious and political, and it can't really be called a country. Other small states or countries which were mentioned were Monaco, seven square miles, and Lichtenstein, 62 square miles. But, we all agreed that no country, big or small, could be more beautiful, romantic, exotic and enchanting than Seychelles.

When the ship left Seychelles' main port and capital, Victoria, on Mahe Island, there was a little sadness, but there was the more powerful attraction of homecoming and Mombasa. The conversation on the deck and the dining room soon turned to the politics of East Africa, which meant a conflict of interests between the colonisers and the colonised. Political agitation for freedom was happening in all three countries of East Africa, but nowhere had it become as dangerous and bloody as in Kenya. The infrastructure of government and civil administration wasn't affected in any significant way: that was the consensus. Trains ran on time. People went about their business without fear of being blown up. There was racial discrimination in clubs, posh hotels and swimming pools, but neither the Africans nor the Asians took much notice of the Europeans' unilateral declaration of superiority.

The hazy outline of the coast of Mombasa appeared in the distance, causing considerable excitement among the passengers. There were some tourists on board the ship, but for most, it was homecoming. Soon after, there was hectic movement all over the ship, with people getting ready to disembark. Aparna, Aparajita and Nondon were there on the deck, asking questions and getting excited. I had a sense of adventure when I set eyes on the coastline of Mombasa because, I think, images of Africa which I'd internalised in my boyhood, images of unknown danger and exciting adventure, lay dormant in my mind. Sudarsana, in the mean time, was putting things together, tidying up, packing and getting organised for disembarking. I gave her a helping hand and the children were efficient too. Finally, I put all the passports together, checked the money, tidied up and was ready to start life again in Africa, the country of my adoption, the country where I'd decided to spend the rest of my life.

The port officials and the customs inspectors were just as efficient as the last time when we were here four years ago – efficient, thorough and polite. We went through quite painlessly and were reassured by the presence of Mr and Mrs Patel, who'd come to receive us and waved to us from a distance and gave us a friendly smile. Clearing our luggage was also fairly painless. We were warmly received, but the warmest reception was reserved for Nondon, who thoroughly enjoyed the attention. We were just as comfortable this time as last time in the Patels' large and affluent bungalow. The accommodation was excellent, the food was home cooking at its best, but the most remarkable aspect of their hospitality was their relaxed friendliness. An additional reason for my enthusing about the hospitality of the Patels is that I've never liked the impersonal atmosphere of hotels.

I think we spent just one night with Mr and Mrs Patel. Unlike the first time, when we were stepping into an unknown and uncertain future, now we knew the place where we were going to work and the people we were going to work with. And many of these people were colleagues whose company we enjoyed. There was also our work. Both Sudarsana and I thought that we'd learnt new skills and acquired new ideas which would make our teaching more creative and interesting. But we wouldn't know unless we'd tried out our skills and ideas in the classroom. I'd missed the weekend meetings between us – Ted, John, Naresh and me. There were quite a few students I was looking forward to meeting again. Sudarsana's aunt and uncle had always been kind, generous and affectionate. We wanted to meet up with them before we met anybody else. We were actually going to stay with them until we moved into our own house, and where our house was allocated would depend on where we worked. Quite a lot was going to happen in the months to come. For reasons which I only partly understood, there was more excitement and expectation than fear, anxiety or uncertainty in the way I looked at my future this time round. I suppose I'd gained in confidence as a result of my teaching as well as incidental, unexpected 'extra-curricular' experiences. Perhaps we take ourselves seriously when others take notice of us.

It was a re-run of experiences we already had four years ago, yet it was going to be different. Mr and Mrs Patel dropped us off at the station and we started our journey. We had an extra player in our team whose curiosity knew no bounds: Nondon. Both Sudarsana and I had to be awake and alert to answer mainly his questions. I think we were less lucky with the animals this time as the train sped through the Savannah. The giraffe was definitely Nondon's favourite animal. I think we also saw antelope, zebras and elephants. Nondon's excitement was immeasurable and a joy to see. Aparna and Aparajita remembered their previous experiences. It was they who were educating Nondon. Both Sudarsana and I noticed that Aparna and Aparajita had taken over from us the responsibility of educating Nondon. Aparajita was five – there wasn't a great deal she remembered. But Aparna knew and remembered facts and figures which surprised us. Then we remembered that whereas this train journey was the second one for Sudarsana and me, it was the third for Aparna and Aparajita. For Nondon, too, it was the second. We were impressed with the way Aparna identified African animals and talked about them. One way we could explain Aparna's knowledge was by the fact that she'd travelled by this train from Kampala to Mombasa the year before in the company of her grandfather, a man of very wide interests.

'You know a lot about these animals,' Sudarsana said, 'I'm impressed.'

'Dadu knows everything about animals,' said Aparna. 'He's taught me a lot.'

It was a great relationship – between Aparna and her Dadubhai. I'm sure my father-in-law loved Aparajita and Nondon just as much, yet there was a difference. He was closer to Aparna. When we first left India for Uganda, Aparna would probably have wanted to continue to live with her Didibhai and Dadubhai. But it wasn't an option available to her. I respected her love for these rather special people, but I never seriously considered leaving her behind. The first time we left for Africa she missed them and did express her disappointment and frustration but this time there wasn't any gesture or remark which indicated reluctance or reservations about leaving her grandparents behind in Tollygunge and coming back with us to Kampala. There was a strong attraction or incentive this time which wasn't there in 1951 – Nondon and Aparna were close. The affection was mutual. Aparna wouldn't want to be separated from Nondon. It was quite obvious that Nondon fully reciprocated. But whereas both Nondon and Aparajita looked up to their *Didi,* their elder sister, the relationship between the younger siblings was one of equals. The other explanation was that Aparna hadn't seen us for a year and had missed us.

There were at least two distinct parts of this memorable train journey from Mombasa to Kampala – the Savannah and the Highlands, both breathtakingly beautiful in their different ways. From Mombasa the train took us north-west to Nairobi and then to Nakura and to Eldoret. We'd soon reach the Kenyan border of Tororo, from where Kampala was a matter of 120 miles. We all had a strong and familiar feeling of homecoming, I was sure. I was looking forward to meeting up with John, Ted and Naresh, to seeing Sudarsana's uncle and aunt, and to going back to teaching. This was that very interesting time – the time of transition. Therefore, while I was looking forward, the highlights of the immediate past were also surfacing from time to time: the warm and friendly Mr and Mrs Patel and their hospitality; the landscapes in Kenya which were arid and inhospitable, as well as lush, green and beautiful. The steep rise of 9001 feet above the sea level to Timboroa, the highest station on a main railway line anywhere in the world; the station at 8716 feet, where the equator runs across the station; the breathtaking beauty of the Rift Valley. We were now firmly on our way home – Kampala.

Other familiar names floated noiselessly into my consciousness – Jinja, the Ripon Falls, Mbale, Mount Elgon, Lake Victoria, Entebbe, Masaka, and the Murchison Falls on the Victoria Nile. But more than anything else, it was the sights and sounds and people in Kampala which were uppermost in our minds. We travelled all the way from the Western shores of the Indian Ocean through a number of exciting places, but the thought of Kampala and the images of the city and its people never left me. Now we were within minutes of reaching the station. So we huddled together round the windows on the side of the station and each one of us looked out for familiar faces. I saw nobody. There was no group of teachers or students, large or small, waiting for us. Others around us were waving with zest, talking excitedly, shouting out names, but we saw no one. Then Sudarsana spoke out excitedly and pointed to a nucleus of four people standing some way behind the excited groups, rushing towards different compartments, shouting names and greetings, waving, laughing and excitedly talking. I looked in the direction in which Sudarsana was pointing and found Sudarsana's uncle, looking with some intensity at the faces in the windows and my three steadfast friends, John, Ted and Naresh, standing around him. I waved frantically, our eyes met, and Sudarsana's uncle and my three friends started walking in our direction. I think that the expression of excitement of my three friends was somewhat muted by the presence of Sudarsana's uncle, Mr K.D. Gupta, the Indian Education Officer, a formidable character. Uncle and John had brought their cars. Sudarsana and the three children got into Uncle's car and I got into John's. Our destination was Uncle's house in Old Kampala where John, Ted and Naresh were also invited for a drink.

We were going to stay with Sudarsana's uncle and aunt until we moved into our own house, Naresh informed me, while John was driving us to Old Kampala. Important changes had happened in Uganda to Indian education while we were in England and in India. Robi Banerji had gone away to Dar-es-Salam as headmaster of a school there. Mr D J Raval, the senior teacher of Physics in Old Kampala School, had become headmaster of a school – a new school – in Kololo, and both Naresh and Ted had been transferred there while we were still in London. John was still at Old Kampala School because Mr B. D. Gupta had refused to part with him. Naresh and Ted had houses in Kololo Hill, and they still met at Naresh's house most weekends – to have lunch or dinner and sit and talk. They had been discussing a lot of politics, Ted informed me, and also a little elementary philosophy. They hoped I'd return to the fold as soon as possible. John was the only person to drive a car among the three of them, so he'd drive up to Kololo Hill and we'd continue our weekend meetings. I responded to the suggestion that we should continue.

'Haven't you found anybody else eligible to join our weekend get-together?' I asked.

'Most of our colleagues are married people who, I suppose, attend to their wives and children. Nobody has shown any interest,' Naresh answered.

'And haven't you thought of tying the knot?' I said.

'That will be the ultimate betrayal,' Ted said, dramatically.

It was past lunchtime when we arrived at Uncle's house at Old Kampala. Ted, John and Naresh stayed for a drink and left. Sudarsana and her aunt sat on a sofa and seemed deeply engrossed in their conversation which, I felt certain, was about the family. The questions were coming mainly from Sudarsana's aunt, and they were, I'm sure, almost entirely about the family. She'd certainly want to know how her four brothers and her elder sister were, as well as her nephews and nieces, including Tutu-da. She'd have shown special interest in Joy, his English wife. I tried to listen. She was pleased and relieved when Sudarsana told her that Joy was a special kind of person. She was intelligent, well-informed, loving and generous.

Aunt didn't have children. I thought she got vicarious pleasure out of the success and happiness of her nephews and nieces.

'And how are your parents?' Aunt asked.

'They're well. They send you their love,' Sudarsana answered.

Sudarsana's cup of tea had gone cold by now. There were more questions and answers. For example, Aunt wanted to know how Mr and Mrs Patel in Mombasa were. She was pleased to hear that they'd treated us well and had sent their love and regards to her and Uncle. At this point, I was summoned by Uncle, who also asked me various questions about the family and about Mr and Mrs Patel of Mombasa. But his chief interest was about the quality of the course of studies at the Institute of Education, University of London. Many of these post-graduate courses, he commented, turn out to be too academic, too theoretical. He said that he'd observed the teaching of quite a few teachers with good teaching certificates and diplomas, and quite often he'd been disappointed, although their knowledge of the theory of teaching was sound. I invited him to come to my classes and observe a few lessons.

'I don't sit in on lessons any more,' he said. 'David does. David has great ideas about making the teaching in the classroom really interesting. I've seen him in action. He gets the complete attention of the class. They listen, they respond, they participate. He has a relaxed, friendly personality. I like his teaching.'

David was one of his colleagues, the Deputy Director of Education. I wondered what he'd think of my teaching. The conversation moved back to the family. So I too, like Sudarsana, got involved in a discussion about this subject of common interest.

We returned to official business. Uncle informed me that both Sudarsana and I were allocated to Mr Raval's school on Kololo Hill. There was no resistance from Mr B.D. Gupta, headmaster of Old Kampala School, he said, underlining the fact that Mr Gupta, junior, was probably quite relieved to part with the Bagchis, one of whom regularly experimented in the classroom, with untested and outlandish methods of teaching. This was good news for me. I liked Mr Raval and he approved of innovations. Sudarsana also would be pleased to work in Mr Raval's school, I was sure.

The children had gone to bed. We were sitting up and talking generally about the state of affairs in Uganda. Uncle thought Uganda would soon be granted internal self-government and independence should follow. Milton Obote of the Uganda People's Congress had emerged as the indisputable leader of the country. Uncle was certain that the transition to independence would be fairly peaceful because Sir

Andrew Cohen, the Governor, was a progressive liberal and his mandate, quite clearly, was to facilitate early independence.

Then we returned to more personal, more mundane matters – where we were going to live, and when we were moving in. At the brand new secondary school – Kololo Secondary School – the reputation of the school depended on us – its pioneers.

The next day, Uncle took us first to see the house on Kololo Hill where we were going to live and then to the school where we were going to work. The house was a bungalow with three rooms – two bedrooms and a living room, with some ground in the front, which wasn't large enough for a car as well as a proper garden. We liked the look of the house and Mr and Mrs Joshi, who were to be our neighbours. Then Uncle drove us to the school, which was shut at the time. The school building was built on two levels of the terraced hill. The classrooms were a level above the street – at level two of the hillside – and the administrative block was at level three. One had to go up some wide flights of stairs from the classrooms to the administrative block. From the street below, a wide driveway led to the first level, where the classrooms were. Between the two separate blocks of classrooms, there was an open space for morning assembly. There was also at one side of the square an open space for cars to park. At the time we visited, it looked pretty desolate. It was difficult to imagine the presence of a few hundred students and quite a few teachers going about their business in this place the next morning.

The hill overlooked a deep valley which stretched below it for miles, a valley of trees scattered all around in a disorderly fashion, and tall grass, shrubs and dense undergrowth in places through which it would be difficult to walk. Although quite close to the centre of Kampala, it had wide open spaces all around it and it was quite obvious that the city would spill over onto Kololo Hill in the years to come. Already there was a hectic building of houses and institutions taking place in Kololo. East Kololo Primary School and Kololo Secondary School were two educational institutions I was interested in because they were concerned with the education of the children of parents from the Indian sub-continent. I was also interested in Makerere University which was to the west of Kampala, where I had made a few friends.

We moved to a house in Bukoto Street initially with two bedrooms and no garden, but with some open space in front where I could park the Morris Minor. There was great excitement as we moved into our new house. Mr and Mrs Joshi, a young couple without children, were our neighbours. Across the road, Mr and Mrs Singh had two boys of between six and ten years. Aparna, Aparajita and Nondon shared one bedroom and Sudarsana and I another. We had someone to cook for us – a young man called Felix and someone to generally take care of the children when we weren't at home, Faisi. We were well on our way to rebuilding our home, our independent establishment, once again. Mary had unfortunately left us, though I can't remember why.

Shelter was organised. Now we had to see to the education of our two daughters. Nondon wasn't old enough for school, so we depended on Faisi to take care of him. From time to time, we'd leave him with Aunt, who'd stopped teaching by then and moved into their house – a large double-storey building on Kololo Hill. A new elementary school had come up in Shimoni, Kampala, called Primary Demonstration School, attached to Shimoni Teacher Training College. The pupils of this school went either to Kampala Secondary School or Kololo Secondary School.

Primary Demonstration school had earned the reputation of being progressive, but exactly what the word meant in this part of the world was difficult to ascertain. I went to have a look one Sunday afternoon. They were new buildings, single-storey bungalows. The playing fields had to be shared with Shimoni Primary School, a much larger school a few hundred yards away. When I went round, the whole place looked desolate. Schools, colleges and churches were normally places where we found congregations of large numbers of people, busy learning or praying. They look and feel like lonely places when there's nobody there. I didn't see or meet anybody, not even the caretaker. But I liked the look of the place and decided that Aparna and Aparajita were going to go to Demonstration School. Our lives were beginning to take shape.

My first day at Kololo Secondary School started with great expectations because the school was new and the teachers were young, by and large: Naresh, Ted, Sukumar, Sudarsana, Nalini, Promila, Mr and Mrs Menon – and me. There were other teachers also who were in our age group – we were all in our early thirties or mid-forties. The students were between 13 and 16 years old. Only a very few teachers were 40 and above. Mr D. J. Raval, our headmaster, was one of them.

Not having to work in the Old Kampala School gave me a sense of liberation because I was sure that if I'd gone back to teach there, the headmaster, Mr B. D. Gupta, would have continued to question both my methods of teaching as well as my pedagogic credentials, despite the fact that I'd done my teaching practice in two excellent British grammar schools and had acquired the Post Graduate Certificate in Education from the University of London.

I was now given the responsibility of making sure that we have an interesting as well as useful morning assembly. We, the teachers, were always there but Mr Raval often stayed away – partly because he had other things to do but also because he believed that leading inconspicuously from behind was quite often more effective. I also found that delegation is a creative and imaginative way of giving my students self-confidence and the incentive to learn and express themselves. One of the senior teachers – and occasionally the headmaster - made the announcements which were necessary or important for administrative purposes. Then one of the senior students read the news – relating to the school, the country and the world.

There were some students from the fourth year whose news reading and commentary were very competent as well as interesting. Peter Nazareth was one of them. Peter used to come to my house sometimes. He tried to introduce me to his kind of music but didn't get very far. I don't know how the other students fared but I know Peter went to Makerere University and then to the University of Leeds and is now teaching English literature at the University of Ohio. Many of my colleagues and students from Kampala and Kololo Secondary Schools are scattered around the world, some of them doing creative and responsible work... Some of these successful people were driven out of Uganda after Idi Amin came into power. Ravinder Maini left Kampala long before the advent of Idi Amin. He went to Cambridge, read medicine, and became professor at the Kennedy Institute, Imperial College, London. He has won several highly prestigious awards for his work targeting rheumatoid arthritis. He was knighted in 2003. There are, I'm sure, many other distinguished men and women among my former students doing immensely important work in various parts of the world, but I don't know where they are.

I was feeling fairly settled in Kololo Secondary School, with Sudarsana also teaching there and Mr Raval as headmaster. I was getting to know my students and beginning to relate to them. My two daughters were going to Demonstration School and Nondon to a nursery school. Our small bungalow was comfortable and our little Morris Minor an excellent car. The rhythm of our life was slow, safe and regular. There were mild surprises, mostly pleasant, and gentle undulations, always negotiable. Once or twice, we all went to the top of Kololo Hill in the evening and looked at the lights sparkling bright and clear on the surrounding hills. It was an incredible and magical sight because Kampala is built on a series of hills at an elevation of almost 4000 feet. Tier after tier of lights on those hills gave the city an amazing festive look. During the day, the sun was strong, but it didn't blaze and burn – the height restrained its tropical ardour. What made the strongest impression on me was the rain in the hills. I don't remember many persistent drizzles, for when it rained in the hills, it poured. The rain came down in torrents. The horizon remained hazy. Exhalations from wet earth filled the air with the scent of rain, especially when the rain stopped. Rain in the hills of Kampala had a different character from the rain in the plains of Calcutta. I was fascinated by both. My life had now fallen into a steady rhythm and I let the notion grow in my mind that we'd settled down – Sudarsana, our three children and I – to a life where everything that happened was expected except for some occasional mild surprises. As it happened, there was a mild surprise.

'Before you go home this afternoon,' said Mr Raval, 'Please come and see me in the office.'

It wasn't often that Mr Raval wanted to see any of us in his office. The extra-linguistic features of the message indicated to me that he had some news for me which was important. When I went to Mr Raval's office at the end of the day's teaching; he was waiting for me with a cup of tea. It was clear that whatever the subject, it was going to take a little time to discuss it.

'I have to collect the children from school, and I haven't managed to tell Sudarsana about our meeting,' I said.

'Sudarsana knows we're meeting after school. My car will collect the children. Sudarsana is going in the car to collect them,' Mr Raval informed me.

Mr Raval was a good organiser.

'Thank you very much,' I said. 'Now I can relax. It's a long time since I've spent any time with you.'

First of all, Mr Raval thanked me for recommending Ted, who I had said, would make an excellent secretary because his English was impeccable and his integrity unquestionable. He also complimented me on my teaching – without sitting in on any of my lessons. I pointed this out. He had talked to people and people had talked to him – teachers, students and parents. The news about good teaching spread in schools quicker than that of the Suez crisis, he said. The Suez crisis was what people were discussing at the time, when Egypt's Nasser nationalized the Suez Canal to raise funds denied to him for his Aswan Dam project with the fees for international oil freight thoroughfare.

'I've been very happy having you here and so have many others. Thank you very much for your contribution to the school,' he said.

There was something not quite right, something valedictory – the formality of the language, the compliments, and the excessive politeness.

'You're kind,' I said, 'and I'm beginning to find this unsettling.'

I laughed and looked at him for his response, a reciprocal laugh or, at least, an amused smile. But Mr Raval didn't laugh. There was a good reason for his behaviour, he said. It was necessary for him to say all that he had said because he wanted me to know that he deeply and sincerely appreciated my contribution to the school before I left. I was puzzled and alarmed. Where was I going?

Then he explained. Mr John Crossley-Hayes had told Mr K.D. Gupta, the Indian Education Officer, that he urgently required a lecturer at his college, the Shimoni Teacher Training College, on methods of teaching, and Mr Gupta had recommended me. I was expected to see Mr Hayes on Monday and start teaching the week after. This was too sudden. I didn't know how to react. What I didn't understand was why Mr Raval, who'd just told me how useful I was, should so readily agree to part with the jewel in his crown.

'What I don't understand, is that one moment you should tell me how much I'm appreciated and then get rid of me soon after,' I said with a smile, although I *was* puzzled.

Again, Mr Raval didn't smile. He answered my question seriously. Mr Gupta had decided that I was the best man for the job and it was his prerogative to make decisions about the deployment of teachers, his responsibility to make the best use of available resources. He wasn't the kind of person who didn't think long and hard before making a decision and administrators of his ilk didn't easily change their minds.

'There's another important reason why I didn't object,' said Mr Raval. 'It's the kind of job that'll suit you. There'll be small classes, dedicated students. Also, a lecturer has a higher status in the educational hierarchy. *And* better pay.'

I felt relieved after this explanation. But uncertainty always compels anxiety unless one's the adventurous kind, which I was not. A chronic sense of insecurity threaded through my days and ways – though I wasn't really afraid, only slightly apprehensive. Here in Kololo Secondary School, I had an intelligent, responsive group of students who made me feel useful, and friendly colleagues with whom I hardly ever had a feeling of unease. Why should I want to go away? There was also the feeling of rude interruption, not easy and natural transition. I wanted to do things which now must remain incomplete. I'd started off with a feeling of total frustration, but after Mr Raval had talked to me, it was mild disappointment. Whatever – a new beginning usually brought with it a sense of adventure.

Mr John Crossley-Hayes was a Scotsman – tall, well-built and bald. He wore thick, round glasses in a steel frame and was probably myopic. He was immaculately dressed grey trousers, white shirt, a modest tie and polished brown shoes. His jacket hung on the back of his chair. He was friendly, welcoming and brisk. He quickly put me in the picture. Whoever was lecturing on methods of teaching was going back to England and he required a replacement. He was standing in, but this arrangement couldn't go on for ever. He hoped I didn't feel disrupted. He welcomed me to the college on behalf of the staff and students. He was delighted to have me on the staff of the college.

I liked Mr Hayes. He gave me the impression of taking teaching and administration equally seriously – you let your students down if you're casual or careless in either of these areas, he said. After that he made a few brief comments on the importance of education in the developing countries and started talking about teacher-training in Uganda. He didn't think enough was being done to improve the standard of teaching in the classroom and complained about bureaucratic red-tape. Complaining wouldn't achieve much. We had to neutralize the deadly impact of mindless bureaucratic intervention with patient, inventive teaching, so that the whole experience of learning became self-generative and addictive. I listened to Mr Hayes's ideas with interest. His manner of speaking wasn't that of a passionate propagandist. It was matter-of-fact, logical and, if anything, understated. He was practical – neither too romantic nor too cerebral.

Without giving me any time to feel apprehensive or nervous, Mr Hayes started asking me searching questions about teaching in general and teaching particularly in Kampala's schools. How did the methods of teaching in England and Wales differ from what I'd seen in Kampala? How did the relationship between teachers and students differ when I compared my experiences in Blaenau Ffestiniog Grammar School in North Wales and East Ham Grammar School near London with what I saw around here? Was I critical at all about the way my subject, English, was taught in the local schools? There was then a quick transformation – the articulate commentator and critic became a patient listener, who seemed genuinely interested in everything I had to say. The final question was what my priorities would be if I came to teach at the college. It was only at this point that I realized that, despite the informality of this meeting, what was going on was an interview. Before Mr Hayes confirmed the appointment, he had to feel that what was on offer was acceptable.

'I'll see you on Monday,' he said. 'We start at 8.30.'

I'd got the job, I thought. I didn't think there was any uncertainty about it – unless Mr Hayes discovered that I was somewhat mentally retarded or our views on education were so different that we couldn't function together in the same institution. I was now a lecturer, although the lecture-mode wasn't the most effective way of teaching in my view. It was too one-sided. One person held forth and others listened. It lacked interaction. The few minutes left at the end of a lecture for asking questions certainly didn't compensate for ongoing interaction between teachers and students. Unfortunately, even in our schools, a large proportion of teachers behaved like lecturers and didn't provide the students sufficient opportunity to express their views and their reactions. Good teaching required the students to be active participants in the experience of learning. With these thoughts in my head I came to Kololo School to tell Mr Raval about my meeting with Mr Hayes.

Mr Raval was pleased but not a bit surprised. I would certainly have felt unwanted and unhappy if I hadn't been given the job. Yet I wasn't particularly joyful or flattered. If anything I was uncertain, apprehensive and generally insecure. As a teacher, I consciously avoided lecturing. Interaction is excluded during a lecture. The short period of time left at the end for a few questions created more frustration than interaction. So lecturing was neither the most rewarding, nor the most exciting way of teaching. Having expressed such views in the past, how was I going to be reconciled to lecturing, day in and day out, now that I was a lecturer?

But I couldn't have found anybody – not even Sudarsana – to sympathise with me in my purely theoretical predicament. Both my daughters were delighted, because their school was next door to the Shimoni Teacher Training College. Their father would be there, three minutes' walk from their classrooms. Even if they had nothing to do with him, the knowledge of his presence in the staffroom, one of the classrooms or the Assembly Hall would certainly give them an extra sense of comfort and confidence. I also liked the idea.

The college was a relaxed institution that set aside very little time for activities which were formal and ritualistic. There was no morning assembly, no sermons from the principal on various special occasions, no determined or dedicated look on the students' faces, no manicured lawns, no uniform. There was no tightness around the place, no determined pursuit of pre-meditated ideals. My colleagues were friendly, helpful, articulate, efficient people who made me feel I belonged to the place even before the month was out. I'd now lost my feeling of uncertainty largely because of the people around me – Mr Shukla, Edith Garvie, Mr Whitfield, Mrs Fermanian, Mr Bird, Mrs Walker, Gwen Poolman and Mr B. H. Patel. It wasn't customary for us to address one another by our first names but Edie and Gwen didn't want people to be formal with them, so I called them by their first names and they called me Ganesh.

Some very intelligent and academically well-equipped students joined the college because a job was assured after the successful completion of the course. Apart from that, there weren't many career opportunities in Uganda, and getting a place in Makerere University was difficult, because the best students from Kenya and Tanganyika also competed with grim determination for a place there. One of the students we had in our college became a lecturer there. Francis Lobo took over from Richard Bird as the PE tutor at Primary Demonstration School – and then he took charge of Physical Education at Makerere University College.

Among the students, who all behaved like responsible adults, there were quite a few potentially excellent teachers. There was very little tension in our relationship because I regularly demanded their active participation. Instead of telling them how to teach poetry, I would ask my students which poems had made an impression on them and why, and let them present to us aspects which had made the poems memorable. After various poems had come up for teaching and discussion, we would do a summing up, each one of us telling the others of our perception and our appreciation. I always made sure that I wasn't carried away, that I didn't appropriate more than my fair share of the discussion. Soon I found that I was greatly involved in the work that I was doing. I soon stopped looking back at Kololo Secondary School with nostalgia.

Gwen was the most friendly and companionable among my colleagues. She was slightly shorter than me but not a lot younger. She taught English through drama, producing short interesting situations, rather than plays. She wore a longish skirt and a white shirt, the sleeves of which she invariably rolled up. She also turned up the collar. All this made her look rather unusual, but it went well with her somewhat unusual temperament. During break and any other free time we might have, I probably spent more time with her than with anybody else. I was aware of this imbalance in my behaviour and wanted to do something about it before my colleagues and the students came to the wrong conclusions. But the problem resolved itself. Gwen's husband was transferred to Jinja, and Gwen, of course, had to go with him. It wouldn't be practical for her to commute 50 miles a day.

There was some excitement at the college – the drama group had won the best production award in a competitive festival of plays meant for various colleges. Behind their success was Edith Garvie, who was an experienced director of plays. There was a celebration of the success in the evening that weekend – dancing, a buffet supper and a congratulatory speech by the Principal: the kind of occasion which never happened in the secondary schools, where the parents were conservative and, by and large, opposed to the influence of 'pernicious' Western culture. In this college, too, not everybody participated in the dancing. Muslim girls wouldn't dream of getting up and dancing with the boys. There was one group of girls who belonged to the Ismaili community, the head of which was the Aga Khan. They called themselves Muslims but they eschewed the orthodoxy and conservative practices of Islam. And there were the students whose parents or grandparents were from Goa. They were Christian and largely subscribed to Western values. It's mainly the boys and girls from the Ismaili community, and the boys and girls who called themselves Goan that kept the dancing going. I joined the dancing sometimes. On occasions like these, I was keenly aware of Gwen's absence. She always participated in the dancing with her usual energy and good humour. I'd begun to miss her. It was a little more than friendship but less than love. I was always happy in her company and laughed at her jokes, was aware of her presence and enjoyed it, but there was nothing obsessive or compulsive in the way I felt about Gwen.

She rang. Some celebrity from the world of education was giving a talk in the town where she lived at the time. Would I be interested to come and listen to the talk on Friday morning, stay with them Friday night, and return to Kampala after lunching out with her and her husband on Saturday afternoon? I said I'd be delighted. Edgar Castle, a consummate speaker, an experienced educational administrator and philosopher, spoke without a script and held us in thrall. Gwen and I had lunch out. We returned to Gwen's house and retired, severally, for a nap, a postprandial luxury in tropical weather. I was rudely startled out of my daydreaming by a distraught and angry voice in the next room demanding various kinds of explanations from Gwen. My name was mentioned – far from affectionately. I hadn't really unpacked. I picked up my travelling bag; rushed to my car, a fairly new Peugeot 403, dumped my bag on the back seat, started the engine and whizzed off.

I arrived back at the Teachers' Training College in Kampala and rang Gwen. Thankfully it was she who picked up the phone at the other end.

'Are you all right?' I asked.

'Yes,' she said. 'I'll explain when we meet again.'

The incident, obviously, had something to do with their relationship. I never found out, because we never met again. There have been many fragments, many unfinished stories in my life.

Apart from teaching at the Shimoni Teacher Training College and occasionally meeting up at weekends with Ted, Naresh and John, there wasn't a great deal I was doing at the time. Once in a while, Sudarsana and I and the children would visit the Carlins on the Makerere University campus, where they had a bungalow. Sudarsana and I got to know Margery and Murray through Professor Alan Warner. At first, we enjoyed spending the occasional evening and weekend with them, but in a matter of months, weekends with the Carlins became almost routine. There was an important relationship there not only for Sudarsana and me, but also for our daughters – Aparna and Aparajita. Margery and Murray had two daughters – Vuyelwa and Aviva – about the same age as our girls, and they too got on very well with our two daughters. For the first time in Kampala we'd made friends – Sudarsana and I, on the basis of mutual affection and interest, with two uniquely sincere people. Apart from anything else, Murray and I had a common interest – English literature. Murray was a poet as well as a good literary critic.

I attended a talk he gave on Nabakov's *Lolita,* which I found both erudite and interesting. What I mean is that life was becoming multi-dimensional. It was no longer restricted to the teacher training college and the Indian schools. I also wanted to diversify my life in other ways. At the request of Professor Warner, Alan Warner, whom I've mentioned before, I gave a talk at a Makerere literary meeting on Tagore. At the end of the meeting it looked as if my friends and their colleagues had taken a genuine interest in the subject and that some of them were already familiar with some of Tagore's work.

Students of the college thought I played football well enough to be included in the college eleven. I was flattered. What's more, I enjoyed playing with the students and felt good if I made an impression on them. That evening we went to Old Kampala School to play against their senior side. It was a formidable team which had won many trophies. It had rained heavily, but now it wasn't even drizzling. The ground was wet but the sun was shining again, bright and clear. The game started. For some time, neither side had the upper hand. The break came and went. Still neither side had scored a single goal. I was playing inside left. Someone passed the ball to me. I dribbled past one player, and then there was nobody between me and the goalkeeper, John Agard, six foot two and lots of muscle. I was about to shoot when John charged. I shot the ball as quickly and hard as I could. At the same time, I felt the impact of the fast-moving, solid mass of John's tank- solid body. I shot up in the air and fell. I got up with difficulty – with help from John, who looked genuinely concerned. I couldn't move my left arm – the forearm had gone totally limp. Then there was cheering and the spectators went quiet, having registered the fact that there was an accident. I lifted my left forearm with my right hand: it was inert. I signalled to Jussa, one of my students, to come to my aid and requested him to drive me to Nakasero Hospital. Jussa drove my car and took me to the Emergency Unit of the hospital.

Dr Makandya, who was on duty, carefully examined the part of the arm where it had broken and said to himself, 'Excellent.'

'I don't understand,' I said.

We'd met before. His wife taught Hindi at Primary Demonstration School.

'What is it you don't understand, Mr Bagchi?' said Dr Markandya.

'What can there be in a broken arm that one can describe as 'excellent'?'

'I'm sorry,' he laughed. 'The break is in the long bone in the upper arm, the humerus. When I said 'excellent', I certainly didn't mean to say that I was happy that you'd broken your arm. I was happy that it was a clean break, not full of cracks and splinters. I'll put you in plaster. It won't hurt a lot but you'll be uncomfortable. I'll prescribe some strong painkillers. This kind of break heals easily.'
'Thank you. Now I feel reassured,' I said.

Jussa drove me back home after that. I felt great relief that though there was a feeling of discomfort, there wasn't any real pain. I asked Jussa how he was going back to the hostel.

He'd walk, he said. Sometimes one had to walk up steep hillsides, but those who'd lived in and around Kampala, a city of seven hills, didn't find this a problem.

'The ball you kicked before you fell and broke your bone,' said Jussa before he left, 'didn't miss the mark. It was a goal. We won! So it was worth breaking a bone!'

'Really?' I said. I truly found it incredible.

'What was the final score?' I asked.

'One goal to nil,' Jussa said.

Sudarsana and the children were all concerned. Nondon was quite tearful before I explained that such accidents were not unusual when you played football and that I wasn't in a lot of pain. I was soon back in college, teaching. There was consensus among my students that I was teaching better with a broken arm than I'd ever done with a whole one.

A few months passed. The damaged arm had healed, but I wasn't playing football yet. I liked the college, its environment, the students and my colleagues. I'd struck up a friendship with Dickie Bird, our PE teacher, who had a real zest for life, which included a healthy interest in attractive women. Our students were doing well at the various schools in Kampala and elsewhere in the country and I had the feeling, a feeling we all have from time to time, that things were going my way.

Though I missed Gwen; her friendly banter, her iconoclastic ideas; and her natural indifference to respectability. But there were obvious contradictions. Why was she so obsessed and possessive about her Persian carpets? It'd rained one afternoon and I was coming in through Gwen's front door and about to step on to one of her pristine Persian carpets, which adorned her living room.

She leapt out of her seat and almost screamed, 'Careful! Hang on! Please don't mess my carpet. I'm afraid I must ask you to take off your shoes!'

Wise men will tell me, with their gentle and tolerant smiles, that such contradictions are only human. But I found it odd, though this didn't detract from the fact that she was a warm-hearted and friendly person. Yes, I missed Gwen.

My greatest worry at the time was the health of my eldest daughter. Aparna was often wheezing badly. Sometimes it kept her awake, and when she fell asleep, it was out of sheer exhaustion. On one or two occasions, I'd driven up to Dr Jayant Thakkar's house at night or in the early morning. Jayant was always there for us. He kept assuring me that Aparna would grow out of it – most people did – and before that happened, he would try and make her as comfortable as possible. But Aparna's suffering was painful to watch, and if it was painful to see, it must have been really difficult to bear. Jayant understood my anxiety. He did his best to relieve Aparna's suffering. We talked about her condition quite often – me, the anxious father and him, the caring healer. Aparna still suffered quite a lot but, as far as I remember, the attacks became less frequent. Under the watchful care of Jayant, Aparna began to feel more confident. Jayant and I became good friends.

I thought that my teaching session with my students that morning had gone well. I was relaxing in the staff room, thumbing through the *Uganda Herald* when Mr De Souza from the office came and told me that Mr Hayes would like to see me.

'Mrs Fermanian is going back to England,' said Mr Hayes. 'I need someone to take over from her. I'm going to recommend you, if that's all right?'

Mrs Fermanian was the Headmistress of the Demonstration School.

He knew it was a bit too sudden, he had said, but he wanted to know if it was all right for him to recommend me for the post of Principal of the Demonstration School there and then. It was obvious he liked me as a lecturer, and was therefore prepared to entrust to me the responsibility of administering the school.

Mr Hayes was a first-rate teacher and administrator himself. It was good to know that I'd won his confidence.

'It certainly is all right. It's no problem,' I said. 'Thank you very much!' I said - scarcely able to believe what was happening.

Chapter 12

Demonstration School, Drama Festival, London

Primary Demonstration School was next door to Shimoni Teacher Training College. For all practical purposes, it was an independent school, administered by a headmaster who made all decisions about the institution's pedagogic approach and method. There were no criteria for selection except age – children had to be six years old to register for admission. Those who were registered would be accommodated first, and then the newcomers would be admitted if there were still places. My two daughters, Aparna and Aparajita, were already in the school and Nondon was going to start the next year. The school building was fairly new and the teaching staff were young, most of them ex-students of Shimoni Teacher Training College. There were six fairly large classrooms, toilets, a staff room and the headmaster's room. Alongside one of the walls of each classroom was the class library. Most of the administrative work was the headmaster's responsibility – though he could count on secretarial help from the college staff. The headmaster of Demonstration School was also referred to as the principal.

Next door to the school was the playing field, which we shared with Shimoni Primary School, a much larger school than ours. It had a well maintained playing field. What Primary Demonstration School lacked was an assembly hall. When we wanted the whole school to assemble, we used the open space opposite classes one to four. The school started off to provide training college students with regular access to the various classes to try out their ideas of how best to teach different subjects. But demand for places in the school grew rapidly because Miss Fermanian and her team of young and creative teachers had built up a good reputation for the school. Young professionals wanted their children to come to Demonstration School, with the result that many of our pupils were highly motivated. Since motivation largely determines the chances of success and failure, most of the pupils of Demonstration School were likely to do well in their schools and colleges, and later in their careers. Most teachers, including myself, found it both exciting and challenging to teach our pupils, especially in forms five and six.

Both my daughters, Aparna and Aparajita, were doing reasonably well in their respective classes, but both were frustrated by the presence in their classes of someone who was always slightly ahead of them: Kiran Phadke in Aparna's class and Saroj Datta in Aparajita's. Nondon was not yet in school. He expected to be there the year after. I thought I was not just accepted but liked by my colleagues in the school. In short, I was now head of a well-organised school with a band of colleagues, who were youthful, imaginative and friendly and pupils, who were intelligent and motivated. I had now the great opportunity of turning a good school into an outstanding one. Was I going to be able to rise to the challenge?

It was the weekend. The children were doing what they wanted to do, and Sudarsana and I were relaxing after supper, probably listening to some music. Someone knocked on the front door. It was Jayant, Dr Jayant Thacker, who'd quite unusually and unexpectedly come to see me. We always saw Jayant in his surgery, and arrived at his doorstep only in an emergency. We visited him – he didn't visit us. I was pleased and curious.

It's good to see you, Jayant,' I said. 'Have a drink. What will you have?'

'I'd love a cup of tea,' he said.

It had rained heavily that afternoon. We talked a little about the weather and about politics, but I felt quite certain that the purpose of his visit was not to make sociable conversation.

'I do apologise,' he said, 'for bursting in on you without warning, but I've come to discuss something important. At least, *I* think it's important.'

Then he explained. For quite a few years now the British Council had sponsored a competitive drama festival which was staged in the large assembly hall of Makerere University College which, incidentally, had a well-equipped stage and a hall with very good acoustics. The expatriate community, mainly British, participated in the festival with several plays. The Goans, infinitely smaller in number than the Indians, always entered a play. The Africans usually entered more than one play. Which community was conspicuous by its absence? The Indian People from India and Pakistan not only failed to produce any plays, leading to a general belief that they were an illiterate community of shopkeepers and clerks, devoid of any cultural or intellectual interest, but they also didn't much care to turn up at this important annual cultural event.

I knew he was a good doctor who took immense trouble to keep abreast of the most recent developments in medical science, as conscientious as he was hard-working, but I had no idea that he felt so concerned about the backwardness of our community in cultural matters.

'What do you think we ought to do?' I asked. 'We can't undertake to educate our community!'

'I've no such plan,' Jayant said. 'But I'd like to enter a play in the forthcoming drama festival.'

'What kind of play do you want to enter?' I asked.

He didn't know, Jayant said, and that's where I came in. Before anything else, we had to choose a play and enter it. The last day for entering the festival was just under a month away. He knew that while I was at Kololo School, I'd translated one of Tagore's plays – *Rakta Karabi* or Red Oleanders - and it had been staged. So I had to find an appropriate play for his group, the Youth League, as soon as possible. It could be a short one-act play or an excerpt from a longer play, but it had to fit into an hour, including the time to set up the stage and clear it. I'd do my best, I promised... Jayant then relaxed, had another cup of tea and left.

I did do my best. I read feverishly, both likely and unlikely plays. We could either produce a short play or an excerpt from a play, the rules said, so long as we didn't exceed an hour. For any extra time we took, we'd be penalised. My frantic search didn't yield any satisfactory results. I saw Jayant and told him that I hadn't found anything appropriate because of various reasons. One of these reasons was that what would be appropriate for a British expatriate group wouldn't be ideal for us. Some of the expatriate English-speaking groups would have a great advantage over us if we chose certain kinds of plays, either classical or contemporary. They would be equally at home with Shakespeare, Shaw, Ibsen, Congreve, Pinter, Ionesco, Wesker or Osborne – because most of them were experienced and took theatre seriously. On top of that, some of them were really good actors and directors. I'd seen their work and been impressed with it, at the last drama festival, for example... Jayant interrupted me. He looked thoughtful and despondent. It seemed to me that I'd almost extinguished his enthusiasm.

'What do you suggest? Do we give up the idea?' he asked, seriously.

Then came my punch line.

'I'll write a play, a play that'll reflect our strength, not betray our weaknesses,' I said.

Jayant didn't look relieved. He didn't jump for joy and shake my hand.

'Are we that desperate?' he asked, looking thoughtful.

He said that not as a joke, not to pull my leg. I could have taken it as an insult, but Jayant wouldn't say anything faintly insulting, even as a joke. But either way, I wasn't quite sure what he meant.

'What do you mean,' I asked.

'Have you written any plays before?' he asked.

'No,' I said. 'But I've been in the business of reading and teaching English literature. There's no reason why I shouldn't give it a go.'

Jayant was kind of convinced. Time was another problem. Two months.

'Have you, vaguely and generally, worked out the story, plot and characters?' was Jayant's next question.

''Vaguely and generally' are the exact words I'd use,' I said.

Then I tried to give Jayant some rudimentary idea of my embryonic play. I'd already chosen the title: *The Gold Diggers of Yaksha Town*. The gold diggers would be the commercial communities. They would be interested in money. There would be a king, behind high walls, in his palace, who'd be more interested in power, in control, in his image more than in anything else, and there would be people who didn't have a say in anything including their own lives. It'd be based on the interaction between these forces.

Jayant listened carefully.

'It's not an epic you're setting out to write Ganesh,' he said. 'It's a one-act play which mustn't exceed an hour on the stage.'

'The play will be a kind of prologue. I'll have to be happy with that just now. I'll write a play of epic proportions only after I've established myself as a consummate writer of one-act plays,' I said, tongue-in-cheek, trying to introduce a little levity into the sombre atmosphere.

After this Jayant looked either relaxed or resigned, I couldn't tell. He asked for another cup of tea; asked how Aparna was, whom he'd often treated for various ailments; discussed politics, which meant the then recurrent subject of Ugandan independence, and left.

I applied myself wholeheartedly to the task and finished the play. My ex-student, Rajat Neogy, who took an interest in creative literature (he was the editor of an avant garde magazine called *Transition*) read and approved of the theme, the treatment of the theme and the dramatic structure. Avtar Singh, known to all by the name of Tari, typed the script. The play was submitted to the committee of the Uganda Drama Society for approval, which was routine. There was a discussion. Of course, Harold Pinter or John Osborne didn't have to be submitted for critical appraisal, but it was different with an original play – it had to be vetted. Jayant objected and pointed out that he'd read the Drama Festival rules and there was no such stipulation there. The chairman said this was because this was the first time a drama group had entered an original play, and it would therefore have to be read and approved by members of the committee. In that case, Jayant insisted, such a condition should be incorporated in the rules. I don't know whether my play was read and discussed by the more knowledgeable members of the Uganda Drama Society, but within a week we were given the green light and we had to get down to casting, rehearsing and organising the stage props. The casting was done without any formal auditioning because we didn't have many potential actors to choose from. Sudarsana, who had some experience in acting, because she was a student of Vishwabharati University, Shantiniketan, was given the main part. One Miss Patel had the part of the narrator. John Carneiro was the rabble rouser with romantic ideas about equality and a non-repressive society and Sudarsana was his admiring comrade. Together, they protested against injustice and inhumanity – through words, singing and dancing, and many like-minded young people joined them. There were *agents provocateurs* who tried to lure them into making compromises but there was a certain purity, a certain innocence in them which had made them immune to temptation. There came, however, a time when their innocence, purity and love of life became a threat to the King, who lived in a palace behind high walls – the palace and the wall beautifully conceived and crafted by Naresh, my artist friend, and placed at the rear left of the stage. Our play was on the third night. There were two more nights of the festival. I was the King behind the wall, so I didn't know how the audience had reacted to the play, I only knew that the applause at the end of the play was long and spontaneous. Although I couldn't tell how our play compared with the other plays in terms of audience reaction, what I did know was that the audience had liked our play, and this knowledge would help me bear the agonizing passage of time between the performance and the verdict of the adjudicator.

One or two of the plays I'd seen were quite professional – the movement, the grouping, the lighting, the set and the acting. It was most impressive to see how skilled some of the performances were – the great clarity of the speeches, the timing and the body language. The two African plays communicated a relaxed sense of enjoyment. There was no self-consciousness, which was especially useful for the kind of play the African groups had chosen. The natural, spontaneous and unselfconscious acting of the Africans was pitted against the professionalism and sophistication of the plays produced by the British theatre groups. A Goan group had entered a play in the festival but it was an instance, quite clearly, of an amateur group producing an amateur play. Where did we come in?

On the fifth and final night, Norman Marshall, a well-known British theatre personality, did a brilliant and erudite summing up of the event. He said he was genuinely impressed with the depth and variety of the plays in production, as well as the histrionic skills of the actors, and briefly discussed the importance of theatre in life and education. Then he did a quick review of most of the plays, and declared that the best play in the festival was *The Gold Diggers of Yaksha Town* by Ganesh Bagchi.

I had a huge sense of pleasure and relief because of a job well done. The tightness in my brain had gone. Jayant went up to take the Spencer Shield for the best production of the Festival from the adjudicator, Norman Marshall, and when he actually received it, the long, sincere and enthusiastic applause indicated that Marshall's decision was approved of. Sudarsana got an honourable mention for her acting – a well-deserved tribute. The evening's images still live on in my memory.

During the week that followed, sometimes a stranger would stop in the street to congratulate me. A woman's magazine praised Sudarsana's acting, her dress sense, her personality and the clarity of her accent. The local English newspaper – I think it was called *Uganda Herald* – sent up its theatre critic to interview me and published the contents of our discussion. An Afro-American theatre group, which was visiting some towns and cities in East Africa, performing most effectively *Our Town* by Thornton Wilder with a minimum of stage props, requested us to stage our play and said how impressed they had been with both the play and the performance. One of the missionary schools on the outskirts of Kampala, where the standard of teaching and the level of academic achievement of the students was high, requested us to stage our play for the benefit of the students and we were delighted to do that because most of us were teachers. We went and presented our play wherever and whenever we were requested, not for the persistent persuasion of fame, but because it made us feel good that we could create some pleasure and excitement during the short time when the house lights were off and the stage lights were on. The attentive silence in the nearly dark auditorium, the occasional laughter, the spontaneous applause, the feeling that what we were able to offer was being enjoyed by so many gave us all a feeling of heightened pleasure and excitement. Then it all stopped. It had to stop.

We returned to our posts – Jayant to his patients, and Sudarsana, Naresh and I to teaching. Not that we'd ever left our posts, but we were probably too engrossed and preoccupied with the drama festival to give our jobs as much attention and care as they deserved. Not everybody took an interest in drama festivals, so not everybody was aware of our success. Those who were congratulated us. There was some discussion here and there; some discussion about the importance of theatre in education; some excitement that Asians, the shopkeepers, had won the best play award in the drama festival... then it was all forgotten, more or less.

Then one afternoon, Jayant rang to ask if he could see me briefly on his way to his surgery. He looked very pleased with himself.

'What do you know about Norman Marshall?' he asked.

'Not a lot,' I replied.

He told me that Norman Marshall was no run-of-the-mill adjudicator. He was a well-known English theatre director and producer, who was particularly interested in innovative theatre and experimental plays. He was the author of the books *The Other Theatre* and *The Producer and Play,* a man right in the front row of experimental theatre.

'To get the best play award from Norman Marshall is no mean achievement,' Jayant commented, looking very pleased with himself. I readily agreed. Norman Marshall certainly knew what he was doing, I said. I must have sounded smug, but to receive his acclaim was, obviously, no mean achievement because he was a man who took theatre seriously. For the first time I began to wonder whether I should put more of myself into the writing of plays.

While we were all engrossed in the effort of producing a credible play for the drama festival, tragedy, real tragedy, nearly struck. We had to concentrate on intensive rehearsals every weekend. We left our children – Aparna, Aparajita and Nondon – with Uncle and Aunt. One weekend Uncle and Aunt had taken the children to the house of their good friends, the Hiras. Unbeknown to everybody, Nondon had wandered off and tried to cuddle the Alsatian who spent much of its time chained up in an adjoining room. Mr and Mrs Hira had no children; therefore the dog wasn't used to children. They didn't cuddle the dog because they wanted a fierce dog to guard the house. In the circumstances, the last thing that Nondon should have done was to offer it affection. It had bitten into the back of his head. He had to be rushed to hospital and needed several stitches. I was told that he was brave, and after the initial shock, cried very little. When we saw him several hours later, he was serene and matter-of-fact, and described the near-tragedy of the morning.

'The dog isn't used to children, so it bit me,' he explained to Sudarsana and me, as he sipped his Ovaltine, a drink he liked.

He was repeating what he had been told. He was calm – he wasn't at all distracted by pain, partly because of the painkillers and partly because of all the attention and affection everybody was giving him.

'The dog didn't bark at me in the beginning, but when I went to cuddle it, it bit me. I cried and ran. There was blood on my cheeks,' Nondon said.

Fortunately, the dog was chained to a post. The other reason why a more serious tragedy was averted was the efficiency of Uncle, who'd immediately rushed Nondon to the accident and emergency department of the government hospital. He was treated by the same doctor who'd attended to my broken arm after a football game some years ago. Then there was Aunt, deeply concerned and caring. Anyway, the worst was over.

I was being taken notice of by people interested in the theatre on account of the success of my play. A visiting drama specialist, whom the British Council had flown out from England to give lectures, suggested to me that to acquire skills and insights into acting and play-writing, I should do a course at the Rose Brueford College of Drama and she could recommend me for admission. I was interested and said I was excited at the prospect of such an experience. The next time I met her she said a place at the college would be available to me for a three- month course and I'd hear from the principal. I did hear from the college and I wrote back to say I accepted the offer. I'd given the college the school address, so Sudarsana didn't know anything about what was going on. It wasn't because I wanted to keep her in the dark, it was a totally unexpected development and I wasn't at all certain about the outcome of my very brief conversation with this theatre personality. It was only later that I gathered that she was well-known in theatre circles for her contribution to drama and I was fortunate to have been taken notice of by her. It's a pity I cannot remember her name.

Sudarsana wasn't a bit pleased. She didn't comment but became quietly alienated, answering my questions with the utmost brevity, keeping out of reach by finding unnecessary things to do with the utmost dedication. When she was like this, neither frankincense and myrrh nor the offer of eternal devotion made the slightest difference. Days later, she explained.

'We haven't lived apart since we got married. Now you're expecting me to arrive in Calcutta with three children and spend three months there without you. Is this fair?'

I explained that it had all happened too quickly. But I could still write to the college, cancelling the course.

'Do you really want to do this course?' she asked.

'Yes, I do,' I said.

'In that case, we'll manage,' she said. Peace was restored.

One of the reasons why I thought it would be all right for Sudarsana and the children to go to India on their own was that travelling by train to Mombasa and then by ship to Bombay was now no longer necessary. Now the administration had decided that everybody would fly to their countries of origin and fly back. There was uncertainty in the minds of both of us about this separation but I don't think the children had registered anything about the impending separation. I wasn't quite certain that it was such a good idea. Of what relevance was a drama course in England going to be for me? I was neither a professional playwright, nor a highly gifted actor inspired by great ambition. Why was I going? Was there an undefined subconscious desire for adventure, further reinforced by a home-sickness for London where, four years ago, I had a sense of liberation, although I had done nothing to make me feel guilty or uncomfortable. Whatever the reason, the decision to go our separate ways and stay apart for three months was made; flights booked; preliminary packing done; interested people at both destinations informed. The die was cast.

Sudarsana and the children were going to stay at Golf Club Road. Sudarsana's parents were incredulous to begin with about my separating from the family to go to London to do a drama course but were soon reconciled to the idea. There was no uncertainty about Sudarsana and the children's food, shelter, comfort and care in Calcutta, and Sudarsana's parents were inordinately fond of their daughter and grandchildren.

There was a difference in Sudarsana's attitude in the beginning between when I was first selected to go to England for the Post Graduate Certificate of Education and now. Taking up that offer would have meant better job prospects. That would make a difference to my career and our lifestyle. But a term's crash course at a drama school wasn't going to help either me or the family in any practical way. I'd never thought of myself either as an actor or a director. So why was I going? Why did I organise my separation from the family for three months? This question must have occurred to Sudarsana. What answers she was going to find I didn't know. What conclusion she'd arrived at I didn't know.

It was soon after their leaving for Calcutta that I set out for London. The flight was from Entebbe to Khartoum, then Cairo, finally London. I went to the post office in Khartoum to buy some stamps for picture postcards to send to India. The post office staff were sitting around a large bowl of meat and eating their lunch. It was communal eating. They were dipping their bread in the gravy of the curry and eating with their hands. They invited me to join in because, one of them explained, it was a long-established tradition with them to invite people if they turned up at mealtime, and I was expected to eat with them. I sat with them and ate. I couldn't stay until the end of lunch because then I'd miss my plane. I was touched by their friendly, relaxed behaviour and their generosity. The meat curry was excellent, but the conversation limited and the time I spent with them short.

Murray Carlin, a friend, had fixed up my accommodation in Golders Green with a friend of his, who was a teacher, and owned a basement flat where she usually rented out two rooms. It was a friendly place but my room was damp, cold and sunless.

There was a heater in one corner of the room, struggling to keep itself going. Apart from the bed, there were a couple of chairs, a small bookcase and a table. It was almost Spartan but what worried me most were the damp and the cold. The bed was also uncomfortable; only the thick quilt kept me warm.

Apart from this, there was a living room which was shared by all three of us – Micky Kidron, the landlady, and the other lodger, who was a designer of jewellery, and me. This was a comfortable room and I started spending most of my time there – reading and writing and dozing off from time to time. Quite often, especially over

346

the weekends, I had company.   The other lodger, whose name I forget, was an interesting person with radical ideas about life and politics. He came from Israel to live in England. He wasn't too keen on discussing politics. About the Arab-Israel conflict, he said 'A plague on both your houses,' more or less summed up his attitude. Politics wasn't a popular subject of conversation, nor was literature or art. Micky called herself an anarchist but I found it difficult to work out what exactly it consisted of and she and her like-minded friends only succeeded in making it appear even more obscure to me than it was already. Most institutions – whether it was the monarchy, the parliament, the United Nations, the church, the synagogue, the World Monetary Fund or the World Bank – were flawed because they served the interest of the rich and powerful. I began to understand some of their objections to established institutions and values, but I had no idea what they wanted to put in their place and exactly for what purpose. Their approach struck me as nihilistic and, quite often, rather obscurantist, although some of their ideas appealed to me. The insidious inroad of power and money into every department of human activity was something that had always worried me. But, I argued, we had to work out what we'd replace the established institutions with before we organised their destruction or disappearance.   But such discussions were few, and none of Micky's friends impressed me as dedicated anarchists. One positive development was that I'd now met a few people who were intelligent, articulate, interesting to talk to and young and enthusiastic about life and ideas.

My initial sense of isolation had now gone. I wanted to do things, meet people, and explore Golders Green and other areas of London.   I began to feel less like an outsider. I was more relaxed in my relationship with those around me and felt less threatened by people who seemed indifferent or hostile because I was less unsure of myself even among strangers. Only the bedroom with the smoky heater continued to be damp and cold, although the thick quilt provided warmth and a sense of shelter.

I had an appointment with the Principal of Rose Bruford Training College for Speech and Drama. The Principal was Rose Bruford: the college was named after her because, I suppose, she was the founder. I went to Sidcup, saw Rose Bruford, and was impressed with her friendly informality. Teachers who were interested in drama and teaching were precisely the people who gave her institution its unique character, so she was happy that I'd chosen to come to that college. There could be a place for me because I was a teacher, a playwright and an actor. I pointed out that the person who'd recommended me had based her remarks on one one-act play and about ten minutes on the stage. It's the interest that counts, she said. However, she wanted me to spend three weeks in the college before I paid the fees and was enrolled as a student. She gave me an appointment after three weeks. In the intervening period, I was to sit in on the rehearsals of Eliot's *The Family Reunion,* which was going to be produced by a professional West End director for the college on the college stage. I think the name of this director was Frost, but I can't be sure. Watching the rehearsals was a great educational experience, and the director's comments on the delivery of the lines, the movements, the gestures, the use of silence and stillness were exciting. The director of the play as well as the students of the college talked of Stanislavsky with utmost respect, but I hadn't even heard of him. Quite often I was out of my depth when the students talked of method acting, of understatement, of the psychological basis of gesture and movement. Shakespeare never came up for discussion but Chekhov did, especially *Uncle Vanya* and *The Cherry Orchard.*

In many of the students – most of them were quite a few years younger than me – there was a dedication bordering on the religious. Another name which was often mentioned was that of Bertolt Brecht. Some students were planning to work on *Mother Courage* and *The Threepennny Opera.* It wasn't even a fortnight since I'd come to this college, but I felt I belonged because the younger people around me – men and women – were so friendly and helpful. There was a student, Penny, who seemed so intelligent, articulate, charming and attractive that I sought her company single-mindedly. I admitted to myself that Penny was attractive and I was attracted – but there the matter ended. Apart from that, she was much younger and could have been perplexed by my attention. In any case, events which followed pre-empted any further development of the relationship.

The Principal wanted to see me. The idea was that I'd sit in on the rehearsals of *A Family Reunion,* interact with the students and attend a few lectures and then see her to express my views and describe my reactions. If I liked the place and decided to stay on with my group and do the kind of work I was doing, she would organise a course suitable for me – a course which would both teach me a few skills as well as give me insights which would make me a better teacher of language. I knew she'd taken a great deal of trouble to accommodate me and I expressed my appreciation. I also told her how much I liked the students I worked with and the teachers who took a special interest in my reactions and responses. Towards the end of the interview, Ms Rose Bruford gave me a form to fill up. All was well – except the fees. I forget exactly how much it was, but it was way above anything I could afford. I think, then as now, the fees that overseas students had to pay were much higher than what British students paid. That might or might not have been the case. All I knew was that I couldn't raise that kind of money. I came out of the principal's office feeling depressed and disorientated.

Penny thought I looked preoccupied, 'Are you all right?' she asked.

All was well, I assured her. Nothing was lost, I kept telling myself. But that wasn't true. I did look forward to enjoying the warmth and affection of these young, intelligent people as well as their cheeky irreverence about the establishment – for about nine more weeks. I'd have to miss out on that. Nor would I have agitated discussions about Grotowski's poor theatre or Brecht's alienation effect. So what? What difference would that make to my teaching or educational administration? Was there any real reason why I needed a profound understanding of Stanislavsky's Method?

That reminded me. I'd have to go back and return a few library books.

I didn't want to go and say farewell to people in the college who liked me and whom I liked and tell them I didn't have the money to do the course, even the extremely short course devised especially for me. I'd just go the next day, return the library books, behave as if it was a day like any other day and then go away and stay away. After all, how important were the likes of Stanislavsky, Grotowski and Brecht in my life in Uganda, where teaching was my passion and my profession? The only involvement with dramatic art which Sudarsana and I had was in the production of the play, *The Gold Diggers of Yaksha Town*. Sudarsana had more theatre experience and histrionic talent. Yet, it was I who had had the opportunity to come to drama school. Now I was angry and frustrated that I couldn't afford the course. Did I tell Ms Bruford that I'd come to England for some training in acting and producing and now I'd have to go back without doing the course because I found the fees were more than I could afford? No, I didn't, and I was going to do no such thing. That was my reaction.

Micky declared that my pride was absurd. I didn't argue. Some friends of Micky's turned up in the evening. Micky brought up the subject of my quitting the college and there was another discussion about the logic of my decision. Basically, Susan said, it was my inability to ask for a favour, and she fully sympathised with me. She also found that she couldn't ask people for favours. Susan was a highly sensitive and intelligent woman. I was pleased as well as relieved to find that she understood why I didn't want to plead for concessions on account of my indigence.

Susan had been to see *My Fair Lady* a few months back at Drury Lane Theatre with Rex Harrison as Professor Higgins and Julie Andrews as Eliza Doolittle. It was hugely entertaining, she said, and she was in favour of theatre as entertainment.

Experimental theatre bored her witless. I pointed out that Shaw's *Pygmalion* was a serious play with a serious message. She had no objection, she said, to serious messages so long as they were good theatre. Micky and others also got involved in the discussion. They were all in agreement that *Waiting for Godot* was far from entertaining, and *Krapp's Last Tape* was boring. Someone suggested that we went out to eat. We ended up in an Indian restaurant and were chock full of curry and cold beer by the time we'd finished.

The conversation at dinner turned to politics. Susan, who'd thoroughly enjoyed *My Fair Lady* and had no time for *Waiting for Godot* or committed intellectuals or pacifists or communists surprised me when she started talking with passion and conviction about the Campaign for Nuclear Disarmament formed earlier that year. She urged us to join the movement because she couldn't think of anything more mindless than investing vast quantities of human resources to ensure the extinction of the race. Micky was more worried about the hatred and nastiness of white youths who taunted black immigrants with racist slogans. Not so long ago a gang of young white men also were attacked by black people at Notting Hill Gate. They'd hurled milk bottles and petrol bombs at them and attacked them with iron bars. Similarly white youths in certain other areas had ambushed black people, old and young, and quite mercilessly beaten them up.

The police were finding it increasingly difficult to control racist violence. The politicians and the media had discussed the problems but nothing tangible had been achieved. We agreed with Micky but none of us had any constructive suggestions to offer for containing or eliminating the menace. I think that part of the reason why this discussion wasn't energetically pursued and rather abruptly came to an end was that it was getting late. Most of the tables were empty, and it was a cold November night when curling up in bed beneath a quilt was a more attractive proposition.

One of Micky's younger friends, Rachel, lived in a two-room ground-floor flat about a mile away from where we were. She was about five-foot four, slim, darker than the white Israelis. Israel is a nation largely of immigrants but it never occurred to me to ask where she or her parents came from. Micky had already warned me that most Israelis don't like the implication of that question. Israel is their country and they are Israelis: that's the beginning and the end of the story. Do we ask an Englishman whether he originally came from: Denmark, Sweden or France? It was infallible logic. Anyway, I had no intention of asking Rachel where she or her ancestors came from. Nor did I know whether she'd come to England to settle or for a break of a few months from whatever she was doing in Tel Aviv.

I'd met her in the living room which was shared by the three residents of the flat, met her and liked her. Micky said to me one day that Rachel was looking for a teacher who could make sure that she didn't make too many obvious mistakes in grammar and pronunciation, for English wasn't her first language. I had noticed that certain sounds she used didn't quite belong to English phonology, that the singular subjects in her idiolect didn't always take singular verbs, nor plural subjects plural ones. She also used a disproportionate number of sentence fragments. Would I teach her and help her to overcome the irregularities which had become such a habitual part of her spoken English? I said I'd be very happy to give it a go... Rachel came to find out how soon I could start and I said, immediately. She insisted that she was going to pay me and I didn't object. Only the previous week I had to write to Alan Warner for money. Alan was at the time in Cambridge, writing a book on English style. Alan was a friend.

I enjoyed teaching Rachel. She was intelligent and motivated and never failed to do her assignments. She was relaxed. I found her attractive, but she wasn't bothered one way or another. We worked in the living room. The other residents of the flat were at work, so we had the flat to ourselves. The situation contained a certain amount of tension but Rachel was too focussed on grammar and pronunciation and I was unsure of myself and unprepared for any romantic involvements. I took my teaching seriously – probably too seriously. I decided that although Rachel's spoken English was improving by leaps and bounds, her written work betrayed ignorance of basic English grammar. Therefore I proceeded to teach her, quite relentlessly, all about verbs and sentence types and discourse functions. I was probably over-enthusiastic and tried to teach her topics which were neither relevant nor particularly useful, but Rachel didn't show any signs of boredom and I pressed ahead. She took it all very seriously. I was convinced she was making reasonable progress, which meant I was rather pleased with myself.

'How's Rachel doing?' Micky asked one weekend.

'I think she's a good student. She takes her lessons seriously,' I said.

'A little too seriously,' Micky commented.

I didn't understand what she meant by 'too seriously', if it was some kind of innuendo. But I thought it was best to treat the remark casually.
'And because she takes it seriously, I really enjoy teaching her,' I said.

'I'm glad to hear that,' Micky said.

Micky was fond of Rachel, so she asked me about her progress and commitment, and I had no hesitation in giving her a positive report. There were times when she appeared too serious, too intense – as if her future depended on how well and how soon she acquired a good control of English, especially spoken English. She usually came for her lesson after I had finished breakfast. This particular morning she turned up as usual but I wasn't waiting for her in the living room, because I was still in bed. I was breathing with difficulty, coughing quite frequently, and had a fairly high temperature. Rachel called out my name and I answered from bed.

'Come in Rachel,' I said, 'I'm sorry, but I'm not feeling well.'

She came in, looked alarmed, placed the palm of her right hand on my temple like my mother used to do and declared, with the confidence of an experienced nurse, that I had a high temperature.

'You must be feeling pretty rotten,' she said.

I *was* feeling weak, had a headache and muscle- pain. Earlier that morning I just couldn't stop sneezing. My nose was running and my eyes were heavy with sleep, but I couldn't sleep for the coughing.

'I'm feeling <u>very</u> weak and miserable, Rachel. I don't think I can teach you this morning,' I said.

She was surprised that I could even think of teaching when I was so ill. She wasn't so sure that I had the full-blown flu virus but the symptoms looked pretty serious. Then her expression changed. She'd made a crucial decision. It just wouldn't make sense for me to be on my own in the flat from about 7.30 in the morning to about 7.00 in the evening. So I had to go and stay with her in her flat which wasn't all that far away – so that she could make sure that I wasn't struggling alone in a damp basement room without food and medicine when I was so ill.

What she said made sense. It would bring me immense relief if someone like Rachel was around to see me through this debilitating and quite unexpected bout of illness. I was feeling very ill – totally devoid of energy and quite depressed. To move in with Rachel in her flat, which had two bedrooms, one large and one small, was unquestionably a great solution.

Now, although I felt quite miserable, and greatly relieved at the prospect of food and shelter and tender care, I quite suddenly felt concerned about Rachel. I came from a conservative Bengali background where marriages were arranged and husbands and wives *usually* lived with each other through thick and thin. How happy or miserable they were didn't come into it. What would people say if Rachel, who lived alone in a flat, took a man, a young Indian, as a lodger? Wouldn't she be up against convention and racial prejudice? She'd always given me the impression that she was a strong-minded person who knew exactly what she was doing, but I felt concerned that she mightn't have considered the implications of her action. Rather hesitantly, I said.

'But Rachel, you live alone in your flat.'

'What's that got to do with it?' was her casual response. 'I think I know what I'm doing.'

That shut me up. Rachel was entirely businesslike.

She dragged my case out from a corner of the room, packed it quickly and said, 'I'm going to get a taxi. You can throw in the rest of your stuff – your toilet bag, for example. I'll do a little shopping apart from getting a taxi.'

She looked confident and resolute. I got out of bed, brushed my teeth, washed and got dressed. I looked around to make sure I wasn't leaving anything behind. Then I quickly wrote a note to Micky, briefly explaining why such precipitate action was necessary.

I also left the week's rent in an envelope. I thanked her, of course. When Rachel returned, we put my things in the boot of the taxi and arrived at Rachel's flat in another part of Golders Green. Rachel continued to be businesslike. We sat in the living room, had some tea and toast, and then she organised the spare bedroom for me and insisted that I quietly rested. Once I was installed, she left, carefully closing the door of my bedroom. A doctor from the local surgery visited me in the afternoon the next day and prescribed some medicine, expressing the opinion that the infection would take about a week to disappear. I think that was about as long as it did take for me to feel reasonably normal.

I resumed teaching Rachel English grammar and syntax. We practised speaking, reading and comprehension, and went shopping regularly for the morning paper and a few household items.

Soon it was only a matter of weeks before it was time for me to return to Kampala. This was when Rachel turned up in my bedroom quite early in the morning in her dressing gown and informed me that she was feeling poorly and I should be prepared to fend for myself the next few days. She didn't look at all well – her eyes looked watery and swollen, she was coughing and sneezing and running a temperature. I felt guilty. I felt responsible, though there was at least a two week gap between my illness and hers. I was nothing but trouble to her, I thought, blaming myself for her distress. But what would I have done, sick and alone in my damp basement room at Micky's? Yet, I couldn't avoid feeling that I'd brought this upon Rachel and she was now paying the price for her kindness to me.

I'd more than once wanted to take her in my arms and thank her but I wasn't at all certain that she'd welcome that. It was the obvious thing to do and she'd done it, so what was all that fuss about? That would be her reaction. The first day of her illness, she felt thirsty a few times and wanted hot drinks. She rested most of the time, and slept. She didn't want me to ring the doctor because she said this kind of cold and fever could only be treated with analgesics. She didn't need a doctor to tell her that. She started eating a little from the second day – Heinz tomato soup and a few pieces of toast, things like that. She was quite addicted to Kit Kat and I bought her a few packets of these. After a few days, I felt she was definitely getting better. This particular morning when I entered her room with her morning cup of tea, she was sitting at the edge of the bed.

I put down her cup of tea on the bedside table and asked her how she was. She sat up, put her arms round me, and rested her head on my shoulder and stayed like that for a few minutes. Then she let go, looked up at me and thanked me for my care and concern. I said I hadn't done a lot. I didn't tell her she'd done a lot more for me, because I knew she'd dispute that.

'Did you know I was married?' she asked.

'No, I didn't,' I said. 'I'm married too and have three children, two daughters and a son, ten, eight and five.'

'Where are they?' she asked.

'They're in Calcutta. I've missed them. I hadn't realised how much I'd miss them,' I said.

She said that her husband was coming the next day and his name was Simeon. She didn't feel well enough to go to Heathrow to meet him, but Micky was going instead.

'You'll see him tomorrow evening when he gets here,' she said.

I was sitting down on a chair by her bed and stood up to leave. Rachel was sitting at the edge of the bed. She too got up, put her arms round me and kissed me long and hard. I responded body and soul. After that Rachel just stood there, her arms round me. Then she turned round and went back to bed. Her eyes were moist. Nothing was said. Meeting, loving, parting. It's all happened before – both to emperor and clown.

I felt close to Rachel, not only because of her natural concern for me, but because of who she was – a young woman, affectionate, warm-hearted, human, who very naturally cared for people. And she'd just given me something I'd always remember and treasure, something warm and spontaneous, something which indicated that she'd remember me not only as the man who taught her English grammar and phonology, but also as a good friend. I should have probably taken that more casually. But it affected me deeply and the memory of that spontaneous and totally unexpected kiss will always remain with me. It was unexpected, but by no means unwelcome.

Simeon, Rachel's husband, arrived – a pleasant young man with curly hair, average height, bushy eyebrows and bright, intelligent eyes. He was amiable and articulate, but not particularly sociable. At first, he treated me like any other lodger, spent some time with Rachel after breakfast and then went away, usually returning in the evening, when he often took Rachel out for a meal and sometimes to the cinema. I wasn't included in these outings. I did hear them discussing *My Fair Lady* with interest but I don't know whether they'd any plans to go and watch it. I don't remember exactly whether it was on at the time.

Our English lessons continued. Rachel was serious and attentive as usual. And I was getting ready to return to Kampala – to Sudarsana and the children, and my job at the Demonstration School.

Simeon was greatly interested in politics. It was an important time in contemporary history, he said. About this time Fidel Castro, Che Guevara and Raul Castro were in the news for their onslaught on the Batista government in Cuba. Mao Zedong had firmly established his authority in China – he was President. In Vietnam, there was the rise and fall of the Communist Vietminh, who a few years ago had decisively defeated the French troops in the Battle of Dien Bien Phu. And in 1958, the same year that I'd travelled to London, Uganda, a British Protectorate, was granted internal self-government. We were approaching the sixties, the years of social, cultural and political unrest, and the pain and upheaval of the Cultural Revolution in China. Fundamental and historically significant changes were beginning to happen. London in 1959 was a good place to live in or visit because it was here that you felt the winds of change blowing away many of the no longer relevant established beliefs, values and morals. Most of the time, Simeon and I were on the same wave length... except when it came to discussing Israel.

Many of the issues which were important to Rachel, Simeon and me weren't relevant in East Africa. Nobody had ever talked about the right to be gay in Kampala or the urgent need to halt nuclear proliferation. Rachel was obviously interested, but only occasionally participated in the discussion, mainly on account of her lack of confidence with spoken English.

On the whole, the three months that I spent in Golders Green in the autumn of 1958 were without any sense of purpose... I'd found it frustrating. I'd got interested in theatre because of the unexpected success of my first play, but when I tried to learn more about the subject, I found that I needed to pay for the course with money which I hadn't got and couldn't raise. Added to the frustration was regret. Had I gone back to the Principal, explained the circumstances which were compelling me to opt out of the course, wouldn't she have waived the fees, or given me a concession which made it possible to complete the course? Couldn't I have raised a loan? But I couldn't bring myself to do either.

Then there was the great city of London to explore and to absorb the spirit of a place which had weathered fire, the plague and the blitz. I could visit places which I hadn't visited in 1954-1955 and revisit landmarks of the city which had impressed me – St Paul's Cathedral, Westminster Abbey, Buckingham Palace, Drury Lane, the streets, the theatres, the parks, the monuments, Canary Wharf at night, Mayfair, Kew Gardens, Hampton Court, Covent Garden, Piccadilly Circus, Regent Street... I could go on and on without being able to produce a comprehensive list. But in actual fact, I spent very little time exploring the city or participating in its cultural life. I may have actually spent the time I had left – after my three weeks' flirtation with theatre-craft and almost two weeks of illness – at first I was ill and then Rachel's illness followed and then after Simeon arrived, I didn't see Rachel most of the time – just gazing at the River Thames, which gave the city its distinctive appearance and character. If I were asked to locate the soul of this great metropolis, I would unhesitatingly point to the River Thames.

So my homesickness, which was always there, dormant much of the time, surfaced, and I wanted to be back in Kampala, reunited with Sudarsana, Aparna, Aparajita and Nondon, and return to Demonstration School to take charge of its administration. By and large, I decided, my trip to England in the autumn of 1958 was unsuccessful. I derived some consolation, however, from the fact that it wasn't disastrous, thanks to Rachel's timely and generous intervention. Getting to know Rachel was the most important part of my 1958 visit to London.

When I recount my experiences in London in 1958, I don't usually publicise my failure or ineptitude or lack of resourcefulness or excess of false pride. Nor do I go out of my way to inform friends and relations that coming to London to do a course in theatre craft was a bad idea because I hadn't thought things through. Since I left Golders Green in 1958, I've rarely been completely honest about my failure. I don't tell people that I did three weeks of observation at the college of drama on the understanding that I was going to attend a term's lessons and rehearsals, and then just left without attending the regular course. I don't admit that the whole idea was ill-conceived and ended in a fiasco.

I tell people that I did a very short course at Rose Bruford College of Drama. I don't tell them how short the short course was.

What saved the trip from total failure was my very special relationship with Rachel and the three weeks at the college with younger students, who were friendly, helpful and generous, many of them with a somewhat special iconoclastic sense of humour. Another minor but positive event was a talk I was asked to give by the BBC on their overseas broadcasting service. The talk was about Uganda. Exactly which aspects of Uganda I talked about I don't clearly remember but politics and education came into it – education because I was playing my part in the education of Ugandan children, and politics because education and politics were inseparable in a developing country. The fee I received was unexpectedly generous. I bought a woollen suit with the money, my best suit for very special occasions.

The time of departure often gives rise to mixed feelings – about separation and union – if one has a strong emotional bond with the place one is leaving and also looks forward to where one is going. It could have been three exciting and profitable months in London but they weren't. Rachel's friendship was something I'll remember and recall in future years – her care and concern which put me back on my feet, the hot cups of tea in the cosy living room, with winter outside and the warm glow of gas fire within.

Rachel's relationship with me had all kinds of potential, but it never really broke the bounds of conventional morality. A brief relationship, if it's serious, is painful. If it's adventure, it seems irresponsible. What I can honestly say is that the occasion of my leaving London was dominated by my longing to re-engage with Sudarsana, Aparna, Aparajita and Nondon.

I left the way I came – on a BOAC VC Ten – and arrived in Uganda via Cairo and Khartoum, feeling like the prodigal son, regretting the misadventure of the past three months, but determined to put a good face on it. I wasn't going to admit that the drama course in England didn't really work, or that the end was just as frustrating as the beginning was exciting and full of promise. I'd already decided on a half-truth: it was a very short course but it'd given me insights into drama that I didn't have before.

Then I'd say, without the feeling that I was holding anything back or manipulating facts in any way, that I wished I hadn't decided to go my separate way because I missed the children and Sudarsana very much – though meeting Rachel had taken away some of the sense of futility and frustration.

All was well at school. I felt that the children as well as my colleagues were genuinely happy to see me back. There were no problems in the school in my absence – either pedagogic or administrative – but they felt better when I was around. I also had missed the school, I said, and was glad to be back. What I didn't talk about was the absence of my three children, which made me feel there was something missing. Sudarsana and the children were, however, due to arrive at Entebbe airport in a few days. Friends assumed that I was missing the children and Sudarsana and invited me over. There was one noisy and boisterous party in which some of my old students tried to demonstrate how liberated they were from bourgeois values – with the result that I left much earlier than I'd intended. One evening I went to the cinema with Valerie Vowles, and another evening I had dinner with the Carlins. Then one Sunday morning, they were all there – Sudarsana, Aparna, Aparajita and Nondon, back from their three months' holiday in Calcutta. There were gentle hugs and happy smiles, and excited exchanges of bits and pieces of news – more between me and the children than between Sudarsana and me. Sudarsana looked preoccupied, devoid of the excitement of home-coming, as she stepped into the light drizzle and onto the wet asphalt and walked towards the car park. The luggage went into the boot of the car, the children sat at the back and Sudarsana and I in front.

'Are you glad to be back?' I asked.

'Yes, of course,' she answered readily, but with an uncharacteristic lack of warmth in her voice. It sounded almost as if she was speaking with resentful reluctance.

'How are your parents?' I asked.

'They're well. They send you their love.'

There was nothing wrong with her responses; there was nothing strange or hurtful in what she said; yet the manner of her speaking created a sense of unease within me. There was a sudden cloudburst, a downpour with the rain hitting the windscreen like lances. We were all quiet, the windscreen wipers frantically trying to keep out the rain water to make it possible for me to drive.

'Would you mind singing one of my favourite songs?' I said to Sudarsana.

She began to sing. It was one of the songs I'd heard her sing when she first came to Calcutta University as a fifth year student. The river was in spate, the song said, and both its banks were flooded. Love, like a river, couldn't always be contained within its banks. It was a highly emotional song, a song of love, and Sudarsana sang it very well. Whenever she sang this song, I felt very close to her.

But on this occasion, I didn't feel she was singing to me. It was as if she was singing to somebody else a long way away. The rain had stopped, and the tropical sun was ablaze overhead. Sudarsana stopped singing. I drove on silently. I registered the sound of the moving car on the wet road, the children's intermittent dialogues from the back seat, the sunshine after the downpour and the familiar landscape of Entebbe Road with a certain sense of happiness. But Sudarsana continued to be quiet.

Chapter 13

Shimoni Teacher Training College

Back from our sojourn – I from Golders Green and Sudarsana and the children from Tollygunge, Calcutta – we were settling down to life in Kampala. It was mainly now home and school and, occasionally, weekend socializing. It was amazing how quickly we readjusted and started living as if we hadn't gone so far away from each other for more than three months. The feeling that this was where we belonged was quite strong in all of us. We were glad to be back. Returning to Kampala was homecoming even for Aparna, who'd left Calcutta and her grandparents most reluctantly when we first left the shores of India in 1951. Now we also had among us someone who was African by birth – Nondon. What's more, I now had some African students at the Shimoni Teacher Training College. This sense of identity had grown slowly – my African identity – but now, more than before, I really had a sense of belonging, which was further strengthened when I returned to work at Demonstration School, where I was warmly welcomed back both by the pupils and my colleagues.

But there was something in my immediate environment which was creating a sense of unease. Sudarsana seemed casual, off-hand, preoccupied and distant. She was also quite restless at times, unable to concentrate on what she was doing. We'd both acquired the lethal habit of smoking, but Sudarsana had been an amateur smoker who indulged in the habit on high days and holidays, and often out of a sense of camaraderie; but now she was smoking almost as frequently as I did.

'Is everything all right with you?' I asked one evening after dinner when we'd both lit up our postprandial cigarettes.

'Yes, of course,' she answered casually. 'Why do you ask?'

'You've been looking rather preoccupied recently,' I said.

She didn't respond immediately, looked pensive and changed the subject.

'You haven't told me a great deal about your holiday in England, have you?' she said.

'You're absolutely right. On the whole, I think I acted in haste. The unexpected success of my play and the spontaneous praise of someone of the stature of Norman

Marshall made me think I might go places. I didn't think things through. I didn't do the drama course in the end and I missed you and the children,' I said.

Sudarsana looked absent-minded once again, as if she was many miles away. I wasn't sure she had registered what I'd said. Then she came out of her trance and started talking about her holiday in Calcutta. Both Aparajita and Nondon fell ill.

The doctor was certain that their illness had to do with their tonsils, which needed to come out. This meant hospitalisation, and care and attention during the time of recuperation. But more than anything else, she said, her suffering was psychological – a feeling of crisis, of loneliness and of being abandoned.

'But you were with your parents,' I said. 'And our children were with you, not with me.'

'They missed you. They didn't understand why you weren't with us,' Sudarsana said, in a matter-of-fact way, without wanting to make me feel guilty.

But I did feel guilty. I did want to say that it was the wrong decision. I missed them. My world at the time consisted mainly of the four of them. After the success of my play, the very first play I'd ever written for the Uganda Drama Festival, I'd had delusions of grandeur. So I'd responded with alacrity to the opportunity of spending a term at a drama college in England. The drama college hadn't worked. I'd also spent a few miserable days in bed, suffering from a cold and fever, though it was a relief to be looked after by a generous young woman who, unexpectedly, made a difference to my otherwise lonely holiday. These were the thoughts going through my head – I wouldn't for the world talk about either the failure of my project or my feeling of loneliness to Sudarsana to arouse her compassion. I kept quiet, but Sudarsana went on, quietly and with restrained emotion.

'And do you know who stood by me, gave me strength and confidence? Our mutual friend, Ronu. He came with me to the hospital. He amused the children, first Aparajita and then Nondon, when they felt unhappy or were in pain. I shall never forget the way he stood by me throughout the crisis.' Sudarsana's voice wasn't quite steady.

'I must write and thank him for his help,' I said.

'That reminds me,' Sudarsana said. 'Have you received any letters from him at the school?'

'No, I haven't. Letters from India normally come to our home address,' I said.

It was usually Sudarsana's parents who wrote to us from India. They usually wrote in Bengali and it was Sudarsana who wrote back on behalf of all of us. So why should Ronu write to my school address? There was some confusion or problem which I didn't understand. It was obvious she was feeling generally let down – first by me and then by Ronu.

'Ronu lives for the moment. He's easily distracted,' I suggested, trying to find an explanation for his not writing. 'It's also possible he's away on business.'

'It really doesn't matter all that much,' Sudarsana said, suggesting that she didn't want to talk about it any more. What worried me was her obvious distress.

Life for the Bagchis went on without any major upheavals. I was getting a taste, I thought, of a bourgeois lifestyle, of which I had spoken so contemptuously in my youth. All my three children were in Demonstration School, where they were doing well. Sudarsana was Senior Mistress in her school. Demonstration School, where I was Headmaster, was well thought of, and there were always many more applications for admission than there were places in the school.

Mr Hayes had retired and returned to England. A new Principal, Mr Braithwaite, had taken charge and was running the college almost as efficiently as Mr Hayes. Demand for places in the Teacher's Training College was just as great as before – if not greater. Now quite a few African students had joined the college, making life on the campus richer and more complex. Apart from doing the administration of the school, I was still taking some classes at the college, talking about various approaches to teaching in general, and teaching English in particular. I also taught fairly regularly at Demonstration School because I believed the classroom is the laboratory where our pedagogic ideas must be tested.

Nondon was quite obviously enjoying being at school. He had a friendly temperament and got on well with the others in the class. Nondon's closest friend, Kuldip was also his rival. They competed on the playing field as well as in the classroom. Most of the boys and girls in his class came from an affluent business or professional background and the boys were interested in cars from quite an early age. Nondon had gathered from them that German cars – Mercedes Benzes, Audis, BMWs – were some of the most fashionable and desirable cars, and had asked me on several occasions why we couldn't have one of them. I'd said our car – Peugeot

403, a French car – was as good as his German cars. It had given us such good service, taken us to so many places, I'd said, that we shouldn't suddenly discard it or talk slightingly of it.

We'd seen a white Mercedes, 190B petrol, in the display room of one of the car dealers on the High Street and admired it. Nondon was especially enthusiastic about it. He'd asked me several times why we couldn't have it. One afternoon, when regular classes were over and the school's football eleven was kicking a ball around in the playing field, I strolled across to the dealers just across the road to have a look at Nondon's car. For some reason that I don't clearly remember I had a free afternoon. I talked to the car dealer. How much was that white Mercedes, I asked, pointing to the object of my desire, for what had started as Nondon's boyish enthusiasm for the car had transformed itself into his father's very keen desire to own the vehicle.

The dealer, a smart, middle-aged Gujarati, was an articulate and well-informed salesman. He started off by telling me that I was a connoisseur of cars. Then he explained that Mercedes Benz 180D was a special model but it was soon going to be replaced by one with a smarter and slicker look. This was, however, the car he loved because of a whole host of reasons. Then he talked for several minutes, rapidly and compulsively, about the body of the car, the engine capacity, the transmission, the clutch, the 4-cylinder engine, the suspension, the steering, the brakes, the wheels, the tyres and much more. What I could look at if I turned my head a little to the left, in other words, was a machine of extraordinary efficiency and the salesman fully understood and appreciated my interest in it. And then came a dramatic announcement.

'Do you know,' he said, 'because the company is soon going to replace it with a new model, it is offering a large discount on the old model.'

I asked how much discount was on offer. I had to admit it was rather attractive. It was beginning to look like I could afford to buy the car. There was also my Peugeot 403 to sell. I should get some money by selling it, I thought, which would come in handy for the purchase of the new vehicle.

'I am interested,' the salesman said when I told him that I had a grey Peugeot 403 sedan to sell, and I'd like to sell it first before I clinched my deal with his company. I was seriously considering buying the Mercedes.

Everything moved with extraordinary speed after that. I took my Peugeot 403 to the car dealers. They made an offer which I found acceptable. Now I had to raise the amount payable to the dealers – the price of the Mercedes minus the amount I was going to receive for the Peugeot. I went to the accounts section of the Department of Education to borrow this money. Without any fuss and without asking many questions, the chief accountant sanctioned the required amount with the condition that it would have to be paid in instalments within a time limit. Within the week, the car was mine – the white Mercedes 180D – and all I had to do was drive it home. I didn't even have to wait for the number plates because it had been fitted with them for another buyer, who had exchanged this car for another after three months; I was also given a large discount for that.

I took delivery of the car at the end of the day, drove it around and took it back home a little later than when I usually returned home. The children were busy reading or doing their homework or just chatting. I'd deliberately left my briefcase in the car. Sudarsana was in the living room, sorting out her teaching programme. I said hello to everybody and then asked Nondon to fetch my briefcase from the car. I could hear his cry of surprise and delight. Then he burst into the living room carrying my briefcase.

'Have you bought the Mercedes?' he asked in an agitated voice with surprise and delight.
'Yes, I have,' I said.

'It's ours then?' he asked.

'Yes, it is,' I answered.

'We'll go to school then in the Mercedes tomorrow?'

'Yes, we will,' I said, giving him a hug.

Nondon rushed away to inform his sisters, who followed him to the garage to check the veracity of his report. They were all excited and happy. All my three children approved, but it was Nondon who just couldn't contain himself. Twice he went out through the front door to make sure that he wasn't dreaming.

'I like our car,' he said.

'So do I,' I said.

Sudarsana had registered all the excitement around her over the Mercedes but hadn't participated in it. She'd neither approved nor disapproved. It was only after the children had gone to bed that she asked me whether it wasn't a rather impulsive act to buy such an expensive car with borrowed money. I explained that I'd got a good price for the Peugeot and a large discount on the Mercedes. Therefore the loan I had to raise wasn't so large that we'd have to lower our standard of living in any way, or face financial embarrassment. My incentive, I think, was a mixture of pleasure of driving and pride of possession.

'In any case,' Sudarsana said, 'I'd have liked to be consulted.'

'Everything happened too quickly and I wanted to give all of you a surprise, especially Nondon. We live in an affluent society. Nondon and his friends discuss cars quite a lot. Apart from that *I* was tempted. It was hasty. But the deed was done.' That was the truth.

Sudarsana accepted my explanation. Then Nondon came along and said he was looking forward to being driven in that car. I said I'd be delighted.

The car wasn't a sensation when we took it to school. In an affluent world, a new Mercedes goes unnoticed, though some showed interest and some had a close look at it, more out of politeness than curiosity. Nondon had persuaded some of his friends to take an interest, and they crowded round the car and asked each other questions about cars in general – most boys were interested in cars – and Nondon's Mercedes in particular. But, on the whole, the excitement didn't measure up to Nondon's expectations. One of his friends had told him their family had *two* such cars, both bigger and better than ours. I said it didn't matter, and Father and son tried to be philosophical.

Something exciting had just happened. Demonstration School, just six years old, had done outstandingly well in the Secondary School Entrance Examination and Aparna Bagchi had scored the highest marks in English. She had also scored the highest marks on the aggregate and come first in the country. Kiran Phadke, who'd always been a perennial rival of hers, was beaten into second place, but wasn't many marks behind. This meant disappointment for Kiran, who was both highly intelligent and highly disciplined. But for the school, it was an all-round triumph, and that too in the very first year of its entering the competitive arena of Uganda's junior schools' external examination!

And now it was now time to get started on the new play for the annual Drama Festival. Jayant reminded me that the expectations of the audience of our standard of performance would be high – after last year's success – and he hoped that we would be able to live up to it. I did take it seriously but I had strayed into an area which was unfamiliar ground.

Independence had been in the air, the previous year. Uganda had been granted internal self-government. It would be appropriate, I thought, to write a semi-political play with the central theme of multi-racial co-existence to be staged with a multi-racial cast. Peter Carpenter was the adjudicator that year. What we got was mild praise from the adjudicator and a lukewarm response from the audience. One of its main drawbacks, I think, was that it was uniformly didactic with few occasions of relief. The Governor of Uganda had come on the night my play was staged. His secretary rang me the next day to say that he had liked it. *Soma and Synthesis* – for that was the name of the play – quietly disappeared into oblivion because it was an ambitious play, and my ability didn't measure up to the challenge. We were all disappointed, especially Sudarsana, Jayant and me.

'Who collects your post at the college?' Sudarsana asked.

'The caretaker does – from the post office,' I said. 'I do too, occasionally, from our post box.'

'I still don't understand why Ronu hasn't written,' Sudarsana looked really unhappy.

'Why don't you write and find out if all's well with him, Reba and Runki?' I suggested.

'I did,' Sudarsana replied, looking very distressed.

Disappointment was writ large on her face. I was beginning to get worried and hoped she hadn't fallen in love with Ronu. Ronu was naturally charming, generous, helpful, loving and giving, and a few naive and vulnerable women had succumbed to his lethal charm, only to discover that my dear friend had the special gift of attracting without being attracted. People like him often caused heartache and suffering without meaning to do so. It was an unequal situation. I sympathised with those who let down their defences and discovered, only when it was too late, that Ronu loved being loved but hated the thought of extra-marital involvement, because he loved his wife, Reba, and his daughter, Runki. My present worry was that Sudarsana was at least half in love with Ronu, who had driven her around, taken her to the doctor, the surgeon, the hospital; held her hand at times of anxiety; amused her children when they were in pain. And more than anything else, he'd given her his friendship and his company.

At a time of anxiety and helplessness, both distressing emotions, further aggravated by a feeling of being abandoned by her husband, Sudarsana found an old and trusted friend making it a point to do his best to help her in spite of being a busy man, a caring husband and an affectionate father. He also had an important executive job with KLM. Anyone in a similar situation would have an overwhelming sense of gratitude and a deep feeling of admiration for whoever so helpfully stood by them. It happened to be my wife, Sudarsana.

I didn't weep, fast or pray, but I hoped that Sudarsana's affection, admiration and gratitude hadn't added up to love.

'Give him time,' I said.

'Do you really think I care?' Sudarsana said rather unexpectedly.

'It's not a question of caring or not caring. I want you to understand that this is purely a matter of temperament. Ronu attends and responds to everything around him and finds it difficult to relate to whatever moves out of his orbit. He never writes to me, but if I turned up in Calcutta next week, he'd drop everything to spend time with me. I've been a teacher all my life and the differences of temperament among my students have always fascinated me...' I stopped. I noticed Sudarsana was looking frustrated and angry.

'I don't see why you have to be such an apologist for your friend. I'm disappointed. That's a fact. But I'm not crying my heart out. So, will you please stop feeling sorry for me?'

She sounded cross. I felt quite certain that Sudarsana meant what she said. I resolved not to mention the subject again.

Outside the orbit of our private lives, major changes and upheavals were taking place in Uganda. The order deporting the Kabaka was challenged in the High Court. This paved the way to the return of the Kabaka in 1955 – to a hero's welcome, and an agreement ensuring a unitary government instead of a federal one, and the beginning of a sense of nationhood in the country. Erissa Kironde was a friend who created in me a sense of involvement in the politics of Uganda, and I had a feeling of personal triumph when I felt certain that the idea of an East African Federation was abandoned. The Kabaka's deportation and his return and restoration to power created a countrywide political consciousness which could be the basis of nationhood and independence. It <u>was</u>, as subsequent events in the political history of Uganda doubtlessly proved.

Another significant development which was taking place in the background was the political maturing of a young man, who could be trusted with the governance of a sovereign, independent Uganda. Milton Obote, who was born in the Lango District and was a student of Makevere University College in the latter part of the 1940's, did his political apprenticeship in Kenya during the days of the Mau Mau and the Emergency. When he appeared on the political scene of Uganda later as a member of the Central Legislative Council for Lango District, he impressed both people and politicians with his character, confidence and charisma. After that, he first became the President of the Uganda National Congress and then the President of the Uganda People's Congress. His admirers called the manner in which he achieved the leadership of these parties bold and confident. His detractors criticised him for his unscrupulous ruthlessness. At the time I am talking about, there was ample evidence of his leadership qualities, but he hadn't risen quite to the top yet.

In the wider world beyond Uganda, events with far-reaching significance were happening, of which we tended to take little notice because we were looking forward to the day we'd live in independent Uganda. In the affluent West, people and the media were excited over various changes which were happening in the lives of people, especially young people, which had a positive and transformational quality. And when they talked about the swinging sixties, it was this transformation which they meant. The new spirit of the sixties was clearly in evidence in art, literature and music, and in the way people dressed, spoke and thought about life. The rigour and trauma of the war years were forgotten and there was a sense of freedom, which led to the feeling that life was beautiful and joyful, as well as to some excessive self-indulgence, including drug-taking and free love-making.

For Africans and those of us who lived in Africa, the expectation was that the age of colonialism was over. It was now more than 13 years after India had won independence, India – the jewel in the crown. It was unlikely that the colonisers in Africa were going to drag their feet on and on. That, anyway, was the general belief.

The excitement about an independent Africa wasn't merely a matter of expectations or speculation. Commitments had been made by colonisers which couldn't be withdrawn.   The crumbling of empires had begun; it had to go on.   What we expected was a peaceful transition.   There were African leaders – Jomo Kenyata, Julius Nyerere, Milton Obote – quite capable of heading their own governments, we said, so what were we waiting for?

Kenya became independent in 1960, but we were going to have to wait. I forget exactly why.   News from elsewhere was very varied – both good and bad.   There was fear of civil war in Algeria between the indigenous Algerians and the French settlers.   Albert Camus was dead.   At Sharpeville the police had shot dead 56 Africans and injured 162 others.   The Congo became independent.   John Kennedy was elected American president.   Uganda was getting ready for independence.

The imminence of Ugandan independence didn't affect everybody positively.   Very few British expatriates were ready and willing to continue working in an independent Uganda.   In any case, it wouldn't make sense for them to hold all the key positions in the country's administration, which is what they did now.   Quite a few of them liked Uganda, got on well with their African colleagues and the Africans generally.   Now they were getting ready to go.   Among those who'd decided to return to England was Mr Branthwaite, the Principal of Shimoni Teacher Training College.   I wasn't going anywhere.   I liked it here.   I got on well with my students and my colleagues.   I was the youngest Asian headmaster.   My play had won the Uganda Drama Festival two years ago.   I was full of positive feelings – love, hope, confidence.   My friends approved of my faith in myself and the future of the country.   My critics possibly said I was too full of myself.

Mr Branthwaite didn't believe in fraternizing with his colleagues.   He was efficient. He was businesslike.   But he was remote.   Mr Hayes, the previous Principal of the college, would sometimes, after discussing the business in hand, turn to the political situation, or ask unexpected questions like, 'And what do you think of Tolkien's *The Hobbit* or *The Lord of the Rings*'?

But Mr Branthwaite usually restricted himself to immediate business which had to be dealt with.   He had asked me to come and see him.

He said he had put in his papers, and asked for early retirement like many of his compatriots.   He said he'd recommended me as a suitable candidate because of my long association with the college, and my fairly adequate handling of the administration of the Demonstration School.   The job was going to be advertised, and he knew there would be others competing for it.   He'd gathered that at least two teacher training college lecturers were going to apply for the post of Principal.   He hoped I'd be selected.

'Are you interested? Are you going to apply?' he asked.

'I'm quite happy doing what I'm doing,' I said. 'I like my school, and I like teaching here at the college, especially the history of education in Uganda. But I'll certainly apply for the Principal's post,' I said. 'And many thanks for your recommendation.'

I duly applied. But at that particular time I was more involved in preparing a play for the Uganda Drama Festival, an exciting annual event. I'd written a play, *The Deviant,* a play for three characters. Francis Lobo, an ex-student at Shimoni TTC, now a colleague, was one of the characters, and Sudarsana and I were the other two. Jayant Thakar, my doctor friend, was full of energy and optimism as usual and was directing the play that year. He was rather fortunate this time in that one of my colleagues, Edith Garvie, got interested in the play and would, fairly regularly, sit in on the rehearsals, which usually took place in the evening and over weekends. These were intensive rehearsals, which lasted several hours, with a short break or two, for tea or coffee. Edith had years of experience in directing amateur plays and Jayant valued her comments and criticism, which were constructive. Directors of plays were usually sensitive people, who resented interference of any kind with any aspect of the work they were doing, whereas Jayant acknowledged the fact that Edith's advice and suggestions were valuable, and made considerable difference to the way the play now worked on the stage. And it was not just Jayant who benefited from Edith's advice and guidance; the actors too learnt a few things about voice projection, interaction, grouping, variation and timing. Jayant was a conscientious director. He thought carefully about interpretation, and plotted every move on the stage. Edith's contribution was a few refinements.

It worked. For the second time in the last three years, we were awarded the Spencer Shield for the best production in the Festival. What was especially significant was that it was the same adjudicator – Peter Carpenter – who hadn't even given us an honourable mention the previous year, who gave us the highly prized award this year. We considered Peter a great adjudicator – not because he'd decided that our play was the best that year, but because his adjudication was full of significant and creative suggestions about various aspects of acting, production and playwriting.

An ex-student of mine, who had returned to Kampala after spending a few years in England, had started a magazine called *Transition*. Rajat published *The Deviant* in his magazine. Later on, it was published by Heinemann in an anthology of African plays edited by Cosmo Pieterse.

Soon after our winning the award, we were invited to Mbale by a drama group there to do a weekend production. On our way to Mbale we encountered torrential rain, but although it slowed our progress, it was difficult but not impossible to drive through it. There were six of us in the car: the three actors and our three children. So far there was no real problem. Then in the distance we noticed a group of about 20 African men milling around a bridge and getting drenched. When I got near the bridge, I got out of the car to investigate why they were hanging around the bridge and getting thoroughly wet. Water was rushing across the bridge and there was a car in the stream below. It had been swept away. Fortunately the car had a driver but no passengers, and he had suffered only minor injuries. I gathered this information from the assembled Africans.

I wondered why so many young African men were there in spite of the pouring rain. It couldn't be to watch cars plunging into the stream below as a result of the strong wind and the flooded bridge, could it? I asked one of them why they were there. He explained that they were there to prevent cars being swept off the bridge. Some of them would push from behind while the car moved slowly across the bridge and others would be on either side of the car to prevent the wind and the fast-flowing water sweeping across the bridge from pushing the car into the stream. Did I want their help? It would cost me a certain sum of money, the man said, but he'd undertake to prevent any tragic accident. Was I interested? The amount he mentioned wasn't astronomical, and we needed to arrive at Mbale by a certain time to put on our play at the appointed hour. I thanked the leader of the group and requested him to get his men organised to push the car across. It was still raining, but the downpour was now a drizzle, and I wanted to make the most of what was probably an interlude before the sky opened again. A car _had_ been washed off the bridge and the sky _was_ darkening. There was a certain amount of risk. But with these strong young men to push the car across, there was, I felt certain, little risk of a disaster. I sat at the wheel after giving them the go-ahead and within a few minutes, we reached the other side of the bridge.

The children seemed to have quite enjoyed the experience. What was going to be a routine drive from Kampala to Mbale, turned out to be a bit of an adventure for the children, at no great extra expense? I had a certain feeling of anxiety, followed by relief. Sudarsana dealt with it all with perfect equanimity. I thanked the young men for their help, paid their leader more than the agreed amount to express our appreciation, and we were on our way. Francis Lobo, one of our actors travelling with us, had gone out with the young African men and pushed the car, so I thanked him too. Soon the heavy rain resumed, beating down on the roof of the car, while the windscreen wipers worked frantically to make it possible to move steadily towards our destination. Jayant was spared all this, for he hadn't come.

By the time we arrived at the theatre, the rain had, conveniently, stopped. There wasn't much time before the beginning of the plays – our play *The Deviant* and the Mbale Group's play. The response to our play was moderate; there was louder and more enthusiastic applause for their play. We didn't mind that. There could have been something partisan about the response, but it didn't matter. It was an enjoyable comedy which provoked a few good laughs, and the acting was more than just competent. We were provided with some supper, after which we drove back to Kampala, much later than we expected. It was, all in all, an enjoyable day out for us and the children.

On returning to work on Monday morning, I received a letter from the Department of Education informing me that I'd been short listed for an interview, for the post of Principal of Shimomi Teacher Training College, and I should be available for an interview in about a fortnight at the Deputy Director's office. The first thing I did that morning was to acknowledge the letter and confirm that I'd be there for the interview. During the break I went across to see Mr Branthwaite and told him that I'd been requested to come for an interview. He knew but he was a believer in bureaucratic correctness, so he hadn't told me. Now that I'd been officially informed, he said, casually, that it wasn't news to him and he wished me good luck. I think I've said this before – that examinations and interviews were occasions I didn't look forward to. And I disliked interviews more than examinations, because if I did badly in examinations there would be weeks, even months before I knew the outcome; I could make a fool of myself without anyone finding out anything about it. But in an interview, the wise men arrayed in front of me could make me feel like an idiot, by asking questions on topics about which I didn't have a clue. There were no restrictions on questions which tested your general knowledge, because nobody could define how general is general. Where is Honolulu? What was the real name of Mark Twain? Who was the mother of Elizabeth I? What is the year of the Battle of Plassey? Any question was legitimate in these job interviews. They didn't have to be relevant.

We were a small group of people being interviewed for the post of Principal, Shimoni TTC – an African, a Briton and an Indian. I had one advantage over the others: my close association with the institution for six years. But the other two candidates also had their advantages. The African was a teacher with quite a few years experience in secondary schools and since the day of independence for Uganda, as everybody knew, was around the corner, the wise men interviewing us might consider him the most appropriate choice for the post, all things being equal. The British man had history on his side – the two previous principals of the college were fellow countrymen.

My turn came. I was uncharacteristically relaxed for two reasons: I didn't expect to be selected and I liked being the Principal of the Demonstration School. Mr Wood was one of the interviewers. He was a Deputy Director. Then there was Mr Philip Acaye, Education Secretary, an African. There was also, I think, one of the Assistant Directors of Education. There were no general knowledge questions. The interview began with some friendly, personal questions. What did I do in India before I came to Uganda? Did I like teaching? Why did I like teaching?

After that, questions were more focused on the history and principles of education and the methods and approaches to teaching – subjects I had been teaching for a few years. It was, therefore, not a question of whether I knew the answers but whether the panel agreed with my ideas. I had all the information – correct and up-to-date. Where there could be disagreement was in the conclusions I'd arrived at and the generalizations I was making. If anything, I was glad that some of my ideas were challenged, because that gave me the opportunity to defend, explain and justify the conclusions I'd arrived at after ten years of teaching. I talked with conviction, guarding against making the discussion too one-sided and breaking into the lecture mode. Mr Wood and Mr Acaye wouldn't be pleased if I mistook them for my students, subjecting them to a stream of ideas and information which they were familiar with. It was a good feeling when you knew that you had the attention of your interviewers. The tension soon came to an end. Mr Wood smiled and Mr Acaye said thank you and goodbye. The interview was a positive experience because it seemed to me that wrong-footing the people they were assessing wasn't the panel's objective but to let them express their ideas and to exchange views. I emerged from the room feeling that this was how interviews should be conducted.

About the same time I was participating in an extra-mural teaching session at Makerere University College. I was in charge of a group which was going to write their one-act play and produce it. I was to discuss the subject, choose a theme, give it dramatic form and then produce it. At the time, the transfer of power from the British to the Ugandans was a given: the details were being discussed. The participants worked out a play of contemporary political relevance and produced it successfully. Other groups had other objectives. A very good friend of mine, Carol Harlow, ran a course in law, and various others ran other courses. At the end of the course, there was a party in Makerere University College Hall and I was having a drink and talking to Carol, when Mr Wood was going past. He stopped and walked up to me.

'Hello, Mr Bagchi,' he said. 'I thought I'd let you know that you have been selected for the post of Principal. The letter's in the post. Congratulations.'

I don't remember the exact words. We shook hands. I thanked Mr Wood. He was a friendly and informal man. We had a common interest – the theatre. I told Carol what Mr Wood had just told me. She was genuinely pleased and congratulated me. Sudarsana was delighted. The children were asleep. It wouldn't really make any difference to them, especially to Aparna, who was now in secondary school. For Aparajita and Nondon, I'd move out of the headmaster's office at Demonstration School – but I'd be just next door.

Changes happened quickly. A farewell party was arranged for Mr Branthwaite and his wife. I attended the party as the headmaster of the school and a lecturer at the college, but not as the next principal, because my appointment wasn't official yet. Speeches were made by the President of the Students' Council and by Mr Branthwaite. It was a pleasant and friendly occasion.

Soon after that my appointment was officially confirmed, and I started spending a little time at the Principal's office, discussing the guiding principles of Mr Branthwaite's administration, and his ideas for the expansion and improvement of the college. I gathered at the time of his handing over, that he was going back to England because it made sense for expatriates to make way for indigenous people, on the eve of independence, which was going to happen the following year. I'm not sure he was worried about what I did. Anyway, the handing over was not a complex or formal affair. It happened over a few hours spread over a few days. I was then installed in the office of the Principal.

Why was Mr Branthwaite talking about Ugandan independence? This is the background. Sir Andrew Cohen, the Governor of Uganda, took up the administration of the country in 1952, within a year of my arrival. It was quite clear to those who understood Uganda's political conflicts and complexities, that he was in the country to oversee its transition to independence. The powerful and the rich do not usually want a change in the power structure and the Kabaka was soon in conflict with the Governor because he had a lot to lose when a democratically elected leader ruled the country. It soon became clear that the Kabaka and the others close to him were reluctant to let Buganda degenerate into a province, an integral part of a sovereign democratic Uganda. For Edward Mutesa II, the Kabaka of Buganda, nothing could be more abhorrent than the idea of playing second fiddle to elected leaders who had always had to bow to his undisputed authority. In 1952, the Kabaka's disagreement with Sir Andrew Cohen led to the Kabaka's deportation. Later, in 1955, an agreement between the Kabaka and Sir Andrew Cohen was reached on the basis of which the Kabaka returned to Uganda in 1955.

All this was happening backstage. I had very little interest in the country's politics to begin with, but I got to know Erisa Kironde through my friends Murray Carlin and Valdo Pons, both lecturers at Makerere University College, and became involved in Uganda's political future. At the time I became Principal of Shimoni TTC in 1961, preparations for Uganda's independence were well on the way and African students had a wider choice of schools and colleges. There was an influx of African students, mainly male; with the result that we had more male African students than Asian. There were about 40 per cent African men and 40 per cent mainly Asian women. At the time there was also a small group of young African women doing a special course in Home Science with Mrs Pullman.

One interesting feature of the college was its Students' Council. It met at regular intervals, organised various student activities, discussed student welfare, and made representations to me and my colleagues about their needs and grievances. At the time they were involved in organising a reception for me, because the Students' Council had established a tradition of welcoming new members of academic and administrative staff, and the new intake of students. It also organised a farewell party for lecturers and principals when they left. The Student Council's most important function was commenting on the running of the College and making suggestions which, however, were discussed, but not always accepted or incorporated in the administrative policy. I'd attended some of the Students' Council parties; most recently it was a farewell party for Mr and Mrs Branthwaite. I was delighted to have the opportunity to meet the students informally. Sudarsana, who often kept out of social and official occasions, connected with Demonstration School and Shimoni TTC responded positively, especially because she was going to have the opportunity of meeting some African students. She was a convinced supporter of African independence.

The education system which we had known from the time Sudarsana and I arrived in the country until now was a segregated one. The result was that there was very little communication between the young people of different races in schools. It was with enthusiasm that Sudarsana joined me on this occasion, which was a special one for me. The Assembly Hall was tidied up and tastefully decorated with flowers and balloons. The students were looking good in elegant outfits. The organisers had managed to create a genuinely festive atmosphere. I went up to some of the members of the Students Council and congratulated them. Sudarsana also told them how impressed she was. After that Sudarsana and I joined in the dancing. Sudarsana was a good dancer and, because of our long partnership, I could not only keep my end up but was able to dance fairly effortlessly and with enjoyment. The lessons we'd taken in London came in useful now.

But there was a certain disturbing aspect of the event to which Sudarsana drew my attention.

'What proportion of your students are African?' she asked.

'African men are in a majority – say 40 per cent. Indian women are about 30 per cent and Indian men 20 per cent. There's a small group of African women students – say 10 per cent. These are not exact figures, but close enough. Why do you ask?'

'Look at your students who are dancing. The African women are dancing with the African men. Most African men who want to dance are dancing by themselves. The Asian women are either dancing with the few Asian men who can dance or with other Asian women. It's a case of never the twain shall meet. There's just one Indian woman dancing with an African bloke. Why is that?' Sudarsana said.

I wondered why Sudarsana made these observations. I explained that Indian women didn't usually dance, and those who danced, often avoided dancing with men. Then she suggested that we sat down and observed for a few minutes. If we did, I'd understand what she meant. We found that quite a few of the Asian women students did dance, but they were either dancing with Asian men or women or not at all. We did know that orthodox Muslim women didn't dance. But why did those who were dancing, deliberately and scrupulously avoid dancing with African men? We both came to the conclusion, unavoidably, that the conduct of the Asian women students was racist. I suggested that we leave the party in protest, but Sudarsana pointed out that the racist prejudice or orthodoxy of a few students should not upset me so much that I should spoil the party for ourselves and others. Sudarsana was right. Although I felt depressed, I also appreciated the fact that we weren't impervious to social pressure and conditioning. Most of the students were born in a country colonised long before they were even thought of, and racial prejudice was endemic to a colonial situation. Apart from that, there was the fact that the British, the Africans and the Asians had very little social contact. I was quite prepared to try and understand why the women students of my community behaved in a way which betrayed their racism, but what I couldn't do was to condone or ignore it.

The week after the party, I met the members of the Students' Council and expressed my disappointment with the way some of the students behaved the previous weekend at the party. I had no control over how they behaved in social environments elsewhere, I said, but at our college I expected my students to do better. I requested the Students' Council not to organise another party of that kind. They mustn't get me wrong, I said. It was a great party. My wife and I had enjoyed it very much. I thanked them. But, at the same time, I didn't want to encourage discriminatory racist behaviour. So – no more parties. There was general agreement about my decision, and we moved on to other matters.

The next morning a group of Asian women students came to see me. They wouldn't object to dancing with their fellow students, they said, but their parents had laid down the law and they had to conform.

'What do you think is right?' I asked.

'But how can we disobey our parents?' said one of the students.

'I haven't asked you to disobey your parents. I've decided to deny you the opportunity to obey your parents and discriminate against some of my students,' I said.

'Isn't who I dance with my affair?' one of the more articulate students retorted. It was defiant and cheeky, some would say, but it was one of my conscious objectives to encourage such cheekiness. If I could, through example, reduce or eliminate their fear of authority, I'd have achieved something. Therefore, instead of saying something like, ''Don't be impertinent,' I seriously engaged in the debate with her.

'If one or two of you, for reasons of personal preference, danced with Peter instead of Paul, nobody would even notice it, let alone object to it. But when practically all the Asian women students blatantly avoid dancing with all the African men, I suspect that they have been brainwashed into believing in stupid ideas. You behaved badly and I will not again provide you with the opportunity to repeat racist behaviour. I have been thinking about it a lot. There is a positive alternative. I've also thought about that. If the Students' Council is prepared to have the next party without any dancing, I won't object.'

We agreed to discuss the alternatives at the next meeting of the Students' Council. The conversation between the women students and me had some unexpected repercussions. One of the parents rang me and argued that I was putting unfair pressure on his daughter to dance with African men. She chose who she danced with, not I. If that was what he thought, I said, he'd have to complain to the Director of Education and see what happened. If there was no redress, he could always take his daughter out of the college.

'Would you treat one of your African students in the same way if she didn't want to dance with Asian men?' he asked.

'I'd certainly deal with her similarly. If there's racism of any kind in the college, I'd have to deal with it. The student's being African wouldn't make any difference,' I said.
'I'll have to take your word for it, I suppose,' said the parent and hung up.

The voice didn't mention any names. It didn't disclose the identity of my student, so I had no way of finding out who I had spoken to. But a Guajarati parent actually came to see me in my office and brought up the same subject. When I explained that values and attitudes were as much a part of education, especially in the education of teachers, as teaching skills and knowledge, he started showing signs of moral indignation.

'I'm not going to be told what my moral values ought to be,' he said.

'You're right. It would be impudent for me to dictate to you about your values. But, equally I couldn't stand by and let one of my students behave badly because she has acquired the prejudices of her community,' I made sure I didn't sound agitated.

The man was probably in his middle forties, spoke good English, and had an air of authority. He was, obviously, used to having his way.

'I still think that you are being high-handed,' he said.

I know that this parent had a point. It was presumptuous to tell a woman who she ought to dance with. But since I suspected that race came into that decision, I had to challenge it, bring it out in the open. It was an all-pervasive problem in this part of the world, and by no means one-sided. If one of my African students refused to dance with one of the Asians – man or woman, and I suspected that this was racist behaviour, I'd certainly want to bring it out into the open and discuss the pernicious business of racist paranoia. But I wasn't ready to engage in a long, perhaps not very rational discussion, about a complex problem, with this man. So I said I thought we were speaking at cross purposes. I pointed out that I'd made certain decisions which I thought were fair and I wouldn't change them. We were wasting each other's time, so maybe we should go back to what we normally did at that time of day.

This meeting ended abruptly. The Students' Council meeting was due in a week. I was usually invited; this time I wasn't. Requesting the Principal wasn't obligatory according to their constitution, so they hadn't even officially informed me about the date and time of the meeting. I knew that they were having a meeting because I made it my business to find out what was going on, which wasn't difficult because it was a small college and my students weren't trying to hide that they were having a meeting. In the course of the next fortnight or so, a Students' Council meeting did take place and one afternoon, the bearers of office and two or three of the women students came to see me.

'We've decided to have a party just before the end of this term,' said the President of the Students' Council.
'I see,' I said, waiting for clarification, because I'd told them there would be no more parties. 'But didn't we agree that there wouldn't be any parties until we'd dealt with certain issues, certain matters of principle?' I asked.

'We have discussed racism in Uganda and in this college, and we have agreed that it isn't acceptable. Some of our parents, and friends and relations are racist. They live here without love and loyalty and influence their children and relations. Many African parents also resent our being in this country. But we think it's wrong. We'll have a party. Racism won't come into it. Can we go ahead?'

This was a Guajarati student about whom I didn't know very much and today I can't even recall her name. This was the first time that I'd realised what a sensible and articulate young woman she was.

'You certainly can,' I said. 'I'd be very disappointed if you didn't go ahead. Can we come, Sudarsana and I?'

'You certainly can,' said the President of the Students' Council. 'We'll look forward to your being at the party.'

I felt good on this occasion. I've spent a lifetime with much younger men and women – a few thousand of them – and I know that they're generous; the meanness happens later in life. They aren't naturally selfish, narrow-minded and prejudiced people. It's a pity that quite often the values of their families and friends are wrong. What I've said here applied equally to my African and Asian students.

There was no question of arm-twisting anybody into coming to the party. One option was open to all – they could stay away. On this particular occasion everybody came and it seemed to us that they were enjoying themselves. Nothing was happening which could be interpreted as sexist or racist. My relief and pleasure was immense. Sudarsana said she was really enjoying herself. It was very different, she said, from the last time she was here.

'I don't know what your input was in bringing about the change, but change there is, and it's change for the better,' she said.

'I'm glad,' I said, 'that you approve.'

We didn't stay till the end of the party, but we were there long enough to know that it was going well. I'd decided that these young people had a natural concern for what was just and fair. The way the students behaved confirmed my belief.

Among my compatriots I was beginning to get the reputation of bending over backwards to please the African bureaucrats on the eve of independence, when power was changing hands. I came by this kind of information or speculation during my occasional meetings with Mr D J Raval, Headmaster of Koloto Secondary School and my friend and mentor. Because of my interest in writing plays and acting, I had got to know some of the top administrators in education who treated me as a friend. This had also caused people to make adverse comments: I knew how to get on in life, I was a go-getter. One of my erudite colleagues in one of the secondary schools had also commented that I was flying too close to the sun. We laughed about it, Mr Raval and I, but I found such criticism painful.

I was beginning to worry that the college had moved right into the centre of my life. I was, I'd convinced myself, engaged in the pursuit of excellence. I wasn't spending any time with the children or with Sudarsana. I was reading very little. My social engagements were few and far between. At staff meetings, I started holding forth with proselytizing zeal about dedication and excellence, expecting my colleagues to notice the circle of light around my head. And, incidentally, had my colleagues noticed that I hadn't missed a single day's work either at the Demonstration School or at the College? Nobody got up and clapped, but it distinctly looked to me as if my colleagues were all impressed.

Then it happened. I'd started feeling very tired at the end of the day, and even in the morning when I got out of bed and drove to the college, the world did not appear bright and beautiful. It was most unusual for me to have headaches, but they became my constant companions. Passing urine was painful because I experienced a burning sensation, and one morning I found blood in my urine. I hadn't had any illness to keep me away from any of the schools in which I had worked since my arrival in Kampala more than ten years ago, or from the college. Only a few days ago I had bragged about it – uncharacteristically. Now I regretted having said what I had said about never being absent from work. A slightly different version of a nursery rhyme kept going round and round in my head –about someone sitting on a wall and having a great fall. Bragging, I realised, got you nowhere.

I regretted having held up my noble example to shame those colleagues who, for one reason or another, had had to take time off. Now I was feeling really miserable. I had a short staff meeting and explained that I'd have to go to hospital for treatment for a condition which might be serious. My doctor friend, who'd directed my play, did a thorough check-up and decided I'd contracted bilharzia and for confirmation referred me to the Government Hospital.

At the hospital, I had to be anaesthetized for a thorough check-up, which was carried out by a British surgeon, who asked me several questions, including one to find out whether I was in the habit of indulging in extra-marital sex relationships. After the testing and the questioning, the surgeon informed me that I had *schistosomiasis,* popularly known as *bilharzia,* a parasitic disease which affected vast numbers of people in Africa, Asia and South America. The treatment would begin immediately and continue for a certain number of days, during which I'd have to stay in hospital for medication and observation. At the end of the treatment, I'd be examined again under anaesthetics. I was allocated a clean little room on the third floor, a room of which I was the only occupant.

The treatment would take ten days or more. There could be side effects. Whether they were mild or severe would depend on various factors, the most obvious one being my physical condition. But the surgeon didn't think there was any real danger of my young life being cut short. I had no serious apprehension myself, and the very confident assurance of an older and wiser man, who was a respected specialist, helped.

I wish I could remember the name of the surgeon, but I can't. He told me that he was treating me with a drug called *Astiban,* which I would have to take for about a week. After that, I would be kept under observation for a day or two, because some side effects like vomiting and rashes might cause me some distress. He warned me that minor suffering might happen, but he didn't expect anything too unpleasant or life-threatening.

The treatment had started as soon as it was confirmed that I had bilharzia. When I gathered that I'd have to spend much more time in hospital than I'd expected, I requested Sudarsana to bring along a pen and some writing paper when she came to visit me. I started writing a play for the annual British Council Drama Festival, which was due in a few months. The title of the play was *A Recurrent Theme,* in which three unemployed young men, unable to pay the rent for their flat, try and keep out of the way of the landlord; but make up to his charming daughter, hoping that if push came to shove, she'd prevent their eviction by mediating between them and her father. At one stage of the play some complication happened on account of the bachelors not meeting the deadline for the payment of rent, and some rivalry between the friends for the attention and affection of the landlord's daughter, but in the end things came right. In my first three plays I'd dealt with social and political problems. Relief was provided through the light-hearted treatment of some aspects of those problems but in a way that didn't take away from the seriousness of the central theme. This was different. Sudarsana listened to bits of the play during the visiting hour and found it interesting. Incidentally, I now realize that my story resembled that of a famous opera, but at that time I didn't know it. The main inspiration and encouragement came from an attractive young woman who had come to the hospital for an operation. Whereas I talked at length about my affliction as well as the causes, symptoms and treatment of bilharzia, Sarah was reticent about what had brought her to the hospital.

Every evening after supper – we had supper early at the hospital – she came to listen to whatever I'd added to the play during the day. She was a sensitive and friendly person whose suggestions and criticism I valued. Sarah had a high-powered job at the Government House at Entebbe. One evening she was particularly enthusiastic about the play. We met many times. We talked about race, sex, politics, plays and related topics. This very temporary relationship had two very positive results – it made the unpleasant reaction to the drug appear quite bearable and helped my playwriting.

'Can you think of any reason why I should flatter you?' Sarah asked one evening
'Not really,' I replied, intrigued by the question.

'I like your play very much. It works. It has a great sense of fun. You ought to finish it and enter it in the British Council's Drama Festival,' she said, with conviction.

I thanked her for her unequivocal praise and explained that there could be no question of my not completing the play, because my friend Dr Jayant Thacker had twice visited me at the hospital, to make sure that I wasn't dragging my feet and letting this *minor* affliction affect the writing. Only incidentally did he ask me how I was and expressed confidence in Astiban, which was the drug that was being administered to rid me of 'snail fever'.

I was soon discharged. I returned home and resumed my work at the college. At the next staff meeting, we laughed about the certainty with which I'd talked about my unbroken record of attendance, which was so rudely disrupted by bilharzia. We decided at the meeting that this situation should be exploited for perfectly legitimate educational purposes. Someone who was well-known both at the school and the college had bilharzia or schistosomiasis, a disease which had a devastating effect on a very large number of people in Africa, including children. So the science teachers' first duty would be to tell the students what the nature of the disease was and what precautions should be taken against contracting it. I was fairly certain that I'd acquired it by swimming in Lake Victoria at Entebbe. To begin with, therefore, the students had to be warned against swimming in that vast and beautiful lake, where, it was now established; the fresh water snails carried the parasite. The better solution, of course, would be to get rid of the infested water-dwelling snails. The idea was generally popular, the science teachers being particularly enthusiastic. This was, one of my colleagues suggested, a case of adversity being the mother of invention.

An unmistakable change had happened to me of which I wasn't aware at the time. The affairs of the college, the achievements of the students and the direction in which we were moving had all become quite central to my life. I had a team of capable and creative colleagues who had earned the respect and affection of the students. Our college continued to be most of what I cared for in life. Our contribution to the education in the country was quite small because we were a small college and there was the possibility of its being amalgamated with an older and well-established college. Sir Edgar Castle, a well-known and respected educationalist, was at the time at Makerere University College. He might have been there in an advisory capacity. He was, I think, asked to submit a report on the college. He had said ours was a unique college, I was told, and it would be a pity if it were to lose its separate identity. This was, as far as we were concerned, an off-the-record investigation. Otherwise, why should such a distinguished man in the world of education suddenly visit our college and spend time sitting in on the teaching, looking with interest at the collection and quality of books in the library, and talking to students and teachers? It gave me a good feeling that Sir Edgar had visited our college – a learned man, gentle, human and kind.

Uganda was approaching independence in a unique manner – with the consent and co-operation of the colonial masters. There were problems, but these were mainly indigenous, the dominance of Uganda being one of the main sources of resentment to the other four kingdoms. Then there were deep divisions between the Nilottes and the Bantu, the Protestants and the Catholics, the Democratic Party, the Uganda People's Congress and the Kabaka Yekka, which didn't want to accept any plan to share the Kabaka's sovereign power with any other party. In the end, the close collaboration between the Governor and the political parties worked and elections were held, so the government of an independent Uganda could take over. The Democratic Party, which represented the Catholic population of the country, emerged as the majority party but they didn't have absolute majority. Milton Obote, the leader of the Uganda People's Congress, then proposed a coalition with Kabaka Yekka, and the country was now ready to rule itself. We were going to be residents of an independent Uganda. The price paid for independence by Uganda was so small – in comparison with India or Kenya, for example, ruled by the same colonial masters – that it seemed unreal. It was incredible that the millions of the residents of this country of some 240,000 square kilometres were at last going to wake up in an independent Uganda.

While we at the college were getting all excited at the prospect of celebrating independence, some of my friends and well-wishers were worried about the advent of independence in a country where trade and commerce had been, by and large, taken over by the Asians, who were referred to by the Ugandans as the *Mahindi*. *Mahindis* in East Africa evoked more resentment and anger than affection or respect.

We, the Asians, were the accomplices or partners in crime of the British imperialists. How were my African students going to behave after independence? I was running an educational institution with a majority of young African men. Next to the African men, were the young Asian women. And they lived in hostels next door to each other. The young Asian men were a minority because teaching wasn't one of the most popular of professions in a commercial community. A mixed group of students with different values and expectations from life – but at no time did I consider the situation unmanageable. The other problem was that the Africans had been second-class citizens in their own country for nearly 70 years. When their confidence and self-respect are restored to them, aren't they likely to feel liberated? And wouldn't some of them decide that it was pay-back time? Such questions were being asked, but they didn't worry me.

'And how are you going to deal with this?' asked my well-wishers.

'I don't know,' I answered honestly. I hadn't really thought of a strategy.

When I told some of my advisers and well-wishers that I didn't think of my students as African men and Asian men and women but simply as my students, some of them thought I was deluding myself. Others found my naivety quite incredible. They didn't *want* me to come to grief, but they were almost certain that I would.

The 9th of October, 1962, the day power was going to be officially handed over by Britain to Uganda, was almost upon us. Before all special occasions for the college or the country which was likely to significantly affect the students, it was customary for us to call a meeting of the Students' Council. The students took the initiative most of the time, but from time to time, I or one of my colleagues also could suggest that a meeting should be called. Since we were on the threshold of an independent Uganda, and we were looking forward to attending the ceremony marking the occasion, a meeting was arranged. We decided that our students would be divided into mixed groups of men and women, Asians and Africans, and a man and a woman would be in charge of each group. It was their responsibility to ensure that nobody got hurt or lost.

The makeshift pavilions of Kololo heaved with men, women and children. There were high-ranking officials in their well-pressed suits and their wives, elegantly dressed. Some of them were outgoing administrators and some successors – and their wives or husbands. Then there were invited guests from other countries – heads of states or their representatives, celebrities, friends. In hierarchical terms, the most important guests were the Duke and Duchess of Kent, who were representing the Queen, and the Governor of Uganda, Sir Walter Coutts. They were the representatives of the outgoing government, the colonial set-up.

For the incoming government, there was the Kabaka, Muteesa II, who was to become the President of Independent Uganda after midnight, and Milton Obote, the Prime Minister. The venue of this historical occasion was Kololo airstrip, which was for a time used for the landing and take-off of light aircraft in some distant past.

This evening, it was in a blaze of light, with music playing, and eager, expectant faces waiting and watching for history to happen.

Then various events followed, one after another, the exact order of which I don't remember, evoking feelings of excitement and elation. Milton Apollo Obote took the oath of office. Uganda's national anthem was sung. The Union Jack was lowered. Uganda's national flag was raised. Sixty-eight years of colonial administration ended. We would all wake up the next morning in a free Uganda.

It was the early morning of 10th October. We went to the women's hostel to see whether everybody had returned from the ceremony. We were ready to wait, but that wasn't necessary. Our students had all returned and were in the Common Room of the women's hostel, talking animatedly about their experience. Some of the students from the men's hostel were also there. They had organised their own transport, arrived at the ceremony punctually, left soon after it was over and were now going over some of the highlights of the ceremony. Wednesday, October 10, was, I think, a holiday. We said goodbye and left. It was a great and memorable day and my trust in my students was vindicated.

When we returned to college, business was as usual. We organised a ceremony of our own to emphasise the incredible fact that Uganda was now an independent country – with Obote, the Prime Minster, Kabaka Muteesa II, the President, and Sir Walter Coutts, the Governor General. Everything looked the same. The structure of power and privilege had not drastically altered, but there was all around us an air of friendliness, a sense of achievement and a forgetting of failure and remorse. Here and there, during the break, students stood in small groups, discussing the events of the celebration. What did you think of Obote's independence speech, one asked? Another worried about the Kabaka's role, now that the nation's independence was a reality. Would he be content with his mainly ceremonial role in the government? I stopped and talked to some groups. Some of the students in a group behind me were beginning to sound quite frustrated and angry – exactly why I never found out.

The women rarely joined the men's groups. And politics was never the dominant subject for discussion among them. One of my pleasures in the college was engaging in informal discussions with my students, whenever an opportunity presented itself. I found them rewarding. Quite some time had now passed since I became the Principal. During this time there were minor challenges, temporary worries but nothing had worsened, nothing had got strange or strained, nothing had disturbed the harmony of our small community.

The students who were Africans weren't all from the same tribe. The Asian students were Hindu, Muslim and Christian – Indian, Pakistani and Goan. Of my colleagues, three were British, one American, one African, one Canadian and four Asian. There was no lack of variety, but the diversity hadn't led to any conflicts, at least none that really mattered. Sue and Edith taught methods of teaching. There were differences in their approach and I was sometimes called upon to ensure uniformity. I didn't think uniformity was of the essence. It was better for the students to make their own decisions – to choose one or the other, or to take from each what they thought acceptable, or to invent or devise their own teaching approach or method. The college, by and large, had developed its own dynamics. I felt that I was part of a fairly integrated community. The college had acquired a good name in the teaching community. Our students, after they had left college, had no problem finding jobs. We mattered, and I identified myself very closely with my college. Thinking of the college, I often had a feeling close to euphoria. One aspect of our situation, however, worried me. We were surrounded by well-wishers and admirers, but there were none to censor our lapses and shortcomings. We had capable and erudite people on our Board of Governors – Mahendra Maini, Norman Godinho, Peter Marsh and others. They occasionally made suggestions, but never criticised. This, quite overwhelmingly, persuaded me that I was doing a good job at the college.

But that afternoon, I was in for a shock, a rude awakening. I had taken Nondon and Aparajita home from school, had a quick cup of tea with Sudarsana and come back to the office to finish some work which couldn't wait. Miss John, the warden of the women's hostel, walked in, an anxious look on her face. Her uncertain aspect worried me.

'I don't know if it is true but what I've heard from one of the students of the women's hostel is quite alarming,' she said.

Only a little while ago, I was congratulating myself on running a place which had brought me happiness and confidence. Now alarmed, I asked, 'What is it, Miss John?'

'Some of the African men have been bringing women prostitutes into their rooms... Sometimes they are noisy and rowdy. If the parents of my girls suspected what was going on in the men's hostel, they wouldn't let them stay here another day.'

Miss John said what she had to say with great restraint. She was a most efficient hostel superintendent with traditional values, and she didn't believe in fraternizing with the girls. She kept her distance. The women students of the hostel respected her.

I listened to Miss John with great attention. I knew this was serious because Miss John had found it necessary to report the matter to me in person. Apart from that, she looked deeply distressed. I assured her that I, too, considered the situation unacceptable.

I'd act immediately, I promised, and make sure that the students who had taken such liberties were punished. But I couldn't take any action against the offenders on the strength of information given to us by students, however reliable they might be. Miss John left, but her frown, always a sign of deep anxiety, hadn't disappeared.

If what Miss John suspected was true, then I was living in a fool's paradise. Students whom I trusted, who had given such a good account of themselves only recently at the Independence Day celebrations and had proved responsible and totally trustworthy, were actually doing things behind my back which I couldn't allow to happen on the college campus! I couldn't accuse, far less punish, the deviant group, without some reliable evidence. Even Miss John had witnessed nothing. It could be malicious gossip. Race did play an evil part in our relationships in this country. As for the Africans, they also didn't have a lot of time for the *Mazungus*, which is what they called the white colonisers, or the *Mahindis*, the Asians. It was our amazing good fortune, or the result of good governance, that we never had any loss of lives or damage to property as a result of race riots. Asians in remote African villages plied their trade without fear of losing their life or business. But below the surface, resentment seethed. It was unlikely that the Ugandans were going to weep for the colonizing British, or for the Asians, if they too decided to go. Therefore, any high-handed, hasty action by the head of a mixed-race institution in the heart of the capital could have unforeseen repercussions. At the same time, it would be wrong to ignore any blatant flouting of a decent tradition in an academic institution. The resident students were all told that women were not allowed to visit men in their rooms, nor were men supposed to visit women. According to Miss John, some men weren't taking any notice of that rule. I decided I had to do something. Maybe, I thought, we should have a warden at the men's hostel also.

One Saturday evening I drove up to the college about eleven at night; parked my car near my office and walked a few hundred yards to the men's hostel. Quite a few rooms were shut. The men were out visiting friends and relations or watching films in cinemas or eating out. Some were in the common room, reading newspapers and magazines before going to bed. At the end of the corridor, in one of the rooms, there were lights blazing and people noisily enjoying themselves. I walked up, knocked on the door and entered. It was clear that a party was in full flow with music, dancing and drinking. I was greeted without any self-consciousness or signs of guilt or embarrassment. Someone even offered me a drink. There was nothing crude, unpleasant, vulgar or compromising that anyone could object to, except perhaps that the music was loud and some of the women looked too relaxed, their eyes glazed. I left soon after I had entered the room. Mrs John had said that the women who came to visit were not the right sort, but how could one tell? As I was driving back, it struck me that it was past 11 o'clock, there were no cars in the drive and it was much too late for any kind of public transport.

There could be only one conclusion: the women were going to spend the night with the three students who had invited them. What I didn't understand was why none of the students, not even those who were such responsible members of the Students' Council, had reported any of this to me. Sudarsana was still awake reading when I returned home. I made a cup of tea and told her about my recent experience.

'I don't understand,' I said, 'why none of my most trusted students, or members of the Students' Council, have told me anything about what's been going on. They must know!'

'I can think of a reason,' Sudarsana said. 'To tell on people is against the culture of the people here. Nobody is guiltless. If we revealed each other's secrets, where would we be? None of the Africans I know indulges in reporting other people's lapses. It's against their culture.'

Sudarsana might be right. I wouldn't make a generalisation like that on the basis of the few Africans I knew. But now I didn't need any informers. There could be no doubt that at least three of my students had ignored codes of conduct and something had to be done about it.

I wrote to them. I didn't beat about the bush. I said that what they were doing was against the rules, and I'd like them to leave. I gave them a fortnight to reorganise their lives. I didn't for a moment think that my letter was the end of the story, but the beginning of a protracted battle. They knew, for example, that they could come and see me; make representations through the Students' Council; write to the Director of Education; present my high-handed action as an act of racial discrimination and turn it into a political issue. As for me, I'd done what I'd done –

not only because there was in me a combination of obstinacy, fatalism and a certain respect for conventional moral values, but because I acted instinctively rather than impulsively.

My friend and well-wisher, Mr Raval, warned me that this was independent Uganda, and my action might have far-reaching consequences. Hairline cracks slowly began to appear on the facade of my conviction. In the meantime, there was no representation from the Students' Council and no request for an interview from the victims.

Mr Philip Acaye, an African, one of the education administrators, was somebody in whom I had confidence. I trusted him because of the way he related to people. He, I sincerely believed, didn't allow his judgement to be clouded by race or politics. I rang him and made an appointment. When I saw him, he listened to what I had to say, read the letter I had written to the three students, thought for a minute and said without any hesitation,

'What you have done is right. If there are problems, I'll deal with them'.

Mr Acaye had always shown interest in the college. He told me that teachers trained in our college were well-thought-of. He was glad I'd referred the matter to him. He thought I'd acted appropriately, and that I shouldn't hesitate to see him if I had any problems. The meeting had lasted no more than 20 minutes. My relief was immense. When I returned home from work that day, Sudarsana, a keen observer of my changes of mood, asked what transformational event had taken place in my life. I explained.

There was no further development from what had happened that evening when I visited the men's hostel. I was expecting tense discussions and debates at specially convened meetings of the Students' Council. That didn't happen. No representation of any kind was made on behalf of the three non-conformist students. They didn't attend classes and they didn't complain to anybody as far as I know, unless someone on their behalf had seen Mr Acaye, who was in charge of teacher-training colleges – and had got short shrift from him.

One of the Asian students who lived in the hostel had this explanation: those three students stuck together because they came from the same small town and belonged to the same tribe. It was clear from the alacrity with which they left that they weren't particularly serious about the work they were doing at the college, or about a career in teaching. This incident was a gentle reminder of the fact that one couldn't expect an uninterrupted run of good fortune: it was likely to be broken occasionally by unpleasant and unwanted incidents. The good news was that the crisis turned out to be minor and short-lived although it had had the potential to be long-drawn and serious.

A few months went by. The new group of students arrived. When Charles Kabuga joined the college, there was no place for him in the hostel and he wouldn't be able to enrol unless he found some cheap accommodation in Kampala. I liked Charles and didn't want him to go back to his village and miss the opportunity to be a teacher. He'd set his heart on a teaching career, had good grades, and I'd decided at the interview he would make a good teacher. So what was the solution? I asked him to bring his suitcase along with him to our house in Kololo at the end of the day. I introduced him to Sudarsana and the children. While he was having a cup of tea and talking to the children, I withdrew into our bedroom with Sudarsana and told her about Charles's predicament.

Attached to the garage there was a room with a small window, just large enough to take a bed and a small desk. I wanted to offer that room to Charles to sleep in at night. During the day he could use the living room to do his college work, to read his books and the newspaper when we had no visitors. Not many people visited us, so he'd have no problem. He could withdraw to his room whenever he wanted to be on his own. Did she think it was a good idea? She thought it was.

After that I explained to Charles why I had asked him to bring along his suitcase and meet my family. It now depended on whether he thought the small room attached to the garage, normally used for storing garden implements or spare tyres – was habitable and whether he wanted to live with us and complete his course at the college.

Charles accepted my offer with a sense of relief. Within a fortnight, Sudarsana, the children and I were convinced that the arrangement which I had suggested and Charles had accepted was working to our mutual advantage. Charles related well to the children, who loved listening to his stories. Sudarsana and I found him a friendly, mature and relaxed person with no hang-ups of any kind, and equally comfortable in the company of both adults and children. Within the month, he had started playing the role of the older brother, the group leader and mentor with my son and daughters.

It was soon after independence. The atmosphere was chock full of patriotism. One evening, I returned from a meeting at the college later than usual and found Charles and the children standing upright, singing the Ugandan national anthem. Later I gathered from my younger daughter that Charles had a little transistor radio, which he'd named *Lily*. Whenever the national anthem played on the radio, Charles would stand up bolt upright and sing:

'Oh Uganda, Land of Beauty
Oh Uganda, may God uphold thee
We lay our future in thy hand
United, free, for liberty
Together we'll always stand!'

And the children would sing with him. One of my students had had an existential problem. On the spur of the moment, I'd offered a solution. It worked. Charles did well in his theory papers and his practical teaching. That wasn't all. Later he applied for a place at Makerere University College and was accepted. I lost touch with him for a long time but learnt later on that he had done well, got his degree and had a good career in education. It always gives me great pleasure to remember and narrate Charles's story. Goodness, intelligence and integrity, I sincerely believe, are related qualities. This doesn't mean, however, that sharp-witted crooks do not abound in our society.

Independence brought other problems in its wake. It wouldn't make sense to let the Europeans and the Asians hold the key administrative positions in the different government departments. They would have to go. If on account of their expertise they were irreplaceable, the government would request them to stay, but they couldn't be compelled to do so. Now, the terms and conditions for the departure of a large number of expatriates had to be negotiated with the independent Ugandan Government.

To discuss the terms and conditions of the expatriates' departure in the wake of the Africanisation of government jobs, the President of the Asian Civil Servants' Association, Mr Siddiqui, was going to London. But what about the terms and conditions of service for those who had been given the option to stay? We found the notification circulated by the Ugandan Government really discriminatory. It said, quite explicitly, that all things being equal, Africans would be preferred for new appointments as well as for promotions. I was then the Vice President of the Asian Civil Servants' Association and Mr Siddiqui, the President. The two of us and the Secretary of the organisation requested an appointment with the Prime Minister, Milton Obote, and got it.

Mr Obote made quite sincere remarks about the contribution of the Asian community. It was necessary, however, to correct the imbalance that existed in the Civil Service, he said.

'Do you think that if you go to England, as some of you are planning to do, you won't come across discrimination? If you and an English person have the same qualifications and personality, wouldn't the English person get the job?' he asked.

He shouldn't, I said. The criteria for selection should be purely objective, I insisted. Mr Obote then said that it was good to be idealistic but real life didn't follow the ideal pattern. In the end, on this and other points, we totally disagreed. We left Entebbe without winning a single concession. It was a disappointing meeting from which we took some time to recover.

Milton Apollo Obote was about the same age as me, confident, articulate – and inflexible. I had the impression that he'd decided in advance what the outcome of our discussion was going to be. That made nonsense of our marshalling of facts and presenting our arguments. I wasn't even quite certain that he was listening to what we had to say. It was a charade, a travesty of democratic discussion and debate. It was so depressing that the idea of packing it all in and returning to India crossed my mind for the first time.

It struck me suddenly that the college had become so central to my life, that there was very little else that really mattered. This was a situation which had occurred before. It was important to restore some kind of balance, I said to myself. The Uganda Drama Festival wasn't too far way; so I fished out the play which I'd written during my stay in the hospital after being afflicted with bilharzia. Naresh, Francis and I were going to take the parts of the three young men – one an artist, one a musician and one a writer. Sudarsana was allocated the part of the landlord's daughter. The young men couldn't pay the rent but loved the landlord's daughter. Their problem was partly emotional, partly financial. This was the situation which led to complications which resolved themselves in the end. The plot couldn't be simpler. The three young men devised various means of amusing themselves. On one occasion the situation really got out of hand. They had invited Keya, the landlord's daughter, but when she arrived for her evening out they hadn't organised a meal for her – because they had no money to buy the food and drinks. But they pretended to have a really great meal. They talked about the quality of the champagne and caviar and various exotic dishes, drinking non-existent drinks and eating fantasy food. Quite a bit of miming was involved in this scene and there was evidence that the audience found the action amusing. Some suspected that I'd taken the story from Puccini's *La Boheme*. But I didn't know anything about Puccini or *La Boheme* at the time. *A Recurrent Theme,* and *The Deviant* before that, were staged at the National Theatre, which had come into existence at the end of 1959.

The adjudicator at the festival was Clifford Williams. He praised the play and awarded Sudarsana the best actor prize. This was no ordinary evening for us and no ordinary achievement for Sudarsana, for Clifford Williams was no ordinary theatre personality. Clifford Williams hadn't yet become a household name in the theatre world, but what he'd already achieved in his mid-thirties was most remarkable. He'd produced new plays, experimental plays, Shakespeare and Marlowe, all the time evolving new styles by using new approaches. When he came to Kampala to adjudicate plays at our fairly new National Theatre, he'd already directed a most impressive production of *The Comedy of Errors*. He rang me to suggest that we went out with him to have a meal at a restaurant before he left. His company was magical. It was an evening both Sudarsana and I recalled several times in the years that followed. We never understood why he chose to spend an evening with us when he'd had so many options.
'Clifford Williams must have been very impressed with your acting,' I suggested days later.' He gave you the best actor prize and wanted to meet you to seriously consider whether he could use you on one of the productions he's thinking of directing,' I suggested.

'I was truly disappointed,' said Sudarsana. 'I was dreaming of giving up my job, living in London and acting. You could look after the children, especially when I was on tour.'

'Maybe there's a letter in the post,' I said.

'A career in acting would suit me fine,' said Sudarsana

'Not when you have three growing children and a husband who's getting on,' I said.

'Hem,' said Sudarsana. 'Back to earth!'

We laughed about it, but I did think that Sudarsana could have had a good career in acting. We've very rarely talked about this evening, especially with friends who know about the theatre world, for fear that they might think we were either having them on or indulging in fantasy. My play, *The Recurrent Theme,* had been praised by Clifford Williams, but it hadn't won the Spencer Shield for the best play in the festival. Rebecca Njau had won it with a play with an African theme and an

African cast. Rebecca Njau was an artist as well as a playwright, and she'd used a large canvas and many characters. It was an impressive play, an authentic presentation of village and tribal life. I was completely absorbed in it because, apart from the rich spectacle and the authentic theme and characters, the histrionic aspect of it was outstanding. But the highlight of the festival for us was what happened after the festival – a few hours in the company of Clifford Williams. I've always been prone to idolatry.

Our conference with Milton Obote was not the end but only the beginning of the story about the transfer of administrative and educational control from the expatriates to the sons of the soil. If the Africans took over, we'd have to leave and return home, or find a job somewhere else. What was independence for the Africans was disruption for us expatriates. The African rulers had a responsibility to those who had come out to Africa – not always and entirely to make a living. Many came out of a sense of adventure and some, probably a small minority, to help, to relate to the people of the country and to have new and exciting experiences. What I'd gained from my African experience, was much more than my salary and accommodation, security and comfort, during the previous twelve years. I'd identified with so much that was African that I believed I was partly African, for ethnicity wasn't the only criterion! My relationship with my colleagues and students at Demonstration School and the Teacher Training College was much more than mercenary. Charles Kabuga had, within months, lost the self-consciousness of the outsider and become one of us. We knew we'd make Charles unhappy if we suddenly upped and returned to India. We had African friends who wouldn't want us to leave, I was sure. Yet, after the interview with Milton Obote, I'd felt very strongly that, however much we might identify ourselves with Uganda, there was little chance of us being accepted as citizens of this newly independent country. The African perception was that we were on the side of the colonisers and would never be able to change our spots. Why should they think differently about me?

My leave in India was due at this time. We flew, leaving Charles in charge of the house. Calcutta was just as exciting as always for me, but unlike our other holidays, this time I was looking at Calcutta through the eyes of the prodigal son wanting to return home at the end of his adventures or misadventures. Yet I was very much in two minds. We'd certainly have to go back and wait and watch before irrevocably making up our minds.

But while I was in Calcutta, I was looking at Shambazar, Park Circus, College Street and Tollygunge with tentative eyes, always speculating whether returning to

India was either practical or desirable. Uganda was for me a new country, full of promise, full of excitement, where Sudarsana and the children had settled down, made friends, done well in their different spheres of activity   And so had I. Sudarsana, as a teacher and actor, was widely admired. Aparna was a good student and had come first in her nationwide entrance examination to secondary school. Aparajita loved her ballet classes, she and Nondon had won elocution prizes and made good friends in Kampala and showed no special urge to leave Uganda and return to Calcutta. Then why was I thinking of going back to Calcutta on the basis of a brief encounter with Milton Obote, who hadn't really been long enough in his job of Prime Minister to know what was good for him and his country? Was I over-reacting?   Shouldn't I wait until this new Prime Minister, who was about my age and too young to be the chief executive of a newly independent country, found his feet? Should I throw tantrums because I had the impression that Obote didn't value the potential of Asian contributions, material and intellectual?

All this was internal conflict, which was for me and me alone to resolve. I looked around, met friends and relations. Father had died. My eldest brother and his family were still at Congress Exhibition Road. His eldest daughter had died when I was still at school; the second daughter had got married. Mejda, my second oldest brother was doing some kind of business which required him to travel to Orissa from time to time.   His daughters didn't go to school but his son, a rather unmotivated student, was soldiering on in a secondary school. My sister, Hena, had got married to Sudarsana's uncle and had borne him a daughter.

We spent some time with Ronu and Reba, who were excellent at hosting, apart from being our best friends in Calcutta. This was one of our most restful and low-key holidays.

It was soon time to return to Uganda, independent Uganda, where changes were happening quite rapidly in various departments of public life. In Indian education, however, there seemed to be very few changes. The British expatriates, including teachers, were leaving in large numbers, but not the Asians.   That was partly because many of the Asians had no plans to quit, and as far as I could see, the Uganda Government had no plans to throw them out of the country. Nobody was yet thinking of the residential or citizenship status of the Asians.   The resident Asians had British passports. Those who came out to teach short terms or do other jobs from India and Pakistan had Indian or Pakistani passports. We used to travel at the time on British passports.

When we returned to Uganda from Calcutta it was again time for the Drama Festival. I had so far written six one act plays – The *Gold Diggeres of Yaksha Town, Soma and Synthesis, The Deviant, Of Malice and Men, A Recurrent Theme I* and *A Recurrent Theme II*. All of them had received some award – except *Soma and Synthesis*. Sudarsana was awarded the best actor prize on two occasions, on one of which, we also bagged the best play award. Two of my plays – *The Deviant* and *Of Malice and Men* were later published by Heinemann. I'm not quite certain of the year of production of *Of Malice and Men,* nor of who adjudicated at the Drama Festival that year. Finally, it was *A Recurrent Theme II* which had four characters, the same as in *A Recurrent Theme Part I.* I remember it was a good drama festival with many interesting plays. The adjudicator that year was Denis Carey and the Representative from the British Council was Peter Marsh. Denis Carey was a well-known and highly respected theatre director. While he was director of the Bristol Old Vic Theatre Company, he directed 30 plays, including *The Cocktail Party, Two Gentlemen of Verona, Romanoff and Juliet.* One of his most notable commercial successes was *Salad Days.* He was a prolific and profoundly knowledgeable man of the theatre. I was greatly impressed with his witty, articulate and incisive assessment of the plays and the acting. I was awarded the best actor prize that year. That however, was *not* the reason why I was impressed with him.

While we were fiddling, Rome wasn't burning, but crucial decisions were being taken by leaders and administrators in London, Delhi and Kampala. Mr Siddiqui, the then President of the Uganda Asian Civil Servants Association, and he and the Secretary of the Association were in London to negotiate the terms and conditions of voluntary retirement and redundancy. There were various other issues relating to the transfer of power. It was agreed that there would be a compensatory element to induce civil servants to leave their jobs if it were possible to Africanise those jobs. Where it was not possible to replace incumbents – specialists, for example – they would be requested to stay on in their jobs. But should they also decide to quit, they would be entitled to the same terms and conditions as the others. What I thought was an important part of the agreement was that our pension would be index-linked.

My father had retired from his job in the Collector's office in Faridpur in the 1930s. By the latter part of the 1940s, his pension was worth nothing. Rising prices had destroyed much of its buying power. I hadn't decided to retire. I saw no reason to retire. My depression was the result of my brief encounter with Mr Obote. It was highly unlikely that I'd meet him again. The college had come to mean so much to me that starting life again without the challenges of that responsibility didn't at all appeal to me.

Apart from the students, there were my colleagues with whom I related well. Sue Mason had returned to America. Dickie Bird was seriously thinking of leaving. But Edith Garvie was still there and Francis Lobo. There was also Mr Thakore and Mr Patel…

During this time, Miss John, the ladies' hostel warden came to see me in the office one day. She had something to report. One of the ex-students of the college was now teaching methods of teaching science in junior schools. He demonstrated how to carry out simple scientific experiments in our small science laboratory. I liked Dinkar. There were others too, students and colleagues, who liked him for his friendly and helpful ways. I let him borrow my car on at least two occasions because he was picking up some disabled relative, he'd said. But it was not really for any relative at all, either healthy or disabled. Miss John told me something I didn't know, and would never have suspected. Dinkar used to take his girlfriend out for a spin in my car! It was about that that Miss John had come to see me.

'I don't like what's going on, and there's nothing I can do about it,' she said. I waited.

'Dinkar Mehta is no longer a student. He's joined the staff of the college. So he has no business going out with one of my resident students,' she said.

'But they're both adults,' I said.

'That doesn't matter in the culture of the girl's family. They're conventional; they're orthodox, they're religious, they're Sikhs.' she said. 'This is not a relationship which is likely to work. *And* I don't want to have to answer for it.'

'Why don't you talk to the girl?' I said.

'I have; it hasn't worked,' she said.

'Please leave it with me. I'll have a word with Dinkar,' I said.

Miss John didn't look too happy when she left, but profoundly anxious. She probably hadn't told me the whole story.

398

I didn't have the chance to talk to Dinkar.

It was Sunday morning. We'd finished eating our late breakfast. I was reading the Uganda Herald and listening to some music. Francis Lobo and Shabanali Jaffer, two of my younger colleagues, both my students before they joined the teaching staff of the college, had come to see me. They were looking sad, thoughtful, and serious.

'Dinkar is in hospital,' said Francis. 'He came to the college last night, went to the laboratory, collected some lethal acid and took it when he returned to his rented accommodation in town. He was soon screaming with pain. He was taken to the hospital by tenants in an adjoining flat.'

'How is he?' I asked.

'He's heavily sedated. We thought he recognised us but we weren't sure,' said Shaban.

I went to the hospital with Francis and Shaban. I wasn't sure that Dinkar cared any more. As he looked at us, there was no light of recognition in his sightless eyes. The acid had burnt his insides but hadn't killed him instantly. His screams had rent the air, I was told, when he was brought to the hospital. Without really heavy sedation, the pain would have been unbearable.

Dinkar died that night.

The student with whom Dinkar had been in love quietly left the hostel and the college.

We had a meeting of remembrance in which we talked about the tall, handsome and intelligent young man who had successfully completed his course at our college and had become an excellent teacher. He had perfectly legitimate expectations from life, one of which was to love and be loved. But our society had created unnatural and inhuman barriers in the way of young people's right to be themselves. In Asian society, caste, religion, sect and similar other considerations kept people apart. One of our friends, an ex-student of the college and later on a valued colleague, had paid the price for our narrow sectarian values. If our values had been more rational and human, this tragedy wouldn't have happened. There was a real sense of loss among our students.

My experiences at the college had so far been positive and fulfilling. I was surrounded by colleagues and students who were creative, and related well to each other. This unexpected tragedy showed that we exploited and restricted the young people in our society in a way which could lead to tragedy.

I had to attend the coroner's inquest and answer several questions about how accessible the different chemicals were at the science laboratory, how accessible the key was and how I was going to make sure that such tragedies didn't happen again. It was not a pleasant experience. There was something menacing about it. This was the most tragic experience I'd had since I first arrived in Kampala, the most tragic experience of my life so far.

There was a minor problem I had to attend to. A few weeks before Dinkar's tragedy, the caretaker of the college had run away with the office keys and tried to open the safe where, quite often, sums of money were kept. He'd had no success because I never parted with the safe-key. I'd reported the matter to the police. The caretaker was caught, and the office keys retrieved and I was summoned to attend a court hearing to identify the accused and give evidence. I had to attend court at ten in the morning and turned up a little before time, when another case was up being sorted. I thought it would soon be my turn to stand at the witness box. But more than an hour went by and there was no indication that I'd be asked to do anything at all. I was carrying a paperback edition of Jean Paul Sartre's play *In Camera* in my pocket. So I took it out, started reading and soon got so absorbed in it that I didn't notice the passage of time.

An *askari* or policeman tapped me on the shoulder and startled me out of the complex world I'd entered. I thought my turn had come to stand at the witness box but another man was already there, so where was I supposed to go? The policeman signalled for me to follow him. We went past the witness box and down some steps. He opened an iron gate and asked me to step into an enclosed area behind grills where a rather noisy group of Africans were waiting, I suppose, to be summoned. They asked me what crime I had committed. They were intrigued by the fact that a *Mahindi* or Asian, in a suit and tie, was in the same cell as them, waiting for trial. Some laughed. Some made comments, which I didn't understand, and laughed. They laughed because they found my predicament hilariously funny. Completely perplexed and somewhat anxious, I took a cigarette out of a new packet and lit it. Like hungry vultures my cell mates swooped down on the packet and a cigarette was dangling out of practically every pair of lips. Then one of them *borrowed* my box of matches, which also disappeared. The room filled with smoke. My eyes were watering. I could see through the iron grills of the gate that there was no policeman posted outside the door. Was it fair to throw me to these people, most of them probably hardened criminals? I squatted on the floor and started reading *In Camera*. I'd hardly made any progress when the *askari* returned and announced that I was now going to have to go up to the witness box.

The magistrate – who I gathered later on was Welsh – first subjected me to a mini-lecture, which sounded like a rebuke, in an indignant attempt to bring home to me that in reading a book while he was dispensing justice, I'd shown disrespect to the system and was guilty of showing contempt for the head of state and the head of government. I was head of an educational institution and I should have known better. He would have carried on a little longer but he stopped when I said sorry. After that what I had to do was simple: I had to identify the man, the caretaker, who had stolen the office keys in the hope of stealing public money. He got a jail sentence and I got back the office keys. This was one of the magistrate's last flings. The country was now independent and magistrates like Mr Jones or Mr Lewis or Mr Thomas were on their way out.

Back at college, business was as usual, except that beneath the casual exterior there was a sense of proud achievement in the citizens of the newly independent Uganda. Before very long, I said to myself, I must do something about our citizenship. Ours was a rather dubious situation – Indians, living in Uganda, holding on to British passports. There was a long period of time over which I seriously considered becoming a Ugandan citizen and settling down in the country which had treated me so well.

Mr Gupta, Sudarsana's uncle, had retired. He had got to know the Indian High Commissioner in Uganda. I first met him in Uncle K.D. Gupta's house. The conversation was about the new environment created by Uganda's independence and how we could help the country. According to the High Commissioner, there were two categories of Indians – those who ought to stay and those who ought to go. The Indian entrepreneurs in business and commerce are a valuable asset for the country – they need not, must not leave, nor the doctors and scientists. But people like us stood in the way of the Africans. There were many excellent African teachers and teacher trainers who could do my job at least as well as I did. If I went back to India, my contribution to the African cause would be far greater than if I stayed.

'I know our Prime Minister, Jawaharlal Nehru, is strongly in favour of us doing everything we can to facilitate Africanisation,' he said.

'This is the first time I've heard anything about this,' I said truthfully.

"If the government of India weren't really serious about Africanisation, why should it offer the concessions it's offering to those who're leaving Uganda to facilitate Africanisation?' the High Commissioner said.

I didn't know anything about the Nehru government's interest in rapid Africanisation, nor the concessions which were on offer and said so. What Nehru wanted to do was to let the Africans run their country and not depend on expatriates even after *Uhuru*. That would reduce the quality and significance of independence. In other words, a quiet exit by people like me would be appreciated by the Nehru administration and to provide an incentive to leave, it was offering certain concessions. What were these concessions, I asked. I could ask for help with re-employment. I would be given preferential treatment if I asked for materials or concessions which would help my rehabilitation. There were heavy import duties on foreign goods. These would be waived for those who were returning to India to promote the rapid Africanisation of government posts.

'I happen to have a Mercedes Benz,' I told the High Commissioner. 'Will I have to pay import duty?'
'Is it more than a year old?' he asked.

'Yes, it is,' I said.

'No, you won't pay *any* duty on condition that you don't sell it for five years,' he said.

I told Sudarsana about my conversation with the Indian High Commissioner. She was unexpectedly excited at the prospect of returning to Calcutta.

'My father looked frail last time we were in Calcutta. I know he'd like nothing better than having us back. He's really, really fond of his grandchildren,' she said.

'What about the children?' I asked.

'They'd like nothing better than going back to Dadubhai and Didibhai,' she said.

'I don't think either the children or I have bonded with this country the way you have. But one-sided love can have tragic consequences.' The philosophising was a little heavy, but I saw her point.

'But what about jobs? We're getting a bit too old, don't you think?' I said.

'Don't be a defeatist,' she said, admonishingly.

I was encouraged by Sudarsana's certainty. Early next week I put in my papers. Sudarsana was on a different kind of contract and didn't have to give notice of quitting her job so early.

This was 1964. There was an exciting possibility of Sudarsana and me getting involved in the celebration of the quarter-centenary of William Shakespeare's birth. The celebration was to be in April, and Peter Carpenter, the Director of the National Theatre, had decided to produce *A Midsummer Night's Dream* with a cast drawn from the African, Asian and European theatre groups. We thought it was a great idea and an ideal way of showing our love for the bard. We were auditioned. Sudarsana was cast as Titania and I was Oberon. The fairies were young Asian girls – Yasmin, Aparajita and a few others from our Demonstration School. Theseus, Hippolyta, Hermia, Helena, Lysander, Demetrius and others were all from the British drama groups, and so were Quince, Snug, Bottom and Flute. Puck was a mercurial young African, who was unusually short for his age and very nimble on his feet – an ideal Puck. Sudarsana and I liked our parts, rehearsed with might and main over weekends and any spare time we had, including after dinner, and were truly word-perfect. If you're interested in acting and are reasonably good at it, there's no better way of enjoying your part, I discovered, than knowing your lines really well and being able to say them effortlessly. We played to a packed house on the large, well-equipped stage of the National Theatre for three nights. The applause each night was too spontaneous and long not to be genuine.

There was also a matinee for senior school children whose enthusiasm for the play more than matched that of the adult audience. It was a highly rewarding finale to our theatre experiences in Kampala. And what Sudarsana and I knew, and not the others, was that for us, it was an appropriate and 'dramatic' way to say goodbye to Uganda.

Aparna had finished her secondary school and was now ready for university education. Aparajita and Nondon were still in school. They weren't too happy having to leave their friends and Charles. Felix, who looked after us in various ways and Feisi who looked after the children, were not convinced that it was at all necessary for us to leave Uganda and said so whenever they thought the situation was appropriate. They didn't like our decision to leave at all. Charles had left us by then. Then there was Ebony, our black dog, who expressed no disappointment and continued to chase cars driving past our front door. Ebony was in many ways more Felix's dog than ours – because it was he who fed him regularly, gave him a bath, and took him out for a walk. It was a great relief when Felix proposed that he'd like to take Ebony to his village after we left.

It's something rather incomprehensible to me even today that we were all suddenly and almost totally focused on the return journey – Kampala, Mombasa, Bombay, Calcutta – after more than 13 years in a country where we were treated well, where we made good friends, and where we lived comfortably and with dignity. We continued to do our work, meet our friends, watch sunsets from Kololo Hill, but the sights and sounds and problems of Calcutta increasingly began to dominate our thoughts. My affection for Uganda, I believed, remained undiminished – but we slowly began to wind up. We said goodbye to friends – to some several times – but that neither advanced the day of departure, nor delayed it. And then it started happening – everything pointed in the direction of the exit door. Quite a few farewell tea and dinner parties happened. The students at college gave us a farewell party in which they proved that they had forever buried their segregationist past. The food and music were excellent. There were other parties – one for Sudarsana at her school. There was a tea party organised by the Board of Governors – Mahinder Maini, Norman Godinho and Peter Marsh among them – in which the friendly members of the Board wished me *bon voyage* and presented me a first print of David Shepherd's beautiful *Elephants*.

I handed over the car to the Public Works Department, the PWD, for shipping to Calcutta, and we arrived at Mombasa by train through the same exciting terrain that we had travelled through 13 years ago. Yet it wasn't quite the same, and we had certainly changed. There couldn't be any question, however, about the majesty of the mountains, the glory of the Savannah, the diversity of animals, some of whom seem to have stepped out of our Palaeolithic past. Another difference between the two journeys was that the first time we passed this way, the country was unknown but the jobs certain; during the journey back, and the destination was known but jobs uncertain. We knew where we were going but not what we were going to do. But there could be no question about the fact that we were all excited – though apprehensive.

Nairobi station didn't look any different from the one we'd passed through before. It was just as clean, busy and efficient. After all, it was the same people who were required to do the same work after independence as before in the lower categories of the hierarchy. It was the super-structure which had changed radically. The engine driver and the ticket collector were the same people; an African must have replaced the British Director or Commissioner of Railways.

From Mombasa railway station we took a taxi to Oceanic Hotel, a fairly new luxury hotel with more than 200 rooms and a large swimming pool. Sudarsana and I were impressed with the affluence of the place, but it didn't impress the children. They moved around confidently in that vast place and found their way around without any problem. They felt no anxiety and caused us no anxiety. They made an excellent team whose leader, undoubtedly, was Aparna. Their favourite place of pleasure and relaxation was the swimming pool, which was a great attraction for me also. There had been a few occasions before Oceanic Hotel when I'd stayed in big hotels frequented by faceless, affluent people, I'd felt lonely and uncomfortable, because of their impersonal atmosphere. This was different. The fact that Sudarsana and the children weren't overwhelmed by the largeness and affluence of the place but thoroughly enjoyed their brief stay in the hotel pleased me and gave me a great sense of relief. It turned out to be a week we'd always remember.

I do not remember in which ship we travelled from Mombasa to Bombay – SS Uganda, SS Kampala, SS Kenya or SS Karanja. I've never been able to recall their names. What was important for us all was that we were on our way back to Calcutta in a friendly ship that was sailing through the vast expanse of the Indian Ocean.

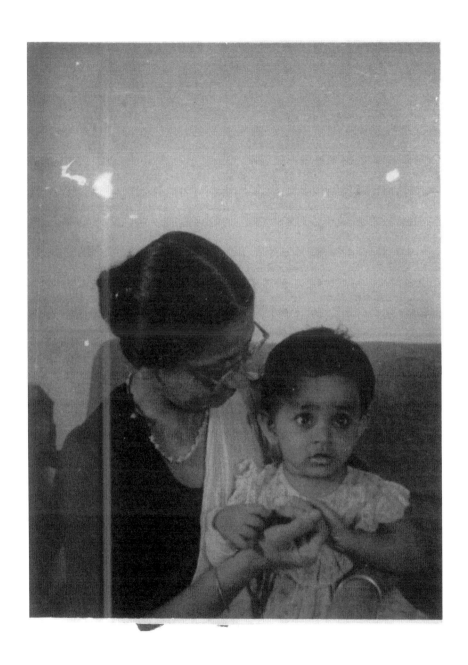

408

Chapter 14

Return to India, Julia

There was a consensus between the five of us that travelling by sea was more enjoyable than travelling by train or plane. Standing on the deck and looking out at the sea and the sky at any time of the day or night was a profoundly peaceful experience for me. During our several voyages we never had any experience of a turbulent sea. The sun, the moon, the stars and the dolphins travelled with us. The clouds tirelessly changed their shapes and colour. And all through the day and night, we felt the living, moving presence of the sea. Then there was a sense of community on board the ship which wasn't there on a plane or train, because the free association of so many people wasn't possible there.

Because so many of us met so many times – on the deck, at the breakfast table and at lunch and dinner – we didn't feel isolated from the rest of the world. We were, practically all of us, from newly-independent countries – India, Kenya, Uganda and Tanzania; so we tended to talk about our colonial past, our transitional present and our unknown future. The assassination of John F. Kennedy, the 35th president of the United States, was still fresh in our minds. More recently, Jawaharlal Nehru, the first Prime Minister of India, had died at the age of 74. Lyndon Johnson had signed the Civil Rights Act and it had become law, ending racial segregation, but the United States was getting more and more sucked into an unending war with North Vietnam. American casualties were rising but the number of dead and wounded Vietnamese was vastly greater. I think the Asians in East Africa, by and large a commercial community, was highly politicised, because neither the British nor the East Africans had a loving-and-giving kind of relationship with the Asians. They had to understand politics to keep out of it.

They were also interested in discussing East African politics with me because they were staying and I was going. We, the Asians, had everything to gain and nothing to lose by staying, they felt. The economy of a country was central to its power and prosperity, and without the Asians, the financial stability of East Africa would be irreparably damaged. The people who ran the country couldn't possibly fail to understand this simple truth. I pointed out that my situation was rather different. Whereas Africans hadn't had much experience in trade and commerce, the number of African teachers and education administrators was much greater among the Africans than among the Asians. I felt that the people who'd come from the Indian sub-continent and Britain should return to their countries to facilitate Africanisation.

I explained how and why I'd changed my mind because at one time I had decided to stay on in Uganda, a country and people I'd come to like. My fellow passengers were mainly Gujarati but a few were also from the Punjab. We talked about vegetarianism – the Gujaratis were nearly all vegetarians – arranged marriages, the dowry system, the film industry in Bombay and various other matters, but invariably returned to the subject of politics. In Africa, South African politics was a subject for recurrent discussion, despair and anger. The discussion of Mandela's sentence to life imprisonment on Robben Island and the *apartheid* policy in South Africa took up much of our time, but there was no discussion about the totally unjust, undemocratic and repressive white South African settler regime that had no right to be there in the first place.

In India, Lal Bahadur Shastri was the new Prime Minister. Would he measure up to the charismatic and internationally respected Jawaharlal Nehru? None of us was disappointed with Churchill's retirement from politics, because, among other reasons, he was fiercely opposed to the idea of India's independence. Privilege and power had depleted his humanity.

The long and fairly relaxed discussions among us fellow passengers created a sense of community. If one of our more articulate members – like Mr Desai or Mr Nayak – was absent from our discussions, we missed him and made it a point to find out whether all was well with him. Ours was the kind of spontaneous, all-embracing and informal discussion which was highly addictive. It had no beginning or end. It had no structure, no agenda. We looked at a whole spectrum of human ideas which had to do with politics, religion, sports, human occupations and pre-occupations. We weren't too worried about the depth and quality of these discussions. There is a Bengali word for it – *adda* – a palindrome, a word of two syllables, with a juncture in the middle, which, I think, should find its way into the world's most widely used languages. First the word, then the practice.

The voyage from Mombasa to Bombay was a re-run of the same play with mostly new actors, but the total impact on me was different. It was a different voyage from those I'd made before and a unique one because it was the last of several voyages. I was returning to India from Africa for good. And quite often, as the ship moved towards the shores of India, it was as if past voyages, train journeys, the flora and fauna, and the people and events of Africa were thrown on a magic screen in front of me. The images which floated across were partly induced by memory and partly by the blue sky, the tranquil sea and the steady monotone of the thudding engine. Then the excited shouts and laughter of children or a familiar voice brought me back to whatever was happening around me.

Time had passed quickly. We were fast approaching the shores of Bombay. My excitement and happiness were mixed with a growing sense of uncertainty about the future. We had a little money but not enough to see us through more than a year or two. Sudarsana and I would need jobs to feed ourselves and educate the children. We talked about it, Sudarsana and I, comforted ourselves by referring to the statistical fact that the demand for teachers tended not to diminish either in the developed or in the developing countries. The financial rewards of a teaching job are not comparable to those in some other professional fields of activity, but by and large, there was greater job security in teaching.

For whatever reason, I was in no great hurry to get off the ship this time.   I remember the quality of the early morning light at sea and the tranquillity. I could just sit in a deckchair and look out at the sea, the horizon, the sky, and never tire. And when I wanted company, it was there. The children were happy. They enjoyed each other's company, and they were as accessible to us as we were to them. For a time, life at sea seemed like the best of all possible lives. I wanted it to go on. It was euphoria. What did the lotus-eaters have that I didn't? But I knew it couldn't go on. The ship was steadily and inexorably moving towards the coast of Bombay.

But that too was exciting. That was also the moment we were waiting for – our arrival.

Nothing memorable happened in Bombay. At Howrah Station, my parents-in law and Sunanda, Sudarsana's sister, were all there. They were all happy to have us back, but it was, for reasons I didn't understand, a quiet homecoming, with very little demonstration of enthusiasm. There were the usual greetings and embraces, but things seemed somewhat muted. It was because I expected an explosion of pent-up feelings. Such expectations are unrealistic. We don't show all we feel. Just as well...

'I don't think any sensible group of administrators, especially in a newly independent country, would want to get rid of their teachers, especially good teachers,' my father-in-law commented. 'You were doing so well. Why did you leave? It looked like precipitate action.' Now I realised that my father-in-law looked pensive because he thought I'd made a hasty decision.

I felt good that Sudarsana's father was so certain about our teaching abilities. At the same time, I wanted him to understand that I hadn't acted in haste, and it was more a matter of principle than a careful consideration of personal profit and loss. Then I mentioned our meeting with Milton Obote, which had caused me frustration and unease.

'We have enough money to manage a modest standard of living for about a year,' I said. 'During that time a job or two are bound to come along.'

I understood my father-in-law's anxiety. When Tutu-da, Sudarsana's cousin and a very good friend of mine, had turned up in Calcutta with an MRCOG, there was very little work for him and he ended up accepting a job in a tea garden.

'I'm sure something will turn up, but it may not be ideal to begin with,' Father-in-law commented. Then we turned to other matters. My father-in-law was an affectionate man, but also a practical one.

Sudarsana's uncle and aunt owned the top flat in the building where we also had a two-bedroom flat. But our flat was rented to one of Sudarsana's cousins. The top flat was vacant because Sudarsana's uncle and aunt hadn't returned yet from East Africa, and it wasn't certain when they were coming back, though they too were coming back.

In the interim, we had the run of the brand new top-floor flat at 37 Golf Club Road. I was also able to collect my car from Kidderpore Docks, a fairly new Mercedes Benz, which would make us mobile. The life of the Bagchis was taking shape again. The next big challenge was going to be in the job market. But that could wait.

A few months went by. We were looking out for jobs but the search was casual and occasional. There were so many other matters of importance which couldn't wait that both Sudarsana and I were unable to concentrate on the quest for jobs. Then there was the unexpected news that Sudarsana's uncle and aunt had sold their mansion on Kololo Hill and were returning to Calcutta to settle for the rest of their retired lives. They were flying and were expected to be in Calcutta in a matter of weeks. I don't think they realised that this would disrupt our lives just when we were settling down. We had to look for another place to stay straight away

I didn't have to search for long. A few miles north of Golf Club Road, we found a three-bedroom bungalow at a reasonable rent and moved in. This was in Moore Avenue, in an area not far from Regent Estate, in which Sudarsana's uncle, her father's eldest brother, had a large property. Sudarsana had lived there and I had visited her half a dozen times, so it was familiar ground. But once again, just when we were beginning to feel at home, Aparna fell seriously ill. Our usual doctor in Tollygunge, Dr Dasgupta, started her treatment immediately, but a week passed without any encouraging signs of recovery. We had a family conference and decided we should turn to a specialist that Dr Dasgupta had recommended. He came and examined Aparna, went into a huddle with Dr Dasgupta, said a few reassuring words to Sudarsana and me, and left. The specialist had diagnosed Typhoid. The medicines he prescribed made a difference and Aparna showed signs of recovery quite quickly. There are doctors whose professional expertise and dedication make it possible for us to live a safe and healthy life. They deserve our respect and gratitude. This doctor was one of them. Aparna slowly but steadily recovered, although she continued to look very frail. I'd been fortunate and hadn't experienced many traumas; but this was certainly one of the few I've had. It was one of the few times in my life that I'd actually prayed.

We had managed to organise shelter. Now the big challenge was getting a job. With a Post Graduate Certificate in Education from the University of London, both Sudarsana and I were qualified to teach, but there had to be vacancies and there seemed to be none.

Sudarsana made an appointment with the Principal of Modern High School in Calcutta. She saw her and was impressed with her. Unfortunately, there was no teaching post available just then. However, the post of Librarian – the school had a big library – was going a begging. The Librarian of the school was about to retire and there was just about enough time for a leisurely handing over, if Sudarsana was interested. She accepted the offer without hesitation and with relief. My anxiety about reorganising our lives – with both of us in regular employment and the children in schools and colleges – diminished somewhat, but far from disappeared.

Not many days after that, I found an advertisement by the British Council for an English Language Officer. The teaching of English as a second language was what I'd specialised in at the Institute of Education in London. I had learned English as a second language myself; therefore, I was familiar with the trials and tribulations of learning a second language. I felt strongly that the British Council ought to invite me to an interview, particularly because I really needed a job. I applied. My two referees were Professor Bruce Pattison of the Institute of Education, London, and Peter Marsh, the British Council Representative in Kampala. My application and C.V. were all written by hand and sent away within hours of my discovering the advertisement. I was also most impressed with the quickness of response: I was requested to come for an interview the week after.

The British Council was appropriately housed in an old, two-storey, colonial building with large rooms with high ceilings, a wide staircase and polished wooden balustrades. The lawn outside was meticulously manicured, green, spotless and large, occupying twice the space of the building, with flower-beds bordering it all around. Inside the building, the atmosphere was quietly efficient and businesslike. I was the only candidate being interviewed that morning. The representative, Mr Mackenzie-Smith, was the only person in the room. He got up to shake hands, greeted me in a businesslike manner, and started a friendly conversation about East Africa and my ideas and experiences, educational and existential. He was especially interested in how I had got to know Peter Marsh, who was the British Council Representative in Uganda. I told him that Mr Marsh was on the Board of Governors at the college of which I was the Principal. I also told him about the British Council Drama Festivals and my interest in writing plays and acting. Then, not unexpectedly, he wanted to know why I left Uganda, a country I liked, and gave up a job which, obviously, meant so much to me. I explained, as best I could, the initial certainty and the later change of mind. It didn't at all feel like an interview. I had a job interview over a cup of tea – an unusual experience for me.

The defeatist idea that Mr Mackenzie-Smith probably didn't take me seriously – because of the informality of the interview – did cross my mind. Soon, what had flitted across my mind as a possibility became a certainty when more than a week passed and I hadn't heard from the British Council. Why didn't I ring? I was an escapist and the near-certainty of being told in a *pukka* English accent by a *pukka* Englishman that he regretted that I hadn't got the job was something I didn't want to face up to.

My friends, Pradip Sen whom I'd got to know when I was at St. Xavier's College and his wife, Alo, lived just round the corner from the British Council. Sudarsana and I decided to visit them one weekend. They had another friend visiting them. The five of us, apart from discussing the hazards of smoking, which was in the news at the time, and the recurrent topic of Vietnam, also discussed the successes and failures of friends and relations. At one point the discussion turned to the topic of the rehabilitation of the Bagchis. They congratulated Sudarsana and said reassuring words to me.

I thanked them about their concern. The conversation then returned to Vietnam, Martin Luther King, Cassius Clay and astronauts.

It was nearly time to go when one of Pradip's other visiting friends said that his father was retiring from the post of Principal of Delhi Public School. The school wanted a new Principal. He thought I should give it a go. We came home, put my papers together, wrote an application and generally spent the evening in the excitement of expectation.

'These public schools have very good accommodation for teachers and staff. The Principal's house is likely to be large, and beautifully furnished. We won't have to worry about renting houses for some years,' I said.

Sudarsana was neither impressed nor enthusiastic about the prospect of being the Principal's wife again.

'Haven't you seen these private schools? Haven't you said the system is unfair? Now how can you apply for a job in Delhi Public School?' Sudarsana said.

'If I get the job, I will make radical changes,' I said.

'The Board of Governors will change you before you change the noble traditions of an Indian public school,' Sudarsana said. She was being obstructive when I desperately needed a job!

The discussion soon became an argument. The next day, when we went over to see Sudarsana's parents and sister, they too joined the discussion.

'It's not fair to expect that Ganesh should indefinitely sit on his hands and you should live on your savings. I think he should take the job,' my father-in-law said.

Then he asked me if I'd applied. When I said I hadn't but was about to go and post my application, Sunanda, my sister-in-law laughed.

'Here we are, debating whether you should accept the job and you haven't even applied!' she said.

It was Sunday morning. We left the children with their grandparents, went shopping, put the letter in a post box and returned home.
In the evening Sudarsana brought up the subject again. 'What about my job? The Headmistress has told me that as soon as there is a vacancy, I'll be teaching. It'll be a permanent job,' she said.

I pointed that just then it was all speculation. I needed to work. Rent, the rising cost of living, the education of three children, running a Mercedes – all this required two incomes, not one. A teaching job is easier to find than the post of Principle. So if Delhi Public School wanted me to go to Delhi for an interview, I'd certainly go. I'd also be able to see my very good friends, Khuku and Mutu De. There, for the time being, the matter rested.

It was just over a week after that. I took Sudarsana to school and came home. There was a letter for me. The Board of Governors would like me to attend an interview in a few days' time. If I started off the next day by train, I'd make it. I wrote off immediately to inform the Secretary of the Board of Governors that I would attend the interview. In the evening I rang Mutu in Delhi and told him about the interview. He said he'd like me to stay with them. Sudarsana didn't rejoice.

I wasn't at all certain about moving to Delhi. I, too, like Sudarsana and the children, wanted to live in Calcutta, but if this was not to be, Delhi was a well-organised, metropolitan city and my good friends, Ira – whom we called Khuku – and Kritish De, whom we called Mutu – lived there. Khuku and Mutu were delighted to see me. Mutu was a friend from my college days. Khuku was a friend of Mutu's sister, no more than a nodding acquaintance of mine. I got to know her really well after she got married to Mutu. I'd come to Delhi primarily for the interview but without much hope because, although jobs had to be advertised, quite often decisions were made well in advance of interviews, reducing them to a formality. I'd thought things over and come to Delhi – at the expense of the Delhi Public School – hoping to get the post of Principal, but also fully prepared for a negative outcome.

The panel of interviewers looked impressive, with the well-known educationist, Anil Chanda, as its chairperson. One of the difficult questions to answer was what I thought of public- school education. I made the point that it didn't matter whether a school was public or private. Education should not only aim at academic excellence. It should also encourage students to be independent and generous. I would encourage them to use the library and reference books and do their own research. I would introduce a strong measure of consultation between my colleagues and me, between us and the students, and between the students themselves. I held forth for a few minutes but was careful not to lecture my audience. After that Mr Anil Chanda asked me some down-to-earth questions about organisation and administration and asked me to wait in the library.

I was sent for after about an hour.

'We've decided to offer you the post,' said Mr Anil Chanda. 'How soon would you be able to come and take over your responsibilities?'

'Thank you,' I said. 'I should be able to start in a fortnight.'

'That sounds just about right. Thank you for accepting our offer. Congratulations.' Mr Chanda, though friendly, was businesslike.

I told Mr Chanda that Sudarsana was a student of Vishwa Bharati and he remembered her. It was difficult to believe: I was no longer unemployed, anxious about the future of my family and myself. Not only that, in my new incarnation, I was Principal again!

I hurried back to Ira and Kritish's house in Defence Colony by taxi. It must have been the school holidays because Ira was at home. She was very pleased that I had been offered the job and had accepted it.

'But there's a problem,' Ira said. 'You've now got two jobs – one in Delhi and one in Calcutta. Therefore, you've got to make up your mind - quickly.'

I only half-understood the situation. I'd been interviewed for two jobs – one in Calcutta, one in Delhi. I'd accepted the Delhi job because it was offered. 'If the British Council, after dragging its feet, has now decided that I will do, they shouldn't be surprised if I turn down their offer,' I said to myself. I felt peeved. If they'd offered me the job earlier, I needn't have come to Delhi. I was fairly certain what had happened, but I said,

'Which is the other job?'

'The British Council job for which you were interviewed. Sudarsana rang after you had left. Mr Mackenzie-Smith has written to you, offering you the job for which you were interviewed' Ira replied.

I rang Sudarsana. She was waiting for my call. She was happy, she said, that I'd got the British Council job. She sounded excited and jubilant.

'We'll work again,' she said, 'just a few miles away from one another, just like in Kampala. And the children's schools and colleges will also be within easy reach from the British Council.'

'We're incredibly lucky,' she concluded. 'Within just a few months of our return to Calcutta, we've both landed the kind of job which, I think, we will enjoy doing. We'll celebrate when you're back. Congratulations! When are you coming back?'

What was I going to do? I'd accepted the offer to be Principal of Delhi Public School. Khuku and Mutu had arranged a mid-week party with a few friends because I'd got a job which would make it necessary for Sudarsana, the three children and me to move to Delhi. We were already planning all kinds of exciting activities, both social and cultural, after we'd settled down in Delhi, and I to my new job.

'Look Sudarsana, there's a problem. Immediately after the interview, I was offered the job at the school in Delhi and I accepted it,' I said.

Sudarsana was amazed. How could I do a thing like that? Didn't her job matter? Did I think she had returned to India to live in Delhi, away from her parents, her sister and her friends? There was no way she was going to give up her job and leave her parents. This was in the nature of an outburst. Yet she never once raised her voice. I'd come across only a few people who could do that – never raise their voices even when they were really angry and agitated. Confronted with such cool characters, I tended to sound frustrated, angry and agitated.

'You're not being fair. You didn't seriously object when I was offered an interview and came to Delhi. We both agreed that I couldn't indefinitely go on without a job, both for financial and psychological reasons. It's mainly because the British Council dragged its feet that we're in a muddle. I'll cancel the party here and leave for Calcutta tomorrow,' I said.

I explained what the confusion was to Khuku and Mutu, who understood the problem at once and agreed that the sooner it was resolved the better. Therefore, my decision to leave the next day was the right decision. Two jobs were on offer. Both employers were expecting that I'd work for them. I should accept the job I preferred and inform the other prospective employer about my decision. The sooner I did this the better. That was Mutu's opinion.

'But I've accepted this job unconditionally and undertaken to report for duty in a fortnight,' I said to Mutu, who had been my friend, philosopher and guide from our college days.

'You can't put at risk the happiness of Sudarsana and the children by being an uncompromising man of principle. First, I should spend some time with Sudarsana, discuss the situation face to face, and then make my decision objectively. And once the decision has been made, there should be no regrets, no recriminations.'

Mutu took my question seriously and answered it seriously. That was his way. He'd helped me in various ways but most of all by being a good friend.

I took the train to Howrah the next day. When we met my father-in-law to discuss the problem of two jobs, he was strictly non-partisan. He would give us his full support whatever decision we took. He'd like to be near his daughter and his grandchildren, but much more important than that was our future. I'd by then more or less decided that I couldn't be inflexible. In terms of the gross family income and accommodation, we'd certainly be better off in Delhi. But didn't I always say that Calcutta was my city? There was yet another matter that I'd forgotten and Sudarsana hadn't.

'Haven't you always called them bastions of privilege? How can you so easily compromise?' Sudarsana asked in her usual clear and quiet voice. I found it difficult to answer. She'd asked that question before and I'd prevaricated.

I made my appointment with the Representative, British Council, Calcutta.

I arrived a little earlier than the appointed time and waited. A little later Mr Mackenzie-Smith came out from his office. We shook hands, exchanged greetings and entered his office. He got straight to the point.

'I hope you've decided to accept our offer?' he said.

Without the slightest hesitation, I said, 'Yes, I have.'

'Good,' he said, 'I'm sorry we've taken much longer to confirm your appointment than we meant to. We were waiting to hear from your referees.'

I confessed that at one point I did feel fairly certain that I hadn't been selected. I didn't tell him anything about the Delhi Public School's offer of a job and my acceptance. That could wait.

'Professor Bruce Pattison replied fairly quickly, but my colleague, Peter Marsh, was slow to respond because he'd gone away on business. But when he responded, he made you sound quite irresistible,' he said, laughing.

'Peter was a member of the Board of Governors of Shimoni Teacher Training College. He was also a friend. Maybe friends shouldn't be referees,' I said.

For some reason that I never quite understood, Mr Mackenzie-Smith addressed me as Ganesh Chandra Bagchi, my full name, which appeared on official documents. Others called me either Ganesh, Mr Bagchi, or Ganesh Bagchi. I haven't to this day found an explanation.

Having first welcomed me, Mr Mackenzie-Smith then proceeded to give me a description of my job. For a few weeks, I'd be working in the British Council Office in Shakespeare Sarani. Mr Jacob would give me some administrative tasks to keep me busy, but my real assignment would be teaching later on at the Institute of English in South Calcutta. I was appointed Assistant Professor at the Institute. The Director of the Institute was Dr Nirupam Chatterji.

I liked Mr Mackenzie-Smith. I liked the general atmosphere. I liked Mr Jacob, the Administrative Officer. I returned home, drafted a carefully-worded letter to the Chairman, Board of Governors, Delhi Public School, explaining why I'd decided to opt out, offering my sincere apologies. Both my father-in-law and my mother-in-law were pleased that I'd decided to take the British Council job. When Sudarsana returned from work, she was both relieved and pleased and said so more than once. The tension which everyone had felt for days suddenly disappeared. It was pleasant to be able to live again without uncertainty and tension which had frayed our nerves.

The letter from Delhi was critical of my irresponsible conduct, but there was nothing really unpleasant in it – no threat of legal action, no page-long enumeration of the problems my irresponsible behaviour had caused. The very dignified response of the Chairperson made me feel most uncomfortable. Mixed with the discomfort was a certain amount of disappointment as well. Being Principal would mean much wider responsibilities than I'd have at the British Council. I'd also be able to give the students – with the help and co-operation of my colleagues – a sense of direction and purpose. To be involved in the hopes, aspirations and development of young people was something I always found important. Their success in whatever they wanted to do and their development into people of integrity and humanity were rewards devoutly to be wished.

But being a leader has its problems. Anxiety, tension, sleepless nights and fear of failure are the price of leadership. Here I'd be one of three Assistant Professors at the Calcutta Institute of English, accountable to its Director. The Institute was a collaboration between the Department of Education of the Government of West Bengal, and the British Council. To begin with, the Director of the Institute was a British Council Education Officer. Later on, Nirupam Chatterji took over. I'd work for the Institute of English, where the Director was appointed by the Government of West Bengal, but I'd be paid by the British Council.

I would have a flat on the second floor of the Institute, a spacious flat of two bedrooms and a very large living room, which could be divided into a bedroom and living room.

When the college term started at the Institute, I moved from my bungalow in Regent Estate to the flat at the Institute and started my life as Assistant Professor, Calcutta Institute of English, where my responsibility would be to teach teachers of English how to teach English as a second language. It was a small, academic institution of about fifty students, all teachers or lecturers, who wanted to teach English better in their schools and colleges and we, a band of four or five, were expected to help them. This was in the mid sixties of the 20th century, when we were still very much under the influence of language teachers who were trying to present language, which is infinite, as a system of finite structures. We called it the 'structural approach'. It over-simplified language. But to those who objected that we conveniently simplified what was complex to the point of distortion, we offered the justification that when the objective was teaching vocabulary of a few thousand words, and sentences which weren't too complex, the structural approach worked. I found that it was not an efficient way of teaching English for a different reason. The approach was quantitative and simplistic. Some of us dared to suggest that to ensure a higher level of interest, we should present to the learners units of communication in real situations. The suggestion wasn't too popular. What was of interest to me was that I was dealing with mature students for the first time, most of them experienced teachers. There were a few lecturers as well.

Teaching was rewarding to me because I was in the company of mature and intelligent students and some of them became good friends and remained good friends as long as I was in Calcutta. There was one tragic accident not long after I left the Institute. Keya, one of my brightest and most talented students, a college lecturer, was also a brilliant actor. She normally acted on the stage, but for the first time, she was acting in the leading role in a film. It was an emotionally-charged scene and took place while she was travelling by boat on a river. She threw herself into the water. She was wearing a sari which restricted her movement and either she didn't swim at all or wasn't an expert swimmer. In any case, it was customary, I understand, to set up elaborate and expert arrangements to prevent any accident. Nets were strategically placed and expert swimmers were at hand. Nothing worked. Keya drowned.

My Institute of English assignment was a limited one, lasting a couple of years. I was really an employee of the British Council and I returned to Shakespeare Sarani, to work as an Assistant Representative or English Language Officer. I had three colleagues whose work was directly connected with education: John Blackwell, Nigel Hudson and Michael Vodden. John Blackwell was helping the West Bengal Board of Secondary Education to reorganise some aspects of the curriculum. Another colleague, who I had got to know in Kampala, Roland Hindmarsh, worked for some time at the Institute of English while I was there. All of them had experience in setting up various educational programmes in the countries where they had worked before. Now they were using their expertise to help education in India.

I had worked with all of them on various occasions and enjoyed doing so. But it was Michael Vodden with whom I had to work most closely. We were colleagues and friends. We liked each other and learned from each other. We represented the British Council on various occasions when the teaching of English came up for discussion, especially at the college level. Each year the UGC – the University Grants Commission – organised Summer Institutes, where various methods and approaches to teaching English – both the written and the spoken forms of it – were tried and tested by those who were lecturers in various parts of India. I was a resource person at one of these summer institutes at Calcutta University and one at the Institute of English. The Summer Institutes were largely based on the theories of teaching English, with some seminars on the practical aspects.

A great deal of interest was generated by groups of very competent teachers. Their erudition was unquestionable, but both Michael and I found that the emphasis was solidly on theory – with some peripheral concessions to the practical aspects of teaching and learning. For example, quite a few of the lecturers were able to hold forth on phonetics, phonology, morphology, syntax and semantics, but when it came to teaching their students how to express themselves in speech and writing, the extent of their success wasn't impressive. So when Michael and I were organising the Summer Institute in Poona, we devised a new model: the Three Phase Summer Institute. This put much greater emphasis on participation.

In the first phase we would try to isolate the problems in groups. There were group leaders – Michael Vodden, John Strover, Shiv Verma, Dr Mikherji and myself. The Director of the Summer Institute was the Professor and Head of English, Poona University – John Strover. He was from the University of Leeds, a friend of Michael's. Each day the five groups would discuss a topic and report the essential points of their discussion to a general meeting at the end of the day. All these topics would relate to practical aspects of teaching. Because the groups were small, we were able to ensure the participation of practically all the lecturers, although some were more creative and articulate than others.

After the debates and discussions of the first phase, we agreed on some basic principles. The lecture mode has a place in the education system, we decided, but there is a time and place for it. It should be used on some occasions and for specific purposes. For example, if the audience is so large that individual participation is just not practical, the lecture mode offers a practical solution. But in our colleges the classes are not usually so large that lectures are the only solution. Some colleges, our participants pointed out, did have very large classes. When classes are large, a talk or a lecture might be unavoidable. But even then it could be divided into sections and the students encouraged to ask questions and discuss various points. In short, we ought to do everything to ensure the participation of our students in the learning process. Apart from questions and answers, we discussed various other strategies which could be used to ensure such participation.

In the second phase, the participants of the Poona Summer Institute went out to different colleges to put into practice the ideas which had been generally accepted. John Strover and I went to two rather small towns where the accommodation and other facilities were basic and where the students sat in ranks on hard benches, and listened to their lecturers in silent awe, admiration – and boredom. When our participant from the Summer Institute tried to encourage the students to ask questions, initially there was an atmosphere of confusion and non-comprehension. It was a strange thing for the lecturer to interrupt their lecture and ask the students what they thought of a character in a play or novel, or a line or lines in a poem. Our lecturers from the Institute had to be fairly persistent and resourceful to get responses from the class. But when they did get a few sensitive and intelligent responses, they felt rewarded. They were beginning to believe that all stimuli and no responses make teaching a dull business. Our hare-brained ideas were beginning to be taken seriously. Some of the lecturers confessed that whereas the traditional lecture mode was tidier, the participation of students in the learning process made the experience of teaching more rewarding. The interactive situation was important because little or no time was provided in our colleges for seminars and tutorials. And even in colleges which provided tutorials, there was always the need for inter-active teaching.

The third and final phase, which was shorter than phases one and two, was for the lecturers and the Summer Institute tutors to report back and compare notes about their various experiences. The different groups had separate sessions and met up to compare notes. It was heartening to note that there was consensus that the Poona Summer Institute had experimented – and discovered some valuable facts. It would probably be truer to say that we'd tried out an educational idea which had always been there and which made good sense. The impact on the students was positive and the enthusiasm among the participating lecturers was heartening. I understand that in the community of those who were involved in the summer institutes organised by the University Grants Commission, the three-phase model with special emphasis on student participation, was often referred to as the Bagchi-Vodden model. John Strover was impressed with the way we approached and dealt with the challenges of second language learning at the Poona Summer Institute.

When John returned to Leeds, he convinced his professor and head of department, Professor Mitchell, that I should be invited to teach at Leeds University for a term. Professor Mitchell consented and I spent three months at Leeds in 1968-1969. Michael Vodden saw to it that the British Council released me, and I was in Leeds, staying at John Strover's house with him, his wife and his adopted son, who was two or three years old. I'm not sure what kind of impression I made as a lecturer but my suggestions on teaching approaches and methods were widely and seriously discussed.

I benefited greatly from the visit because, apart from John Strover, I got to know Martin Banham, who was director of the drama department, and A. P. Cowie, who went on to be one of the two authors of the *Oxford Dictionary of Current Idiomatic English,* published in two volumes. I gave Martin my play, *A Recurrent Theme* to read, and suggested that I produce the play with the help of two students from his department, a man and a woman. I was the third actor, apart from being the director. It was well-received by the audience and Martin said he liked it. I also gave a talk on the teaching of English through drama, which was well-attended, and, I think, well received.

It was a most rewarding three months of my career. I did some teaching, gave a talk, produced and acted in a play that I'd written. I also met a few interesting and highly intelligent people who became good friends. There were opportunities to improve various teaching skills because the people I fairly regularly met were genuinely interested in all aspects of teaching in general and the teaching of language in particular.   Tony Cowie and John Strover were good friends and discussing pedagogical problems with either of them was always rewarding.   I didn't spend much time with Martin Banham, head of drama, but he made it possible for me to attend the drama festival at Reading University.   I watched as many plays as I could fit into the few days of the festival.   The play which particularly impressed me was Samuel Beckett's *Krapp's Last Tape*, because it was a young actor who was doing the part of a much older man.   He was entirely credible as Krapp.   A one-man play without any action in which the actor nostalgically looks back and recounts events of the past offers very little suspense. And an old man's interaction with an old tape recorder isn't the stuff that drama is usually made of. Yet the play worked. We made the journey from youth to old age with Krapp and shared his joy and sorrow. It was clear to me that the audience was totally sympathetic. The young man who did Krapp received the best actor award. There were other plays – some run-of-the-mill, some good and some impressive: a standard distribution of quality. I was fortunate to be there. Professionals usually have expertise and polish; amateurs may lack these but they quite often make up for that by their freshness of approach.   A surprisingly large proportion of amateur plays that I had watched measured up to professional productions.

Refreshed and renewed by my theatre experience in Reading, I was returning to Leeds by train. A middle-aged English gentleman in the next seat wished me good morning. I reciprocated. Usually, that was as far as my conversations with fellow passengers went, especially if they were English. But this morning, uncharacteristically, the middle-aged man in a suit and tie asked,

'What do you do?'

'I teach at the university,' I said.

'What do you teach?' he asked.

'I teach linguistics, and discuss its relevance to the teaching of English,' I answered.

'Hmm,' he commented, 'carrying coals to Newcastle!' and went back to his newspaper.

That was the end of our conversation. After that the gentleman read his newspaper with an intensity of interest which surprised me.   We didn't talk at all from that moment on until the train reached Leeds, when he grunted goodbye and left. I haven't to this day been able to puzzle out how exactly I had offended him. There was an all-pervasive resentment against non-white immigrants at the time. Could it have been that? It didn't really worry me. I wasn't planning to stay anyway. It was nearly time to return to Calcutta. After the teaching and the other educational activities in Leeds, the British Council provided me with some time at the end of my stay in England for acquainting myself with what was going on in London at the time, especially in the world of theatre. So I said goodbye to John and his wife, told them that the last few months had been some of the most useful and productive months of my life, in spite of a rampant Enoch Powell, crying doom and gloom which some people took seriously. I took part in a protest march against racism in which some of the Leeds University students shouted strongly-worded slogans against racism. One that I remember is 'disembowel Enoch Powell'. It was meant to be hyperbolic and funny; figurative language which wasn't meant to be taken literally. But I disapproved. There was at least one voice which remained silent when the marchers shouted that particular slogan – mine.

I stayed with my friends in Richmond, with Michael and Carol Harlow. We – Sudarsana, the children and I – had spent a wonderful holiday at the foot of the Mountains of the Moon, the Ruwenzori Mountains, long ago in East Africa. We discussed Powell's racist speech, in which he talked dramatically about the 'River Tiber foaming with much blood' to warn the British public of impending racist violence, came up for discussion. We approved of Edward Heath's earlier sacking of Powell from his post of Shadow Defence Minister. We also talked about the great happening in London, the musical *Hair,* which had exploded onto the London stage. It was a love-rock musical. The nudity of a large cast of young men and women in it was made possible by the relaxation of censorship laws.

Because of my interest in the theatre and my job in the British Council, I was given a ticket to *Hair*. But the day I was going to see it, a volunteer- teacher, whom I had got to know in Calcutta, turned up in the afternoon. If I went to the theatre, he couldn't spend any time with me, after having taken the trouble to come and see me. What was more, we couldn't meet another day because he was going to be away. Sometimes people who couldn't make it to the theatre sold their tickets. Richard came with me to try his luck.

We had no luck. So I sold my ticket to a grateful young man who couldn't believe his luck. Richard and I ate out and spent the evening together.

I was now preparing to get back to Calcutta. This was the time when thousands of Asians with British passports were getting ready to get out of Kenya and set out for the UK. The US was getting ready for its first moon landing. Nixon was sworn President of the USA. Harold Wilson was the Labour leader and the Prime Minister of the UK. The Vietnam War was still raging and taking toll of a huge number of human lives, Vietnamese and American.

Although it was exciting to live in Leeds and London, the prospect of returning to Calcutta was always exciting – Calcutta with its crowded streets; sultry nights with frantic fans whirring overhead; cooling rain and memories. Carol drove me to Heathrow. After getting rid of the luggage, I sat down and had a conversation with her about her time in Uganda, about politics, relationships and other matters, both serious and trivial. Reminiscing as well as speculating is an absorbing occupation. We didn't notice the passage of time nor register announcements about the departure of my plane.

Then Carol interrupted the conversation, pricked up her ears and said, 'Ganesh, you must hurry. The plane is about to take off.'
I grabbed my bag and ran, without even attempting to say a proper goodbye to Carol. When I arrived at the entrance, I realised that another few minutes and the plane would have left without me. I wasn't popular. The looks I received from the stewardesses weren't full of loving kindness as I was silently ushered to my seat, and the unspoken message on the faces of my fellow passengers was definitely *not* one of approval.

'Sorry,' I said to the air-hostess, who was checking the luggage-rack to stow away my hand luggage.

'Don't worry,' she said. 'It does happen from time to time.' She smiled.

The plane took off soon after the various rituals connected with safety. I had a window seat. As I looked down, the streets narrowed to wide ribbons and the cars, coaches, buses and buildings looked like toys in Meccano sets, and then disappeared. Drinks on a trolley arrived just in time and I asked for a long, cold drink, which I drank quite quickly and relaxed.

The flight was uneventful, the way I liked flights to be. Between spells of fitful sleeping, I fitted in breakfast, lunch and dinner, without really registering their quality. What mattered to me when I flew was the beginning and the end; I just about tolerated what happened in between. Being stationary, tied to one's seat for so long, without much scope for movement isn't a particularly enjoyable situation. And usually, neither the food nor the conversation is of a memorable quality. But there is really no alternative way of travelling between continents. It's quick and convenient. It's different when you are travelling with a friend or a member of the family or the person sitting next to you turns out to be interested in talking to you about subjects which are meaningful. On one occasion, the man sitting next to me talked about cheeses, and on another, about flying kites. I didn't notice the passage of time because his conversation was interesting.

It was good to be back home, although Leeds, Reading and London were memorable experiences. At the office I was welcomed back with friendly warmth. Soon it was as if I hadn't been away at all and my life a seamless continuum.

Not long after returning from Leeds, we moved to a flat in Dover Road. This was a flat that my friend Kalyan had reserved for himself with a co-operative society and then had it transferred to me. It was exciting to move into our own flat. We didn't have to spend large sums of money on furniture because we had already acquired most of what we needed. Both our previous flats were unfurnished and we had to buy the furniture. Not long after we had moved to our new flat, Aparajita got married to Ian Zachariah. Her relationship with Jimmy Chowdhury hadn't worked. I wasn't impressed with Jimmy, so I didn't regret the break-up. I didn't know Ian; therefore I could only hope that he was a man of intelligence and integrity. Ian was Jewish. They had some kind of Jewish ceremony which we didn't attend because we weren't invited. But the Zachariahs and the Bagchis had a joint wedding ceremony at the Dalhousie Institute. Ian's parents were pleasant people, whom I never got to know very well. Our relationship with them was cordial, but never very close.

Our relationship with Dubby's parents was worse– it was fraught to begin with and then it was non-existent. Dubby was Rajinder Singh Bhagat's nickname. Aparna and he married when they were both very young. Dubby's father was a Lieutenant-General in the Indian army. We were not considered to be of equal status and were not invited to the reception given after their wedding – without any frills – at a registrar's office.

Apart from teaching at Modern High School, Sudarsana was now involved in acting in Bengali plays. Aparna Sen was the leading light of the group and there were other good actors – Sohag Sen and Ashit Bose – all of them innovative members of the group, more than just competent.

I was fairly busy at the British Council, planning cultural and educational events, attending to their organisation, and making sure they were adequately advertised.

The tickets for free entrance had to be collected from the library – to ensure that the number of people interested could be accommodated in our small British Council Hall. On all such occasions, I was there, whether or not I was actually participating. My two daughters were married; Nondon attended college during the day and played his drums in the evening; Sudarsana took both her teaching during the day and her acting and rehearsals in the evening seriously. And I was focused on organising other people's cultural activities at the British Council. We were all busy with our different interests, briefly communicating when we met at meals. Our family life was fragmented.

Our social life in Kampala had always been active and sometimes frantic. In Calcutta social engagements were occasional. Although Vera and Michael Vodden did invite us over and we invited them, the meeting- up of friends for dinner was infrequent, more in the nature of a pleasant surprise. When Julia and John Blackwell entered our lives, that changed somewhat, though not dramatically. But in the short time we had known them they'd already invited us more often than any other British Council couple in the five years that I had worked for them. There was an invisible red line between the expatriate British and the local Indian employees of the British Council. But nobody was particularly troubled by this. On the surface of our daily relationship, there was little or no tension, and nobody was paranoid about what complexities existed in the deep structure of people's minds. Mr Mackenzie-Smith had now left and Mr Tim Scot was our representative. Tim was more accessible. He frequently engaged in the discussion of administrative topics which were taboo in the days of Mr Mackenzie-Smith. We received only a fraction of what our British colleagues were paid. They were provided with houses, we weren't. They had entertainment allowances and free medical treatment, including hospitalisation, oversees leave and many other concessions and privileges. They could also buy imported drinks and groceries at subsidised prices. Why was such blatant discrimination necessary? Michael Vodden didn't like it. Other British colleagues were embarrassed by it. But the discrimination carried on. The establishment's justification was demand and supply.

Tim Scott was a quiet, civilized and sympathetic character. I trusted him. But he didn't make the rules. They were made in London and part of his briefing from the head office was that he'd make us accept those rules, mainly by not letting them come to the surface. And we did accept because the terms weren't bad by Indian standards.

Two issues had come up during our lunch breaks and other occasions: a pension scheme and a canteen. Mr Jacob, an assistant, suggested that we shouldn't just discuss these issues but form a union. We did, and I was elected the first President. Although neither Mr Jacob nor I was supposed to join Unions, there were no rules against it. We'd signed no undertaking that we'd accept the status quo. I wrote to the London Office and requested Tim to forward it with his comments. Within weeks we were given permission to go ahead with the canteen and a certain amount of money was provided.

It wasn't entirely satisfactory, but the limited facilities of our newly-acquired canteen were widely appreciated. On the question of pension, we had an unequivocal thumbs-down. I didn't give up and pressed on with tireless communication, protesting against the lack of fairness of the present arrangement – a one-off payment of a month's salary for a year's service. I was at the time on a salary of 2,300 rupees per month. This meant that if I retired after ten years, all I'd be entitled to was 23,000 rupees. How long would that last? My pursuit of a reasonable retirement scheme was so relentless and persistent that the representative in Delhi was heard to declare, I'm told, that he couldn't take it any more. This could have meant that I'd have to go. But the sacking of a senior Indian official for demanding what was both common practice in both state and private sector organisations – either a pension or a provident fund – would certainly have been considered a most unreasonable act for a cultural public-relations organisation like the British Council. Whatever the reason, no action was taken against me and I continued to be the President of the Union and I didn't stop pointing out that the British Council was losing its credibility by denying its Indian employees fair treatment. Tim Scott continued to be friendly. He appreciated my contribution to the British Council's reputation as a cultural organisation in Calcutta. I believe he made positive recommendations. He would have liked to see considerable improvement in the terms and conditions of our service. But during the time I was President, I won no major concessions. The canteen remained the only little gift from the Administration, a token gesture which cost the establishment very, very little.

Michael went back to England. After that, the nature and quality of my working life changed. I wouldn't say it was worse. Many interesting cultural and literary events had taken place since Michael had left. Tim, my other colleagues and the regular and loyal members of the public were all appreciative of our activities. But the really serious care and concern that Michael had about the quality and output of our teaching was very rarely in evidence. Tim was a good administrator –

effortlessly efficient – but he always managed to be an involved participant one moment and a detached observer the next. As time went on, my feeling of being an outsider increased. I cared more and more that the British part of the British Council was infinitely more privileged than its Indian counterpart. 'Isn't it humiliating to accept such overt discrimination?' I began to ask myself. At the same time, I told myself that I shouldn't allow this growing sense of alienation to affect the quality of my work.

We organised a one-act play competition about this time on behalf of the English Language Society. I did Krapp in *Krapp's Last Tape*. There was another play, *Happy Days*, also by Samuel Beckett, in which both Sudarsana and I acted. The group of young actors which produced various plays and play readings for the British Council also participated in a festival with an original play. It was a competitive drama festival. The judges – Satyajit Ray was one of them – awarded the prize for the best play to the one written and directed by Jayant Kripalani, who richly deserved the award though there were other interesting plays as well.

I began to feel frustrated with my work at the British Council, although the output of various cultural activities was impressive. There were two reasons that I could think of. Michael had warmth, humanity and enthusiasm about teaching and a great appreciation of the contribution I made to the teaching and teacher training sessions in which we both participated. I didn't feel the same way about my present colleagues who had most to do with education: John Blackwell and Nigel Hudson. John and I did participate in a teaching session at Loreto School, but for the rest of the time I was on my own. I did get some satisfaction in organising various cultural activities, quite a few of which won public acclaim, but I found it difficult to derive the same kind of satisfaction from organising events as from participating in them. I was struggling to keep down a growing sense of dissatisfaction.

At home the children had their own lives. Aparna and Aparajita were both married. Aparajita was expecting her first baby. Nondon was busy with music, girlfriend and college, in that order. Sudarsana worked hard all week and rehearsed in the evening with the drama group of which she was a leading light. She acted with confidence. Her contribution was highly valued by other members of the group, with the result that she got more and more involved in its activities. Three of its other luminaries were Asit Bose, Aparna Sen and Shohag Sen. The group had made a name for itself, so its productions were popular, and the more they were in demand, the busier Sudarsana became during evenings and weekends. There were times when I felt, probably without any real justification, that it was time to pack it all up and hang my hat on a pension. But there were problems. The British Council had generous retirement schemes for their British employees but practically no retirement benefits for their Indian counterparts. And even if they'd had any, I had worked too short a time to benefit substantially. I would have to wait before I took the curtain.

There was a positive alternative, a creative option. After Michael had left, classroom teaching wasn't as much a British Council priority as it had been during his time. So I decided to develop the cultural activities, many of which had to happen in the evening. I'd got to know Utpal Dutt during a production of *Waiting for Lefty* by Clifford Odets. I persuaded him to give a talk. The title of his talk was *Shakespeare's Kings*. It was original, brilliant and very popular. Professor Ghosh from Vishwa Bharati University gave a talk on T. S. Eliot's poetry, which was both erudite and interesting. Being a teacher of many years of experience, he was able to present his insights into Eliot's poetry in language which was perfectly comprehensible to the audience. The versatility of Shamik Banerji also proved an asset to me because he too was a teacher and able to assess how far and how deep he could go with the audience.

Apart from these talks, there were other popular activities. We did a family production of Jean Anouilh's *Antigone* with Aparajita in the lead role, Aparna as Ismene, Sudarsana as the nurse and me as Creon. Aparajita also took the part of the student in Eugene Ionesco's *Lesson,* which was very well received by the audience. Victor Bannerji, Vijay Krisha and Aparna acted in our production of *The Deviant,* a play I had written many years ago. We also produced *The Bald-Headed Prima Donna*, in which Aparna acted. There were many other events which made the British Council during my time with them a powerhouse of cultural events. There were many creative and erudite people around. I managed to bring them together.

The few plays we had produced in the small hall of the British Council had attracted a group of young actors and a young teacher by the name of Zarin Chowdhury. Zarin was a great asset for all of us interested in the theatre. The younger people, many of them still university students, learned a great deal about acting and production through informal discussions with her and the pantomime workshops she ran on behalf of the British Council. Zarin related well with both men and women of a younger age group, thus making the British Council an attractive rendezvous for them, leading to some enjoyable theatre sessions.

The result of all these frantic activities was that Sudarsana and I met in between the various exciting happenings in which we were engaged. We ate together and ended up in the same bed at the end of the evening to say hello and good night, but our lifestyle wasn't helping our relationship at all. Quite often in a lifetime, we get our priorities wrong. Sometimes we pay a heavy price for it, sometimes we escape the consequences.

It was only a few months before all this was happening that we had moved from Kabir Road to our new flat in a large multi-storey building in Dover Road. This move was an instance of precipitate action which was necessary because of a proposal my very good friend, Kalyan Sen had placed before me one Sunday morning. He had decided to buy a three-bedroom flat in Dover Road in a seven storey building through a co-operative society of which he had become a member by paying an advance of several thousand rupees. But quite unexpectedly he had been transferred to Bombay as the Income Tax Commissioner there. If I paid him the money he had advanced on the flat, he said, he could transfer the right of ownership to me. Was I interested? I said I was and thanked him profusely, and then proceeded to raise the money.

While I was still in East Africa, I had bought a piece of land in Shantiniketan. My brother-in-law – Sunanda's husband Tublu – had supervised the building of a two-bedroom bungalow built on the land which measured one-third of an acre. We had also had a well dug there, as there was no central water supply system in the village. The idea had been to take up a post at the Visvabharati University in Shantiniketan, which had been offered to me on our last home leave from our jobs in East Africa in 1962. This job had unfortunately not materialized. The offer had casually been revoked – as spontaneously as it had once been made. So we had rented out the house and now I sold this property to raise money. I also sold my Mercedes. After a year or so, we moved into our new flat – No 405 Dover Court – Sudarsana, Nondon and I. Aparna and Dubby now lived in a rented flat near Shakespeare Sarani. Aparajita and her husband, Ian, did occupy one of the three bedrooms in the rented flat in Kabir Road for a time but moved into their own flat later. Now I had a stable job, a flat of our own, two married daughters, and a son in St Xavier's College. I was really beginning to feel secure – perhaps too secure.

Life, on the face of it, was getting fairly organised. I lived in a world where I didn't have to look over my shoulder; the trains ran on time, people kept their promises and the left wing CPM state government continued to be in power in the federal state of West Bengal. But there was a certain restlessness within, a feeling of stagnation. Sudarsana, I suspected, had very little idea of the crisis creeping up on me. Where do I go from here? I asked myself. Was I dramatising my situation?

It was at about this time that I got to know Julia Blackwell. I'd seen her before when she'd flitted in and out of the British Council office either to see John Blackwell, her husband, or on account of some maintenance problem. She was about five foot six, slim, with auburn hair – plenty of it – and blue eyes. She was partial to a bouffant hairstyle and mini-skirts. My colleague, Nigel Hudson, thought her sartorial outfit, hairstyle and make-up were all unworthy of a British Council wife. He wanted Indians to have a different image of British women.

I was in England in the late sixties. Women in their twenties and thirties were wearing their skirts short and trying out various hairstyles. Fashions weren't the innovation of any individual. They were usually dictated by fashion houses. But once an idea had caught on the followers of fashion had a sense of belonging and they wore short skirts and long hair, or long skirts and short hair, just like the others did. I wasn't ready to sit in judgement over followers of fashion.

'What do you think of this new look?' asked Nigel one morning when Julia had come to the British Council office to sort out some problem, probably to do with her house and garden, air-conditioning or water supply.

'I quite like it,' I said.

'I think it's bizarre,' said Nigel.

There wasn't a lot of friendly conversation between Nigel and me that morning. He was convinced that young, trendy British Council wives gave the organisation a bad name. The British Council, Nigel thought, should encourage the spread of the best traditions of British culture and the mini-skirt and the bouffant hairstyle weren't ideal British exports.

Quite early on, I had noticed the pointed formality of Nigel's relationship with Julia Blackwell. I thought it was unfortunate. But at the same time, it didn't matter because I didn't really know her. Her husband, John Blackwell, was young, energetic, friendly and unorthodox. At the time John was the only British Council colleague who had a personal relationship with me. He was down-to-earth, matter-of-fact and businesslike. John was also somebody, since the departure of Michael Vodden, with whom I'd spent time in the evening because he'd invited us to dinner. And we'd reciprocated.

Julia had decided that she wanted to learn Bengali. And since I was a language teacher and a Bengali and, by now, a friend, I was requested to teach her my language. I started spending some time with her trying to communicate with her in Bengali, and incidentally comparing the sounds of Bengali with those of English. It looked for a time as if we were making reasonable progress when John was invited to join a seminar at St Paul's school in Darjeeling and our Bengali lessons had to be interrupted. Julia and John's son, only about seven, was going with them. For anybody residing in Calcutta, Darjeeling was an irresistible attraction with its well-organised urban infra-structure, its height of 7,000 feet above the sea level on the slopes of the Himalayas, and the majestic beauty of the snow-capped Kanchenjunga, 28,170 feet high, south east of Mount Everest. I knew Julia was particularly interested, and asked me many questions about it. Michael and I had gone up to North Point College in Darjeeling two years in succession to discuss how to make the teaching of English effective and interesting in Indian schools and colleges.

After Julia, John and Mark had returned from Darjeeling, we learned that they'd had an unpleasant experience on the train on the way back to Calcutta. They'd got on to the train in Siliguri. The train had stopped in the middle of nowhere a few hours after that and a whole crowd of young people had boarded the train, shouting revolutionary slogans. What followed had shaken her.

It was a weekend. Quite a few people had turned up from the British Council office to demonstrate solidarity. After some time, most of them had gone. Julia had asked us to stay and have some lunch. We were dancing, Julia and I, and Julia was giving me an account of her experiences in Darjeeling. It started pleasantly. John's contribution to the seminar was generally appreciated. The scenery around Darjeeling was quite stunningly beautiful, the most dramatic and memorable spectacle being the Kanchenjunga, a Himalayan mountain on the Nepal-Sikkim border. When the sun shone on the peak, it was a magical spectacle.

'In the years to come,' said Julia, 'I am sure I'll look back on those few days in Darjeeling with pleasure. But what followed on the way back, when we were travelling by train from Siliguri, was very frightening...', the expression on her face changed. 'A noisy crowd of young men entered our compartment, shouting slogans. I didn't understand most of what they were shouting. But I could tell they weren't trying to be friendly. Some carried clubs and spears. A young man was pointing a spear at me. Mark most indignantly shouted at him. 'Don't you dare hurt my Mum'.'

A couple came to say goodbye. We stopped dancing. After they'd gone, Julia continued the account.

'A young man harangued us while the others in the crowd made supporting noises. There was something menacing about them. The slogans were in Bengali – I could tell, and they weren't friendly slogans. It sounded as if John and I were responsible for all their suffering and humiliation. If that's what they were saying, then the idea was absurd. But I found their voices menacing and I was afraid.' Julia looked and sounded distressed.

'At no point,' Julia said, 'did John look ruffled. He calmly spoke to those in front of the group and with the loudest voices. He explained that he and his wife and son had only recently come to India, and Mark and I had come with him to St James's School, where he was taking part in an educational seminar. It was inconceivable that he and his wife and son could have had a hand in the exploitation of the poor people who depended on tilling the soil for their survival. Then one of the young men talked to the others in Bengali and the crowd dispersed. John thought they dispersed when they realised that he was a teacher.'

'I'm glad,' I said, 'you're all back in one piece.'

'Yes,' said Julia, 'so am I.'

We continued dancing. I was telling Julia about the Naxalite movement. Naxalites, I was saying, were far-left radical communists, who also called themselves Maoists. There was a village, Naxalbari, in the State of West Bengal. That was where the movement had started. Later it had spread to other parts of India. The central idea was to stop the exploitation of the poor and vulnerable tillers of the soil by the rich and powerful land-lords. The students of West Bengal, Tamil Nadu and elsewhere had taken up their cause.

'Young people are always looking for a just cause so that they can fight for it,' I said

I think Julia was listening to me with interest. We were still dancing. She moved closer to me. We kissed.

'I think we could do with some food,' said John.

'You're quite right,' said Julia. 'It's really past our dinner time.'

We stopped dancing and joined the others.

John and Sudarsana were discussing the various chaotic aspects of life in Calcutta. I told Sudarsana that Julia, John and Mark had had a terrible experience on their way back from Darjeeling. This time John narrated what had happened, making light of the menace of the situation. But Sudarsana was visibly upset and John decided she needed a strong drink to calm her down. The conversation then turned to our lives in East Africa, theirs in Dar-as-Salam and ours in Kampala. Julia and John had also spent some years in Africa and were great admirers of Julius Miserere, the Tanzanian President from 1964-1985, who called himself a socialist, was a great speaker and was genuinely loved and admired by his people and respected by the colonialists. Milton Obote, who was our Prime Minister while we were still living in Uganda, and later became the country's President, wasn't, we agreed, quite in the same league as Julius Nyerere.

We discovered during the evening that both the Blackwells and we knew the Njaus – Rebecca and Elimo Njau. They were Tanzanians who lived on the campus of Makerere University College – highly gifted teachers and artists. Rebecca wrote some excellent plays. It was an exciting and eventful evening. Both Sudarsana and I left the Blackwells' Alipore house feeling that it was an evening well spent. There is always a certain joy in getting to know people whose expectations from life are similar to yours.

A few days after that evening, the teachers, the students and the Director of the Institute of English were celebrating the last day of the academic year, when students were awarded their certificates for the successful completion of the course. Professor Vernon George, from Wellington University, New Zealand was going to give a talk. This was to be followed by the presentation of certificates. After that the students were going to present a short, one-act play, and the morning was to conclude with some light refreshments. Professor Vernon George had given his inaugural talk and the certificates were duly distributed. Vernon walked up to me and asked if I could go with him to Chitpore almost immediately because he had urgent business there, and he could do with my help. What was the business? He was interested in Indian music and he had had a sitar crafted for him according to his specifications by one of the craftsmen in Chitpore. He had to collect the instrument and wanted to leave almost immediately. So we left – without any explanation and without saying goodbye to anyone. I felt confused by his precipitate action, but wanted to help.

Our work done, we returned to the Institute. The main business of the day was over, but quite a few of the students and lecturers, including Nirupam Chatterji, the Director of the Institute, were still around, talking about education and politics, two very popular subjects at the Institute. I joined in. Soon we all got involved in talking about contemporary events, education and politics. Nirupam's secretary interrupted me in the middle of some observation I was making. Someone was on the phone, wanting to talk to me.

It was Julia.

'Hello,' I said.

'Hello,' she said. 'What happened? Where did you disappear to? I looked for you. I asked Nirupam Chatterji. Nobody knew.'

'Vernon had some important business in Chitpore. I went with him,' I said. 'He doesn't know his way around in Calcutta.'

'I was disappointed,' she said. 'I came especially to see you and talk to you. Then I looked everywhere but you weren't there.'

Julia's voice broke. Was she crying? Our friendship was only a few months old. I found her warm, friendly, attractive and loving, but I hadn't told her anything, hadn't confessed to the fact that I was always aware of her presence if she was anywhere around. I had felt attracted to Julia without wanting to admit it to myself. Julia sounded tearful, but I couldn't be sure.

'I'm sorry. Vernon hadn't said anything to me before and we were in a hurry. But I'm sure we will meet again quite soon. It's your turn to come to us,' I said.

'I'm going shopping tomorrow about ten. Why don't we meet up somewhere near New Market?' Julia suggested. Julia knew our academic year had just ended.

We met up on the first floor of a small restaurant near New Market. Downstairs was noisy, full of weekend shoppers, who talked compulsively and laughed loudly. Julia was sitting next to me, looking perfectly calm.

'I was overwrought yesterday when I rang you. I'm sure you registered,' she said. 'Yes, I did. If I hurt you, I'm sorry,' I said.

After that we tried to be casual, had another cup of coffee and talked about subjects which were topical at the time. We sat close, held hands and talked about unconnected news headlines in a desultory fashion but steering clear of what might be more relevant for us to discuss: what was happening, which way were we going, do we stop and turn around or keep moving without any idea of the direction or destination? It seemed as if we had reached a tacit understanding not to force the moment to its crisis. The direction in which we were moving was unmistakeable, but at the time I had no idea exactly where it was leading; I don't think Julia had either.

My time with the Institute of English was now over. I returned to the British Council office in Shakespeare Sarani. It meant my having to deal with ESL problems during the day, and dispensing British culture in the evening. My evenings were often more demanding than my working hours from nine in the morning to five in the afternoon. But, quite often, I'd go back to the office in the evening for various cultural activities for promoting the dissemination of the English language and culture. A group of actors – Vimal Bhagat, Junie Bose, Kabir Seth and my daughter Aparajita were rehearsing a play which I had written – *Tomato Ketchup.* The play was going to be staged in the basement of Kala Mandir, where we'd had a festival of one-act plays earlier that year. Julia and a friend of hers were helping us occasionally with the sale of tickets. We sold all the tickets and, if the audience reaction was anything to go by, the play was a success. At the end of the third and final performance of the play, there was going to be a party in the evening to be hosted by Mr and Mrs Blackwell on behalf of the British Council. John and Julia Blackwell had already acquired a modest reputation for hosting excellent parties.

Sudarsana and I, and members of the cast of *Tomato Ketchup* were all enjoying themselves. The music was chosen carefully by Julia so that it inspired people to dance. I danced with Sudarsana, Julia and a friend of Julia's, Margaret. Then I circulated for a while, talking to those involved in the play. I don't know why but I was beginning to feel detached and without any urge to get involved in a conversation. I didn't want to dance either. Between the long and fairly wide garden shed and the lawn, there was a high hedge, which ran parallel to the garden shed. I walked along the hedge and turned right on the green lawn. My mood and the scene were just right for a cigarette, I decided. I put my hand in my pocket and fished out a packet. I was about to light a cigarette, when I noticed two shadowy figures standing close to the hedge – a woman in a man's arms. It didn't take me any time at all to see that the woman was Julia – but who was the young man? I quietly returned to the bar in the garden shed and asked for a drink. Sudarsana joined me there and then Pradip, Alo and Ranajoy – all good friends. They said there were too many unknown faces at the party and they'd rather go to Ranajoy and Sadhana's flat in Kidderpore and have a party there. Finding Julia in the embrace of another man had upset me, so I readily responded to the idea.

'You're very quiet this evening,' commented Sadhana.

'I think I ought to go back to Alipore. After all the party was to celebrate the successful staging of my play,' I said. Apart from the personal, I had an official obligation as well.

After some time, I returned to the party, which looked different from the one I had left. Some had left and others were going. There was no dancing. Those who were still thinking of leaving had congregated in the living room. Julia walked up to me and led me through to the door at the side of the dining room.

'Where did you disappear? I looked for you everywhere. I even walked up and down the street outside the house,' she said. It was obvious she was trying to hold back her tears.

'I left because some of my friends, who didn't know many people here, wanted to leave. I went with Ranajoy and Sadhana, to their flat in Kidderpore,' I said.

'That's not the whole story, is it?' Julia asked.

'No, it isn't. I saw a young man hugging you behind the hedge. I didn't like it. I overreacted,' I said.

'I have to tell you, loudly and clearly, you didn't see me in the embrace of this young man. He was dancing with me and trying to see how far he could go. I took him to where others couldn't hear me and I was telling him to behave himself. My problem is that I shrink from everybody's embrace but yours.' She couldn't go on and walked away towards the kitchen. I stood there, almost in a state of shock, and returned to the living room where the remaining guests had assembled.

Julia was back in the living room, brightly smiling and carrying a silver beer mug. 'Ladies and gentlemen,' she said, 'there is unfinished business which we must now attend to.' Then John made a short speech, thanking me and the cast of the play. He was particularly happy that the British Council had sponsored the play. Julia presented me with the silver mug with *Tomato Ketchup* engraved on it. Everybody clapped. The party was now over and everybody ready to go home.

Sudarsana was saying goodbye to John, and some of the other guests were saying their final few words to Julia before leaving. I too was getting ready to go when Julia came along and said, 'Can we meet up tomorrow where we last met?' I said yes. She said, thanks, and left to attend to her obligations as the hostess. Soon after, Sudarsana and I said goodbye and left. Sudarsana told me on the way home that Julia had taken my absence from the party very badly.

'What made you do a thing like that?' she asked.

'Alo and Sadhana insisted that I went with them,' I said.

Sudarsana warned me that Julia was getting rather too fond of me. She pointed out that in my mid-forties, I couldn't risk my career to have an affair with a colleague's wife. It certainly wasn't the best way of improving my prospects in the British Council. Sudarsana was serious.

'No, it hasn't come to that yet,' I said.

'Not yet. But there's more to come.'

Sudarsana liked Julia. She didn't want her to be hurt, nor did she want any complication in her own life or mine. We were both quiet on the way home.

The next morning I met Julia at the appointed time and place. There were few customers in the restaurant, except for some unemployed young men and late-morning shoppers, stopping for a cup of coffee or a pot of tea. Julia looked her usual self. Whatever had upset her the previous night was forgotten, irrelevant. Her blue eyes looked unhurriedly for me, our eyes met; she came and sat next to me on the first floor of the restaurant, her face as relaxed this morning as it had been tense the night before. Our conversation was casual and impersonal. She talked about the British Council protocol. She mentioned, light-heartedly, John's inordinate love of parties and pretty women. I was puzzled as well as intrigued by what almost amounted to transformation. Quite cautiously I broached the subject.

'I am glad you sound so different this morning. You looked desperately unhappy last night and said things which you've probably forgotten,' I said.

'What did I say last night that you think I've forgotten?' Julia said.

'You said you shrank from the embrace of men,' I said.

'I think you've got it wrong. I said I shrink from the embrace of men other than you. Now I'll say it more simply: I'm in love with you.' She sounded so casual that I wondered whether she realized the implication of what she'd just said. I squeezed her hand which was lying on the table.

'Please don't think,' she continued, 'that I want to disrupt your life in any way. I've moved to Margaret's cottage. Mark is with his father. I'll stay with Margaret till I've got my flight to England organised.'

'I'll be there whenever you want me,' I said.

I saw Julia regularly at the cottage. Margaret and her partner were going to Digha, a seaside town of great beauty, a major tourist attraction. By now I had no doubt at all that I was in love with Julia. So I took some leave and Julia and I went with them to Digha for a week. Digha at the time had a most unspoilt beach and at no time did we see huge crowds of people there. It was as peaceful as it was beautiful. But what made the difference was being with Julia. What made the difference was being in love. I knew the feeling, but this time round it had happened quietly and taken hold of me. There was no dramatic declaration of passion, devotion or loyalty, but there *was* a difference. Julia had made a difference.

It wasn't difficult for Sudarsana to see that I wasn't connecting too well with what was going on around me. She knew now what accounted for the change. But she was amazingly in control. She didn't demand an explanation or indulge in any recrimination. What surprised me most was that she behaved as if she was deeply sympathetic, as if she knew the nature of my conflict. I wondered whether the way she felt about me had anything to do with her unrequited love for Ronu. Ronu's commitment to his wife and daughter was real and he basked in their love and admiration. What he had on offer wasn't love, but Sudarsana had hoped it was. Their relationship was emotional rather than physical, but she was deeply hurt.

Sudarsana was worried that I'd got myself into a situation in which considerable suffering lay in store for me. Her problem probably was ambivalence. It was strange, but the near certainty of my relationship with Julia running into sand gave her a sense of security; on the other hand, her conviction was that if I was stupid enough to take the relationship seriously, I would be badly hurt – and this made her unhappy.

For Sudarsana there was an unexpected solution. The relationship between John and Julia deteriorated. John, not unusually, was having an affair with someone who was a good friend of Julia's, but Julia insisted that this was incidental. She made these points without betraying any emotional distress: she loved me; she was leaving John and going back to Stanmore, not far from London. She believed that I loved her but she'd understand if I was too involved in my life and work in Calcutta to begin a new life with her somewhere else. She realised that both my family and Calcutta were central to my life. It would be unrealistic and unfeeling for her to expect that I'd end more than 25 years' relationship with Sudarsana, and also abandon my children, for someone I'd known for such a short time.

'But if you should want to come to England, or ask me to come to you in India or elsewhere, I'll come,' she said, with quiet confidence.

Julia was leaving the next morning. We met up in Hotel International on Lower Circular Road for dinner the evening before. Outwardly, she was calm but she was talking compulsively. Her effort to be matter-of-fact and casual wasn't succeeding. Her conversation was fragmentary: one moment she talked about some relationship she had in Dar-es-Salaam, and the next moment she was asking me to take care of myself and not be upset by her sudden departure. She kept going quiet, looking pensive.

'We *are* going to meet up again, aren't we?' she asked.

'Yes, we are,' I said reassuringly, although I had no idea when and where.

Julia talked more than was usual for her. It was as if she found silence oppressive. She talked about her life in Tanzania – love affairs, intrigues, socialising, excitements and disappointments. She had loved the country, liked the people. She was happy in Calcutta to begin with but she had been very ill for longer than was good for her confidence and general sense of well-being. Now she was leaving with a pervasive feeling of unfinished business. She didn't mention John's chronic need for adventure in his sex life.

'Maybe we can come back to my city at some time in the future?' I said.

'So we *are* going to meet up?' Julia said.

'Isn't that the idea?' I asked.

'Yes, it *is*,' she said. 'But isn't it too much for you to give and me to take? I know how close you are to your family. You always talk lovingly of Calcutta – of the river, of Tagore and Roy, its art and culture, its humanity.'

'Wherever I go, whatever I do, I'll keep in touch with both my family and friends and with Calcutta. And I don't think you'll stand in the way,' I said.

'No, I don't think I will,' she said, taking my hand.

What else did we talk about? I was tense. I didn't quite understand what impact this separation was going to have on our lives. Nor did Julia. All we knew just then was that Julia was leaving the next day for England with her son Mark, and John was going to stay in Calcutta until his leave was due. As for Julia and me, we were sailing the seas but didn't know whether we'd come to the holy city of Byzantium.

Julia left with Mark. I went to work as usual. She wrote to tell me about her safe arrival and her immediate preoccupations – putting Mark in school and finding herself a job. She wrote regularly and I did too – except that she had a lot more to write. She'd now got fairly organised, she said in one of her letters later on, had put Mark in a school Mark liked, and found herself a job in London, promoting the sale of hair products, for which she had to travel to London by tube, six days a week. Life, for various reasons, wasn't ideal, but she was coping. She hoped I was well and the atmosphere in the office wasn't too stifling or unfriendly.

Attitudes weren't unfriendly, the air wasn't stifling, but I had a feeling of unease. Then, one day, Tim Scott wanted to see me. The Deputy High Commissioner had asked him what my plans were.
'I don't understand,' I said.

'He thinks it's embarrassing – your relationship with Julia, when her husband and you are colleagues,' he said.

'Is it against the British Council's constitution that two adults should be allowed to change partners if they were British Council employees?' I asked. I could ask Tim such questions. He was fair minded. He was quite unusual.

'Come, come, Ganesh,' Tim said. 'You aren't comfortable, nor is John. Do you really want to continue?'

'I thought you might ask me that question. I *will* resign and go, and this is my schedule,' I said.

I told Tim that I wanted to leave and exactly when I'd hand in the required notice. I couldn't tell whether my certainty saddened him or brought him relief. As for me, considering the fact that I was at a crossroads, at the end of one journey and the beginning of another, I was fairly focussed on what I wanted to do. I wanted to meet up with Julia in Delhi, begin our life there, and then see what happened.

I resigned. There was no official or unofficial farewell party, no polite words of appreciation of my contribution to the British Council, not even a cup of tea and a polite handshake from the Representative to say goodbye. My behaviour was an embarrassing departure from the norm, so the British Council had decided to ignore my resignation. It was something I didn't quite understand, but I was at the time too preoccupied to be seriously affected by the attitude of the British Council.

I sold my car and put the money in Sudarsana's account. I was going to stay with my friends, Kritish and his wife, Ira – Mutu and Khuku. I had my last month's salary of 2,300 rupees to cover the immediate expenses, and after that was gone, what was I going to do? I hoped to find some kind of job in Delhi, but I had no idea what it was going to be or how soon I'd get it. I'd started saying goodbye to friends and relations. One of my friends was Jagdish Gopal, whom I'd got to know when I lived in East Africa. He knew of my plans but I'd no idea whether he approved. I saw him in his office. He was the Secretary of the Bata Shoe Company. Jagdish was a practical man and he asked me practical questions. He used to call me *Dada,* which means elder brother in Bengali.

'Have you got a job or promise of a job in Delhi?' he asked.

'No, I haven't,' I said.

'How much money have you got to fall back on?' he asked casually. He was alarmed when I said that I was taking about 2,500 rupees with me.

'Two thousand and five hundred rupees and no job, and Julia's arriving on the twelfth? You're being unrealistic,' he said.

Jagdish then called his Secretary, asked her to give me 4,000 rupees in cash. He made me promise that I'd let him know if there was any problem or crisis. It was only after I'd discussed the situation with Jagdish that it was brought home to me that there were practical aspects of my new beginning which I couldn't afford to ignore. Jagdish's concern made a deep impression on me. I left his office quite overwhelmed by his generosity.

There was something else which had caused me deep unhappiness. I'd handed in my notice of resignation, but I was still attending office. Nondon was then in St Xavier's College. One afternoon he came to my office and sat in a chair opposite me.

'Is it true, Baba? Are you really going away?' he asked.

'Yes, Nondon, I am,' I said.

Nondon's face registered disbelief, shock, profound unhappiness, but he didn't let himself break down. He held his head between his hands and lowered it as if to pray. He had long, shoulder-length hair then and a longish beard, which gave him a spiritual look. He stayed like that for almost half a minute. Then he threw back his head, opened his eyes.

'See you later, Baba,' he said and left.

Nondon's visit was short, but it brought home to me the certainty of the profound emotional insecurity, helplessness and misery my action was going to cause those who had always been able to take my protective love and care for granted. It wouldn't make sense to Sudarsana, Nondon, Aparna and Aparajita that there are times in people's lives when they aren't in control of what they do, or of their destiny. I was in love. So what? Did I have the right to set fire to the house that sheltered those I loved, and those who loved me? If it hurt me to hurt those who loved me and those I loved, why was I going away? Nondon and Sudarsana were confident, self-reliant and resourceful people. Our daughters were married. Nobody was actually dependent on me. But was that the point?

Why did I do it then? Retrospective rationalisation of our actions which have hurt people or damaged them one way or another is a waste of time. But I had come to terms with what I was doing, and in so doing I had to have several dialogues with myself. And as far as I remember, it wasn't just, 'I'm in love with Julia, therefore, I'll leave everything – my family, my friends, my city and my job and go wherever Julia wants me to go.'

In terms of my personal relationship with Sudarsana and the children, I was beginning to feel redundant. Sudarsana's interest in me, I thought, had diminished to the lukewarm. Aparna and her husband, Raj Bhagat or Dubby were in England. Aparajita, newly married, was expecting her first baby. Nondon had his music and his studies, in that order of importance. I was busy with my British Council work. It was at this time that Julia came into my life. Before she left, on her last evening in Calcutta, after our dinner at the hotel, Julia had said a few simple words of farewell.

'I do hope to see you again, Ganesh. I'll wait for you. But if you can't come, I'll understand.'

The simplicity of those words had moved me. In the end, however, the closest I can get to the truth is: something really important had happened to me, I'd decided, and I *had* to take notice of it. We all talk of love, nobody understands it, and there are as many different kinds of love as there are lovers. Sudarsana waited and watched, asked few questions, and wondered, I suppose, which way things would go.

After Julia left, we wrote to each other about what was happening in our lives and how we were adjusting to each other's absence. Implicit in every letter was that we would meet up somewhere and spend the rest of our lives together. Did I not ask myself how I could break up a relationship which had meant so much for so long and leave my children and my grandchild soon to be born? Yes, I did. I also admitted to myself the possibility that my ego had obscured my reason. But amateur psychology doesn't really show one the way. All I knew was that I believed in my relationship with Julia, and not once did I think of opting out.

During the time that I was preparing to go, there wasn't one word of recrimination from Sudarsana. It was something I couldn't explain, but greatly appreciated. She became very attentive. It was as if she felt that I was letting myself in for certain pain and disappointment. If we thought of all the novels we had read – both Sudarsana and I were students of literature – and the films we'd seen, and the couples we'd met in East Africa, and at home, did we find much evidence of loyal, monogamous relationships? That was probably the kind of thinking which explained why she was just then more apprehensive about the suffering which was lying in wait for me. I was stepping into a world with a different system of values. I was surely going to be hurt, leaving behind me my newborn grandson, my son Nondon, my daughters Aparna and Aparajita, my friends, and Calcutta.

Sudarsana wasn't the only one who thought that the future of my relationship with Julia was fraught with all kinds of danger, including those which come from a clash of cultures and a conflict of values. Extra-marital relationships – both overt and covert – were more the rule than the exception in Western culture, an erudite friend of mine gently warned me. This, however, wasn't what worried me. My problems at this point of time were much more existential and mundane – job, shelter, Julia's ability to adjust to the uncertainty of a new beginning and the weather in Delhi. But none of these problems were strong enough to make me change the direction in which I'd decided to go.

In order not to cause unnecessary pain, I'd quietly packed my case and put it away. When the day came for me to leave, I said goodbye to Sudarsana before she left for school and to Nondon before he went to college. I then waited for my friend Subroto, who was going to come with me to Howrah Station. I was on my own now, about to leave my wife, whom I had loved, and whom I'd married 24 years ago. I was also leaving my three children, whose love and good opinion I valued. But was I really leaving them? I certainly wouldn't let myself lose touch with them. These and other thoughts came crowding into my head as I was preparing to go. But I wasn't afraid of a new beginning, although I wasn't sure what the new beginning was going to be like. So much began to crowd into my mind all at once that I began to feel oppressed. Mercifully, the doorbell rang. Subroto came in.

'All set?' he asked.

'I'm packed and ready,' I said.

Subroto had all along avoided discussing what was happening in the lives of his somewhat older friends, Sudarsana and me. He had met Julia, liked her and had visited her in Alipore a few times. He hadn't once tried to dissuade me from going the way I was going. He was still a bachelor, who lived alone but had many friends, who found him caring and helpful. He had strong likes and dislikes, but he rarely took sides. He could be playful, mischievous and obstinately partisan, but I found him, at crucial times, mature and detached. He asked me some practical questions on the way to the station.

'When is Julia coming?' he asked.

'Twelfth February,' I said.

'That's only a week after you get to Delhi!' he said.

'It's how we arranged it. I'll have to get a flat, but my friend Mutu says there shouldn't be any problems,' I said.

'But setting up home in a new place takes time,' he said.

'I've friends in Delhi,' I said, 'who will help.'

'I hope all goes well,' he said.

We went to a restaurant in Howrah Station to have a cup of tea. I was avoiding expressing concern about Sudarsana and Nondon because it might seem hypocritical. But Subroto was a sympathetic friend who had had a few knocks himself. Only the year before, his Canadian girlfriend had left for Toronto when he was expecting her to stay in Calcutta and be his love. He'd cried, standing in the middle of a crowd of strangers at the airport. So I thought he would understand.

'Sudarsana will need company, understanding, friendship,' I said. My concern must have sounded hollow, but Subroto said, 'Yes, she will.'

'I could move into the middle room in the flat, now that Aparajita and Ian have got their own place,' he suggested.

'I think Sudarsana and Nondon would like to have you around,' I suggested.

'Nondon has already asked me to think about it,' Subroto said.

We were now walking along the station platform. A porter was carrying my case. We were approaching my train compartment and I was talking to Subroto rapidly and loudly; rapidly because we'd soon part, and loudly because the noise and the crowd around us were growing apace.

'I've given you my friend's telephone number, haven't I? If at any time you should want to contact me, please ring,' I said, raising my voice as I got into the train.

'Of course I will,' Subroto shouted back.

'Goodbye, Subroto, goodbye,' I said.

I entered my compartment and settled down in my seat. As the train began to move very slowly, responding to the guard's whistle, the changing of the light from red to green and the lowering of the flag, there was in my head a jumble of images that related to the past. I also tried to visualise what lay ahead. Julia was meeting up with me in Delhi on the 12th of February and I was arriving there on the 5th. Ira and Kritish, better known as Khuku and Mutu, were going to put us up until we found affordable accommodation. But I had no idea whether we could hire reasonable accommodation for affordable rent. That was one of my immediate problems. Then, before everything else, I'd need a job, a steady source of income; for the little money I had with me would run out in a matter of months. I'd been fortunate so far, moving out of one job and moving into another, but providence can't be taken for granted. At the next station, where the train stopped, I got out of my compartment and bought a few *rotis* and potato curry and had my supper and felt refreshed. I'd always enjoyed the food they sell at Indian railway stations.

It was a fairly cold February evening. I returned to my seat, made sure that the window was tightly shut, wrapped a blanket round me and picked up the newspaper I'd collected from a vendor. The idea was to read a little and gently drop off to sleep.

But I couldn't sleep and I couldn't read. There was someone very important in my life whom I didn't understand. How could Julia, after getting to know me for a few months, leave a highly intelligent and capable husband with a secure job and a well-paid career?

And how could she, without any discernible hesitation, throw in her lot with a married man who had neither a job nor shelter? What made it possible for her to want to come to a city she didn't know and to people she hadn't met before? There were other small matters too – religion, culture, background. These considerations didn't even seem to count with Julia, and if they did, she managed never to give me the slightest inkling of her anxieties. Yes, she was flying in on the 12th of February, 1972, from Heathrow to Delhi airport, and she hoped I'd be there to meet her. It was all pretty matter-of-fact, cut and dried and businesslike. We were crossing into a new life in Delhi. For me, too, it was fairly straightforward. It didn't feel like a revolutionary change. There was no drumbeat signalling disaster, no premonition of danger, no feeling of insecurity – only the memory of a few months ago and a persistent wish to be with Julia – a wish likely to be fulfilled in a matter of days.

It was a grey winter morning, misty and cold, with the sun not achieving very much by way of providing light and warmth, when the Rajdhani Express trundled into New Delhi Railway Station.

Looking out of the window, I saw my friend Kritish – Mutu – casually walking towards my compartment with his characteristic stoop, smoking his trademark pipe. It was a reassuring sight.

Chapter 15

Teaching, Oxford University Press, Getting married, England

It was February 1973. Before this I had visited Delhi only for a few days at a time on business, stayed with Ira and Kritish, and returned to Calcutta. This time it was different, because I had come to meet up with Julia and live in Delhi. The idea was that I would come to Delhi, stay with my friends briefly, and then look for a place to rent, and Julia would come down from England and join me. Rather uncharacteristically, I had given myself only a week to find a place for us to hire. As it happened, Julia rang to say that because of unfinished business, she'd had to postpone her departure by a week, which meant she'd arrive on the nineteenth of February instead of the twelfth.

In the meantime, my frantic search for a flat had yielded no results. Then one morning I found an ad in the paper of a ground-floor room with a small bathroom and a kitchen not far from where Ira and Kritish lived in Defence Colony. The flat consisted of a room which, after accommodating a double bed, left enough space opposite the front door for a multi-purpose, not very large round table. The attached toilet was adequate, but the kitchen was so small that only a determined, resourceful and innovative cook could function in it. It was part of the landlord's own house, which was well-built and well-maintained, with a clean environment. What is more, the Defence Colony market square was five minutes' walk from where the flat was.

Julia was flying in the week after. The rent was affordable. The address was also convenient – B Block, Defence Colony. The area in which Ira and Kritish lived was called Defence Colony because it was earmarked mainly, but not exclusively, for defence or army personnel. My landlord, if I hired the room, would be a retired army captain. Ira and Kritish would be neighbours living in the next block – a powerful incentive for acquiring the flat. So, after looking at what was on offer and carefully weighing up the advantages and the shortfalls, I went up to see the prospective landlord. Captain Singh was affable and businesslike. He was glad I liked the flat. I was required to pay two months' rent – one month's rent as deposit and one month's rent in advance. I made out a cheque for the required amount and handed it over. Captain Singh looked at it casually and put it in front of him on the table.

'Thank you, Dr Bagchi,' he said. I had told Captain Singh that my profession was teaching and that I had taught school children as well as young men and women at the post-graduate level, but I had never said that I had a Ph.D., so I had no idea why he had decided to address me as 'doctor.'

'You're welcome, Captain Singh,' I said, 'but incidentally, I am not Dr Bagchi. I never had a Ph.D.'
Captain Singh took no notice of what I said.

There was something else I decided I ought to mention. During the evening's conversation, I had mentioned Julia several times and told Captain Singh that she was in England and due to arrive in Delhi in a few days to share the room that I was renting. He'd assumed, I was sure, that Julia and I were married. I was aware of middle-class values, especially Indian middle-class values. I couldn't pretend that whether Julia and I were married or not would be a matter of indifference to Captain Singh. He should know, I decided.

'There's something I ought to have mentioned at the beginning of our meeting this evening: Julia and I will eventually get married, but at the moment we are not. If that makes any difference to you, I'll have to look for accommodation elsewhere.'

Shock and surprise were written all over Captain Singh's face. He picked up my cheque from the table and handed it back to me without the slightest hesitation.

'I am sorry, Dr Bagchi,' he said, 'I would like you to look for a place elsewhere. I wish you the best of luck. I appreciate your honesty, but...'

Captain Singh wasn't able to finish his sentence. From behind the door which led to the adjacent room emerged a tall lady, probably in her middle fifties, and stretched out her hand to me.

'I will take your cheque, Dr Bagchi,' said the lady, presumably Mrs Singh.

'Your relationship with Julia is your business, not ours. In telling my husband that you aren't married to Julia, you showed your respect for our traditional values. Now it is our turn to show our appreciation of your honesty. Please move into the little flat when you want to and we'll do our best to help you in any way we can.'

I said thank you to the tall, dignified, elegant Mrs Singh.

This was a unique experience: a middle-class, Indian woman, defying tradition, and standing up for what she considered right and fair and probably risking the wrath of her husband. I left the company of Captain and Mrs Singh, feeling immensely relieved that we wouldn't have to impose on Ira and Kritish and would have the privacy of our own place. I told Ira and Kritish, and our mutual friend, Surajit, of my experience. They confirmed that it was also their experience – Sikh women usually had a strong personality and character. The turbaned husbands didn't always have it their way. Whether this was true or not I had no way of knowing. What I did know was that Mrs Singh had stood up for me to relieve some of my anxiety at a crucial time of my life.

Surajit Sen was a friend of my friends Ira and Kritish, better known by their other names, Khuku and Mutu. Surajit lived with Khuku and Mutu as a paying guest, but he was very much part of the family. Surajit was a celebrity because he had been a news reader on All India Radio since the days of the Second World War, and his name – and his voice—were well-known to every household where there was a radio. When I arrived from Calcutta, Surajit was specially helpful and caring. He was the only person who seemed to be aware of the practical challenges inherent in the situation.

'I've decided to save you the taxi-fare. I'll drive you to the airport to meet Julia when she comes,' Surajit said.

And so he did. Julia arrived at the airport in New Delhi on the 19th of February, 1973. Surajit stood a little apart while I welcomed her, then I introduced them. Polite enquiries about the flight and health and well-being followed. I asked how Mark, Julia's son, was doing and whether he liked his school. We soon reached Defence Colony. Surajit, Ira and Kritish put Julia completely at ease through their naturally friendly and charming behaviour. It's not only my experience but also the experience of many other people, I'm sure, that some have the extraordinary gift of putting others at their ease, even in difficult circumstances. These friends of mine in Delhi were such people. It was remarkable how, from the moment they met, there was an obvious and pleasant rapport between them. Ira insisted that Julia and I spent a couple of days with them while she and Julia attended to some of the essential problems to do with the flat and the kitchen which they had already identified during their brief conversation. It was a practical offer and we accepted it most gratefully.

Julia proved to be not only efficient but also extremely innovative from the moment we moved into our one-room accommodation in B Block, Defence Colony. Every square inch of space was made use of. Each article, useful or ornamental, was put where it belonged. The bed was the largest item of furniture, and then there was a round dinner-table at one side of the room and four chairs. Since it was the only table in the room, it had multiple functions, a wide spectrum of usefulness. The kitchen had an electric stove; the bathroom had a shower that worked well, the Defence Colony market was a stone's throw from where we were; our friends lived just round the corner; we had a sympathetic and helpful landlady. What else did we want out of life? What was especially heartening for me was that Julia didn't show the slightest signs of anxiety or distress. She cooked and cleaned, ate and slept and related to people around her without showing strain or self-consciousness, and behaved as if she belonged to Delhi. And Delhi belonged to her.

We were just about beginning to feel settled when Kishen turned up and offered to work as a cleaner. He was a little above five feet, slightly built, with a small round face and alert, friendly eyes. He spoke Hindi but had enough English for basic communication. Julia liked the look of Kishen and so did I. He started working for us immediately. His work at this stage consisted mostly of cleaning the house and carrying the rubbish to the public dustbin. Quite soon, however, other responsibilities were added to his daily chores: posting letters, shopping, washing up. The more he had to do, the happier he seemed to be. In just a few weeks, Kishen became a trusted member of our team, efficiently attending to his jobs, finishing his tasks and asking for more. My vocabulary of Hindi words was comparable to Kishen's stock of English words – it was quite limited. But we managed to communicate. A rather unusual aspect of this life for me was that at no time was I oppressed by its limitations. We lived in one room but this didn't interfere with our feeling of well-being. We were spending out of the small sum of money with which I had arrived in Delhi. Yet we had no real sense of insecurity.

Except for one uninterrupted week in Digha, Julia and I had met and parted many times in Calcutta but hadn't really lived together. Yet I had little sense of insecurity about our relationship. Julia also betrayed no feeling of uncertainty. Before very long we got sufficiently organised to start entertaining. We invited Charles Lewis, a friend I had first met in East Africa, and Shanti Chaudhuri, a friend from Calcutta. Charles was now the Managing Director of a well-known publishing company, the Oxford University Press in Delhi, and Shanti, a mutual friend, was just visiting. We sat round our little dining table and ate steaks. Shanti and Charles declared that that was the best steak they had had in years. Samik Banerji, another good friend, also spent an evening with us. In fact we were really beginning to feel settled when it was time for Julia to return to England. There were aspects of her personality which caused me concern, but what I found remarkable was the completely un-selfconscious manner in which she related to people she met in Delhi, most of them for the first time.

Julia had put Mark in boarding school, worked in London for a few months and then flown to Delhi. She hadn't been able to spend more than a few days with him. Now, during his Easter break, she was going to be able to spend some time with him and hoped to lessen his sense of insecurity, which children almost invariably feel when parents separate. So we were back at the airport and I waved to her from the visitors' gallery to say goodbye. I felt no anxiety. I knew she'd be back. When I came back, Kishen was waiting for me. When was madam coming back? What was I going to do for my meals? Did I know how to cook? I answered his questions. Then he revealed what his questions were about – he could cook Indian meals and would be delighted to take charge of the kitchen as well as keep the place clean. The transition was simple. I liked what he cooked *and I* liked Kishen as a person – unobtrusive, efficient, pleasant company.

Our conversation was mainly in English, because I found that Kishen's English was more effective than my Hindi. I decided that Kishen would be good to have around not only for what he could do but also because of the kind of person he was. It was really most fortunate that Kishen turned up in our life in Delhi. I knew Kishen would stay with us as long as we chose to live in Delhi.

We'd all agreed that we needed a larger place. The present accommodation had provided us with emergency shelter and we had been happy here, yet there was no way we could manage to fit in even bare essentials into the available space. I talked things over with Kishan, informed Captain Singh, my landlord, went to the house agents in Defence Colony and requested them to find me a place for a rent of between 250 and 300 rupees. The house agent looked up the list of flats and suggested that I look at a *'barshati'*, which is a small flat on a terrace. I thought it was a good idea. The house agent showed me a *barshati* in Defence Colony, Block A, which appealed to me. It consisted of a large room, a small kitchen and a bathroom outside on the terrace. The room was large, more than twice the size of the room we had in Block B. The kitchen and bathroom were basic. I took the place. I hired furniture. Kishen and I went out and bought odds and ends and set up our new home in Block A, Defence Colony. No curtains and carpets, table mats or lampshades to create aesthetic pleasure; no state-of-the-art domestic gadgets. But we did our best and hoped that Julia would find the place habitable.

Julia's return to Delhi was postponed by more than a fortnight as she had a bad cold. This delay in Julia's return to Delhi wasn't welcome news by any means, but it gave me some time to go job-hunting with renewed energy. Finding a job with a reasonable salary was becoming increasingly urgent because the money with which

I'd arrived in Delhi was slowly but alarmingly disappearing. In most major cities there were tutorial colleges where teachers prepared students for passing examinations through courses specially designed for the purpose. These institutions had little to do with education and learning and everything to do with passing examinations. I was given to understand by some of my friends in Calcutta and Delhi that those teachers who were temporarily out of work or wanted to earn some extra cash could always turn to these colleges. I did. I went from one tutorial college to another. There were no vacancies. I answered an advertisement in one of the Delhi newspapers for an English tutor for a fifteen- year old. The father either worked in the embassy of an Arab country or was actually the ambassador. I was paid reasonably well for a few hours' tuition every week, but the money was nowhere near what I needed for survival. There was another problem: the teenager was more interested in my listening to some of the popular Arab songs which he particularly liked than in learning English. I usually turned down the invitation, but when I did, he became all pensive and remote, so I had to give in sometimes.

Julia was back. She looked frail. One could tell that she hadn't been well. But there was no hesitation in the way she walked towards me. There was confidence and trust in her blue eyes. I welcomed Julia with an embrace which was brief because public demonstration of affection made me self-conscious. It was also unusual in our culture.

'I was miserable,' she said. 'First the separation and then the misery of the cold and the days in bed. I'm so glad to be back.'

'I'm glad too,' I said.

Then, quite unexpectedly, I felt deeply distressed. I remembered the parting with Sudarsana. How brave, how strong she was. There were no words of recrimination or supplication. But wasn't it hypocritical to remember her with admiration?

You've suddenly gone very quiet,' Julia remarked.

I tried to tell her the truth as simply as I could.

'Do you regret leaving Sudarsana?' Julia asked.

'It hurt her deeply. She was too proud ever to talk about it,' I said.

Julia became thoughtful and quiet. I didn't feel like talking for some time. Then I asked her about her parents and Mark and she wanted to know what changes had happened in the life of the nation and the lives of friends in India. One of her main interests, of course, was the *barshati* which I'd hired. At least equally important was the news of Ira and Kritish, Surajit and Kishan. She wasn't particularly perturbed that I hadn't yet landed a job.

Julia liked our *barshati* at A Block, Defence Colony. Both Kishan and Julia were pleased to see each other. Kishan had made tea and organized s*amosas*. Having served the tea, he disappeared to see to the next meal, dinner. We didn't go out, didn't see friends, but stayed at home and talked and talked, Julia showing no sign of jet lag or the illness which had laid her low. Britain had joined the European community. Whether it was Edward Heath's great achievement or failure, we agreed, only time would tell. Mujibur Rahman was now the Prime Minister of the new state of Bangladesh, I said. The bombing of North Vietnam under Nixon continued unabated. Julia's parents and Mark were well. She'd missed me. How was I? What were my plans? We switched from one subject to another. It was time to go to bed. That night Julia slept peacefully.

A feeling of transience marked our previous meetings, when we met for only days or weeks or a few months. This meeting was expected to last longer because, from now on, we were going to live together, for better or worse, unless something happened to change the course of our lives. Julia started off with her customary zest, organising the flat. She liked the *barshati* for various reasons – a large room and a larger terrace where a lovely little garden was a distinct possibility. The kitchen and the bathroom were below par to begin with, but by the time Julia finished with them, they were adequate. Our friends visited our place and were impressed with the transformation.

Julia bought a round stone table for the terrace. Carrying it to the terrace was like one of the ten tasks of Hercules. The man who had sold it to us was himself carrying it. The stairs were steep and narrow with a bend in the middle and the man was really exhausted by the time he reached the top of the stairs. We were very pleased with it. Sitting around it in the evening under the stars was a pleasure we looked forward to. Soon our *barshati* began to look very comfortable and elegant. Balbir was one of the sons of Mr Singh, the landlord. He was so impressed with the transformation of the flat that he brought a friend along to show it off. We'd started our life together, Julia and I, at A32 Defence Colony.

We had no plans at this stage to go anywhere else or look for new adventures. It was a clean, pleasant environment; our *barshati* was more than adequate; our friends and neighbours were helpful and sympathetic. It was summer, and summer in Delhi is hot, but not unpleasantly so because, although the temperature oscillates between about 97°F and 77°F, it's dry heat and dry heat was less oppressive than the heat of July to September, when the monsoon brought humidity. It was especially unpleasant between one spell of rain and another.

Mark came down from his school in England to spend his summer holidays with Julia. Mark's summer holidays coincided with Delhi's rainy season. I'd decided to stay away while Mark was in Delhi so that he didn't have the trauma of finding his father having been replaced by another man. I went away to stay with Sumanto and Bizeth, two of our friends in Delhi. The heat and humidity of Delhi didn't trouble Mark but he was unhappy that I was staying away. He knew me. He also knew that his parents had separated and I was his mother's new partner. So why was I not there? He demanded that I came back to stay with them, which I did with alacrity. Mark didn't have any difficulty settling down and fitting into the pattern of our lives.

Julia had often experienced a sense of guilt during her time with John, who wasn't ready to let life slip by without providing him with ample excitement. He loved parties, interesting conversation, attractive women and relationships which were enjoyable but not demanding. He worked hard for the British Council during the day, but the evenings were for relaxation and that involved going out several evenings every week.

This meant leaving Mark with a babysitter. Julia didn't like it and Mark hated it. During his holidays with us, Mark had his mother all to himself whenever he wanted and Julia didn't have to go away to parties, leaving behind a tearful Mark. I had little doubt about the fact that Mark was enjoying his holidays with us and he looked forward to his next holiday. It was important for both Julia and me that Mark accepted the new set up without showing any signs of trauma or disapproval. He was really enjoying himself being with us – going out in auto-rickshaws, eating out, and meeting our friends. At the end of the holidays, Mark returned to England – reluctantly.

I couldn't afford to remain unemployed any more. The Arab diplomat's music-loving teenage son wasn't learning much English and the money I earned was only a fraction of what I needed to earn. I did get short-listed for a job at Jawaharlal Nehru University – JNU – but I wasn't selected. A much younger person, a young woman who'd passed out from the same university, was selected. My quest for a job continued. I was short-listed for an interview at Hindu College, a college affiliated to Delhi University, but I had the impression that I wasn't taken seriously. My desperation was growing apace. Then Sumanto, whom I've mentioned before, told me that he'd learned from a friend of his at Kirori Mal College that they were going to advertise for a lecturer and I should look out for their advertisement. I did, but unfortunately, one of their requirements was that the mark sheet of my MA examination should be enclosed with the application. This was rather a tall order as I had left university 26 years ago. But there were two aspects of this job that mattered – it was a department with some erudite lecturers and a head of department of outstanding ability. Sumanto thought it would be a job well worth trying for. So I discussed the problem of trying to come up with at least a duplicate of my M.A. Certificates with all my friends and acquaintances. Nirupam, the former Director of the Institute of English in Calcutta, was now working for Oxford University Press in Delhi. His determined efforts and research produced the desired results – and he was able to obtain from the archives of Calcutta University a certified mark sheet which I was now able to enclose with my application.

I was short-listed and received the letter after a very tense week of waiting. The interview was friendly. There were no questions to assess my knowledge of the English language or literature but almost an hour-long discussion about my teaching experience. I got the impression that the professor was particularly interested in the work that I'd done for the University Grants Commission, which ran refresher courses to improve the teaching of English in colleges. At the end of the interview, I was asked to wait in the staff room. A much younger person from Tamil Nadu, who had been interviewed before me, was also waiting there. We sat and talked until we were summoned – first I went in, and then the young man. We'd both been selected. We were both expected to join the teaching staff of the college at the beginning of the next term. I forget the name of my young colleague – let's call him Anand. Anand and I congratulated each other and celebrated our success at the college canteen with *samosas* and cups of tea, though it wasn't the highest point of my career.

My salary would be several hundred rupees less than what the British Council had been paying me. All the same, it was an important day. I felt like shouting, and running in the warm air and bright sunshine.

Julia hadn't shown much anxiety over the steady depletion of our meagre resources. One could see that she'd been in one or two tight corners in her life and had acquired some real experience of coping with lack of money. But she too would much rather not live in the shadow of uncertainty. So we celebrated. We went to an open-air, outdoor restaurant in Defence Colony market square and had *rogan josh* and *parathas,* sitting under a clear blue sky. Our friends were also delighted that my jobless days were over. Something else happened at about this time, pointing to the truth which some believe – that there's a tide in our affairs. The road doesn't wind uphill all the way. Things like that.

Changes for the better began to happen. I'd arrived in Delhi with about 7,000 rupees. Our financial situation was reaching a point of crisis when I received a letter from Mr Jacob, the Administrative Officer of the British Council, with the most welcome news that according to the British Council regulations I was entitled to receive seven months' salary for my seven years of service. My salary at the time of my resignation was 2,300 rupees a month. A cheque for 16,100 rupees was enclosed with the letter. I wasn't yet in the grip of paranoid anxiety, but first the lecturer's job at Kirori Mal College and then the seven months' salary made a difference. At a crucial point of time, the changes were significant; they brought me a sense of security.

I started teaching at Kirori Mal College and found the work both challenging and rewarding: challenging because some of the 'pass-course' students – doing a general course of undergraduate study – had very little English and even less interest in learning English; and rewarding because most of the students who were doing an honours course in English were able, intelligent and hard-working. I wasn't able to create enough interest in English among the pass course students – that was frustrating. But teaching those students who were in the English *Honours* classes gave me a sense of satisfaction and a feeling of homecoming. Keval, Gautan, Kasturi and several others, whose names I've forgotten, brought home to me that I wasn't really fit for any other profession except teaching. Travelling to the University campus from Defence Colony was time-consuming and tiresome, but it didn't constitute a major problem. The changes in my circumstances were not only positive but quite dramatic. Both Julia and I now faced life without the spectre of penury and it made a difference in various other ways. A particularly significant aspect of our period of uncertainty for me was that Julia was put to the test and wasn't found wanting. At no point of our period of uncertainty, did she panic. Before one Christmas, she painted some children's pictures – she had trained and qualified as a commercial artist – and sold them to a store where people who worked in foreign embassies did their shopping. We were going to manage somehow – whether I found regular employment or not. We were prepared for the uncertainty. The Kirori Mal College job changed all that.

Significant changes started happening. We bought a fridge – a landmark in our lives. We also bought a pair of parrots – George and Georgina – in summer. The cold killed Georgina in winter, although Julia had tried to reduce the severity of the cold by covering their cage. George had already managed to fly away. The winter in Delhi was quite severe, and we didn't have adequate heating.

One weekend, we averted a serious accident. Mark had come for Christmas. It had become so cold that we had prepared a charcoal fire, shut the doors and windows, and were sitting round the fire to ward off the cold. After some time we'd begun to feel warm and comfortable – all three of us – and a little after that rather drowsy, quite pleasantly so. At this point of time, Balbir, the landlord's son, knocked on the door and entered. He was horrified to see what we'd done and surprised at our ignorance. The build-up of carbon monoxide in a closed room, according to Balbir, could have had lethal consequences. It was providential that he'd come to see us. We opened doors and windows and walked about on the terrace. Soon we felt better. We thanked Balbir for his timely intervention. According to my friend, Kritish, if we'd all dozed off and then fallen fast asleep, it might have been curtains for two Blackwells and one Bagchi.

Winter in Delhi was November to January, with average temperature not a lot higher than 10°C. Cold waves could push the temperature to below 2°C. Normally, however, the sun shone and going out in an auto-rickshaw to Connaught Circus to do a little shopping and sight-seeing and to eat out was a particularly attractive proposition for all three of us. It was rather pleasant for me to find that Mark really enjoyed spending his holidays with us. When it was time for him to return to England, there was a noticeable lack of enthusiasm.

I'd been almost totally focussed on my problem of getting a job. Apart from that there was another worrying problem – Julia's health. Julia hadn't been very well in Calcutta. While she was away in England, she'd fallen ill. She seemed to be coping fairly well with the climate in Delhi, where temperatures varied from 32°C (90°F) in summer, to around 12-13°C (54-55°F) in Winter. If there were cold waves from the Himalayas, the temperature could approach the point of freezing and even go below that. Life could be really trying. In spite of various difficulties and problems, however, I had a certain sense of security after I got a job and received a few thousand rupees from the British Council. Now I started worrying about Sudarsana. She must feel betrayed and insecure. I decided to go to Calcutta and find out for myself what was happening to Sudarsana, Nondon and Aparajita, but mainly Sudarsana.

I took a room in a hotel in Shakespeare Sarani, Calcutta, not far from the British Council. I rang Sudarsana and told her that I was in Calcutta and would come and see her the next evening. During the day I went to see my lawyer and requested her to draw up a preliminary document undertaking to legally transfer the ownership of the flat to Sudarsana. I'd let her down by leaving her, so she might worry about the security of her shelter. And when I arrived at the flat that evening, my intuition was proved to be right. Sudarsana's very articulate sister, Sunanda, her husband, Rajib, and Sudarsana were sitting round the large dining table. They looked rather serious and businesslike. They greeted me and continued to look serious.

'Did you come by plane?' Sunanda asked.

'No,' I said, 'I came by train.'

'Are you all right?'

'Yes, thanks. Now I've got a job. I'm a lecturer at Kirori Mal College.'

'Congratulations!'
Rajib and Sudarsana asked various questions about the kind of accommodation we had, the weather and the people. Only Rajib asked how Julia was. After that Rajib broached the subject which was uppermost in their minds: the ownership of Flat 405, Dover Court. The flat's sole ownership was mine. Sudarsana didn't for a moment doubt that I'd ever question her right to live there, but she'd be happier if I transferred the ownership to her.

'Would you like a cup of tea?' Sunanda asked.

'That'll be nice,' I said.

I said that I'd expected Sudarsana to feel anxious about the ownership of the flat and had had a lawyer draw up a preliminary legal document pledging that I'd transfer the flat to her. Rajib read the document, signalled his approval and handed it over to Sudarsana, who put it away without reading it. Sudarsana looked apologetic. She wanted to say, I thought, that she was sorry that she felt insecure although her husband had left her after nearly 25 years and with three grown-up children. She wanted to know whether the hotel room was comfortable and then suggested that I moved in for the next three days into the spare room in the flat. I agreed to move in the next day. Sudarsana didn't talk much. She was friendly but distant. She seemed to be asking why all this had had to happen.

I returned to the hotel quite late. The manager, a fairly young man of thirty-something, wanted to see me. Ira had rung his brother in Calcutta to give me the message that Julia wasn't well and I should return to Delhi immediately. Ira and Kritish were friends who'd always stood by me. They had to ring several people in Calcutta to contact me, but they hadn't given up. The hotel manager watched my reaction. It wasn't difficult for him to see that I was distressed and he asked if he could do anything to help. When I explained why I looked lost and helpless, he said he could arrange a seat on the morning flight to Delhi because a friend of his, who worked for Indian Airlines, would see to it.

He arranged the reservation and even lent me some money without the slightest hesitation. It was an experience which was as incomprehensible as it was overwhelming. The manager was a fairly young man from Kerala. I've never met him again.

Back in Delhi, I went to see Ira and Kritish, for Julia was in the private nursing home of Dr Nundy. She hadn't been feeling well even before I left for Calcutta but hadn't said anything because she didn't want to disrupt my plan to visit Calcutta. Kritish and I had a mutual friend, a doctor who Kritish had gone to medical college with: Tapas Roy. Tapas had seen Julia and treated her for dysentery when her problem was hepatitis. This incorrect treatment was responsible for a steady deterioration in her condition. Kritish had suggested that a second opinion should be taken and Tapas had brought along Dr Nundy. Ira and Kritish had moved Julia from our flat at A32 Defence Colony to their house in C Block to begin with, and then Dr Nundy had admitted her to his nursing home because she needed constant care, efficient nursing and round-the-clock medication.

Kritish wasn't at all pleased with me. What made me leave Julia to go back to Calcutta to see Sudarsana at a time when Julia must have been emotionally insecure? Couldn't whatever business I had to transact in Calcutta wait for a few months? A young woman from another country leaves her husband, and is separated from her only child, ten years old, for most of the year, and I leave her to see my ex-wife! Was this fair, compassionate or realistic? I'd never seen Kritish so agitated before. I knew that he was a deeply sympathetic person and he was genuinely fond of both of us. I had great respect and affection for Kritish. His outburst increased that respect and affection.

I tried to explain, as best I could, the reason why it was important for me to see Sudarsana. Kritish calmed down and we turned our attention to the immediate challenge of Julia's illness. We visited Julia. She was beginning to feel better. Dr Nundy decided that it was now safe for her to come home. First she stayed with Ira and Kritish and then returned to our *barshati* at A Block Defence Colony. Before long, she was cooking, cleaning and shopping with her usual zest. Amelita was an Italian friend. We'd met her at Ira and Kritish's house – a warm-hearted and slightly eccentric woman, a few years older than Julia but younger than me. She'd visit us fairly regularly. We liked her outspoken and generous nature. Her husband was an English actor with whom she'd parted company some years back. She had a grown-up son in Italy. She was critical and affectionate, a combination which seemed natural in her case. Our relationship with our landlord's family was also very cordial. We were beginning to feel that we belonged.

Then one morning there was a commotion in the landlord's house downstairs. One of the landlord's three sons – the middle one, Balbir, who was still at college – didn't return home at the end of the day. His family waited all night but he didn't turn up. The next day also he didn't turn up. His father was rushing round, making police reports, taking the advice of friends and relations; and his mother was crying her heart out. We were all distressed, anxious and unhappy. Julia also hadn't shown much interest in cooking, shopping and eating. In the evening, I was preparing my lecture, and Julia was attending to some plants in our modest terrace garden. I was startled out of my task because the door opened noisily and Julia entered in an agitated state. Although she was excited, she was in control and she told me with quiet conviction that she'd just seen a sign in the sky which had convinced her that Balbir was alive and well. Julia believed in the supernatural; therefore, she received messages which weren't available to non-believers like me. While tending the plants, she'd looked up at the evening sky. She said, with tears in her eyes, that if Balbir was alive and well, the Supreme Being in whom she believed should give her a sign. And the heavens had split with a huge flash of lightning. She was then convinced that no harm had come to Balbir. Since she had no doubt at all that the sign had communicated a positive message, she said, she was going to tell Mrs Singh what she had experienced. It could have been a rare coincidence. But it didn't matter, I said to myself.

When Julia told Mrs Singh, she held Julia in an embrace and sobbed with relief. The very next day, Balbir rang from somewhere on the borders between India and Pakistan to say he was safe and well, but he had a story to tell. He couldn't communicate very well, partly because it wasn't a good line. What was important was that he was safe and he was on his way home. Our landlord and his family had always treated us well, but after Julia's message had proved to be true and Balbir returned home, mentally shaken but unhurt, both Julia and I were treated by the

Singh's with special affection and respect. Balbir had seen us briefly, but after a day or two, he came to tell us about his extraordinary experience.

He was returning home from college when two men in a large, new car stopped by his side and offered him a lift to Defence Colony. Without a moment's hesitation, he accepted. One of the men had moved from the front of the car and sat next to him at the back. Quite soon after this, Balbir realized that the car wasn't going in the direction of New Delhi at all. But when he wanted to know what was happening, he was intimidated with a knife and asked to keep quiet. If he behaved himself and did what he was told, the man said, he'd be rewarded, but if he raised an alarm or tried to escape, he would endanger his life.

His assignment was simple. He'd have to carry a rucksack on his back across the border into Pakistan. He would be told where to cross the border. He was required to keep walking in a certain direction until he was stopped and relieved of his rucksack. It sounded like something out of a spy story but too simple to have come out of Le Carré. Did it happen as the man had said? Yes, almost exactly. The plan had worked and he wasn't at any time bullied or treated with rudeness or cruelty. Food was simple fare but he never went without. The large sum of money he was promised never materialised, but it was too large in any case to be true. But he was given enough money to keep him going until he returned home. We speculated about why it was necessary to get him to do their dirty work but couldn't come up with any credible conclusions. We thought his being a turbaned Sikh might have had something to do with it.

Mark came to us for his holidays in the summer of 1973. I enjoyed having Mark around mainly because he was a naturally gentle, pleasant and fun-loving ten-year-old, who loved and trusted his mother and had no difficulty in accepting me as part of her life. We decided that it would be a sensible thing to go for a swim in the humid sub-tropical climate of Delhi and it would be more exciting to go to Badkhal Lake in Faridabad, which is about 32 kilometres from Delhi, than to go to one of the Delhi hotels. We didn't swim in the lake but in a swimming pool close to it. The Badkhal Lake is quite spectacular – with the Aravalli hills around it. On one occasion we took a hotel room and on another we stayed in a small cottage. Apart from swimming and walking, there were other exciting activities one could indulge in. Various species of local and migrant birds were around. Landscaped gardens were beautifully designed, shady and restful. The sunset across the lake was memorable. We looked forward to the experience of spending a few days in summer at Badkhal Lake.

There was at this time a crisis in the life of Aparna, my daughter, the eldest of my three children. She had separated from her husband, Raj Bhagat, and come to live in Delhi. Our mutual friend, Chris Stocks, was then in Delhi, working as an editor for the Oxford University Press. He had a spare room in his *barshati;* Aparna stayed in that spare room. While Aparna was staying temporarily in Chris's spare room – Chris was a friend from her Calcutta days – Mark was with us and he came along when Julia and I went to see a landlord, Colonel Ahluwalia, about renting a *barshati* at Defence Colony, Block C.

It had two rooms – a bedroom and a living room with an attached bathroom; a kitchen, larger than the one in Block A, and a large terrace. It was both larger and better-appointed than our previous accommodation. Colonel Ahluwalia, a turbaned, bearded Sikh gentleman, was most affable. He'd love to have us as tenants. Julia asked him what the rent was, and he told us. Julia and I looked at each other and smiled – disappointed. I thanked Colonel Ahluwalia and said that it was a lovely *barshati,* but not affordable on a lecturer's salary. We got up to leave without finishing our tea and turned towards the door. Mark turned around and said to the colonel, 'We like the *barshati.* We'd love to live in it. Why are you being mean? Why won't you let us have it?'

'Am I being mean, my son?' said Colonel Ahluwalia, affectionately. Then he turned towards me and said, 'How much can you afford, Professor Bagchi?'

I mentioned a sum of money, slightly more than what I could afford at the time. It was really an attractive and comfortable place. It'd be great to be able to live there.

It's yours, *beta*,' Colonel Ahluwalia said to Mark, smiling affectionately. *Beta* in Hindi means 'son'. Then turning to us, he said, 'I hope you'll enjoy living here, Mrs Bagchi and Professor Bagchi. Please drink your tea.' I didn't at first understand why Colonel Singh, like our first landlord, called me 'Professor' when |I was just a lecturer. Then I realised that it was customary in Delhi – as well as in Calcutta – to address and refer to college lecturers as professors.

We shook hands, Colonel Ahluwalia, me and Julia. Mark got both a handshake and a hug. We left Colonel Ahluwalia, feeling happy and excited at the prospect of living at our new address. We told Mark that without his positive intervention we wouldn't have got the flat. He was pleased. That evening we went to our favourite restaurant at Defence Colony, Market Square, and ate *rogan josh* and *rumali roti,* sitting under the summer sky. It was fascinating to watch *rumali rotis* being cooked.

'Why did Colonel Ahluwalia keep calling you 'Professor'?' Julia asked.
'In many parts of India it is customary to call lecturers professors,' I explained.

The open-air restaurant at the Defence Colony Market Square was called Moet's. It was one of our favourite eating places, especially on long summer evenings. While we were eating at the restaurant, we decided that we would suggest to Aparna that she move into the flat at A32 Defence Colony. She did.

Aparna had separated from her husband and started life on her own. I was happy that she'd decided to live in Delhi because I missed my children and, apart from loving her dearly, I respected her. It had baffled me, her falling in love with Raj Bhagat, but neither by word nor deed had I indicated that I found him rather glib and much too clever. Aparna had two MA degrees in English – one from the University of Jadavpur in Calcutta and another from the University of London. Now she wanted a job.

She went for an interview at Miranda House, a women's college affiliated to Delhi University, and was selected. So we both worked on the University campus. I think Aparna enjoyed teaching just as much as I did. Our lives were beginning to look a little more organised. I started taking part in various campus activities. I played cricket for the staff against the students; judged an elocution contest at St Stephen's College; spent an hour at Miranda House, explaining what linguistics was about; was one of two judges at another women's college for a debate. I was beginning to be discovered. Aparna was also settling down at Miranda House.

One late afternoon, after I had finished teaching, I was in the staff room, getting ready to return to Defence Colony. A group of five students came in and stood round the chair where I was sitting. I remember four names – Keval, Kasturi, Niranjan and Gautam. I don't at all remember the name of the fifth student – a bright young man from Orissa in second year English Honours. They had come on a mission. They had heard –probably from one of my colleagues – that I was interested in the theatre, I'd written plays, acted and directed in East Africa and Calcutta. I confirmed that what they'd heard was true. Then Keval, the main spokesperson in the group, explained why they'd surrounded me and prevented me from returning home. There were several drama competitions on the campus every year and the most imminent one was at St Stephen's College. They would like to enter a play. They were hoping that I'd help. I said I would be delighted. It was quite exciting for me, the idea of getting involved in the theatre again. It was also interesting how my minor achievements were catching up with me.

While the other students left, Kasturi stayed back. It was late. The university buses had left. She knew I lived in Defence Colony and she lived in the next colony, a few miles further on. Would it be all right if she came with me? Her parents worried if she returned home on one of the crowded Delhi buses alone. Young women travelling alone on crowded Delhi public buses had often experienced unwelcome behaviour from faceless male passengers, which made them reluctant users of this form of transport.

When I lived in Delhi, Defence Colony was a fairly small ex-army officers' colony where other civil servants of the middle ranks also had houses and flats. Greater Kailash, where Kasturi lived, was to the south of Defence Colony. I said I would be delighted to have her as a travelling companion. When we arrived at Kasturi's Greater Kailash house, her parents were at the door. They looked relieved and thanked me profusely. We had tea together and then I left. Kasturi's parents were affectionate, middle-aged and protective. When I told them of the possibility of our reviving the old Kirori Mal theatre group, they were interested. But the moment I said that Kasturi would probably be an active member of the group, they became quiet and pensive. Rehearsals would mean coming back hours after the regular students' buses left the university campus, so the life and security of their young daughter would be exposed to the rogues and rascals of the shadowy world of Delhi. This would completely rob them of their peace of mind.

I was at the time already planning a production for the St Stephen's College Drama Festival, which was taken very seriously on the university campus. To produce a play, one usually needed both men and women. Kasturi was the only female member of our drama society just then; so she was indispensable. It was important that Kasturi should have the permission of both her parents to participate fully in the activities of our drama society.

'We'll need Kasturi to act in our plays. We'd really like her to participate fully in the drama society's activities. I'll come with Kasturi right up to your doorstep every time there's a rehearsal, performance or meeting,' I said.

Kasturi's parents must have decided that I was a reliable person. They knew of Kasturi's interest in acting and then a man, one of her teachers, comes along and says he'll not only make it possible for her to act but also be her chaperone whenever necessary! Both parents were happy with the arrangement.

In trying to forestall the anxiety of Kasturi's parents, I'd caused a lot of it to Julia. Julia, as always, tried to create the impression that she was in control but she'd worried and wanted to know what exactly had happened. The lack of a telephone in our *barshati* caused us inconvenience and, at times, anxiety. But we had to think carefully before we undertook to do anything that cost money. So the telephone had to wait.

While I was in East Africa, I'd written a play – *The Deviant* – a one-act play with three characters – which, I decided, was an appropriate choice for the competitive drama festival at St Stephen's College. It had a special advantage – it had three characters – Lalit, Shikha and Dibu. I'd cast Keval as Lalit, Kasturi as Shikha and Gautam as Dibu. Its production didn't involve change of scenery and the costumes were contemporary everyday wear. The conflict wasn't anything abstruse or intellectual. It was the recurrent one – between individuals and institutions.

We read and discussed the play and went into rehearsal. We found that setting aside a little time to talk about the play helped its interpretation. When we put on the play on the second or third night, it was well received. This was our first attempt after a gap of many years. We weren't too ambitious. This festival always attracted good plays which were produced not just competently but often with great creative imagination.

The Deviant, quite clearly, had made an impression on the audience. We'd lived up to the high standard of St Stephen's College Festival. People had shown their appreciation and enjoyment with enthusiastic clapping. What more could we hope for? We hadn't fallen short.

The Deviant was staged on a Friday. Other plays were presented over the weekend. I didn't have a car in Delhi, so I didn't take a bus and go to the campus to watch the weekend plays. If the festival plays finished after a particular time, the last bus would have left and I would be stranded. I was interested in the results but didn't have a phone. I decided to wait until Monday morning before I got a detailed account of the adjudication. I'd just stepped into the college compound, when Kasturi, Keval, Gautam and a few other friends and well-wishers met me. They looked unhappy, great disappointment was writ large on all their faces. 'What's the matter?' I asked. Keval said, 'Sir, we're terribly sorry to tell you....' (Long pause, everybody looking miserable…) 'that Kirori Mal College won the best play award.' They all laughed – spontaneously. The timing was good. I was delighted.

'Where's the crowd of admiring students gathered round the shield awarded for best production?' I said.

Kasturi then informed me that the Principal of the College was waiting to congratulate me. The St Stephen's College Drama Festival Award – a silver-plated shield – was in the Principal's office. The Principal got up from his chair and walked up to shake hands with me in appreciation of what we had achieved and said words of genuine praise.

Aparna was settling down at A32 Defence Colony. In the Christmas of 1973, Mark was back in Delhi on holiday. Ira and Kritish threw quite a lavish Christmas party in which at least five others participated – Julia, Surajit, Dean, Mark and me – and were quite high-spirited at the end of the festive occasion. Mark had a special surprise – *Salami* – a dachshund we'd acquired with the help of Surajit, who'd drawn Julia's attention to an ad that dachshund pups were for sale. Julia and Surajit had gone and collected a pup one weekend. We called her *Salami* because dachshunds were sometimes referred to as sausage dogs. But as she grew up, she developed quite a personality. On festive occasions – and moonlit nights – we called her *Salome,* though she didn't dance like the daughter of the King of Galilee.

Our break in winter was just a little more than a fortnight – so there wasn't much we could do. John Blackwell – my former colleague and Julia's former husband, Mark's father, was working for the British Council in Delhi. Mark spent a few days with him, but I liked to think that he preferred our set-up to John's. One important reason for this, I think, was that both Julia and I were there during his holidays to spend time with him and do things together. I was on holiday about the same time as Mark, give or take a week, and Julia did her work – illustrating books – from home. Mark came back in the summer of 1974. We did our usual round of activities, most of which Mark enjoyed. The facilities at Badkhal Lake were not easily accessible, but Hotel Oberoi, 15 minutes ride by auto-rickshaw, had a very popular swimming pool – popular because it was good. We went there from time to time and enjoyed ourselves very much. Mark and I also flew kites from our terrace and from the roof of our bedroom. Mark found kite-flying an exciting experience.

Jill Christie was a friend of a friend of Julia's. She was a teacher. She had come from Reading to teach at Rishi Valley School by arrangement with the Krishnamurthi Foundation. She'd found a room at YWCA to begin with, but soon realized it was expensive and inadequate. Julia's friend, Diana, had given her our Delhi address. Jill wrote to Julia about her predicament. Julia contacted Colonel Ahluwalia, our landlord at C116 Defence Colony and found out that the small room with an attached bathroom above the garage was available for renting – the perfect solution.

The Christies moved in – Jill, Anna and Vicki. Jill went away to teach at Rishi Valley School, while Anna and Vicki stayed with us. Later, Jill returned to Delhi and found herself a teaching post at Delhi International School. She was an interesting and intelligent person. This was obvious when she discussed some of her teaching strategies with me, which were carefully devised to encourage student participation and independent research. I remember the enormous trouble she'd taken to prepare two lessons on D. H. Lawrence's Snake.

Although Jill could at times be unaccountably self-centred, she could also be helpful and efficient. We had a memorable Christmas in 1974 when Anna, Vicki and Mark gave us a carol concert and organised much of our entertainment. Between Julia, Jill and Kishen, they organised a barbecue which was greatly successful. Many friends turned up at the party, which wound up well after midnight. There are occasions in our lives which we like to remember because they make us feel good and it was one of them. There are occasions, of course, which we don't want to remember and wish they hadn't happened. Julia and Jill took Anna, Vicky and Mark to the zoo. It was a pleasant day, and although it was cold, the sun was bright and strong. All was well, but while they were standing quite close to the elephants, one of them whipped away Jill's handbag, scattered whatever was in it and casually rested one of its feet on whatever was near it. The loss wasn't enormous, but Vicki and Anna were frightened and Julia and Jill were shaken – though in retrospect, they also saw the funny side to it.

We enjoyed having the Christies with us, although there were brief moments of stress. There were times when Jill was too laid back, too self-absorbed and remote. She was too involved in radical, intellectual problems to take any interest in mundane activities like cooking and cleaning. I think Jill really believed that she was an intellectual. She very much regretted the fact that her life hadn't provided her with sufficient opportunities to exploit her intellectual potential. This didn't really interfere with our relationship. She was good company and her two daughters were mature for their age. They left a few weeks after the incident with the elephants at the zoo. We missed them.

Our dog Salami, alias Salome, was a dog with unmistakable human characteristics. I didn't like the idea of her being in bed with us. Somehow she'd managed to register this. She'd creep into bed and lie quietly but only after I'd gone to bed, invariably by Julia's side, not mine. It was a well-kept secret between Julia and Salami for some time. Once she fell off the balcony wall, but survived because the grass in the lawn below was thick and wet. She'd sometimes escape into the street below if the door to the terrace – our front door – was left open. Then we had to find her and bring her back and explain to her why it was dangerous for her to run away. She listened patiently but never missed the opportunity to escape. On one such occasion she was hit by a car and died. We missed her. We didn't get another dog. Salami was irreplaceable.

I continued to enjoy my life and work at college. The Kirori Mal College drama group continued to win accolades and prizes in various competitive drama festivals. Sometimes we had rehearsals at our *barshati,* usually out on the terrace. The students in the group were intelligent, sensitive and companionable. Both Julia and I enjoyed their company. There was, however, a problem which we had to face up to. I was teaching, and also writing for Oxford University Press, Julia was doing illustrations for Orient Longman, and editing a book of poems. She was also writing a children's book for Thompsons Press. But we had a sense of insecurity about the money supply. I looked forward to the teaching and felt greatly involved in the production of plays. Yet when Ravi Dayal, who was then the General Manager of the Oxford University Press, proposed that I should join his organisation at a higher salary, I accepted the job of an editor without giving it a second thought.

The Oxford University Press at the time was full of interesting and erudite people – Ravi Dayal, Nirupam Chatterji, Chris Stocks and Adil Tayabji – who were not only exceptionally good at their jobs but also very good company. So although, initially, I felt the wrench, I soon settled down. The fact that some of the books I was editing were interesting and scholarly also made a difference. After the initial upheaval in my professional life, problems disappeared. I found that, apart from the editors, there were others who were well worth getting to know – Ashok Roychowdlhuri, Shampa Banerji, Urvashi Butalia, for example. But we rarely met outside the office. I regret that I didn't get to know any of them really well.

We had now lived in Delhi for four years. Important events had taken place around us, generating discussions and excitement. The impact of political events was probably greater here in the capital than anywhere else. But we registered the news of these events without getting in any way involved in them, although we rejoiced when India and Pakistan signed the Bilateral Simla Agreement to settle future disagreements, not through armed conflicts but through peaceful discussions. This was only a few months after Julia and I had arrived in Delhi to live together. Pope Paul VI visited India in 1973, but it made no impact on us. We registered the fact that India did its first nuclear test explosion at Pokhara in May 1974 and became a nuclear nation, but with mixed feelings. The West Indian cricket team's visit later that year was more important for me. When in April 1975 the first Indian satellite began to orbit in space, I was much more excited. It made a profound impact on the national psyche, because for a country in the developing world, so far behind Europe and the U.S. in science and technology, it was a remarkable achievement.

It was about this time that an Indian government experiment had bizarre consequences. Most Indians accepted that population growth was at the heart of many of our problems, including poverty. Birth control wasn't part of the national culture, so that Indians had large families and the population grew by leaps and bounds. One disturbing feature of the population growth was that the lower the income of the family, the larger the size of the progeny. Something obviously had to be done. Sanjay Gandhi, one of the two sons of Indira Gandhi, introduced a family planning initiative which involved vasectomy for men and tubal ligation for women. For the success of the programme launched, persuasion and reward were the two most frequent methods employed with a modicum of initial success. But persuasion quickly changed into persecution and rewards promoted greed. Then there was the quite powerful consideration of culture. Family planning was an alien concept to most couples. This wasn't a subject one publicly discussed. People – except for a small minority – resented interference with what they considered to be their private domain. Sanjay Gandhi's family planning initiative affected the popularity of Indira Gandhi and the acceptance of the Congress Government.

I was looking back at the years we had lived in Delhi because we were seriously thinking of settling in England, primarily because we'd told Mark we would, and Julia was missing him more and more.

But after the influx of some 30,000 Asians from Uganda in 1972 and more than 20,000 from S.E. Asia, immigration had become a political and emotive issue. I could, however, get permission to live in the U.K. if I was married to Julia. We hadn't got married but lived as partners in Delhi because everybody treated us as husband and wife. They treated us as a married couple because they took it for granted that we were married. I felt that there was an element of deception in our behaviour. On one occasion, when a friend's Muslim wife had invited us to a party and Julia had casually said that we weren't married, there was sudden silence followed by a quick change of subject. Consternation was writ large on the faces of the older women.

It made sense in all kinds of ways to get married. So I went to find out about the registration of our marriage. The official I saw made getting married by registration a complex and tedious business, so I turned to my friend Amal Dutt, who had helped me before. Amal was going away to South India on official business. We fixed a date after his tour was over. Ira and Kritish enthusiastically suggested that the wedding should take place in their house and it did. It was informal. Amal had arranged for one of the registrars of marriages to come to attend the wedding. We signed the book, were given a certificate of marriage and declared man and wife. Amal and Surajit signed as witnesses. Everybody enjoyed the food cooked on the premises by two professional cooks. There was music and dancing and a general feeling of relaxed enjoyment. On the 27th of November, 1976, Julia and I were married in the house of Ira and Kritish De. Apart from Ira and Kritish, the other friends who attended the wedding were Amal, Surajit, Adil Tayabji, Dean Gasper and Chris Stocks. Of my women colleagues only Pronoti came. We managed to create a sense of occasion in which people fully participated.

We'd been married for about a month when Julia went to England to spend Christmas with Mark and her parents. Mark wanted us back and we'd promised that we'd return to England as soon as we'd managed to organize a few preliminaries – like getting married. For me there was another important reason – Julia hadn't been keeping at all well. She'd suffered from various painful diseases including pleurisy, pneumonia and hepatitis and her life had been at risk. Dr Nandy had steered her through some dangerous times. When I told him that we were planning to go away to England, he thought the move might help Julia physically and emotionally. Dr Nandy's approval was most welcome, but our decision to live in England was not influenced by it. We'd made up our minds some time ago. The wheels had been set in motion.

In the Easter of 1977, Julia's mother Freda came over from England and spent six weeks with us in Delhi. Mark came later, on his own. We visited the Taj Mahal, and thought that it richly deserved its reputation as an architectural masterpiece. We also visited Fatehpur Sikri, King Akbar the Great's new capital near Agra, where the emperor had had a great mosque built in red sandstone in memory of Sheikh Salim Christi, a Muslim saint.

Apart from the Taj Mahal, the world-famous mausoleum, there are many other historical sites we might have visited in and around Agra. We used various means of transport, but the most popular of them was the *tonga,* a light, horse-drawn carriage with the same name as the South Pacific Ocean archipelago, Tonga. A *tonga* can be drawn by one or two horses: ours was drawn by one, with whom the *tonga-walla* had a most affectionate relationship. He talked to his horse and I felt certain that the horse understood and responded. The *tonga* ride in Agra was Mark's most exciting and memorable travel experience at the time.

About two and a half kilometres north-west of the Taj Mahal is the historic walled city of Agra Fort, where the Mughal kings lived most of their lives. Very few historic sites have made such an impression on me as this walled city with its palaces, wells, forts and its quite complex system of water supply and drainage. Its sewer system was very advanced for 450 years ago, the methods used for air conditioning in summer and heating in winter were, I gathered, innovative as well as effective. Much of the urban planning was surprisingly modern in its concept.

Mark returned to England at the end of his school holidays, Freda stayed on. One evening I came back from university later than usual. I was hoping to have a relaxed time with Julia and Freda, but they weren't around. I read the newspaper, had a cup of tea and waited for them more than an hour, but they didn't turn up. We had no telephone. Although it was a futile exercise, I went out into the streets of Defence Colony and walked around aimlessly, hoping to catch sight of two English ladies, one with red hair and the other whose hair was beginning to grey. It was getting dark and the street lights came on and I wondered why they didn't leave a note. I can't get away from the fact that I have a tendency to worry whenever life leaves the beaten path – it was almost dinner time and there was no sign of my wife and mother-in-law and no note on the centre table!

Happy and excited chatter was moving up the stairs. I opened the door to see mother and daughter in a delighted frame of mind, laughing and talking, waiting to share some great experience with me.

'Where have you been? I was really worried,' I said.

I realised that it was the wrong thing to say. But I *was* worried. There was an arrangement between Julia and me – because we were new to the city, Julia more than me – that if we had to go out for more than an hour or so, on some unscheduled assignment, we'd leave a note, explaining the situation. It was, however, soon clear why they'd come home late without being able to tell me about it.

They were returning home after some routine, minor shopping from the Defence Market, when a wedding party, with the groom on horseback, ceremonially dressed, and the horse heavily and comprehensively decorated – got in the way. They had to wait until the whole procession moved out of the way. Julia and Freda weren't exactly waiting impatiently for the procession to get out of the way – they were watching, quite fascinated. A middle-aged Punjabi man, part of the wedding party, having noticed their interest and excitement had suggested that they came with him to watch the beginning of the ceremony. They hadn't needed too much persuasion. They were really, really glad that they'd gone.

They didn't understand the language in which the ceremony was conducted – Punjabi, for it was a Punjabi Sikh wedding. But the customary celebration of these weddings – Hindu or Sikh – has some common popular features – ritual singing, dancing, special food and wedding costumes. In a Sikh wedding, the turbans also add to the sartorial extravaganza: turbans, saris, *kameezes* and shawls of many colours as well as Western-type suits and ties. The music wasn't quite their kind of music. They weren't initially impressed with it, but they enjoyed the dancing and realized that the music and the dancing were very much made for each other. They weren't just interested, but fascinated, entranced. And the fact that they were treated as two very special guests had added to the pleasure of their adventure. I listened with real interest to Julia and Freda's account of the wedding. Then we sat down to eat our dinner, during which I did the eating, and Julia and Freda, the talking.

Freda left a few days later, and we turned our attention to preparing for our new adventure – setting out for and settling in England. Was it going to be easy or was it going to be difficult? Having been in uncertain situations twice already – once when I landed in Calcutta in 1966 without a job at the age of 42, and then in Delhi at 48, and having found regular employment on both occasions – I'd gained a little confidence. But there was a much greater challenge in the situation this time round – an Indian teacher of English having to compete with teachers of English who had not only spoken the language all their lives but had also learnt to teach it as a second or other language – was a much harder proposition. Anyway, worrying about such problems so much in advance was quite futile. What was important just now was to apply for a visa to enter the United Kingdom. Being the husband of a United Kingdom citizen, my entitlement couldn't be questioned. How soon I got it was the question. The British High Commission then, as now, was in Shantipath, Chanakyapuri, New Delhi. I applied for my visa and in due course Julia and I went to the Visa Department of the High Commission for my visa interview. Since my entitlement to enter Britain was as husband of a British citizen, Julia was also being interviewed.

While we were waiting in the visitors' room along with one or two others, a young man in his late thirties walked up to me and asked me, very politely, what I was waiting for. When I said I'd come for a visa interview, he pointed in the direction of the sheds outside, which were hot and crowded, and said we should go and wait there.

'My wife isn't well and the sheds are hot, crowded and uncomfortable,' I said.

'That is where all visa applicants are supposed to wait,' the young officer repeated, raising both his eyebrows, staring straight into my eyes and looking somewhat confrontational.

'The heat and the crowd in the sheds won't do my wife any good. So we'd like to stay here until we're called for our interview,' I repeated.

'I see,' said the young diplomat and disappeared. He didn't reappear with a warrant of arrest.

I wasn't being obstinate or awkward. The British High Commission in Chanakyapuri had built very basic sheds for those who came for visa applications or interviews. They were basic and uncomfortable, designed, I thought, to discourage immigration. Julia was recovering from hepatitis and it could do irreparable damage to her fragile condition. Both Julia and I were relieved that there was no further confrontation. I know people who look for confrontation and enjoy the experience; I don't. We were left alone until we were sent for to appear for the interview.

The diplomat who interviewed us was charming and businesslike. He assured us that there wouldn't be any problems with my entering Britain and residing there as the spouse of a U.K. citizen, but the problem was that the influx of immigrants had to be carefully controlled to forestall too much pressure on employment, accommodation, goods and services. How long was the likely period of waiting? I asked. It could be as long as a year. We knew that the High Commissioner wouldn't block my entry to the U.K. and it might be a month or two before we were actually able to meet up with Mark, but a year's wait would certainly be trying for us and disappointing for Mark.

Accidents, broken promises, disappointments – and anything else that catches us unawares – require adjustment, both practical and psychological. In our case, no great readjustment was necessary in our day-to-day living. I continued working for the Oxford University Press, travelling to the office pillion-riding on Adil Tayabji's motorbike. Julia continued with the work of illustrating English textbooks for schools and attending to her domestic duties.

And we waited – for the pleasure of Queen Elizabeth II to let me travel to and settle in the United Kingdom as the husband of a U.K. citizen. The legal hurdle was overcome but I had to wait for my turn. Waiting can't always be taken out of wanting, but the uncertainty of a few months ago was now gone. We were able to tell everybody, especially Mark, that we were now getting ready to come across in a matter of months. For me, the new beginning wasn't exactly the fulfilment of a deeply-cherished ambition. I'd liked the time – almost a year – which I'd spent, mainly in London, as a student. But I didn't have to go looking for jobs or sign up for unemployment benefits. However, the anxiety was peripheral.

Julia and I began to pay more attention to whatever was happening in England. 1976 was a hot, dry summer, the driest in more than two hundred years, we gathered. And, in spite of the economy being far from robust, there was a feeling of well-being and a general and pervading sense of safety.

But dramatic changes followed: the heat led to drought and drought was the forerunner of widespread floods. The country's economy was also on the verge of collapse and had to be propped up by the international bankers with loans running into billions of pounds.

Whatever the political and economic situation might be in Britain, it wasn't going to affect our decision to settle in England, because the reason for the move wasn't either political or economic. It was Mark, who had been separated from both his parents and one of them was going to move closer to him. And Julia would certainly feel better, both physically and emotionally. But when exactly we could travel depended now on the British High Commissioner, whose responsibility was to ensure that immigration to Britain didn't cause serious demographic imbalance and popular resentment at a time when the average wage was around £72 a week and it was not at all easy to get a mortgage.

Was 1977 going to be any better? Labour was still in power as a result of a coalition with the Liberals. David Steel and James Callaghan were just about managing to hold back the Tories, but there was a general feeling of uncertainty and restlessness in the air and little indication of political stability. Inflation, political unrest, anxiety and insecurity were all part of 1976 and 1977 in the UK, yet there was no sign of total despair. Yes, the people seemed to say, there's enough hope to keep us going, for this can't go on for ever!

India is rather a long way away from England, so we weren't at all certain of our assessment. Our efforts to find out what was happening in England were natural interest rather than anything else, because we'd have wanted to live in England even if a bloody revolution was on the way. But a revolution wasn't on the way. What was really happening – and more was on the way – was economic decline. There were, however, some feel-good events: the Queen, Elizabeth II celebrated her Silver Jubilee, and Virginia Wade won Wimbledon.

The issue of immigration at the time was real because the United Kingdom had to accommodate about 30,000 people of Asian origin who'd made Uganda their home but were thrown out by Idi Amin in 1972. They had British passports, acquired during the time Uganda was a protectorate and administered by the British. It was really a British colony, with the Kabaka of Buganda retaining some autonomy. When Uganda became independent in 1962, we all rejoiced, we all celebrated, but I left about two years after that.

Just seven years later, the Ugandan Asians were expelled by Idi Amin, and the majority of those hapless people found shelter in the United Kingdom. I was now going to join them – after having spent nearly 12 years in India. We all look back, sometimes in anger, sometimes with satisfaction, but most often with mixed feelings. By and large, I looked upon my years in Uganda with nostalgia, because I liked those I'd got to know – some Ugandan, some British, some South African and one or two Americans – apart from those from my own sub-continent.

I want to mention a few people here because I'd like their names to be associated with mine – Charles Kabuga, a student at the teacher training college; Erisa Kironde, a Ugandan friend; Marge and Murray Carlin; Naresh Sengupta and Jonathan Kingdon; D.J. Raval and Dr Jayant Thacker were all friends whose company I enjoyed. Some of my other friends were Meriel Watkins, Carol Harlow, Carol Fry, Paul and Valerie Vowles, Sheila Fordham, Don and Joyce Mann. The list is by no means complete. Sudarsana and I had many good friends in Kampala.

England was a country I first knew as a married and mature student. When I came to do a Post Graduate Certificate in Education at the Institute of Education in London, Sudarsana and I were both there. After that, when I came to England on three other occasions, I was on my own for two or three months, on specific educational assignments, I didn't have to pay the air-fare and I didn't have to earn a living in England.

This time it was different. I was going a long way away. Would I be able to keep in touch with Sudarsana, my children and grandchildren? These thoughts did float around in my mind. I was unhappy about the fact that I wouldn't be able to visit

Calcutta and keep in touch with Sudarsana, Nondon, Aparna and Aparajita regularly. I'd also lose touch with my two grandchildren – Benjamin and Sharon. Sudarsana hadn't once made a scene or accused me of being selfish and worthless. On the contrary, she'd given me the impression that she welcomed my visits to Calcutta during the long summer holidays. But now that I was going to be more than 4,000 miles and almost ten hours' flight away, there wouldn't be the same opportunity to see family and friends in Delhi and Calcutta.

Well, a new beginning almost always has its uncertainties. It usually gives one a sense of adventure. But it also means, quite often, separation from friends and family. All kinds of thoughts were going through my mind, but the fact that we'd already set out for England, mentally, was undeniable.

It wasn't really the best of times, the fragile coalition between Labour and the Liberals wasn't likely to hold for long and Mrs Thatcher, the leader of the Tories, was quite confidently waiting in the wings to take over. A life-long socialist, I didn't like the sound of Margaret Thatcher and her politics. I wasn't particularly impressed with contemporary India either.

The Indian Emergency had come into operation at the end of June, 1975 and ended in March 1977. It had created tension, anger and frustration. George Fernandes, the fiery socialist trade union labour leader, along with others who opposed the Indian Congress government's reactionary policies, was arrested. Widespread protests had led to the declaration of an Emergency, which enabled Indira Gandhi to stay in power, but not for long. Before Julia and I left India, both Indira Gandhi and Sanjay Gandhi lost their Lok Sabha seats and the Janata Party President, Morarji Desai, became India's Prime Minister. Was this government going to last? Was much needed economic recovery going to happen? There were many uncertainties both in the country we were leaving – Julia and I – and the country we were heading for.

But more than the future of James Callaghan and Labour, and Indira Gandhi and the Indian National Congress, what concerned me was my separation from people in India – mainly Calcutta and Delhi – which was getting closer each day. There was a sense of solidarity among those who were in Calcutta. Nondon and Sudarsana in Dover Road had settled down to life without me. Aparajita and her husband, Ian Zachariah, didn't give me the impression of being deeply involved in each other's life and interests. There was something in their relationship which worried me. I also felt that Ian didn't want to get too close to us. Much of the time in the evening, when we were together after a day's work, Ian would read thrilling paperbacks like

Le Carre's novels rather than talk to any of us. I was impressed with his concentration. He could sit in the middle of a group of noisy talkers, discussing politics, literature or the rising price of things, and calmly read Le Carre. When I was preparing to go to England, Aparajita and Ian, with their child, Benjamin, were staying with Sudarsana at Dover Road. I was happy about that.

It was Aparna who was being amazingly and quietly brave. She'd left family and friends in Calcutta, got herself a job at Miranda House – a women's college with a good academic record, affiliated to Delhi University – entirely on her own initiative. She'd moved to A32 Defence Colony when we moved to C116, and now that we were moving to England, I proposed to our landlord that Aparna should be his new tenant, a proposal he accepted unhesitatingly. This *barshati* had two rooms – a living room and a bedroom with an attached bathroom and toilet and a spacious terrace. Julia had always been a good home-maker and Aparna appreciated tidy, elegant surroundings. Some academics have a natural indifference to dust and cobwebs. Aparna certainly wasn't one of them. We felt good that Aparna was going to take over our little flat.

My visa had come through. The worst phase of the Indira Gandhi government – with its forced sterilization of men and women, unlawful detention of people and undemocratic treatment of political dissent – was now over. The Janata Party, along with some members of the Lok Sabha, formed the government and for the first time since India had become independent, we had a Prime Minister who wasn't the leader of the Indian National Congress. Was it a good outcome of the turbulent and undemocratic years of the early seventies? I had no idea at the time. But it was a significant political development because the people of India had said an unequivocal no to undemocratic governance. I wanted the new government to work because the decision to oust dynastic rule was spontaneous and popular and the Indira Gandhi regime militated against my values. Though it was a pity that I was going away, without experiencing the results of the change.

I got married to Julia in 1976 and was leaving for England in 1977. I ought to acknowledge here that Sudarsana was both generous and co-operative. She was quite incapable of doing anything spiteful or malicious. I'd visited Calcutta many times during my five years' stay in Delhi, and spent time with her, Nondon, and my two grandchildren – Ben and Sharon. Sudarsana had also taken the initiative in getting a divorce, which had cleared the way to my being married to Julia and leaving India to settle in England. It may be incredible but it was indisputably true that we rarely argued or indulged in any kind of recrimination after we had decided to go our separate ways. Equally remarkable was the fact that Julia never asked me questions about why I regularly left her during the long summer vacations while I was working at Kirori Mal College to go to Calcutta. I think most of us experience generosity during our lifetime which we often either fail to notice or acknowledge. Julia had accepted, without the slightest hesitation, that I would not only keep in touch with Sudarsana but also visit her and the children and grandchildren in Calcutta. And Sudarsana had rarely felt embarrassed or resentful when I'd spent most of my summer holidays at the Dover Road flat in Calcutta. If either of them had any inner conflicts, they didn't reveal them by word or deed.

I had three sisters living in and around Calcutta, but I had little contact with them. I didn't take any special trouble to let my friends and relations know when I was leaving and where I was going – the only decisions we'd made so far. We were leaving in the second, possibly the third week of July, and we were going to stay with Julia's parents in Stanmore. Once again I'd be without a job and so would Julia. My longest period of joblessness since I'd come back from Uganda was in Delhi. I had also to wait almost as long in Calcutta before I was offered a job by the British Council. I didn't like the waiting but I didn't panic. I think I'd learned not to be too agitated and insecure because of my optimism. Sudarsana used to call it insanity.

At the time I didn't know any more about Stanmore than Julia had told me. It was in Greater London, part of the Borough of Harrow, between ten to twelve miles north-west of London. A fairly affluent and mixed population lived there – mainly Christian, but also Muslim, Jewish and Hindu. Julia's parents lived in an area of Stanmore called Kynance Gardens to which they moved from Sidcup after the sustained bombing of London – the *blitz Krieg* had started, and continued night after night. Julia was just over a year old when these sudden and devastating air raids were reducing London to rubble. Wave after wave of fighter planes and bombers flew over London, night after night, dropping their lethal cargo on one of the most densely populated cities of the world. History books tell us that there were 76 consecutive nights of bombing in London at some point between 1940 and 1941 and more than a million buildings were destroyed. By the end of May 1941, more than 20,000 civilians had lost their lives in London and a similar number had died elsewhere in adjacent areas. The house in which Julia, her brother Paul and her parents lived was destroyed by a bomb in 1941. Fortunately, they were all away at the time. It was after that, that the Rose family – Julia, Paul and their parents – moved to Kynance Gardens in Stanmore. That was the house we were destined for, a house in which Julia's parents had lived for 36 years – first as tenants and then as owners.

We were travelling Delhi-Moscow-London with the Russian airline company, Aeroflot. The airport in Moscow – Domodedoro – didn't impress us. The Russian women – most of them overweight and sullen, and the men, coldly efficient – certainly didn't give us a feeling of homecoming. I hoped Heathrow would be better – Heathrow, our destination, which we hoped to reach in a few hours.

I was excited. There were various reasons why I found London exciting. What was uppermost in my mind just now was the certainty of meeting up with some of my old friends – Naresh, Ramenda, Sachinda, Pravin and others – victims of the expulsion of Asians from Uganda by Idi Amin in 1972. The Asians thrown out of Uganda – around 30,000 of them – had been accommodated in Britain, although other countries also accommodated them in smaller numbers. Quite a few returned to India and Pakistan, but they also went to Canada, Australia, West Germany and the United States.

Because of the large number of Asians in Britain, this group of people was often the victim of racial discrimination and prejudice. For me, however, the prospect of meeting up with old friends was an important incentive. So when Julia and I landed in Heathrow, I was full of excitement and expectation as well as fear and trepidation. Julia, however, showed no sign of uncertainty. It was the culmination of five years' planning, for she had wanted to return to England to reunite with Mark. We were in different queues because I had an Indian passport and Julia had a U.K. one. After the immigration officers had dealt with our passports, we met up for baggage reclaim and customs. All this meant more waiting and a few more questions, but we didn't mind. We'd soon be meeting up with Julia's brother and mother, who were waiting to meet us.

Now there was an anti-climax, not for Julia but for me. While Julia wheeled our baggage towards the exit, I had to go to the health control room and get checked for tuberculosis, a disease which affected a very large number of people in developing countries. It is understandable, therefore, that there should be concern in the U.K. about immigrants from the third world carrying the disease, putting lives at risk in the U.K. All this I understood and accepted. Yet I felt disappointed that I had to wait in a depressing environment with three others to be tested for tuberculosis. The nurse was a pleasant, middle-aged woman and the doctor was a Bengali, probably from my city, Calcutta, who was quite young – maybe in his late thirties. They were doing what they were supposed to do, quickly and efficiently, and yet I resented being held up at the end of a long flight.

The test was painless. The friendly doctor did his tests and smiled a friendly smile. He didn't think there was anything wrong with me. Then he shook hands and said, 'Welcome to Blighty. You'll find it a friendly place – by and large.'

He also told me that I would receive a letter in about two weeks, requesting me to go to a clinic in the area where I lived to undergo a chest x-ray. It didn't matter what I'd have to do in a week, a fortnight or a month. I was at last free to meet up with Julia and her brother, Paul, and her mother, Freda, who'd been waiting for me for a long time. We exchanged greetings: I shook hands with Paul; and Freda welcomed me with a cordial hug. I was back in England after a lapse of eight years. But there was a significant difference from my previous visits and this one: I wasn't just visiting. I was going to live and work here for the rest of my days. At least, that was the idea. In other words, a significant change had happened in my life: I'd left India and I was going to live in England.

My life as an immigrant had just started at a time when immigrants weren't the best-loved people in England. When I was in Leeds in 1968-69 for about four months, Enoch Powell was trying to cause panic among the white British citizens by warning them about the dire consequences of immigration. It was clear that he wasn't worrying about white American, Canadian, Australian or South African immigrants when he made his 'Rivers of Blood' speech. Although it has come to be known as the 'Rivers of Blood' speech, he never actually used those words. He said 'the River Tiber foaming with much blood'. He continued to use provocative racist language long after I left Leeds, warning that the white people of the country would be 'made strangers in their own country'. The list of impending disasters that he predicted was long and frightening.

Fortunately Enoch Powell's racist speeches didn't make any real difference to the lives of the immigrants. Politically, however, his speech didn't do *him* any good. It demonstrated that he couldn't be trusted and Edward Heath sacked him from his post of Shadow Defence Secretary. That was a long time ago. What concerned me was what was happening *now*.

I was somewhat apprehensive because this was the time when James Callaghan's Labour Party was still in power, thanks to David Steele's Liberal Party, which had kept the Government from falling. But Margaret Thatcher, the first woman ever to lead a British political party, was waiting in the wings to be centre-stage in British politics. Callaghan wasn't going to last very long, I thought. What's more, I'd gathered that Margaret Thatcher was a strong leader. I didn't like the sound of her at all. But then I knew very little of the actual situation and thought who became the next Prime Minister of Britain wasn't really going to make any amazing difference to the lives of Julia and Ganesh Bagchi. As it happened, it did.

'You're very quiet,' Paul said. Paul was driving and I was sitting next to him in the front seat.

'I was thinking of British politics and the new leader of the Tory Party – a most confident woman with a strident voice,' I said.

'Margaret Thatcher is absolutely the right leader for the country. The Unions are getting out of hand and the only person who can deal with them is Margaret Thatcher,' Paul said, with confidence.

I pointed out that I'd spent only a few hours in the country this time round, so I couldn't offer any informed view on the current political situation. Then I kept quiet, by and large, while Paul proceeded to educate me about the country's politics. There were various problems – the utterly self-interested and short-sighted unions, the economic downturn, the rising unemployment. Then there was this quite massive problem of immigration. Only a few people, in particular Enoch Powell, understood the enormity of the problem. Apart from anything else, his country was a small island, so it couldn't be expected to host countless immigrants, especially from underdeveloped countries.

'Immigrants can make a difference in a positive way,' I suggested.

'They can, I suppose, but they don't,' was Paul's confident reply. Paul is all together a confident sort of person.

We were travelling a distance of about ten miles. Paul wasn't, therefore, able to present to me all the most important reasons why immigration should be stopped forthwith. It wasn't a good beginning for me.

Paul spoke with conviction. I wondered whether he realized that he was actually speaking to an immigrant and, if we looked back far enough, we might find that his ancestors were also immigrants. It was never easy to stop immigrants – sometimes they came in broad daylight – killed, raped, plundered – and then settled down. No passports demanded.

It was different now. Paul's conviction that the evil of immigration was blighting the lives of his people set me thinking.

The Romans left after about 400 years, but the Jutes, the Angles and the Saxons didn't. People from Denmark and Norway also came and settled and didn't go away. And how about 1066 and all that? For better or worse, this island-country has attracted immigrants – hordes of them. Some came through the front door, armed: that's history. Some have come legitimately for work, some through marriage. There's also a large number that live here illegally. For one reason or another, immigration will always happen. William the Conqueror didn't need a visa. I did. I also had Her Majesty the Queen's official permission. When official permission is withheld, determined and highly motivated people try to find a way round it. And desperate people find desperate remedies. This is how it's been in the past and this is how it will be in the future.

It was good to meet Fred, Julia's father. He was about 5 foot 10 inches tall, with a healthy tan all over his bald head and long, lean face. He had a short pointed beard with streaks of white, a moustache, also more black than white, and friendly eyes. I felt comfortable with him almost instantly.

'How do you feel?' Fred asked. 'Tired?'

'I should feel tired, but I don't,' I said.

'Jet lag often waits before it hits. I don't fly across continents, so I don't know a lot about it... Would you like a cup of tea? I'm going to make some,' he said.

I said I'd love a cup of tea, and Fred got up and left. I liked my father-in-law. He was gentle, soft-spoken and generally low-key. In the short time I'd spent with him, I was already convinced that I'd get on with Fred. What had already endeared him to me was that he was just as apprehensive as I was that Mr Callaghan's coalition with Mr Steele wasn't going to last and Mrs Thatcher would become the U.K.'s new Prime Minister. It was a good thing, we agreed, that we were at last going to have a woman Prime Minister but it wasn't such a good thing that this new Prime Minister was inflexible and over-confident. We also thought that socialism in Britain was in for a rough ride.

Julia was with Freda, probably working out the practical aspects of our living together. Freda had some idea about our preferences already because she'd spent some time with us in Delhi. Probably they were also discussing other important matters – like how to make the separation of his parents as painless as possible for Mark.

Fred returned with the tea. It was clear that he took the making and serving of tea seriously. The tea was excellent, made by a connoisseur.

He said he hoped that I'd soon settle down, although, politically, Britain was going through uncertain times. He was a socialist and had always voted Labour, but it looked as if the Tories were going to be voted into power at the next election. It was when a nation despaired that it entrusted their future with some blustering, over-confident leader. That leader was going to be Margaret Thatcher, he said. I was pleased because I was a socialist and would certainly vote Labour, and I too didn't like the sound of Margaret Thatcher. On the subject of immigration, Fred was an outspoken critic of his countrymen. He disliked political parties exploiting prejudice and regretted the government's failure to educate people politically.

'We have tea and political ideology in common. That should keep us going,' he said.

Julia and Freda joined us. Julia was excited because Mark was coming home from boarding school to spend the weekend with us. Another of my new beginnings was happening in Kynance Gardens, Stanmore, Harrow, England. When we begin, we often think of a middle and an end. But I don't think I did. Instead, events from the recent past crowded into my head. I wondered how Sudarsana, Aparna, Aparajita, Nondon and I were going to make our adjustment to the fact that I was now going to live so far away. But then the human animal has an incredible capacity to make adjustments, I thought. And I hoped that nobody had been laid low by the hurt I'd caused.

'Is it true' Nondon had said, 'that you're going away?'
'Yes,' I'd said.

Nondon had said nothing except 'See you later, Baba'.

'Would you like another cup of tea?' Fred asked.

'Yes, please. I'd love another cup of tea,' I said.

1977 was an eventful year. Idi Amin had thrown out thousands of Asians from Uganda. Most of them had come to Britain to start a new and uncertain life. Stephen Bantu Biko, the anti-apartheid activist had died in custody in South Africa. It was fairly certain that his death was caused by the repressive government's brutal police.   Egypt had broken ranks with other Arab countries to make peace with Israel.   The Soviet Union had celebrated the sixtieth anniversary of the Bolshevik Party.

In Britain, the Queen's silver jubilee and Virgina Wade's victory in Wimbledon were good news.   What wasn't good news for me – and Fred – was that the Labour government seemed to be on its last legs, a rampant Margaret Thatcher was waiting to take over, and Britain's economy, after a steady decline, was heading for a crisis.

It was at this point of time that Julia and I arrived in England, in July 1977, for another new beginning in our life together – new beginning number two.

Chapter 16

Living in England, Mark, Robert, Play

The longest I'd lived in Britain before now was about a year in 1954-55, of which I'd spent six weeks in North Wales and the rest in Finchley Central in Greater London. But in July 1977, I was back in England to live with Julia, presumably, for the rest of my days.   We were going to live in Stanmore, Harrow, with Julia's parents to begin with. Harrow was then an outer borough of London and Stanmore was part of it. A large number of Asians lived in Harrow, most of them immigrants, cast out by Uganda's insane dictator, Idi Amin. I hadn't personally encountered any racism during my previous visits, but there had been quite an influx of immigrants, especially Asian immigrants, since the last time I was here.   Resentment against immigrants was strong, especially non-white immigrants.   One of the reasons for this was that white immigration was invisible, and just as white Australians or South Africans came in, white Britons went out.   What's more, the number of economic migrants among the white Australians or South Africans wasn't creating an imbalance. At least, that was the current conviction. There lurked within me a slight feeling of apprehension. Will my presence here be resented?

I liked the feel of Stanmore – friendly people, peaceful environment, large, leafy trees lining the streets, open spaces, parks, and gardens. It was an affluent borough, with a good shopping centre near the railway station, a medieval church, St Mary's, on Harrow Hill, and, not far from there, the well-known public school, Harrow. There were some Asians near where we lived, most of them fairly well-to-do – a chemist, a teacher of Mathematics in a local school, some traders. The chemist was a pleasant young Gujarati man – Mukund – thrown out by Idi Amin from Uganda. Mukund became a good friend – Julia's and mine.

For me, an attractive feature of living in Harrow was that London was easily and quickly accessible. Apart from the fact that London is a great city, lying astride a great river, I had a personal relationship with London, the nature of which is difficult to define.   There was something liberating in the air of England for me. Apart from that, I found London attractive because I thought that it had a lot in common with Calcutta, where I grew up from a boy into a young man, and from a young man into a married man with two little daughters. The quality which the two cities most significantly shared was humanity. Both cities were densely populated; both were people's cities, though Calcutta didn't have quite the diversity of people that London had.   When I thought of Calcutta, it wasn't so much Chowringhee or Esplanade, Tollygunge, Ballygunge, or Shambazar that came to my mind: it was the people – people I knew and people I didn't know. Similarly, London wasn't 'the Square Mile' or 'the City'. Nor was it the 'City of Westminster'.

It was the people, who lived and loved and did ordinary things in an ordinary way, as well as people who'd written immortal plays, painted immortal pictures, in which light, colour and space had created a new and exciting world. There were also the people who'd built great churches and cathedrals, picture galleries and museums. London always reminded me of Calcutta – another great, vibrant and human city, full of creative people.

There were places I'd visited in London before, which I wanted to visit again – the street market in Portobello Road, for example, and other places in and around Notting Hill Gate. In the fifties, the West Indians had come and settled there, and my impression was that their informality, loud laughter and love of fun had made a difference to the place. A culture at the heart of which there is love of fun and which is inclusive is highly attractive. Our idea of Portobello Road might have been somewhat romantic. But I would certainly want to go there again with Julia.

How exactly I'd managed to push my existential problems – a job, accommodation and transport to the back of my mind, I don't know. But on my arrival back in England, my head was full of all the exciting things I'd do in one of my favourite cities. London has earned many epithets. It has been called an unreal city, an eternal city, a vision, a dream. For me, above all, it was a human city. I was a beneficiary of its warmth and humanity for a short time 23 years ago. I'd come back, hoping for more.

High up on my agenda was employment. But before I applied for a job, I had to, or was expected to, register as unemployed and claim unemployment benefits. Whatever might be the case, Freda and I went up to the appropriate place one morning and queued up. The man standing immediately behind me was tall, lean and unshaven, dressed in shabby clothes. He tapped me on the shoulder from behind and said, 'Hi mate, where do you come from?'

It wasn't yet the middle of the day, but he'd already imbibed enough alcohol to make his speech sound like a drawl.

'Kynance Gardens, Stanmore,' I said.

'I don't mean that. I meant which country do you come from?' he said.

'I come from India,' I said.

'Then what are you doing here?' he asked.

'I'm doing the same as you,' I said.

'Why don't you go back to wherever you come from,' he said, 'and grow bananas?'

'Why bananas?' I asked. 'Calcutta isn't famous for growing bananas.'
I moved on and attended to the business in hand, which was registration. The man behind me in the queue was now awaiting his turn, but still going on about too many people coming into this small island. Some people around us were amused, some embarrassed. None of us took him seriously. A small island and too many black and brown immigrants, however, was as an popular idea then as now.

I think I got one cheque from Social Welfare while I was looking for a job. Julia had already landed one as a sales person. She was selling Bontempi electric organs. I'd go with her from time to time. Once she got an order for a dozen instruments, which was worth quite a lot of money. Since she'd earned a sizeable commission, we went to a pub which had an old-world atmosphere and had a good lunch. I liked going out with Julia in our second-hand Skoda, which was in fairly good condition. It gave us a certain sense of freedom. We bought the Skoda because Julia had to have a car for her sales job and she also had to go for a week's training. While she was away, I looked frantically for an appropriate job, but I was beginning to despair when Freda suggested that I saw someone – a fairly senior executive – in the Department of Education in Harrow. Freda had worked in Harrow's Education Department a long time ago and therefore she had a fairly good idea of how to go about the business of finding employment there.

'Hang on,' she said. 'Let me ring the secretary and see if I can fix an appointment.'

Freda believed in precipitate action. 'What have we got to lose?' she asked and rang. Without any difficulty, she fixed me an appointment with one of the Education Officers. It would be ideal, I thought, if I could teach in one of the schools around here. After all, I had more than 25 years' teaching experience in Uganda and India, and a Post Graduate Certificate in Education from the University of London – requisite qualifications, as well as years of experience. The Education Officer, about 40 years' old, was formally dressed, relaxed and friendly. He was most reassuring: he didn't see any reason why I shouldn't be offered a job in one of Harrow's many schools. The problem was that right at that moment, he couldn't think of any school which was looking for my kind of teacher. But I should check the appropriate papers for vacancies in local schools.

I didn't have to wait long. Canon's High School in Edgware was looking for a teacher who could help some pupils, whose mother tongue was Gujrati, with learning enough English to communicate with others in English.

It'd also help if they understood the language well enough to follow what the teachers were saying in the classroom. Not all immigrant pupils needed this help, but there were enough of them to justify the employment of an ESL (English as a Second Language) teacher at Canon's High School. The post was advertised and Harrow Education Department had forwarded my application to Margaret Thorne, who was the person in charge of ESL in Harrow. I was short-listed for an interview at Canon's High School and received a letter asking me to attend.

I had attended quite a few of these interviews because I'd changed jobs several times. But the idea of being asked questions by several men and women sitting on the other side of a table has never appealed to me. I knew it was unavoidable, so I did my best to be reconciled to it. I remember four of my tormentors – Margaret Thorne, head of ESL; Mr Becker, headmaster of Canon's High School; the deputy head of the school – a woman – and one of the education officers from Harrow Education Department. There was no problem. The interview was based on mutual respect. There was no attempt to show me up or catch me out. The panel was more interested to know what I considered to be the most efficient way of teaching a second language and what I thought were going to be the most likely problems. They also wanted to know whether I thought the problems and challenges of teaching ESL here were likely to be different here from those I had encountered in Uganda and India. It was quite a long interview, but hadn't seemed very long, which I thought was a good sign.

I returned home feeling relieved that it was over and that at no point of the interview did I feel out of my depth. But getting a job was so crucial – Julia's work was temporary – that it was goodbye to the tranquil mind until I'd heard from the Harrow Education Department. Even if I'd failed, I'd rather know as soon as possible. But the panel of judges was in no hurry to fulfil my expectations. I waited for what seemed to be an inordinately long time, but nothing happened. No letter arrived from the Department of Education to put my mind at rest. Words like patience, fortitude and optimism came to mind. I reminded myself of Alfred the Great and his legendary patience at the time of the Danish invasion. But nothing helped. Nobody rang. No letter came by post saying whether or not I had been selected. When I was satisfied that I'd waited long enough, I started looking again at the advertisements for jobs. There was one for a tutor of ESL in an English language school in Eastbourne. I looked up Eastbourne on the map. It was in East Sussex on the English Channel coast. Julia told me that it was a modern resort town with spacious and attractive residential areas. I decided to apply for the post of tutor at Eastbourne English Language Teaching School. Since I'd had several copies of my C.V. typed out already, sending in an application took no time at all, and the Director of the School also asked me over for an interview quite quickly. Our newly acquired Skoda was very useful because we were able to drive up to Eastbourne to meet Roger on the appointed day, in a relaxed and leisurely way.

Roger had arranged to interview me over lunch in an upmarket restaurant. He was businesslike, friendly and knowledgeable. From the questions he asked, it was clear that he understood both the academic and the practical aspects of teaching English as a second language. This was not surprising because he'd run his school fairly successfully for a few years. Most of his students came from Arab countries, he said, and only a few from mainland Europe. He'd asked me to come for an interview because he'd found my C.V. impressive, but he also knew that C.V.s didn't always tell the whole story. Anyway, he was happy to be able to offer me the job, although he had always employed an Englishman or English woman before. It also made sense, he said, to have someone English or British to teach English because his students expected to be taught by someone whose vernacular was English. However, he was sure that he'd made the right choice. So, welcome to Eastbourne and his English Language College!

Why did Roger have to say all that? Was he making the point that he'd gone against the tradition of the institution in asking me to teach there and he sincerely hoped that I'd teach at least as well as my English colleagues? I didn't know what to make of it.

After I'd spent nearly an hour with Roger, Julia joined us. She found Roger pleasant and helpful. The language teaching classes, he told us, took place on the ground floor and the first floor of the school building. I'd have a room on the second floor. For meals, I'd have to come down to the ground floor. Julia was most welcome to come and stay with me whenever she wanted. Roger hoped that the arrangement would be adequate and I'd enjoy living and teaching there. I thought it was a successful day: first I'd got a teaching post in an ESL institution, and then I was expected to do the kind of work I'd been doing for years in different countries and with different age groups. Not only was the environment where I was going to work pleasant, but so also was the surrounding area. Beyond the town, further south, were the high cliffs at Beachy Head, 534 feet high, and beneath that, the sea. After saying goodbye to Roger, we drove up to the Channel coast and then drove back to Stanmore. There was still no intimation from the Department of Education, Harrow.

Teaching at Roger's Eastbourne School of English was a real pleasure for me because the students were friendly adults, most of whom were focussed on what they were doing. They were spending a substantial sum of money, each one of them, and they were also very generous. Roger's establishment provided me with breakfast, but I had to organise lunch and dinner. I'd normally eat out. My favourite meal in the afternoon was ploughman's lunch and a cup of coffee. Quite often groups of my students would wander into the pub I went to and insist on picking up the bill. I thought the best part of my job was my relationship with my students. Roger was most affable and accommodating and expressed his appreciation through casual, throw-away remarks but maintained a certain distance, partly because he was the employer, and partly, I think, because he was English.

Julia was selling her Bontempi electric organs in the Southern counties. This was most convenient for me because not only was she able to drive me to Eastbourne for my job interview without much trouble, but she would also spend a few days with me in Eastbourne from time to time. She would peddle the electric organs during the day and spend the evening with me. Sometimes Mark too would come along. Our lives were getting organised. There were times when I had a great sense of relief. Mark was in a public school which had a good reputation – although he wasn't entirely happy there. Julia had a job, though it was temporary. I liked the work that I was doing. I also liked Eastbourne, an attractive residential town, where one didn't have to go too far to experience great natural beauty – the sea, high cliffs and leafy suburbs.

There was, however, a nagging worry at the back of my mind – how secure was this job? Yet another question was – how adequate was our joint income if we set out to run our own establishment? We decided that it wasn't going to be too hazardous to rent modest accommodation and start life on our own. After all, we'd encountered a very similar challenge in Delhi when Julia and I met up to start our life together. There was no reason why we should cower this time round!

Julia was with me in Eastbourne at the time. Freda rang. The Headmaster of Canon's High School had contacted her to say that the job was now on offer and he would like me to tell him as soon as possible when I could begin. This was a weekend, so I had time to think things over, and since Julia was with me, to discuss the advisability of giving up what I'd got. I liked my students here; I had a pleasant bunch of colleagues; I liked Eastbourne. But equally important were other considerations which came to my mind. If we lived in Harrow, Julia's parents, as well as her brother and his family, would be easily accessible. Mark's school would also be much nearer – though my career was at least as important for me as the family was important for Julia. Which job offered greater security and better prospects? Which employer was offering me the bigger salary and retirement benefits? Where would there be greater continuity and a sense of purpose? I thought about all that long and hard and decided I would be much better off teaching in a large state comprehensive school in Harrow than in a language school in Eastbourne. I told Julia what I thought, and she approved. I rang Mr Becker and accepted his offer – he was delighted. I told Roger – he *wasn't* delighted. He hardly ever spoke to me after that. From then on, I also avoided meeting him. Discussing teaching strategies and the future of the language school wouldn't make sense anyway. The way Roger deliberately avoided my company was beginning to be rather oppressive for me, so I too made sure our paths didn't cross. I did attend a staff meeting in which my colleagues were officially informed of my impending departure. Roger did say that he was sorry I was leaving and wished me well in a perfunctory fashion. Then he moved on to other more important matters. I was no longer relevant.

Doreen, one of my colleagues, noticed my discomfort and offered to put us up – Julia and me – in her house outside Eastbourne in a village which had all the charm and peace of the English countryside. I accepted her offer. Doreen was friendly, pleasant and helpful – without ever being obtrusive. We enjoyed our last few days in Eastbourne, mainly on account of Doreen's quiet understanding of my embarrassment at having to let Roger down, and my need to put some distance between him and me. I did feel unhappy to have to abandon my students and let Roger down. I liked Roger. He was a disciplined man whose practical common sense and entrepreneurial zeal had helped him to organise a successful institution, where students from abroad from middle-class families could improve their skills in English. Roger related well with them. It was a pity that during my last few days at the school he kept his distance, and refused to give me an opportunity to explain why it was really important for me to work in Harrow. In the end I decided to leave quietly – without even saying goodbye to Roger or my students. Julia and I thanked Doreen for making our last few days in Eastbourne both pleasant and comfortable. We took her out to a restaurant, not far from where she lived – a clean, well-appointed, upmarket establishment. The food, the wine and the service were of excellent quality. The evening cost me a week's wages, but I thought it was well worth that and more.

I'd started well in Eastbourne; I'd related well with my students and colleagues; I'd started planning a future for the school in which I'd play a significant part. Roger had said to Doreen that he was considering the idea of a partnership in which he would take care of the administration and I'd be responsible for what went on in the classroom. All that had changed in the last few days. It was all set for an unfortunate anti-climax when Doreen intervened and prevented that from happening. We'll always remember Doreen's spontaneous act of understanding and generosity. I certainly felt sad at the time of saying goodbye to her.

We left Eastbourne and drove back to Stanmore. Julia wasn't particularly communicative when she was driving. I was thinking of my short experience of teaching in Eastbourne. My students were all men – I wondered why there were no women. How useful were these short, intensive courses? How did they ensure continuity? I was born a Bengali. The only language that I used for speaking to people around me was Bengali until I was almost 20 years old. It seemed unnatural to express myself in any other language. And yet here I was teaching Arab students English – mainly spoken English. Most of my life I'd spent teaching English at different levels of proficiency, to different age groups – In India and Africa. Now I was going to teach this amazing language, used by millions, in the country to which the language owed its origin. Julia turned to me and asked why I was so quiet.

'You don't like talking when you are driving,' I explained.

'I don't like silence either,' she said.

'It *is* difficult to please some people,' I said. 'I was quiet because I was thinking of what this small island and its insular people have given to the world,' I said.

'What's that?' she asked.

'The English language,' I said.

I explained why I thought English was such an amazing gift. Science and technology had rapidly moved us all in the direction of one world. This one world needed a common language. English was that language. The empire wasn't built to unify the world – to rule the world, the empire builders had to devise devious means to divide the world. But the people who went out to rule the world either lacked the aptitude to learn other peoples' languages or were too arrogant to do so. The result was that the inhabitants of India, Arabia, Africa, America and elsewhere had to learn the language of the colonisers. Vast numbers of Indians learned English either because they had to or wanted to. I think the negative attitude of the colonisers regarding learning the languages of the colonised produced a significant result – English, a world language, a means of communication across national, ethnic, linguistic and cultural boundaries. It is true that we can use this language to curse or bless, to unite or divide. And the more powerful the language and the greater its reach, the greater its potential for quickening the pace of progress or slowing it down. For me one of the achievements of our civilization is that it has evolved a language like English. I was glad that I was doing my modest bit in promoting the use and understanding of the language. How can we promote mutual understanding without communication, and how can we communicate on diverse issues without a common language?'

Julia listened patiently to my long spiel, and then said,

'You're forgetting something important.'

'What's that?' I asked.

'We wouldn't be here today if you didn't know English.'

That's true,' I said.

'Are you glad we are returning to Harrow?' Julia asked.

'Yes, I am,' I said, 'for reasons both personal and professional.'

'For personal reasons – yes, of course. We both want to be closer to my parents and Mark. But why is the Harrow job better professionally?' Julia asked.

I pointed out various aspects of what my new teaching situation was going to be. For one thing, this teaching assignment would be a greater challenge. In Eastbourne all my students were between 20 and 25 years old and almost entirely Arab. In Canon's High School, the students were going to be mainly from the Indian sub-continent, predominantly Gujarati-speaking, but there would be a wider range of age-groups. Apart from Gujaratis – immigrants from East Africa – there would be some Pakistanis. Their respective language-learning abilities would vary much more widely and greater variety meant greater challenges. Julia was glad to hear the reasons for my preference. She wouldn't have liked the idea of my making sacrifices so that she could be nearer Mark and her parents. I was entirely honest when I said that I was hoping to get greater satisfaction from teaching at Canon's High School.

I didn't critically examine the reason for the feeling, but from the very beginning of my return journey, I felt that I'd made the right decision. The reactions of Mark, Freda and Fred told the same story – they were happy to see us back in Stanmore. Now the most important next step was contacting Mr Becker.

Mr Becker welcomed me – not with bureaucratic formality but genuine warmth. He was glad, he said, that I hadn't made any commitments which I couldn't get out of. The reason why I wasn't notified was that another person was selected for the job, a young woman with the right qualifications. Mrs Thorne, the Head of ESL teaching in Harrow, was particularly impressed with her. She had the right personality and the right qualifications. But for some reason, which Mr Becker didn't go into, she couldn't continue and Mr Becker sent me the message which had brought me there. I got the impression that Mr Becker had wanted me all along, but Mrs Thorne had preferred the woman candidate. Mr Becker hadn't made any overt statement to that effect. I'd made that deduction, but I wouldn't be able to establish, step by logical step, how I did it. It was a great relief that the head of the institution where I was going to work thought that he'd chosen the right person. Now it was up to me to live up to his expectations.

Apart from practical and relational considerations, there were ideological reasons why I'd rather teach in a comprehensive school. Privilege distorted social and personal relationships and grammar schools and the English public schools further promoted the interests of the privileged. It was socialist initiative which had produced both the idea and the reality of the comprehensive schools and I wanted these schools to achieve such excellence that the most privileged families would want to send their children there. What Labour in Government had tried to do was to democratize the education system at the school level. I wanted the system to stay and get better every year and provide equal opportunity for pupils from different strata of British society. The problem was that the public schools and the grammar schools had, long before comprehensive schools were even thought of, established a tradition of capturing, through totally unfair competition most of the places in the best universities. Schools outside the state system, run by the privileged and paid for by the privileged, produced students who went to universities which produced successful men – and a few successful women – who ran the country. Dustmen's sons never go to Eton and Harrow. Oxbridge isn't overwhelmingly peopled by Brick Lane boys and girls. When we talk of universities, of people in high places doing extraordinary acts of creation and innovation, lavatory attendants don't come into it. The rock-solid structure of power and privilege is built to last. The creators of the comprehensive system had the idea of providing equal opportunities to both the privileged and the underprivileged. I liked the idea and felt excited that I would be able to participate in the experiment, which I hoped would become the national norm. One has to be extremely naïve to dream such dreams. I'm talking about more than thirty years ago. Nothing has changed. Power and privilege is restricted to an even smaller section of our world community than ever before.

My first pupil was Govind. He was so far behind the others of his age group that he needed one-to-one attention to begin with. Govind read English better than he wrote it, and both read and wrote it better than he spoke it. After a few lessons, he was able to provide some information about himself, his friends and his family, his environment, his likes and dislikes, and what he wanted to do and who he wanted to be. When he'd gained some confidence, he joined other pupils. When the class timetable said English, my pupils came to me. They had to be divided into groups according to how much English they could cope with. Govind now joined the general groups, so he had the opportunity to interact with the others – something of great importance. An activity which all my pupils enjoyed was miming followed by story-telling. First, one group would decide, through discussions between themselves, on a situation, event or story. Then they would present it non-verbally, through miming. Then the other groups would have to guess what was mimed and describe the situation or the event, or tell the story. This simple strategy generated a great deal of natural, motivated communication between the groups. There were innovations and experiments as well as traditional and structured lessons.

Both my colleagues and I were most interested in the spontaneous, natural and purposeful communication between our pupils and between our pupils and us. We found that it was an effective way of learning a language.

The pupils from East Africa, mainly Uganda, were greater in number in our school than from any other part of the world, and their first language was Gujarati. Their English wasn't non-existent but inadequate. They accepted the authority of the teacher without any difficulty because they were conditioned to believe that a teacher's role in society was significant and they deserved respect. The only really disrespectful and disruptive pupil in my class was a 14-year-old Gujarati boy who had lived in England longer than the others and spoke English more fluently. But neither his reading comprehension, reading speed or writing skills had reached anything like the appropriate standards.

A Chinese girl of 13, with amazingly good handwriting, was my pupil for just over a year. Her reading speed, as well as reading comprehension, was also above average. She was quiet, soft-spoken, and intelligent and had a pleasant nature. I was disappointed when she left. The most successful of my students was a Greek girl of 15. Her English was fairly good to begin with, but the progress she made was amazing. Then there were two Turkish sisters, most pleasant and co-operative by nature, who always took their work very seriously. They were naturally friendly and helpful. At least twice a year, the two sisters would give me a gift of Turkish Delight, a sticky confection which came in little cubes, each lightly coated with powdered sugar – a fairly large box of it. My classes didn't look anything like the United Nations General Assembly, but they looked fairly heterogeneous.

There were two of us after about three months of my appointment. A much younger colleague, most likeable, pleasant and efficient, joined me and shared the teaching. She had quite a few good ideas and I thought we made a good team. Unfortunately, she didn't stay for long, but left after only a few weeks at the school. I neither remember her name, nor the reason for her sudden departure. I liked her and believed that the work we did was helping our pupils; therefore, I was unhappy at her sudden departure. Fortunately, I didn't have to wait long. Richard, who took her place, was full of enthusiasm about teaching in general and language teaching in particular. He was a student of foreign languages. Apart from English, he knew French and Italian. He particularly admired Marcel Proust and carried around his great autobiographical work *A la Recherche du temps perud – Remembrance of Things Past.* He said that he'd read that tome more than once – in the original French, of course. I was truly impressed.

Richard settled down quickly. He took his work seriously. He had a special talent for innovative teaching, which made him popular with the pupils. He particularly liked the miming and story-telling routine that some of the pupils did, and which they'd learned to do well. I felt more involved in my work now than I'd done before. Not only did Richard teach well – he also related well to those he taught. A good teacher usually does.

There was comfort, a general sense of security and a feeling that our living with Julia's parents was mutually enriching. But, at the same time, there was a need to have a home of our own, to make our own choices about how we lived our lives, what we ate at meal-times, what programmes we watched on the telly and who we invited to dinner.

We started thinking about it, making tentative plans and vaguely and generally looking around. Right then there wasn't a great sense of urgency about money because my job was secure and better paid than any job that I'd done before. But Julia seriously started looking round for work which was better paid, more stable and more challenging and interesting. She didn't want to sell electric organs for the rest of her working career. And in any case, we'd always agreed that two jobs were better than one.

Ward Blenkinsop, a small, British-owned chemical company with headquarters in Wembley, had advertised a vacancy for an executive sales person. If selected, the employee would be provided with a car, because the job involved quite a lot of travelling. Julia applied for the job, got an interview and was selected. There was a period of training, after which her work would really start. She would then be given a company car, which would be hers to keep.

Our search for a house of our own seriously started. Fortunately we didn't have to look for long. We found the proverbial 'lovely little cottage' on Harrow-on-the-Hill, just below Harrow School on Middle Row. We had to raise some of the money for the initial payment which we were able to borrow from Julia's parents. Carol, a friend, also sent me some money, which I returned many years later. When we moved to our house in Harrow-on-the-Hill, nobody was happier than Mark, who had been waiting to get out of the public school to which he was going, a school he didn't like. He disliked the residential part of his school life even more. In the house on Middle Row there was really only one proper bedroom. There was a second room, which was really too small to be called a bedroom, but Mark wasn't particularly concerned either about the size or the shape of the room. His priority was moving in with us, close to his mother. One of the reasons for which he was unable to accept his public school was that it stood between him and Julia. The day he actually moved in with us was obviously and unquestionably, a very important day. He said so many times, and his body language confirmed the message.

When I approached Mr Becker, the Headmaster of Canon's High School, about Mark's admission, he said that this wasn't going to be a problem at all. But he was somewhat perplexed by my decision. The public school had a special place in English society and anybody who came out of a public school could count on various advantages for university entrance, in the job market, and in life generally, some fair and some quite unfair. Very rarely did anybody who came out of a public school fail to find a place in a good university. Oxbridge and public schools were made for each other. Mr Becker felt quite certain that Mark would find it difficult to accept the lack of facilities in our school which a public schoolboy took for granted. I thought it was kind of Mr Becker to express genuine concern about the wisdom of moving Mark from a public school to a comprehensive. I thanked him for his concern and assured him that there was no question about it. Mark wanted to join this school because he wanted to live with us and he wasn't happy where he was. After a fortnight Mark confirmed that he preferred Canons High School.

I was no admirer of public schools – those bastions of privilege, the breeding ground of empire-builders. I much preferred the comprehensive system of education and told Mr Becker what I thought. Mr Becker was delighted. Mark was in and he was delighted too. We'd go to school together by car, either ours or Pauline Ibbotson's. Pauline was a colleague who lived a few hundred yards up the road, quite near Harrow School, who mainly taught GCSE (General Certificate of Secondary Education) English. She lived on her own – I didn't know her well enough to ask whether she was ever married. Her house was larger than ours, but not a lot larger, but she had a garden at the back which I was greatly impressed with, partly because we had no garden to speak of, and partly because Pauline released her creative energy there to make it impressive wit its variety. On the very few occasions we had tea with Pauline, we sat outside and admired her garden. But more than English Literature, which she taught at school, more than her garden, more than theatre and ballet, Pauline loved opera. She'd travel to London regularly to go to an opera wherever she found it. There were quite a few operas she loved, but there was really one opera singer she admired above all singers – the Spanish tenor, Placido Domingo. Her attitude to him could be compared to that of a votaress of some Greek or Roman god in ancient times. She was very knowledgeable about opera. Julia was, and always had been, interested in opera too, with the result that she and Pauline would from time to time get engrossed in discussing *The Magic Flute, Carmen, La Bohème, Othello, Rigoletto* and other well-known operas, with me listening – much of the time, with simulated interest. They discussed the qualities, the strong points and the special features of the performances of the great opera singers – Enrico Caruso, Luciano Pavarotti, Placido Domingo, and others. But always, and with relentless regularity, Pauline would return to her favourite – Placido Domingo, whom she had actually met on one occasion.

I was discussing Mark's reactions to his new environment when I digressed. Mark reacted so positively to the change that he made it all worth it – coming out to England, organising our own habitat, getting him out of his boarding school and into Canon's High School. He had no problems and fitted into the comprehensive school routine without showing the slightest sign of distress. I was told by some of my colleagues that English public schools encouraged in their pupils a quite obvious form of delusion of grandeur, which made them behave like superior human beings. And they were uncomfortable except in the company of other public school pupils, because they grew up to believe that they were a class apart. In the case of Mark, however, it wasn't difficult to see that public schools had left him quite unscathed, that there was nothing snooty, superior, arrogant or excluding in Mark's attitudes.

I was pleased to see how easily Mark settled down both at home and school. The room he occupied at home was quite small, but he didn't once comment on its size. He wasn't particularly tidy and that made the room look even smaller. Yet nothing interfered with his general feeling of well-being, which I thought was the result of his sense of belonging. We did things together. On a few occasions we even managed to smuggle him into cinemas with us to see adults-only films. At school he related well to the pupils in his class and made a few friends – both to Julia's and my relief.

We lived in Middle Row, Harrow-on-the-Hill, and if we trudged up a few hundred yards, there was Harrow School, the famous independent or public school, founded under the Royal Charter of Elizabeth I about 400 years ago. Churchill went to Harrow – the great hero of the British people. Nehru, the first Indian Prime Minister, also went to Harrow before he went to Cambridge. Many other heroes and leaders of modern times were nurtured by Harrow. But it was also an exclusive establishment, a bastion of privilege. I didn't approve of it. I preferred Canon's High School.

About this time I began to feel a little relaxed, and felt able to look back at the months I'd spent in England because some of our all-important objectives had been achieved – jobs for both of us until we reached the age of retirement, a house of our own, Mark out of boarding school and living with us. At least, I thought so. It was time to lean back, close my eyes and take stock. And I did at weekends, sit on a comfortable sofa in our comfortable little room and look back with some satisfaction and a lot of relief at what we'd achieved.

It was a quiet Saturday morning after a restful Friday night. Mark hadn't emerged from his room and Julia was nowhere to be seen. She's gone shopping, I said to myself, although it struck me that it was rather early for that. I made myself a cup of tea and sat down to drink it as I read the morning paper.

It was clear that Labour was losing its grip on power while Margaret Thatcher was well on the way to convincing the nation that with her in power the nation had nothing to fear. By and large, the newspaper conveyed to me the not-too-exciting information that the world I lived in wasn't either particularly peaceful or prosperous at the time. Nor was England. Just as my mind was filling up with visions of a world falling to pieces Julia entered.

'I went out on a mission,' she said

'What mission?' I asked

She'd taken a sample of her urine to the chemist's for a pregnancy test. I was startled, excited.

'What's the result?' I asked, eagerly.

'I don't know yet. Vipin's doing the test,' Julia said in an incredibly matter-of-fact voice. I think she was *trying* to appear calm.

Vipin ran the chemist's shop in Stanmore, where Julia's parents lived. Julia said he would ring as soon as he'd done the test. I sat by the telephone, hoping Vipin wouldn't keep us waiting too long. Only about half an hour ago I had felt that the major events of our new venture had already happened – now we were going to consolidate our position and live a settled life without any major excitement. All that might now change in the next half an hour. At the age of 54. I don't think the possibility had once crossed my mind. I had no uncertainty at all about how I was going to respond: there would be joy abounding if it was *yes*, and disappointment, the like of which I hadn't experienced for a long time, if it was *no*. I asked Julia when she thought it might have happened. Aunty Ethel lived in the seaside town of Worthing in West Sussex. It's a beautiful place at the foot of the South Downs, not far from Brighton, and Julia and I were visiting her. Aunty Ethel was Fred's sister, a widow, who had no children, and she made sure that we had a really enjoyable time while we were with her.

'I'll ring Auntie Ethel and give her the news if the result is positive,' Julia said.

'Would you like a cup of tea?' I asked Julia.

She said yes. All roads led to tea – both stress and relief from stress; expectation and disappointment. There had been some variations. When Nondon was born, and I'd just got the news, I'd triumphantly punched the door in front of me so hard that I'd had a swollen wrist for weeks.

'Yes, please,' she said.

Tea for me was the great tranquilliser. The telephone rang. It was Vipin, the chemist. Yes, he said, Julia was pregnant. There was no doubt about it.

Nondon, the youngest of my three children, was born 26 years ago. Julia and I had now lived together seven years. And then, one Saturday morning, in the summer of 1978, not long after I had had a quiet cup of tea, I was told that, at the tender age of 54, I was going to be a father again. Was it any wonder that I felt dazed, elated, euphoric? What would be the right word to describe my feelings? After all it happened a long time ago, so I'm really speculating about how I must have felt. Just knowing that another son or daughter was on the way made a difference to the way I thought and felt, but life went on as before.

On Monday morning, I went to school with Mark. Julia climbed into her brand-new Hillman Minx and drove off to sell Ward Blenkinsop's pharmaceutical products. At Canon's High School, my life and work was becoming more interesting. My colleague, Richard, was good company and an excellent teacher, and he was one of the reasons I enjoyed going to school. Then, there was Dave and Roger. Dave was the teacher-in-charge of Religious Instruction and Roger dealt with pupils with reading disabilities. Talking to them and observing their relationship with their pupils, I felt certain that they were excellent teachers and they had earned their pupils' respect and affection because they cared for them. I was now equally comfortable at home and at Canon's High School – at home because the uncertainty of starting in a new country and on a new career had now gone, and at the school because I enjoyed my teaching more than at the beginning and had made some good friends there.

At school there were, in the summer of 1978, at least three good friends. I enjoyed teaching but also looked forward to spending a little time with Dave, Roger and Richard. Outside school also I'd met someone quite different from anybody I'd got to know before – Jack Haikon. Jack liked talking, laughed loudly, and lived positively. He worked in a factory, making machine tools. He was a union man with strong socialist views and we were united in our dislike of the Tories and their current leader, Margaret Thatcher. Jack was a champion cyclist at one time and had taken part in various competitions, winning prizes – but that was in his youth. Now he had put on weight, which I thought suited his personality. It would be absurd for him to have a lean and hungry look and earnestly discuss Kafka or existentialism. He had that special gift which enabled him to make people relaxed and happy. At the same time, he was a serious critic of the establishment and the monarchy; but his criticism was good humoured, rather than bitter. Both Julia and I thought of him as one of our closest friends.

Julia rang Jack to give him the news that she was pregnant. He arrived with a bottle of champagne to celebrate. Right opposite our house, on the other side of the road, lived Margaret and one of her two daughters. We liked Margaret. She had a pleasant and friendly personality. We liked spending time with her. At the time we got to know her, she had a problem. She had a friend whom her daughter disliked. Margaret was more amused than angry about her daughter's total rejection of her friend. At this point of time, Jack entered Margaret's life. The result was positive, human. They got married in the end. Margaret's daughter fully approved.

My life was taking shape, falling into a pattern, without being either too predictable or repetitive. Never once had I come across any slight, insult or rudeness yet which could be described as racist.   As a matter of fact I hadn't encountered any unpleasantness at all, in spite of not being white, Anglo-Saxon or Protestant. Although there was widespread resentment against non-white immigration, especially after 1971, when Milton Obote was overthrown in an army coup and more than 50,000 people from Asian countries, many of whom had lived in Uganda for generations, were expelled from that country, About sixty per cent of those thrown out of Uganda had come to Britain to settle.   This sudden influx of non-white immigrants had caused panic in the indigenous population, but as I've said before, I hadn't directly experienced the slightest act or gesture which implied racial discrimination.   What did upset me from time to time were the discussions, some learned, well-informed and compassionate, and others deeply prejudiced and openly, defiantly racist, which the yellow press encouraged.   My impression was that the strident voice of prejudice could be heard more clearly than the quiet voice of reason.

Julia had always said that I had a predilection for anxiety that I loved to worry. If there was nothing to interfere with the tranquil mind, I'd invent some disaster, dream up some crisis. She pointed out that my present anxiety about Margaret Thatcher heading the British Government was totally irrational, totally unnecessary. I insisted that she was going to be a problem, whereas Julia thought she might be the solution.   The unions were getting out of hand; the economy was in deep decline; Labour's majority was paper-thin. The country had to find some kind of solution, some sort of alternative.   That solution wasn't Margaret Thatcher, I insisted, although I didn't see any other possibilities of a radiant future either.   It was fairly certain that she was going to be the next Prime Minister, the first ever woman Prime Minister of Britain, if the Conservative Party won the next general election.

Sixteen years ago, when I was in Kampala, Uganda, I'd written a play with the title *The Golddiggers of Yaksha Town.* It was about the political and economic exploitation of a people presided over by a ruthless king. I looked for it, found it, re-read it carefully, and decided that I could keep the basic structure of the play and re-write it, keeping in mind some of the problems that Britain was facing. I persuaded Richard to write the words of songs with which the play was going to be interspersed and Neil, the music teacher, to compose the music. A narrator was going to introduce certain scenes and the school choir, at appropriate intervals, was going to sing the songs, the lyrics of which were written by Richard and the music composed by Neil. Woven into the story of *The Land of Yaksha,* were a few dances. These were choreographed by an African pupil in her final year at school. She was part of a dance group which practised dancing for pleasure – a group of about a dozen African girls. Now that both music and dancing were taken care of, the next exercise was casting the play. The main protagonist of my play was Mary, who was young and vibrant and romantic, but was somewhat naïve, because she thought that by agitating for a world in which everybody could live with dignity and freedom from oppression, she could change the world. The purity of her vision of a just world attracted many followers.

At first the king, who lived behind high walls in a magnificent palace, and his advisers and other people of wealth and power, took lightly what Mary and her followers did and preached. They were even somewhat amused by her belief that she and her followers could usher in a just world of equality and freedom. But when more and more people started to take her seriously, they began to discuss between themselves a plan of action in the event of the situation getting out of their control. I found Mary without having to look high and low for her. Andrea Wilder came for an audition and I knew at once that she was just the person I was waiting for. I welcomed Andrea with a great sense of relief. The Narrator was a young Indian in his final school year with a good presence and clear and confident speech. One of Mark's friends was Mary's friend and admirer, and an articulate rebel whom the establishment looked upon with great suspicion. Mark was going to appear in a street scene or two. The Head of English obviously had produced and directed a few plays himself. This was clear from the way he commented on the acting and movement when he sat in on one or two rehearsals. I was flattered by the fact that this very knowledgeable colleague of mine came along to show solidarity as Head of English. More and more of my colleagues were getting involved in the forthcoming production of *The Land of Yaksha.* The teacher of art came along to watch the rehearsals. As the time for the production drew near, his team often painted scenery and constructed sets while we rehearsed the play. The most amazing part of the production was the number of people who voluntarily got involved.

Quite often when we produce a play, there are plays behind the scenes, plays within the play. I am quite certain that the bravest of the brave – be they actors or directors, make-up men and women, or people doing the lights and music – come to the opening night of a play with fear and trepidation. The anxiety of the playwright is probably even greater. If the audience miss the jokes, they feel frustrated. If they aren't moved by the misery of the characters that they have created, they feel they have failed. There is joy abounding if the audience laugh loudly and spontaneously when they think they have created a situation in which laughter is the only natural reaction. They also feel vindicated when tears roll down the cheeks of the audience – because the characters they have created are caught in a cycle of frustration, misery, isolation and emptiness.

Most human reactions to reality within and without, are predictable, and playwrights count on this predictability of human reactions. If audience reactions belie these predictions the playwright is in trouble. When I was in Uganda, between 1951 and1965, an English friend told me of an experience which I found difficult to believe at the time. He had gone to a performance of *Macbeth* by a professional British team of actors in a large East African town. It was a predominantly African audience but there were quite a few Britons and Asians as well. It was quite obvious that the performances of the actors and the production as a whole were being greatly appreciated. When Lady Macbeth called Macbeth "infirm of purpose," and stomped off looking frustrated and angry, and Macbeth was alone, disorientated and in conflict with himself, the audience reacted with sympathy. They listened in hushed silence, and one could see Shakespeare was making a predictable impact on the audience.

Later on came the fifth and final act: the Scene is Dunsinane, and A Room in the Castle. A Doctor of Physic is discussing Lady Macbeth's condition with a Waiting Gentlewoman. Both are deeply concerned about Lady Macbeth's condition. Lady Macbeth is out of touch with the world around her. She is obsessive, schizophrenic, full of guilt, quite unable to handle that burden. She had, not so long ago, found Macbeth "infirm of purpose'. Yet, now, *she* had lost control. She was seen trying endlessly to wash blood out of her hands – blood and guilt. She wasn't succeeding. She was distraught. The audience was left in no doubt that her suffering was real. It is certainly one of the most moving scenes in Shakespeare. Yet the audience – or most of the audience – *laughed!* We can't question that significant cultural differences exist between people. But I found this incredible.

Before going into production, most playwrights, directors and actors suffer from nightmares and one of the most recurrent ones is the audience laughing when they are expected to shed silent tears. Another source of anxiety for them is the general reaction of the audience. I thought I'd written a serious play and I wanted it to be taken seriously.

And to be taken seriously, the main components of the play had to hold together – what was being presented and how it was being presented. I cannot deny that I was anxious.

Evenings and weekends were full of agitation, speculation, hopes and fears. There was the play, but more important was the baby who was expected to be born about the same time that the play was going to be staged. What were we going to call our child? If a girl, Julia wanted her to be called *Shona,* which means 'gold', but was regularly used in our language as a term of endearment. It meant the Loved One. What if we had a son? I suggested V*almiki,* the author of the *Ramayana.* 'Hmm' said Julia. She didn't like the sound of it. What was wrong with it? She just didn't like it. It was instant rejection. When pressed to give me a reason for it, she said that in England, *Balmiki* would be an alien sound and it would lead to Micky, and she didn't want her son to be called Micky. I didn't give up. Valmiki, I pointed out, was the sage who wrote the *Ramayana.* It was he who created epic poetry. I held him in the highest regard. Valmiki is the name in Sanskrit and Hindi. In Bengali, the *V* has been replaced by *B*. So *Valmiki* is *Balmiki* in Bengali. I didn't know anyone in Calcutta or anywhere else who is Bengali and bears the name of Balmiki. This neglect wasn't acceptable, I said, and I'd like our son, if we had one, to be called Balmiki. It would be a most original name. We've carelessly neglected it.

'The Bengalis are sensible, so there are no Balmikis,' she said, making an unexpected concession to Bengalis. I wasn't getting anywhere, and having remembered from past experience that going about in circles wasn't the best way to reach the destination, I abandoned the discourse. The naming of our unborn child mustn't become an issue, I decided. And, in any case, I'd always defended the mother's prerogative in making decisions about children. We let the matter rest.

This was February 1979. Our child was due to be born towards the end of March or early April, but Julia was still working for Ward Blenkinsop and driving many miles every week without showing any disturbing signs of wear and tear. There were the obvious indicators of pregnancy, but I don't remember her having complained. Nor did she demand extra attention and care. Mark was now 14; so the memory of her last pregnancy must have somewhat faded. Good fortune played a major part in ensuring her general sense of well-being – no fatigue, no heartburn, no backache, no swollen breasts, no painful shortness of breath, no dramatic changes of mood; or so it seemed. It just isn't credible that there was no major discomfort during the entire prenatal period of pregnancy. But Julia was too excited and happy to complain, although she did suffer from time to time and did feel apprehensive. She received special attention and care from the gynaecologist because of her age. She was pushing forty. But the gynaecologist thought she was doing very well; it wasn't a pregnancy fraught with any real problems.

At the end of February, 1979, Julia gave up her job with Ward Blenkinsop. For me the next few weeks were going to be tense – full of anxiety and expectation. It was at the end of March that my play *The Land of Yaksha* – was due to be staged. It was about that time that the baby was going to be born. Nobody knew which event would happen first. There was first the writing of the play and then the casting and the rehearsals. All of this took a few months, but the baby was on the way well before the preparation of the play had begun. I'd come back home quite late because I used to stay on for rehearsals after school. There were times when I felt pleased with the rehearsals; at other times I was quite depressed about the quality of the play and the histrionic competence of the cast. But I found a kind of tranquillity talking to Julia about the baby. She remembered enough from her first pregnancy, although it was many years ago, to educate me about the way the baby was growing inside her. I'd had three children before, but each time the whole experience is powerful and unique. Waiting for my children to be born, holding the new-born babies, watching them grow into adults was for me the most significant part of my life. When we lose respect for life, we cause immense misery. Life *has* to be about preserving and promoting life.

When Julia and I went to bed, it was most important for me to talk a little about our baby, waiting to be born. I liked putting my ear to Julia's bulging belly, because, quite early in her pregnancy, I thought I could hear the heartbeat of the baby. We speculated about the baby's size, shape, colour of hair and weight. To begin with trying to hear the heartbeat was a regular ritual; then it was feeling the movement. Feeling the movement was most exciting – and reassuring. But as the baby grew larger, it moved less frequently. Then one morning Julia decided it was time to go to hospital to wait because the baby wasn't going to keep her waiting for very long.

Julia was being looked after by a competent and caring gynaecologist who'd inspired her confidence from the very beginning. She had kept in regular contact with her and moved in when she'd advised her to do so. Julia had moved into Northwick Park Hospital after I'd left for school, so I went to see her on the way back, hoping to see our newborn child. The baby had announced its impending arrival, but was still holding back. The nurse came in, asked routine questions, checked what had to be checked and then left. Contractions were taking place, but these contractions, I gathered, didn't signal the imminence of the baby's advent. It was good, however, that I was there. It took Julia's mind off the anxiety, discomfort and pain—just a little. In the end we decided that nothing was going to happen then. And I couldn't afford to miss the train.

I said whatever I could think of to reassure her that all was going to be well, although I was probably more worked up than Julia. I said goodnight and returned. Mark was beginning to feel left out. The attention of both Julia and me had shifted away from him in recent days. He must have noticed the change, but neither Julia nor I had noticed any perceptible change in his mood or attitude. He was helpful with housework and could rustle up a basic meal. On the way to school, he asked,

'When is the baby coming?'

'In a day or two, I think,' I said.

'How do you feel about the play tonight?' was Mark's second question.

It was the first night, the opening night of the play. I was nervous, full of fear and trepidation about a week ago. Y et this morning, I felt inexplicably calm.

'I feel it's going to be all right. After all, what's the risk? The audience will suffer and say that it was a waste of time. But parents often come to school plays to show solidarity. They don't mind suffering,' I said.

'The cast likes it,' Mark said.

That was welcome news, I said. If the cast really liked the play, that was half the battle already won. We'd find out later that day about the other half, I said.

After the morning assembly, the Headmaster, Mr Becker, asked the same question: was I looking forward to the opening night of the play? Yes, I was, I said. Then he remembered about the baby and asked when it was due. I said that the baby was due any time now.

'What are you doing here, then?' was Mr Becker's next question.

'I've quite a few classes to teach today,' I said.

'You've no classes to teach today,' he said. 'You go back to hospital and attend to the more important business of the day. I'll get Roger to engage your classes.' Mr Becker meant what he said.

I thanked Mr Becker, collected my bag from my room and set out for the hospital.

It was indeed a most important day in my life. There could be no doubt about it – the first night of the play, and the baby on the way. Although I was hurrying to the hospital, I noticed the daffodils, hosts of them, swaying in the wind by the roadside.

I arrived at the hospital, half expecting to see a baby asleep in its cot and Julia, lying in her bed, relaxed and reading a woman's magazine. But she wasn't in her room. A nurse, finding me looking anxious and disorientated, volunteered to take me where I could find her – the labour ward. The nurse went into the room while I waited outside. A young man, wearing the outfit of a surgeon, came out. He asked, very rapidly, if I wanted to see the birth of my baby.

'Yes, please,' I said eagerly, surprised and excited.

'Please put these on and follow me.'

I put on some gloves and a white gown and followed him. He was obviously the gynaecologist who was going to deliver the baby – a tall, gentle and friendly person, who believed in a father's presence at his baby's birth. This wasn't an option which existed in India and Uganda, where my other children were born. It was work as usual during the day for me. When Aparna, Aparajita or Nondon was born, they'd already arrived when I got to the hospital.

Although Julia was in labour, she registered my presence and then went on to focus on what was important for all of us – the birth. Contraction followed contraction. There was an intense concentration on Julia's face. Peter, the friendly young gynaecologist, was watching every heave of Julia's belly. From time to time he uttered a single word of exhortation: push! The top of a small head with black hair appeared where all eyes were focused. 'Push,' said Peter with great urgency in his voice. The head, the shoulder and the rest of the body appeared in quick succession. 'A boy,' declared Peter. There was probably a general sigh of relief, but I didn't hear it. Relief was also writ large on Julia's face, but she was quite obviously tired. The baby must have cried at birth and later but I don't remember. It was the 29th March, 1979 – a cold but sunny morning in Harrow, and a son was born. This was Julia's second child and second son. This was my fourth child and second son. We haven't had any children after this son, who remains our youngest. I held Julia's hand briefly and gave it a tight squeeze to say many things. I left soon after.

Later that day I went back to school. A group of senior pupils were putting the finishing touches to the set. The palace of the tyrannical king was at the back, stage left. The king could not be seen but only heard, for he ruled with tyranny, which often bordered on cruelty and inhumanity, from behind high walls. The art teacher and his team had made quite a spectacular set. The cast arrived one by one, and in twos and threes, and soon everybody was there. I went around, saw Andrea and others, I tried to reassure everybody that it was going to be a great first night, although I needed that reassurance myself as much as anybody else.

Then I stood around and met people – parents, colleagues and their friends and family – who came to watch the play. I told Mark that the baby was born and it was a boy. I also told Mr Becker that I had a son and Julia was well. I thanked him for having urged me to go back to the hospital because I was present at the birth of my son. 'Congratulations!' said Mr Becker with real warmth.

There were people I liked who I wanted to be at the first night of the play – my cousin, Tutu-da and his wife, Joy, who had both in the meantime also moved back to England; Ravinder, a student of mine from Uganda, now Professor of Immunology at Charing Cross Hospital and his father, Sir Amar Maini. They'd all come. After the customary greetings, I informed them about the birth of my son and was duly congratulated. Then, just before the beginning of the play, Mr Becker made a short speech welcoming the audience and pointing out that the play and the songs were entirely original, and the production was the result of teamwork, in which a large number of my colleagues and pupils were involved. He knew that many hours of dedicated work had gone into the preparation of the play. At the end, he mentioned the birth of my son that morning. There was warm and spontaneous applause.

The audience responded well to the play. Some parents waited and looked out for me. When I met them, they told me how much they had liked the play. Usually school plays were predictable – comedies, musicals, Shakespeare badly done, said one of the people I met, who looked too young to be a parent. He was about 30, with long hair and carelessly attired. He seemed genuinely interested in the theatre. This play was different, he said: an original play with a large cast, and it had worked. He liked the play. The Headmaster had arranged a small drinks party for a few guests. I invited him to come to it. The young man accepted. He talked to several people, including Mr Becker who said the young man looked scruffy but had a good mind. Mr Becker was also enthusiastic about the play. He said he had deliberately kept away from rehearsals because they would give him an incomplete picture, and reduce its impact when he finally watched it. He approved of the idea of the narrator. That helped. The singing and dancing had enriched the play without causing any distraction from the theme. Sir Amar Maini also made positive remarks and Tutu-da and Joy said they were glad they had come. I genuinely valued their comments.

Then there was Ravinder, who had been the mainstay in Old Kampala Secondary School of the Debating Society and the Drama Club. He said he was 'bowled over'.

The next day I was able to tell Julia about the play and the various comments made by people who had watched it. She congratulated me and regretted that she wasn't there. I touched my son but don't remember having lifted him out of his cot, probably because he was asleep. I went back to school for the second and last performance of the play, after which the cast and everybody else connected with the production of the play, had a party. We had a very pleasant time. Photographs were taken.

What was particularly important for me was that a large team of teachers and pupils – some 40 of them – had worked together and produced a play without any misunderstandings or conflicts. There was involvement. There was a sense of purpose. There was creative co-operation between individuals and groups. All in all, it was a most memorable experience for me. Mark and I returned home quite late that night. Mark was tired whereas I think I was still too excited to be tired – the day before my second son was born, and tonight we celebrated the success of the play.

Julia was back from hospital with the baby. My initial excitement was replaced by a mixture of tenderness and concern. There was also a certain insecurity because the experience of being with a newborn baby was a distant memory. Julia had Mark

15 years ago, but I didn't notice any signs of lack of confidence. She knew exactly what to do and when. What about Mark? I had the impression that he was somewhat disorientated. He wanted to show interest but it wasn't particularly convincing. I don't think young men of 15 in any country or culture would find the 'muling and puking' of an infant really riveting. There wasn't, however, any overt expression of jealously or rejection. There wasn't any major difference in our lives or in our lifestyle. A pram was added to our earthly possessions and various other minor infant accoutrements. Julia took care of every need of the baby.

The second and final performance of the play happened on a Friday. When I went back to teach on Monday, I was sent for by Mr Becker after morning assembly. He greeted me with a smile and asked me to sit down.

'Have you seen this?' he asked, holding up a newspaper.
I hadn't. It was the local weekly newspaper, *Harrow Times,* or something like that. It was clear that the theatre critic of this paper was the same long-haired young man who had talked to us after the play and was so enthusiastic about its originality and production. The reason why Mr Becker and I felt certain about who wrote the article was that it wasn't only the content but also the language that was similar. We thought his review of my play was reminiscent of Kenneth Tynan's critical assessment of John Osborne's *Look Back in Anger*. He was almost as enthusiastic.

It read like a panegyric. I was relieved. I was happy. It was a whole week of excitement and a certain sense of achievement. At the same time, even in my most unguarded moments I didn't indulge in self-deception. I hadn't become an eminent playwright overnight. The headline in the local weekly read, 'This play should run and run'. The relevant page was posted on the main notice board of the school. At home, Mark confirmed that the actors and the members of the production team were all very pleased with the critical acclaim accorded to the play.

There was a general feeling in our little family of four at Middle Row that life was exciting and eventful. At that time, it certainly wasn't standing still. There was Mark's GCSE examination looming ahead, although I seemed to be more anxious about how well he was going to fare than anybody else. I wanted him to do Advanced Level GCSE and go to university but we hadn't discussed his education at that stage. Apart from my preoccupation with the regular teaching, there was the excitement of the newborn and Julia's gradual return to daily life – cooking, cleaning and minding the baby.

More than a week had now passed. During one of my free periods, Mr Becker sent for me. Harrow School had written to him to request that we took our play, *The Land of Yaksha,* for a performance there. Quite obviously, it was the result of the extremely favourable review of the play in the local weekly. Did I want to take the play to Harrow School? Was I flattered? My answer to both these questions was unequivocally positive. When I talked to Andrea, the heroine of the play, and the young man who was the Narrator, they both said it would be a great experience. The opposition to the idea of taking the play to Harrow School did not come from the actors or stage hands, but from the teachers of the final-year students. It would be irresponsible to let their students get involved in another lot of rehearsals and then the staging of the play when the GCSE examinations were imminent. We had to have our priorities right, they said. The reason we were all so excited, they insisted, was that Harrow School, no less, from its Olympian heights, had granted us this unique offer of presenting our play on their stage. So lowly Canon's Comprehensive was so flattered and excited that it had to go and perform and be patted on the back and patronised. 'Not bad, for Canon's Comprehensive,' was the highest praise we could expect from them! I was quite taken aback. The force and venom of the attack surprised me. Andrea was especially disappointed. So was Mark, but for different reasons. Andrea had loved her role in the play. She'd been able to identify herself with the role she was playing, and because she loved acting, she'd excelled in it. It would have been another opportunity for her to appear in that role; Mark thought that comprehensive schools felt inferior to public schools. He hadn't liked public schools. Yet he felt very strongly that we should have accepted Harrow School's invitation.

My particular friends in the school, Dave and Roger, thoroughly disapproved of public schools as those were institutions which perpetuated the domination of the few over the many. They groomed empire builders. They created a divided society. And so on. But they didn't approve of the belligerence of some of their young colleagues. Dave joked that knowing one's enemies was strategically important. What about me? I was deeply disappointed. Apart from anything else, plays are written to be performed and watched by an audience. I'd have liked to see how the Harrow School staff and students reacted to the play.

If the baby was awake, I quite regularly picked him up, held him in my arms and talked to him, mainly in English, but also in Bengali from time to time – for variety and because it came to me naturally. He did everything that babies were expected to do – laughed, chuckled, exercised his limbs and made noises to indicate that he found life great fun - and slept. He didn't cry. It's unlikely that he never cried, but I have no memory of him crying. He was, however, far from placid or apathetic.

He enjoyed eating, sleeping, being cuddled, grinning, making noises which were probably profound comments of the outsider on the world where he had recently landed. The weekends brought back the memory of nappies, baby food, the milk bottle, baby-in-the-bath, baby-in-the-pram. What I also remember is that our little son behaved in a manner which caused very little stress. And Julia, being an extremely efficient mother, took such good care of the practical problems that I had most of the pleasures of being a father again, after a lapse of 26 years, without any of the pain. I enjoyed being quietly happy in our little house at the bottom of Middle Row, where I lived with my stepson, my little son and my wife, and I was happy being where I was and working at Canon's High School during the day, and sleeping at Middle Row during the night, with our little son in a cot beside our bed. I keep referring to the baby as our little son because we couldn't think of a name which sounded right to both of us. I was trying to convince Julia at the time that I'd found just the right name for our son – *Ranjan.* It was a Bengali name which meant, *he who pleases, delights.* How about it? I asked Julia. She didn't reject it outright. She said she was thinking about it

It was about this time that Freda, Julia's mother, arrived to see her grandson. Julia's father hadn't come, but for Julia's mother it was too important an occasion. She couldn't wait any longer. Julia's parents had sold their house in Kynance Gardens and moved to Bardney in Lincolnshire, a village not far from the city of Lincoln. We welcomed Freda, sat round in the living room after dinner, discussing people and politics. Then Freda quite casually asked whether we had decided on a name for our newborn son. Julia said we had. It was my choice. She had initially hesitated but had now decided that she quite liked it. It was a Bengali name, Ranjan, I said. My other son, who was in Calcutta, was Nondon. What did she think of it?
Freda went very quiet and looked disappointed. When she spoke, I had the impression that she was holding back tears; for when she spoke, her voice nearly broke. She wanted to call her grandson Robert. It was a name she had always liked. But she couldn't question the prerogative of the father to name his son, could she? When Freda had arrived about half-an-hour ago, she had a bright smile on her face, and at the sight of her grandson, the smile became even brighter. She held him, talked to him, laughed and made her grandson chuckle. Now the change was sudden. She looked tired, unhappy and disappointed.

I was thinking about the name – *Robert,*' I said. 'I like the name. I don't insist that the name I suggested is the best name for my son...' Then I turned to Julia and said, 'What do you think?'

Julia was never particularly keen on *Ranjan,* so she happily accepted my suggestion. As for Freda, there was now light where there was darkness, happiness where there was misery. Dinner followed. After that we sat around and talked mostly about subjects which didn't matter. Mark was by now asleep in his bed and Robert in his cot. I got my son's birth registered the next day or the day after, and Freda returned to Bardney, having achieved her objective of spending some time with us, seeing her newborn grandson and making sure that he would be known by the name of *Robert.*

Julia's agenda was rapidly filling up with new plans which I hadn't thought of. It was no longer realistic to live in our small Middle Row cottage, she'd decided. She contacted agents and we put our house up for sale. The same day or the day after, a middle-aged couple came to have a look, liked the house, agreed on the asking price and said they would like to complete the deal immediately. This development created a problem for us because we didn't expect such precipitate action. Julia explained to the prospective buyer and his wife that we were caught unawares, that we had to find a house and buy it before we could move out and they could move in.

Our search began and we found a house in Watford quickly – a three-bedroom house in a leafy suburb of Watford. A special attraction for me was the study in the attic, which overlooked the sylvan landscape of Cassiobury Park. The walls were lined with bookshelves. The books were read, for they weren't gathering dust. The owner of the house was a teacher of English while I was a teacher of English as a second language, so there were areas of common interest. He was one of those people who knew their minds, making it easy to transact business with him. We got down to the timetable of when they could move out and we move in and similar practical matters, and didn't allow ourselves to get involved in discussing the pleasures and the trials and tribulations of teaching. We said we really liked the house and agreed on a price.

The likely date of completing the paperwork and moving in couldn't be fixed because the vendor had a few problems to sort out. We did all the negotiating with the husband; the wife remained in the background the entire time.

Relieved of our anxiety, we came home and rang the couple who were waiting to buy our house. All was well, we told them. We had found a house in Watford and decided to buy it. They could now expect to move in before very long.

Events, however, didn't exactly go our way. The wife of the man with whom we had negotiated rang to say that the deal was off because she and her husband were getting divorced, and her lawyer had advised her not to move from that house. They weren't going to sell the house and go their separate ways. She and her two children were going to continue to occupy the Watford house and what her husband did was not her business. Vacant possession wasn't going to be available now because *they* were going to be there. The husband wasn't even available to confirm what his wife had so emphatically told me. I accepted that we would have to begin our search all over again.

The couple who had made us an offer were staying in a hotel, waiting for us to buy our new house and move. The problem was that now nobody knew when that was going to be. Our search for a house was fairly urgent all along, because we felt responsible for causing anxiety to two very reasonable people. The search for a house was now resumed with greater urgency. Then a property came up in Watford and we went to look at it. There was nothing salubrious about it, but Julia decided that, since it met our basic requirement of space, she was going to opt for it. She wasn't put off by the gloomy surroundings; shade-less, low-watt bulbs hanging from the ceiling; hideous and dusty carpets on the floor; furniture that had seen better days, and two windows in the living room boarded up for privacy, shutting out the light. I was expecting Julia to turn round and run; instead of which she engaged in a serious discussion with the vendor about price, vacant possession and various other terms and conditions.

'Thank you very much,' she said, 'for showing us round. We like the house and would want to move in as soon as the formalities are completed. We'll get in touch.'

Mr Ali looked pleased with the outcome, but I must have looked puzzled, even bewildered. I don't remember having thanked Mr Ali. Thank him for what? He'd just offloaded his dark, dingy house onto us. I'd never before suffered from claustrophobia, but now my wife had ensured that I would. Anyway, there was nothing that we had done to make it legally binding. Decisions aren't irreversible. I decided, however, to let Julia explain, because she couldn't have failed to notice puzzlement writ large on my face.

She didn't keep me waiting and dealt with my anxiety. She had noticed the same lack of regard to hygiene and aesthetics in Mr Ali's house, but the deficiencies were all man-made. Therefore, when the Alis moved out and the Bagchis moved in, the

Augean Stables would be cleaned, and she assured me, it wouldn't take very long because she was a lot more efficient than Hercules.

I said I didn't want her to make light of the enormous problem of making the Watford house habitable. It was then that Julia began to explain seriously that she hadn't made a hasty decision. She had experience of making an uninhabitable house habitable. Her brother had bought a run-down building in Bristol and she and John, her first husband, had moved in. She had then created a pleasant environment there through careful planning and hard labour; and she would do it again. She wouldn't be able to do now what she'd done before because she was older *and* had a little baby, but what she would be able to do would make a difference. Her next reason for the decision was the price, which was reasonable for a house with one fairly large bedroom and two smaller ones, and a really large living room. The kitchen was a good size and the garden occupied more space than the house itself. And finally, she pointed out, two people were patiently waiting in a hotel room to move into our house.

Therefore, waiting was *not* an option. I agreed.

After Kynance Gardens and Middle Road, this was the beginning of Chapter Three.

Chapter 17

Thatcher - 'Immigrants go home!' - We go home

Winning a war is, almost always, a matter of national rejoicing, sometimes excessive, sometimes muted by a sense of loss, especially personal loss. I didn't rejoice. I thought wars should be banned, not only because of their enormously destructive nature, but also because they represent the ultimate failure of reason, compassion and humanity. There was jubilation in the streets of Britain, and in most British homes, after the victory in the Falklands War. There was certainly a great deal to feel relieved about – there could have been a greater loss of lives; the war could have dragged on; Britain might have lost, and a dishonourable treaty might have been imposed on this country. But I had to accept the fact that the war which Michael Foot, the Labour leader, had described as a 'monstrous gamble', had been won, and in the forthcoming election next year, Margaret Thatcher was certain to win, and prolong my misery. My choice was between my job and my self-respect.

Elsewhere also, there were problems and confrontations. Menachin Begin ordered Israeli troops into Southern Lebanon. The troops, supported by the Israeli air force, reached Beirut, the Damascus highway. About this time, the United Nations intervened. A ceasefire agreement was accepted by Israel and within three days broken again. Hostilities continued without showing any signs of slowing down or stopping, although within Israel, a peace movement, which called itself Peace Now, was growing in strength. But the problem was that the pro-war Israeli population was much bigger. I didn't think at any time that peace based on understanding and a genuine desire for reconciliation was ever just around the corner in Israel. But it would have given me genuine relief if somehow peace came about in this region. But there was no sign of it; only peace proposals and counter proposals, leading to what is called a stalemate.

Then the massacre of Sabra and Chatila happened – the massacre of 2,300 Palestinian men, women and children. What was happening around me and in the Middle East depressed me and made me feel desperate. I had started well. I had friendly colleagues at work. My teaching had generally proved effective. I had produced a play which was well received. Robert was born. Mark had made his adjustments to the new environment fairly well. Why then had I begun to feel restless and unhappy? I thought the world around me had much to do with it.

I expressed my sense of frustration to Julia a few times but she looked at me with incomprehension. After nearly a decade of uncertainty, we had our own house; I had a permanent and pensionable job; we had made good friends. Then there was my daughter, Aparna, and her second husband, Ian Jack, both of whom mattered a great deal to me, and they lived in London. And I shouldn't forget that after years of uncertainty, Mark was beginning to find his feet. He would feel lost and unloved, even betrayed – if we got up and left.

Julia had registered the beginning of my conflict but she wasn't sympathetic. Aparna might not like the idea of my leaving but she would understand. Ian would give me a detached and balanced view. My friends, Jack, Roger and Dave wouldn't like the idea of my leaving either, but I did expect them to give me their honest opinion.

I had my own personal conflicts too. I was now 56, not exactly the ideal time of life to start a new career in India, where the retirement age was 55. And, as I was turning over in my head the reasons for and against our returning to India to start life afresh, I thought of the friends I had made in and outside the school. There was Jack and his partner, Margaret. Jack was a machine-tool maker in a factory, an old friend of Julia's, helpful and generous by nature, an unmistakeable romantic, who liked to think of himself as a down-to-earth, hardcore realist. The morning when Julia's pregnancy was confirmed, he had arrived forthwith with a bottle of champagne. Then both Dave and Roger at work were really good friends. My colleague in the ESL group of teachers was also someone whose company I enjoyed and without whose creative contributions, our small department wouldn't have acquired the modest reputation it had for interesting and effective teaching. Then there was Robert growing up into a good-looking and articulate little boy. The disruption of Mark's life and studies would be an immediate consequence of my departure.

A secure present, an uncertain future. A little boy, not yet four years old. A wife totally opposed to the whole idea of returning to India and starting afresh, because she was just beginning to hope that she had left behind her nomadic and insecure past. Was it at all reasonable to expect that she would go back to India and start life afresh?

I turned my attention to school, family and friends. I produced another play with more or less the same cast as in *The Land of Yaksha* – Jean Anoulth's *Antigone*. It got a lukewarm review from the same critic who had raved about my other play. I wasn't surprised – a half-hearted production received half-hearted praise. The young actors found the long speeches of Creon and Antigone difficult to handle. Apart from that, the quality of the acting was affected by the response of the audience. Quite obviously, it was not the kind of play our audience enjoyed: I had made a wrong choice. Some parents suspected that I had an unfortunate predilection for the gloomy and the tragic, and they said so to some of my colleagues. One of the parents was so frustrated that he wrote to Mr Becker, the headmaster, that they had come to be entertained but had returned home depressed. 'I suggest,' said Mr Becker, 'that the next play you produce is a comedy.'

Once events in one's life start going wrong, they seem to go on going wrong. Mrs Margaret Thatcher was back in power, with an overall majority of 144 Members of Parliament – the largest majority since 1935. Labour won 209 seats – not my dream result. I had to keep saying to myself that it couldn't go on like this. The tide *has* got to turn! The question was only when... The lady who'd built a stone wall of rigid Tory convictions around herself and her party so that she was unable ever to turn – bored me and made me angry.

A Tory government with a ruthless Prime Minister, huge unemployment, racism, riots – first in Brixton in April 1981, then in Liverpool, London, Hull, Wolverhampton, Birmingham and Chester. The only saving grace of those riots was that they weren't racist, directed against the immigrants – not white youths fighting black immigrants. These were black *and* white youths, protesting against the massive poverty and unemployment in the less privileged communities of England, innocent victims of Margaret Thatcher's mindless monetarism. It really looked and felt like a very different England from the one to which I came in 1977 – the year of the Queen's Silver Jubilee. Worried above all about the unpleasant events taking place around me, I don't think I took much notice of the Prince of Wales' wedding to Diana Spencer in St Paul's Cathedral – a ceremony watched worldwide on the television screen by a record number of viewers in July, 1981. The pattern of events *outside* the cathedral continued unchanged – destitution, unemployment and mass demonstrations against a government which protected privilege and inflicted hardship on the poor. The sense of frustration among the jobless underclass and a small minority of compassionate people was enormous.

Though there were some redeeming developments also in the world around me. The Shah of Iran was driven into exile. Egypt and Israel signed a peace treaty in the U.S. Thousands of CND supporters formed a ring round the Greenham Common airbase to protest the proposal that 56 U.S. cruise missiles should be sited there. These were determined, dedicated women. The Campaign for Nuclear Disarmament was also gaining ground and at one point had gained majority support within the Labour Party. The anti-nuclear movement had my full moral support. At a time when I was beginning to feel rather low, the pro-life movement organised by the CND and Greenham women lifted my spirits.

Among the positive happenings I must also include the advent of Francine in the ESL department of Canons High School. Francine was quite a few years younger than me. Tall, elegant and efficient, she took no time at all to figure out the situation and fit in. She was one of those people who not only did what she was supposed to do but also what she thought she ought to do. She had been teaching children in primary schools. She fitted in excellently well and gave me the impression that she had been teaching all her life. She related well to her pupils in the class as well as outside. A change of environment is often recommended by specialists for a general improvement. It helped in language learning also. Francine organised educational trips. We enjoyed our days out. We went to various interesting places in and around London – most of them predictable – like the Tower and Madame Tussaud's – but we also did some random exploring. Francine was an asset for various other reasons also; she had initiative and she had ideas, an ideal combination.

The learning experience for our pupils became more exciting after the advent of Francine. Richard, who was my ESL colleague before Francine, was also highly creative. I had a pleasant time at the school partly because of some of my colleagues.

Because Francine also lived in Watford and drove to work and back, I had started going with her. She would usually drop me off on her way back. She got to know Julia, Mark and Robert, because she often stopped off to spend time with us. Apart from Jack and Roger, I had now made another good friend – Francine. Richard had gone to Rome to teach English as a second language. After six years of a sense of adventure, followed by a period of stability, minor achievements and good fortune, culminating in the birth of my son, Robert, I should have been a positive and forward-looking person, wanting to take life to new heights. But I began to feel restless, unhappy and insecure. I wondered why...?

First, Margaret Thatcher's return to power for another term was a major disappointment. The politics of the right had come to stay and I didn't believe Neil Kinnock was the man capable of turning things round. Then, there was the whole issue of immigration, which was on every British *WASP*'s lips and on every television screen. It was now almost universally believed that the immigrants – not white immigrants from Ireland, America, Australia, New Zealand and South Africa

– but immigrants with dark skin pigmentation from Asia, Africa and West Indies – were responsible for all the problems Britain had. Asian immigrants – except for the Chinese and Japanese – were generally referred to as Pakis, which became a term of abuse. At Canons High School, Mark's classmates found it most incongruous that an English lad, who had gone to public school for education, had a *Paki* stepfather. They often made snide remarks about this and caused Mark irritation, even distress. I began to feel like a stranger. I started asking the fatal question, *'What am I doing here?'* I wondered why I continued to live in a country where the majority of the population resented my being there, and politicians standing for election for a seat in the parliament or the local county council in most parts of England, Scotland and Wales did better if they promised to rid the country of Asian, African and West Indian immigrants. Where was my self-respect?

I talked to Jack, Dave and Roger, and they accepted that people in this country were, by and large, racist and against the immigrant underclass. This didn't mean that people who were against immigration were necessarily racist but there was a significant overlap. I didn't discuss my distress about British people's attitude to non-white immigration either with Julia or Francine because I didn't think they would be at all sympathetic. They would argue that the right action would be to stand up to prejudice, not to give in to it. If people could achieve foul objectives by being nasty and unpleasant, there would be more of that rubbish, not less! But the white Britons' objection to non-white immigration couldn't be adjudged nasty, unpleasant or racist because this island couldn't accommodate more than a certain number of people. What was rarely discussed was that number wasn't the issue – culture and pigmentation were at least equally important considerations. And ignorance and prejudice was endemic among large sections of the British community when it came to the subject of immigration. If I were a billionaire, I fantasised, I would spend most of my money rehabilitating Indian immigrants back in India– doctors, nurses, teachers, small businessmen, those running corner-shops, toilet-attendants and any other Indian who felt insulted and humiliated having to live in this country.

Ireland in 1982 had already been an independent sovereign country for more than 40 years, but no English man or woman was particularly anxious about the number of Irish immigrants who lived and earned a living here. In certain areas of England – London, Leicester, Birmingham – the concentration of people from the Indian sub-continent was so great that it created widespread resentment. Whether the resentment against non-white immigration was legitimate or not was not the most important question for me. I wasn't white; I was an immigrant; and the general, unthinking resentment against the likes of me affected me deeply. The failure of the

Labour Party to offer credible opposition to the rise and rise of the Tories under their strident leader, Margaret Thatcher, also made me quite miserable, so that the idea of going back to India began to take root in my mind. And quite often, when I was on my own, I found myself carefully weighing up arguments for and against this recurrent and irrepressible idea.

I was unhappy but not desperately so. My salary from the Canons High School job was higher than any salary I'd ever earned before. Its security was unquestionable. I enjoyed doing what I was doing. I wouldn't be entitled to any employment pension or severance pay if I voluntarily quit my job. I couldn't afford to do that. I had worked for an organisation – the British Council – which discriminated against Indian employees recruited in India in various ways. They paid them much smaller salaries than their British counterparts and they paid them no pension. There was no substantial retirement benefit. I was paid a month's salary for each year's service. Also, I hadn't worked long enough at Kirori Mal College or Oxford University Press to be entitled to any retirement benefits. It was, therefore, really unthinkable for me to hand in my resignation to Harrow Education Department and go back to India. I couldn't afford to be sensitive. Once again, I concluded that I should stay – although I couldn't get rid of the feeling that I was here on sufferance. *'Ignore that lot,'* I kept saying to myself.

Yet the feeling of being an uninvited guest, persisted. It was now a question of choosing between living in England with the feeling of being uninvited and unwanted, and not being able to provide food and shelter to my four-year-old son Robert, and my wife, Julia.

The choice was obvious. I was going to stay; help the children of mainly Asian immigrants to speak, read and write English. I was going to live here until I grew old enough to retire, see Mark settled, and watch Robert grow. Pragmatic surrendering to good sense seemed then the most reasonable alternative. I decided to stay.

Then something unexpected happened. During the lunch break at school, quite a few of the more experienced members of the teaching staff were discussing a document with a certain amount of excitement. I sat down in a chair near them to find out what it was about. I asked Neil, the music teacher. The document, he explained, was a circular which spelt out the terms and conditions for early retirement. Margaret Thatcher's government, having created massive unemployment, was now trying to create jobs, and one of the ways it could do that was by letting some people retire, so that their places could be filled by some of those who were now unemployed.

Whether that made economic sense for this country wasn't my concern. What I wanted to know was the terms and conditions. A minimum of five years in employment was the first condition and the second was that the applicant had to be more than 50 years old. I fulfilled both conditions. Then, as an additional incentive, those who opted to retire would be paid an enhanced pension. The addition wasn't going to be substantial, but it wasn't negligible. Suddenly, there was quite a lot to think about. I could not only take early retirement and go back to India, but I would also be awarded an enhanced pension! It was all very incredible, but my colleagues assured me it was true.

I noted down the terms and conditions and returned home, feeling excited but not euphoric. When I told Julia, she looked unhappy and apprehensive. Another new beginning? She had already had more new beginnings than she had bargained for. In 1970, she had left John and returned to England. In 1972, she had left England and come to Delhi to live with a man she had not known for very long. In 1977 she had returned to England at the age of 38, hoping for stability, security and continuity. She did not want to disrupt Mark's studies and the prospect of a settled career. She wanted Robert to grow up in an organised society, which she knew and trusted, and take advantage of good English schools and universities. And, finally, she herself had no desire for travel, no *wanderlust*. She was quite happy to leave exploring to younger people – reincarnations of Marco Polo or Dr Livingstone. She was in control while she stated her reaction to the prospect of another new beginning.

'Can I go now?' Julia said, looking anxious and weary. 'It's a hot day. Robert would appreciate a bath,' she added.

Weekends invariably brought up the subject of returning to India. I hated living in England with all the *Paki-bashing* and Margaret Thatcher at 10 Downing Street. British politics wasn't compatible with my self-respect. But Julia insisted that I was being unnecessarily sensitive. It seemed quite absurd to her that I should find the racist prejudices of a bunch of under-privileged hooligans so unbearable that I wanted to leave a country where we had put down our roots and where we could expect to live without any major upheaval for the rest of our lives. The privileged *and the* underprivileged wanted us out, I insisted. We had now reached the worst time in our 12 years' relationship. Yet I hoped she would come round, see my point and co-operate – if she was really convinced that I no longer liked it here.

'Whether we live in India or England, I would like to live with self-respect. I can no longer feel part of this country,' I declared.

Julia refused to understand. She became remote, didn't want to discuss the subject of leaving, and the distance between us grew by the day. It wasn't as if she was trying to punish me. She was disorientated. She also thought that I was out of my mind. And I thought Julia didn't care. An impasse!

I despaired of getting her consent or co-operation. If I waited for it, I wouldn't be able to return to India. So I put in an application for early retirement and handed it over to the new Head of the school, who was a woman, and whose name I can't recall.

I waited for the official response to my application. It didn't come and it didn't come, and then when it came, it seemed to me totally incomprehensible. Yes, said the letter, I did fulfil the conditions for early retirement. There was, however, a problem: the Department of Education wouldn't be able to find a replacement for me, so they couldn't let me go. I was doing very well. The Education Department and the Head of my school thought that the work I was doing was most valuable, and hoped that I'd continue to help my pupils to do as well in the future, as they had done in the past. Flattering words but they were quite shattering for me. Early retirement was an option others could exercise, but *I* couldn't because I was irreplaceable! In other words, I was being punished – denied what I wanted and was entitled to – because I was doing my work well! The logic of it struck me as unquestionably lopsided. The decision to turn down my application was unjust, unreasonable and unexpected. I found it difficult to come to terms with it.

For the first time in more than six years, going off to work to meet my colleagues and the pupils stopped being attractive. A kind of lassitude descended on me, so that preparing lessons, assessing written work and travelling to work seemed to require colossal effort, and totally exhausted me – five days a week, week after week. Then came a time when I felt I couldn't take it any more. I saw my General Practitioner, Dr Barham, who took it all very seriously. He asked me many questions, and came to the conclusion. He diagnosed a serious depression. He said I should stay off teaching for a time and see him again.

Julia was concerned for the first time. She had noticed distinct signs of depression herself but hoped it would pass. When it didn't, she reluctantly accepted that I wasn't the same man, physically or mentally, that I was a few months ago, and became more sympathetic. I applied again for early retirement on the grounds of depression. The Harrow Education Department wanted an independent opinion, so I was referred to a specialist of their choice. I saw him and waited anxiously for his verdict. I didn't hear from him but received a letter from the Department of Education that I was eligible for early retirement, the terms and conditions of which had been made available to us by a circular earlier that year.

I wasn't just relieved, I felt liberated. I wanted to throw away the anti-depressants which had been prescribed earlier that year by Dr Barham. But Julia said I should do no such thing. She knew a little about depression and it was important for me to stay on those pills which made me feel like a zombie!

Preparation for returning to India now started in real earnest. The first and most difficult task was also the one which was causing me the greatest discomfort and guilt. Mark hadn't started his career yet. His apprenticeship would take more than another year or more to complete. He would feel uprooted and disrupted. A lot had happened since we had moved to Watford. The most unexpected and untimely death of Tutu-da, Sudarsana's first cousin and a dear friend of mine, Joy's husband, was certainly the most tragic event of our lives – Julia's and mine – since we had arrived in England. He, with Joy, was our travelling companion when in 1955 Sudarsana and I had travelled back to India, by car, train and ship, via France, Italy, Yugoslavia, Turkey, Syria and Iraq.

There were other experiences, too, which had caused me great anxiety. Julia had to have a lump removed from her right breast. Fortunately, it turned out to be benign. Robert had his tonsils and adenoids removed. I had a hernia operation. Nothing untoward happened, but I had a pervading sense of insecurity. So much could still go wrong. And there was also the inescapable question which so many had asked and so many more were going to ask. *Was it going to be worth it after all, was it going to be worthwhile?*

Mark, who was by now 19, was offered a room in the house next door by a lady who was somewhat strange and eccentric. She lived alone. Nobody ever seemed to visit her and she never seemed to go away anywhere. I caught her on a few occasions talking to herself. Both Julia and I were in two minds about accepting her offer. But Mark had no objection and we all found it convenient. The arrangement wasn't quite satisfactory but we settled for it.

We had in the meantime, sold our house without any difficulty at all. We arranged for some of our stuff – mainly books – to be shipped to India and started going round saying goodbye to friends, relations and colleagues. This wasn't the first time I had left one country or continent to go to another.

Was I more worried about my future this time round than on previous occasions? There *were* worries because I was older and now had a son just over four years old! But it is difficult to compare one situation with another. Despite similarities, each event is somehow different. If it wasn't, we would die of boredom. There was, however, quite a strong feeling that I had over-reacted. I was treated well by friends and colleagues. I wasn't personally at the receiving end of intolerance or racial discrimination. London was my favourite city after Calcutta – because of its history and diversity. And it's people – such a wonderful collection of race, colour, creed and so much else. But I was going – returning to India – without completing the major mission of our coming to England – providing Mark with love, care and a sense of shelter, which he had missed for the last five years. Yet, I had to go.

Why did I have such a sense of desperation? I had 15 years in Uganda – 11 years under colonial British rule and four in independent Uganda. At no time did I have a sense of belonging. I was being told in a language – which had no words– that I didn't belong. Here, again in England, especially in Enoch Powell's England, in Margaret Thatcher's England, I had the same feeling. It was a feeling that militated against my self- respect. Aparna, my daughter, was here. Ian, my son-in-law, was here. Mark was here. Jack, Roger, Dave and Francine were here. *But I had to go.*

India won the World Cup that year, playing in the finals against a very strong West Indies side. Sir Richard Attenborough and Ben Kingsley won Oscars for *Gandhi*. In spite of another Tory victory, positive events were happening. *But I had to go.*

In October 1983, when Robert was four years old, we flew out to Delhi by Thai Airlines. One of the air hostesses gave each of us a pink orchid. The plane flew smoothly beneath a clear blue sky above banks of white clouds. The formalities before getting on a plane have always been tiresome. So people always had a sense of relief after they had settled down, and the plane was steadily speeding through space at high altitude. Eyes drooped, there was relaxed conversation. I shut my eyes and wondered why I was doing this, why I was returning to India. I liked living in England and had made friends. I had a secure future; I decided some questions had no satisfactory answer. Was life going to be better? Was it going to be worse? All I knew for certain was that it was going to be different.

After the initial excitement of boarding and take-off, Robert was soon fast asleep and Julia had dozed off. Both looked vulnerable. Was I hasty? Was my decision going to cause them hardship? What if my money runs out and I still haven't got a job? Anxiety can be relentlessly persistent. The drinks trolley rolled up.

'Would you like tea or coffee?' the very pleasant and attractive air-hostess asked, interrupting my thinking.

'Tea, please. I'll have some tea,' I said.

When we arrived at Delhi International Airport, the first familiar face we saw was that of Nondon, my eldest son.

6707079R00294

Printed in Great Britain
by Amazon.co.uk, Ltd.,
Marston Gate.